PHILIP'S

STREET ATLAS
North
Essex

First published in 1999

Philip's, a division of
Octopus Publishing Group Ltd
2–4 Heron Quays, London E14 4JP

First colour edition 1999
Third impression with revisions 2003

ISBN 0-540-07289-3 (hardback)
ISBN 0-540-07290-7 (spiral)

© Philip's 2003

This product includes mapping data licensed
from Ordnance Survey® with the permission of
the Controller of Her Majesty's Stationery Office.
© Crown copyright 2003. All rights reserved.
Licence number 100011710

Printed and bound in Spain
by Cayfosa-Quebecor

Contents

III   **Key to map symbols**

IV   **Key to map pages**

VI   **Route planning**

VIII   **Administrative and Postcode boundaries**

1   **Street maps** at 3½ inches to 1 mile

222   **Index** of towns and villages

223   **Index** of streets, hospitals, industrial estates, railway
stations, schools, shopping centres and universities

Digital Data

The exceptionally high-quality mapping found in this atlas is available as digital data in TIFF format, which is easily convertible to other bitmapped (raster) image formats.

The index is also available in digital form as a standard database table. It contains all the details found in the printed index together with the National Grid reference for the map square in which each entry is named.

For further information and to discuss your requirements, please contact Philip's on
020 7531 8439 or ruth.king@philips-maps.co.uk

Street Atlases from Philip's

Philip's publish an extensive range of regional and local street atlases which are ideal for motoring, business and leisure use. They are widely used by the emergency services and local authorities throughout Britain.

Key features include:

◆ Superb county-wide mapping at an extra-large scale of 3½ inches to 1 mile, or 2½ inches to 1 mile in pocket editions

◆ Complete urban and rural coverage, detailing every named street in town and country

◆ Each atlas available in two handy sizes – standard spiral and pocket paperback

'The mapping is very clear... great in scope and value'
★★★★ BEST BUY   AUTO EXPRESS

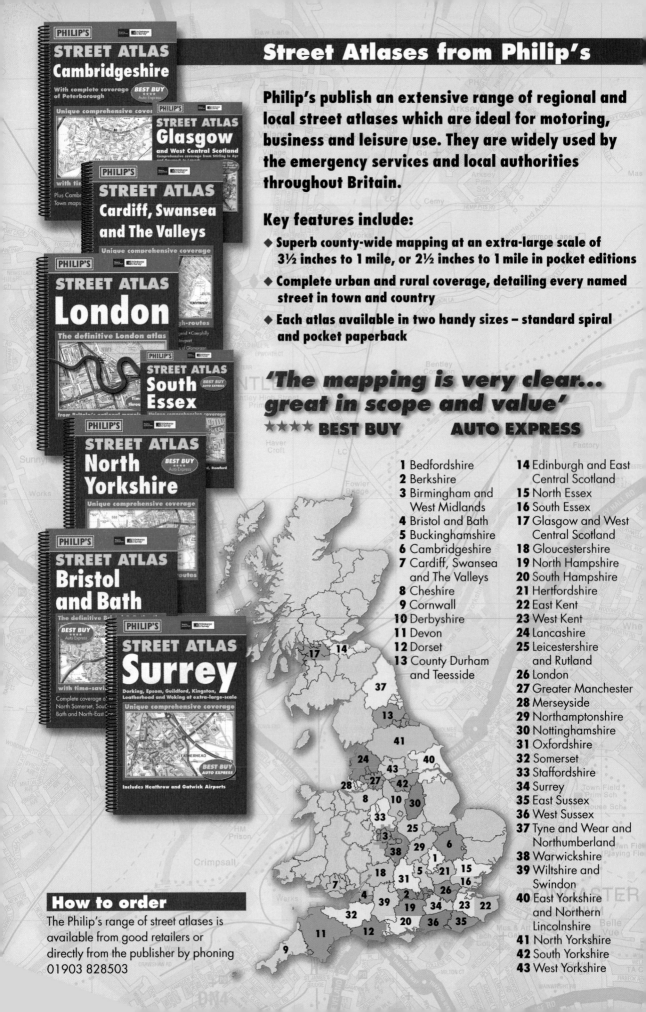

1 Bedfordshire
2 Berkshire
3 Birmingham and West Midlands
4 Bristol and Bath
5 Buckinghamshire
6 Cambridgeshire
7 Cardiff, Swansea and The Valleys
8 Cheshire
9 Cornwall
10 Derbyshire
11 Devon
12 Dorset
13 County Durham and Teesside
14 Edinburgh and East Central Scotland
15 North Essex
16 South Essex
17 Glasgow and West Central Scotland
18 Gloucestershire
19 North Hampshire
20 South Hampshire
21 Hertfordshire
22 East Kent
23 West Kent
24 Lancashire
25 Leicestershire and Rutland
26 London
27 Greater Manchester
28 Merseyside
29 Northamptonshire
30 Nottinghamshire
31 Oxfordshire
32 Somerset
33 Staffordshire
34 Surrey
35 East Sussex
36 West Sussex
37 Tyne and Wear and Northumberland
38 Warwickshire
39 Wiltshire and Swindon
40 East Yorkshire and Northern Lincolnshire
41 North Yorkshire
42 South Yorkshire
43 West Yorkshire

How to order

The Philip's range of street atlases is available from good retailers or directly from the publisher by phoning 01903 828503

Motorway (with junction number)	**Railway station**
Primary route (dual carriageway and single)	**Private railway station**
A road (dual carriageway and single)	**Bus, coach station**
B road (dual carriageway and single)	**Ambulance station**
Minor road (dual carriageway and single)	**Coastguard station**
Other minor road (dual carriageway and single)	**Fire station**
Road under construction	**Police station**
Pedestrianised area	**Accident and Emergency entrance to hospital**
Postcode boundaries DY7	**Hospital**
County and Unitary Authority boundaries	**Places of worship**
Railway	**Information Centre** (open all year)
Tramway, miniature railway	**Parking**
Rural track, private road or narrow road in urban area	**Park and Ride**
Gate or obstruction to traffic (restrictions may not apply at all times or to all vehicles)	**Post Office**
Path, bridleway, byway open to all traffic, road used as a public path	**Camping site**
The representation in this atlas of a road, track or path is no evidence of the existence right of way	**Caravan**
126	**Golf course**
Adjoining page indicators	**Picnic**
94	**Important buildings, schools, colleges, universities and hospitals** Prim Sch

Acad	**Academy**	Meml	**Memorial**
Crem	**Crematorium**	Mon	**Monument**
Cemy	**Cemetery**	Mus	**Museum**
C Ctr	**Civic Centre**	Obsy	**Observatory**
CH	**Club House**	Pal	**Royal Palace**
Coll	**College**	PH	**Public House**
Ent	**Enterprise**	Recn Gd	**Recreation Ground**
Ex H	**Exhibition Hall**	Resr	**Reservoir**
Ind Est	**Industrial Estate**	Ret Pk	**Retail Park**
Inst	**Institute**	Sch	**School**
Ct	**Law Court**	Sh Ctr	**Shopping Centre**
L Ctr	**Leisure Centre**	TH	**Town Hall/House**
LC	**Level Crossing**	Trad Est	**Trading Estate**
Liby	**Library**	Univ	**University**
Mkt	**Market**	YH	**Youth Hostel**

River Medway	**Water name**
	Stream
	River or canal (minor and major)
	Water
	Tidal water
	Woods
	Houses
House	**Non-Roman antiquity**
VILLA	**Roman antiquity**

■ The dark grey border on the inside edge of some pages indicates that the mapping does not continue onto the adjacent page

■ The small numbers around the edges of the maps identify the 1 kilometre National Grid lines

The scale of the maps is 5.52 cm to 1 km (3¹/₂ inches to 1 mile)

0		¹/₄		¹/₂		³/₄		1 mile
0	250m		500m		750m		1 kilometre	

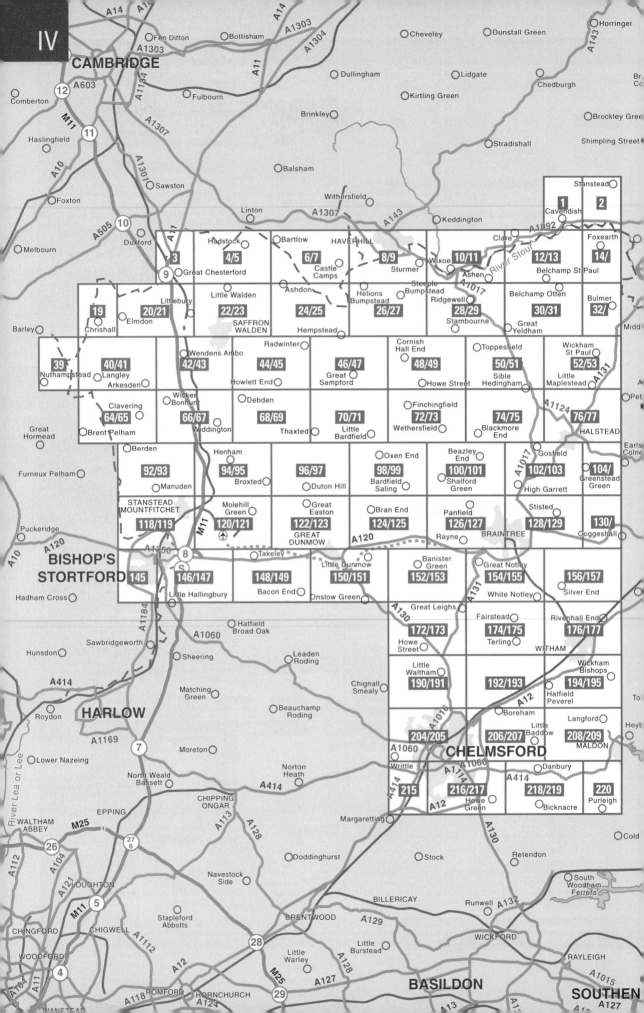

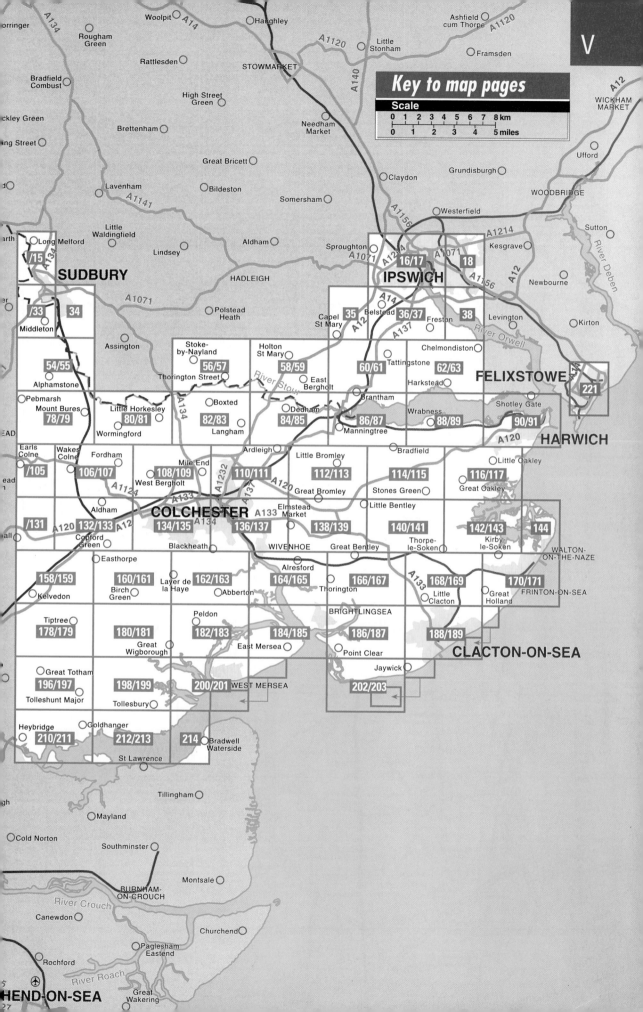

Route planning

Scale

0 1 2 3 4 5 6 7 8 km
0 1 2 3 4 5 miles

Major administrative and post code boundaries

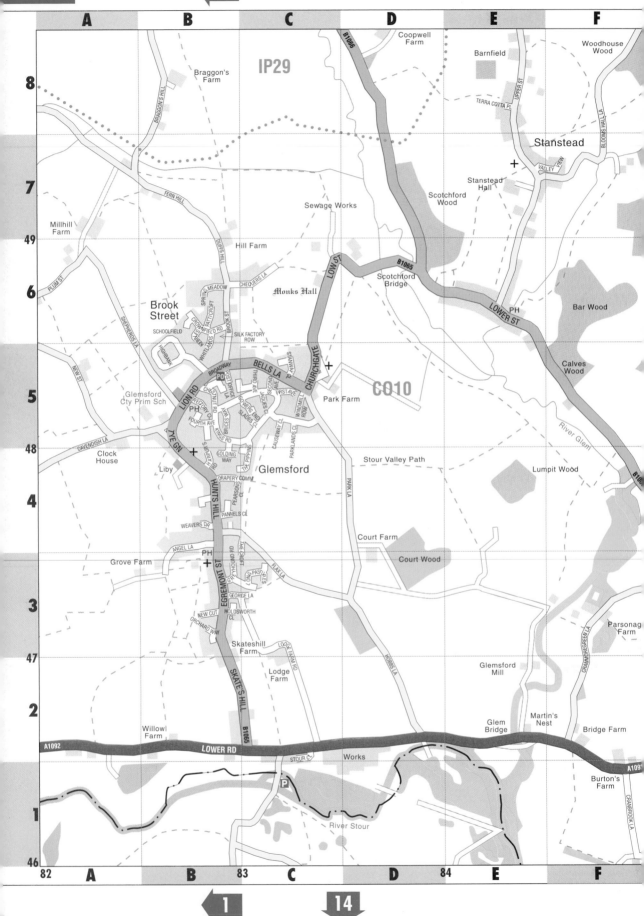

8

IP29

Braggon's Farm

Coopwell Farm

Barnfield

Woodhouse Wood

UPPER ST

TERRA COTTA PL

Stanstead

VALLEY VIEW

BLOOMS HALL LA

7

Stanstead Hall

Scotchford Wood

49

Millhill Farm

FERN HILL

Hill Farm

Sewage Works

PLUM ST

DUFFS HILL

CHEQUERS LA

SPRING MEADOW

B1065

Scotchford Bridge

LOW ST

LOWER ST

PH

Bar Wood

6

Brook Street

SCHOOLFIELD

SHEPHERDS LA

CROWNFIELD RD

WHITLANDS

NEWB RD

PATTCROFT

HIGHBANK

Monks Hall

SILK FACTORY ROW

CHURCHGATE

STANWAY CL

BELLS LA

5

NEW ST

Glemsford Cty Prim Sch

LION RD

REGDAY CL

CHESTNUT RD

POST OFFICE LA

THIRD AVE

Broadway

PO

PH

JACQES CL

BICKERS END

FIRST AVE

WINDMILL ROW

SLADES CL

Park Farm

CO10

48

CAVENDISH LA

Clock House

Liby

TYE GN

FOURTH AVE

KINGS RD

SHRLEY RD

NN BRIDGE

GOLDING WAY

TYE PIPPINS

DRAPERY COMM

PARKLANDS CL

CAUSEWAY CL

Glemsford

Stour Valley Path

River Glen

Lumpit Wood

4

HUNT'S HILL

WEAVERS DR

PEARSON CL

PANNELS CL

PARK LA

Court Farm

Court Wood

ANGEL LA

THE CROFT

LONG PASTURES

RICHMOND RD

FLAX LA

PH

GEORGE LA

HOLDSWORTH CL

3

Grove Farm

EGREMONT ST

NEW CUT

ORCHARD WAY

LODGE FARM RD

CRANMOREGREEN LA

Parsonage Farm

47

Skateshill Farm

Lodge Farm

HOBBS LA

Glemsford Mill

2

SKATE'S HILL

B1065

Willowl Farm

LOWER RD

A1092

STOUR CL

Works

Glem Bridge

Martin's Nest

Bridge Farm

A1092

P

Burton's Farm

CRANBROOK LA

1

River Stour

46

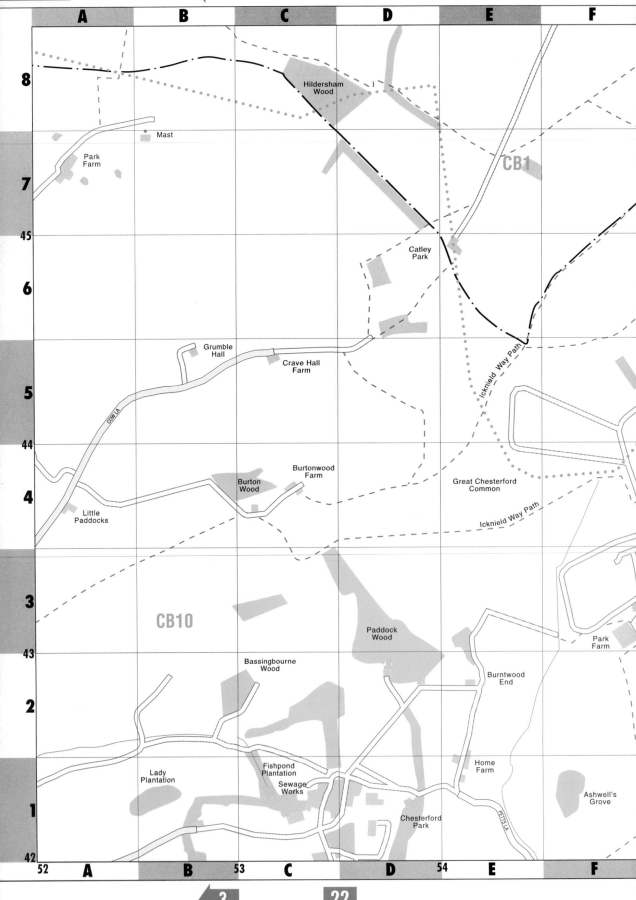

A   B   C   D   E   F

8

Hildersham
Wood

Mast

Park
Farm

CB1

7

45

Catley
Park

6

Grumble
Hall

Crave Hall
Farm

Icknield Way Path

5

COW LA

44

Burtonwood
Farm

Burton
Wood

Great Chesterford
Common

4

Little
Paddocks

Icknield Way Path

3

CB10

Paddock
Wood

Park
Farm

43

Bassingbourne
Wood

Burntwood
End

2

Lady
Plantation

Fishpond
Plantation

Sewage
Works

Home
Farm

Ashwell's
Grove

PETTS LA

1

Chesterford
Park

42

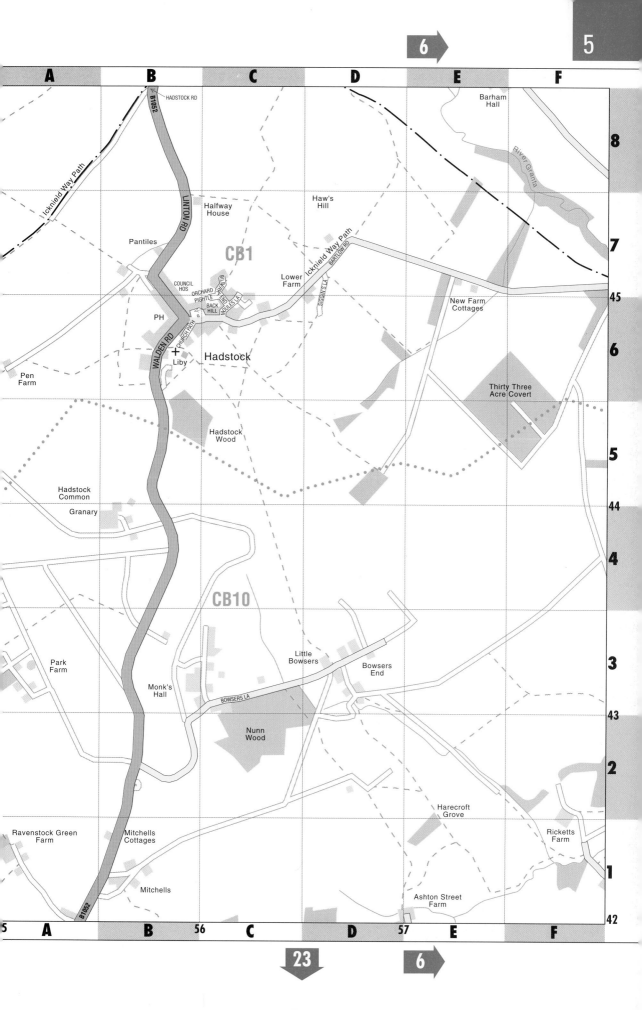

A   B   C   D   E   F

8
7
45
6
5
44
4
3
43
2
1
42

B1052
HADSTOCK RD

Icknield Way Path

Barham
Hall

River Granta

LINTON RD

Halfway
House

Haw's
Hill

CB1

Pantiles

Icknield Way Path
BARTLOW RD

Lower
Farm

SIGGIN S LA

New Farm
Cottages

COUNCIL
HOS
ORCHARD
PIGHTLE
BACK
HILL

BILBERRY END
MOULES LA

PH

WALDEN RD

CHURCH PATH

Pen
Farm

Liby
Hadstock

Thirty Three
Acre Covert

Hadstock
Wood

Hadstock
Common

Granary

CB10

Park
Farm

Monk's
Hall

Little
Bowsers

Bowsers
End

BOWSERS LA

Nunn
Wood

Harecroft
Grove

Ravenstock Green
Farm

Mitchells
Cottages

Ricketts
Farm

Mitchells

B1052

Ashton Street
Farm

A B C D E F

8

Little Barham
Hall

DEAN RD

Bartlow

The
Dower House

7 CAMPS RD

Three Hills
(PH)

PO

45

Bartlow Hills
TUMULI

CB1

Westoe
Farm

6

Hills
Farm

River Granta

MAIN ST

5

44

Harcamlow Way

Aulnoye

River Bourn

4

The
White House

Home
Wood

3

Sewage
Works

Waltons

CB10

Whitensmere
Farm

Woolpack
Grove

43

Ashdon
Place

Whiten's Mere
Grove

The Bonnet
(PH)

2

Newnham Hall
Farm

Knox
End

Steventon
End

OVER HALL LA

Over
Hall

Holden
End

BARLOW ROAD
COTTS

Hops Close
Farm

CARTERS CROFT

The Bricklayer's
Arms (PH)

Windmill
(disused)

The
Grove

Langley
Wood

DOBY'S LA

Rogers
End

1

Ashdon Cty
Prim Sch

PH

PO

Ashdon

RECTORY LA

RADWINTER RD

42

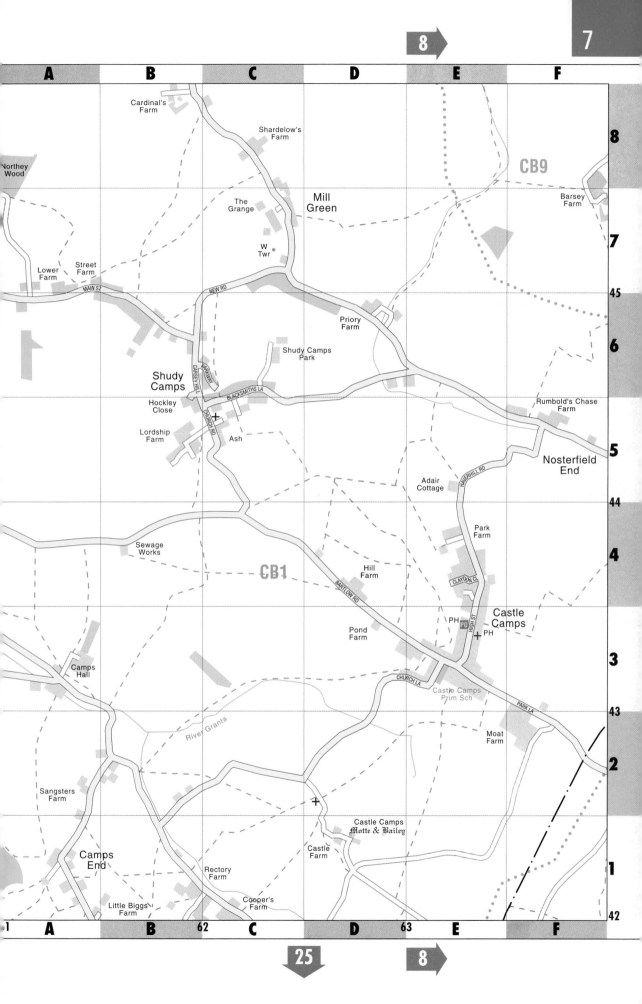

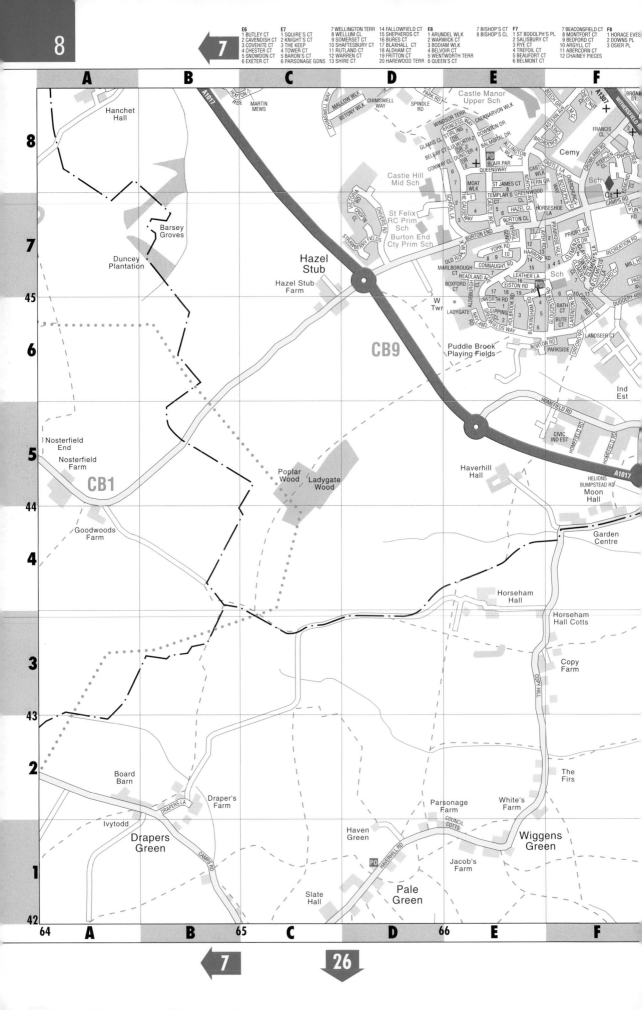

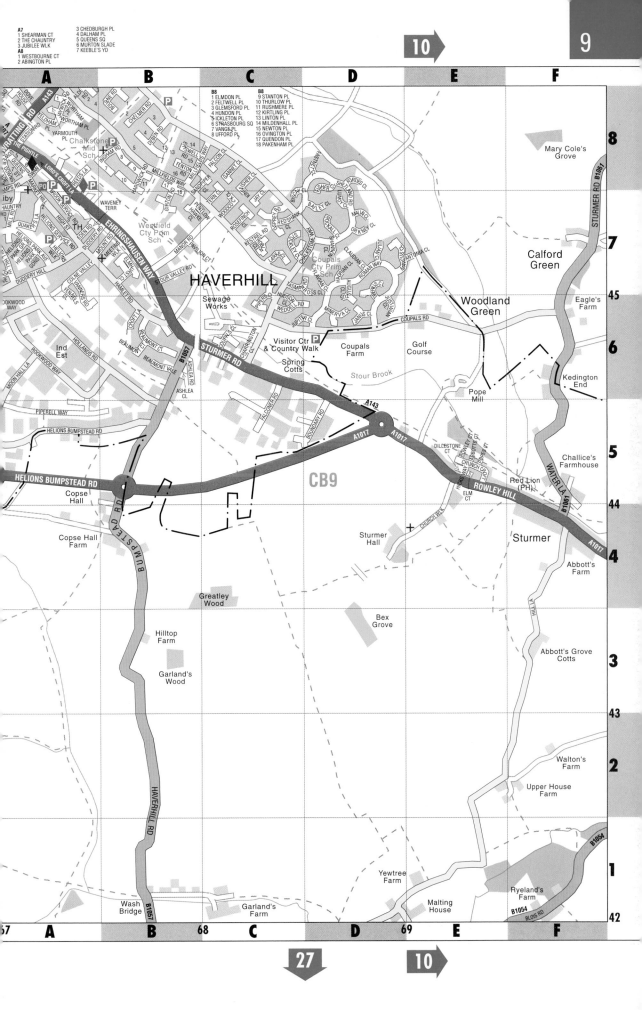

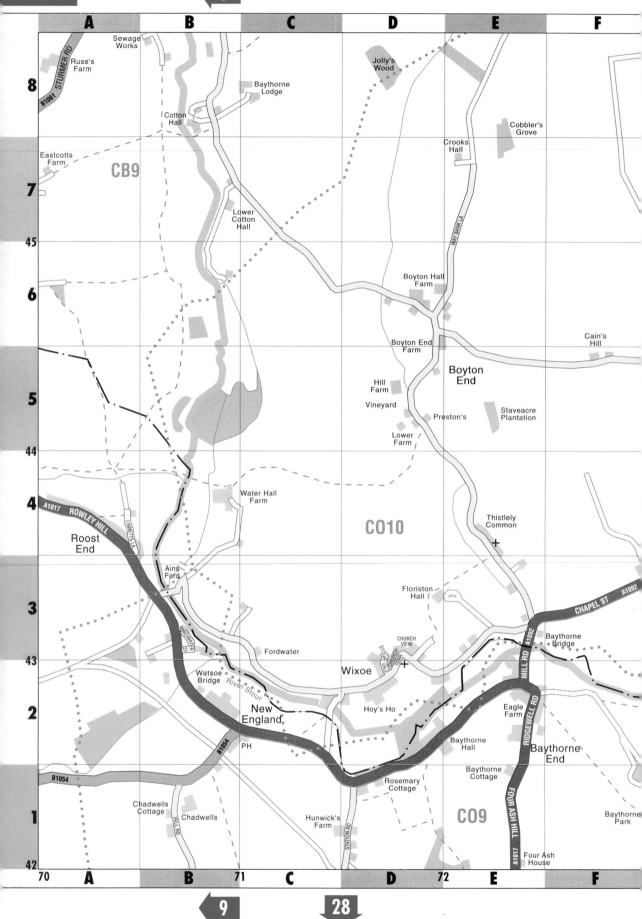

STURMER RD
B1061
Ruse's Farm
Sewage Works
Baythorne Lodge
Cotton Hall
Eastcotts Farm
CB9
Lower Cotton Hall
Jolly's Wood
Crooks Hall
Cobbler's Grove
WAY BANK LA
Boyton Hall Farm
Cain's Hill
Boyton End Farm
Boyton End
Hill Farm
Vineyard
Preston's
Staveacre Plantation
Lower Farm
Water Hall Farm
CO10
Thistlely Common
A1017 ROWLEY HILL
Roost End
LINNETTS LA
Ains Ford
Floriston Hall
CHAPEL ST A1092
FORDWATER LO
Fordwater
CHURCH VIEW
Baythorne Bridge
STOUR VALE
A1092
MILL RD
Wixoe
Watsoe Bridge
River Stour
New England
Hoy's Ho
Eagle Farm
RIDGEWELL RD
Baythorne End
B1054
PH
Baythorne Hall
Baythorne Cottage
FOUR ASH HILL
B1054
Rosemary Cottage
Baythorne Cottage
Baythorne Park
Chadwells Cottage
FELL RD
Chadwells
Hunwick's Farm
STATION RD
CO9
A1017
Four Ash House

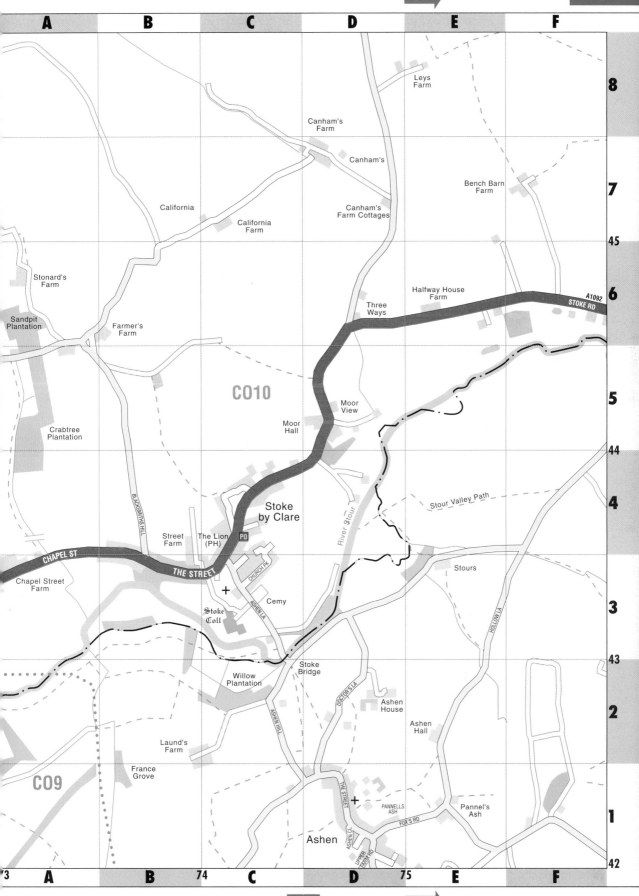

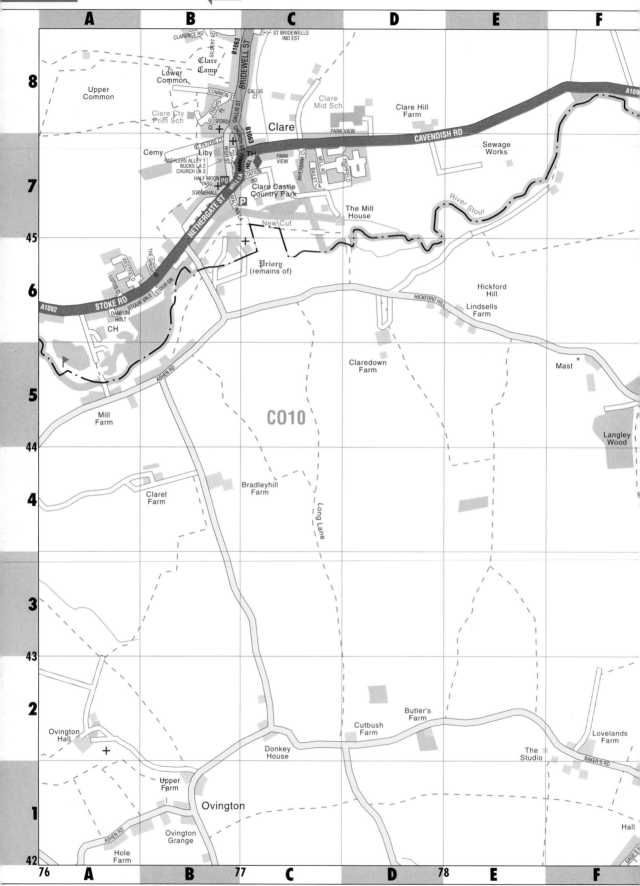

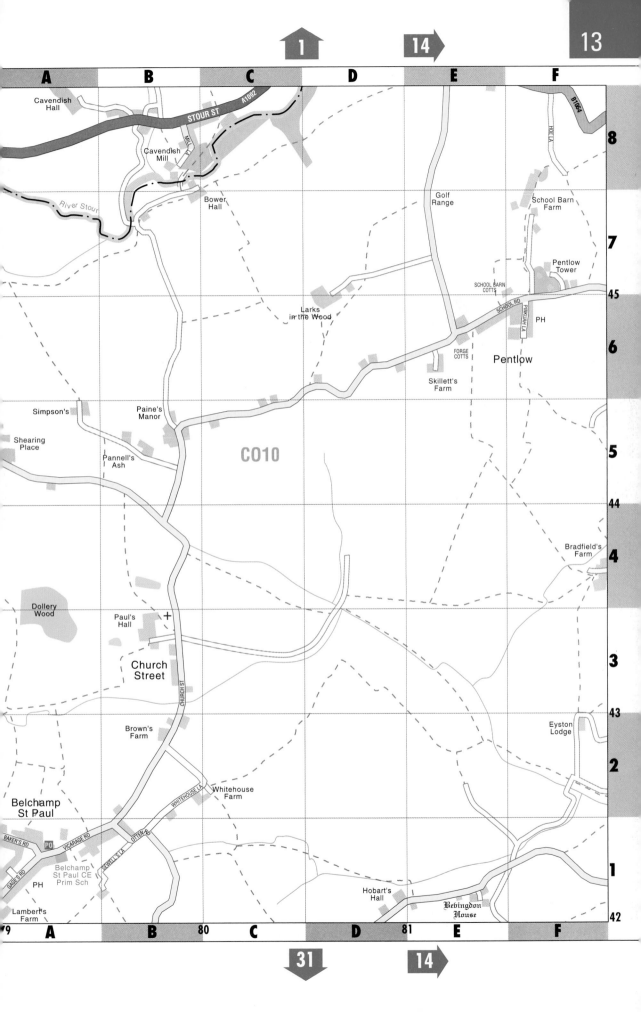

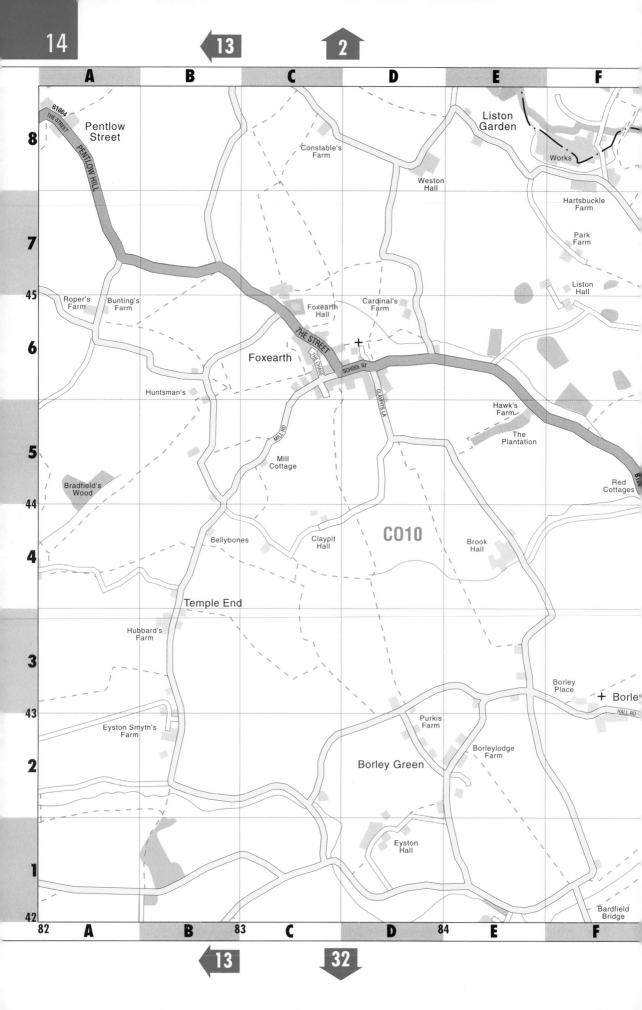

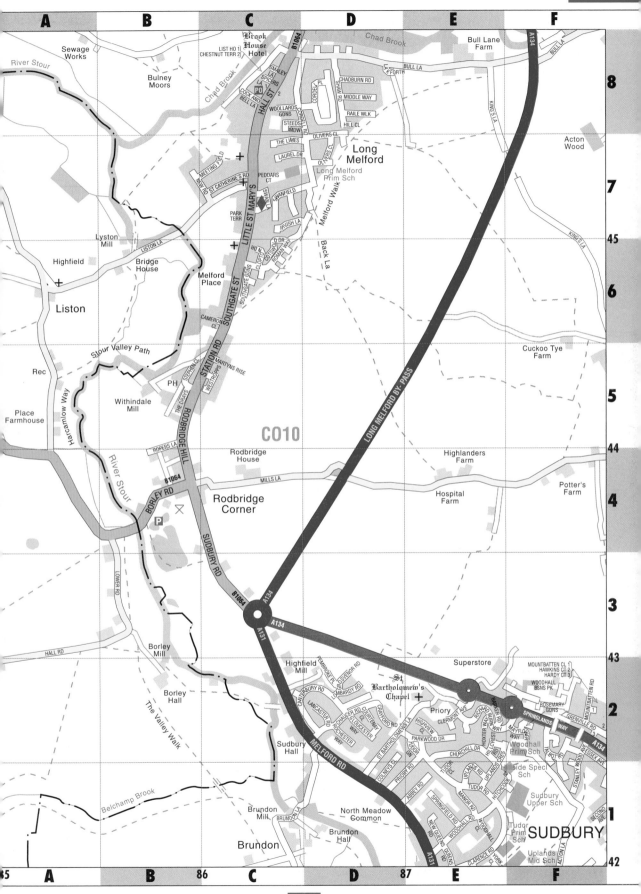

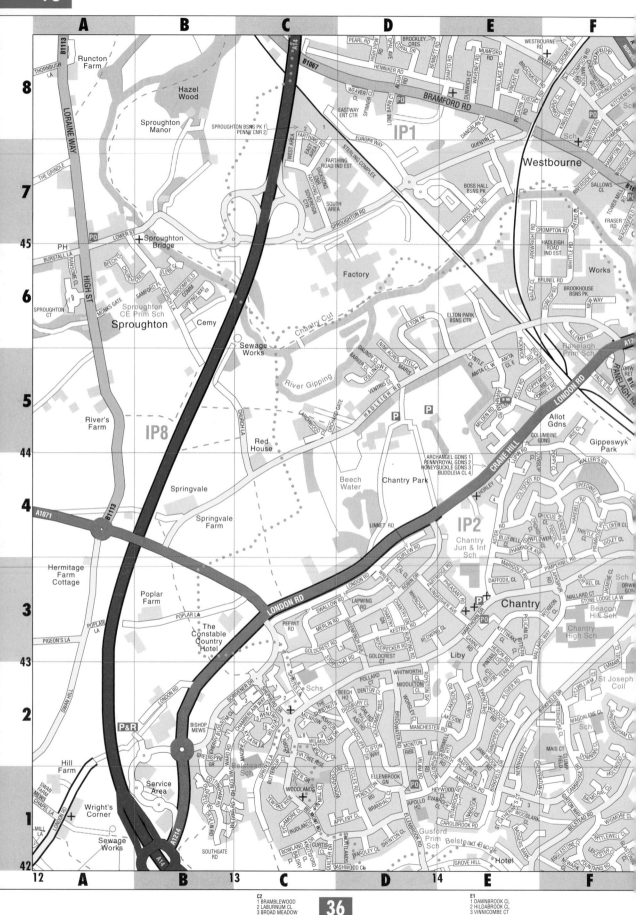

C2
1 BRAMBLEWOOD
2 LABURNUM CL
3 BROAD MEADOW
4 INNES END
5 PEACOCK CL
6 HALFORD CT
7 MERRION CL
8 MATLOCK CL
9 MOTTRAM CL

E1
1 DAWNBROOK CL
2 HILDABROOK CL
3 VINNICOMBE CT

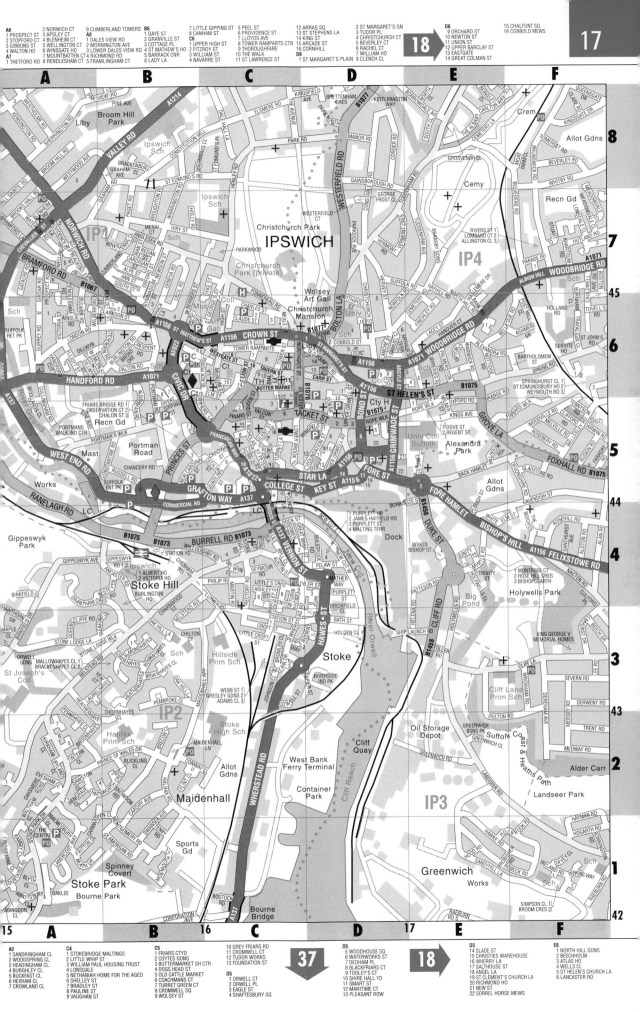

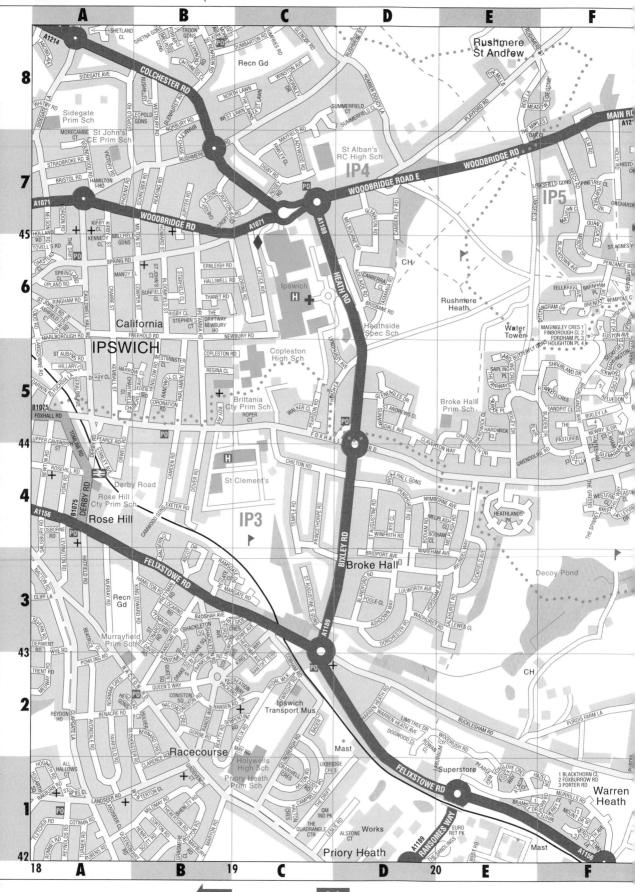

A   B   C   D   E   F

CB10

Ickleton Old Grange

GRANGE RD

The Lodge

Ickleton

8

Welches Wood

Valance Farm

7

41

Lodge Farm

Argers

ROYSTON LA

6

The Poplars

QUICKSET RD

New Jersey Farm

5

Sewage Works

40

Strethall Wood

Strethall Hall

Elmdonbury

Strethall Hall Farm

ICKLETON RD

ELM CT

HORSESHOE CL

4

Strethall

HEYDON LA

HOLLOW RD

Icknield Way

PH

Elmdon

ESSEX HILL

Church Farm

Free Wood

Felsted Croft Grove

Ann's Wood

FREEWOOD LA

Mill Hill

Freewood Farm

3

39

Bradley Grove

Bixett Wood

ESSEX HILL

Lofts Hall

2

CB11

Littlebury Green

Lee Wood

Ash Grove

Green Farm

1

Elmdon Lee

38

46   A   B   47   C   D   48   E   F

A   B   C   D   E   F

8

Emanuel Cott

Emanuel Wood

Petlands

Little Walden

PETTS LA

PH

The Slade

The Slade

B1052

Four Acre Grove

The Hall Farm

7

Joseph Farm

Bell Cotts

41

Springwell

Stone Bridge

B184

CB10

Rowley Hill Farm

Stone Bridge Farm

6

Protection Plantation

Grimsditch Wood

High Balks

Westley wood

Mead Hall

5

Westley Farm

Byrds Farm

WESTLEY LA

LITTLE WALDEN RD

40

John's Acre

Brown's Plantation

SPRINGWELL RD

The Slade

4

Northend Farm

LITTLE WALDEN RD

Northend

Catons La

Harcamlow Way

Byrd's Farm La

Northend Lodge

The Vinyard

ROOKES

LIMES

Spring Wood

WINDMILL HILL

1 DODDENHILL CL
2 CORNWALLIS PL
3 WYNYARD RD
4 COLYN PL

3

CB11

Obelisk

SAFFRON WALDEN

39

River Cam or Granta

St Mary's Prim Sch

USTERDALE RD

Duck Street

2

Home Farm

CH

Sewage Works

Castle (rems of)

Mus

The Common

EASTACRE 1
HATHERLEY CT 2

B1383

CASTLE ST

RADWINTER RD

B184

Sir William's Plantation

YH

Liby

TH

Tea Bridge

Place Pond

EAST ST

CATES CNR

Cemy

Nursery

JOHNSONS YD 1
MARKET PL 2
MARKET ST 3
ROSE & CROWN WLK 4
MERCERS ROW 5
MARKET WLK 6
BUTCHERS ROW 7
MARKET ROW 8
CENTRAL ARC 9
MYDDYLTON PL 10
PRIME'S CL 11
WALDEN PL 11
HANOVER PL 12
PARKSIDE 13
KING EDWARD IV'S ALMSHOUSES 14
PARKSIDE 15
CUSTERSON CT 16
THE MALTINGS 17

PARK LA

PO

HIGH ST

AUDLEY RD

THAXTED RD

B184

1

Stable Bridge

Audley End

Audley Park

ABBEY LA

Margaret

STATION RD

Sch

VICTORIA AVE

VICTORIA GDNS

B184

B1383

Spring Hill

38

52   A   AUDLEY END RD   B   53   C   D   54   E   F

E1
1 NEWCROFT
2 ALPHA PL
3 FARMADINE CT
4 JOHN DANE PLAYER CT
5 FARMADINE HO

F2
1 SAFFRON BSNS CTR
2 BRADLEY MEWS
3 NIGHTINGALE MEWS
4 HAMILTON MEWS
5 HADLEIGH CT
6 ROCHESTER CT
7 LAYENDER FIELD
8 CAVENDISH CT

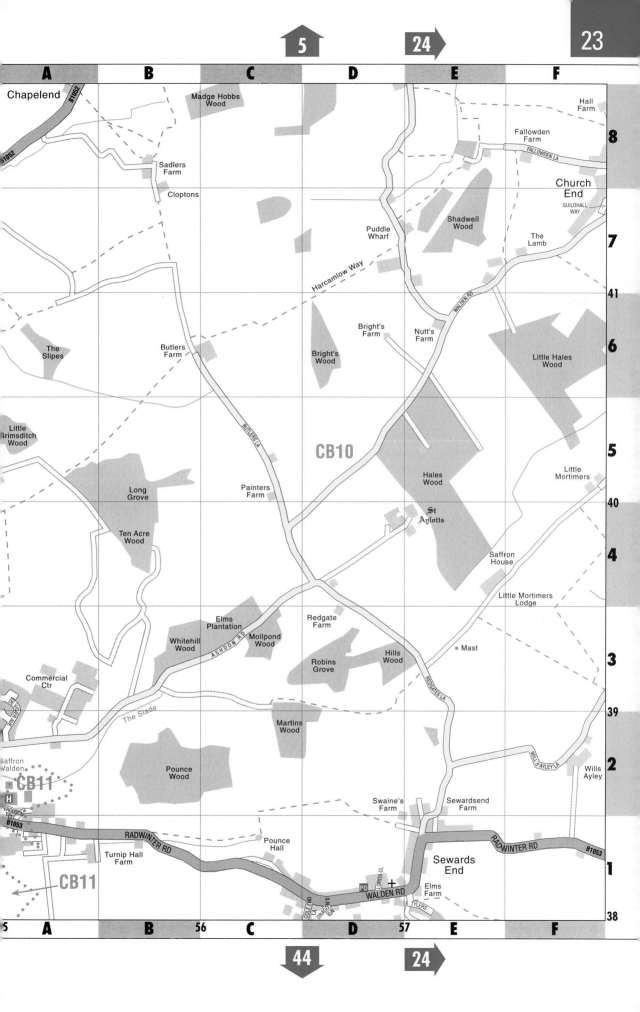

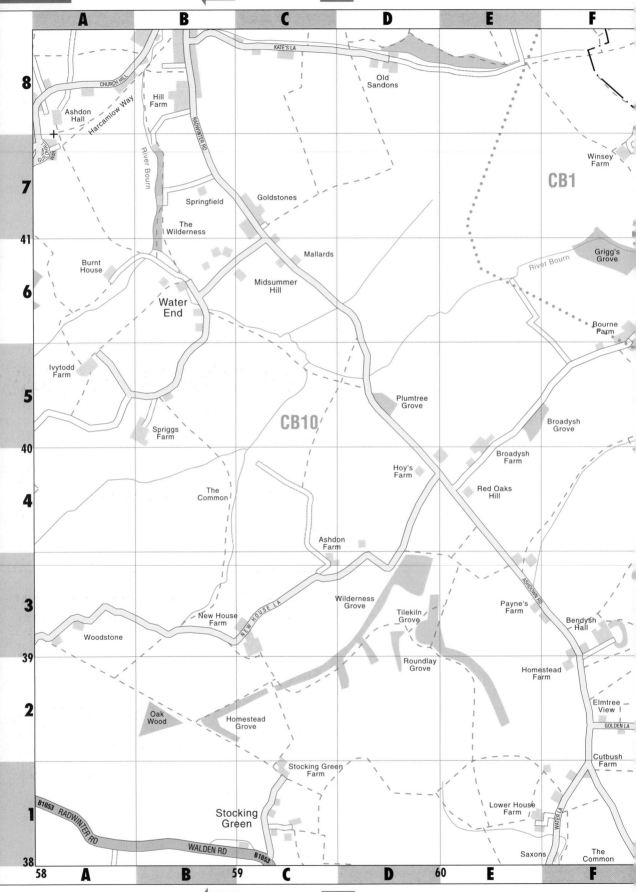

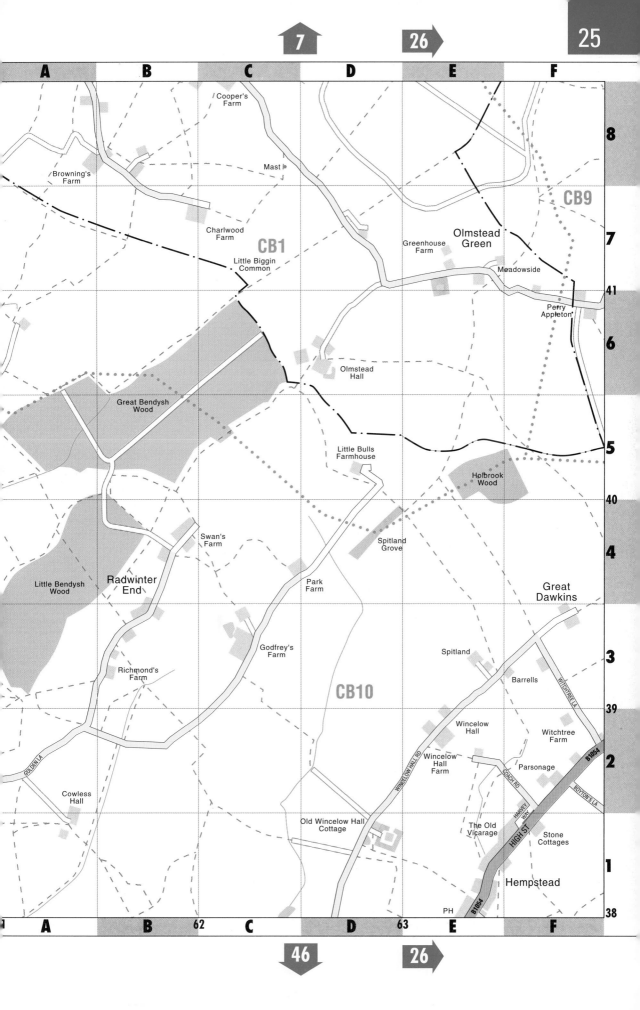

A   B   C   D   E   F

8

CB9

7

Olmstead
Green

Cooper's
Farm

Mast

Charlwood
Farm

CB1

Browning's
Farm

Little Biggin
Common

Greenhouse
Farm

Meadowside

41

Perry
Appleton

6

Great Bendysh
Wood

Olmstead
Hall

Little Bulls
Farmhouse

Holbrook
Wood

5

40

Little Bendysh
Wood

Swan's
Farm

Spitland
Grove

4

Radwinter
End

Park
Farm

Great
Dawkins

Spitland

3

Godfrey's
Farm

Barrells

WITCHTREE LA

Richmond's
Farm

CB10

39

Wincelow
Hall

Witchtree
Farm

B1054

WINGLOW HALL RD

Wincelow
Hall Farm

COACH RD

Parsonage

2

GOLDEN LA

BOYTON'S LA

Cowless
Hall

HARVEY WAY

The Old
Vicarage

Stone
Cottages

HIGH ST

Old Wincelow Hall
Cottage

1

Hempstead

PH

B1054

38

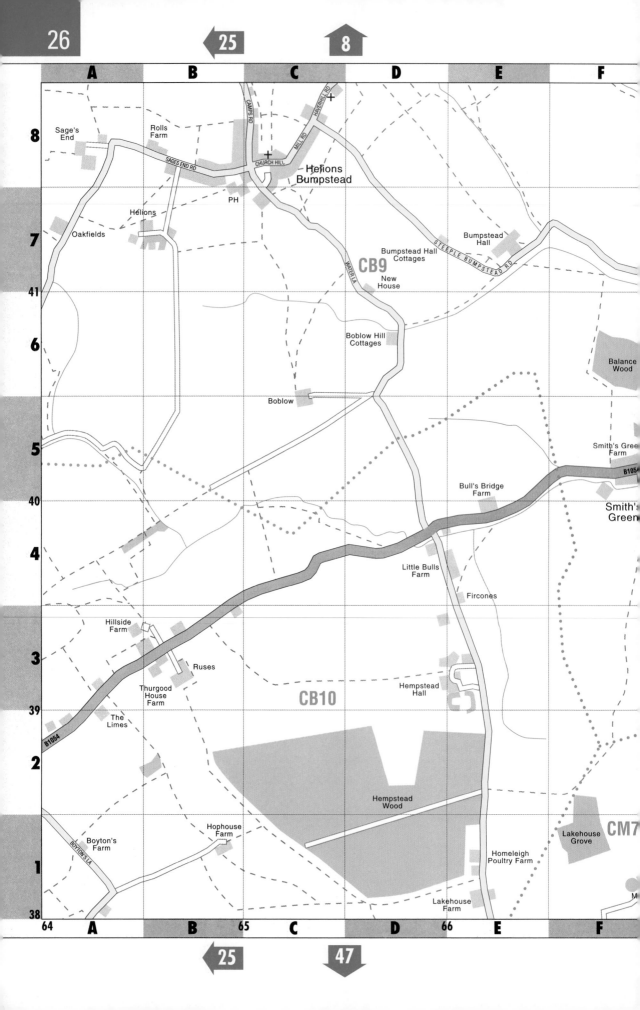

A | B | C | D | E | F

8

Sage's End

Rolls Farm

SAGES END RD

CAMPS RD

HAVERHILL RD

MILL RD

+

+

CHURCH HILL

Helions Bumpstead

PH

7

Oakfields

Helions

WATER LA

CB9

Bumpstead Hall Cottages

Bumpstead Hall

STEEPLE BUMPSTEAD RD

New House

41

6

Boblow Hill Cottages

Balance Wood

Boblow

5

Smith's Green Farm

B1054

40

Bull's Bridge Farm

Smith's Green

4

Little Bulls Farm

Fircones

Hillside Farm

3

Ruses

Thurgood House Farm

CB10

Hempstead Hall

39

The Limes

B1054

2

Hempstead Wood

CM7

Boyton's Farm

BOYTON'S LA

Hophouse Farm

Lakehouse Grove

1

Homeleigh Poultry Farm

Lakehouse Farm

38

64 | A | B | 65 | C | D | 66 | E | F

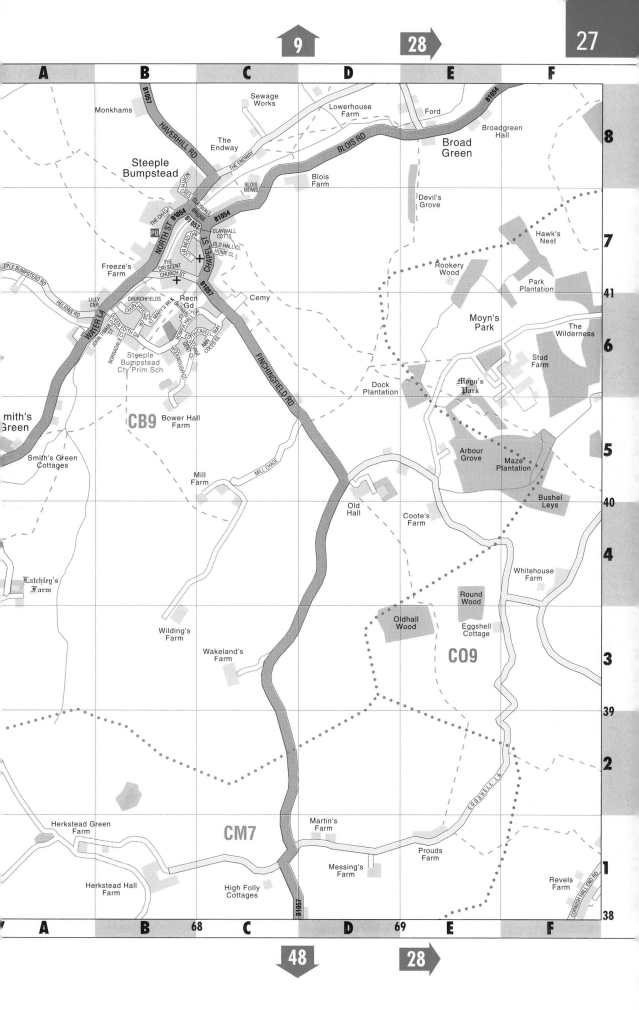

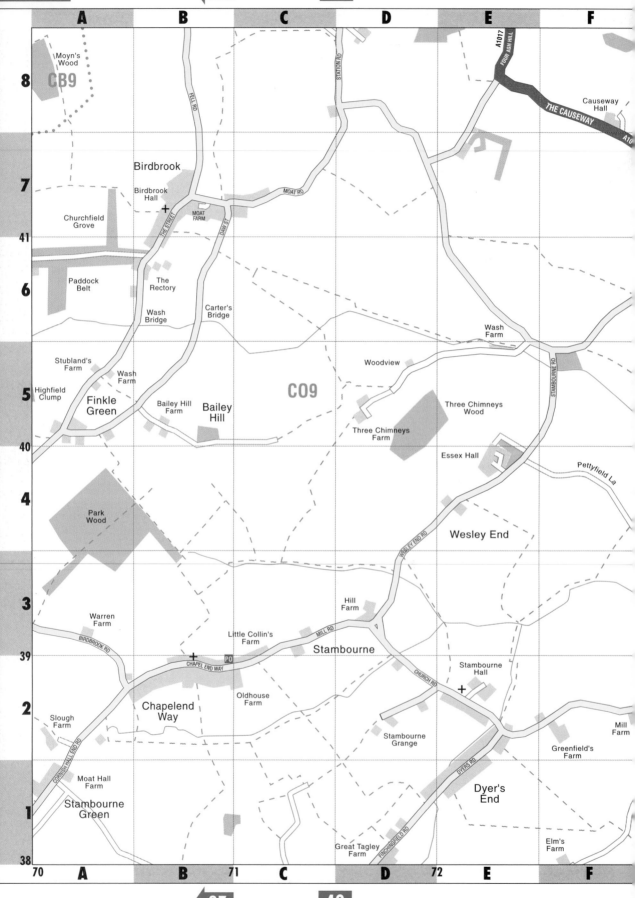

A   B   C   D   E   F

8   Moyn's Wood   CB9

Causeway Hall
FOUR ASH HILL
A1017
THE CAUSEWAY
A10

7   Birdbrook
Birdbrook Hall
MOAT FARM
STATION RD
MOAT RD

41   Churchfield Grove
THE STREET
DAW ST
FELL RD

6   Paddock Belt
The Rectory
Wash Bridge
Carter's Bridge
Wash Farm

Stubland's Farm
Wash Farm
Woodview
STAMBOURNE RD

5   Highfield Clump
Finkle Green
Bailey Hill Farm
Bailey Hill
CO9
Three Chimneys Wood
Three Chimneys Farm

40   Essex Hall
Pettyfield La

4   Park Wood
Wesley End
WESLEY END RD

3   Warren Farm
Hill Farm
BIRDBROOK RD
MILL RD
Little Collin's Farm
Stambourne

39   CHAPEL END WAY
PO
Stambourne Hall
CHURCH RD

2   Slough Farm
Chapelend Way
Oldhouse Farm
Stambourne Grange
Mill Farm
Greenfield's Farm
CORNISH HALL END RD

1   Moat Hall Farm
Stambourne Green
Dyer's End
DYERS RD
HINCHINGFIELD RD
Great Tagley Farm
Elm's Farm

38

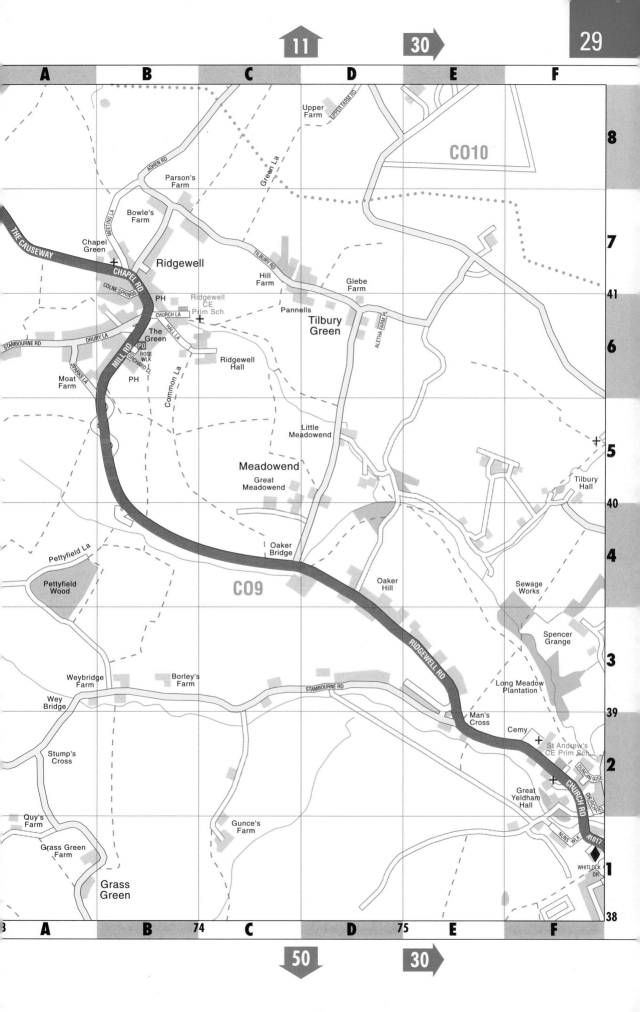

8

7

41

6

5

40

4

3

39

2

1

38

A B C D E F

CO10

THE CAUSEWAY

Upper Farm

UPPER FARM RD

ASHEN RD

Parson's Farm

Green La

Bowle's Farm

MEETING LA

Chapel Green

CHAPEL RD

Ridgewell

TILBURY RD

Hill Farm

Glebe Farm

Pannells

COLNE SPRINGS

PH

CHURCH LA

Ridgewell CE Prim Sch

Tilbury Green

ALETHA FARM PL

STAMBOURNE RD

DRURY LA

The Green

HALL LA

PO

ROSE WLK

ORCHARD CL

MILL RD

SPARKS LA

Moat Farm

PH

Ridgewell Hall

Common La

Ridgewell Hall

Little Meadowend

Meadowend

Great Meadowend

Tilbury Hall

Pettyfield La

Oaker Bridge

Sewage Works

Pettyfield Wood

CO9

Oaker Hill

Spencer Grange

RIDGEWELL RD

Weybridge Farm

Borley's Farm

Wey Bridge

STAMBOURNE RD

Long Meadow Plantation

Man's Cross

Cemy

St Andrew's CE Prim Sch

Stump's Cross

CHURCH RISE

Great Yeldham Hall

CHURCH FIELD

CHURCH RD

Quy's Farm

Gunce's Farm

NURS WLK

A1017

Grass Green Farm

WHITLOCK DR

Grass Green

29

12

A B C D E F

8

CO10

Silver End

Gage's House

Knowl Green

Cane's Cottages

Hole Farm

WAKESHALL LA

Wakeshall Farm

Cherry Tree (PH)

7

Lodge Farm

Park Farm

MASSHLA

Wood Barns Farm

41

Mast

Marshy Wood

Mashay Farm

6

Tilbury Cottage

Twelve Acre Wood

MASHEY RD

5

Tilbury Juxta Clare

Red Barn

Jay's La

40

Tilbury Court

Red House

4

Hyde Wood

CO9

CHURCH GN

Little Yeldham

Lodge

The Hyde

Bendysh House

HYDEWOOD RD

SCHOOL RD

3

Brook Farm

North End

MILL LA

The Hyde Farm

Hall Green

NORTH END RD

PH

TILBURY RD

LITTLE YELDHAM RD

39

2

Armstrong Way

Highfields

Upper Yeldham Hall

LITTLE HYDE RD

GOODCHILD WAY

CARLTON CL

THE COURT

LEATHER LA

NORTH RD

BUTLERS WAY

GREAT OAK

PH

Highlands Farm

WHITLOCK DR

1

A1017

HIGH ST

PO

Great Yeldham

POPLAR CL

Spayne's Hall

Hunts Wood

Priestfields Farm

WHITLOCK GR

A1017

38

76 A B 77 C D 78 E F

29

51

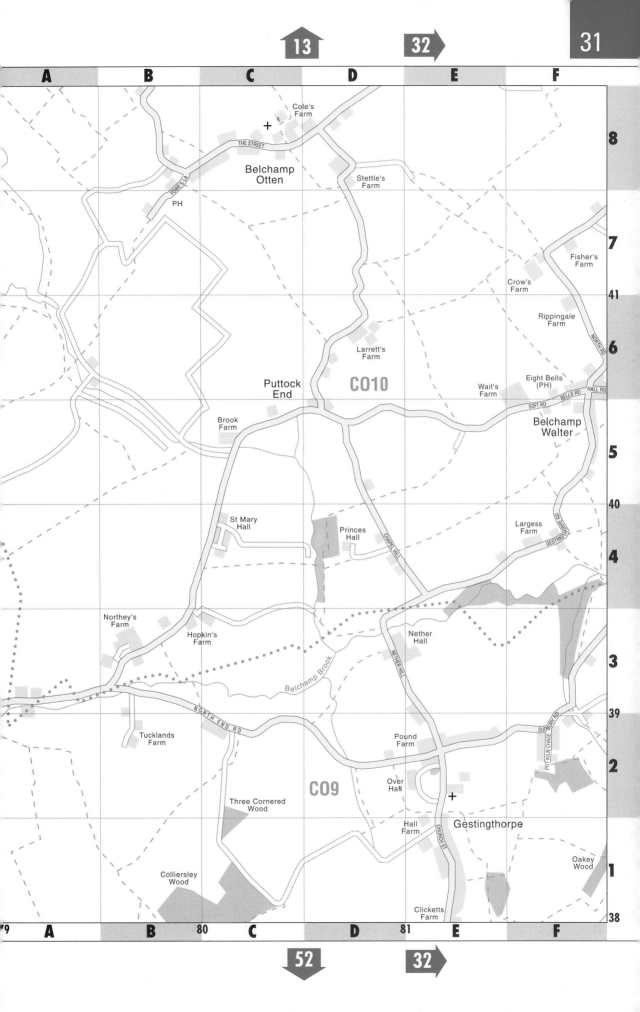

A B C D E F

8

Newbon

The Rookery

Clark's Farm

Smeetham Hall

41

7

Heaven Wood

Smeetham Hall Cottages

HALL RD

Belchamp Brook

6

Belchamp Hall

SMEETHAM HALL LA

SUDBURY RD

Springgate Farm

PH

Blackhouse Farm

Goldingham Hall

CO10

Bulmer

5

New Barns

Grigg's Farm

THE STREET

VICAR'S ORCH

40

BULMER ST

ST ANDREW'S RISE

PO

SANDY LA

Auberies

Lower Houses

St Andrew's CE Prim Sch

4

Brakey Hill

CHURCH RD

SUDBURY RD

Upper Houses

3

OLD CHURCH LA

Hill Farm

New Barn

Hilltop Farm

39

PARK LA

A13

Bulmer Tye

CO9

OLD CHURCH LA

2

Wiggery Wood

Jenkins Farm

BLACKSMITH'S LA

Parsonage Wood

B1058

Wesborough Hill

Tyecorner Farm

1

Hole Farm

A131

38

82 A B 83 C D 84 E F

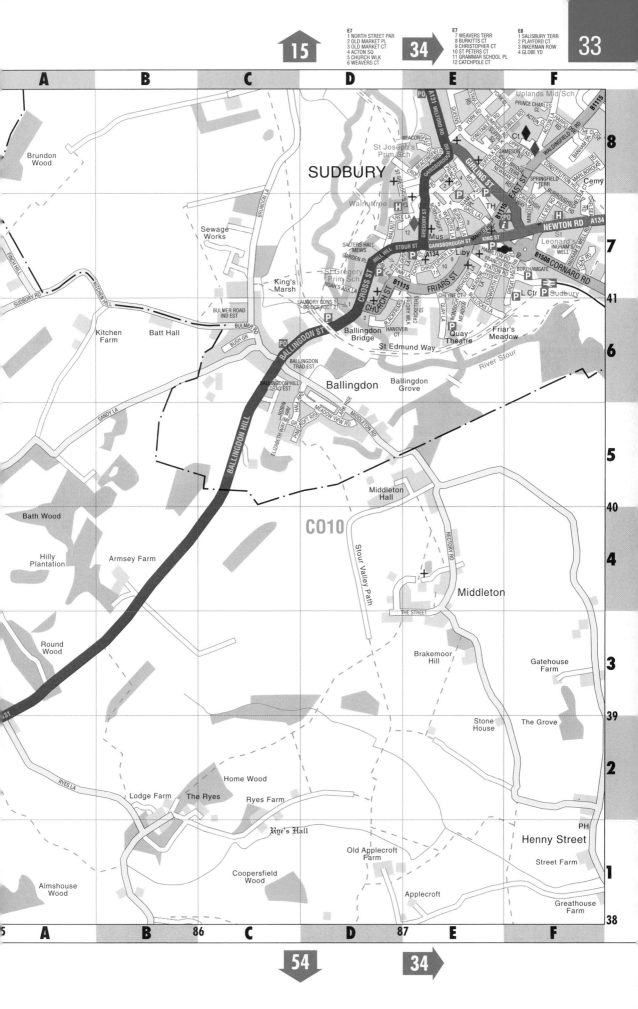

A B C D E F

8 SUDBURY

CHILTON IND EST

GRANGE Farm

CHILTON IND EST

WARNER WAY MILLS RD

WINDHAM RD CURZON RD

Valley Farm

ALEXANDRA RD HILLSIDE COTTS
SOUTH SUFFOLK BSNS PK

NEWTON RD

MALDON CT

Cornard Tye

Lawn Farm

The Elms

A134

Sudbury Rd A1

7 QUEENS TERR WTON CROFT

HILLSIDE RD

WINDSOR PL

HAWTHORN RD

Water Tower

Tye Farm

41 CHILTON LODGE RD CHILTON RD CORNARD RD

B1508

ELM RD SANDRINGHAM CT

CAT'S LA

POPLAR RD CHERRY TREE RD POPLAR CT

SYCAMORE RD SHAWLANDS AVE

CHESWORTH AVE

THE POT KILNS

Cemy
Pot Kiln Cty Prim Sch

KERSEY AVE

6 KINGS HILL

KINGS MEADOW

SCOFIELD CL ORCHARD RD

NORTH RISE

ST ANDREWS WAY

ROWELL CL

RORREL CL

GLENSIDE WAY

KILN DR

BUTT RD

CORNER SCH CT

POT KILN RD

SHELLEY AVE

SPARROW RD

BEECH

HIGHBURY WAY

DAY RD

OAK RD

THE DRIFT

RAYDON WAY

RECK WAY

MINSMERE WAY

CLOVER CL

FARFORD FIELD

LANGUIDEC CL

SHEPSHEAD HILL

Abbas Hall

+ CHURCH RD +

WICKROSE FIELD

PO

RECREATION WAY

QUEENSWAY

CANIHAMS RD

KEMPSON DR

MALLARD WAY

CAUSTONS GREYS CL

PEGOCKES CL

BRANDS CL

PARK LA

WALSINGHAM CL

CATESBYS DR

TUCKENTINE DR

Abbas Hall Wood

CO10

5 Great Cornard

RADIATOR RD

PHILLIPS FIELD RD

HEAD LA

NURSERY RD

BROOM ST

SINK CL

LIONEL HURST CL

LAYZELL CROFT

GUZZOCK CL

E DAVIDSON DR

Little Greys Farm

40 MILL TYE

RED HOUSE LA

STOUR GDNS

PERRYFIELD

RUGBY RD

MEAD DANES CT

MOORSFIELD

WELLS HALL RD

Wells Hall Cty Prim Sch

HORSE POND RD

Great Cornard Upper Sch

Great Cornard Mid Sch

Prospect Hill Farm

Greys Hall

4 BURES RD

Brook Farm

PH

P Great Cornard Country Park

PROSPECT HILL

Moor's Farm

BLACKHOUSE LA

3 River Stour

Little Mere

Blackhouse Farm

39 Nature Trail

Cornard Mere

Holly Lodge

Peacock Hall

+ Little Cornard

2 LC

Stone Farm

KEDINGTON HILL

Sewage Works

CHAPEL LA

Costens Hall

1 Shalford Meadow

Casefields Farm

38 B1508

B　C　D　E　F

Coles
Green

Washbrook

Coles Green
Farm

Fen
Cottages

PHEASANT
RISE
Copdock Cty Prim
Sch

CHURCH LA

DALES VIEW

FEN VIEW

BACK LA

THE STREET

SCHOOL LA

8

Glenfield

CHATTISHAM RD

Westhill
House

Copdock
Hall

The
Covey

HOLLOW RD

ELM LA

POUND LA

SAXON LA

Copdock

7

Barrens
Farm

Mace
Green

Hotel

Felcourt

41

WENHAM RD

THE AVENUE

Rookery
Farm

Cottage
Farm

Glebe
Farm

OAKFIELD RD

Eight Elms
Farm

IP8

LONDON RD

6

The Grange
Farm

Elms
Farm

A12

Apple Tree
Farm

Orchard
House

Redhouse
Farm

5

40

Pippin
Farm

FOLLY LA

Brockley
Wood

4

Lane
Farm

Bentley
Old Hall

C07

Clay Hall

OLD HALL LA

Bentley Long
Wood

3

Station
Farm

39

A1
1 STOCKMERS END
2 CHALKNERS CL
3 SAWYERS CL
4 LITTLE GR
5 RED SLEEVE
6 LITTLE GULLS
7 DODMANS

Capel St Mary

1 ROUNDRIDGE RD
2 JERMYNS CL
3 THE QUEECH
4 FARTHINGS WENT
5 THE SQUIRRELS

Ponder's
Grove

Pond
Hall

Bentley
Park

2

THE PIGHTLE

PENN CL

IP9

Tare
Grove

Fingery
Grove

Pond Hall Lane Tk

GLEBE END RD

LONGFIELD RD

HAMBRIDGE

BROOM WAY

OLD ACRES

PETER'S GR

LITTLE TUFTS

GREAT TUFTS

ASH GR

PENNY MEADOW

CROTCHETS CL

ROYLANDS

THORNEY RD

WINDING PIECE

BARNFIELD

GARROODS

BUTCHERS LA

Pedlar's
Grove

Church
Farm

Bentley
Hall

SCHOOL CL

SNOWCROFT

Liby

Prim Sch

THE STREET

LONDON RD

Motel

Engry
Wood

CHURCH RD

1

PAPEL CL

GATE RD

LEMBROW CL

SMY THERS CL

WANEY CL

PO

PH

WHITE HORSE

HOMEFIELD RD

PLATFIELD RD

LONG PERRY

BUS

Capel
Rig

38

9　A　B　10　C　D　11　E　F

35
16

A B C D E F

8

Copdock
Mill

Belstead Brook

BUTLEY CL
BROOKVIEW
Belstead
Bridge

ST OSYTH
HALESOWEN
NETLEY CL
DOWNSIDE CL
WINCHESTER
STOKE PARK DR
ALDERLEE

GATEKEEPER CL
FRITILLARY CL
ELLENBROOK RD
PLAYING CL
BAWDSEY CL

IP2

Alder
Carr

Ashground
Plantation

POUND LA
Belstead
Rise

OAKFIELD RD

A12

MILL LA

A12

A14

HOLLY LA
GROVE HILL

Belstead
Hall

Belstead

IP8

CHAPEL LA

Spring
Wood

Thorington
Hall

41

BLACK'S HORNS LA

Mill Poultry
Farm

Alder
Carr

A14

7

6

Blacksmith's
Corner

Street
Farm

BENTLEY LA

THE STREET

Charity
Farm

Spinney
Wood

Pannington
Hall

Hill
Covert

5

Wherstead
Wood

Pannington Hall
Cottage

40

Old Hall
Wood

Clubs
Heath

Bluegate
Farm

4

VALLEY

A137

3

Newcome
Wood

Bentley
Manor

Hubbard's Hall
Farm

Tattingstone Trout
Farm

Park
House

Road
Farm

Holbrook
Park

IP9

39

2

1

PH

WHITE HORSE HILL

SCHOOL RD

Tattingstone
White Horse

COXHALL RD

Shrub
Wood

38

LEMONS HILL

A137

12 A 13 B C 14 D E F

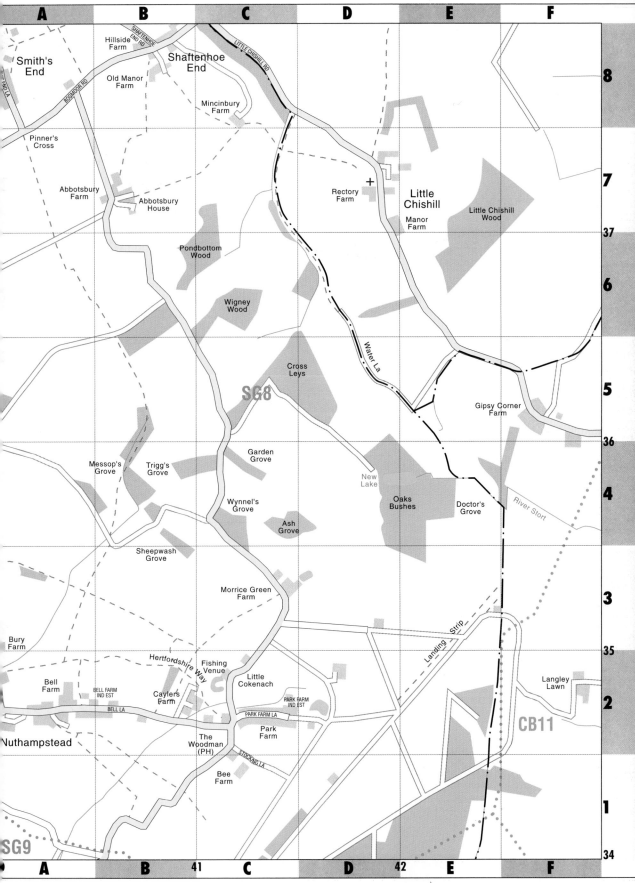

A   B   C   D   E   F

8

Smith's
End

Hillside
Farm

Old Manor
Farm

Shaftenhoe
End

Mincinbury
Farm

LITTLE CHISHILL RD

Pinner's
Cross

7

Rectory
Farm

Little
Chishill

Little Chishill
Wood

Manor
Farm

37

Abbotsbury
Farm

Abbotsbury
House

Pondbottom
Wood

6

Wigney
Wood

Water La

5

Cross
Leys

SG8

Gipsy Corner
Farm

36

Messop's
Grove

Trigg's
Grove

Garden
Grove

New
Lake

Oaks
Bushes

Doctor's
Grove

River Stort

4

Wynnel's
Grove

Ash
Grove

Sheepwash
Grove

3

Morrice Green
Farm

Landing   Strip

Bury
Farm

35

Hertfordshire Way

Fishing
Venue

Little
Cokenach

Langley
Lawn

Bell
Farm

BELL FARM
IND EST

Caylers
Farm

PARK FARM
IND EST

CB11

2

BELL LA

PARK FARM LA

Nuthampstead

The
Woodman
(PH)

STOCKING LA

Park
Farm

Bee
Farm

1

SG9

34

A B C D E F

8

Monkshole Wood

Building End

BUILDING END RD

Lower Farm

Chiswick Hall

Lower Pond Street

Hope Farm House

Upper Farm

BUILDING END RD

COMMON LA

7

SG8

Mead Bushes Wood

Upper Pond Street

37

Wicken Water

B1039

6

Harcamlow Way

Duddenhoe End Farm

Hall

Common La

Pickerton Green

High Wood

White Fria Farm

5

Roughway Wood

Oldfield Grove

Chrishall Common

36

Killem's Green

Lorking's La

4

River Stort

Grange Farm

Cosh Farm

Hall Grove

Duddenhoe Grange

CB11

PARK LA

The Hall

Harcamlow Way

3

Church Farm

THE CAUSEWAY

Hall

Upper Green

35

BULL LA

THE KANGELS

LONG LEY

2

Langley

The Bull (PH)

HIGHFIELDS

Bury Farm

Lower Green

1

WATERWICK HILL

Ford

Roper's La

New Farm

34

43 A B 44 C D 45 E F

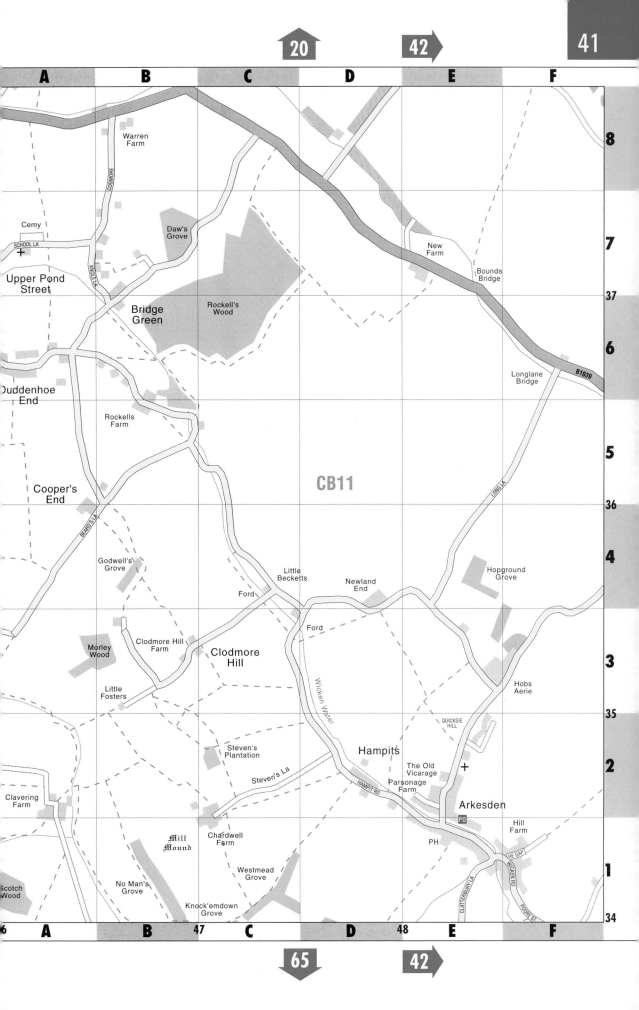

A B C D E F

8
7
37
6

Warren Farm

Cemy
SCHOOL LA
Upper Pond Street

Daw's Grove

New Farm

Bounds Bridge

Bridge Green

Rockell's Wood

Duddenhoe End

Longlane Bridge

B1039

Rockells Farm

CB11

LONG LA

Cooper's End

BEARD'S LA

5
36
4
3
35
2
1
34

Godwell's Grove

Little Becketts

Ford

Newland End

Hopground Grove

Morley Wood

Clodmore Hill Farm

Clodmore Hill

Ford

Hobs Aerie

Little Fosters

Wicken Water

QUICKSIE HILL

Steven's Plantation

Hampits

The Old Vicarage
Parsonage Farm

Steven's La

Clavering Farm

Mill Mound

Chardwell Farm

Arkesden
PO

Hill Farm

PH

THE GAP

No Man's Grove

Westmead Grove

WICKEN RD

CLATERBURY LA

PODRE ST

Scotch Wood

Knock'emdown Grove

A　　B　　C　　D　　E　　F

Bush Pasture Grove

Cups Grove

8

Mast

7

Red Leg Plantation

37

6

B1039

ROYSTON RD

CB11

5

Clanverend Farm

Clanverend Bridge

36

Duddenhoe La

4

Harcamlow Way

Long Plantation

3

35

2

BURY WATER LA

1

Severals Farm

34

The Triangle

Strawberry Close Belt

CHESTNUT AVE

B13

Cornwallis Hill

The Willows

Neville Hill

LONDON RD

The Old Vicarage

Wenden Place Farm

NATS LA

THE BEECHES

RAILWAY COTTS

STATION RD B1039

WALL RD

P

MUTLOW HILL

CHURCH ST

CROSWELL LA

PH

DUCK ST

Mutlow Farm

Wenden Hall

BEARWALDEN BSNS PK

SILV RD

Mutlow Hall

Audley End

Wendens Ambo

Norton End

Rookery Farm

ROOKERY LA

LC

Mill Farm

Bulse Farm

Mill Hill

M11

Whiteditch Farm

Tudhope Farm

WHITEDITCH LA

Newport Free Grain Sch

Nursery

BURYWATER COTTS

BURY WATER LA

TENTERFIELDS

SCHOOL LA

MEADOWCROFT

B1038

WICKEN

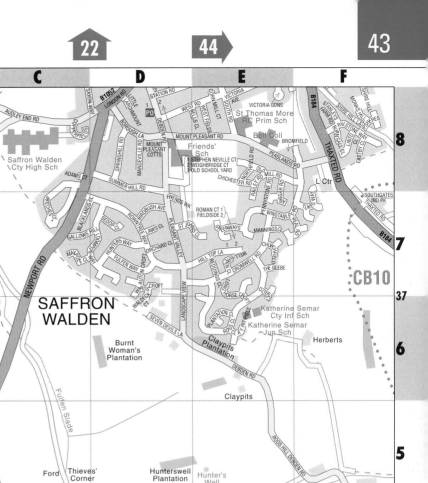

A B C D E F

43
23

8

Shire Hill Farm

SHIRE HILL LA

THE DREYS
Sewage Works

The Towers

Tiptoft Farm

Frogsgreen Farm

Bears Hall

COLE END LA

7

THAXTED RD

B184

Veerman Lodge

37

Brickkiln Leys Farm

Cole End Farm

Cole End

6

Wr Twr

Gunters

Thunderley Parsonage

The Old Pig And Whistle (PH)

COLE END LA

Six Acre Wood

Harrison's Wood

5

Thunderley Hall

CB10

36

Crowney Wood

THAXTED RD

4

New House Farm

Peverel's Wood

Abbots Manor

Parsonage Farm

3

Harleyfield Grove

Pamphillions

Purton End

PARSONAGE L

35

Airfield (dis)

WIMBISH WLK

H WLK

WALDEN AVE

2

Newhouse Farm

CB11

Carver Barracks

ROWNEY AVE

PINKNEY CL

DEBDEN DR

Sewage Works

B1

BROAD OAKS CL

PEVERELS RD

PO

Debden Manor

Ricketts

Freemans

Elder Street

Burnt House

1

WATER LA

IVY TODD LA

34

43
68

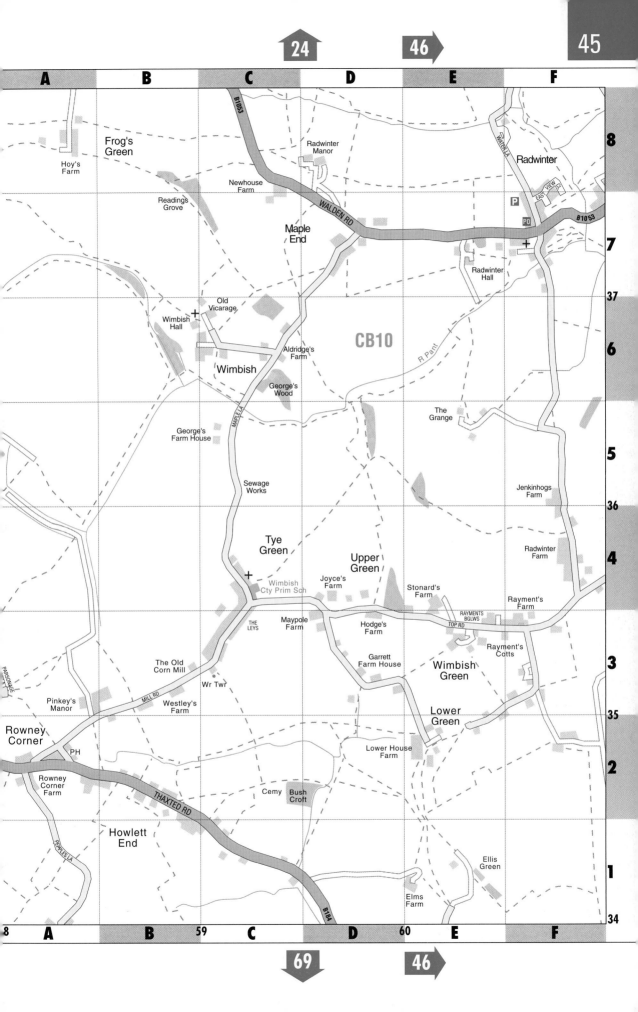

A **B** **C** **D** **E** **F**

WINCELOW HALL RD

HILL RD

B1054

HIGH ST

CHURCH RD

Church Farm

8

Shelland's Farm

Hill Farm

B1054

LONGCROFT

B1055

Equestrian Ctr

B1054

Pant Brook House

Sharp Crofts Wood

Prentice's Farm

7

Hill Farm

Moss's Farm

B1053

PH

37

Anso Corner Farm

6

B1055

Howses

Anser Gallows Farm

5

Mortlock's Farm

Clay Wood

River Pant

CB10

Long Thatch

36

TOP RD

B10

4

Little Brockholds Farm

Different Part Grove

Sparrow's Hall

Moor End Farm

Great Brockholds

Goddards Farm

3

Ivytodd's Farm

Barleyfields

Byeball's Farm

35

Giffords Farm

Longmead

TINDON END RD

BUSH RD

Broadfields

2

Collins Cross

The Dovehouse

Bush Cottage

BUSH LA

Mill Farm House

B10

Blackhouse Farm

South Fields

Hole Farm

Grassy Grove

Tindon Manor

1

Tindon End

Broadcroft Grove

Bush Farm

B1051

Market Farm

34

61   **A**   62   **B**   **C**   **D**   63   **E**   **F**

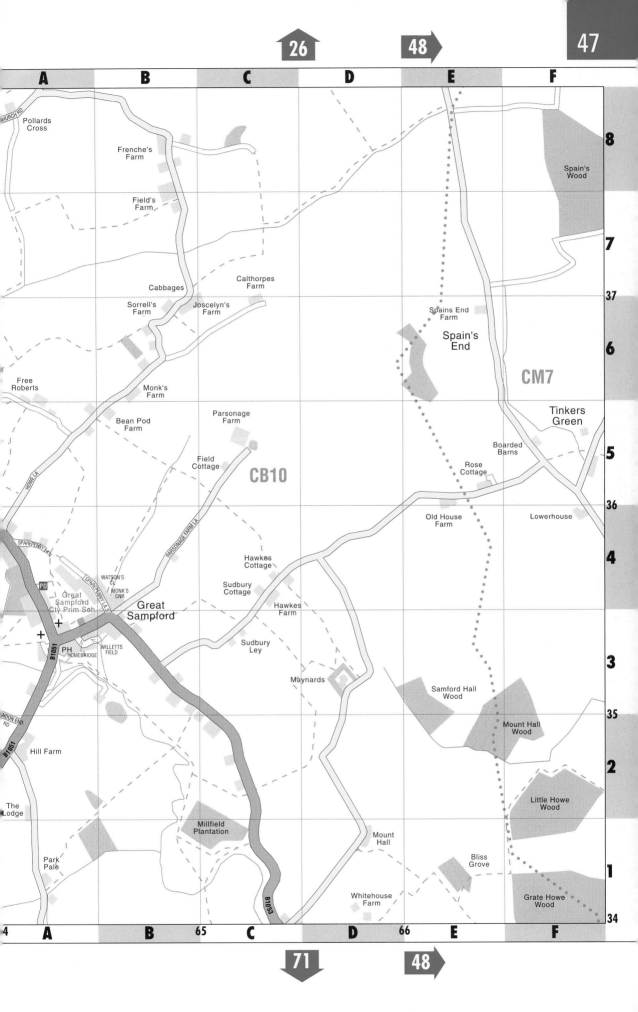

A B C D E F

8

7

37

6

CM7

5

36

4

3

35

2

1

34

Pollards Cross

Frenche's Farm

Field's Farm

Cabbages

Calthorpes Farm

Sorrell's Farm

Joscelyn's Farm

Spains End Farm

Spain's End

Spain's Wood

Free Roberts

Monk's Farm

Bean Pod Farm

Parsonage Farm

Field Cottage

CB10

Tinkers Green

Boarded Barns

Rose Cottage

Old House Farm

Lowerhouse

SPAREPENNY LAN

PO

HOWE LA

PARSONAGE FARM LA

SPAREPENNY LA S

WATSON'S CL

MONK'S CNR

Great Sampford Cty Prim Sch

Great Sampford

Hawkes Cottage

Sudbury Cottage

Hawkes Farm

PH

HOMEBRIDGE

WILLETTS FIELD

Sudbury Ley

Maynards

Samford Hall Wood

Mount Hall Wood

B1051

NDON END RD

B1051

Hill Farm

The Lodge

Millfield Plantation

Mount Hall

Little Howe Wood

Park Pale

Bliss Grove

Grate Howe Wood

Whitehouse Farm

B1053

A **B** **C** **D** **E** **F**

8

CO9

Little Nortons

Old Robin

Great Nortons

CORNISH-HALL END RD

Lopham's Farm

Rockall's Farm

7

Bushy Grove

Howsey Wood

Springlette

37

Shore Hall

The Grove

Sewage Works

Rivett's Farm

6

White House Farm

MILLERS ROW

Briar Cottages

HEARDS LA

PH

Cornish Hall End

Heard's Farm

HEARD'S LA

Hole Farm

5

CM7

Whitleys

36

Cornish Hall

Jekyll's Farm

4

JEKYLL'S LA

Unwin's Farm

Hobtoe's Farm

3

New Cover

Little London

MILL LA

35

Rook Hall

Yeldhams

2

Howe Farm

Obourne's Farm

Howe Street

1

Spainshall Farm

Bumpstead Lodge

B1057

Tridgate Ley

Spain's Hall

34

B1057

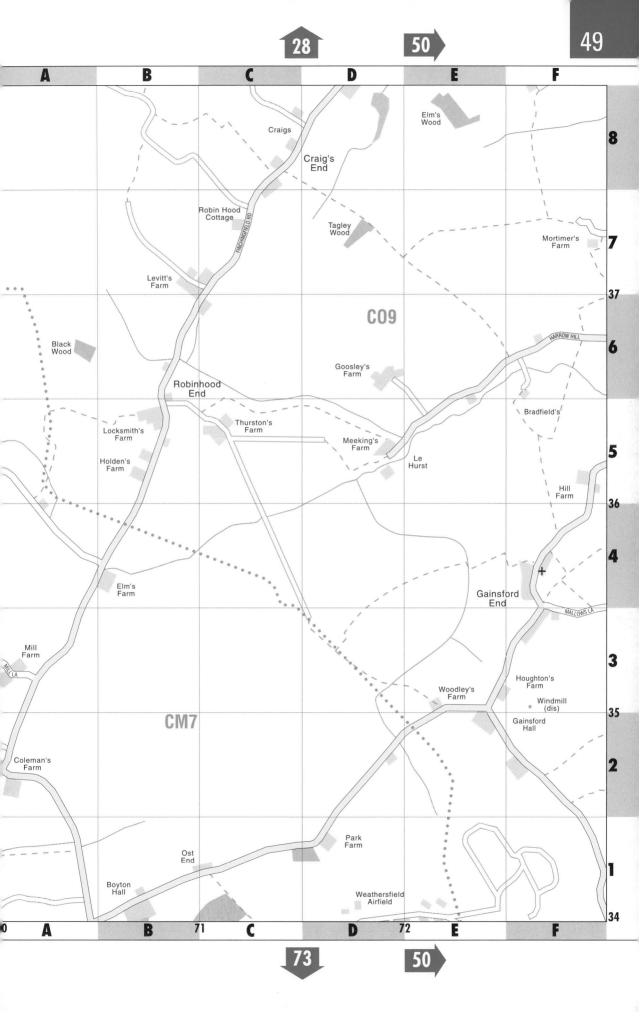

A B C D E F

Elm's
Wood

Craigs

Craig's
End

Robin Hood
Cottage

Tagley
Wood

Mortimer's
Farm

FINCHINGFIELD RD

Levitt's
Farm

CO9

HARROW HILL

Black
Wood

Goosley's
Farm

Robinhood
End

Bradfield's

Locksmith's
Farm

Thurston's
Farm

Meeking's
Farm

Le
Hurst

Holden's
Farm

Hill
Farm

Elm's
Farm

+

Gainsford
End

MALLOWS LA

Mill
Farm

MILL LA

CM7

Houghton's
Farm

Woodley's
Farm

Windmill
(dis)

35

Gainsford
Hall

Coleman's
Farm

Park
Farm

Ost
End

Boyton
Hall

Weathersfield
Airfield

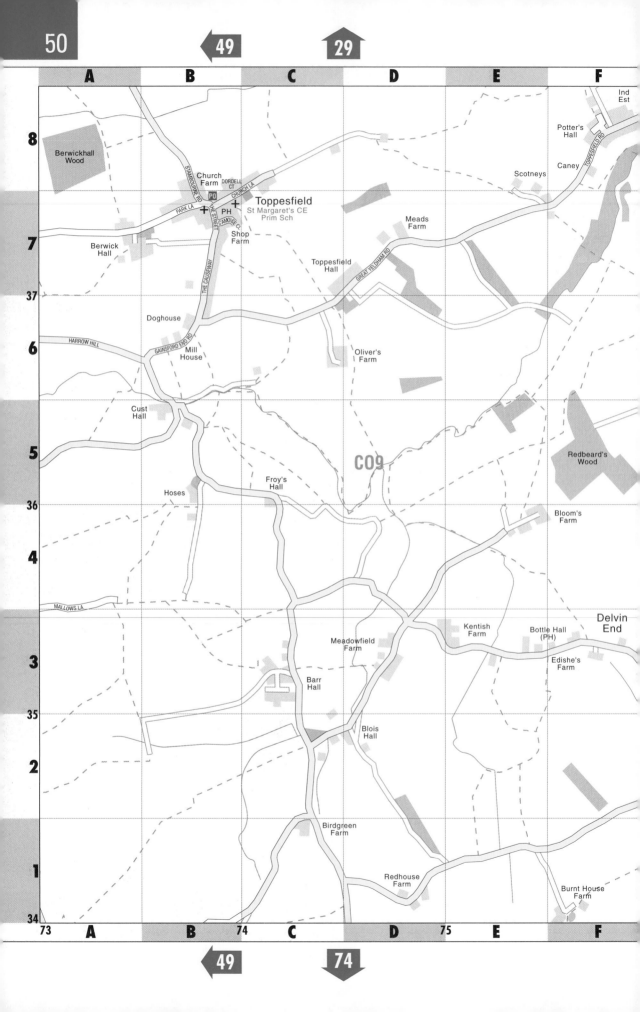

A　　B　　C　　D　　E　　F

8

Berwickhall Wood

Church Farm
STAMBOURNE RD
DORDELL CT
PARK LA
PO
CHURCH LA
THE STREET
PH
CAMOISE CL
Toppesfield
St Margaret's CE
Prim Sch

Potter's Hall
Ind Est

Scotneys
Caney
TOPPESFIELD RD

Berwick Hall
Shop Farm

Meads Farm

7

THE CAUSEWAY
Toppesfield Hall
GREAT YELDHAM RD

37

Doghouse
GAINSFORD END RD

HARROW HILL

Mill House

6

Oliver's Farm

Cust Hall

Redbeard's Wood

5

CO9

Hoses

Froy's Hall

Bloom's Farm

36

4

MALLOWS LA

Kentish Farm

Bottle Hall (PH)

Delvin End

3

Meadowfield Farm

Barr Hall

Edishe's Farm

35

Blois Hall

2

Birdgreen Farm

1

Redhouse Farm

Burnt House Farm

34

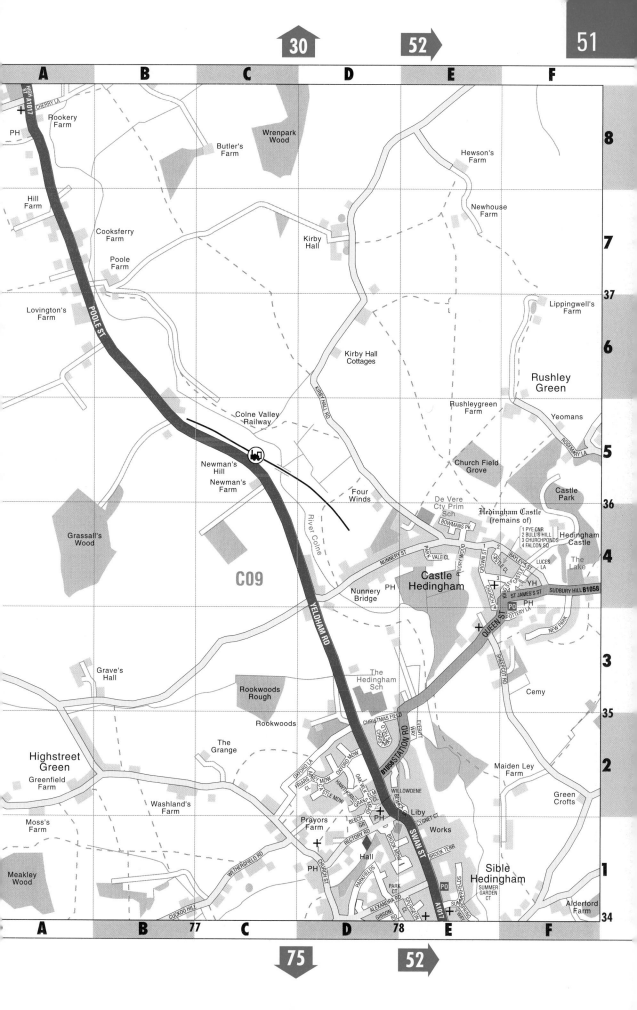

A B C D E F

8

Ridley's Wood

Delvyn's Lane

Delvyn's Farm

CHURCH ST

Audley End

PH

Edeys Farm

Rectory Farm

7

37

Parkgate Farm

DELVYN'S LA

Crouch House

Great Lodge Farm

Branwhite's Grove

The Moat

6

B10

C09

Lawrence's Farm

5

Pannells Ash Farm

Odewells

Rosemary Farm

36

SUDBURY RD

Pantile Cottage

Kendallscroft Grove

Little Chelmshoe House

ROSEMARY LA

4

B1058

ST JAMES'S ST

Bayham Hall

New Barn

Little Lodge Farm

Chelmshoe House Farm

3

Monks Lodge Farm

Monks Lodge

35

Hosden's Farm

MONKS LODGE RD

2

St Giles CE Prim Sch

Link Hills

ST GILES CL

Hopwell's Farm

Great Maplestead

ST GILES COTTS

Lucking Street

Luckinghouse Farm

1

CHURCH RD

Little Lodge Farm

Purls Cottage

Barrett's Hall

34

79 A B 80 C D 81 E F

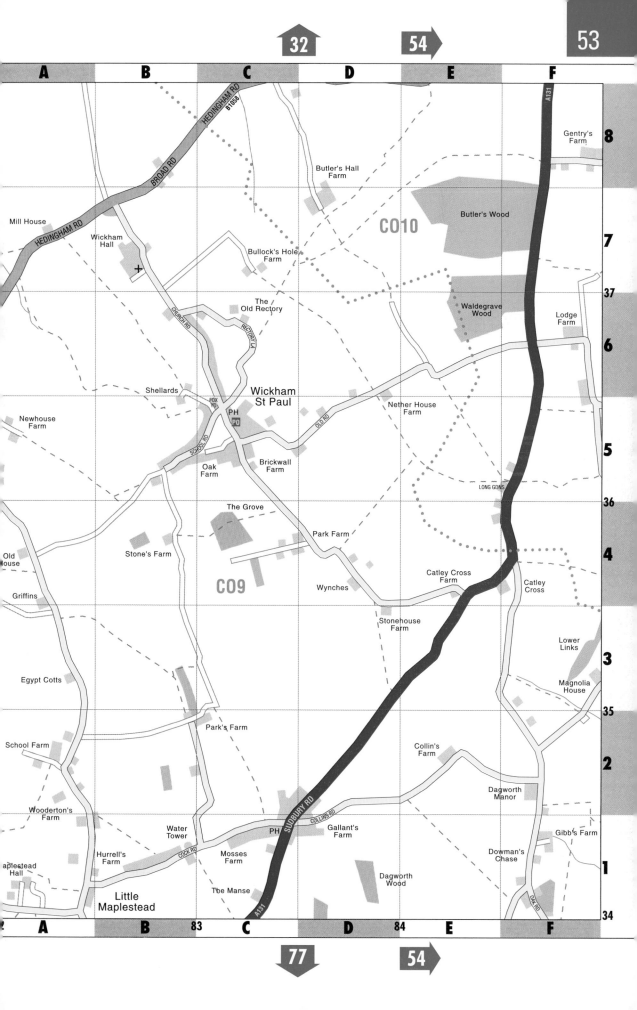

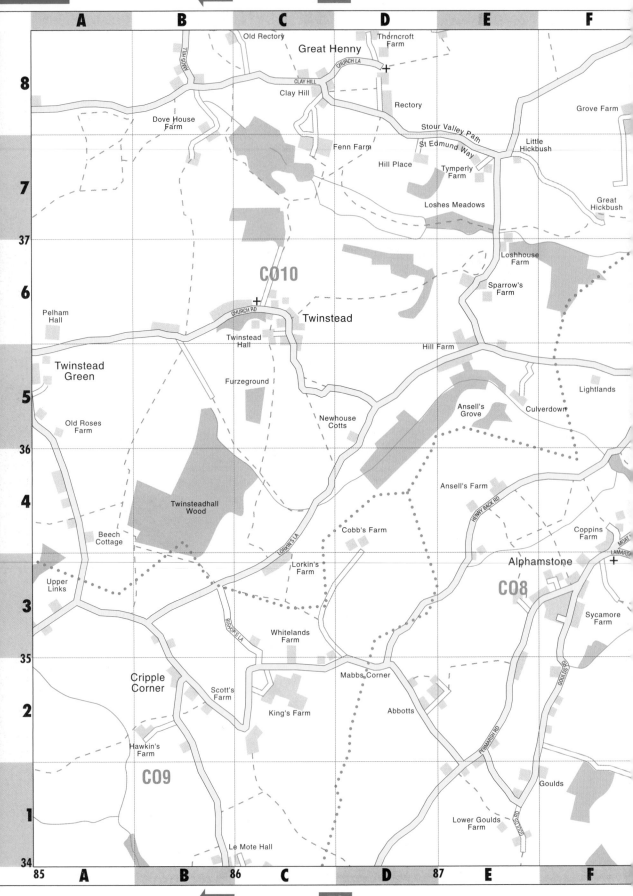

A B C D E F

8

7

37

6

5

36

4

3

35

2

1

34

85 A B 86 C D 87 E F

Old Rectory

Thorncroft
Farm

Great Henny

CHURCH LA

CLAY HILL

Clay Hill

Rectory

Stour Valley Path

St Edmund Way

Little
Hickbush

Grove Farm

AMOS HILL

Dove House
Farm

Fenn Farm

Hill Place

Tymperly
Farm

Loshes Meadows

Great
Hickbush

CO10

CHURCH RD

Twinstead

Hill Farm

Loshhouse
Farm

Sparrow's
Farm

Pelham
Hall

Twinstead
Hall

Twinstead
Green

Furzeground

Newhouse
Cotts

Ansell's
Grove

Culverdown

Lightlands

Old Roses
Farm

Twinsteadhall
Wood

Ansell's Farm

HENNY BACK RD

Coppins
Farm

LAMARSH

Alphamstone

Beech
Cottage

LORKIN'S LA

Cobb's Farm

CO8

Sycamore
Farm

Upper
Links

Lorkin's
Farm

GOULDS RD

Whitelands
Farm

Mabbs Corner

BISHOP'S LA

Cripple
Corner

Scott's
Farm

King's Farm

Abbotts

PEBMARSH RD

Goulds

Hawkin's
Farm

CO9

Lower Goulds
Farm

RUSTLINGS

Le Mote Hall

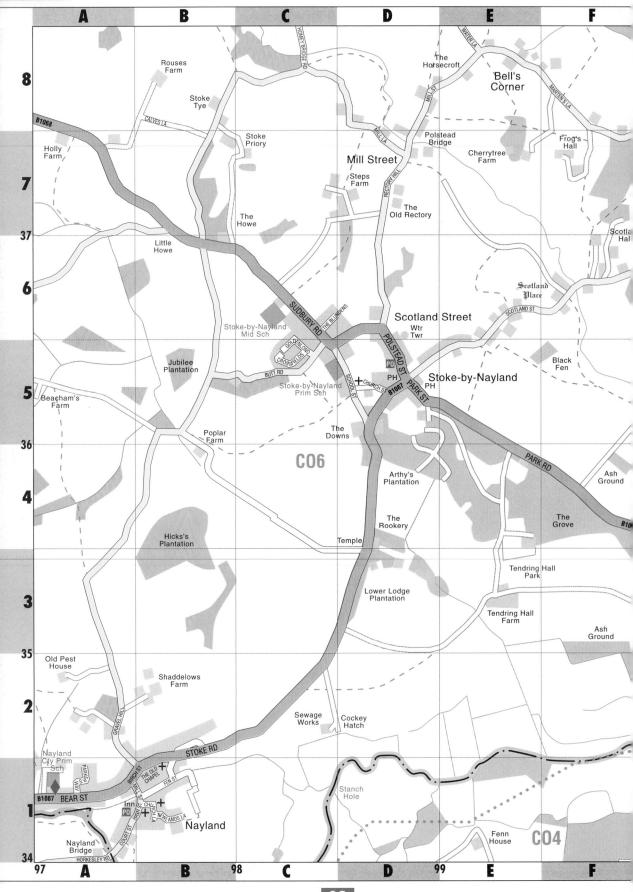

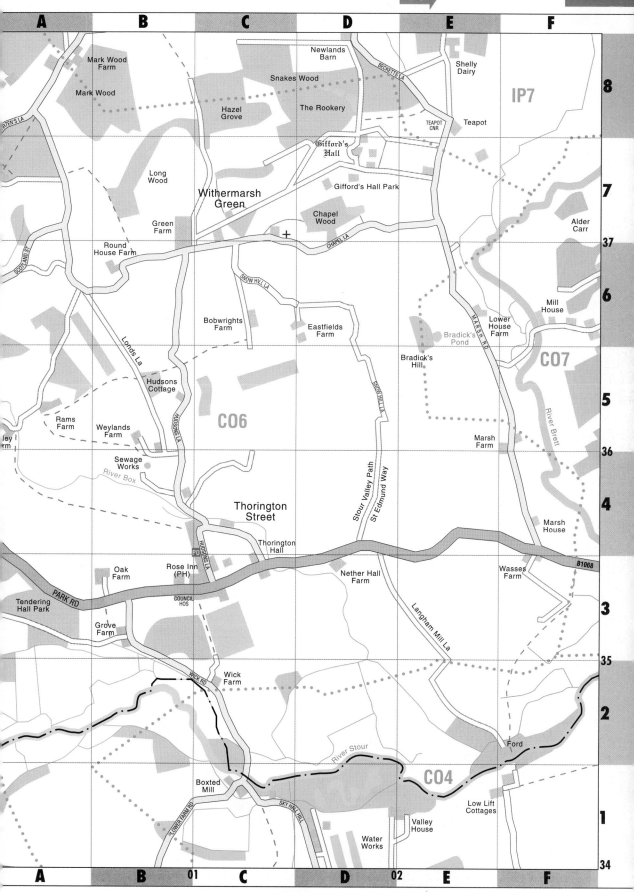

A　B　C　D　E　F

Mark Wood Farm

Newlands Barn

Snakes Wood

Shelly Dairy

BECKETTS LA

Mark Wood

Hazel Grove

The Rookery

IP7

TEAPOT CNR

Teapot

Gifford's Hall

Long Wood

Gifford's Hall Park

Withermarsh Green

7

Green Farm

Chapel Wood

Alder Carr

37

Round House Farm

CHAPEL LA

SCOTLAND ST

Londs La

SNOW HILL LA

Bobwrights Farm

Eastfields Farm

MARSH RD

Lower House Farm

Mill House

6

Bradick's Pond

CO7

Hudsons Cottage

Bradick's Hill

River Brett

5

Rams Farm

Weylands Farm

HUDSONS LA

CO6

Marsh Farm

36

ley Farm

rm

Sewage Works

River Box

Thorington Street

Stour Valley Path

St Edmund Way

SNOW HILL LA

Marsh House

4

Thorington Hall

Wasses Farm

B1068

Oak Farm

Rose Inn (PH)

Nether Hall Farm

PARK RD

Tendering Hall Park

POWS LA

HUDSONS LA

Langham Mill La

3

Grove Farm

COUNCIL HOS

35

Wick Rd

Wick Farm

WICK RD

2

River Stour

Ford

Boxted Mill

CO4

Low Lift Cottages

LOWER FARM RD

SKY HALL HILL

1

Water Works

Valley House

34

57

A   B   C   D   E   F

8

Capelgrove

Springhill

Wenham Place

Sewage
Works

The Robins

Hill House
Farm

7

Wenham
Hill

Orchard
Farm

Manor
House

Bradfield
Farm

Old London Rd

IP9

37

Three Elms

Lattinford
Bridge

Boydland
Farm

6

Oaks Farm

Brick Kiln
Farm

Lattinford
Hill

Hill Farm

Highfields

Hassocks

Chaplain's
Farm

The
Four Sisters

5

Stratford
House

FOUR SISTERS

Kiln
Cottage

CO7

Woodgates
Farm

Hustlers
Grove

36

Rookery

Road Covert

HUGHES
CNR

High Trees
Farm

QUINTONS
CNR

Rookery
Farm

4

Foxhall
Covert

HUGHES RD

The
Lodge

Foxhall
Fields

East Bergholt
High Sch

Parkfield

Lodge
Plantation

Allen's
Farm

GASTON END

HEATH RD

L Ctr

3

Ackworth
House

East Bergholt
CE Prim Sch

Richardson's
Farm

Elm Farm

Gatton House
Farm

East Bergholt

35

Old Mill
House

EAST END RD

Dead La

Cemy

Willow
Farm

Highlands

Warren
House

2

Vale Farm

PO

GANDISH RD

MILL RD

CEMETERY LA

THE STREET

RECTORY HILL

GANDISH CL

WHITE HORSE RD

East Bergholt
Place Gdns

Warren Wood

1

Fishpond
Wood

Old Hall

PH

BURNT OAK
CNR

MANNINGTREE RD

B1070

34

59
35

A B C D E F

8

7

37

6

5

36

4

35

3

2

1

34

09 A B 10 C D 11 E F

RED LA
LONDON RD
FRIARS RD
A12

White Horse Farm

Grove Farm

POTASH LA
POTASH COTTS
Falstaf Manor

Potash

A12
Bush Farm

Great Gilberts Farm
BLUEGATE LA
Tawney's Farm

Windy Farm

CHURCH RD
Bentley CE Prim Sch

OLD LONDON RD
Roynton Hall
Bluegate Farm

Bentley

CASE LA
PH
THE LINK
Woodfield

EAST MILL GN
SOUTH VIEW GN
MILL GN
WEST
STATION RD
HIGHFIELDS

LC

Holly Wood

IP9

LINK LA
GROVE RD
PO
SILVER LEYS

Dingle Dell

Martin's Hill Cottage

Bentley Grove

Teapot Hill

Great Martin's Hill Wood

Kenmure

Hazel Shrub

King's Field

Martin's Glen

Dodnash Wood

Dobnash Priory Farm

Coppery Farm

Little Dobnash Farm

Little Charles New Plantation

Dobnash Fruit Farm

The Grange

CO7

Meadow Cottages

Manor Farm

Alder Carr

Keeble's Grove

CO11

EAST END RD
PH
MISSION LA
FISHER'S LA
THE ELMS

GRAVEL PIT LA

Home Farm

Woodlands Farm

East End

PARK RD
BROOM KNOLL

SLOUGH RD

THE POPLARS
IPSWICH RD
A13

Park House

Brantham
Church Farm

JIMMY'S LA

Barn Hazel

BRANTHAM HILL A137
ACACIA CT
SYCAMORE WAY
BIRCH DR
BLENHEIM CL
CEDAR CO
QUINCE
CHURCH LA
RECTORY LA

Brantham Glebe

THE CHASE

Brookland Farm
PO
SCHOOL LA
VALLEY
ELM CL

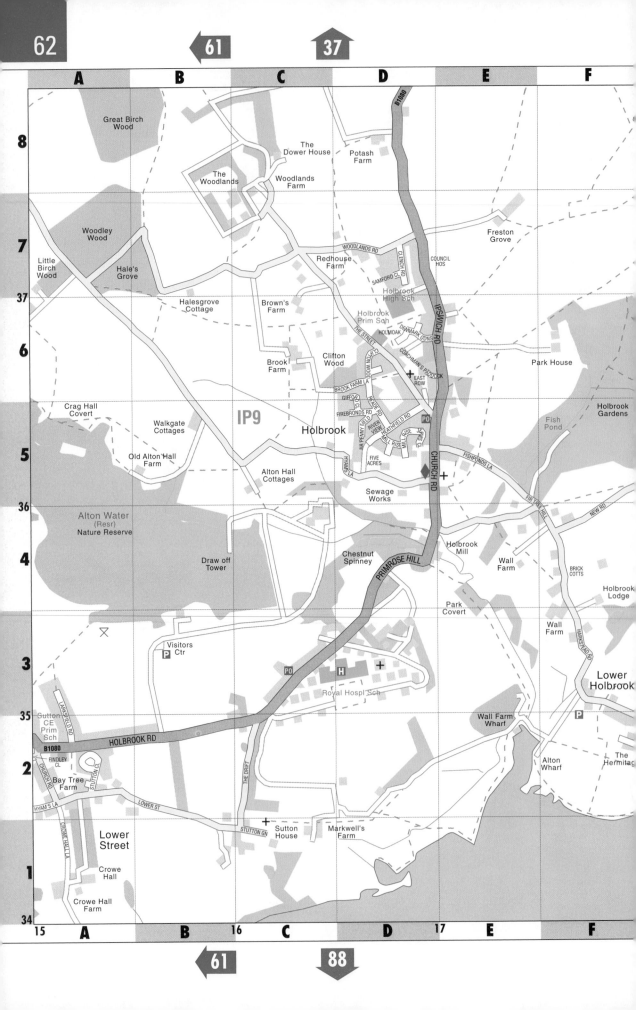

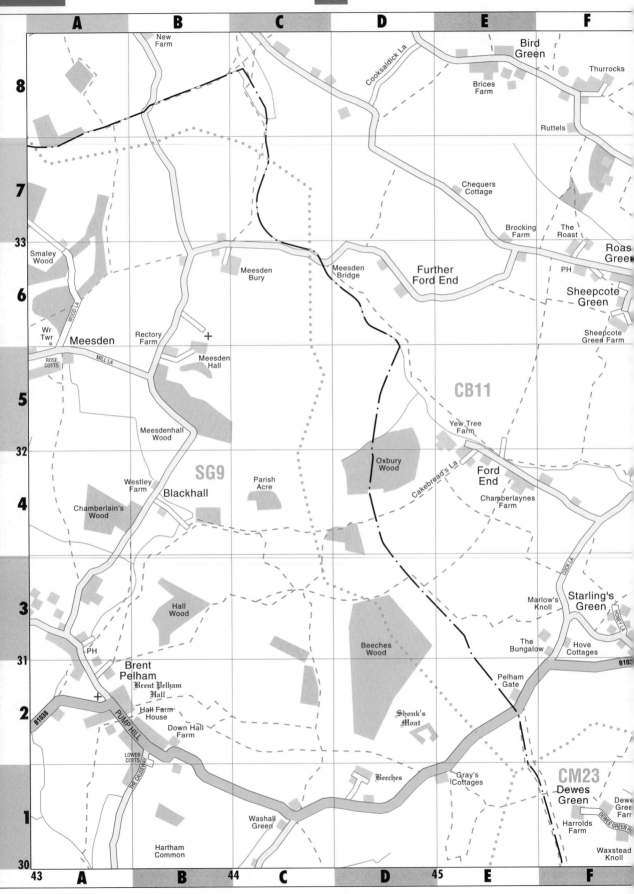

A B C D E F

8

7

33

6

5

32

4

3

31

2

1

30

A B C D E F

43 44 45

New Farm

Cooksaldick La

Bird Green

Thurrocks

Brices Farm

Ruttels

Chequers Cottage

Brocking Farm

The Roast

Roas Green

Smaley Wood

Meesden Bury

Meesden Bridge

Further Ford End

PH

Sheepcote Green

WOOD LA

Wr Twr

Meesden

Rectory Farm

Meesden Hall

Sheepcote Green Farm

ROSE COTTS

MILL LA

CB11

Meesdenhall Wood

Yew Tree Farm

Cakebread's La

Ford End

Westley Farm

SG9

Parish Acre

Oxbury Wood

Chamberlaynes Farm

Blackhall

Chamberlain's Wood

COCK LA

Hall Wood

Beeches Wood

Marlow's Knoll

Starling's Green

HONEY LA

PH

The Bungalow

Hove Cottages

B103

Brent Pelham

Pelham Gate

Brent Pelham Hall

Hall Farm House

Shonk's Moat

CM23

B1038

PUMP HILL

Down Hall Farm

Beeches

Gray's Cottages

Dewes Green

LOWER COTTS

THE CAUSEWAY

Washall Green

Harrolds Farm

Dewes Green Farm

DEWES GREEN RD

Hartham Common

Waxstead Knoll

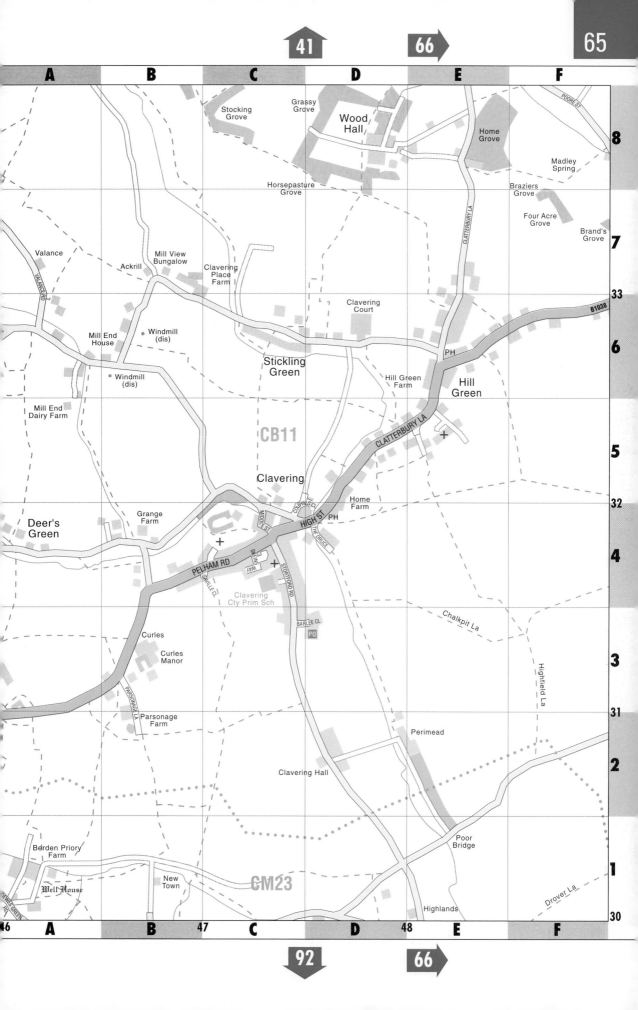

A   B   C   D   E   F

8

Stocking Grove
Grassy Grove
Wood Hall
Home Grove
Madley Spring
Horsepasture Grove
Braziers Grove
Four Acre Grove
Brand's Grove

7

Valance
Mill View Bungalow
Ackrill
Clavering Place Farm
Clavering Court
CLATTERBURY LA
B1038

33

VALANCE RD
Mill End House
Windmill (dis)
Stickling Green
Clavering Court
Hill Green Farm
PH
Hill Green

6

Mill End Dairy Farm
Windmill (dis)
CB11
CLATTERBURY LA

5

Clavering

Deer's Green
Grange Farm
COLDPITS CL
MIDDLE ST
HIGH ST
Home Farm
PH
THE DRUCE

32

4

PELHAM RD
SKEINS WAY
SAVILLE CL
STORTFORD RD
Clavering Cty Prim Sch
Chalkpit La

Curles
Curles Manor
BARLEE CL
PO
Highfield La

3

PARSONAGE LA
Parsonage Farm
Perimead

31

Clavering Hall

2

Berden Priory Farm
Poor Bridge

REVES GREEN RD
Well House
New Town
CM23
Highlands
Drover La

1

30

A   B   C   D   E   F

46   47   48

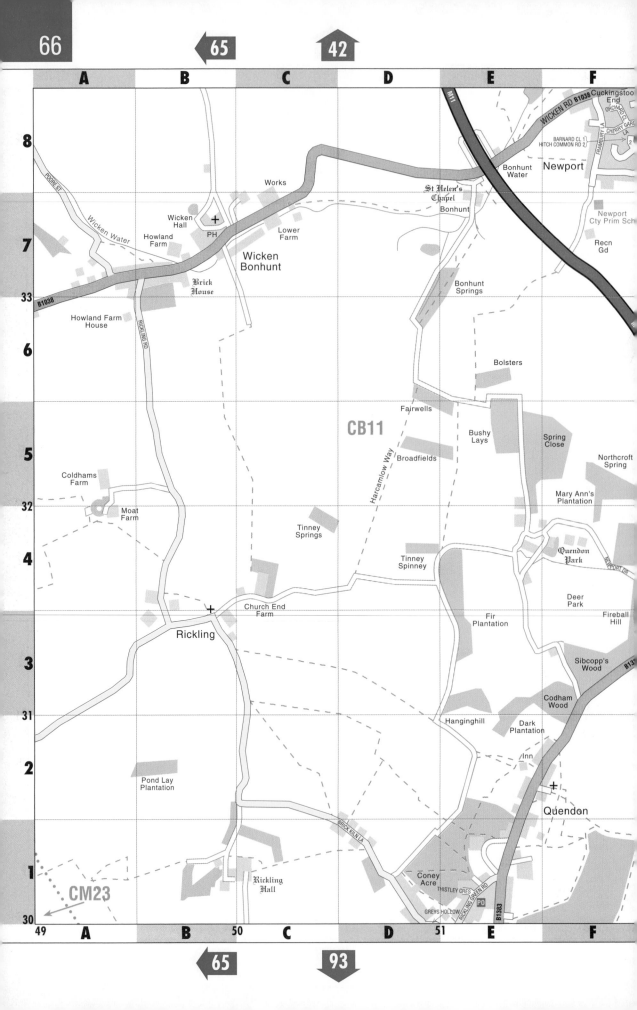

8

7

33

6

5

32

4

3

31

2

1

30

A B C D E F

Wicken Water

POORE ST

B1038

Howland Farm House

RICKLING RD

Coldhams Farm

Moat Farm

Pond Lay Plantation

CM23

Howland Farm

Wicken Hall

PH

Brick House

Works

Lower Farm

Wicken Bonhunt

Tinney Springs

Church End Farm

Rickling

Rickling Hall

BRICK KILN LA

M11

St Helen's Chapel
Bonhunt

Bonhunt Springs

Fairwells

Harcamlow Way

CB11

Broadfields

Tinney Spinney

Bushy Lays

Fir Plantation

Hanginghill

Coney Acre

Greys Hollow

THISTLEY CRES

RICKLING GREEN RD

PO

B1383

WICKEN RD B1038

Cuckingstoo End

ORCHARD CL

CHERRY GARD

FRAMBURY LA

CHERRY LA

BARNARD CL 1
HITCH COMMON RD 2

2

Newport

Bonhunt Water

Newport Cty Prim Sch

Recn Gd

Bolsters

Spring Close

Northcroft Spring

Mary Ann's Plantation

Quendon Park

NEWPORT DR

Deer Park

Fireball Hill

Sibcopp's Wood

B13

Codham Wood

Dark Plantation

Inn

Quendon

49 A B 50 C D 51 E F

A B C D E F

8

7

33

6

32

5

4

3

31

2

1

30

BULLFIELDS
B1383
HIGH ST
POND CROSS FARM
STATION RD
1 CHERRY GARDEN LA
2 CHESTNUT CT
3 CHAPEL LA
4 POND CROSS WAY
5 POND CROSS COTTS
6 FRAMBURY LA
Newport
DEBDEN RD
Harcamlow Way

Dean's Grove
Ringers Farmhouse
Ringers Barn
Ringers
Hanging Grove
Harcamlow Way
Debden Park

Chalk Farm
Newport Pond
THE SPANNEY
LONDON RD

Pig's Parlour
Horseley Wood
Waldgraves
Cabbage Wood
Yewtree Plantation

CB11
Shiptons Farm
Park Wood
Dunstables
ROCK END LA

River Cam or Granta
LC
Springhill
WELLS MEAD

Mast
Prior's Hall Barn
CHURCH LA
SOUTH GN
Widdington Hall
Widdington
Swaynes Hall
PH
Martins Farm
HAMEL WAY
HIGH ST
Mole Hall Wildlife Park
MOLE HALL LA

NORTH HALL RD
HOLLOW RD
CRABTREE HILL
HOLLOW RD
WOOD END
Wr Twr
CORNELLS LA
LC
Newlands Farm

Broom Wood
High Wood
Brickclamp Spring

London Jack Wood
LC
Prior's Wood

M11
North Hall
Jock Farm
Little Henham Hall
Little Henham
Little Henham Lodge
River Cam or Granta
CM22

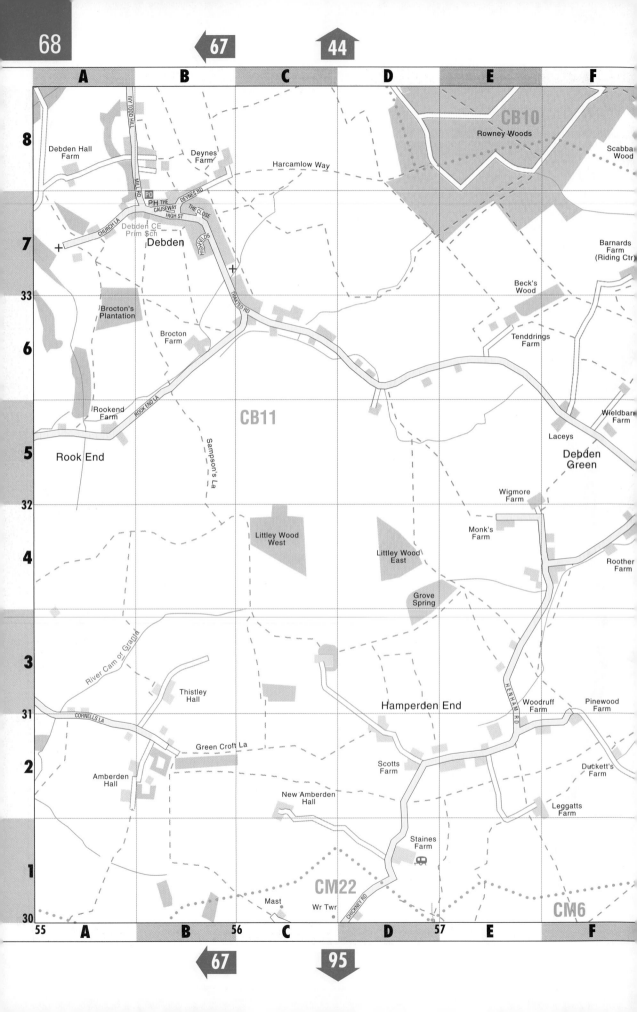

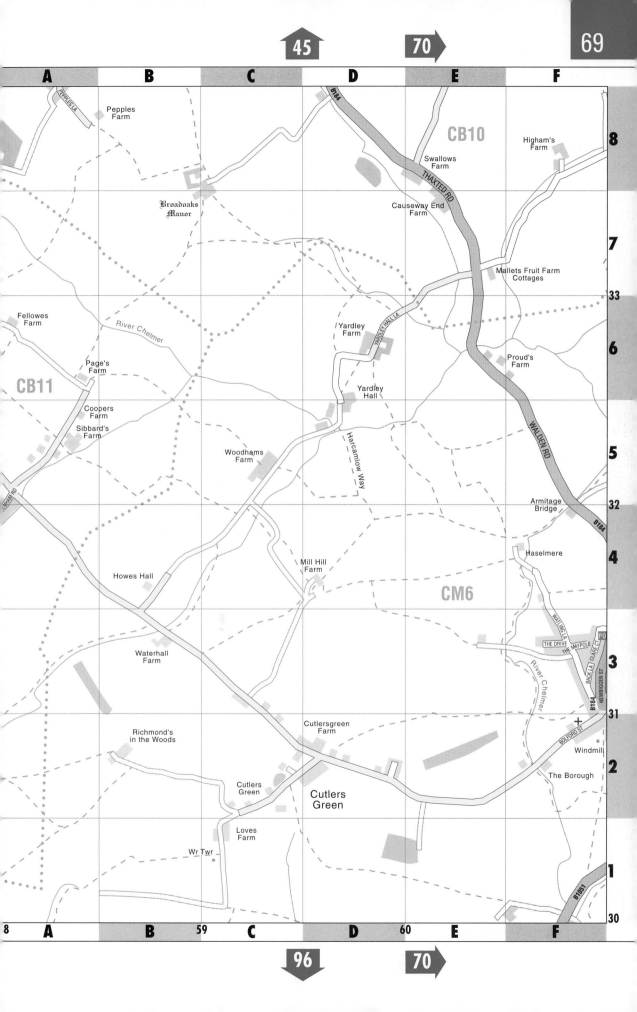

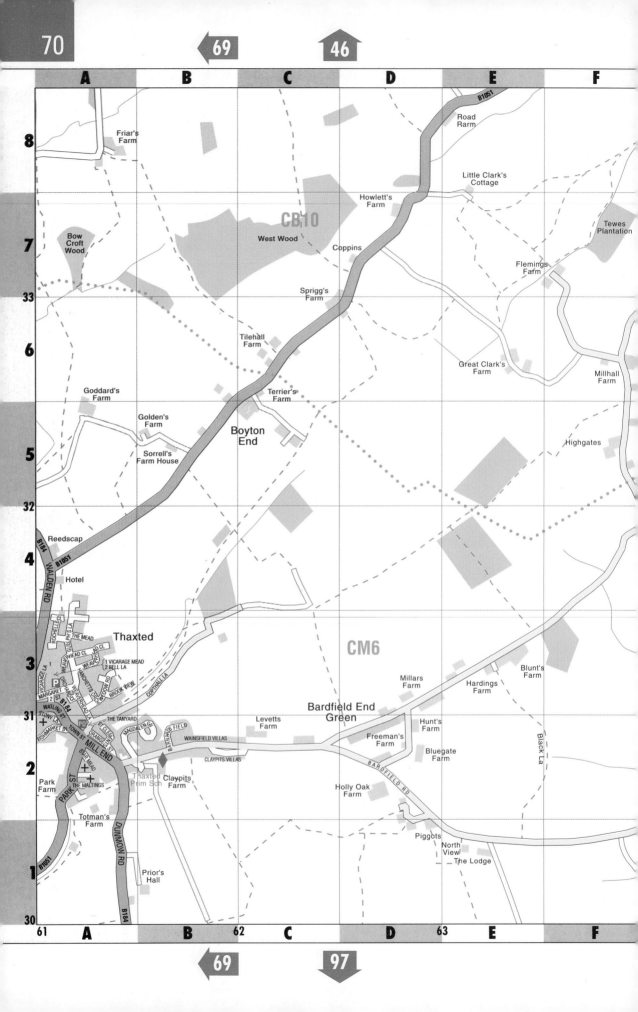

A   B   C   D   E   F

8   Friar's Farm

Bow Croft Wood

7   CB10

West Wood   Road Rarm

Little Clark's Cottage

Howlett's Farm

Coppins   Tewes Plantation

33   Flemings Farm

Sprigg's Farm

6   Tilehall Farm   Great Clark's Farm   Millhall Farm

Goddard's Farm   Terrier's Farm

Golden's Farm   Boyton End   Highgates

5   Sorrell's Farm House

32   Reedscap

B1051

4   WALDEN RD   B1051

Hotel

ROCHELLE CL   THE MEAD

Thaxted   CM6

WEAVERHEAD CL   CL   1 VICARAGE MEAD   Blunt's Farm

3   WEAVER   MEAD CL   2 BELL LA   Millars Farm   Hardings Farm

HANCHETTS ORCH   MEADOW RD   BROOK VIEW   COPTHALL LA

MARGARET   ORCHARD CL   Bardfield End Green

31   THE TANYARD   Hunt's Farm

FISHMARKET ST   MAGDALEN GR   Levetts Farm   Freeman's Farm   Black La

ORANGE'S ST   BARNARDS FIELD   WAINSFIELD VILLAS   Bluegate Farm

2   MILL END   CLAYPITS VILLAS   BARDFIELD RD

Park Farm   Thaxted Prim Sch   Claypits Farm   Holly Oak Farm

THE MALTINGS   Piggots   North View

Totman's Farm   The Lodge

1   B1051   Prior's Hall

DUNMOW RD

30   B184

61   A   B   62   C   D   63   E   F

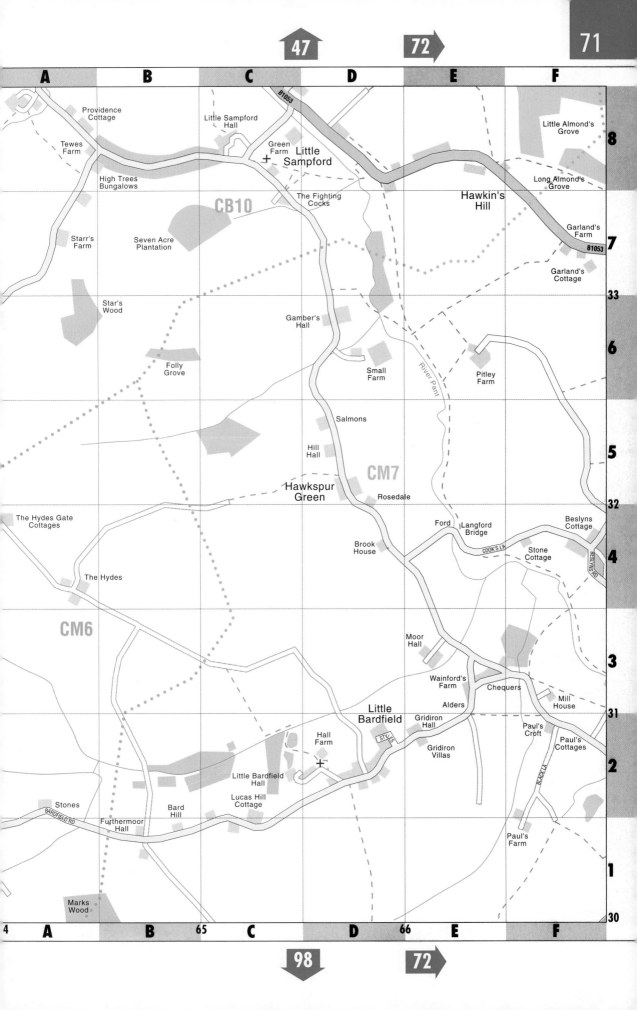

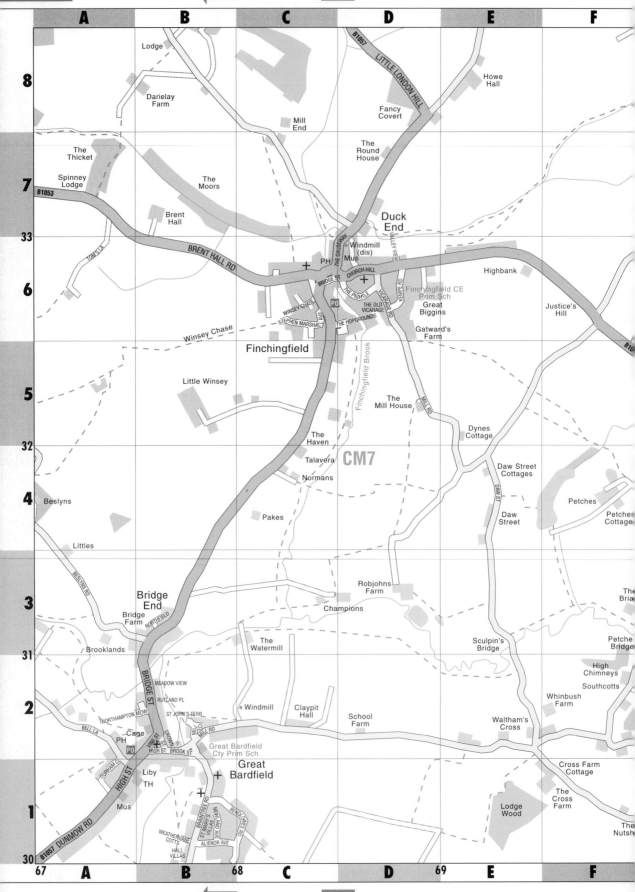

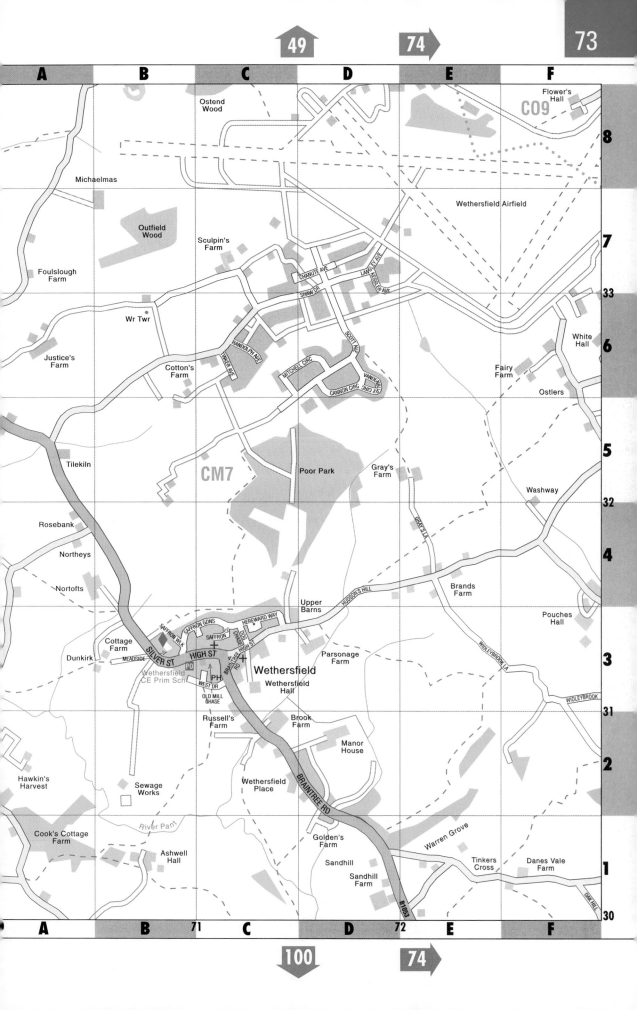

A B C D E F

8

Burnt House Farm

Welcome Slough Farm

Tattersall's Farm

Wethersfield Airfield

Morris Green

Finch's Farm

Almshouse Green

Moss Farm

7

Deek's Farm

SUGAR LA

Sugar Lane Farm

Barnard's Farm

33

Whitehall Farm

Oak House

Runalong Farm

6

Upper Wright's Farm

CO9

Runalong Wood

Thorley Grove

Thorley's Farm

Tredgell's Wood

Cherrytree Farm

5

New Barns

Littley Wood

32

4

Brickkiln Green

CM7

Lower Green

Patten's Wood

Readings

3

Lower Green

School Green

Lealands

Patten's Farm

Hawks Wood

Elms Farm

The Readings Spinney

31

PH

Blackmore End

SYERS FIELD

New Plantation

Baker's Farm

2

Owl's Hall

WIDLEYBROOK

WIDLEYBROOK LA

HYDE LA

Shragg's Wood

1

Hyde Farm

HYDE LA

Summer's Hall

FOUR ASHES

Waver's Farm

Shinborough

30

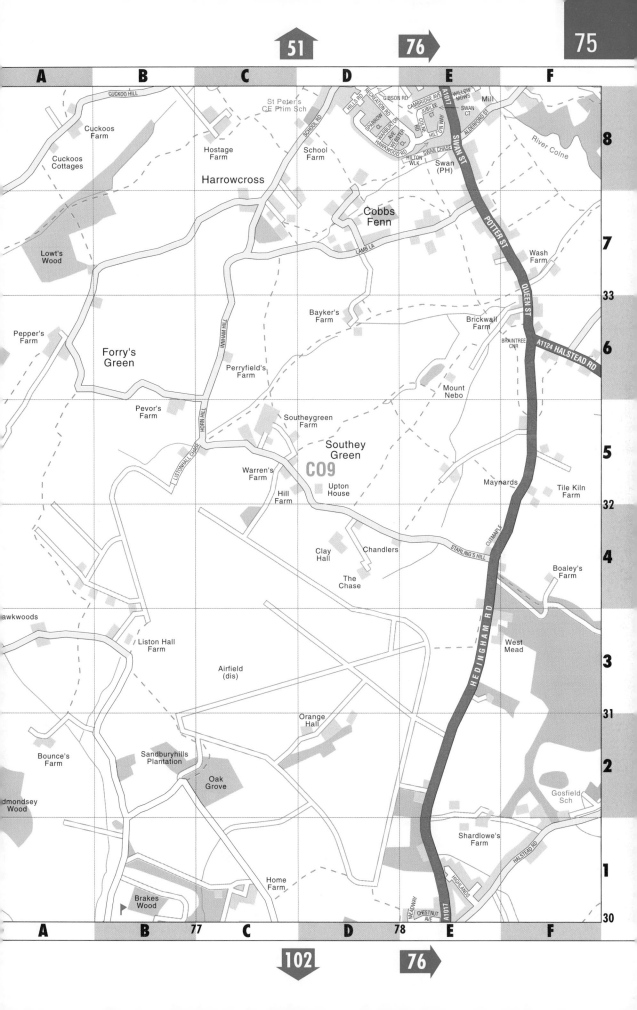

A | B | C | D | E | F

8

Purlshill
Purlshill
Plantation

Barretts
Hall

Toldishall
Cottages

Mill
Farm

7

Hull's Mill
Farm

Chestnut
Grove

Mill

33

Dynes
Hall

Wallace's
Farm

Dog House
Grove

Pearman's
Hill

6

A1124
HALSTEAD RD

Bennett's
Farm

Bennett's
Park

Sewage
Works

Foxborough
Hills Farm

Fitz John's
Farm

5

CO9

Foxborough

Hepworth
Hall

DOE'S CNR

Fitz John's
Grove

32

Brook Street
Farm

HOWE CHASE

The
Howe

4

HEDINGHAM RD

ASHLONG GR

Bradley's
House

River Colne

Wash
Farm

CHURCHILL AVE

Broak's
Wood

Box Mill
Plantation

3

Shardlowe's
Wood

Woodcot

BOX MILL LA

COURTAULD
HOMES OF REST

Halstead

NORTH
MILL PL

H

Greenwood
Sch

Whitehouse
Farm

Sloe
House

BELLEVUE TERR 1
PAPERMILL COTTS 2
TRINITY CT 3

BOIS FIELD
TERR

FINSBURY
PL

SUDBURY RD

31

HALSTEAD

MORLEY RD

Trad
Est

HEAD ST

COLNE RD

2

Gosfield
Sch

SLOUGH FARM RD

STANLEY RD

SLOE HILL

Whiteash
Green

Crowbridge
Farm

HIGH ST

P

COLCHESTER RD

HALSTEAD RD

VICARAGE Sch

Mus

Great Spansey
Wood

TRINITY ST

Liby

1

RUSSELL'S RD

Little Spansey
Wood

PO

P

FAIRFIELD
WAY

30

The
Grange

Russell's
Farm

New
Wood

Blamsters
Farm

MOUNT HILL

A131

79 | A | B | 80 | C | D | 81 | E | F

A B C D E F

8
7
33
6
5
32
4
3
31
2
1
30

OAK RD
SCHOOL RD
A131
Brick's Farm
Seven Acre Wood
Birchleys
Oak Farm
Clay Hills
HAMSPERS CL
Levit's Corner
Hampers
Gage's
The Leys
SUDBURY RD
Byndes Farm
Spoon's Hall
Dean's Hall
Stanley Hall
Poplar Cottage
CO9
Stoneylands
Birch Wood
Hunt's Hall
entall's Farm
Ashford Lodge
Oxley Wood
Worlds End Farm
Abbot's
Constantine's Cotts
The Cangle
Star Style
Rooktree Plantation
BRICKHOUSE RD
NEYWOOD RD
Rooktree Farm
Elm Tree Farm
Threefields Wood
Burton's Farm
CHURCHILL AVE
MATHEWS CL
WINSTON WAY
Abbot's Shrubs
Boose's Green
Andrew's Prim Sch
HAWTHORN CL
BIRCH DR
BEECH AVE
HAWTHORN
The Ramsey Sch
CHERRY TREE CL
PEBMARSH RD
COLNE RD
MAPLE CL
1 COGGESHALL PIECES
2 HAUBOURDIN CT
3 COGGESHALL WAY
Bridget's Wood
my
Mason's Grove
Colne Engaine
UPPER FENN RD
Westwood Farm
CO6
The Ramsey Sch (Priory Hall)
FENN RD
Knight's Farm
SKELLS CROFT
BROOK ST
CRESS CL
COLCHESTER RD
BLUEBRIDGE IND EST
BLUEBRIDGE COTTS
FIFTH AVE
THIRD AVE
FOURTH AVE
Botany Bay Plantation
Bunting's Green
RAINBOW WAY
OXCROFT
STATION RD
CHURCH ST
SYKES CL
PH
Brook Farm
NETHER CL
A1124
BROOK FARM CL
SECOND AVE
FIRST AVE
Coppins

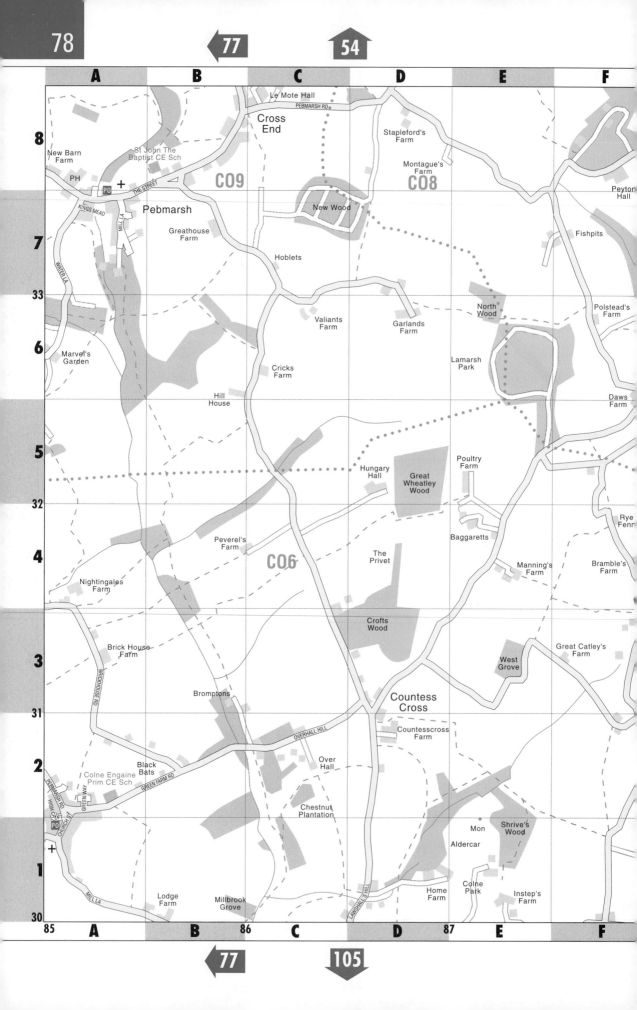

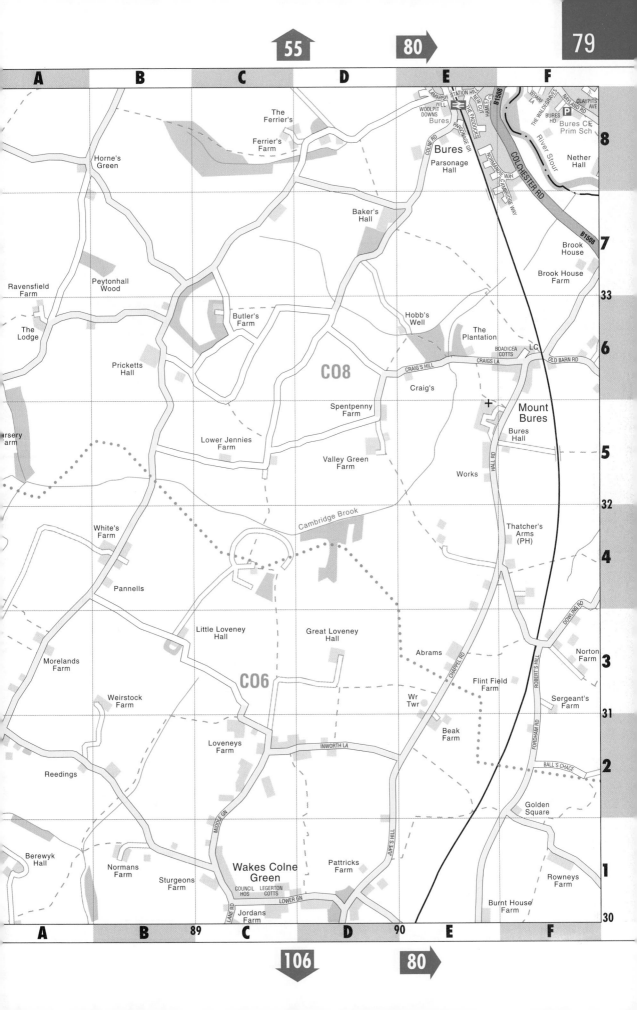

A B C D E F

8
7
33
6
5
32
4
31
3
2
1
30

The Ferrier's
Ferrier's Farm

Horne's Green

LAMARSH HILL
STATION HILL
NEW CUT
WOOLPIT DOWNS Bures
THE PADDOCKS
PARSONAGE GR
COLNE RD
B1508
WHARF LA
THE WALDEGRAVES
NAYLAND RD
CLAYPITS AVE
BURES HO
Bures CE Prim Sch
River Stour
Bures
Parsonage Hall
Nether Hall
B1508
COLCHESTER RD
NORMANDIE WAY
CAMBRIDGE WAY

Baker's Hall

Brook House
Brook House Farm

Ravensfield Farm
Peytonhall Wood

The Lodge

Butler's Farm

Hobb's Well

The Plantation
BOADICEA COTTS
LC
OLD BARN RD
CRAIGS LA
CRAIG'S HILL

Pricketts Hall

CO8

Craig's

Mount Bures
Bures Hall

rsery arm

Lower Jennies Farm

Spentpenny Farm

Valley Green Farm

Works

HALL RD

Cambridge Brook

White's Farm

Thatcher's Arms (PH)

Pannells

Little Loveney Hall

Great Loveney Hall

DOWLING RD

Norton Farm

Morelands Farm

CO6

Abrams

CHAPPEL RD

Flint Field Farm

ROBERT'S HILL

Sergeant's Farm

Weirstock Farm

Wr Twr

BALL'S CHACE

FORDHAM RD

Loveneys Farm

INWORTH LA

Beak Farm

Reedings

MIDDLE GN

Golden Square

JUPE'S HILL

Berewyk Hall

Normans Farm
Sturgeons Farm

Wakes Colne Green
COUNCIL HOS
LEGERTON COTTS
LOWER GN
LANE RD
Jordans Farm

Pattricks Farm

Rowneys Farm

Burnt House Farm

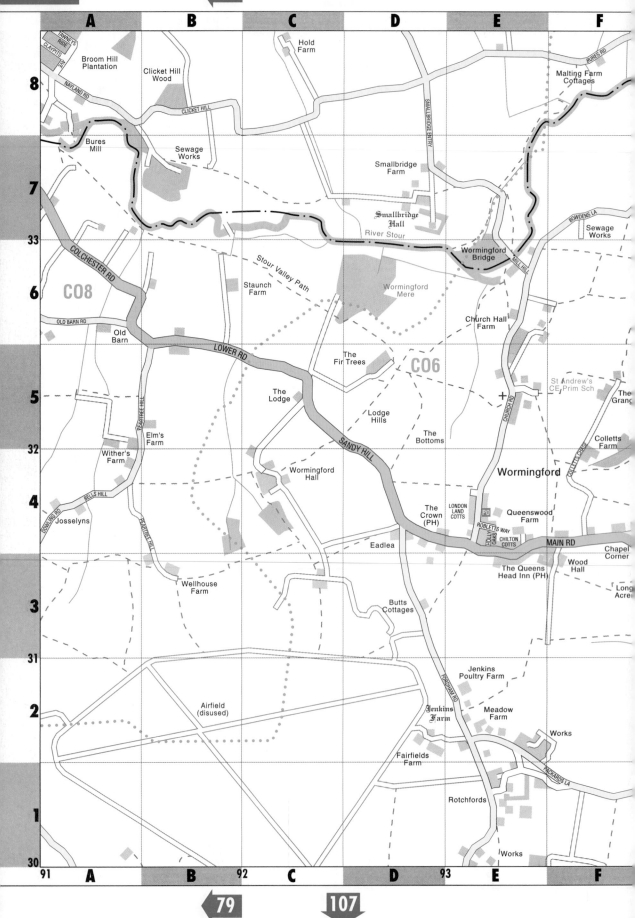

A B C D E F

8

River Stour

WATER LA

PARK RD

Boxtedhall
Great Wood

Gulsons

King's Yard

BURNT DICK HILL

Boxted

7

Windyridge

Valley
Yard

Little Wood

Boxted CE
Prim Sch

CHURCH

HORKESLEY HILL

Whitepark
Farm

Boxted Hall

33

Kerseys

CHURCH RD

Pond House

6

South Lodge

CO4

GREENFIELD
COTTS

WELL LA

The
Chantry

Orchard Farm

Ridgnalls

Potter's
Farm

Vineyard

Brook Farm

+

5

CO6

Coveneys

Carter's Farm

Horkesley
Green

GREEN LA

BROOK
COTTS

Boxted Lodge

Martins
PH

BOXTED CHURCH RD

WORKHOUSE HILL

32

LONDON RD

NAYLAND RD

Holly Lodge
Farm

Workhouse
Hill

4

Mount
Hall

The
Grove

HOLLY LA

Barritts Farm

MILL RD

Noakes
Farm

SCARFE'S
CNR

Nevards
Farm

Enfields Farm

Old Ellis
Farmhouse

ELLIS RD

WINDM

3

TOG LA

Altyre
House

Lodge Farm

BOXTED RD

Frost's
Grove

QUEEN'S HEAD RD

31

Harrow
Corner

REDHOUSE LA

Priory H
Farm

2

Breewood Hall

Essex Way

Redhouse
Farm

STRAIGHT RD

OLD HOUSE LA

THE CAUSEWAY

SCHOOL LA

PO

BROAD LA

Great Horkesley

PH

LINCOLN LA

PEPPER'S RD

LANGHAM RD

Horkesley
Plantation

1

THE
CRESCENT

GR

OLD HOUSE RD

BAS

GL IRELANDS

MORLAND
CT

GLENWAY
CT

A134

Spratt's Marsh

30

97 A B 98 C D 99 E F

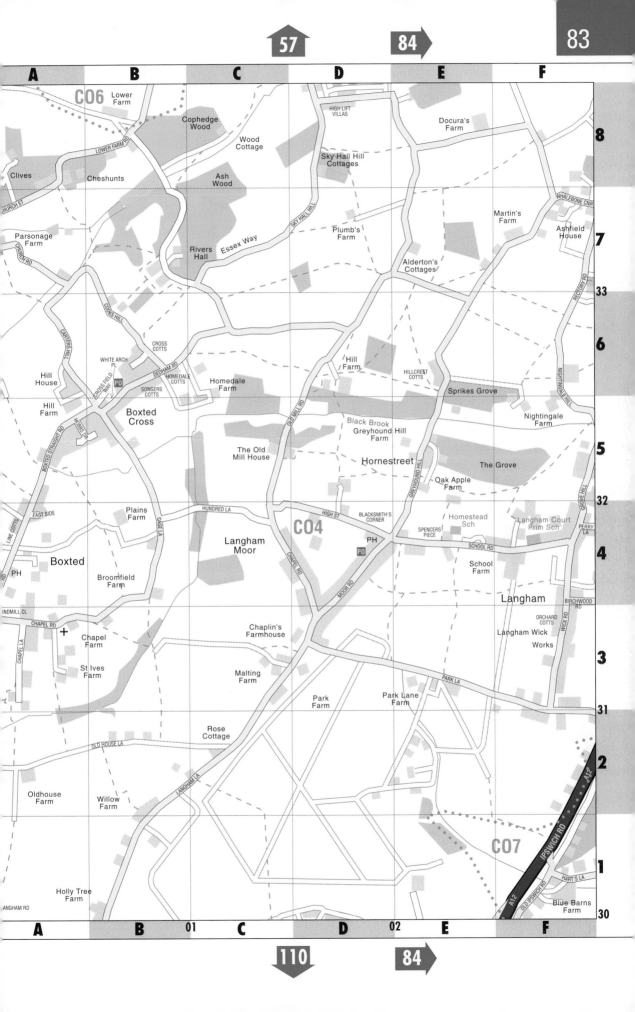

A B C D E F

8
7
33
6
5
32
4
3
31
2
1
30

CO6 Lower Farm
Cophedge Wood
Wood Cottage
LOWER FARM RD
HIGH LIFT VILLAS
Docura's Farm
Clives
Cheshunts
Ash Wood
Sky Hall Hill Cottages
CHURCH ST
SKY HALL HILL
WHALEBONE CNR
Parsonage Farm
Rivers Hall
Essex Way
Plumb's Farm
Martin's Farm
Ashfield House
CHURCH RD
RECTORY RD
Alderton's Cottages
COOKS HILL
CARTERS HILL
CROSS COTTS
Hill Farm
HILLCREST COTTS
NIGHTINGALE HILL
WHITE ARCH PL
DEDHAM RD
HOMEDALE COTTS
Homedale Farm
Sprikes Grove
Hill House
Hill Farm
CROSS FIELD WAY
SONGERS COTTS
Black Brook Greyhound Hill Farm
Nightingale Farm
HOBBS DR
Boxted Cross
OLD MILL RD
The Old Mill House
GREYHOUND HILL
Hornestreet
The Grove
Oak Apple Farm
GROVE HILL
BOXTED STRAIGHT RD
EAST SIDE
Plains Farm
HUNDRED LA
Homestead Sch
Langham Court Prim Sch
LINE COTTS
CAGE LA
HIGH ST
BLACKSMITH'S CORNER
CO4
SPENCERS PIECE
PERRY LA
PH
PO
SCHOOL RD
PH
Boxted
Langham Moor
Langham Moor
School Farm
Langham
Broomfield Farm
CHAPEL RD
MOOR RD
BIRCHWOOD RD
WINDMILL CL
CHAPEL RD
Chaplin's Farmhouse
ORCHARD COTTS
WICK RD
Langham Wick Works
CHAPEL LA
Chapel Farm
St Ives Farm
Malting Farm
PARK LA
Park Lane Farm
Park Farm
Rose Cottage
OLD HOUSE LA
LANGHAM LA
A12
Oldhouse Farm
Willow Farm
CO7
IPSWICH RD
OLD IPSWICH RD
HART'S LA
Holly Tree Farm
LANGHAM RD
A12
Blue Barns Farm

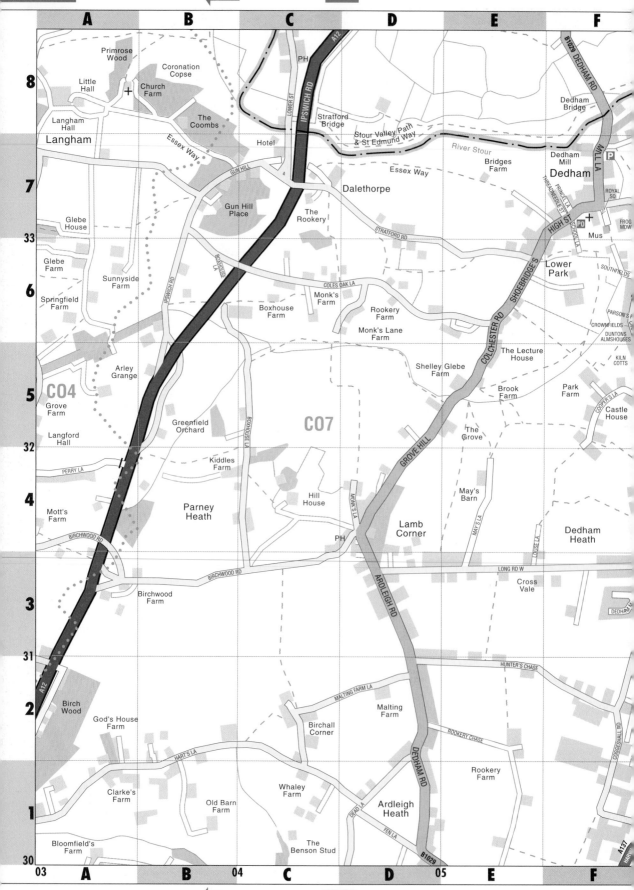

A B C D E F

8

Primrose Wood
Little Hall
Coronation Copse
Church Farm
The Coombs
Langham Hall
Langham
Essex Way
Hotel
PH
Stratford Bridge
Stour Valley Path & St Edmund Way
Essex Way
River Stour
Bridges Farm
Dedham Bridge
Dedham Mill
Dedham
MILL LA
BT029 DEDHAM RD
IPSWICH RD
LOWER ST
A12

7

Gun Hill
Gun Hill Place
Dalethorpe
The Rookery
STRATFORD RD
Lower Park
HIGH ST
SHOEBRIDGE'S
PRINCEL LA
THREADNEEDLE ST
SCHOOL LA
ROYAL SQ
FROG MDW
P
Mus
SOUTHFIELDS

33

Glebe House
Glebe Farm
Springfield Farm
Sunnyside Farm
Coles Oak La
Monk's Farm
Boxhouse Farm
Rookery Farm
Monk's Lane Farm
Shelley Glebe Farm
The Lecture House
COLCHESTER RD
PARSON'S LA
CROWNFIELDS
DUNTONS ALMSHOUSES
KILN COTTS
Park Farm
COOPER'S LA
Castle House

6

IPSWICH RD
BOXHOUSE LA

CO4
Arley Grange
Grove Farm
Langford Hall
PERRY LA
Greenfield Orchard
Kiddles Farm
BOXHOUSE LA
CO7
Brook Farm
The Grove
GROVE HILL

5

32

4

Mott's Farm
BIRCHWOOD RD
Parney Heath
Hill House
MONK'S LA
PH
BIRCHWOOD RD
May's Barn
MAY'S LA
Lamb Corner
LOOSE LA
Dedham Heath
LONG RD W
Cross Vale
DEDHAM LA

3

Birchwood Farm
ARDLEIGH RD
HUNTER'S CHASE
DEDHAM

31

A12

2

Birch Wood
God's House Farm
HART'S LA
MALTING FARM LA
Birchall Corner
Malting Farm
ROOKERY CHASE
DEDHAM RD
Rookery Farm
A137

1

Clarke's Farm
Old Barn Farm
Whaley Farm
DEAD LA
FEN LA
Ardleigh Heath

30

Bloomfield's Farm
The Benson Stud
BT029

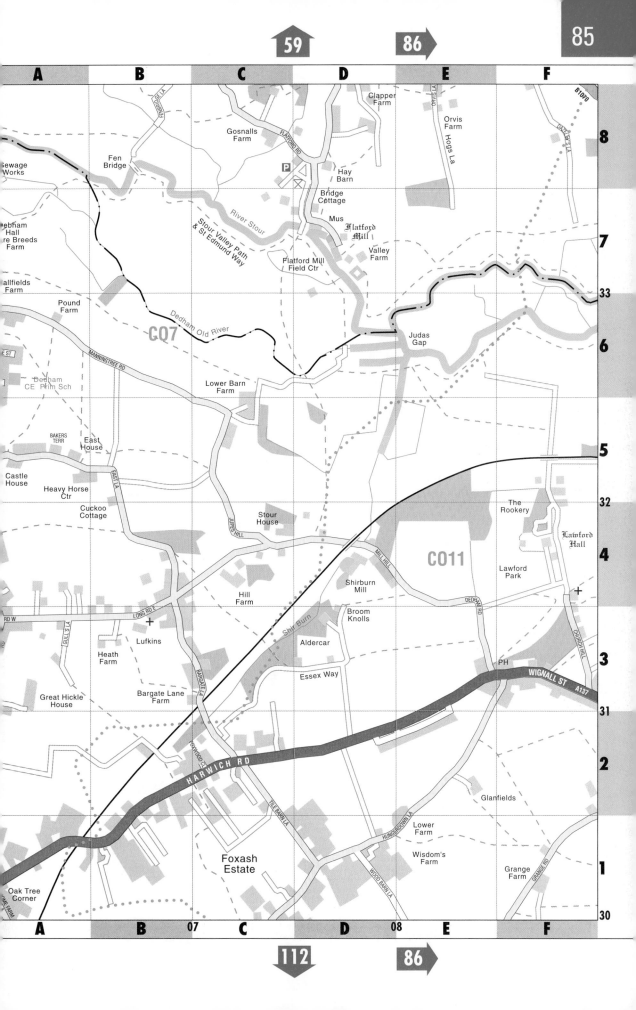

59
86

A B C D E F

8

7

33

6

5

32

4

3

31

2

1

30

A B C D E F

112
86

Sewage Works

Fen Bridge

Gosnalls Farm

Clapper Farm

Orvis Farm

Hogs La

FRITH DE LA

FLATFORD RD

P

Hay Barn

Bridge Cottage

Mus

Flatford Mill

River Stour

Stour Valley Path & St Edmund Way

Flatford Mill Field Ctr

Valley Farm

ebham Hall re Breeds Farm

allfields Farm

Pound Farm

Dedham Old River

CQ7

Judas Gap

B1070

DAZLEY STA

ORVIS LA

MANNINGTREE RD

Dedham CE Prim Sch

Lower Barn Farm

E ST

BAKERS TERR

East House

Castle House

Heavy Horse Ctr

Cuckoo Cottage

EAST LA

JUPES HILL

Stour House

The Rookery

Lawford Hall

CO11

Lawford Park

MILL HILL

Shirburn Mill

Hill Farm

DEDHAM RD

CHURCH HILL

+

RD W

GULL S LA

LONG RD E

+

Lufkins

Heath Farm

Great Hickle House

Bargate Lane Farm

BARGATE LA

Shir Burn

Aldercar

Broom Knolls

Essex Way

PH

WIGNALL ST

A137

FOXWOOD CL

HARWICH RD

TILE BARN LA

Foxash Estate

HUNGERDOWN LA

WOOD BARN LA

Lower Farm

Wisdom's Farm

Glanfields

Grange Farm

GRANGE RD

Oak Tree Corner

YME FARM

07 08

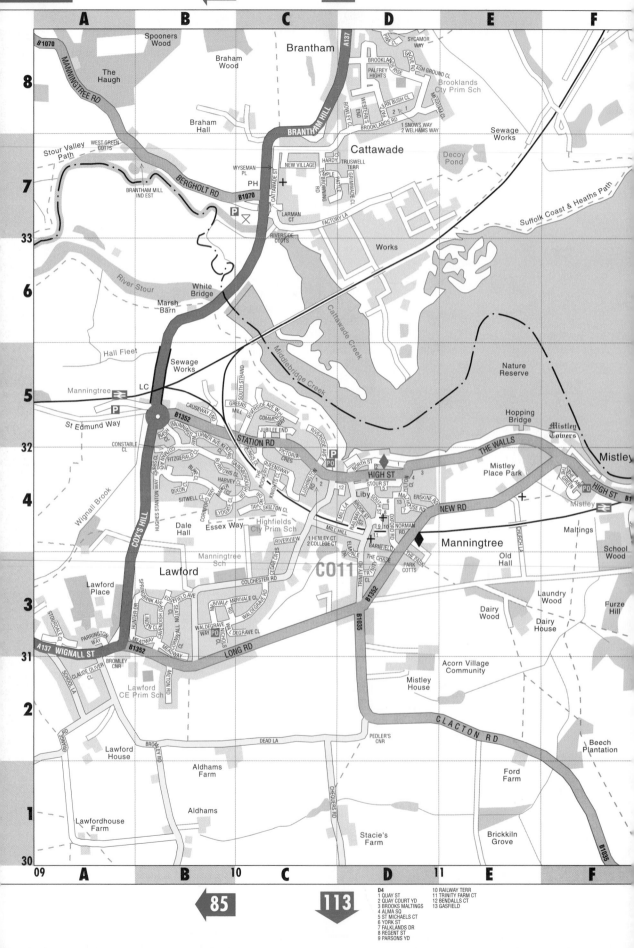

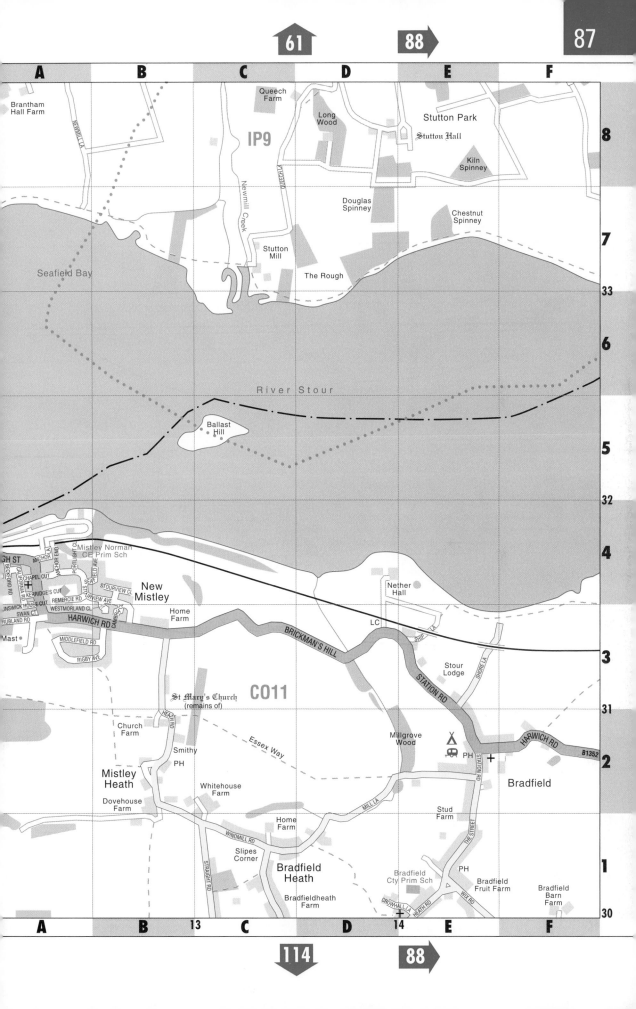

A B C D E F

8

7

33

6

5

32

4

3

31

2

1

30

Brantham Hall Farm

NEWMILL LA

IP9

Queech Farm

Long Wood

Stutton Park

Stutton Hall

Kiln Spinney

Douglas Spinney

Chestnut Spinney

Newmill Creek

QUEECH LA

Stutton Mill

The Rough

Seafield Bay

River Stour

Ballast Hill

GH ST

ANCHOR END

Mistley Norman CE Prim Sch

CALIFORNIA RD

BECKFORD RD

CHAPEL CUT

KERRIDGE'S CUT

SEAT ST

FIELD AVE

PORTLIGHT CL

STOURVIEW CL

STOURVIEW AVE

REMERCIE RD

ANCHOR END

New Mistley

Home Farm

NSWICK HOUSE CUT

WESTMORLAND CL

CAMBRIC A

HARWICH RD

RUBLAND RD

SWAN CT

Mast

MIDDLEFIELD RD

RIGBY AVE

BRICKMAN'S HILL

LC

Nether Hall

SHIP LA

STATION RD

SHORE LA

Stour Lodge

HARWICH RD

B1352

CO11

St Mary's Church (remains of)

HEATH RD

Church Farm

Essex Way

Millgrove Wood

☖ ☕ PH

⚔

Bradfield

Smithy PH

Mistley Heath

Dovehouse Farm

Whitehouse Farm

WINDMILL RD

Home Farm

MILL LA

Stud Farm

THE STREET

PH

STATION RD

STRAIGHT RD

Slipes Corner

Bradfield Heath

Bradfield Cty Prim Sch

Bradfieldheath Farm

CROWHALL LA

HEATH RD

⚔

WIX RD

Bradfield Fruit Farm

Bradfield Barn Farm

IP9

Backhouse Ley

Holbrook Bay

Graham's Wharf

Stutton Ness

Dovehouse Point

River Stour

Stone Point

Wrabness Point

Shore Farm

Jacques Bay

Wrabness Hall

Wrabness

WALL LA

Cemy

CHURCH RD

STONE LA

Wrabness Local Nature Reserve

Lower Farm

P

P

STATION RD

Ragmarsh Farm

WHEATSHEAF CL

Dimbols Farm

Jacques Hall

WHEATSHEAF LA

Brakey Grove

Foxes Farm

Domine Farm

B13

Gateways

CO11

Lonbarn

PH

HARWICH RD

COOK'S CORNER

The Firs

B1352 HARWICH RD

Lonbarn Bridge

LONBARN HILL

SPINNEL'S HILL

Priory Farm

BUTLER'S LA

Butler's Farm

Spinnel's Farm

Windmill

SPINNEL'S LA

Pondhall Wood

Bluehouse Farm

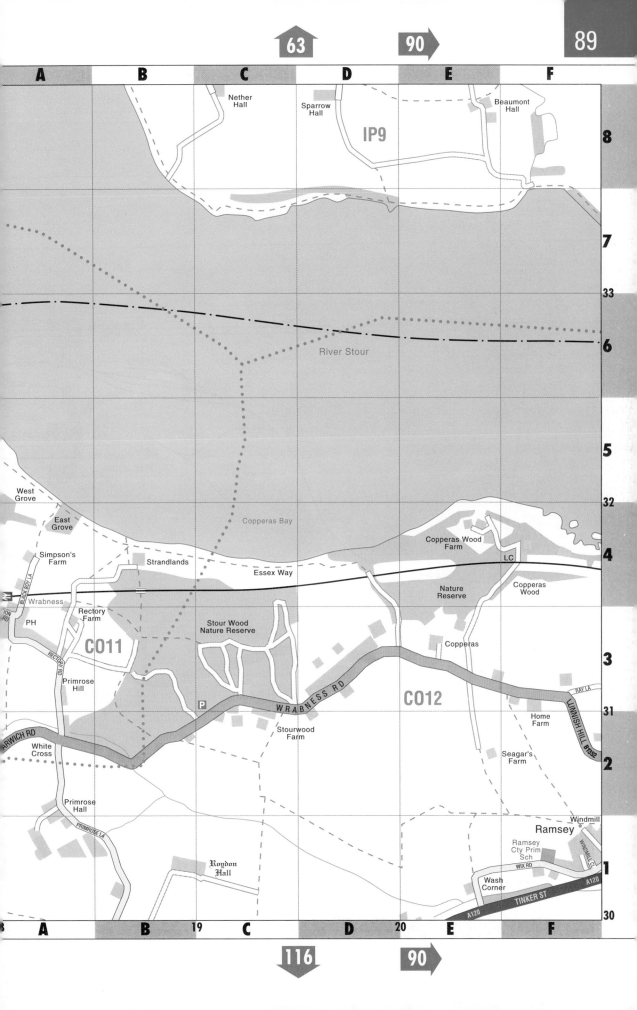

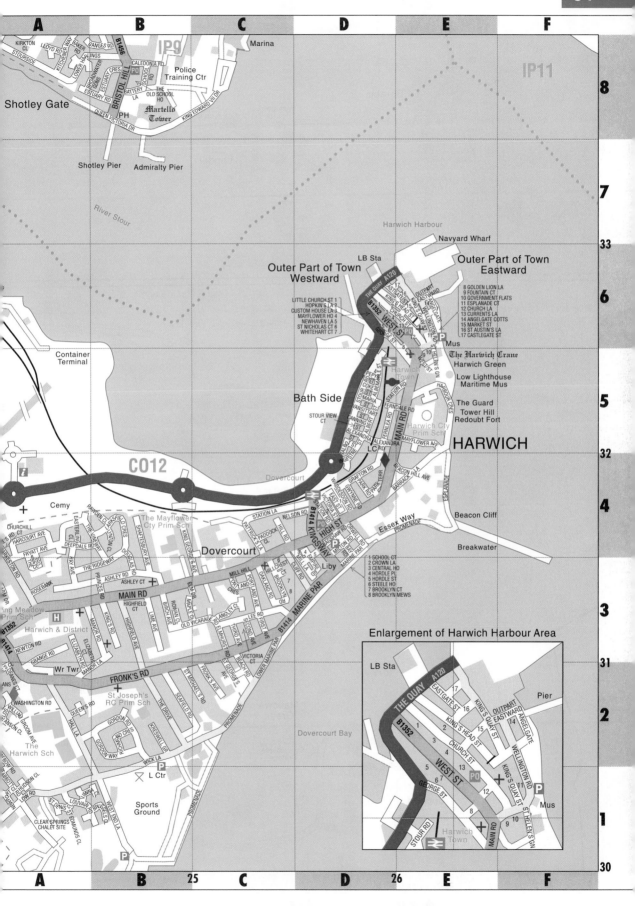

IPg

Marina

Police Training Ctr

The Old School Ho

Shotley Gate

Martello Tower

PH

Shotley Pier

Admiralty Pier

IP11

River Stour

Harwich Harbour

Navyard Wharf

33

LB Sta

Outer Part of Town Westward

Outer Part of Town Eastward

8 GOLDEN LION LA
9 FOUNTAIN CT
10 GOVERNMENT FLATS
11 ESPLANADE CT
12 CHURCH LA
13 CURRENTS LA
14 ANGELGATE COTTS
15 MARKET ST
16 ST AUSTIN'S LA
17 CASTLEGATE ST

LITTLE CHURCH ST 1
HOPKIN'S LA 2
CUSTOM HOUSE LA 3
MAYFLOWER HO 4
NEWHAVEN LA 5
ST NICHOLAS CT 6
WHITEHART CT 7

6

Container Terminal

The Harwich Crane
Harwich Green

Low Lighthouse
Maritime Mus

Bath Side

5

The Guard
Tower Hill
Redoubt Fort

Harwich City
Prim Sch

HARWICH

CO12

32

Dovercourt

Beacon Cliff

4

Cemy

Essex Way

Breakwater

The Mayflower
Cty Prim Sch

Dovercourt

Liby

1 SCHOOL CT
2 CROWN LA
3 CENTRAL HO
4 HORDLE PL
5 STEELE HO
6 HORDLE ST
7 BROOKLYN CT
8 BROOKLYN MEWS

MAIN RD

3

Harwich & District

Wr Twr

FRONK'S RD

St Joseph's
RC Prim Sch

Enlargement of Harwich Harbour Area

31

LB Sta

Pier

2

The
Harwich Sch

Dovercourt Bay

L Ctr

Sports
Ground

Clear Springs
Chalet Site

1

30

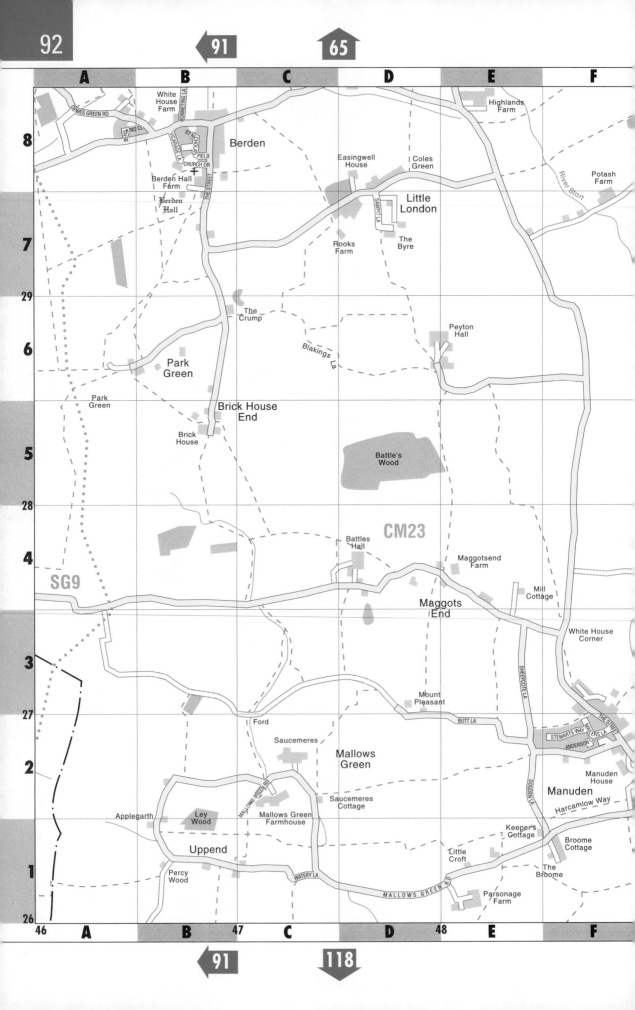

A B C D E F

BEMES GREEN RD

White House Farm

BENSKINS CL

BONNETING LA

ST NICHOLAS FIELD

VICARAGE LA

CHURCH DR

Berden

THE STREET

Berden Hall Farm

Berden Hall

Highlands Farm

Easingwell House

Coles Green

River Stort

Potash Farm

Little London

SAWPIT LA

The Byre

8

Rooks Farm

7

29

The Crump

Blakings La

Peyton Hall

6

Park Green

Park Green

Brick House End

Brick House

Battle's Wood

5

28

CM23

Battles Hall

Maggotsend Farm

4

SG9

Mill Cottage

Maggots End

White House Corner

3

SHEEPCOTE LA

27

Mount Pleasant

Ford

BUTT LA

THE STREET

STEWARTS WAY

MILLERS LA

ANDERSON CL

Saucemeres

Mallows Green

DOGGEN LA

Manuden House

2

MALLOWS GREEN RD

Saucemeres Cottage

Manuden

Applegarth

Ley Wood

Mallows Green Farmhouse

Harcamlow Way

Keeper's Cottage

Broome Cottage

Uppend

Little Croft

The Broome

1

Percy Wood

WATERY LA

MALLOWS GREEN RD

Parsonage Farm

26

46 A 47 B C 48 D E F

A B C D E F

CB11

8

Fivefoot
Bridge

CHs

LC

NORTH HALL RD

The White
House

7

Meadside

River Cam or Granta

Sheepcote La

29

Ugley Hall
Farm Cottages

Birds
Farm

The Cock
(PH)

THE CHASE

6

Ugley Hall
Farm

Down Hall
House

CHURCH ST

CROW ST

Henham

HIGH ST
STA R RD

PO

Parsonage
Farm

HALL CL

HIGH ST

5

Hazelmoor
Common

Bacons
Farm

The
Vicarage

PIMBLETT
ROW

SCHOOL LA

SAGE LA

CARTERS LA

Henham
Ugley Ct
Prim Sch

Birch
Grove

OLD MEAD RD

CM22

28

Old Mead

VERN LA

Playing
Field

4

Church
Common

Mast

OLD MEAD LA

Byculla

Works

MILL RD

The Mill
House

Mill Pond
Farm

Fieldgate
Farm

FIELD GATE LA

MILL RD

B1051

3

Ugley Green

Hudsons
Farm

Bedwell
Common

MAYTREE
GDNS

SPENCER CL

Y GOLD

GOLDS
NURSERY
BSNS PK

JENKINS CL

Ugley
Park

Ugley
Green

BEDWELL RD

Sand Pit

Pennington
Hall

HENHAM RD

27

The
Hermitage

DELLONS LA

NEW RD

ALSA FYG GDNS

P

LC

Elsenham

FENMAN
CT

HUNTERS
CT

CRANMORE
CL

2

SNAKES LA

Harewood

Alsa
Wood

Mast

BROOM FARM
RD

STATION RD

ELM CL

DE MANDEVILLE RD

OTTERS CL

RIDLEY
GDNS

MARKWELLS

CORRIANDER CT

PARK RD

HALES WOOD

The Crown
(PH)

Elsenham
Palace

Stansted Brook

Driving
Range

CH

Elsenham

Playing
Field

FOURWAYS

LEIGH DR

THE CROFT

HIGH ST

Elsenham
Cross

HALL RD

The Old
Vicarage

Elsenham
Palace

1

CM24

MAY TREE LA

Alsa Wood
Cottage

May Tree
Farm

Nursery

STANSTED RD

B1051

GILBEY COTTS

MILL CL

ROBIN HOOD RD

SAUNDERS CL

RUSH LA

PO

GLEBE END

THE GLEBE

Elsenham CE
Prim Sch

Abbotsford
Bridge

26

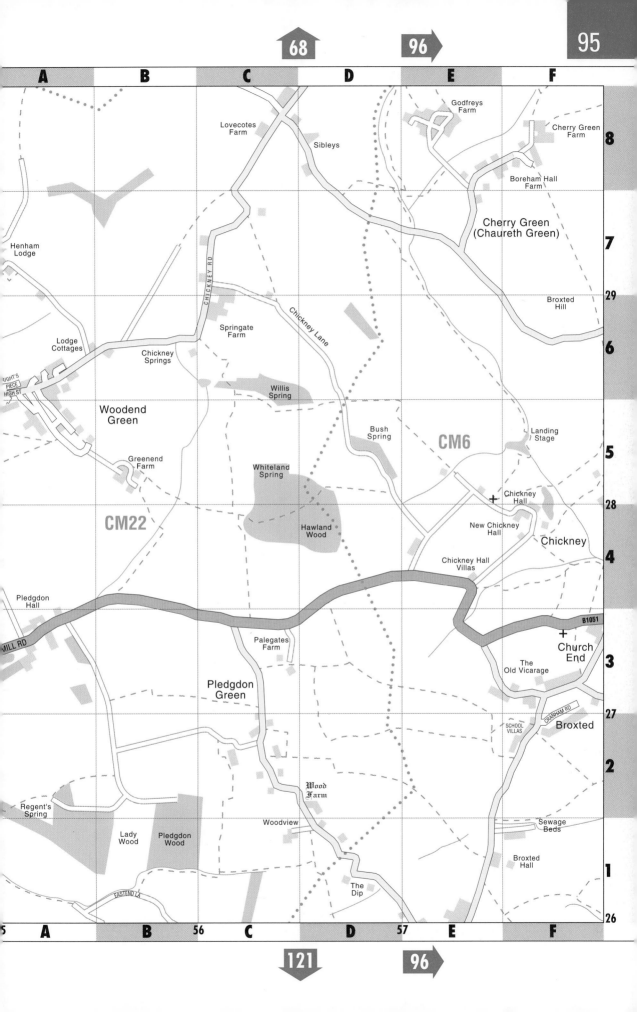

A B C D E F

Godfreys Farm

Cherry Green Farm

Lovecotes Farm

Sibleys

Boreham Hall Farm

Cherry Green (Chaureth Green)

Henham Lodge

Broxted Hill

CHICKNEY RD

Springate Farm

Chickney Lane

Lodge Cottages

Chickney Springs

Willis Spring

Woodend Green

Bush Spring

CM6

Landing Stage

Whiteland Spring

Greenend Farm

Chickney Hall

CM22

Hawland Wood

New Chickney Hall

Chickney

Chickney Hall Villas

B1051

Pledgdon Hall

Church End

MILL RD

Palegates Farm

The Old Vicarage

Pledgdon Green

GRANHAM RD

SCHOOL VILLAS

Broxted

Regent's Spring

Wood Farm

Woodview

Sewage Beds

Lady Wood

Pledgdon Wood

Broxted Hall

EASTEND LA

The Dip

RIGHT'S PIECE HIGH ST

5 A B 56 C D 57 E F

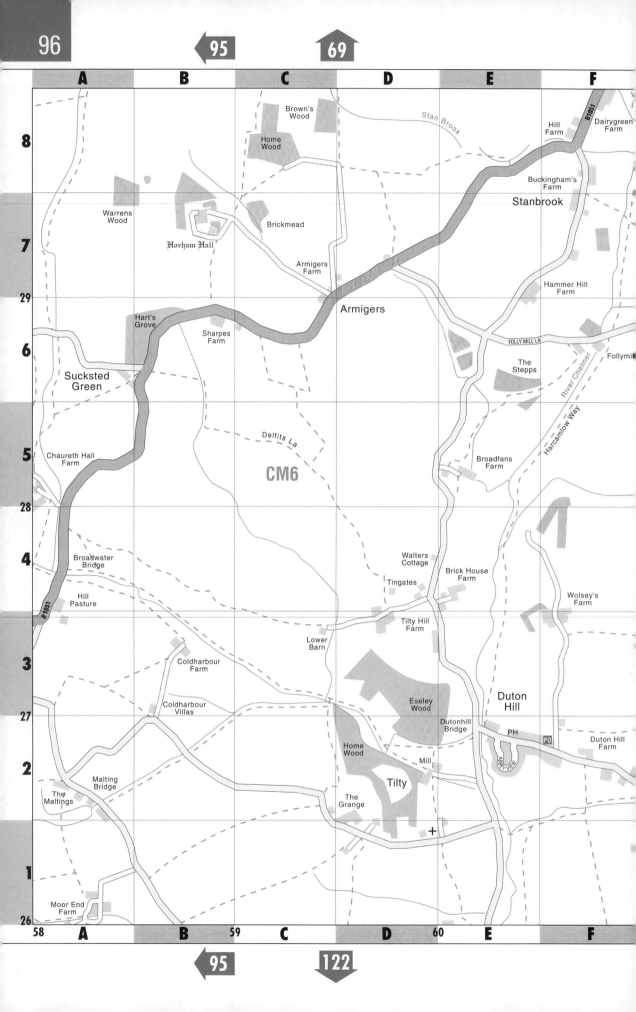

A B C D E F

8

Brown's Wood

Home Wood

Stan Brook

Hill Farm

Dairygreen Farm

B1051

Warrens Wood

Brickmead

Buckingham's Farm

Stanbrook

7

Horham Hall

Armigers Farm

29

Hart's Grove

Armigers

Hammer Hill Farm

6

Sucksted Green

Sharpes Farm

FOLLY MILL LA

The Stepps

River Chelmer

Follymi

5

Chaureth Hall Farm

Delfits La

CM6

Broadfans Farm

Harcamlow Way

28

4

Broadwater Bridge

Walters Cottage

Brick House Farm

Wolsey's Farm

Hill Pasture

B1051

Tingates

Tilty Hill Farm

3

Coldharbour Farm

Lower Barn

Eseley Wood

Duton Hill

27

Coldharbour Villas

Dutonhill Bridge

PH

PO

Duton Hill Farm

2

Malting Bridge

Home Wood

Mill

ABBEY VIEW

The Maltings

Tilty

The Grange

1

Moor End Farm

26

58 A B 59 C D 60 E F

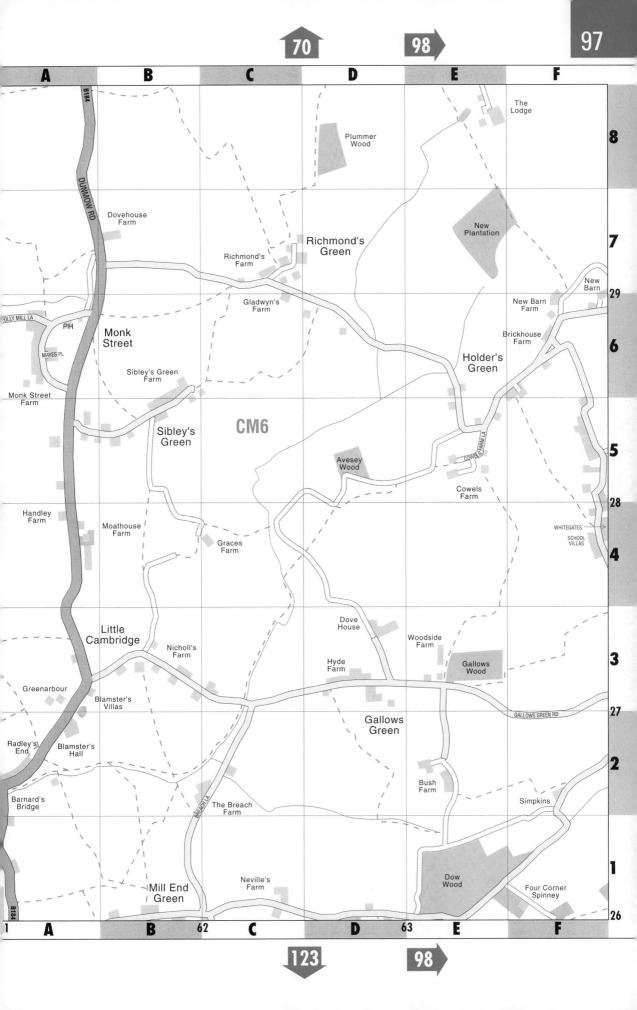

A　　B　　C　　D　　E　　F

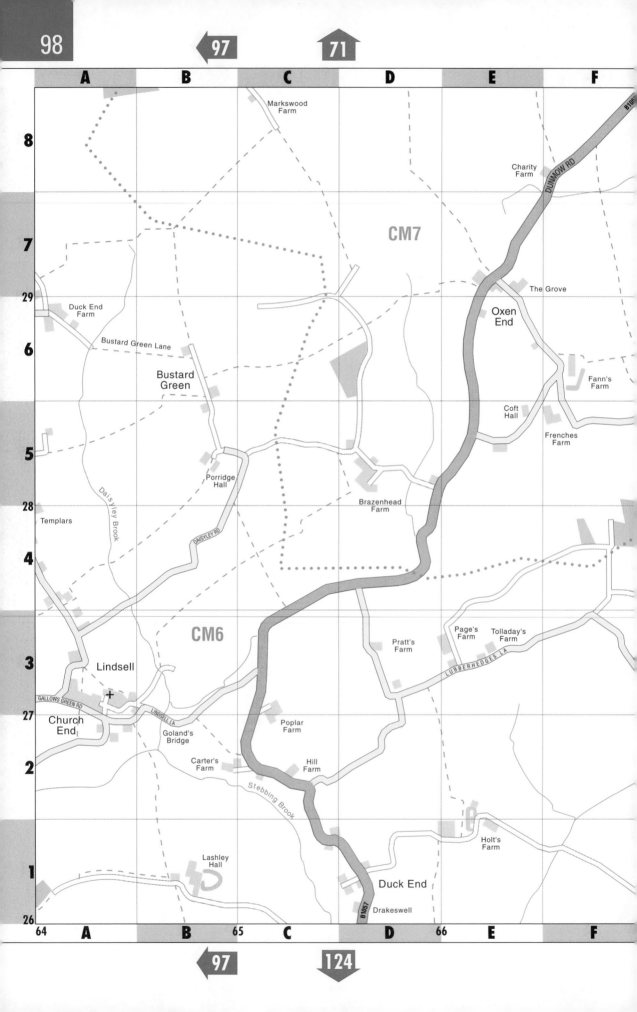

8

7

29

Duck End
Farm

Bustard Green Lane

6

Bustard
Green

Markswood
Farm

CM7

Charity
Farm

DUNMOW RD

The Grove

Oxen
End

Fann's
Farm

Coft
Hall

Frenches
Farm

5

Daisyley Brook

Porridge
Hall

Brazenhead
Farm

28

Templars

DANSYLEY RD

4

CM6

3

Lindsell

Page's
Farm

Tolladay's
Farm

LUBBERHEDGES LA

GALLOWS GREEN RD

27

Church
End

LINDSELL LA

Goland's
Bridge

Poplar
Farm

Pratt's
Farm

2

Carter's
Farm

Stebbing Brook

Hill
Farm

Holt's
Farm

1

Lashley
Hall

Duck End

Drakeswell

B1057

26

64　　A　　B　　65　　C　　D　　66　　E　　F

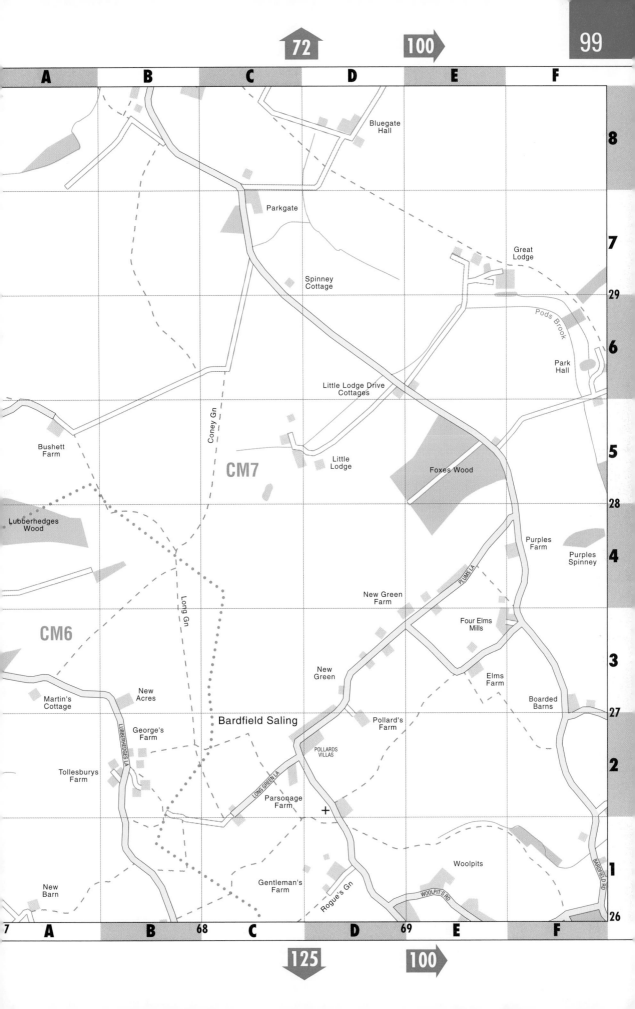

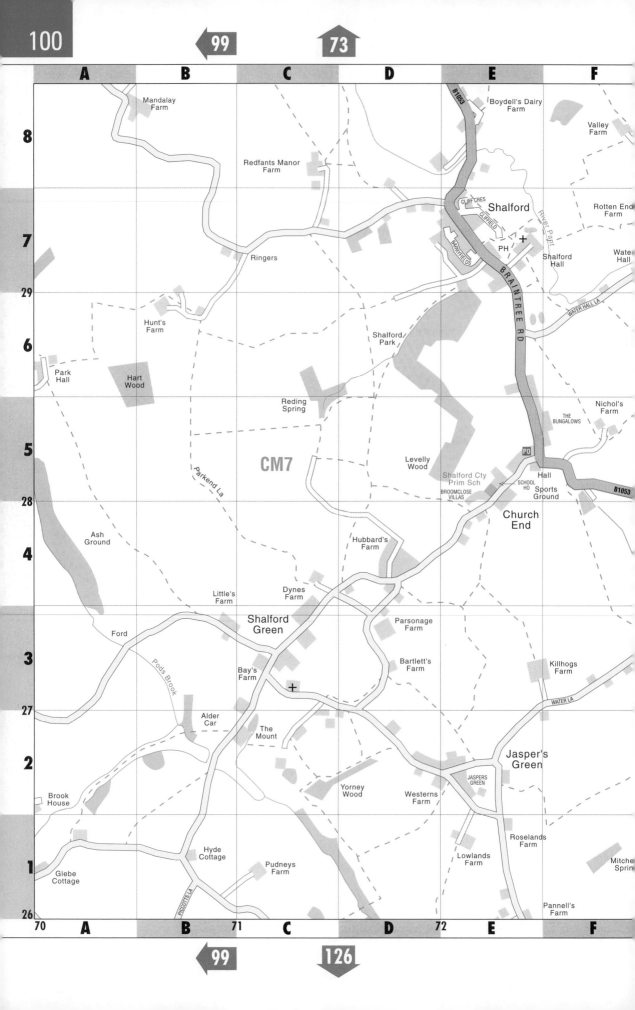

99
73

Mandalay Farm

Redfants Manor Farm

B1053

Boydell's Dairy Farm

Valley Farm

CLIFF CRES

CLIFFIELD

Shalford

Rotten End Farm

Ringers

BARNFIELDS

PH

Shalford Hall

Wate Hall

Hunt's Farm

River Pant

WATER HALL LA

Shalford Park

Park Hall

Hart Wood

Reding Spring

Nichol's Farm

THE BUNGALOWS

CM7

Levelly Wood

PO

Parkend La

Shalford Cty Prim Sch

SCHOOL HO

BROOMCLOSE VILLAS

Hall Sports Ground

B1053

Church End

Ash Ground

Hubbard's Farm

Little's Farm

Dynes Farm

Ford

Shalford Green

Parsonage Farm

Pods Brook

Bay's Farm

Bartlett's Farm

Killhogs Farm

WATER LA

Alder Car

The Mount

Jasper's Green

JASPERS GREEN

Brook House

Yorney Wood

Westerns Farm

Hyde Cottage

PICCOTTS LA

Pudneys Farm

Lowlands Farm

Roselands Farm

Mitche Sprin

Glebe Cottage

Pannell's Farm

99
126

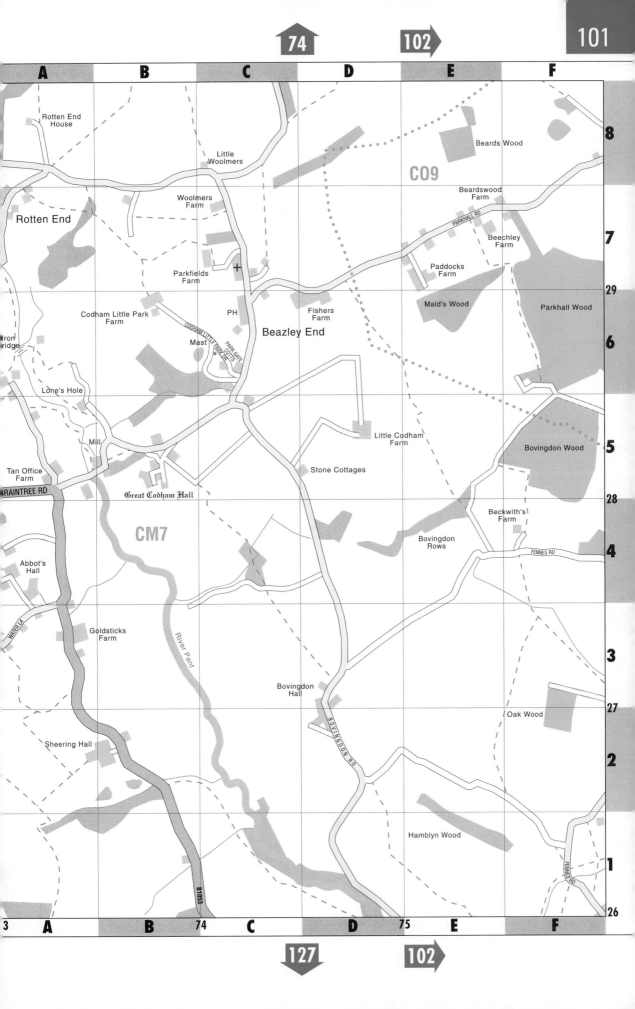

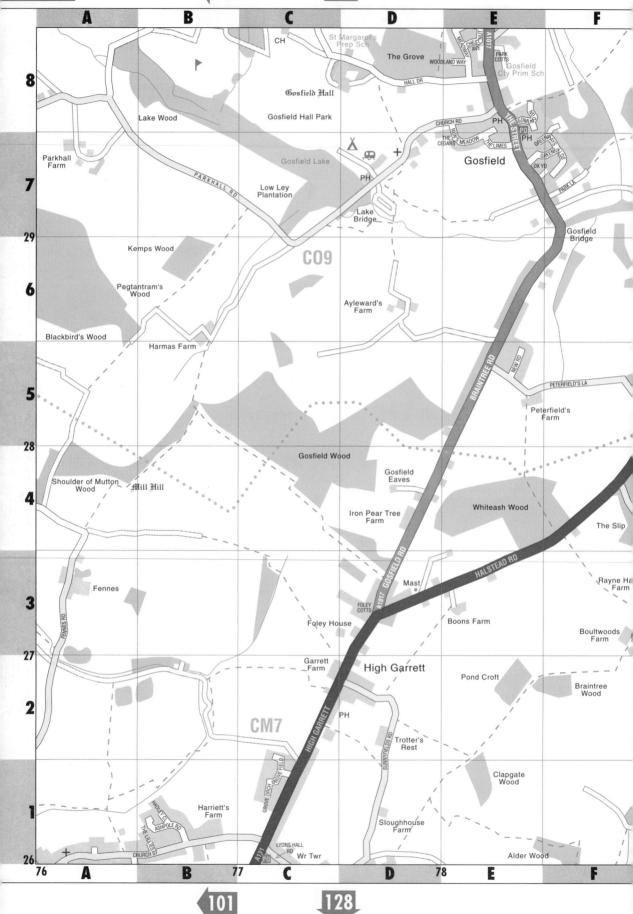

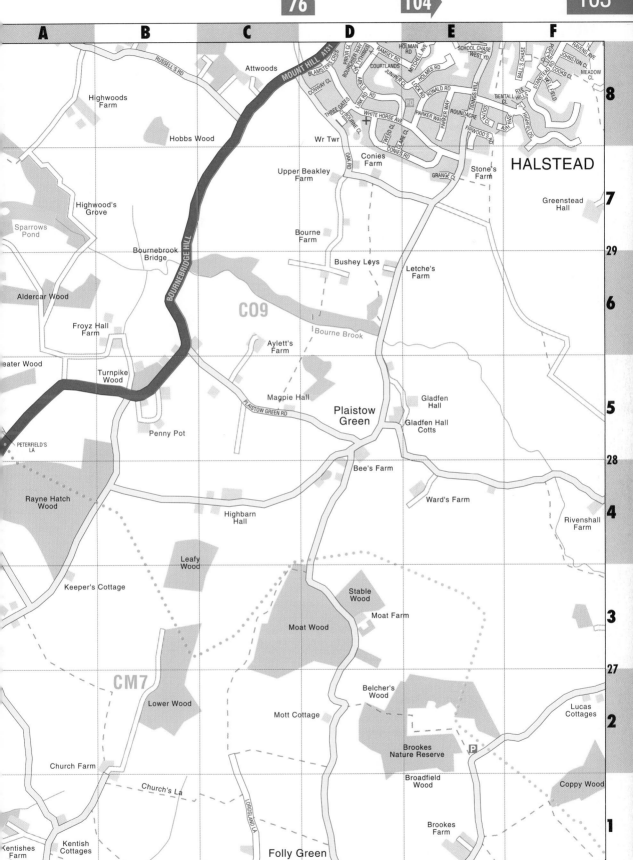

A B C D E F

8
7
29
6
5
28
4
27
3
2
1
26

RUSSELL'S RD

Attwoods

Highwoods Farm

Hobbs Wood

MOUNT HILL A131

BLAMSTERS CRS
CONWAY CL
THREE GATES
C BOURNE CL
BOURNE CL
ABEL'S RD
LINK CL
PRIOR CL
BOURNBROOK WAY
RAMSEY RD
COURTLANDS
JUNIPER CL
LOCK RD
HOLMES RD
MITCHEL AVE
HOLMAN RD
SCHOOL CHASE
WEST YD
RONALD RD
PARKER WAY
WALKER RD
TIDINGS HILL
SOUTH CL
ASH
RYE
BENTALL CL
HIGHFIELDS
RAVENS AVE
PORT
JOHNSTON CL
COOKS CL
MEADOW CL
BALL'S CHASE
STANSFIELD RD
WELL FIELD
FIRWOOD'S RD
ROUNDACRE
GRANGE CL

White Horse Ave

Wr Twr

Conies Farm

CONIES RD

PO

HALSTEAD

Greenstead Hall

Upper Beakley Farm

Bourne Farm

Bushey Leys

Letche's Farm

Stone's Farm

Highwood's Grove

Sparrows Pond

Aldercar Wood

Froyz Hall Farm

Bournebrook Bridge

BOURNEBRIDGE HILL

CO9

Bourne Brook

Aylett's Farm

eater Wood

Turnpike Wood

Penny Pot

PLAISTOW GREEN RD

Magpie Hall

Plaistow Green

Gladfen Hall

Gladfen Hall Cotts

PETERFIELD'S LA

Bee's Farm

Ward's Farm

Rivenshall Farm

Rayne Hatch Wood

Highbarn Hall

Leafy Wood

Keeper's Cottage

CM7

Lower Wood

Stable Wood

Moat Farm

Moat Wood

Mott Cottage

Belcher's Wood

Lucas Cottages

Church Farm

Church's La

LORDSLAND LA

Brookes Nature Reserve

P

Broadfield Wood

Coppy Wood

Brookes Farm

Kentishes Farm

Kentish Cottages

Folly Green

Herbdell

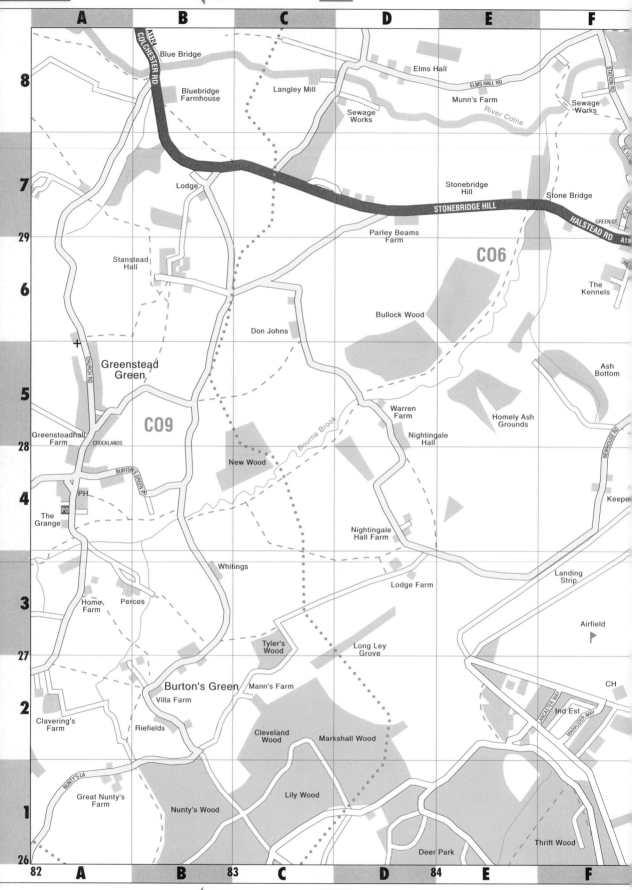

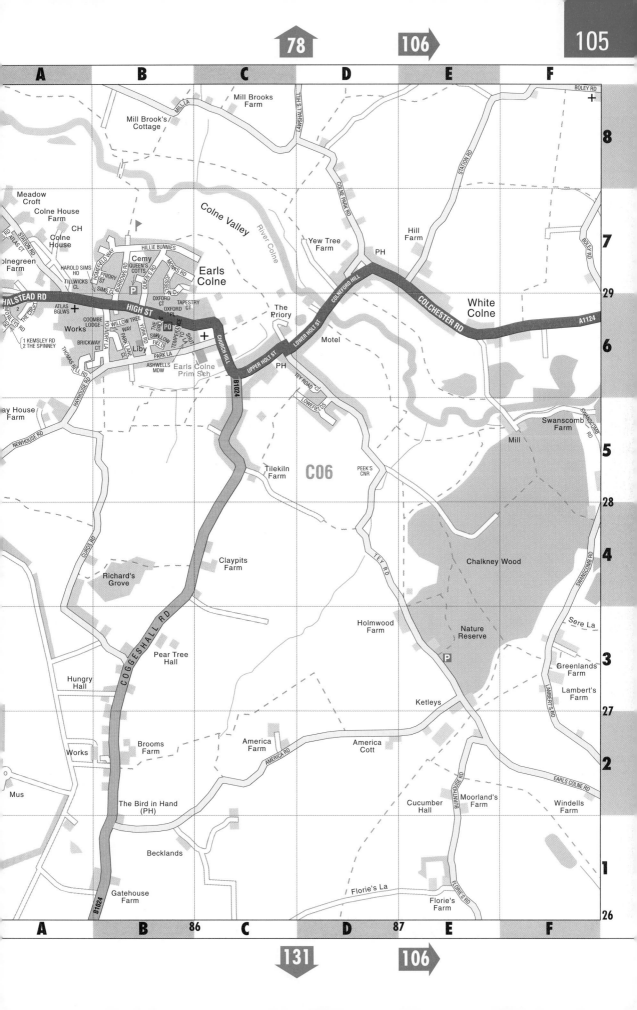

A B C D E F

8
7
29
6
5
28
4
3
27
2
1
26

Boley Rd

Mill Brooks Farm
Mill La
Mill Brook's Cottage
Lawshall's Hill
Station Rd
Boley Rd

Meadow Croft
Colne House Farm
CH
Colne House
Colne Valley
River Colne
Yew Tree Farm
Hill Farm
Colne Park Rd
Colnegreen Farm
Station Rd
Atlas Ct
Harold Sims Ho
Tillwicks Cl
Homefield Way
Priory St
Burrows Rd
Sims Cl
Queen's Cotts
Monks Rd
Queen's Rd
Jessop
CH
Cemy
Hillie Bunnies
Earls Colne
PH
Colneford Hill
White Colne

Halstead Rd
The Croft
Worlds Rd
Atlas Bglws
Coombe Lodge
Brickway
Works
Willow Tree Way
Foundry La
Park Lane
Swallow Field
Temperance
Shut La
Church Hill
Upper Holt St
The Priory
Lower Holt St
Tey Road Ct
Lowerfields
Motel
PH
Colchester Rd
A1124

1 Kemsley Rd
2 The Spinney
High St
PO
Oxford Ct
Oxford Pl
Tapestry Ct
NC
York Rd
Park La
Ashwells Mdw
Earls Colne Prim Sch
B1024
PH

Thomas Bell Rd
Haynhouse Rd
Swanscomb Rd
Swanscomb Farm
Mill

Newhouse Rd
ay House Farm
Tilekiln Farm
C06
Peek's Cnr
28

Curds Rd
Claypits Farm
Tey Rd
Chalkney Wood
Swanscomb Rd
4

Richard's Grove
Holmwood Farm
Nature Reserve
Sere La
Greenlands Farm
Lambert's Rd
Lambert's Farm
3

Coggeshall Rd
Pear Tree Hall
Ketleys
P
27

Hungry Hall
Brooms Farm
America Farm
America Cott
Earls Colne Rd
2

Works
America Rd
Burnthouse Rd
Florie's Rd
Windells Farm

Mus
The Bird in Hand (PH)
Cucumber Hall
Moorland's Farm
1

Becklands
Gatehouse Farm
B1024
Florie's La
Florie's Farm
26

A B 86 C D 87 E F

105
79

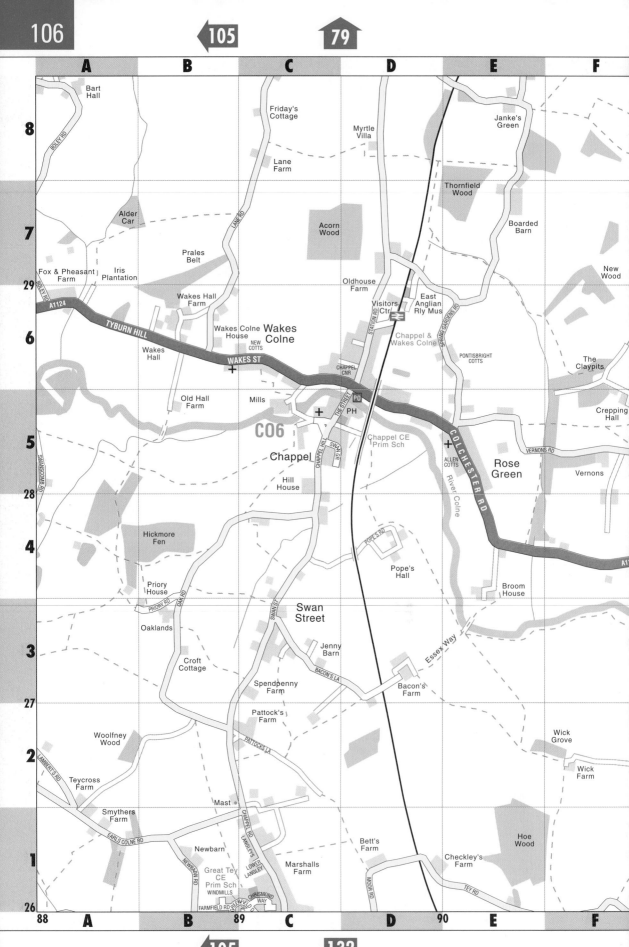

105
132

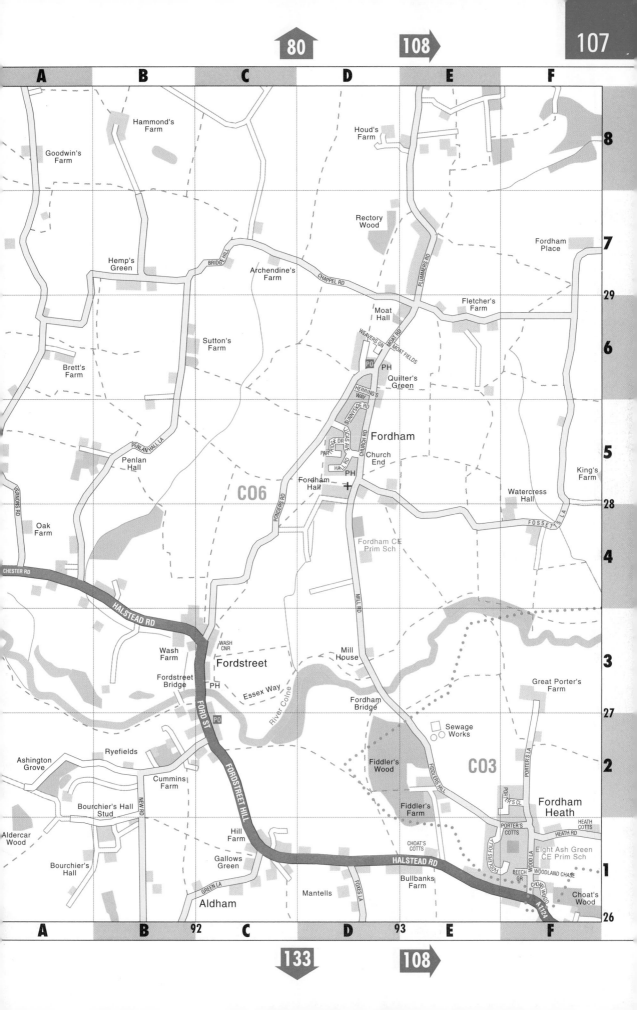

A B C D E F

8

Goodwin's Farm

Hammond's Farm

Houd's Farm

Rectory Wood

7

Fordham Place

Hemp's Green

BRIDGE HILL

Archendine's Farm

CHAPPEL RD

PLUMMERS RD

29

Sutton's Farm

Moat Hall

Fletcher's Farm

6

WEAVERS GN

MOAT RD

MOAT FIELDS

PO

PH

Quilter's Green

Brett's Farm

HERRING'S WAY

SUNNYSIDE RD

Fordham

PENLAN HALL LA

LUCAS AVE

CHURCH RD

Church End

5

Penlan Hall

CE DR AVE

PARK

King's Farm

CO6

HA LT

PH

Fordham Hall

Watercress Hall

PONDERS RD

28

Oak Farm

FOSSETTS LA

4

Fordham CE Prim Sch

CHESTER RD

HALSTEAD RD

MILL RD

VERNONS RD

3

WASH CNR

Mill House

Great Porter's Farm

Wash Farm

Fordstreet

Essex Way

PH

Fordstreet Bridge

FORD ST

River Colne

Fordham Bridge

27

PO

Sewage Works

2

Ashington Grove

Ryefields

FIDDLERS HILL

Fiddler's Wood

CO3

NEW RD

Cummins Farm

FORDSTREET HILL

PORTER'S LA

Fordham Heath

Bourchier's Hall Stud

Fiddler's Farm

PORTER'S CL

HEATH COTTS

Aldercar Wood

Hill Farm

PORTER'S COTTS

Eight Ash Green CE Prim Sch

HEATH RD

Bourchier's Hall

Gallows Green

FOXES LA

FODDERS FOLLY

BEECH GR

WOODLAND CHASE

1

HALSTEAD RD

CHOAT'S COTTS

Bullbanks Farm

GREEN LA

Aldham

Mantells

Choat's Wood

A1124

CHOAT'S WOOD

26

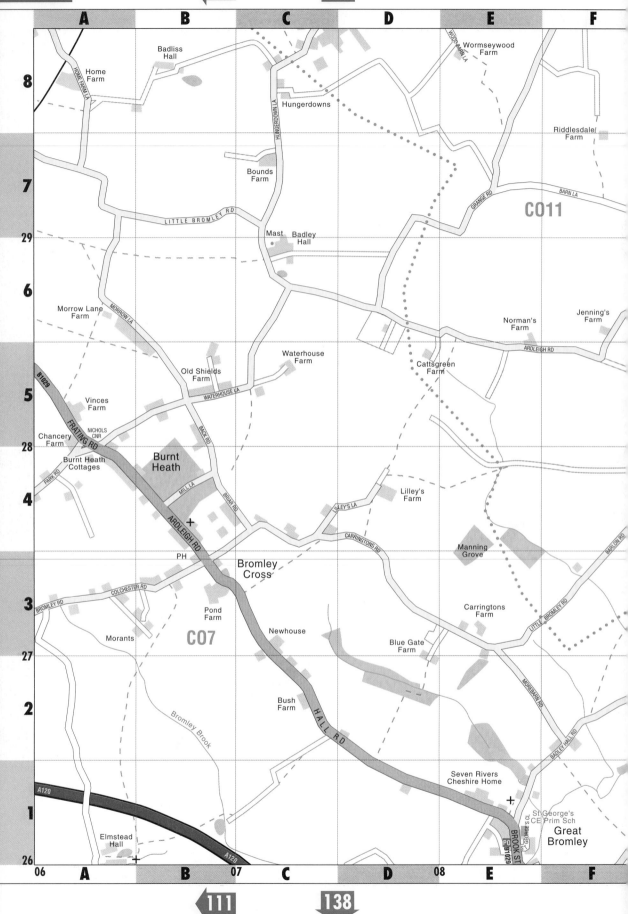

Home Farm
Badliss Hall
Wormseywood Farm
WOOD BARN LA
Hungerdowns
HUNGERDOWN LA
Riddlesdale Farm
Bounds Farm
GRANGE RD
BARN LA
CO11
LITTLE BROMLEY RD
Mast
Badley Hall
Morrow Lane Farm
MORROW LA
Norman's Farm
Jenning's Farm
ARDLEIGH RD
Old Shields Farm
Waterhouse Farm
WATERHOUSE LA
Cattsgreen Farm
B1029
Vinces Farm
NICHOLS CNR
BACK RD
FRATING RD
Chancery Farm
Burnt Heath Cottages
PARK RD
Burnt Heath
MILL LA
BRIAR RD
Lilley's Farm
LILLEY'S LA
CARRINGTONS RD
Manning Grove
BARLOW RD
ARDLEIGH RD
PH
Bromley Cross
Carringtons Farm
LITTLE BROMLEY RD
BROMLEY RD
COLCHESTER RD
Pond Farm
Morants
CO7
Newhouse
Blue Gate Farm
MOREBARN RD
Bush Farm
HALL RD
Bromley Brook
Seven Rivers Cheshire Home
BADLEY HALL RD
A120
St George's CE Prim Sch
Elmstead Hall
A120
ST GEORGE'S CL
BROOK ST
PO B1029
Great Bromley

06   07   08

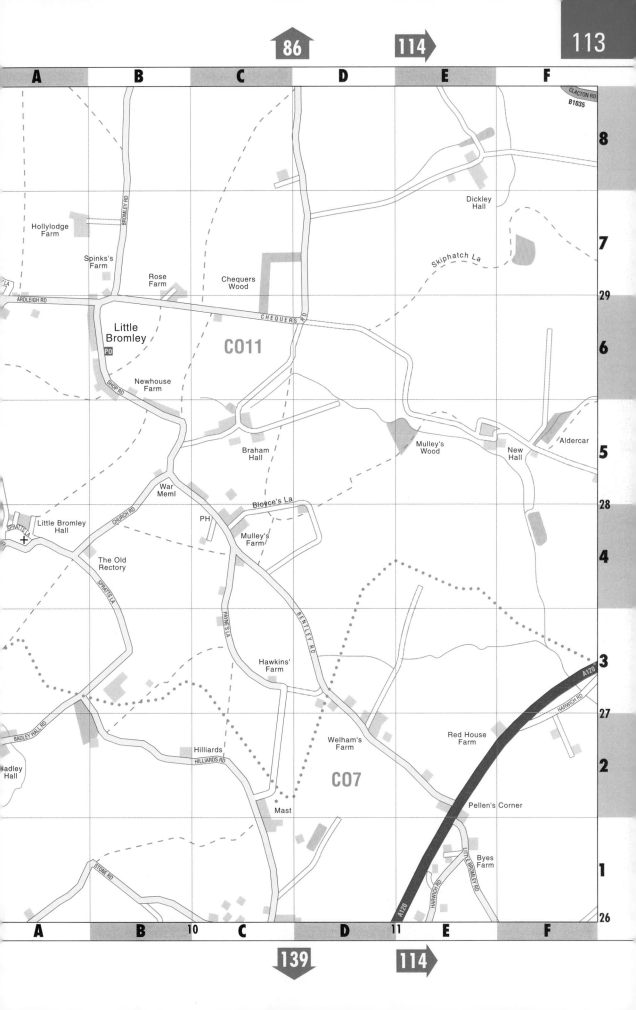

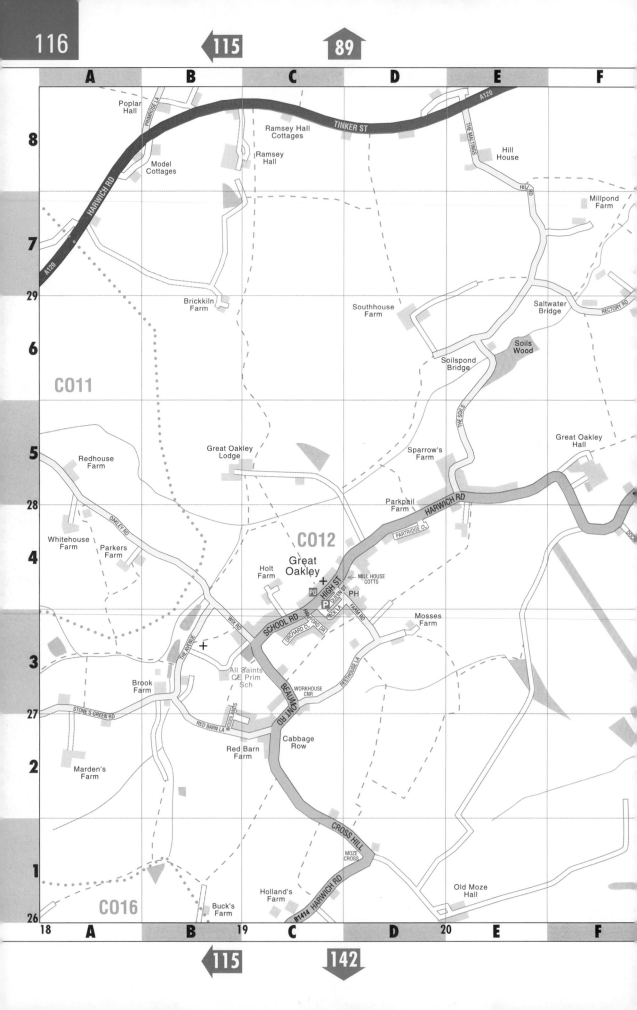

A B C D E F

8
Rectory La
Burnthouse Farm
BAY VIEW CRES
LODGE CT
LODGE RD
OAKLEY RD
MAYES RD
B1414

Little Oakley
Triangle Point
Jubilee Houses
RECTORY RD
HARWICH RD
SEAVIEW AVE
OAK LODGE
BEECH GR
ASPEN WAY
THE HORNBEAMS
Foulton Hall
Essex Way
South Hall Creek
7

29

White House
Little Oakley CE Inf Sch
PH
CHERRY TREE CL
PO
OAKLEY CROSS
Newhouse Farm
CO12
Long Bank
6

Little Oakley Hall
CLACTON RD
Sewage Works
5

28

DOCK LA
4

Great Oakley Dock (dis)
Boat Creek
3

27

Oakley Creek
Dugmore Creek
Great Oakley Works
Pewit Island
2

Bramble Island
Landing Stage
New Island
CO14
Old Moze Dock
Bramble Creek
1

26

A B 22 C D 23 E F

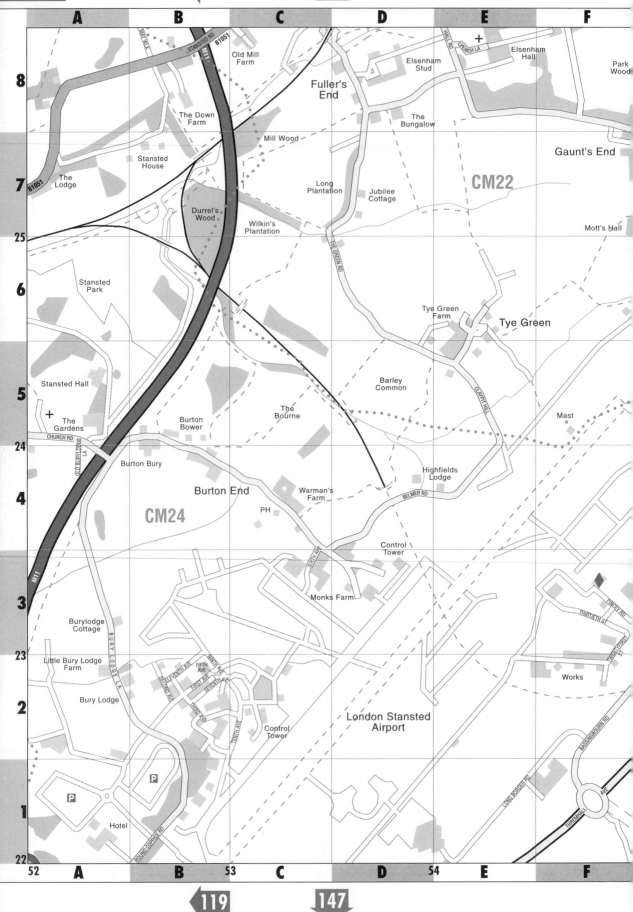

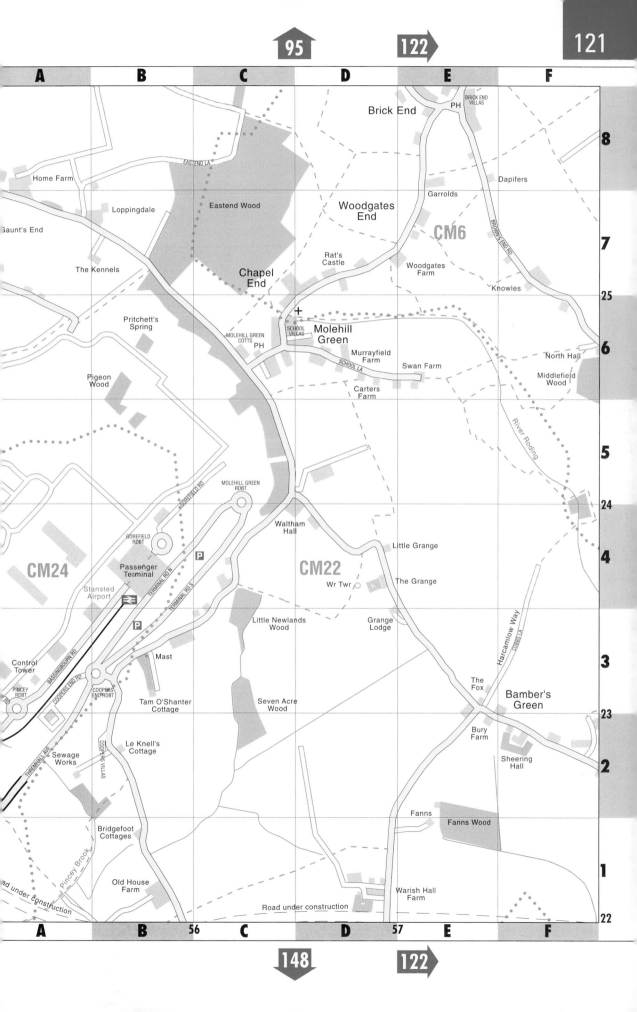

A B C D E F

8

Goodfellows

Broadmead

Little Bullen's

Muscombs

REBECCA MEADS

PH

THE ENDWAY

7

Foxholes

Furrows

Great Easton

WATER LA

South Hill

Croys Grange

BROOKS MEAD

Cherith House

Sewage Works

Cox Hill

25

The Grove

King's Farm House

The Willows

BROWN'S END RD

Broxted Hill

Perryfields

Easton Farm

6

Philipland Wood

Harcamlow Way

CM6

The Gorse

Round House

Little Easto

Flemings Hill Farm

Perryfield Ponds

WARWICK CL

The Lays

Middlefield Wood

The Old Laundry

GLEBE LA

BUTCHERS PASTURE

5

Brookend

Bookend Lodge

Broxted Common Wood

PH

MANOR RD

MAYNARD VILLAS

24

Easton Lodge

Gdns

Easton Glebe

4

Great Pond

Little Easton Farm

Horse Pond

PARK RD

3

River Roding

Lower Bamber's Green

CM22

23

2

The Hoppit

Washlands

White House

Lodge

1

Frogs Hall Farm

Stone Hall

High Wood

Frog Hall

22

58 A B 59 C D 60 E F

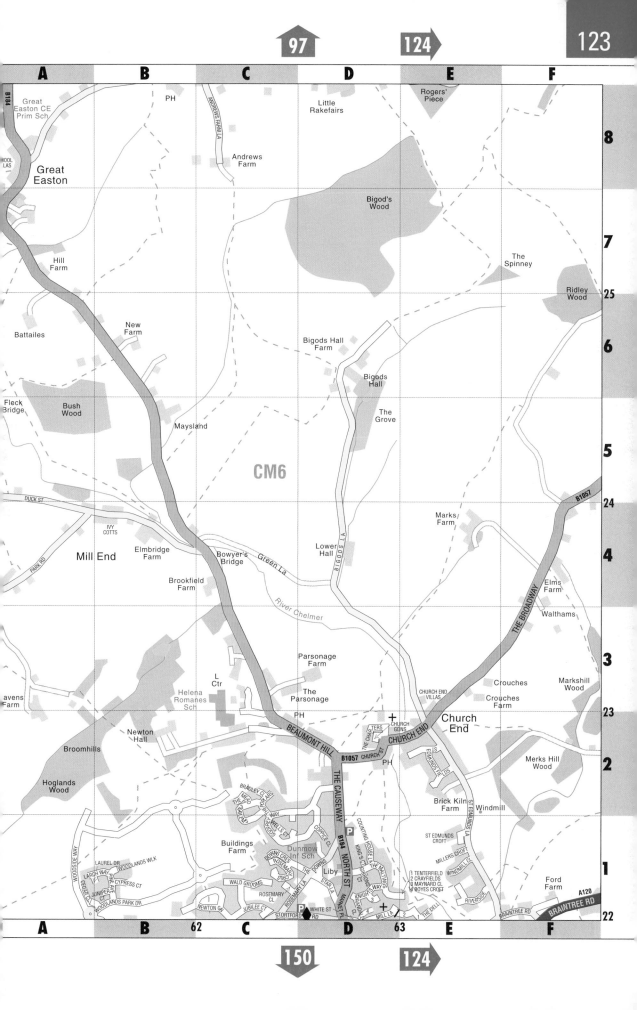

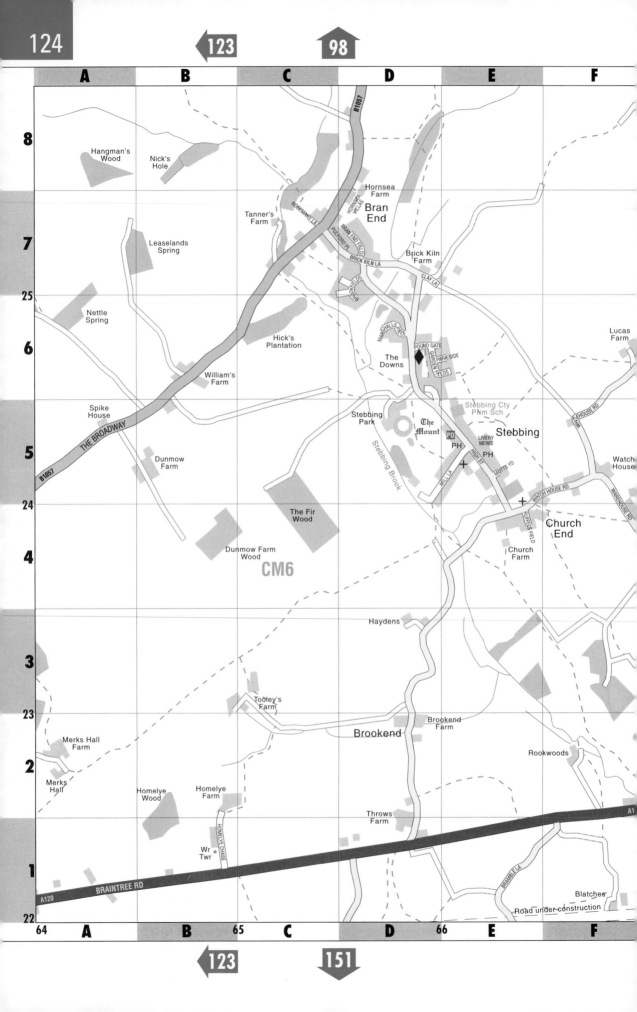

123
98

A B C D E F

8

Hangman's Wood

Nick's Hole

Hornsea Farm

Bran End

B1057

Tanner's Farm

ROSEMARY LA

HORNSEA VILLAS

BRAN END FIELDS

7

Leaselands Spring

PULFORD PL

BRICK KILN LA

Brick Kiln Farm

CLAY LA

BRACKFIELDS

25

Nettle Spring

Hick's Plantation

MARSHALL'S PCE

POUND GATE

GARDEN FIELDS

PARK SIDE

Lucas Farm

6

William's Farm

The Downs

Stebbing Cty Prim Sch

KENHOUSE RD

Spike House

Stebbing Park

The Mount

Stebbing

THE BROADWAY

PO

PH

LIVERY MEWS

PH

Watch House

B1057

Dunmow Farm

Stebbing Brook

MILL LA

HIGH ST

MOTTS YD

5

WATCH HOUSE RD

24

The Fir Wood

RUFFELS FIELD

Church End

WARE HOUSE RD

4

Dunmow Farm Wood

CM6

Church Farm

Haydens

3

Tooley's Farm

Brookend Farm

23

Merks Hall Farm

Brookend

Rookwoods

2

Merks Hall

Homelye Wood

Homelye Farm

Throws Farm

A1

1

HOMELYE CHASE

Wr Twr

BRAMBLE LA

Blatches

BRAINTREE RD

Road under-construction

A120

22

64 A B 65 C D 66 E F

123
151

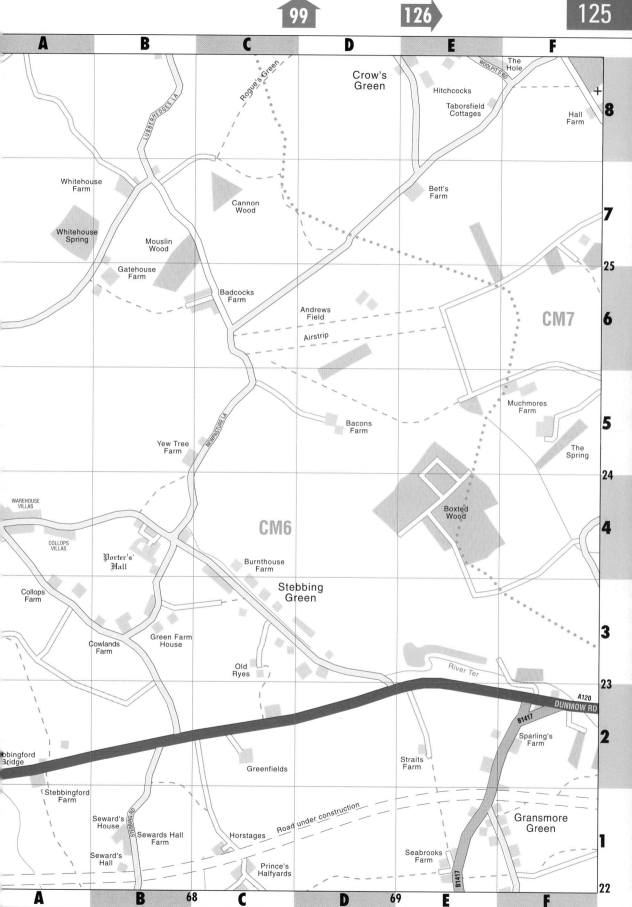

A B C D E F

The Hole
WOOLPIT'S RD
Crow's Green
Hitchcocks
Taborsfield Cottages
Hall Farm
8

Whitehouse Farm
Bett's Farm
Rogue's Green
LUBBERHEDGES LA
Cannon Wood
7

Whitehouse Spring
Mouslin Wood
25

CM7

Gatehouse Farm
Badcocks Farm
Andrews Field
6

Airstrip

NEWPASTURE LA
Yew Tree Farm
Bacons Farm
Muchmores Farm
5

The Spring
24

WAREHOUSE VILLAS
Boxted Wood
4

COLLOPS VILLAS
Porter's Hall
Burnthouse Farm
CM6

Collops Farm
Stebbing Green
3

Cowlands Farm
Green Farm House
Old Ryes
River Ter
23

A120
DUNMOW RD
B1417
Sparling's Farm
2

bbingford Bridge
Greenfields
Straits Farm

Stebbingford Farm
Gransmore Green

STEBBING RD
Seward's House
Sewards Hall Farm
Horstages
Road under construction
Seabrooks Farm
B1417
1

Seward's Hall
Prince's Halfyards
22

68
69

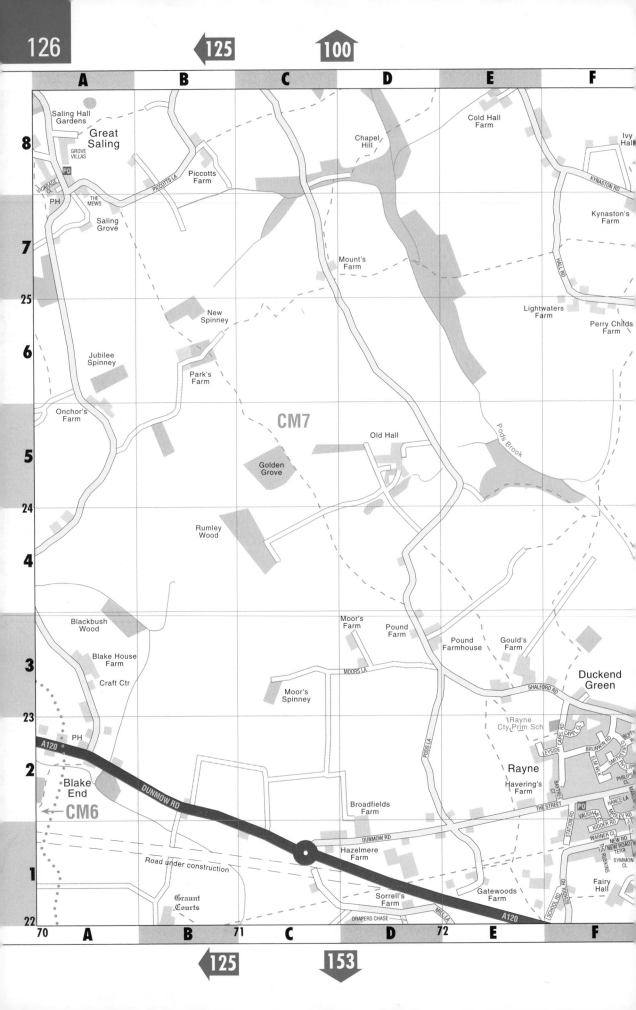

A B C D E F

8

Windmill (dis)
Church St
Mill Gdns Millers Cl
Round Wood
Monken Hadley
BROAD RD
A131
Willoughby's La
Willoughbys Farm

7

Doreward's Hall
THE CHASE
B1053
BROAD RD
Thistley Green Rd
Lyons Hall Rd
Lyons Hall
Bramble Wood
Lyonshall Wood
Woolmer Green Farm

25

Thistley Green
Covenbrook Hall

6

Highfield Stile Farm
Works
Highfield Stile Rd
Highfield Cl
Sewage Works

CM7

5

Braintree Coll.
Mill
CONVENT HILL
Convent La
The Cloisters
Doubleday
Nursery La
River Blackwater
Collingwood Rd
Norris
Cl
BOURCHIER AVE
B1053
Church La
Mus
PO
RIVER MEAD
Phillip's Cl
Bradford St
KINGFISHER GATE
NORTHUMBERLAND
Victory Gdns 1
Trafalgar Ct 2
Falkland Ct 3
Great Bradfords Cty Jun & Inf Sch
St Vincent Chase
Exeter
Boscawen Gdns
Drake
Gilbert Way
CANE
Cavendish
Albemarle Gdns
Rayleigh Cl
Guinea Cl
BRIDPORT WAY
STAFFORD
Jenkin's Farm

24

Bradford's Chase
BAWN CL
BLACKWATER WAY
VALLEY RD
PHILLIP'S CL
WARWICK
BEAUFORT GDNS
RUTLAND GDNS
NORFOLK CL
SOMERSET
ORION WAY
VANGUARD WAY
BEDFORD
ESSEX
Trafalgar Way
KENT GDNS
YORK GDNS
CORNWALL
GLOUCESTER GDNS
WARLEY
WELLINGTON CL
EDINBURGH GDNS
FISHER WAY
BEATTY GDNS
BYNG
NELSON GDNS
HAWKINS WAY
DRAKE GDNS
TINGALE
Sch
FARTHING
SOVEREIGN CL
CROWN GDNS
DEER LEAP WAY
DUNDOW CL
1 Tideswell Cl
2 Snowberry Ct
Hatches Farm

4

LITTLE BRADFORDS
JULIEN COURT RD
BLACKWATER WAY
WESTMINSTER
JOHN RAY ST
CUMBERLAND
PORTLAND
DALLWOOD
ROCHESTER CL
WIGOLD CT
ISHER WAY
JELLICOE WAY
CLAY PITS WAY
B1256
A131

Recn Gd

COGGESHALL RD

B1256
COGGESHALL RD
A120

3

B1256
CROFT CL
MOUNT RD
WOODFIELD RD
RAILWAY ST
KEBLE WAY
ST MARY'S RD
ALBERT RD
EAST ST
PO
TROTTERS FIELD
BEAUMONT
HOWARD CL
BADGER WOOD
AIDS
HAY LA
CUNNINGTON RD
WHEATLEY AVE
BARTRAM AVE
GULLS CROFT
CRABS CROFT
TWELVE AC RES
FORE FIELD
KITCHEN FIELD
CLARKS
WOOD DR
MAXWELL
DAPSER DR

23

CRAIG HO
THE LAURELS
VICTORIA ST
B1018
1 Jacquard Way
2 Groomside
3 The Mulberries
MANOR RD
ENTERPRISE
BENFIELD WAY
CHAPEL HILL
STUARTS WAY
CLOCKHOUSE WAY
BISHOPS AVE
MARKS GDNS
WARREN RD
Ley Wood
Templeborder Wood

2

B1256 SOUTH ST
ROSE
GDNS
Ind Est
STATION APP
Braintree
LAKES RD
ANGLIA WAY
THE CHASEWAY
HAYTOR CL
CRESSING RD
LEYWOOD CL
HUNTER RD
Pyefleet Lodge
BARN MEAD
BRICK KILN WAY
BECKERS GREEN RD
Sch
TANNERS
MDW
1 Cress Croft
2 Punders Field
3 Stilemans Wood
4 Deben Ct
5 Frating Ct
6 Stour Ct
7 Goldhanger Ct
8 Salcott Creek Ct
9 Crouch Ct

1

STEPHENSON RD
HILL SIDE GDNS
APPLETREE WLK
PEARTREE CL
LONGACRES
STRAWBERRY CL
ORCHARD DR
BRUNEL RD
WORCESTER CL
THE LINDENS
BRISE CL
SKITTS HILL
SKITTS HILL IND EST
DUGGERS LA
ROSE
MILL CT
SAXON BANK
ANGLIA
MILL PARK DR
EDESFIELD WAY
MILLENNIUM WAY
The Alec Hunter High Sch
MERSEY FLEET WAY
COLNE
CANT WAY
CHERITON RD
STUBBS LA
RODING CT
SALCOMBE RD
TAPESTRY WLK
THE LEY
MIDDLE KING
PLAINS FIELD
LOWER KING
SLOUGH HOUSE CL
PH
Cressing Lodge
Lanham Wood

22

76 A 77 B C 78 D E F

129
104

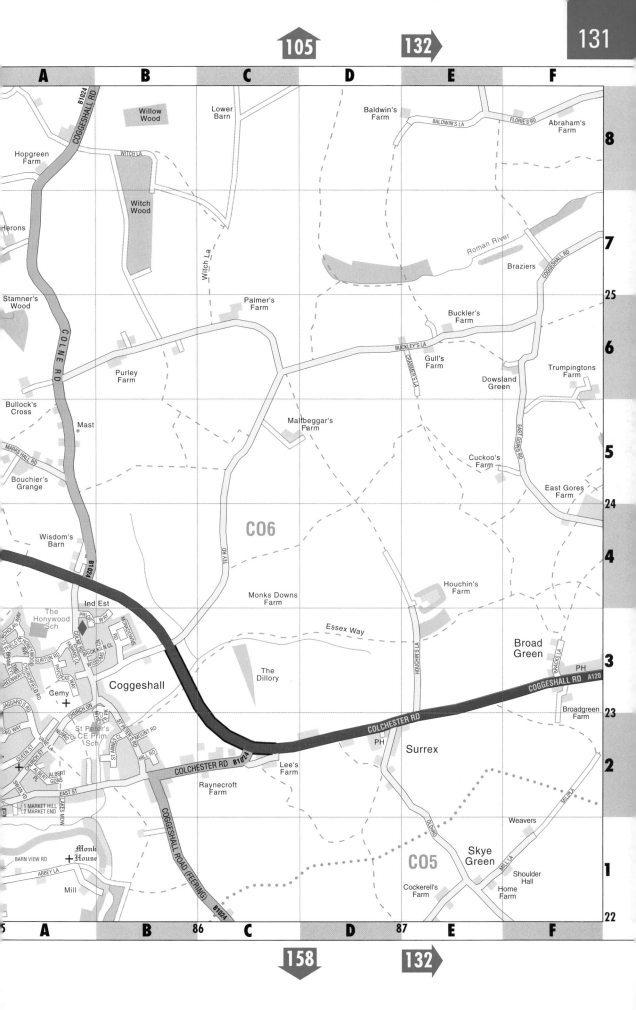

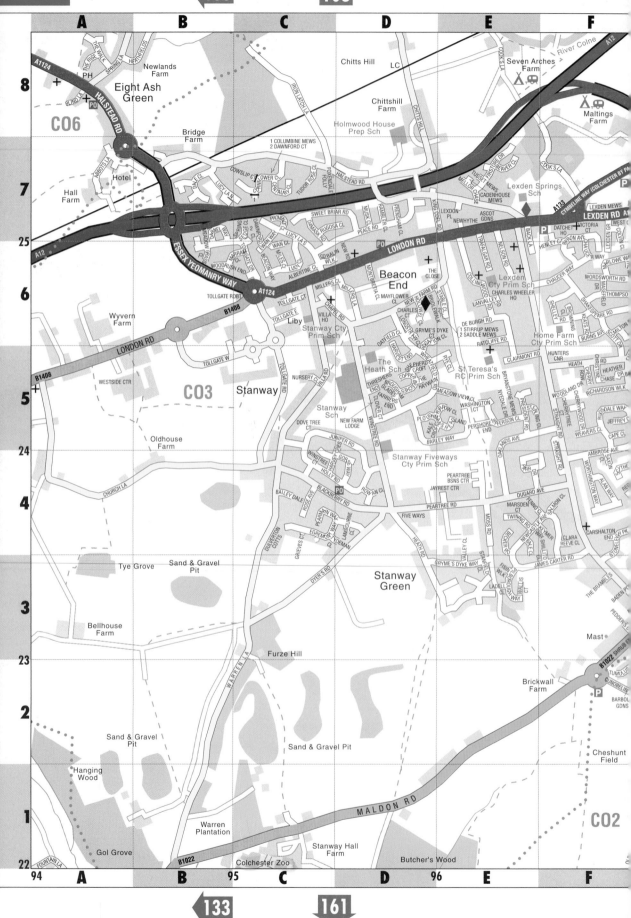

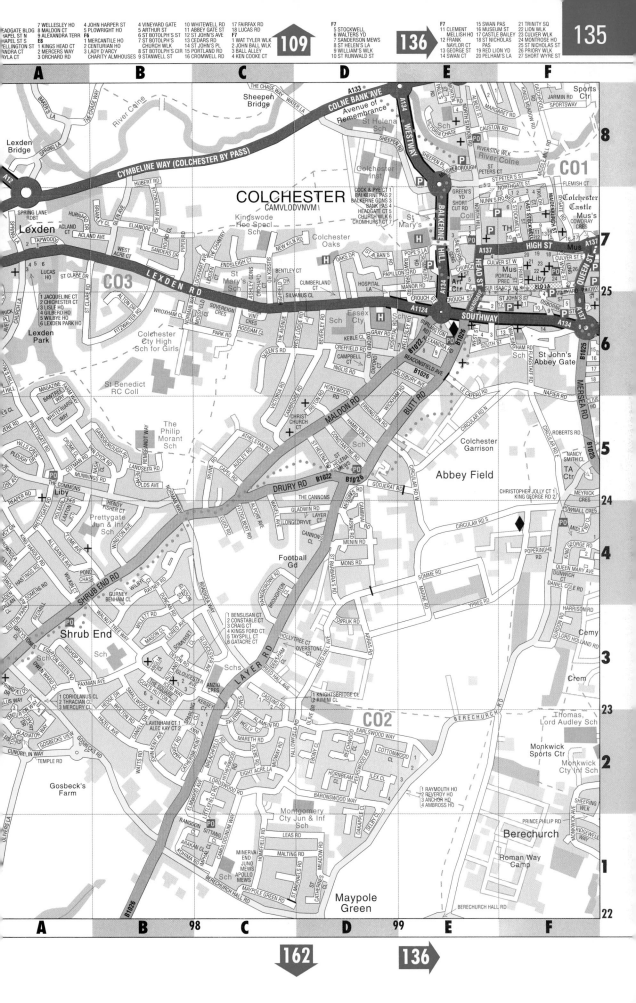

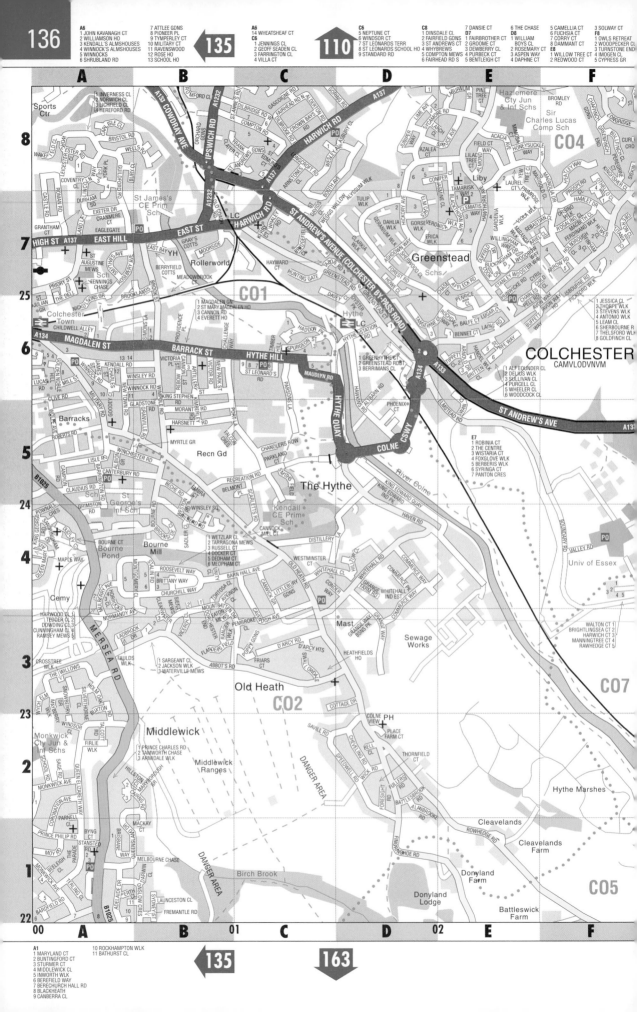

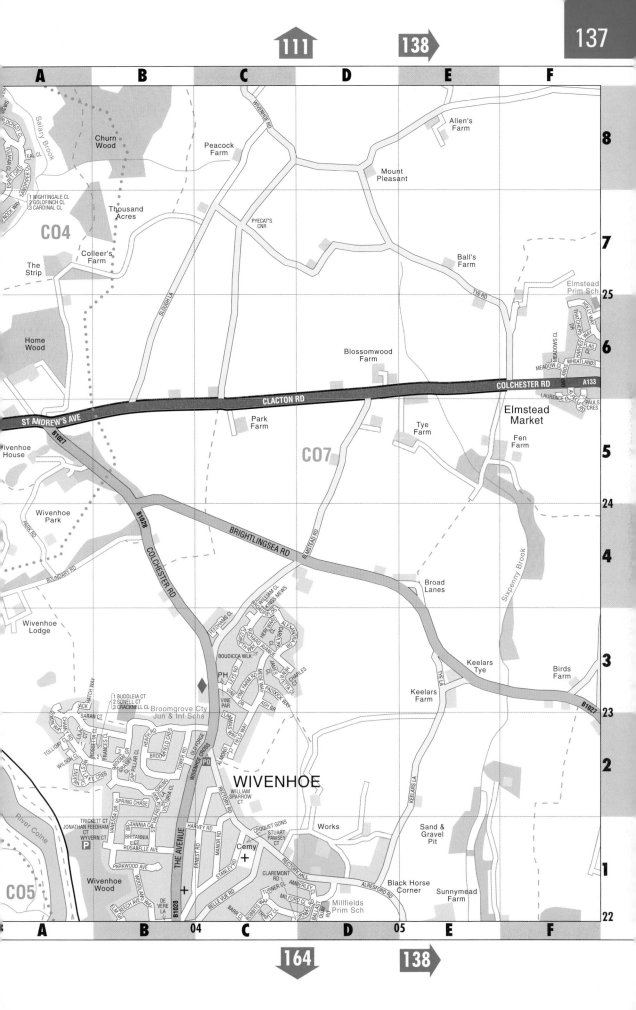

141
116

	A	B	C	D	E	F

8

Oldhouse Farm

Glebe Farm

Potland

B1414

HARWICH RD

B1414

The Horseshoes

New Moze Hall

CO12

Maze Creek

7

25

Northfield Farm

B1414

CHURCH LA

6

HARWICH RD

Lower Barn Farm

Landermere Creek

5

Quay Farm

Quay (dis)

Beaumont Cut

Beaumont Bridge

Beaumont Quay

White House

24

QUAY LA

CO16

GULL COTTS

4

GOLDEN LA

Landermere Hall

Landermere

3

Thorpe Lodge

New Hall

Kentshill Farm

CO13

LANDERMERE RD

WALTON RD

23

2

NEW TOWN RD

PALMERSTON RD

LONSDALE RD

SPENCER RD

KENILWORTH RD

1 HILLSIDE COTTS
2 LANDERMERE VIEW

2

Dale H Farm

ARGYLE RD

NEW THORPE AVE

ROLPH CL

THE SPINNEY

BELDAMS CL

Thorpe-le-Soken

DAMANT'S FARM LA

Damont's Farm

1

ABBEY CRES

B1414

Tendring Tech Coll

OAK CL

Elm Farm

BYNG HO

BYNG CRES

Folly Farm

WHITE LODGE CRES

Sneating Hall

STATION RD

ABBEY ST

B1414

B1033

HALL LA

FRINTON RD

B1033

B1034

SNEATING HALL LA

22

18	A	B	19	C	D	20	E	F

141
169

A B C D E F

8

Stone
Point

Stone
Marsh

Stone Creek

7

25

6

The Dardenelles

Cormorant Creek

The Naze
Nature Reserve

Standcreek
Salts

Salt Fleet

Sewage
Works

5

Walton
Channel

Walton Hall
Marshes

THE NAZE

Hedge-end
Island

24

CREEK
COTTS

The Naze
Nature Trail

CO14

Walton
Hall

4

The Naze
Tower

P

OLD HALL LA

The Twizzle

BUNNY POINT

3

PH

COLES LA

ELISABETH CT

LOUISE CL

P

Titchmarsh
Marina

Mabel Greville
Breakwater

23

HIGH TREE LA

CHAMFORD CL

FIRST AVE

SECOND AVE

THIRD AVE

NAZE PARK RD

D'ARCY HO
2 RIVERS HO

FITTLE CL

ASHD

P

SPENDE
CL

1
2

P.O

FLORENCE RD

CLIFF PAR

2

BRIAR BISHOP CL

Sole Creek

BEATRICE RD

Jubilee
Beach

PERCIVAL RD

COLES LA

TUDOR CL

HALL LA

GREEN LA

WINFIELD
TERR

Walton
Maritime
Mus

Walton
Mere

CH

COASTGUARD
COTTS

EAST TERR

East Terrace
Breakwater

KINGS
REACH

P

1

MILL LA

Walton
Prim Sch

PRINCE'S ESPL

SAVILLE ST

Martello
Tower

NORTH ST

STANDLEY RD

EAGLE AVE

B1034

22

A7
1 THE CAUSEWAY
2 THE OLD MALTINGS
3 FULLER CT
4 LIMES CRES
5 RED LION CT
6 BAKERS CT

7 HOCKERILL CT
8 HARRINGTON CL
9 PRIORS
10 CLIFFORD CT
11 THOMAS HESKIN CT
12 MASTERMAN WHARF

B8
1 BOYD CL
2 HEATH ROW
3 STORTFORD HALL RD
4 GROSVENOR HO
5 EATON HO
6 BELGRAVE HO

← 145   119 ↑

	A	B	C	D	E	F

Collins Cross

Waytmore Castle

Hockerill

BISHOP'S STORTFORD

CM23

CM22

Little Beldams

Grate Beldams

Great Jenkins

Sewage Works

Twyford Bury Farm

River Stort

Twyford Mill

Latchmore Bank

Normandale Kennels

Howe Green

Anvil Cross

Captain's Plantation

Great Hallingbury

The Hall

Hall Farm

Long Plantation

Hallingbury Park

Ladywell Plantation

Morleys

Woodside Green

Start Hill Farm

Birchanger Green Services

Hotel

DUNMOW RD

STANSTED RD

LONDON RD

HALLINGBURY RD

LATCHMORE BANK

CHURCH RD

A1250 A1060 B1383 A1060 A120 M11

1 KIMBERLEY CL
2 MILL ST
3 MILLSIDE

1 BARKERS MEAD
2 GEORGE GREEN

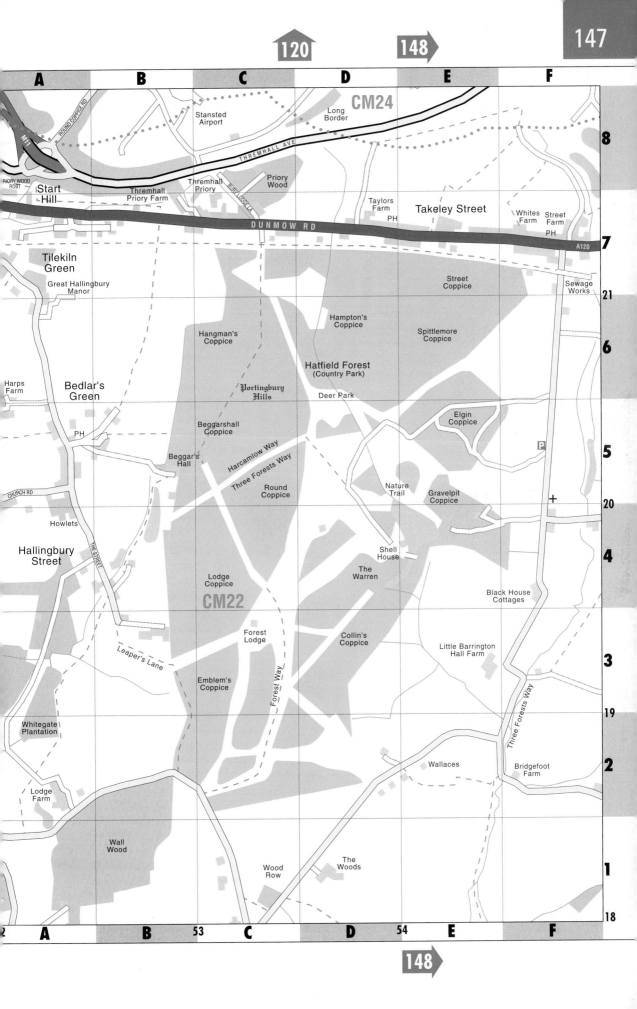

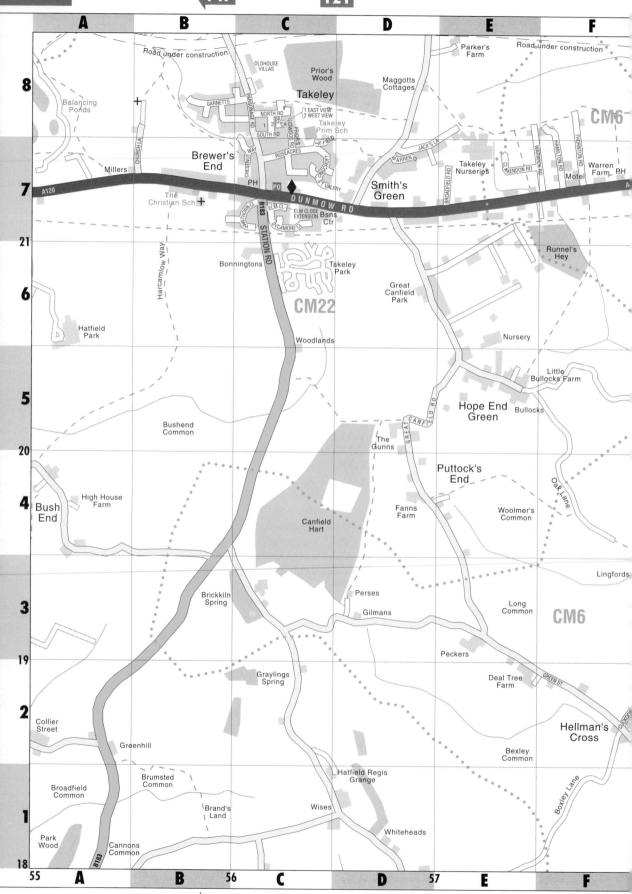

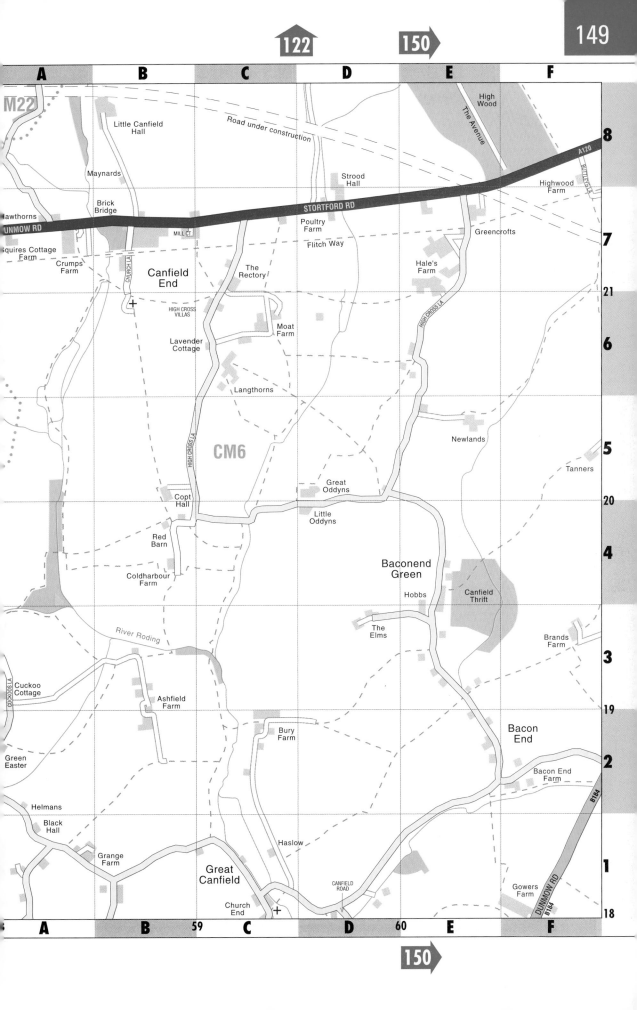

A　　B　　C　　D　　E　　F

M22

Little Canfield
Hall

Maynards

Brick
Bridge

Hawthorns

DUNMOW RD

Squires Cottage
Farm

Crumps
Farm

CHURCH LA

Canfield
End

MILL CT

STORTFORD RD

Road under construction

Strood
Hall

Poultry
Farm

Flitch Way

The Rectory

HIGH CROSS
VILLAS

High Cross La

Moat
Farm

Lavender
Cottage

Langthorns

CM6

HIGH CROSS LA

Copt
Hall

Red
Barn

Coldharbour
Farm

River Roding

CUCKOO LA

Cuckoo
Cottage

Ashfield
Farm

Green
Easter

Helmans

Black
Hall

Grange
Farm

Great
Canfield

Church
End

Bury
Farm

Haslow

CANFIELD
ROAD

Great
Oddyns

Little
Oddyns

Baconend
Green

Hobbs

The
Elms

Canfield
Thrift

High
Wood

The Avenue

A120

Highwood
Farm

BUTTLES LA

Greencrofts

Hale's
Farm

Newlands

Tanners

Brands
Farm

Bacon
End

Bacon End
Farm

B184

DUNMOW RD

Gowers
Farm

8

7

21

6

5

20

4

3

19

2

1

18

A　　B　59　　C　　D　60　　E　　F

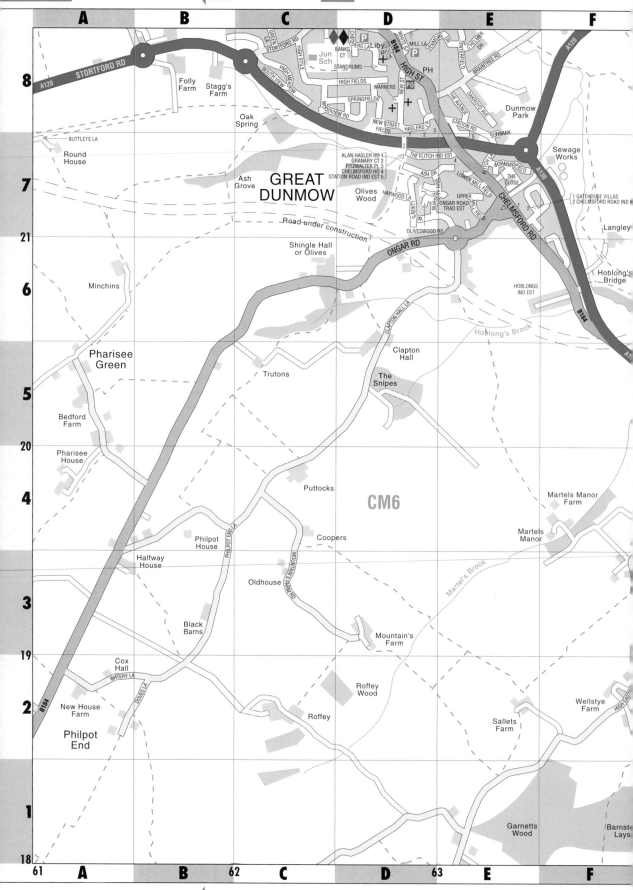

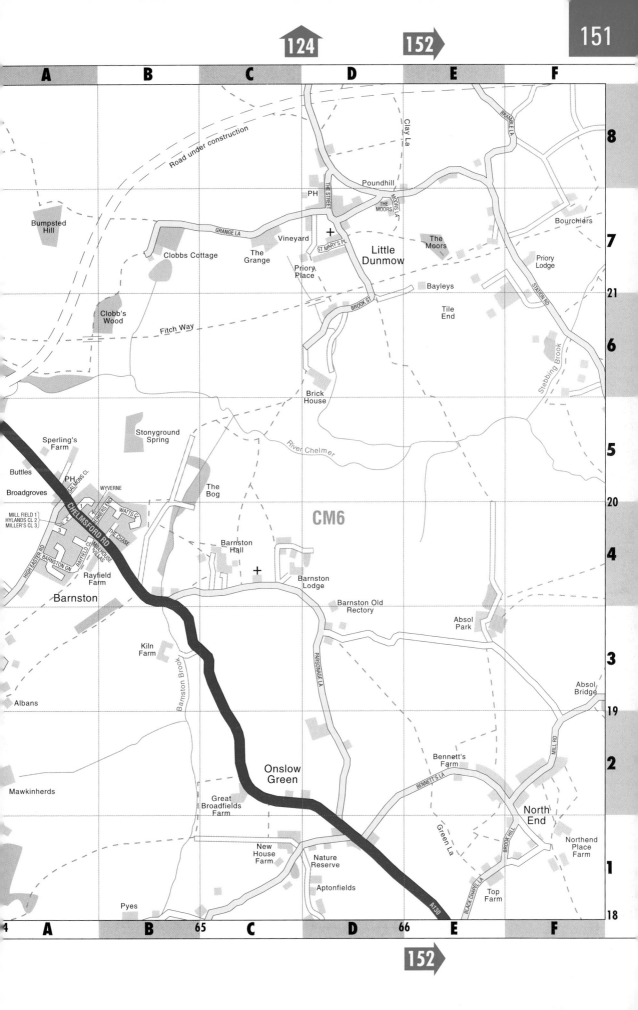

151 125

| A | B | C | D | E | F |

8

Stebbing Brook

Brook Farm

Gifford House

Fitch Way

Great Greenfields

7

Miniature Rifle Range

Stebbing Rd

Weavers Farm

Felmoor Farm

Sunnybrook Farm

Watch house Green

Felsted Cty Prim Sch

21

Water Tower

CHESTNUT WLK

Chaffix CL

CHAFFIX

GARNETTS LA

Chaffix Farm

OXNEY VILLAS

RAVENS CRES

Bannister Green Villas

CRESSAGES

STEVENS LA

6

PLAYERS CT

Felsted Sch

ALDERTON CL

BRAINTREE RD

Chaffix

Oxney's Farm

BURNSIDE RD

THE CO

PH

Bannister Green

Bury Farm

FELSTED ALMSHOUSES

GARNETTS VILLAS

THE ORCHARD

JOLLYBOYS LA N

GARNETTS BGLWS

5

STATION RD

BURY FIELDS

PO

RICHE CL

CROMWELL PK

Felsted Pl

Hotel

The Jun Sch Felsted

Playing Field

CM6

Cleveland's Farm

20

Mariskalls

THE TERRACE

Felsted

BAKERS LA

Jollyboys

JOLLYBOYS LA

Cock Green

Brick Hous Farm

Mill Moorings

CHELMSFORD RD

Potash Farm

4

MILL RD

BRICKBURN CL

Cobler's Green

Pondpark Farm

Mill House

LADYSMITH COTTS

CAUSEWAY END RD

3

River Chelmer

Causeway End

Glanfield's Farm

19

Millbank's Farm

2

LEEZ LA

CM3

1

The Gate House

Prior's Green

B1417

CAUSEWA

18

| 67 | A | 68 | B | C | 68 | D | 69 | E | F |

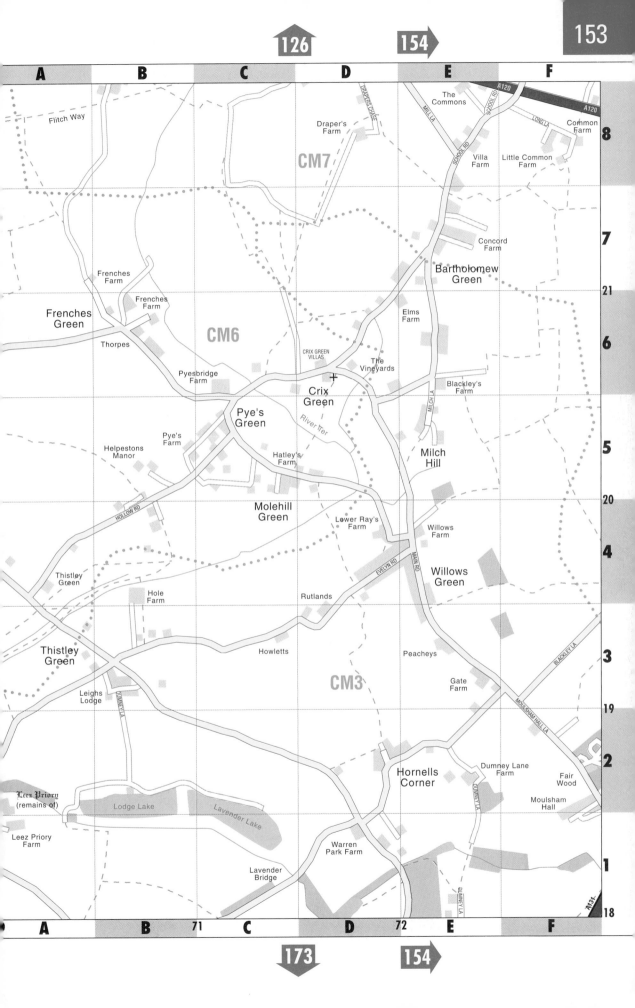

A B C D E F

126
154

Flitch Way

The Commons

Draper's Farm

CM7

MILL LA

SCHOOL RD

A120

A120

Common Farm

8

Villa Farm

Little Common Farm

Concord Farm

7

Frenches Farm

Frenches Farm

Bartholomew Green

21

Frenches Green

CM6

Thorpes

Elms Farm

6

Pyesbridge Farm

Crix Green Villas

The Vineyards

Crix Green

Blackley's Farm

MILCH LA

Pye's Green

River Ter

Milch Hill

5

Pye's Farm

Helpestons Manor

Hatley's Farm

HOLLOW RD

Molehill Green

Lower Ray's Farm

Willows Farm

20

Thistley Green

EVELYN RD

MAIN RD

Willows Green

4

Hole Farm

Rutlands

Thistley Green

Howletts

Peacheys

CM3

BLACKLEY LA

3

Leighs Lodge

DUNMEY LA

Gate Farm

MOULSHAM HALL LA

19

Hornells Corner

Dumney Lane Farm

Fair Wood

2

Leez Priory (remains of)

Lodge Lake

Lavender Lake

DUNMEY LA

Moulsham Hall

Leez Priory Farm

Warren Park Farm

1

Lavender Bridge

DUNMEY LA

A13t.

18

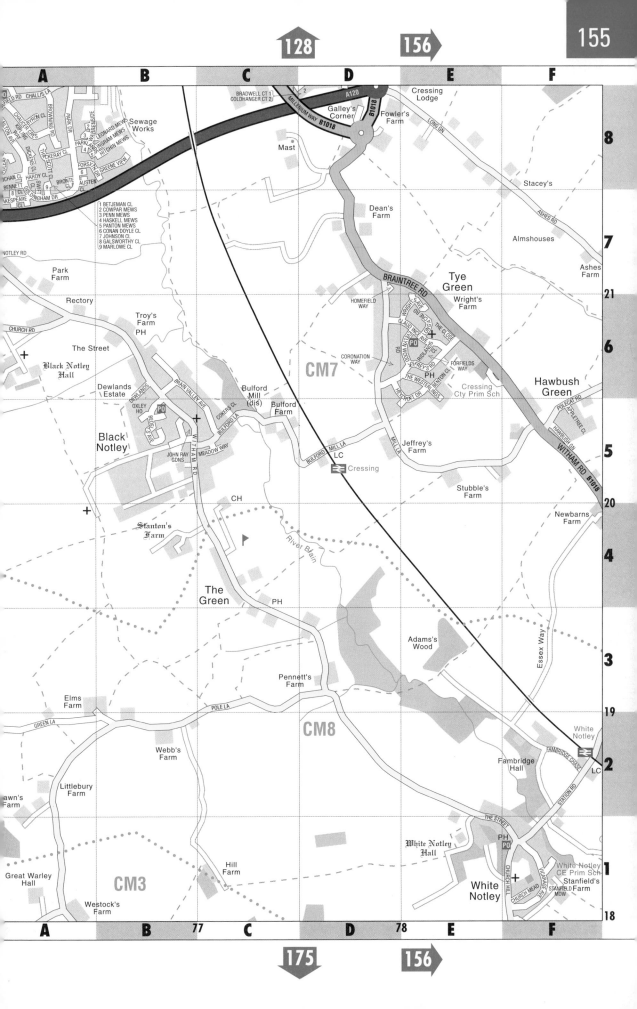

A **B** **C** **D** **E** **F**

8

7

21

6

5

20

4

19

3

2

18

BRADWELL CT 1
COLDHANGER CT 2
Galley's Corner
Fowler's Farm
Cressing Lodge
MILLENNIUM WAY
B1018
A120
B1018
Sewage Works
Mast
Dean's Farm
Stacey's
Almshouses
Ashes Farm
ASHES RD
LONG GN

1 BETJEMAN CL
2 COWPAR MEWS
3 PENN MEWS
4 HASKELL MEWS
5 PANTON MEWS
6 CONAN DOYLE CL
7 JOHNSON CL
8 GALSWORTHY CL
9 MARLOWE CL

NOTLEY RD
Park Farm
Rectory
CHURCH RD
Troy's Farm PH
The Street
Black Notley Hall
Dewlands Estate
OXLEY HO
DEWLANDS
PO
BEDDY'S AVE
BRAIN VALLEY AVE
COKERS CL
BULFORD LA
Black Notley
WITHAM RD
JOHN RAY GDNS
MEADOW WAY
Bulford Mill (dis)
Bulford Farm
CH
Stanton's Farm
BRAINTREE RD
Tye Green
Wright's Farm
HOMEFIELD WAY
WRIGHT'S AVE
CLAUD INCE AVE
WOOD FIELD RD
THE CLOSE
PO
JEFFREY P'RD
PH
THE WESTERLINGS
REXPROFT DR
FENTON CL
FORFIELDS WAY
Cressing Cty Prim Sch
CORONATION WAY
CM7
Hawbush Green
POLECAT RD
APPLETREE CL
HAWBUSH GN
WITHAM RD
B1018
BULFORD MILL LA
MILL LA
LC
Cressing
Jeffrey's Farm
Stubble's Farm
Newbarns Farm
River Brain
The Green
PH
Adams's Wood
Essex Way
Pennett's Farm
CM8
Elms Farm
GREEN LA
POLE LA
Webb's Farm
White Notley
FAMBRIDGE CHASE
LC
Fambridge Hall
STATION RD
Littlebury Farm
awn's Farm
Great Warley Hall
CM3
Hill Farm
Westock's Farm
THE STREET
White Notley Hall
PH
PO
CHURCH HILL
VICARAGE AVE
White Notley
CHURCH MEAD
White Notley CE Prim Sch
Stanfield's Farm
STANFIELD MDW

	A	B	C	D	E	F

8

Lanham Manor Farm

Wr Twr

Lanham Green

Jubilee Plantation

Sand & Gravel Pit

7

Links Rd

Clapdog Green

Gosling's Farm

Ashes Farm

Ashes Rd

PH

Link's Farm

Link's Wood

Schills Farm

LANHAM GREEN RD

THE STREET

21

Essex Way

6 Cressing

Wright's Farm

Airfield (disused)

POLECAT RD

Egypts Farm

Mast

Sheepcotes Farm

BOARS TYE RD

Rolph's Farmhouse

CM7

CHURCH RD

SHEEPCOTES LA

5

CO5

BROOMFIELD

THE GOSLINGS

BROADWAY CT

Silver End

20

B1018

WEAVERSFIELD

RUNNACLES ST

BROADWAY

RACHAEL GDNS

FRANCIS CT

WALTER WAY

SILVER ST

REBECCA GDNS

CONCIL HOUSES

PETTIT LA

MANORS WAY

FRANCIS WAY

Liby

DANIEL WAY

4

MANORS

Hotel

PO

THE SHOPS

CRICK LA

GROOM WY

GROOMS LA

JOSEPH GDNS

New House

Works

VALENTINE WAY

Bower Hall

WESTERN RD

3 Sheepcote Wood

WITHAM RD

TEMPLE LA

MAGDALENE CRES

LEICESTER CT

STRETFORD CT

BRISTOL CT

SCHOOL RD

BOWERS CT

PH

WESTERN CL

WESTERN LA

Park House

STATION RD

Silver End Cty Prim Sch

CM8

19

Rivenhall Pl

2

Cressing Temple Barns

Old Court Room

Cressing Temple

Essex Way

1 Sewage Works

B1018

Hungry Hall

Rivenhall Thicks

18

| 79 | A | B | 80 | C | D | 81 | E | F |

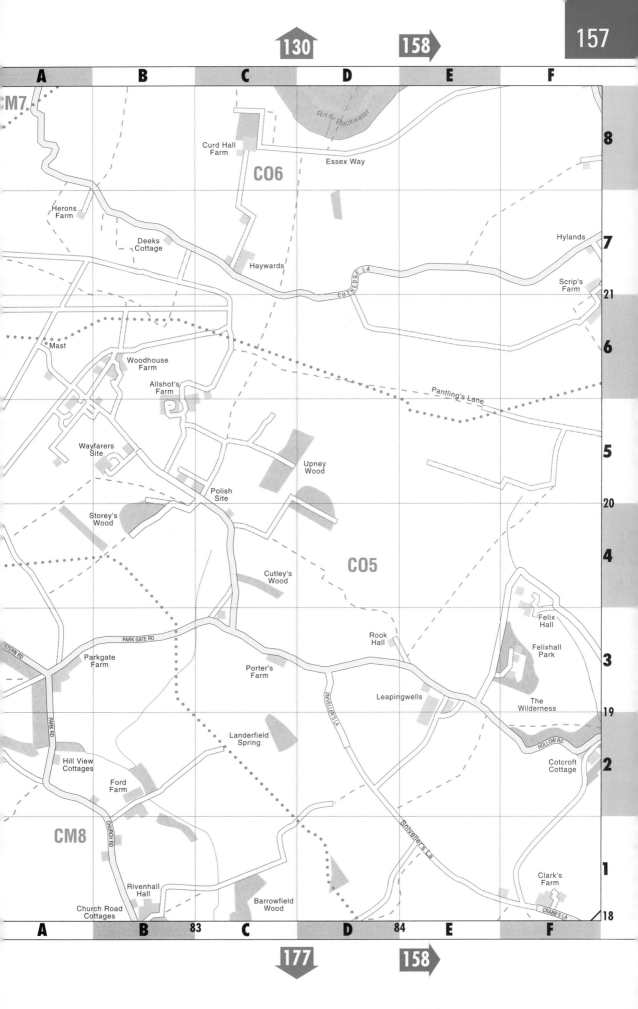

157
131

A B C D E F

8

Pondwick

Coggeshall
Hamlet

CO6

Langley
Green

Langle
Farm

Feeringbury

Kelvedon Rd
Pointwell La
Pointwell
Mill

Littlebury

Old Rd

Outhedge La
Scrip's Rd

7

Gull
Hole

Sewage
Works

Mill
Cottages

Old Mill La

Little Tey Rd

+

Ced
Cotta

21

Scrip's
Farm

Halfway
Cotts

PH

COGGESHALL ROAD (FEERING)
B1024

Frame
Farm

Stocks
Green

Wills
Gn

+

Hanover
Sq

Long Acres

6

Coggeshall
Hall

Feering
Place

Church
Farm

5

Monk's
Farm

White
Barn

Farm Hill
House

Pantlings La

Coggeshall Rd

Glebe Gdns
Moorfield
PO
+
PH
The Street

Hanover Bridge

Hanover
Bridge

New La

B1024
LONDON RD

Feering

Feering CE
Prim Sch
Cemy

London Rd

Little
London

20

CO5

River Blackwater

Harvest Ct
Rye Mill La
Waterman Rd
Mill Crs
Mill Mead

Hall Farm Cl

B1024

B1023

Gore
Pit

4

Windmill
Farm

Observer Way

Sherwood Way
MR
Packway Cl
Driffield Cl

PH

Inworth Rd

Thresherfords
BSNS PK

Newtown

Kings Meadow Ct

Barnwell

Feering Hill
Greenways
Raven Ct

Brick Kiln
Farm

3

Park
Farm

Kelvedon

Station Rd
Rosslyn Terr
Swan St

Hollow Rd

Dowches Cotts 1
Peters Ho 2
Spurgeon Pl 3
Braddy Ct 4
Western Ho 5
Argyle Ct 6

Cherry
Tree Ho

Dowches Gdns

Mallard's
Heron Pl
Tern Cl
Tern Cl

Worlds End La

Park
Farm

19

Lingwoods
Churchill

Rolleylane
Bridge

Church Rd
New Rd
Glebe Rd
Croft Rd
Thorne Rd

HIGH ST

St Mary's Rd
Rolley La
6
The Chase

Orchard Rd
Doucecroft
Sch

Gadwall Reach
Moorfield Rd
Avocet Cl
Curlew Cl
Lapwing Dr

Kelvedon
CANONIVM

LC
Cemy

Ratcliffe
Ct

Casterford Rd

St Mary's
CE Prim Sch

Wigeon Way
Dunlin Ct
Godwit Ct

+

2

+

+
St Mary's Sq
PH

Brockwell

Riverside Way

1

Church
Hall

Liby & Feering Mus

Malden Rd

Grey's
Mill

Ewell
Hall

Inworth
Hall

B1024 LONDON RD

Ewell Hall Chase

A12

18

85 A 86 B C 87 D E F

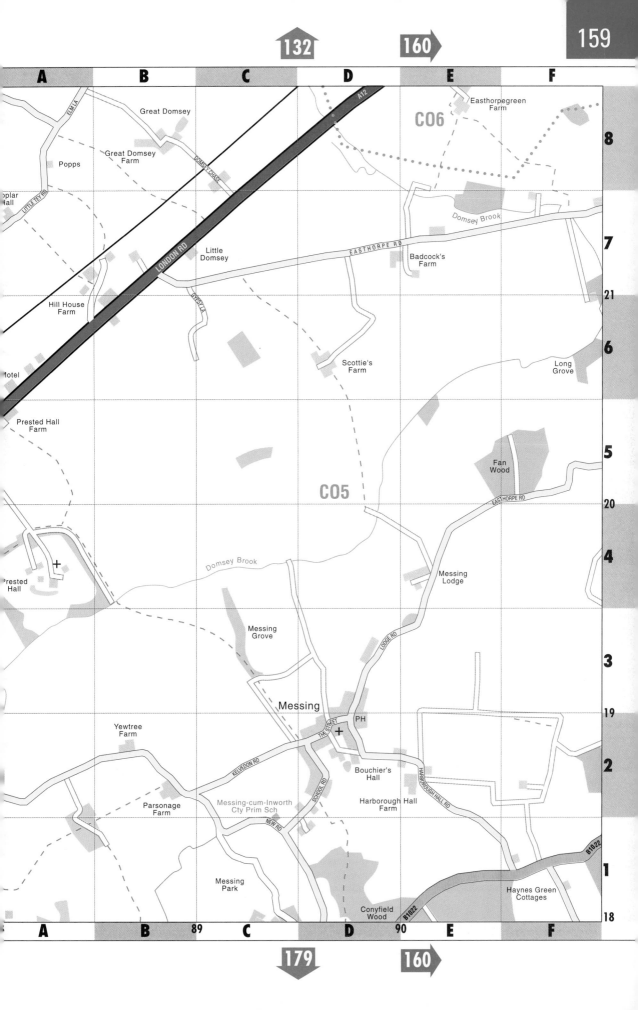

A   B   C   D   E   F

A12

CO6

Easthorpegreen
Farm

Great Domsey

ELM LA

Great Domsey
Farm

Popps

8

Domsey Brook

Poplar
Hall

LITTLE TEY RD

DOMSEY CHASE

Little
Domsey

LONDON RD

EASTHORPE RD

Badcock's
Farm

7

Hill House
Farm

B1024

21

Motel

Scottie's
Farm

Long
Grove

6

Prested Hall
Farm

Fan
Wood

5

CO5

EASTHORPE RD

20

Prested
Hall

Domsey Brook

Messing
Lodge

4

Messing
Grove

LODGE RD

3

Messing

19

Yewtree
Farm

PH

THE STREET

KELVEDON RD

Bouchier's
Hall

HARBOROUGH HALL RD

2

Parsonage
Farm

SCHOOL RD

Messing-cum-Inworth
Cty Prim Sch

Harborough Hall
Farm

NEW RD

Messing
Park

B10 22

B1022

Haynes Green
Cottages

1

Conyfield
Wood

18

A   B   89   C   D   90   E   F

A B C D E F

8

Little Birch
Holt Farm

St Mary's
Grange

Boarded
Barn

CO6

Eastorpe
Hall

EASTHORPE RD

Bockingham Hall
Farm

PH ONSLOW
COTTS Eastorpe

CHURCHWELL AVE

Seller
Wood

7

Whitehouse
Farm

Potash
Wood

WELL LA

21

Hogget's
Farm

6

Porters
Green

Hellens

Hardy's
Green

Winterflood's
Farm

Beckingham
Hall

Round
Grove

Sandfordhall
Green

Shemmings
Farm

Cantfield's
Farm

EASTHORPE RD

Radar
Spinney

Glebe
Farm

CO2

5

Greenacres

20

Brake's
Farm

4

BLIND LA

MALDON RD

Sewa
Work

CAPEL LA

Sand
Pit

3

Palmer's
Farm

ROUNDBUSH
CNR

19

Birch
Holt

2

Birch Holt
Cottages

CO5

ROUNDBUSH RD

Roundbush
Farm

Smythe's
Green

Pond
Farm

B1022

Layerwood
Farm

Duke's
Farm

WINTER'S RD

WINTER'S HILL

1

Grassreasons
Farm

Thorrington's
Farm

Layer
Wood

18

91 A B 92 C D 93 E F

A B C D E F

8

Sodoms
CH
King's Ford Park Hotel

BERECHURCH RD
PH
BERECHURCH HALL RD
BERECHURCH HALL RD
LETH GR

Berechurch Hall Camp

7

Kingsford Farm

Fridaywood Farm

21

King's Ford Bridge

PH

P

6

Friday Wood

Park Farm

Mill House

CO2

Bounstead Bridge

Roman River

HALL LA

CHERRY TREE LA

NEW CUT
HIGH RD
B1026

LES BUS
THE FOLLY
MILL LA
BOUNSTEAD HILL

Wood Field End
2
Old Forge
1
SWALLOW CL
MARTIN END
GRT HOUSE FARM RD
NANTWICH RD
MALLARD CL
ABBERTON RD
Lower End

5

Malting Green
Lower Houses
Wellhouse
LAYER RD
Abberton Manor

20

1 WINSTREET CL
2 GREENACRES RD
Malting Green House
MALTING GREEN RD

4

RYE LA
FIELDS FARM RD
Hill Farm
OXLEY HILL

Rye Farm

Layer Fields House

Abberton Hall
RECTORY

3

Blind Knights

CO5

19

2

Abberton Reservoir

1

18

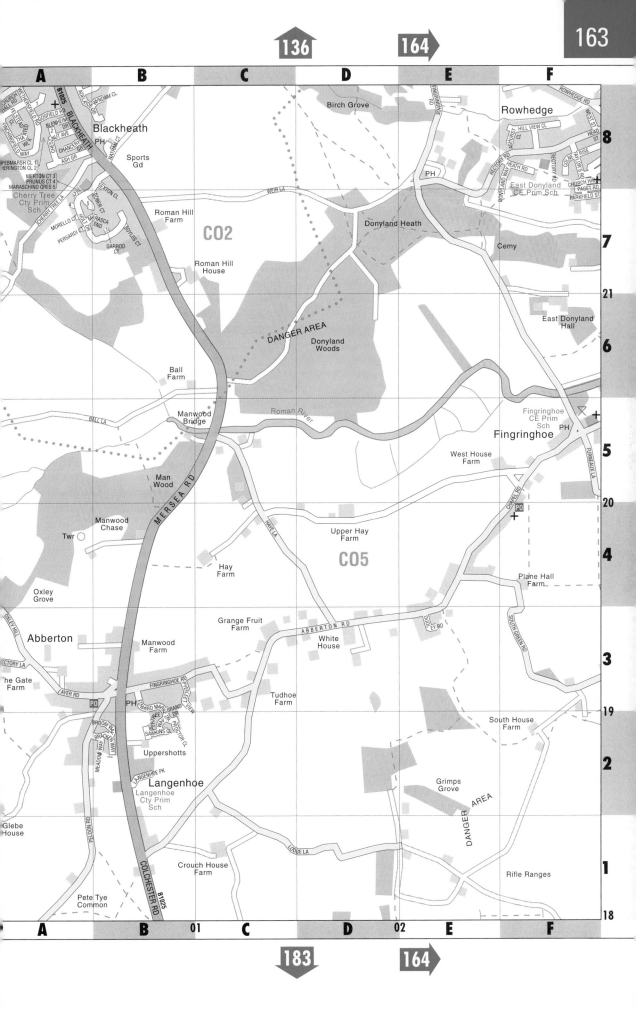

Blackheath

NETHERFIELD
CHURCH HALL RD
CROSFIELD RD
FINCHINGFIELD WAY
THATE WK
BLENHEIM DR
CHESTNUT AVE
CHANCERY RD
ASH GR
B1025
ADELAIDE DR
WYNDAM CL
NATHAN CT
PH

PEBMARSH CL 1
HERINGTON CL 2

Sports Gd

Cherry Tree Cty Prim Sch

MERTON CT 3
PRUNUS CT 4
MARASCHINO CRES 5

CHERRY TREE LA
MORELLO CT
HOLLY DR
PERSARDI CT
MARASCA END
SEXTON CL
BOMER CT
POYLES CT
GARROD CT

Roman Hill Farm

CO2

Roman Hill House

Birch Grove

Donyland Heath

WEIR LA

Rowhedge

ROWHEDGE RD
RECTORY RD
HEATH RD
DONYLAND WAY
HILL VIEW CL
HURST CL
COLNE TAYLORS RISE
RECTORY RD
HEAD ST
WEST LA
CHURCH HILL
PAGET RD
PARKFIELD ST

East Donyland CE Prim Sch

FINGRINGHOE RD

PH

Cemy

21

East Donyland Hall

DANGER AREA

Donyland Woods

Ball Farm

Manwood Bridge

Roman River

Man Wood

BALL LA

MERSEA RD

Fingringhoe CE Prim Sch
PH

Fingringhoe

West House Farm

FURNEAUX LA

Twr

Manwood Chase

Oxley Grove

HAY LA

CHAPEL RD
PO

Upper Hay Farm

CO5

Plane Hall Farm

Hay Farm

20

OXLEY HILL
RECTORY LA

Abberton

The Gate Farm

LAYER RD
PO

Manwood Farm

PH

EDWARD M4
PERTREE M4
WALNUT CT
BRAND CL
PROCTOR CL

FINGRINGHOE RD
PYEFLEET VIEW

Grange Fruit Farm

ABBERTON RD

White House

DUDLEY RD

SOUTH GREEN RD

South House Farm

19

BROOM WAY
BRACKEN WAY
SAWKINS CL

Uppershotts

Tudhoe Farm

MEADOW WAY
LANGENHOE PK

Langenhoe

Langenhoe Cty Prim Sch

Grimps Grove

DANGER AREA

2

Glebe House

PELDON RD

COLCHESTER RD B1025

Crouch House Farm

LODGE LA

Rifle Ranges

1

Pete Tye Common

18

163
137

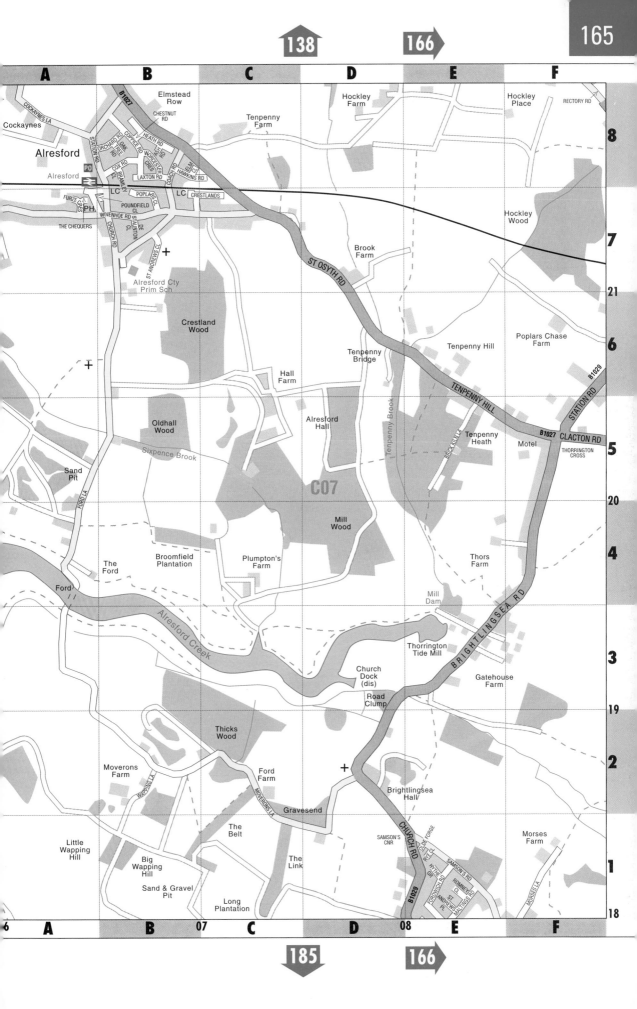

165 139

A B C D E F

8

SCHOOL LA
B1029
STATION RD
Burr's Farm
GREAT BENTLEY RD
Lufkins Farm
Hill House Farm
THORRINGTON RD
FRATING CROSS
DE VERE EST
ROBIN CL
STURRICK LA
CHERRYWOODS
LINNET WAY
THE PATH
HECKFORD RD
Bentley Green
WEELEY RD
ABRALYN CL
BIRCH AVE
PINE CL
ROWAN CL
THE GREEN PH
Great Bentley
SYCAMORE PL
CEDAR WAY
ELM CL
PO
MORELLA CL
NEW CUT
STATION RD
Great Bentley Cty Prim Sch
LC
Great Bentley
Ind Est

7

FRATING RD
GREAT BENTLEY RD
LC
HALL VIEW RD
KEEBLE CT
PLOUGH RD
St Mary's Farm

21
LC
Mast
STATION RD
B1029
The Talbots
Whitehouse Farm
CHURCH RD
Frating Abbey
Bentley Brook
FRATING ABBEY FARM RD
Lodge Plantation
ST MARY'S RD

6

5
B1027
HEATHLANDS
CLOVER DR
HAZEL CL
ACORN WLK
HONEYSUCKLE WAY
PO
CHAPEL LA
ROSEMARY LA
PH
High Barns
Thicket Grove
Aingers Green
WEELEY RD
AINGERS GRN RD
ST MARY'S CL
THE PADDOCKS
Carpenter's Farm

20
Thorrington

4
Glebe Farm
Thorrington Hall
CLACTON RD
CO7
The Lodge
Colles Brook
COLLES BROOK RD
SOUTH HEATH

3
Thorringtonhall Wood
Saltwater Brook Cottages
Saltwater Bridge
HOLLYBUSH HILL
DIAL RD
DIAL CNR
Lady Wood
Kellands Farm

19
MARSH FARM LA
Saltwater Brook
HILL COTTS

2
Crocky Grove
Marsh Farm
Cottage Farm
HILL COTTS

1
FOLKARDS LA
Lowermarsh Farm
Holiday Centre
Dines Farm
FLAG HILL
B1027
CO10

18

09 A B 10 C D 11 E F

167 141

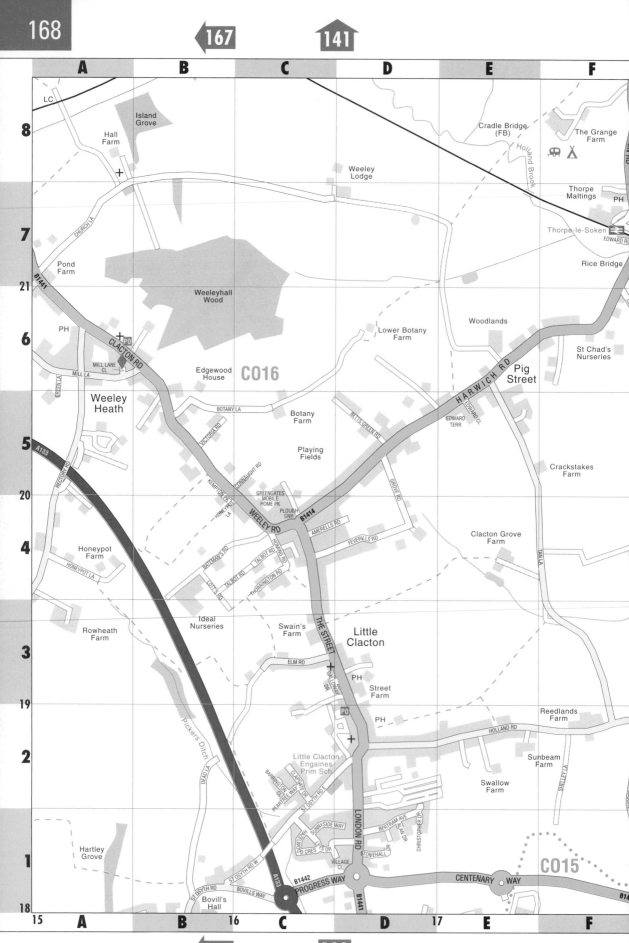

167 188

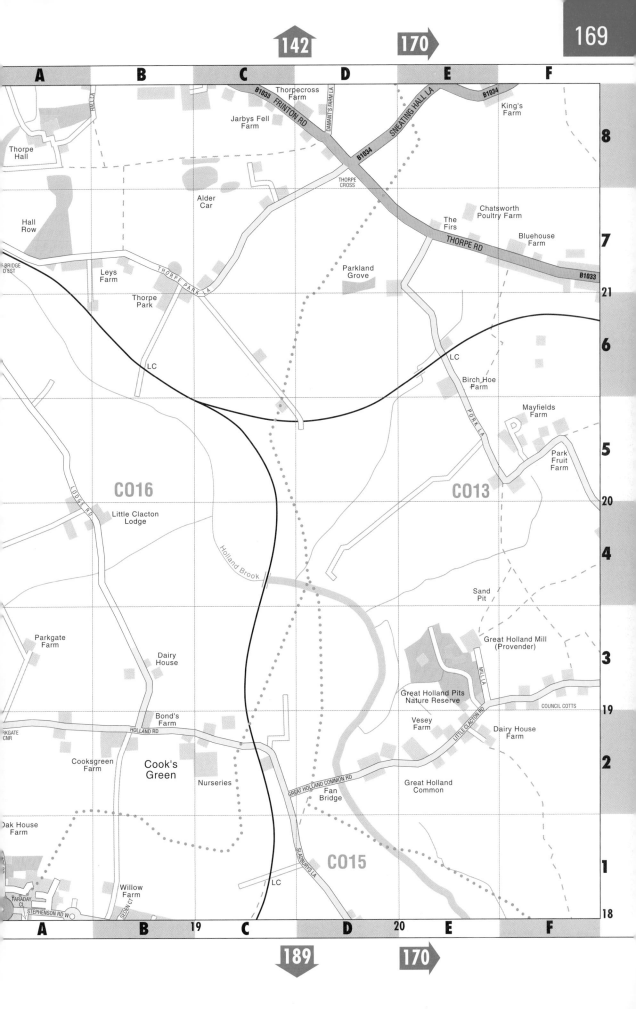

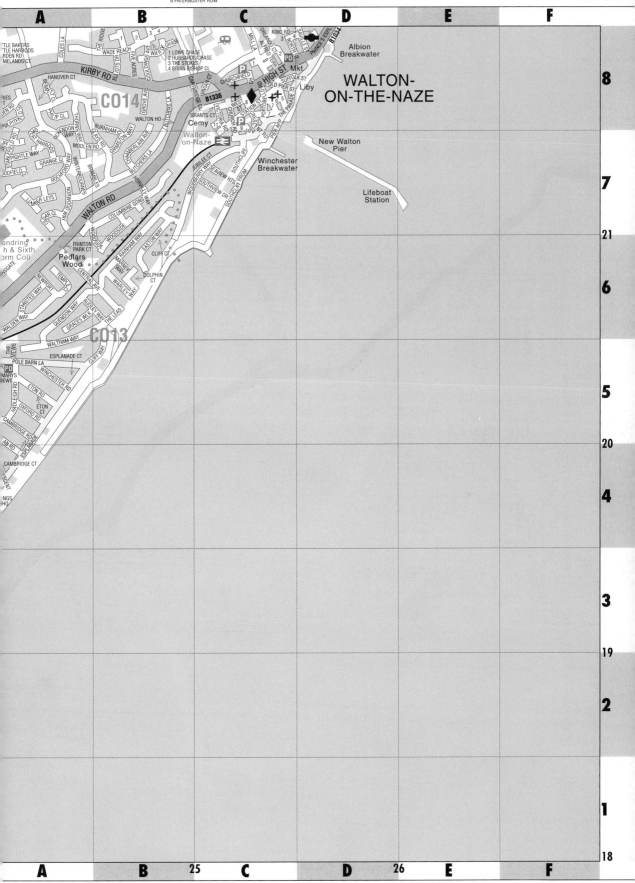

C8
1 MARINA MEWS
2 VICARAGE LA
3 HAVENCROFT CT
4 STRATFORD PL
5 NEWGATE ST
6 PATERNOSTER ROW
7 NEW PIER ST
8 MARTELLO RD
9 AGAR RD
10 AGAR ROAD APP
11 ST BOTOLPH'S TERR

144

WALTON-
ON-THE-NAZE

Albion
Breakwater

New Walton
Pier

Winchester
Breakwater

Lifeboat
Station

CO14

CO13

Walton-
on-Naze

Cemy

Pedlars
Wood

1 LOWE CHASE
2 HUBBARDS CHASE
3 THE STOKES
4 BRIAN BISHOP CL

KIRBY RD

WALTON RD

B1336

B1336

Clendring
h & Sixth
orm Coll

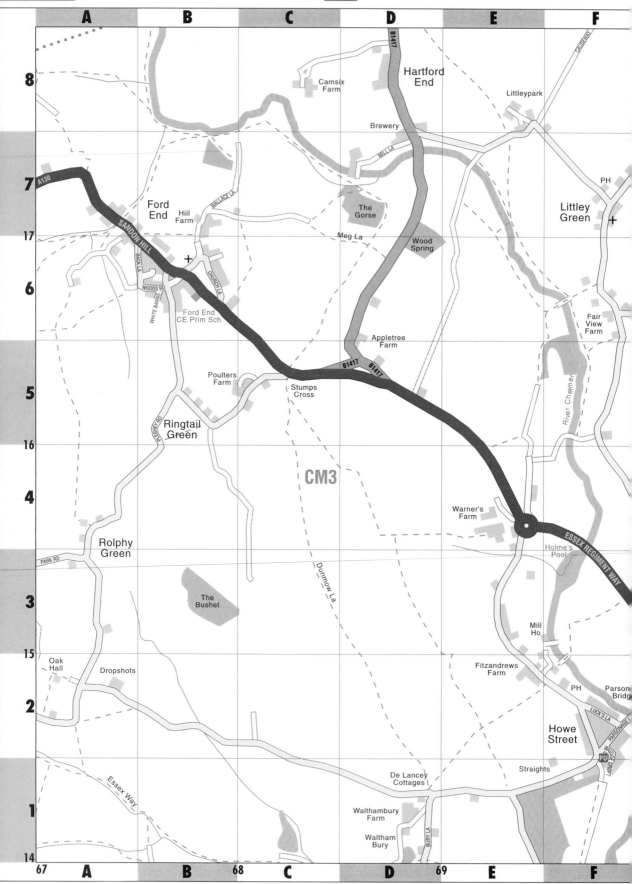

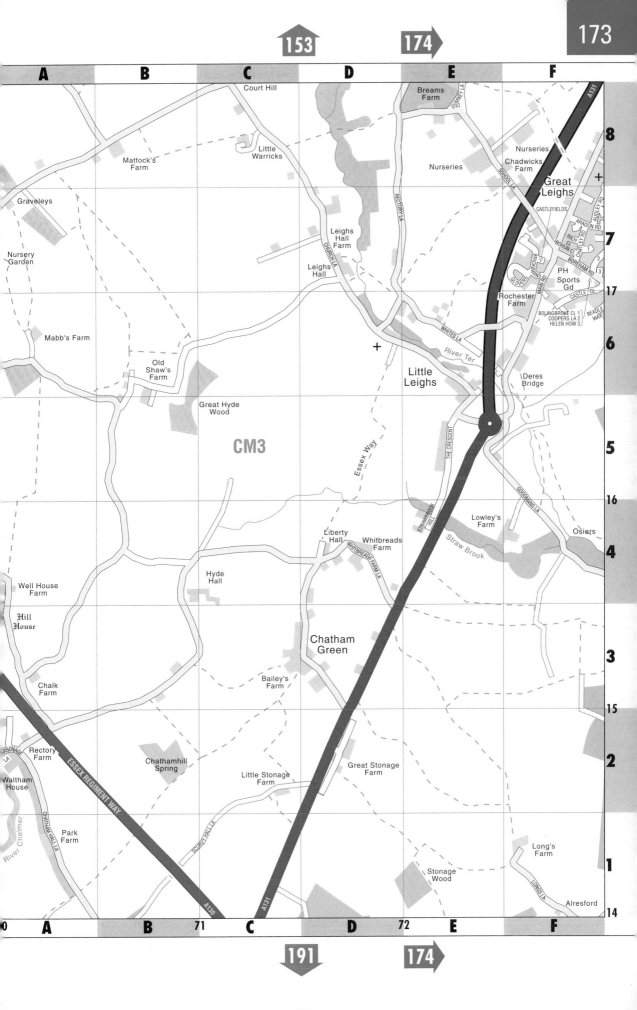

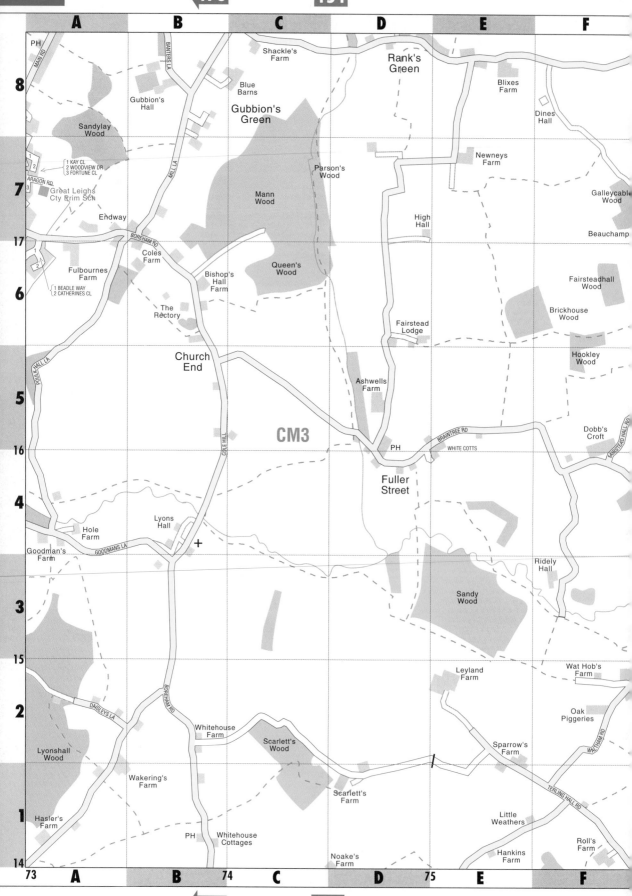

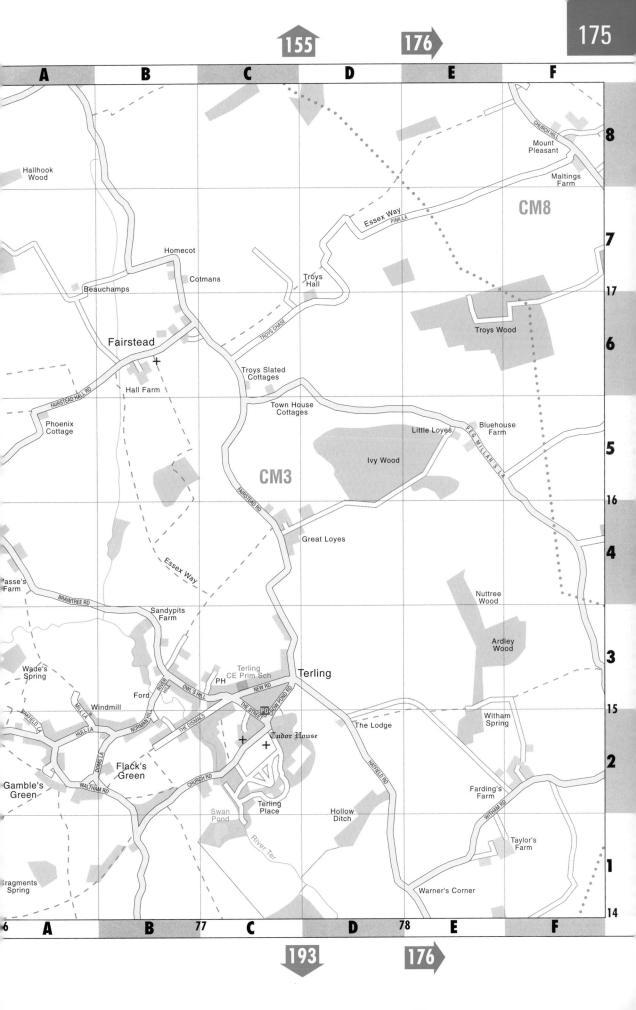

175

156

A B C D E F

8

Whiteways

Godfry's
Farm

Hole Farm

Whitehead's Farm

B1018

CRESSING RD

Tarecroft
Wood

7

Oak Farm

CHURCH HILL

Grove
Cottages

Faulkbourne

Hill Farm

17

COURT ONE 1
COURT TWO 2
COURT THREE 3
COURT FOUR 4
COURT FIVE 5
COURT SIX 6
COURT SEVEN 7
COURT EIGHT 8
COURT NINE 9
COURT TEN 10
COURT ELEVEN 11
COURT TWELVE 12
COURT THIRTEEN 13
COURT FOURTEEN 14
COURT FIFTEEN 15
COURT SIXTEEN 16
COURT SEVENTEEN 17
COURT EIGHTEEN 18
COURT NINETEEN 19
COURT TWENTY 20

The Rickstone
Sch

6

Faulkbourne
Hall

Elm Hall
Cottages

CONRAD RD
LAKE RD
CAMPBELL
VIRGIL RD
MUNRO RD
BRONTE RD
SHAW RD
HEMINGWAY RD
12 8 16
7 15 14
10 9

5

Troys
Farm

Home
Farm

River Brain

Templars
Cty Inf
& Jun Sch
DOROTHY
SAYERS DR
CROSS RD
UPPER ACRES
LONGFIELD
GLEBE CRES

16

The Old
Rectory

Warren
Farm

WITHAM

SOUTHCOTE RD

CM8

LARKSPUR CL 1
LAVENDER CL 2
BRAMBLE CT 3
PRIMROSE PL 4
BUTTERCUP WLK 5
CAMPION WAY 6
THYME MEWS 7

ST NICHOLAS CL

4

FAULKBOURNE RD

HONEYSUCKLE WAY

OXLIP RD

BLACKTHORN RD

ORCHID AVE

TAVERNERS WLK
BRAMSTON CH ST
ST NICHOLAS RD
TEMPLARS LA
BRAMSTON ST
COVERDALE
CHAPPINGHILL

CHURCH ST

CORNEL CL

BYRONY CL

SNOWDROP CL

BRAMBLE RD

PERRY RD
BENTLEY RD
BLUEBELL CL

CHALKS RD

FLORA RD

CALAMINT RD

SPEEDWELL
CL

FOXGLOVE CL
LAVENDER
SAMPHIRE CL

HAREBELL DR

Chipping Hill

Sch

3

The
Grove

Powers
Hall

Powers Hall
End

PH

CM3

Schs

EDEN CL 1
MONKS CT 2
WHITEWAYS CT 3

PO
P

BRAIN RD

AVON
WLK

SAXON DR
THE CL

MONT FARM
CHASE
EARLS RD

WHITE HORSE

CHIPPING HILL

BARNARD
WAY

TEMPLEMEAD

B1018

15

TERLING RD

PEG MILLAR'S LA

WITHAM RD

FIR AVE

DON CT

DART CL

URE DR

CAM
WAY

HIGHFIELDS
FAL
MERSEY RD
TRENT RD

CROMWELL WAY

ARMOND RD

GIMSON
CL

CHELMER RD

CROWN RD

Resr

2

DANCING DICKS LA

HUMBER RD

MEDWAY AVE

OUSE CHASE
DOUGLAS
GR

CROUCH
DR
BRENT CL
COLNE CHASE

SPAN RD

HAMBLE
CL

TEIGN DR

NESS WLK

WHARFE CL 1
AIRE WLK 2
TEES CL 3
DEBEN CL 4
ORWELL WLK 5

GUITHAVON CT 1
OLD PARSONAGE CT 2
MILL VALE LO 3

GUITHAVON VALLEY
NICHOL
CT
LOCKRAM LA
GUITHAVON RD

MILL BRIDGE

Sports
Gd

GUPPERS CL
HIGHFIELDS

GUITHAVON RD
MILL LA

The
Bungalows

HOLLYBANK

2
4

NEWLAND

GUITHAVON
ST

P

1

Wheeler's

Dancing Dicks
Cottages

BLUNTS HALL RD

BLUNT'S HALL DR

Blunt's
Hall

STEVENS RD

1 SUTOR CL
2 PHILIP RD

Sports
Gd

BARNFIELD PL 1
MOORFIELD CT 2

The
John Bramston
Sch
& Sixth Form Ctr

SPA RD
MAVES

Bridge

H

Sports
Ctr

14

ALMA RD

TURSTAN RD

EPPING WAY
TUCKER DR

BRIDGE ST
B1389
TIPTREE CL
TUDOR CL

175

194

A   B   C   D   E   F

8

CO5

Rivenhall CE Prim Sch

Rivenhall

Tarecroft Wood

Hoo Hall

7

Hare Lodge

Hole Farm

17

Stovern's Hall

Durwards Hall

6

Rickstone's Farm

Oak Rd

Henry Dixon Rd

Rivenhall Bridge

Foxmead
Foxden

The Drive

Rivenhall End

Glebe Farm

The Old Rectory

CH

Hotel

Sewage Works

5

1 WIMSEY CT
2 VANE CT
3 HAWTHORNE RISE
4 HOLLY WLK

Whitelands

The Matchyn's

Rose Cottage

Appleford Farm

Cemy

16

CM8

Colemans Resr

Appleford Bridge

4

River Blackwater

Hill Broad Farm

Workhouse Plantation

Coleman's Bridge

Church Chase

Witham Junction

Witham

Coleman's Farm

Elm Springs

3

Little Braxted

15

Lea Lane Wood

2

Ct

1 KYNASTON PL
2 RICHARDSON WLK

Hall

Little Braxted

Liby

Lea Lane Fruit Farm

Broomfield's Farm

1

Briarsford Ind Est

Briarsford Ind Est

Sewage Works

14

A   B   83   C   D   84   E   F

A2
1 GROVE COTTS
2 FOSTER CT
3 DU CANE PL
4 HORNER PL
5 FREEBOURNES CT
6 HEWITT WLK
7 LOCKRAM LA
8 NEWLANDS PREC
9 PENHALIGON CT
10 COACH HOUSE WAY
11 GUITHAVON ST

177
158

	A	B	C	D	E	F

8

Crabb's Farm

CRABB'S LA

LONDON RD

B1024

MALDON RD

A12

London Rd

Koorbaes

Churchman's Farm

7

Ashman's Farm

Lucas's Croft

Highfields

New Barn

HIGHFIELDS LA

17

Kelvedon Hall Wood

Jubb's Row

6

Brickhouse Farm

Merlins

Klevedon Hall

Square Wood

The Glebe House

CO5

New Plantation

5

Fabian's Plantation

CH

Braxted Park

Mason's Plantation

16

Howbridges Wood

KELVEDON HALL LA

GRANGE RD

Inworth Gran Farm

4

Grange Farm

The Lake

The Mount

Ash Plantation

Tiptree Wood

Pine Croft

Prodys

Braxted Park House

Nursery Plantation

CHURCH CHASE

THE AVENUE

3

CM8

BRETTS COTTS

WEST END RD

Pundicts Lodge

PRIORY RD

STONE

15

TEA LA

Great Braxted Hall

Hollytr Farm

2

NOAK'S CROSS

Tiptree Priory

Priory Farm

Noak's Cross Farm

SEXTONS LA

BRAXTED RD

B1

Broadfield Fruit Farm

B1022

1

West Hall Wood

Sexton's Farm

BUNG ROW

PH

TIPTREE RD

PO

Great Braxted

Porter's Farm

BRAXTED LA

Heathgate Farm

MALDON RD

GROVE FARM

LOAMY HILL RD

White Rail Farm

B1022

14

85	A		B	86	C		D	87	E		F

177
196

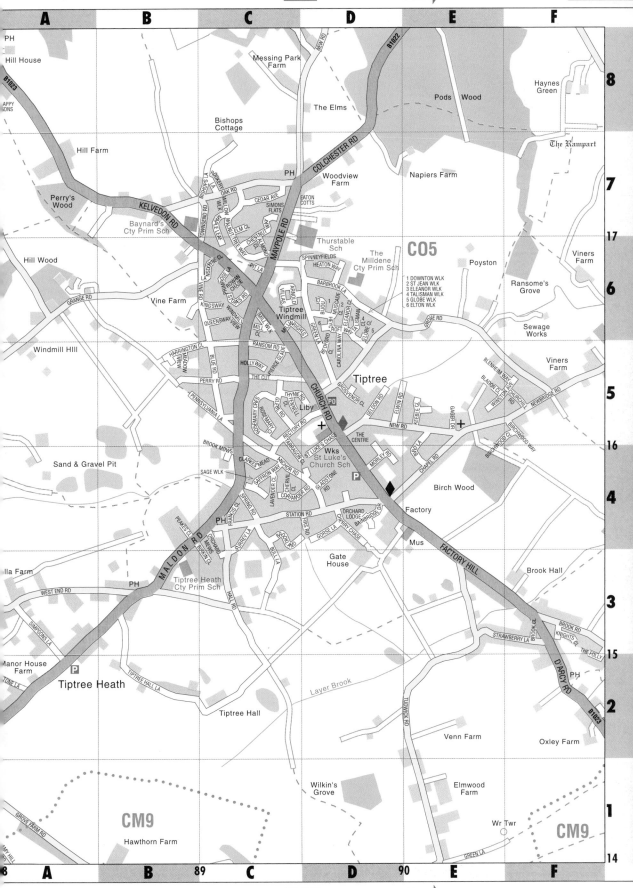

A   B   C   D   E   F

8

Layer Woodlands
Farm

White Lodge

Layer Marney

CO2

HAYNES GREEN RD

STOCKHOUSE RD

Parkhouse
Farm

Layer Marney
Tower

7

Oak Farm

Parkhouse
Farm

Parkgate
Farm

Hall Farm

Wick Farm

17

NEWBRIDGE RD

Layer Brook

6

Stockridge
Farm

CO5

Silverthorn

Rockingham's
Farm

5

Cadgers Wood

16

Long Wood

4

Park Farm

Beatbush
Wood

CM9

PARK LA

3

Paternoster Heath

15

BROOK RD

HAWTHORN RD

THORN WAY

STOCKHOUSE CL

Gobolt's
Farm

Barn Hall Farm

2

Tolleshunt
Knights

ELIZABETH
VILLAS

BARNHALL RD

TOP RD

Palmers
Farm

D'ARCY RD

RECTORY RD

B1023

The
Plough Inn
(PH)

BUNG LA

HONEYPOTT LA

Wigborough
Springs

1

Krissimon
Farm

OXLEY HILL

Oxley Green

Manifold Wick
Farm

14

Lovedowns Farm

91   A   B   92   C   D   93   E   F

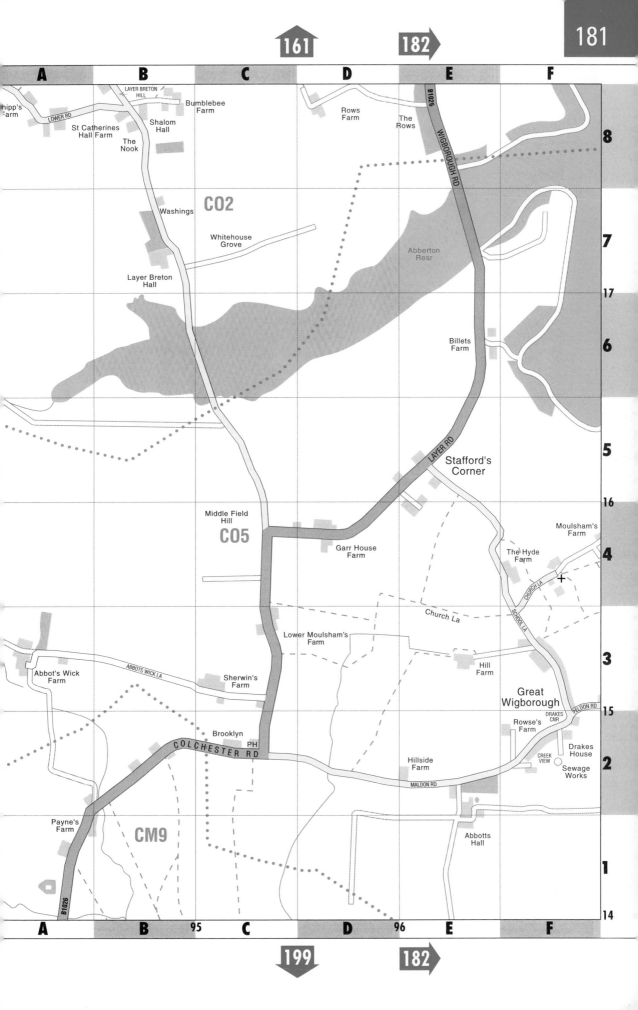

A B C D E F

8
7
17
6
5
16
4
3
15
2
1
14

LAYER BRETON HILL

hipp's Farm

LOWER RD

St Catherines Hall Farm

Shalom Hall

Bumblebee Farm

The Nook

Rows Farm

The Rows

B1026

WIGBOROUGH RD

CO2

Washings

Whitehouse Grove

Abberton Resr

Layer Breton Hall

Billets Farm

LAYER RD

Stafford's Corner

Middle Field Hill

CO5

Garr House Farm

Moulsham's Farm

The Hyde Farm

CHURCH LA

Church La

SCHOOL LA

Lower Moulsham's Farm

Hill Farm

Abbot's Wick Farm

ABBOTS WICK LA

Sherwin's Farm

Great Wigborough

PELDON RD

DRAKES CNR

Rowse's Farm

Brooklyn

PH

COLCHESTER RD

Drakes House

CREEK VIEW

Hillside Farm

MALDON RD

Sewage Works

Payne's Farm

CM9

Abbotts Hall

B1026

A B 95 C D 96 E F

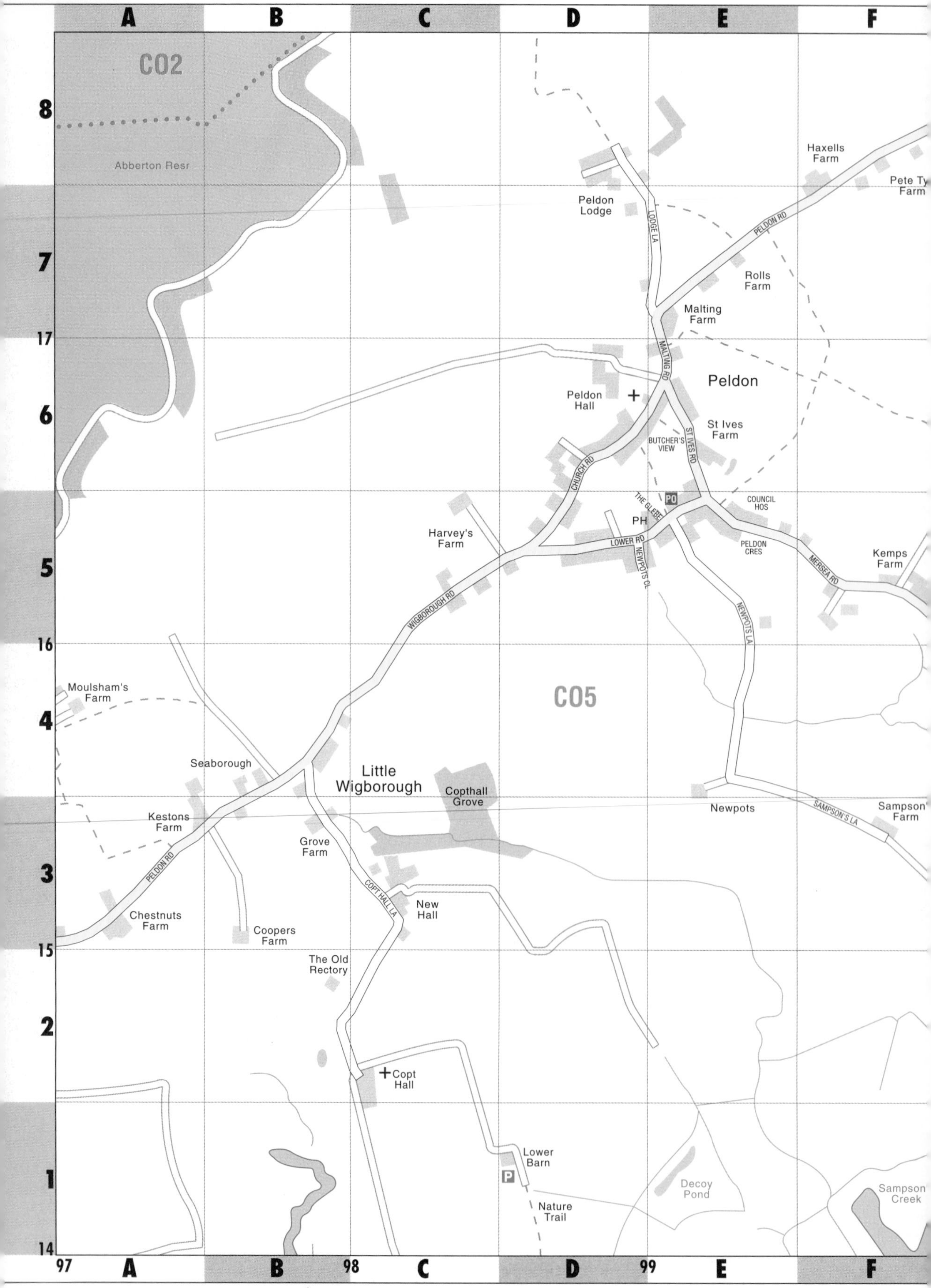

←181
↑162

CO2

Abberton Resr

Haxells Farm

Pete Ty Farm

Peldon Lodge

Peldon RD

Rolls Farm

Malting Farm

Peldon

Peldon Hall

St Ives Farm

BUTCHER'S VIEW

CHURCH RD

THE GLEBE

PO

PH

COUNCIL HOS

Harvey's Farm

Lower RD

PELDON CRES

MERSEA RD

Kemps Farm

WIGBOROUGH RD

NEWPOTS CL

NEWPOTS LA

CO5

Moulsham's Farm

Seaborough

Little Wigborough

Copthall Grove

Newpots

SAMPSON'S LA

Sampson Farm

Kestons Farm

PELDON RD

Grove Farm

COPT HALL LA

New Hall

Chestnuts Farm

Coopers Farm

The Old Rectory

Copt Hall

Lower Barn

P

Decoy Pond

Sampson Creek

Nature Trail

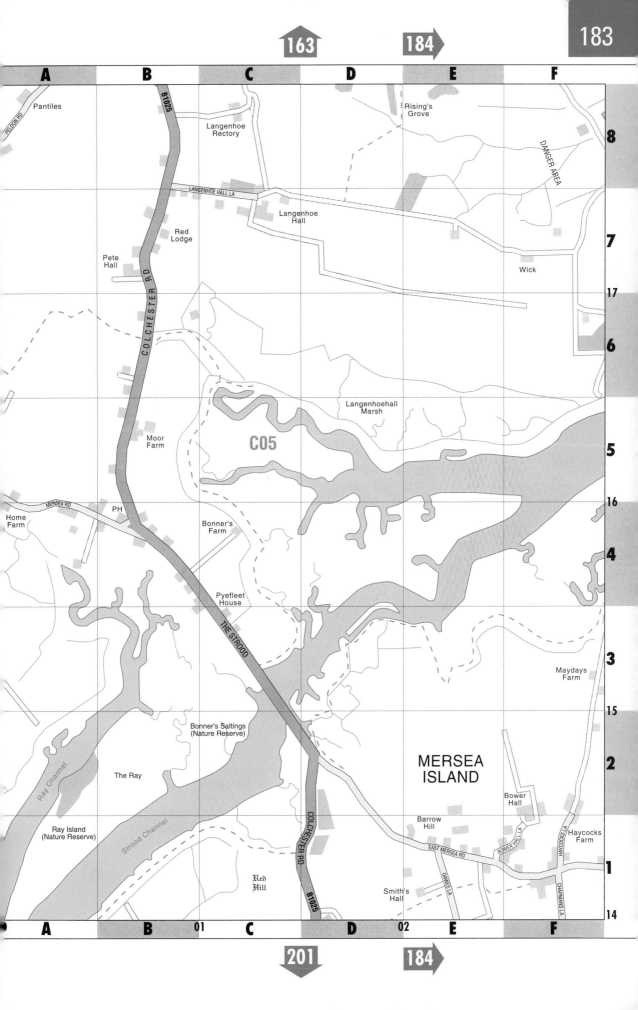

183
164

A B C D E F

8

South Geedon Creek

CO7

River Colne

Fingringhoe Ranges

North Geedon

DANGER AREA

Wick Marsh

Langenhoe Marsh

7

South Geedon

Rat Island (Nature Reserve)

17

DANGER AREA

6

Pyefleet Channel

Pewit Island

5

Reeveshall Marsh

16

Maydays Marsh

Broad Fleet

4

CO5

3

Reeves Hall

May Grove

15

SHOP LA

2

Bocking Hall

MERSEA ISLAND

Works

The Dog & Pheasant (PH)

MEETING LA

PO

EAST RD

Fen Farm

Weir Farm

BARING-GOULD COTTS

East Mersea Hall

East Mersea

1

EAST MERSEA RD

CHURCH LA

Hall Farm

14

183
201

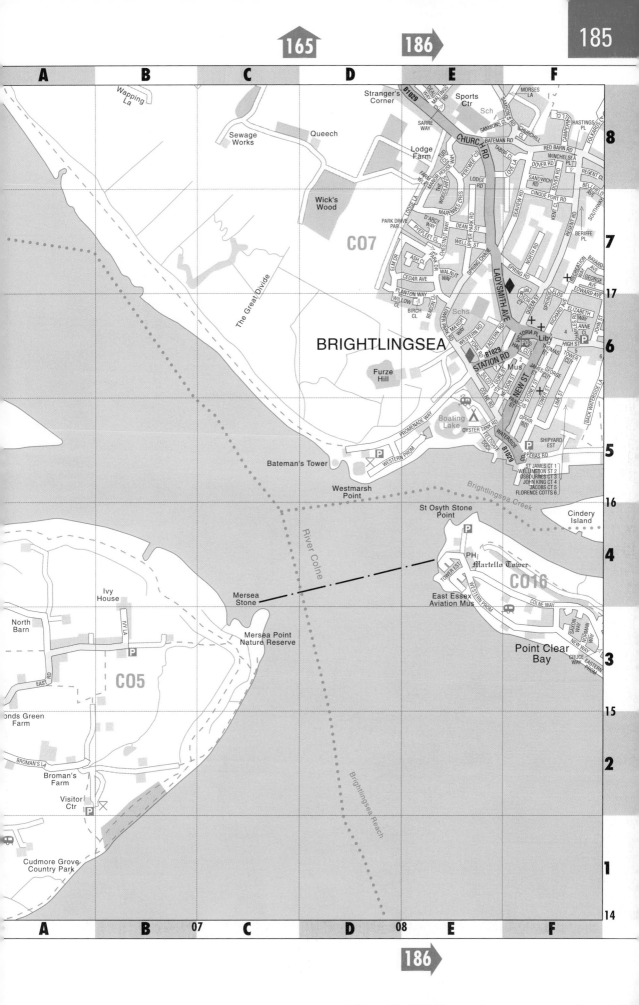

A B C D E F

A B 07 C D 08 E F

8
17
7
6
5
16
4
15
2
1
14

Wapping La

Sewage Works

Queech

Stranger's Corner

Sports Ctr

Sch

MORSES LA

B1029

MALTINGS

DEAL WAY

SAMSON'S RD

HASTINGS PL

CAMPERNE

POLLARD'S

SARRE WAY

CHURCH RD

BATEMAN RD

SAMSON'S RD

CHURCHILL

WINCHELSEA

RED BARN RD

DOVER RD

SANDWICH RD

CINQUE PORT RD

REGENT CL

BELFIELD AVE

SOUTHWAY

REGENT RD

BERIFFE PL

BAYARD AVE

GEORGE AVE

EDWARD AVE

ELIZABETH WAY

ANNE CL

JOHN ST

Lodge Farm

Wick's Wood

CO7

BRIGHTLINGSEA

Furze Hill

Bateman's Tower

Westmarsh Point

The Great Divide

ELM DR

ASH CL

CEDAR AVE

WILLOW

PLANTON WAY

BIRCH CL

BEACON

PARK DRIVE PAR

D'ARCY WAY

PYE-FLEET CL

CHESTNUT WAY

DEAN AVE

WELL ST

UPPER PARK RD

WALNUT WAY

SPRING CHASE

SPRING RD

LADYSMITH AVE

LODGE LA

MAJOR HOUSE WAY

WOODLANDS WAY

THE

PERTWEE CL

MAJOR HOUSE WAY

PARK

MARENIKES CRES

LOVE LA

DOVER RD

KENT CL

SEAVIEW RD

NORTH RD

QUEEN'S

SPRINGFIELDS

CHARLES RD

RICHARD RD

HIGH ST

TOWER CUT

Schs

MARSH WAY

EASTERN RD

LOWER PARK RD

YORK RD

VICTORIA PL

STATION RD

B1029

P.O.

Liby

THOMAS ST

Mus

NEW ST

JAMES ST

GEORGE ST

NELSON ST

CLONE RD

SLEDGE

DUKE ST

SYDNEY ST

FRANCIS ST

TOWER ST

LIME ST

BACK WATERSIDE LA

TELEGRAPH

OYSTER TANK RD

PROMENADE WAY

Boating Lake

WESTERN PROM

OPHIR RD

WATERSIDE

DOCK

B1029

OPPERAS RD

SHIPYARD EST

ST JAMES CT 1
WELLINGTON ST 3
OSBOURNE'S CT 3
JOHN KING CT 4
JACOBS CT 5
FLORENCE COTTS 6

Brightlingsea Creek

St Osyth Stone Point

Cindery Island

River Colne

Mersea Stone

PH

Martello Tower

CO16

East Essex Aviation Mus

WESTERN PROM

COLNE WAY

SAXON WAY

NORMAN WAY

NEW WAY

BRUCE WAY

EASTERN PROM

Point Clear Bay

TOWER EST

Ivy House

North Barn

EAST RD

IVY LA

CO5

onds Green Farm

BROMAN'S LA

Broman's Farm

Visitor Ctr

Cudmore Grove Country Park

Mersea Point Nature Reserve

Brightlingsea Reach

A B C D E F

8

FOLKARDS LA

FLAG HILL
B1027

Marsh Farm House

Eastmarsh Point

STONEY LA

RED BAR RD

BELLFIELD CL

BELLFIELD AVE

BRIGHTLINGSEA

Lower Farm

C07

Flag Creek

Wellwick Wharf

Recycling Ctr

7

GRANVILLE WAY

ROBINSON RD

HILL HOUSE CT

CHAPEL RD

STANLEY AVE

17

ALBERT RD

MARGARET CL

BEAUMONT AVE

KIRKHURST CL

GREENHURST RD

CREEKHURST CL

LINKFIELD RD

HURST CL

FAIR CL

Kiln Farm

East End Green

FREELANDS

B1027

6

BACK WATERSIDE LA

Hurst Green

MILL ST

Nun's Wood

Kitchen Pond

Dolphin Pond

Eng Po

5

Brightlingsea Creek

The Folly

Fred's Hard

St Os Pa

16

Cindery Island

Brightlingsea Creek

4

St Osyth Creek

PH

Pr Fie

MILL ST

3

NORTH WALL

COLNE WAY

NEW WAY

MERSEA VIEW

ALLEN KEW

Point Clear

ROMAN WAY

ALPHA RD

OAKMEAD RD

SNELL LA

C016

Mill Dam Lake

Linley Farm

15

LYDIA DR

SEVEN TERR

COLNE VIEW

BEACON WAY

PO

POINT CLEAR RD

Pightle Court

WIGBORO WICK LA

2

BEACON HTS

DUMONT AVE

LEE WICK LA

1

Sandy Point

RAY CREEK

BEACH RD

Lee Wick Farm

Wigboro W Farm

14

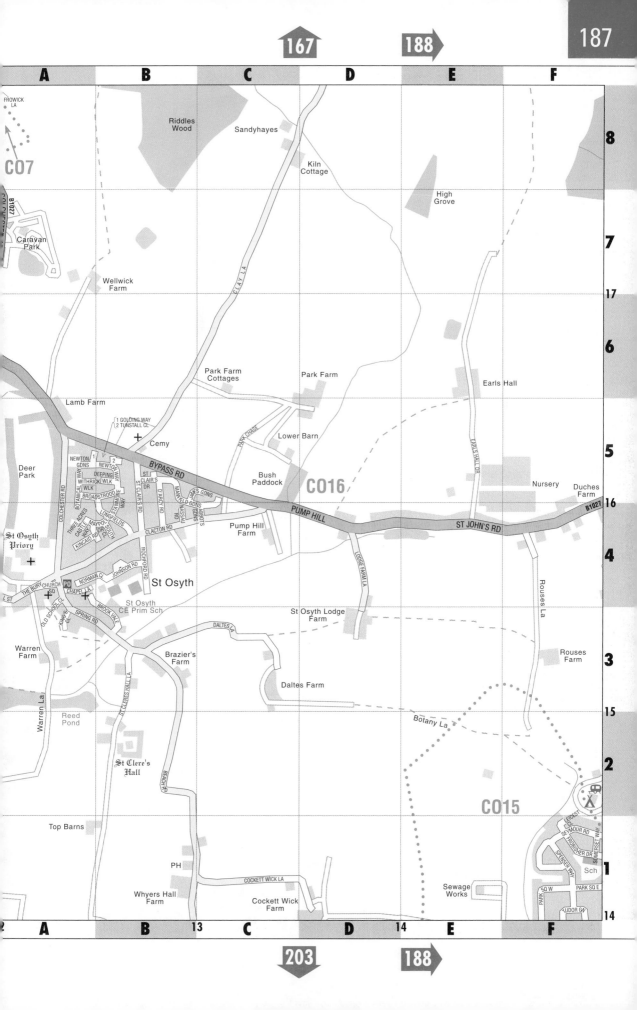

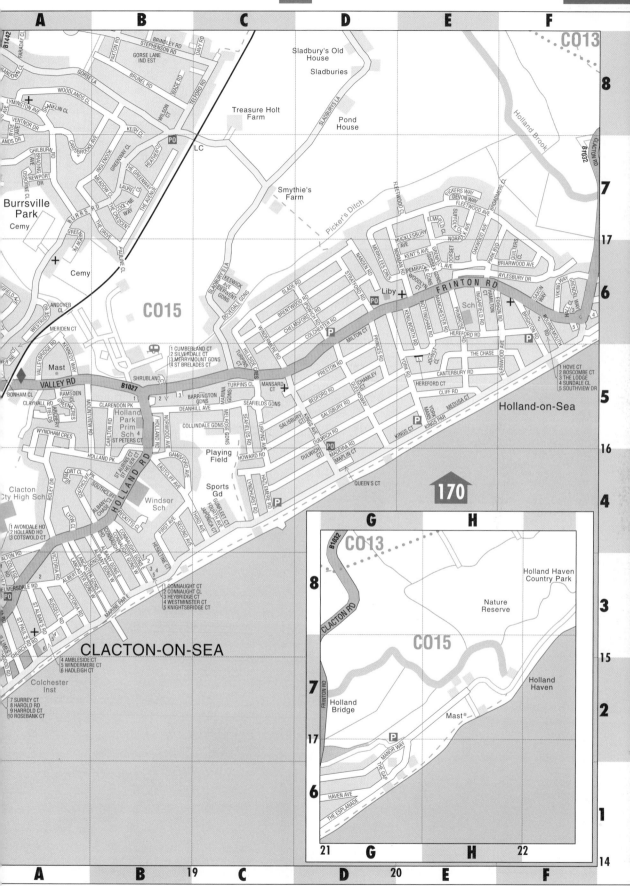

A **B** **C** **D** **E** **F**

CO13

B1142

FARADAY CL

SANDON CL

Woodlands Cl

LYMINGTON AVE

FRANKLIN CL

VENTNOR DR

RYDE AVE

SANDS DR

CHILBURN AVE

BRADING AVE

OSBORNE DR

NEWPORT DR

GORSE LA

PAXTON RD

BRINDLEY RD

STEPHENSON RD

DAISY RD

GORSE LANE IND EST

WADE RD

TELFORD RD

BRUNEL RD

WILSON CT

KEITH CL

CARR AVE

BROOK AVE

INGLENOOK

GREENWAY CL

HEATHER CL

THE GREENWAY

MEADOW RD

LAUREL CL

THE AVENUE

THE COLYNE WAY

THE CRESCENT

THE DRIVE

B U R R S

GREENWAY

PAULINE CL

PO

LC

Treasure Holt Farm

Sladbury's Old House

Sladburies

SLADBURY'S LA

Pond House

Smythie's Farm

Picker's Ditch

Holland Brook

B1032

CLACTON RD

8

17

7

Burrsville Park

Cemy

Cemy

CO15

FIELD AVE

WESTRIDGE

ANDOVER CL

MERIDEN CT

VALLEYBRIDGE RD

KENNEDY WAY

Mast

Bonham Cl

CLAYHALL RD

GREENACRES

RAMSDEN CL

VALLEY RD

B1027

SHRUBLAND

1. CUMBERLAND CT
2. SILVERDALE CT
3. MERRYMOUNT GDNS
4. ST BRELADES CT

TURPINS AVE

SLADBURY'S LA

KESWICK AVE

DERWENT GDNS

DOVEDALE GDNS

HILLSIDE CRES

WINDERMERE RD

SLADE RD

BRENTWOOD RD

CHELMSFORD RD

IPSWICH RD

COLCHESTER RD

MANSON RD

STRATFORD RD

MERRILEES CRES

NORMAN RD

PO

Liby

FRINTON RD

FLEETWOOD CL

HUCKLESBURY AVE

KENT'S AVE

PEMBROKE WOODLYN

GREENE'S

SUSSEX GDNS

MANCHESTER RD

PRIMROSE

PICKERS WAY

DEVON WAY

FLEETWOOD AVE

ELMF

SUFFOLK

NORF

DORSET

OAKWOOD AVE

INGARFIELD RD

PARK RD

QUILTERS

BRIARWOOD AVE

AYLESBURY DR

HAMILTON

EDISON RD

Sch

VIKING WAY

SAXON WAY

GRENFELL WAY

NCL CT

BRIGHTON RD

BURRSMOUTH RD

6

CO15

Mast

WESTBRIDGE RD

MR CT

TURPINS CL

MANVILLE RD

BARRINGTON GDNS

DEANHILL AVE

COLLINDALE GDNS

SEAFIELDS RD

MELROSE GDNS

TURPINS AVE

SEAFIELDS GDNS

PRESTON RD

BEDFORD RD

SALISBURY CT

KINGS AVE

SALISBURY RD

MILTON CT

PRINCES RD

QUEENSWAY

DULWICH RD

CHARNLEY RD

MADEIRA RD

MAPLIN CT

KENILWORTH RD

NOTTINGHAM RD

HEREFORD RD

YORK RD

HEREFORD CT

Liby

CANTERBURY RD

CLIFF RD

THE CHASE

MEDUSA CT

KINGS CT

KINGS PAR

FERNWOOD AVE

PO

JOHN ST

1. HOVE CT
2. BOSCOMBE CT
3. THE LODGE
4. SUNDALE CL
5. SOUTHVIEW DR

Holland-on-Sea

17

6

5

16

4

Holland Park Prim Sch

ST PETERS CT

Holland PK

GAINSFORD AVE

Playing Field

Sports Gd

HOLLAND RD

HOWARD RD

DULWICH

HAZLEMERE RD

LYNDHURST RD

Queen's CT

Queen's CT

170

WYNDHAM CRES

Clacton City High Sch

ALBANY CL

ST AUBINS CT

ST HELIERS CT

ST AUBINS CHASE

BOLEY DR

SOUTHCLIFF PK

SOUTHCLIFF

LYON CL

BRECKETTS CL

FIRST AVE

SECOND AVE

THIRD AVE

JAPONICA CT

GUINFLEET CT

FOURTH AVE

Windsor Sch

CLARENDON PK

MOUNTVIEW RD

CARLTON RD

NORWOOD AVE

EASTCLIFF AVE

1. AVONDALE HO
2. HOLLAND HO
3. COTSWOLD CT

ALTON RD

COLLEGE

ELMERSDALE RD

VICTORIA RD

RUSSELL RD

ST ALBAN'S RD

MARINE PARADE

LANCASTER GDNS W

LANCASTER GDNS E

ALBERT GDNS

CONNAUGHT GDNS E

CONNAUGHT GDNS W

HAZELNE RD

ALBANY GDNS E

1. CONNAUGHT CT
2. CONNAUGHT CL
3. HEYBRIDGE CT
4. WESTMINSTER CT
5. KNIGHTSBRIDGE CT

ST ALBAN'S RD

CHURCH RD

ST PAUL'S RD

LIMES

WELLWOOD

4. AMBLESIDE CT
5. WINDERMERE CT
6. HADLEIGH CT

CLACTON-ON-SEA

Colchester Inst

7. SURREY CT
8. HAROLD RD
9. HARROLD CT
10. ROSEBANK CT

3

15

2

17

G **H**

B1082

CO13

Holland Haven Country Park

FRINTON RD

CLACTON RD

Nature Reserve

CO15

Holland Bridge

Holland Haven

P

Mast

MANOR WAY

THE GAP

HAVEN AVE

THE ESPLANADE

8

7

17

6

1

21 **G** 20 **H** 22

14

A **B** 19 **C** **D** 20 **E** **F**

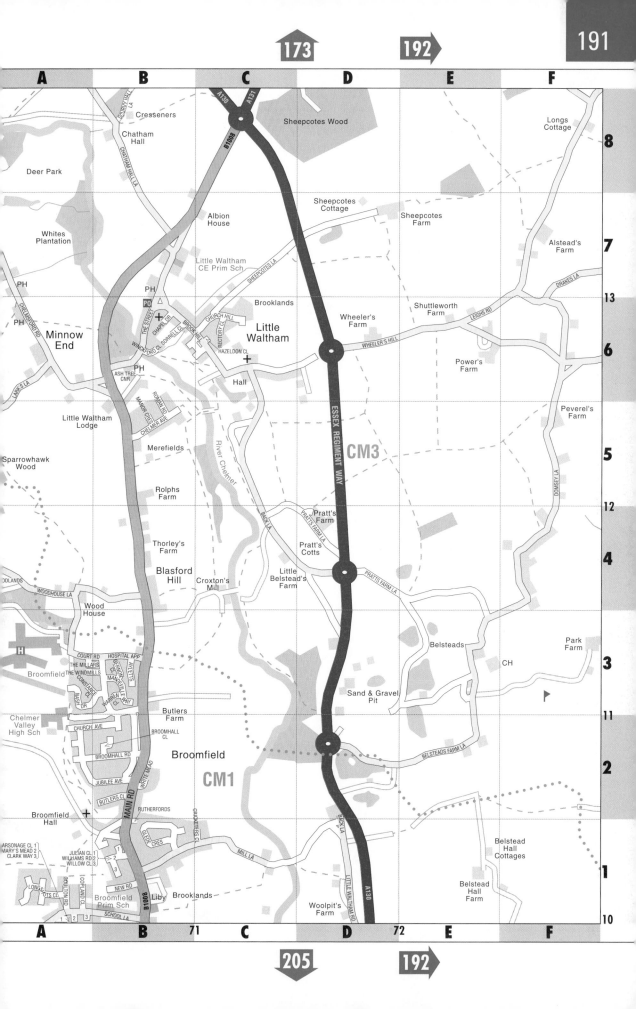

A B C D E F

8

Cresseners

Deer Park

Chatham Hall

SCURVY HALL LA

CHATHAM HALL LA

A130
B1008
A131

Sheepcotes Wood

Longs Cottage

7

Whites Plantation

Albion House

Little Waltham CE Prim Sch

SHEEPCOTES LA

Sheepcotes Cottage

Sheepcotes Farm

Alstead's Farm

13

PH

PH

CHELMSFORD RD

Minnow End

PH
PO

THE STREET

CHAPEL DR

WINCKFORD CL

SORRELL CL

BROOK HILL

CHURCH HILL

RECTORY CL

Brooklands

Little Waltham

Wheeler's Farm

Shuttleworth Farm

LEIGHS RD

DRAKES LA

6

LARKS LA

ASH TREE CNR

PH

MANOR CRES

ROMAN RD

CHELMER AVE

HAZELDON CL

Hall

WHEELER'S HILL

Power's Farm

Little Waltham Lodge

Merefields

River Chelmer

ESSEX REGIMENT WAY

CM3

Peverel's Farm

5

Sparrowhawk Wood

Rolphs Farm

DOMSEY LA

12

Thorley's Farm

BACK LA

Pratt's Farm

PRATT'S FARM LA

Pratt's Cotts

4

Blasford Hill

Croxton's Mill

Little Belstead's Farm

PRATTS FARM LA

WOODHOUSE LA
DODLANDS

Wood House

Belsteads

CH

Park Farm

3

H

COURT RD
THE MILLARS
THE WINDMILLS

HOSPITAL APP

BETHNOLNEVILLE WAY

AYLETTS

MANSE

Broomfield

NASH DR

WARREN LA

Sand & Gravel Pit

11

Chelmer Valley High Sch

CHURCH AVE

Butlers Farm

BROOMHALL CL

BROOMHALL RD

Broomfield

CM1

BELSTEADS FARM LA

2

JUBILEE AVE

WHITE MEAD

MAIN RD

BUTLERS CL

Rutherfords

RETREAT

CRES

Belstead Hall Cottages

Broomfield Hall

PARSONAGE CL 1
MARY'S MEAD 2
CLARK WAY 3

JULIAN CL 1
WILLIAMS RD 2
WILLOW CL 3

CRICKETERS CL

MILL LA

BACK LA

Belstead Hall Farm

1

LONGCOTS CL

GOULTON RD

COPLAND CL

NEW RD

B1008

SCHOOL LA

Liby

Brooklands

Broomfield Prim Sch

Woolpit's Farm

LITTLE WALTHAM RD

A130

10

A B 71 C D 72 E F

191
174

A B C D E F

8

Chopping's Wood

Noake's House

Noake's Farm

Lawns Farm

Ringer's Wood

BOREHAM RD

Little Drakes

Bird's Farm

7

DRAKES LA

Works

Drake's Farm

Russel Green House

13

Russell Green

6

Brent Hall

Stocks Farm

5

CM3

Works

P

Stocks Cottages

Little Holts

Porter's Wood

12

Boreham Airfield (disused)

Holts Farm

4

WALTHAM RD

Sand & Gravel Pit

Wallace's Farm Cottages

WALLACE'S LA

Park Farm

3

Walford House

Mount Maskall

11

2

GENERALS LA

The Grove

Brick House Farm

Centenary Circle

BORE IND

GWYN CL 1
ROSEMARY COTTS 2
ARMONDE CL 3
MEADOWSIDE CT 4
SEABROOK GDNS 5

SHEARE

BE ELYN WAY

B11

BULLS LODGE COTTS

New Hall (Convent)

P

Bulls Lodge

BRICK HOUSE RD

SORRELL DOWN

MAIN RD

ST ANDREWS RD

ALLENS CL

PLANTATION RD

1

VILLIERS PL

ST ELYN WAY

CLEVES CL
OAK COTTS

B1137

CLAYPITS RD

10

A12

A B C D E F

73 74 75

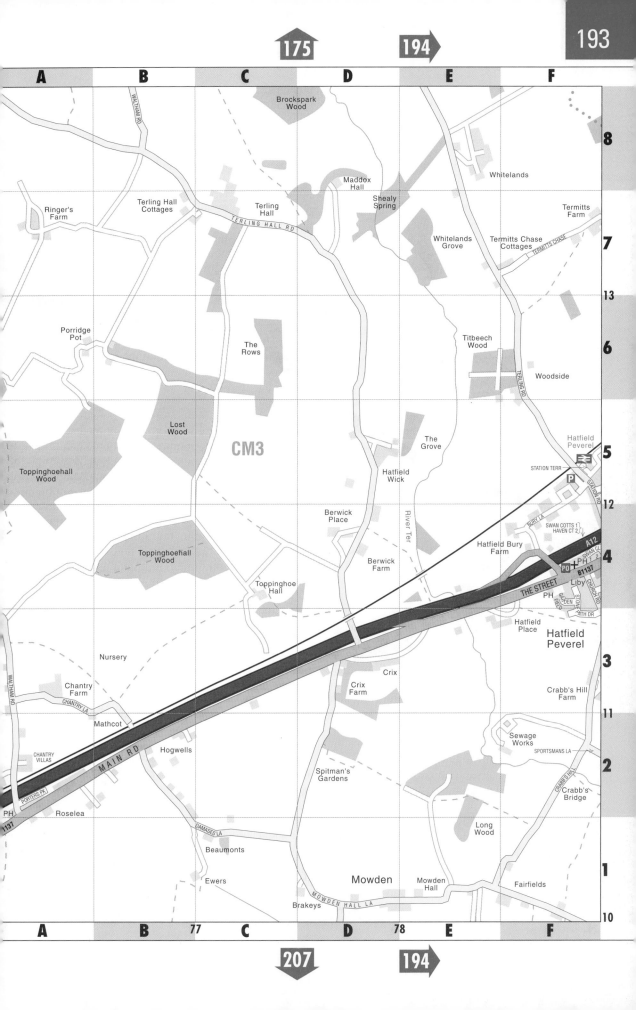

A B C D E F

8

PHILIP RD 1
ALUF CL 2

Dancing Dicks

Bridge H B1389

WITHAM

Holy Family RC Prim Sch

Pondholton Farm

PONDHOLTON DR 1
JUVINA CL 2
KINLOCH CHASE 3

Schs

MALTINGS LA

7

Termitt's Farm

Job's Wood

Lodge Farm

HATFIELD RD

CM8

Home Farm

OLIVER

TERMITTS CHASE

Wood End Farm

13

Mayfield Nursery

B1389

6

Dengie Farm

HOWBRIDGE HALL RD

B1

Latneys

THE TERRACE

MALDON RD

5

The Vineyards

Sand Pit

Sand Pit

Appynest

B1

THE TERRACE

Knowles's Farm

12

THE PINES

Sandford's Farm

ROOKERY

PRIORY CT B1137

THE STREET

B1019

CM3

HATFIELD RD

Barnards

4

A12

B1137

THE MILESTONES

Hatfield Peverel

Lane's Farm

WICKHAM BISHOP RD

Brook Farm

St Andrew's CE Jun Sch & Hatfield Peverel Cty Inf Sch

ST ANDREW'S COTTS PH

Bovingtons

The Nook

Lane's Wood

Sand Pit

3

Crabb's Hill House

Ivy Barns Farm

MALDON RD

11

The Priory

Lower Farm

Hayward's Farm

SPRING LA

2

SPORTSMANS LA

Gray's Farm

Moor Gardens

PH

Priory Farm

PRIORY FARM RD

PRIORY MEWS

ULTING RD

Jenkin's Farm

Moor Gardens

Smith's Farm

LEA GR

1

Nounsley

NOUNSLEY RD

MANOR RD

PEVEREL AVE

Butlers

DOE'S CNR

Works

B1019

Bridge Farm

Middlefield

CM9

10

MOWDEN HALL LA

ASHFIELD FARM RD

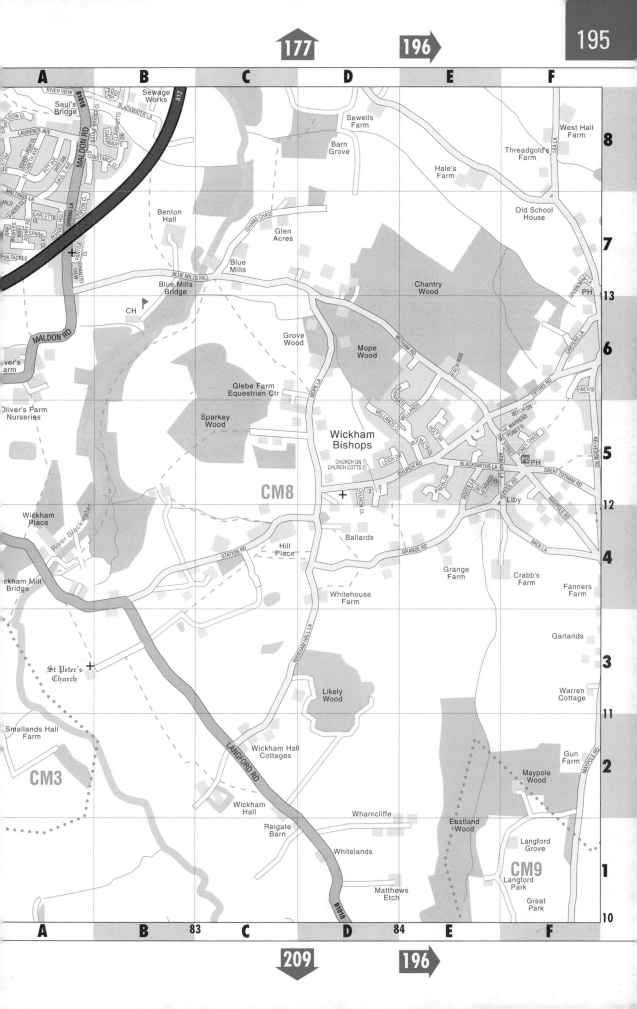

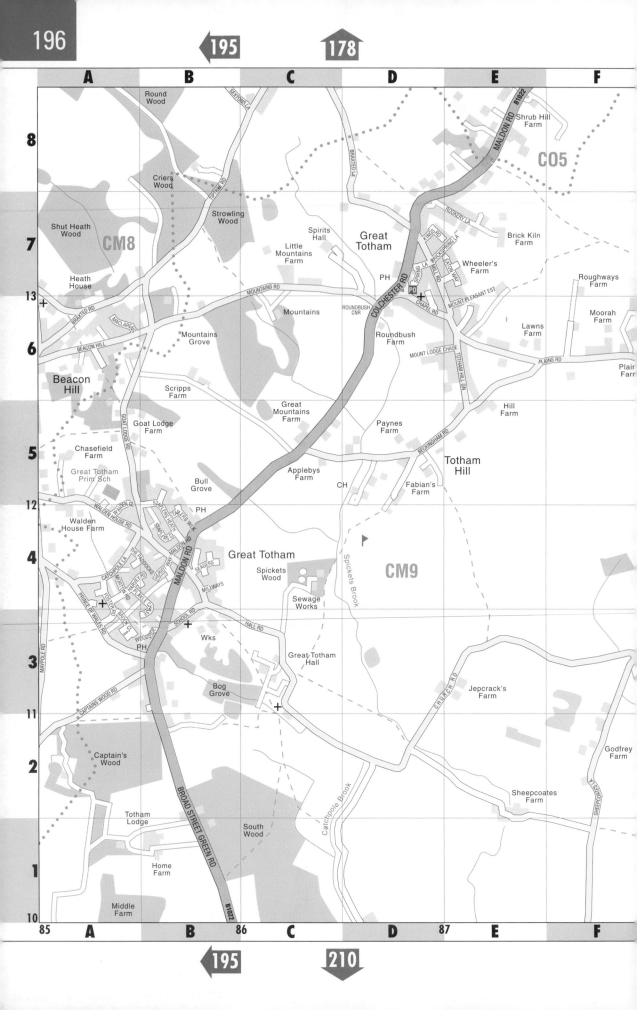

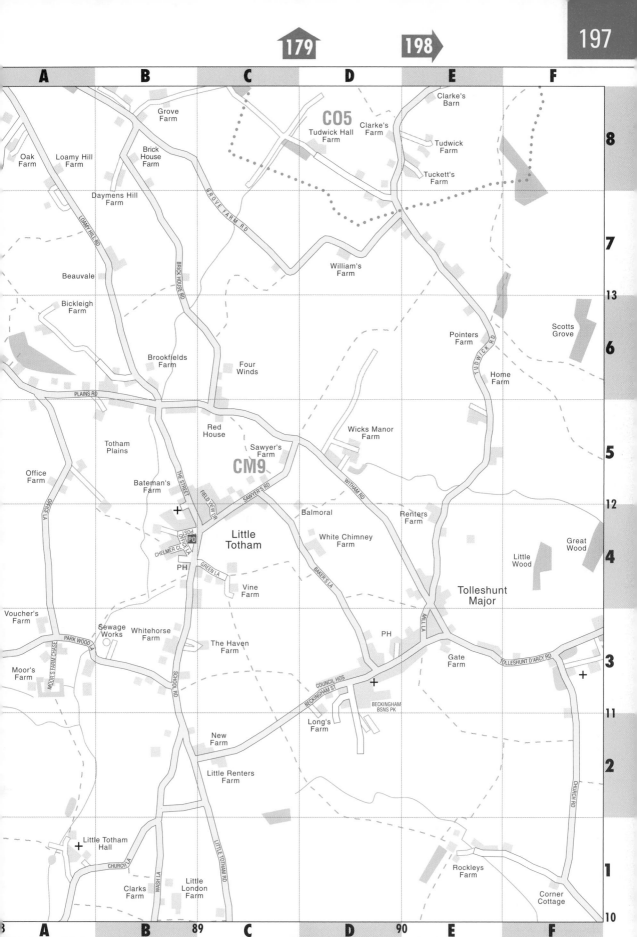

A B C D E F

8 13 6 5 12 4 11 2 1 10

CO5
CM9

Grove Farm
Oak Farm
Loamy Hill Farm
Brick House Farm
Clarke's Barn
Tudwick Hall Farm
Clarke's Farm
Tudwick Farm
Tuckett's Farm
Daymens Hill Farm
GROVE FARM RD
LOAMY HILL RD
BRICK HOUSE RD
Beauvale
Bickleigh Farm
William's Farm
Pointers Farm
Scotts Grove
TUDWICK RD
Brookfields Farm
Four Winds
Home Farm
PLAINS RD
Red House
Sawyer's Farm
Wicks Manor Farm
Totham Plains
Office Farm
Bateman's Farm
THE STREET
SAWYER'S RD
FIELD VIEW DR
WITHAM RD
Balmoral
Renters Farm
POST PO
CHELMER CL
Little Totham
White Chimney Farm
Little Wood
Great Wood
PH
GREEN LA
BAKER'S LA
Vine Farm
Tolleshunt Major
Voucher's Farm
Sewage Works
Whitehorse Farm
The Haven Farm
PH
MILL LA
Gate Farm
TOLLESHUNT D'ARCY RD
PARK WOOD LA
MOOR'S FARM CHASE
GROVE LA
Moor's Farm
SCHOOL RD
COUNCIL HOS
BECKINGHAM ST
Beckingham BSNS PK
New Farm
Long's Farm
Little Renters Farm
Little Totham Hall
CHURCH LA
WASH LA
LITTLE TOTHAM RD
Clarks Farm
Little London Farm
Rockleys Farm
CHURCH RD
Corner Cottage

89
90

197
180

A **B** **C** **D** **E** **F**

8

B1023

Grove Hall

BLIND LA

Lower Farm

High Hall

OXLEY HILL

HONEYPOT LA

RECTORY RD

BARNHALL

Hotel

CH

7

Devonia

Middle Farm

13

6

KELVEDON RD

D'Arcy Gate

B1026

Profits Farm

STATION RD

Station House

5

Limes Brook

Limesbrook Farm

Grout's Farm

Pond Farm

Pond Farm

CM9

12

Frame Farm

THE CROSS

Tolleshunt D'Arcy

SALTER'S MDW

VICARAGE CL

SOUTH ST

NORTH ST

PO

CHAPEL RD

4

Hill Farm

BECKINGHAM RD

CHURCH ST

B1023

Tolleshunt D'Arcy Prim Sch

D'ARCY WAY

PH

Spring Farm

Bowstead Bridge

Cemy

FESTIVAL GDNS

Tolleshunt D'Arcy Hall

TOLLESHUNT D'ARCY RD

Wildfields

Bowstead Brook

Tolleshunts Farm

TOLLESBURY RD

3

11

2

MALDON RD

Brook House Farm

Upper Grove

White House Cottages

B102

White House Farm

PAGES RD

1

Hyde Farm

10

B1026

A **B** **C** **D** **E** **F**

91   92   93

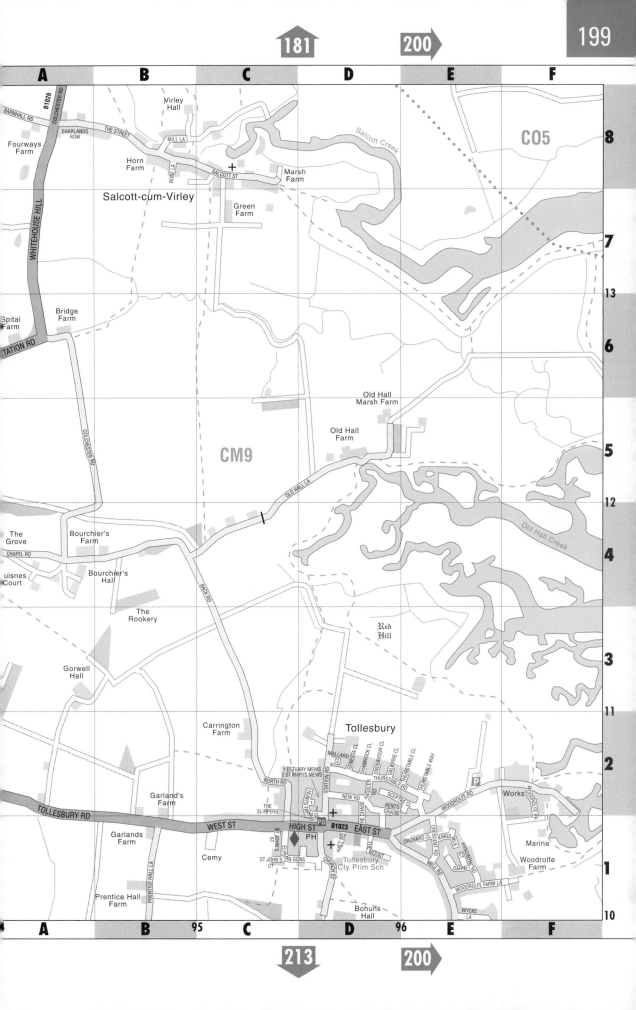

199
182

A   B   C   D   E   F

8

Decoy
Pond

Abbot's Hall Saltings

Copthall
Saltings

Sampson's
Creek

CO5

7

Quince's
Corner

Feldy
Marshes

Salcott Channel

13

Little Ditch

6

Old Hall
Marshes

Sunken
Island

Thorn Fleet

Marsh...

5

Joyce's
Head

Pennyhole
Fleet

12

CM9

4

Old Hall
Creek

Mersea
Quarters

Quarters
Spit

Tollesbury
Fleet

3

Woodrolfe Creek

North Channel

Virley Channel

11

Little Cob
Island

Great Cob
Island

The
Nass

2

South Channel

Shinglehead
Point

1

Tollesbury Wick
Marshes

10

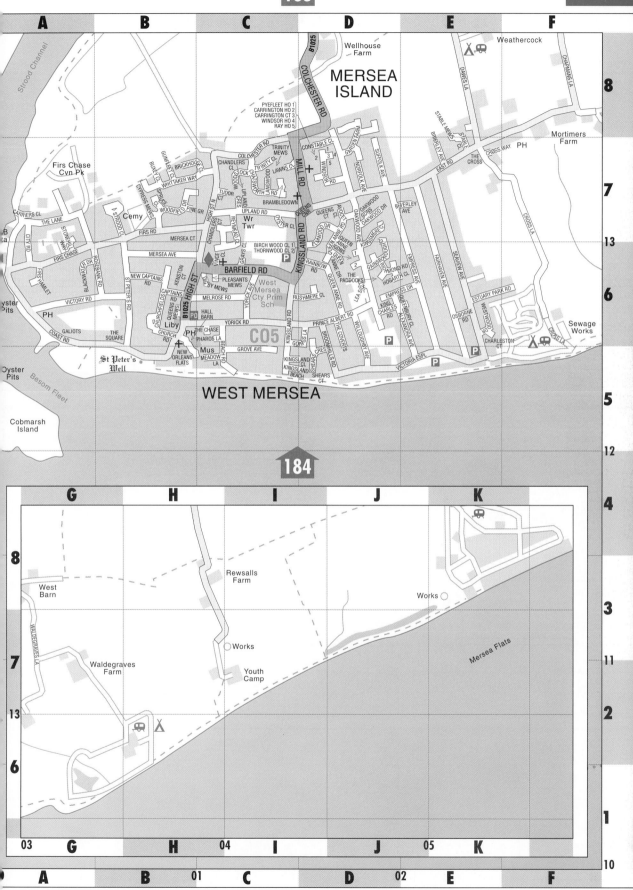

183

184

A B C D E F

MERSEA ISLAND

Wellhouse Farm

Weathercock

Mortimers Farm

Strood Channel

PYEFLEET HO 1
CARRINGTON HO 2
CARRINGTON CT 3
WINDSOR HO 4
RAY HO 5

CROSS WAY PH

THE CROSS

Firs Chase Cvn Pk

CHAPMANS LA

DAWES LA

STABLE MEWS CL

BRIERLEY AVE

STABLE

EAST RD

CARRIERS CL

THE LANE

CITY RD

Cemy

CYPRESS MEWS

STROOD CL

FIRS RD

SPRUCE

WOODFIELD DR

PINE GR

BUXEY CL

GUNFLEET CL

BRICKHOUSE CL

WHITTAKER WAY

CHANDLERS CL

COLCHESTER RD

TRINITY MEWS

CONSTABLE CL

LAWNS CL

LANGWOOD

CHASWYTH

SYMTH

TUDOR CT

HIGH ST N

UPLAND CRES

REYWOOD CL

GRAYS CL

CHANDLERS CT

VINCE CL

GREEN FARM

GYVERN FARM

NORFOLK AVE

SUFFOLK AVE

WINDSOR RD

QUEENS CT

QUEENS ESPL

Wr Twr

OYSTER CL

BRAMBLEDOWN

UPLAND RD

MERSEA CT

MERSEA AVE

MILL RD

KINGSLAND RD

ELMWOOD

QUEEN ANNE DR

QUEEN ANNE RD

AVOCET

OAKWOOD GDNS

OAKWOOD DR

BEVERLEY AVE

EMPRESS AVE

FAIRHAVEN AVE

SEAVIEW AVE

ESTUARY PARK RD

WESTWOOD

CHARLESTON CT

CROSS LA

Sewage Works

BARFIELD RD

West Mersea Cty Prim Sch

PLEASANTS MEWS

TUDOR BY MEWS

MELROSE RD

NEW CAPTAINS RD

CAPTAINS RD

KENISTON CT

ST PETER'S RD

CHURCHFIELDS RD

QUEENS MEWS

HIGH ST

B1025

HALL BARN

Liby

THE CHASE

PHAROS LA

YORICK RD

GROVE AVE

MEADOW LA

BEACH RD

CHURCH RD

PH

Mus

NEW ORLEANS FLATS

RUSHMERE CL

BIRCH WOOD CL 1
THORNWOOD CL 2

RAINBOW RD

QUEEN ANNE RD

LEA RD

KING CHARLES RD

THE PADDOCKS

HOGARTH CL

EMPRESS DR

QUEBURY CL

OSBORNE RD

ALEXANDRA AVE

PRINCE ALBERT RD

THE COVERTS

BROOMHILLS RD

WILLOUGHBY AVE

VICTORIA ESPL

KINGSLAND RD

GOS LA

CRES LA

SHEARS CL

KINGSLAND CL

KINGSLAND BEACH

SHEARS

St Peter's Well

Oyster Pits

Oyster Pits

FIRS HAMLET

ROSEBANK RD

BLACKWATER CL

PH

GALIOTS

COAST RD

VICTORY RD

THE SQUARE

STONEHALL WAY

FIRS CHASE

CO5

WEST MERSEA

Besom Fleet

Cobmarsh Island

G H I J K

West Barn

Rewsalls Farm

Works

Mersea Flats

Works

Youth Camp

Waldegraves Farm

WALDEGRAVES LA

03 G H 04 I J 05 K 10

A B 01 C D 02 E F

186

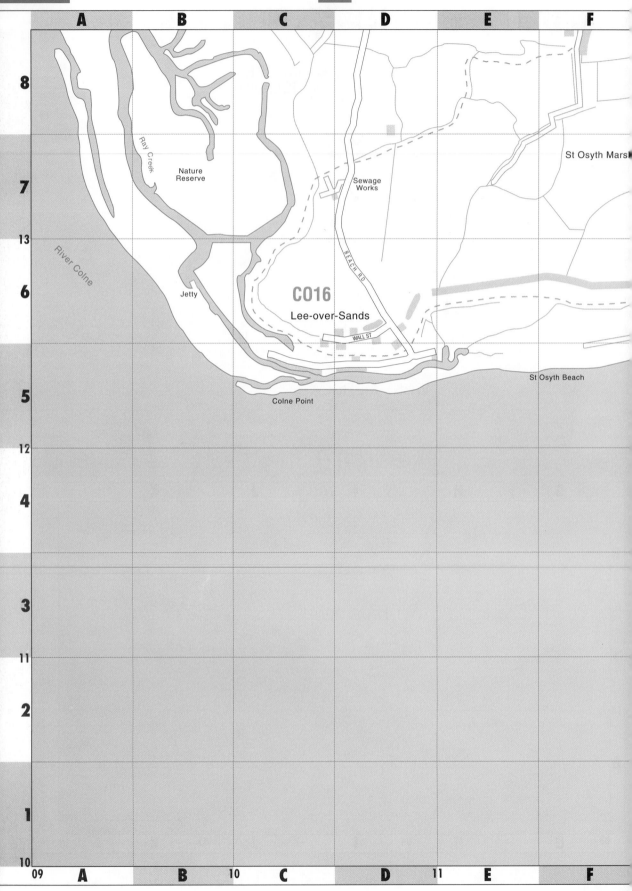

A B C D E F

8
7
13
6
5
12
4
3
11
2
1
10

09 A B 10 C D 11 E F

River Colne

Ray Creek

Nature
Reserve

Sewage
Works

St Osyth Marsh

Jetty

BEACH RD

CO16
Lee-over-Sands

WALL ST

St Osyth Beach

Colne Point

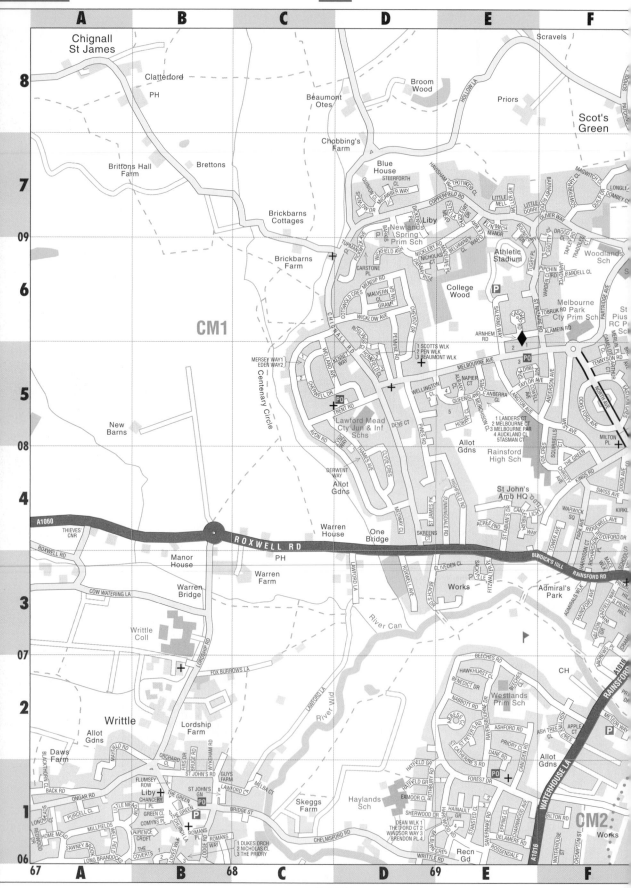

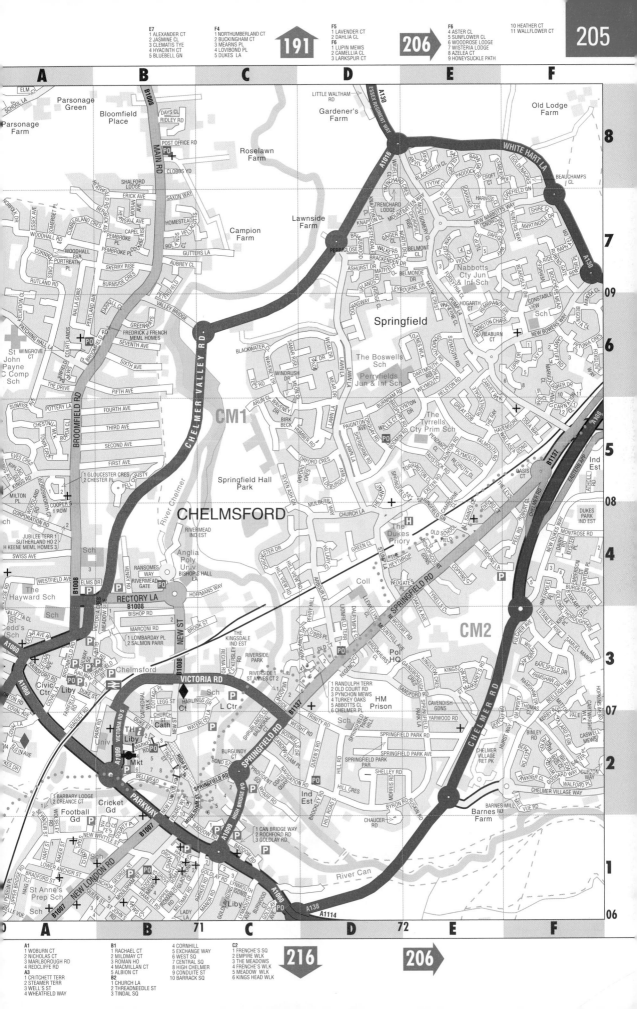

A B C D E F

Rickstones
MOWDEN HALL LA
Gardener's Farm
8

Culverts Cottages
Brakey Wood
Botter's Farm

Mulberries
Culvert's Farm
Belstead Cottages
World's End Cottage
7
Chelmer & Blackwater Navigation

Multum in Parvo
09

Weir
Paper Mill Lock
Paper Mill Bridge
Bassett's Farm
6
River Chelmer
New Wood
Brickwell Wood

Coleraines
Tofts Chase
5
SPRING CL
WICKHAY COTTS
JARVIS FIELD
NORTH HILL
Tofts

Holybreds Wood
Walters Cottage
08

PH
+
Bassett's Wood
Little Baddow Hall
Holybreds Farm
RISLEY
Warren Farm
4
HOLYBREAD LA
CM3
Scrub Wood
The Hoppet
Cuckoos
Little Baddow
Gibbs

CHAPEL LA
PO
+
Duke's Orchard
Burghfields Farm
The Warren
3
Waterhall
HURRELLS LA
COLAM LA
PASTURE WGH
SPRING ELMS LA
Birch Wood
07
Belle Vue Farm
THE RYE FIELD
PH
MILL LA
POSTMAN'S LA

New Lodge
Blake's Wood
Elm Green Sch
PARSONAGE LA
OAKLANDS WAY
2
NEW LODGE CHASE
Long Spring Wood
Old Riffhams
THE RIDGE
Pheasanthouse Wood

Nature Reserve
COMMON LA
Long Wood
Great Graces
GRACES LA
RIFFHAMS CHASE
The White House
DARCY RISE
FIR TREE LA
Poors' Piece
1
Hall Wood
Great Graces Farm
Riffhams
RIFFHAMS LA
Ling Wood
WOODSIDE
CHESTNUT WLK
06

A B 77 C D 78 E F

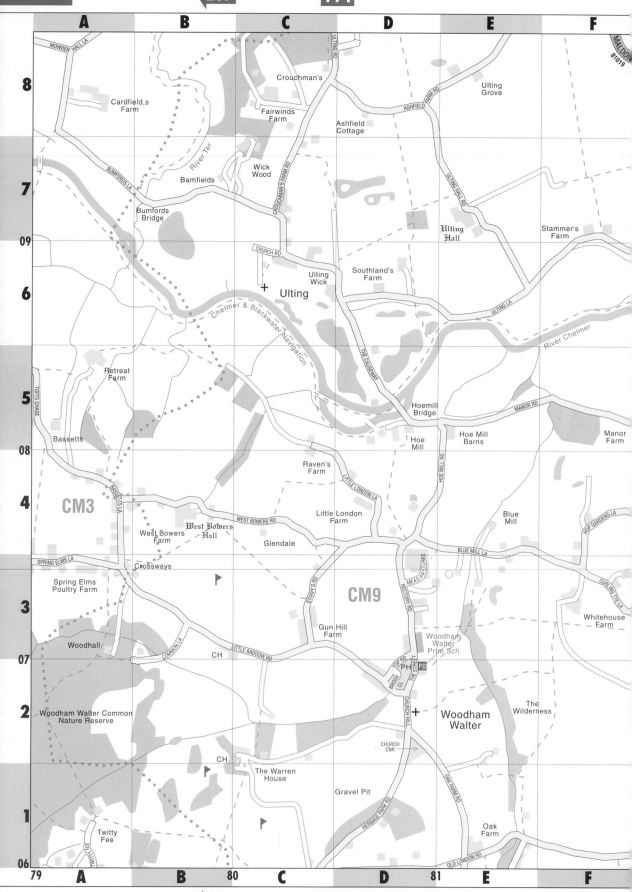

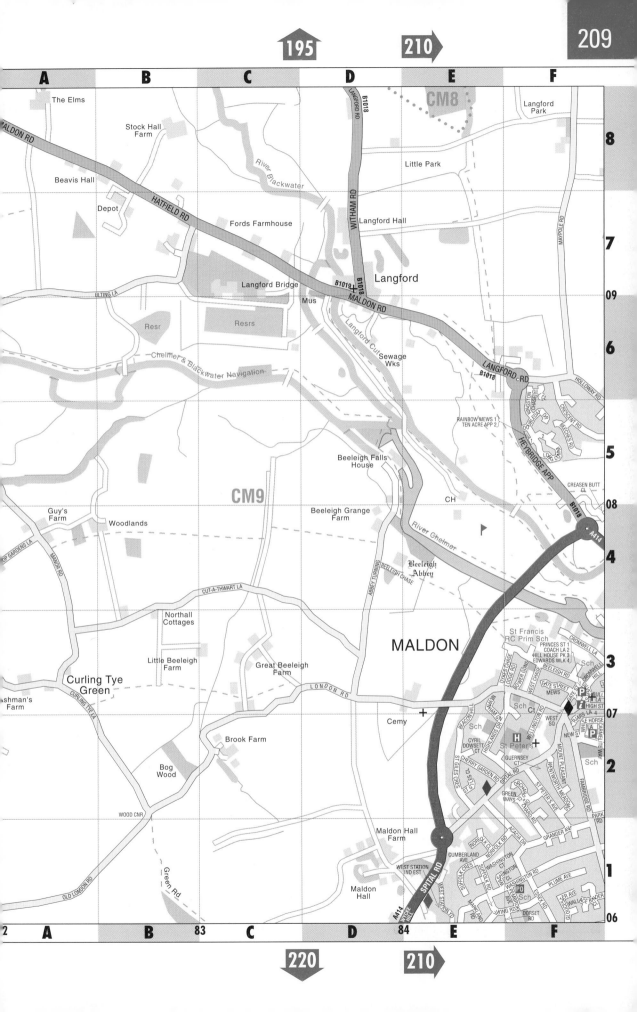

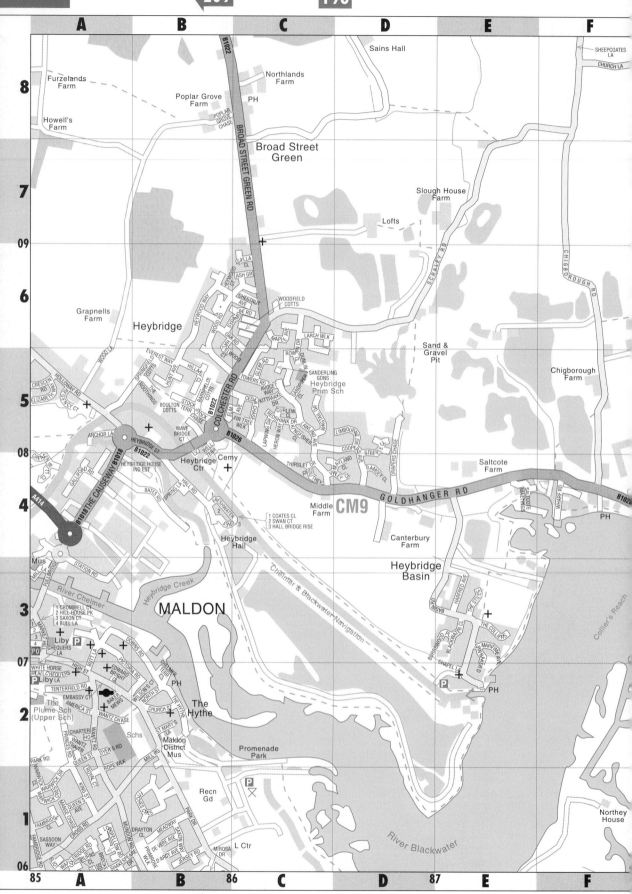

A B C D E F

CHURCH LA

Little London
Farm

Brick
Cottages

Chappel
Farm

WASH LA

BLIND LA

LITTLE TOTHAM RD

Falcons Hall
Farm

Folly Faunts
House

B1026

HIGHAMS CHASE

Goldhanger
House

Agricultural/Domestic
Mus

MALDON RD

PO

HALL EST

SORREL CL

PH

CHURCH ST

Goldhanger

PEARTREE CL

HEAD ST

FISH ST

PH

Rook
Hall

Cobb's
Farm

THISTLEY CL

CM9

Wash
Bridge

Gardener's
Farm

Bound's
Farm

BARROW
MARSH

Vaulty
Manor

GOLDHANGER RD

Red
Hill

OSEA RD

Cvn
Pks

Sewage
Works

Mill
Beach

Collier's Reach

Hilly Pool
Point

Decoy
Point

Causeway

River Blackwater

West Point

OSEA
ISLAND

Northey
Island

8

7

09

6

5

08

4

3

07

2

1

06

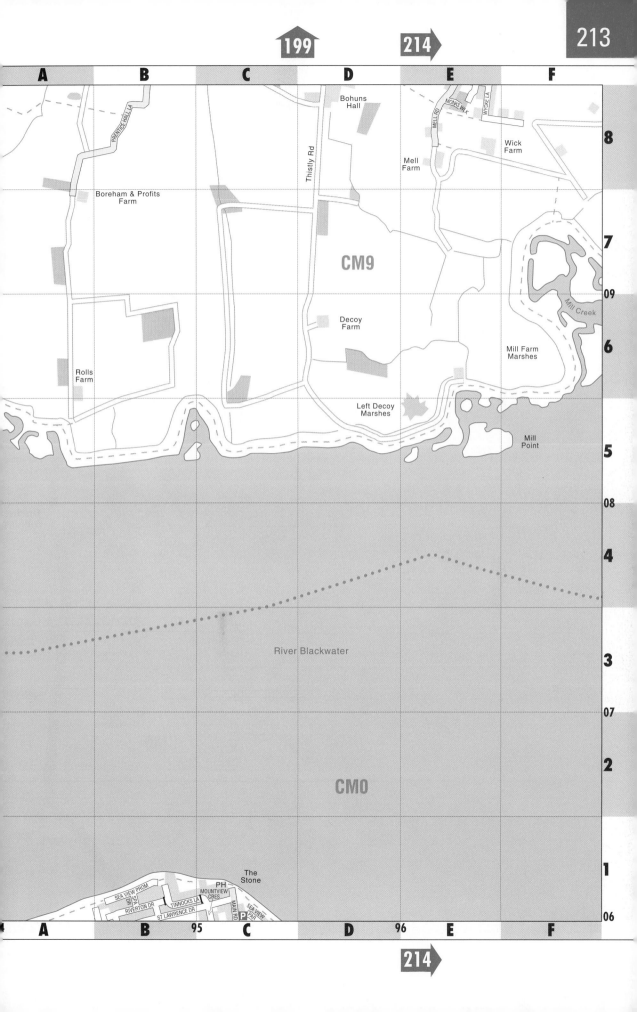

PRENTICE HALL LA

Bohuns
Hall

MONKS WLK

WYCKE LA

MELL RD

Wick
Farm

Mell
Farm

Boreham & Profits
Farm

Thistly Rd

CM9

8

7

09

Mill Creek

Decoy
Farm

Mill Farm
Marshes

6

Rolls
Farm

Left Decoy
Marshes

Mill
Point

5

08

4

River Blackwater

3

07

2

CM0

1

The
Stone

PH
MOUNTVIEW
CRES

SEA VIEW PROM
SPA
RIVERTON DR
TINNOCKS LA
ST LAWRENCE DR
MAIN RD
SEA VIEW PAR
P

06

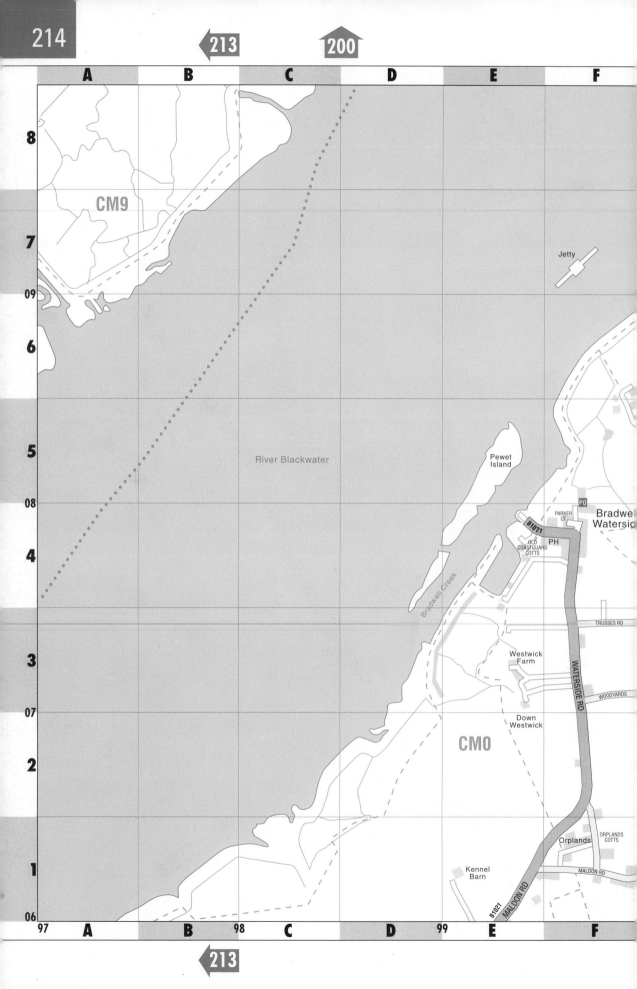

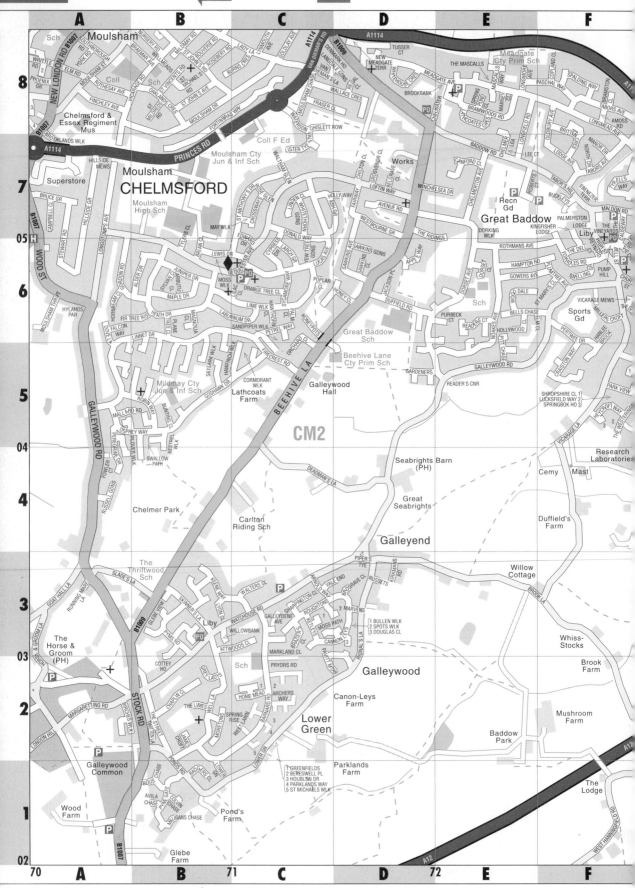

A8
1 CHERRYGARDEN LA
2 UPPER CHASE
3 DOUGLAS WLK
4 LAUREL GR

215

205

215

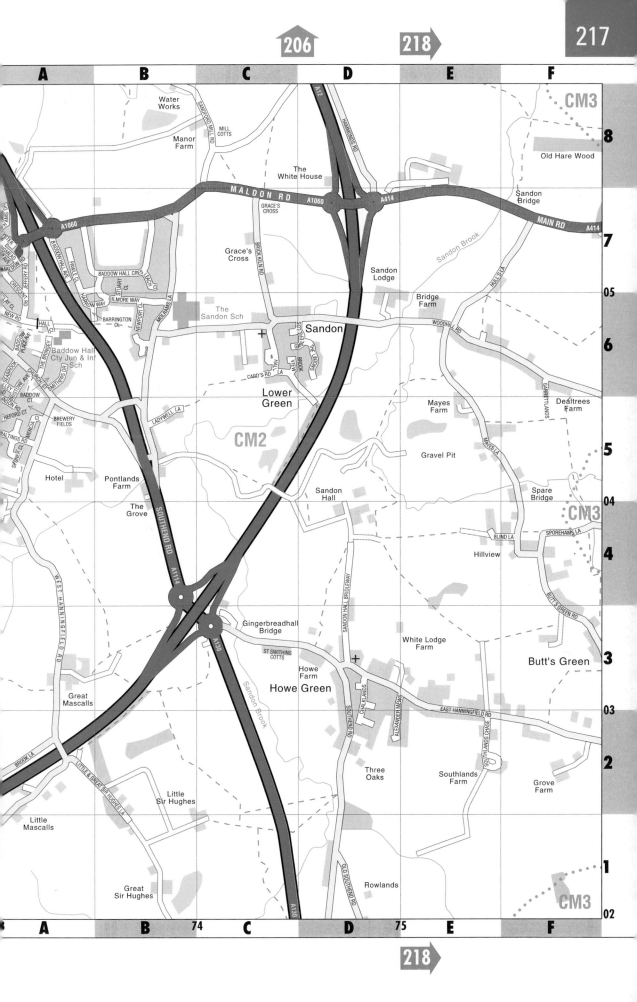

A B C D E F

8

Water Works

Manor Farm

MILL COTTS

SANDFORD MILL RD

Old Hare Wood

The White House

MALDON RD

A1060

A414

Sandon Bridge

MAIN RD

A414

GRACE'S CROSS

A1060

A12

HAMMONDS RD

A1060

7

Grace's Cross

BRICK KILN RD

Sandon Lodge

Sandon Brook

HULL'S LA

05

BADDOW HALL CRES

LEACH CL

Bridge Farm

WOODHILL RD

6

The Sandon Sch

MOLRAMS LA

GILMORE WAY

Sandon

SOUTHEND RD

Lower Green

CARD'S RD

HALL LA

THE LYNONS

BROOK LA

Mayes Farm

GARRETTLANDS

Dealtrees Farm

5

CM2

Gravel Pit

MAYES LA

Spare Bridge

04

CM3

Hotel

Pontlands Farm

The Grove

SOUTHEND RD

A1114

Sandon Hall

BLIND LA

SPOREHAMS LA

Hillview

4

BUTT'S GREEN RD

Great Mascalls

WEST HANNINGFIELD RD

Gingerbreadhall Bridge

A130

ST SWITHINS COTTS

Howe Farm

SANDON HALL BRIDLEWAY

White Lodge Farm

Butt's Green

3

Howe Green

CHALKLANDS

ALEXANDER MEWS

EAST HANNINGFIELD RD

03

LITTLE & GREAT SIR HUGHES LA

Little Sir Hughes

Sandon Brook

SOUTHEND RD

SOUTHLANDS CHASE

Three Oaks

Southlands Farm

Grove Farm

2

Little Mascalls

BROOK LA

Great Sir Hughes

A130

OLD SOUTHEND RD

Rowlands

1

CM3

02

A B C D E F

74 75

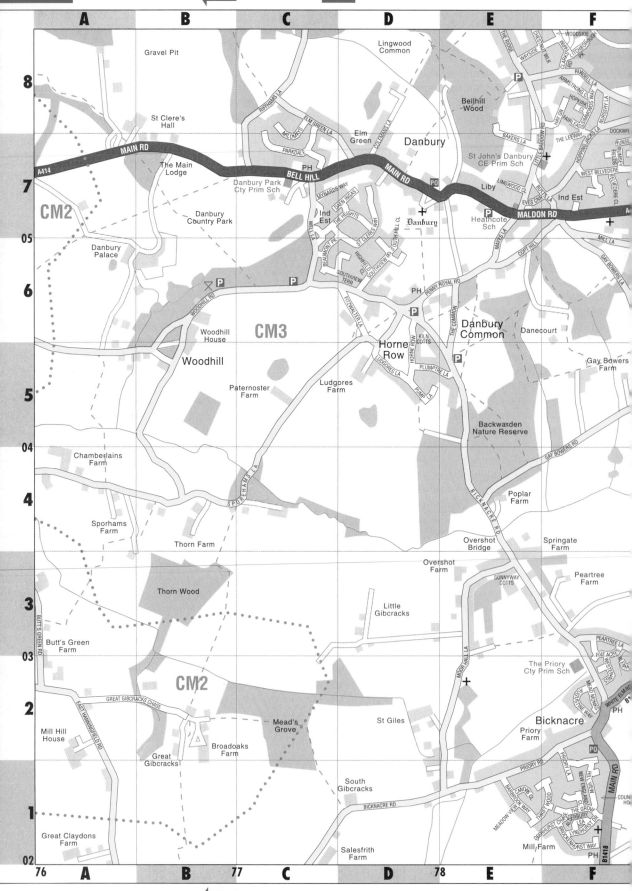

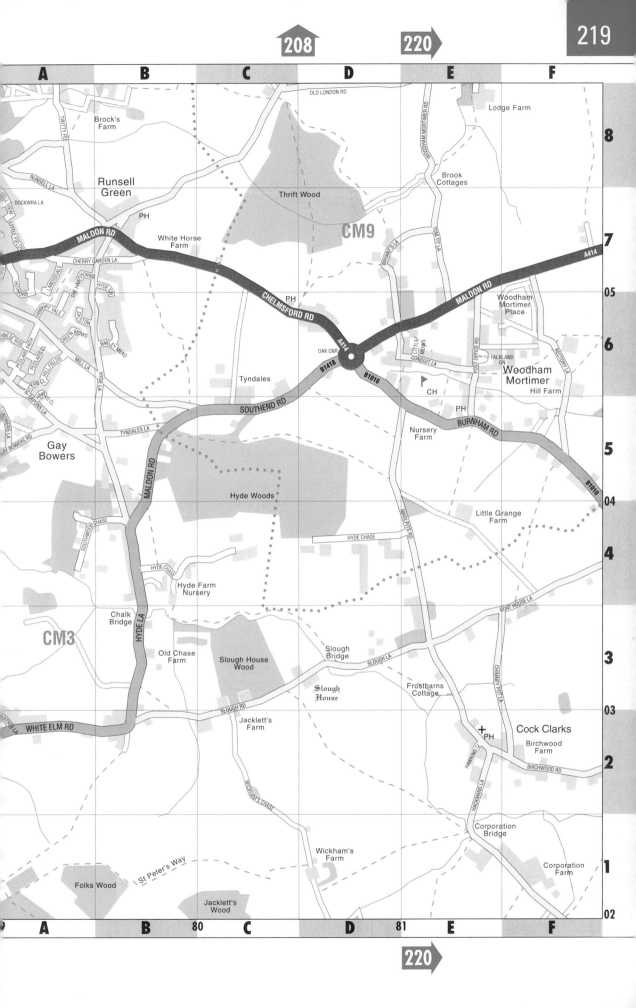

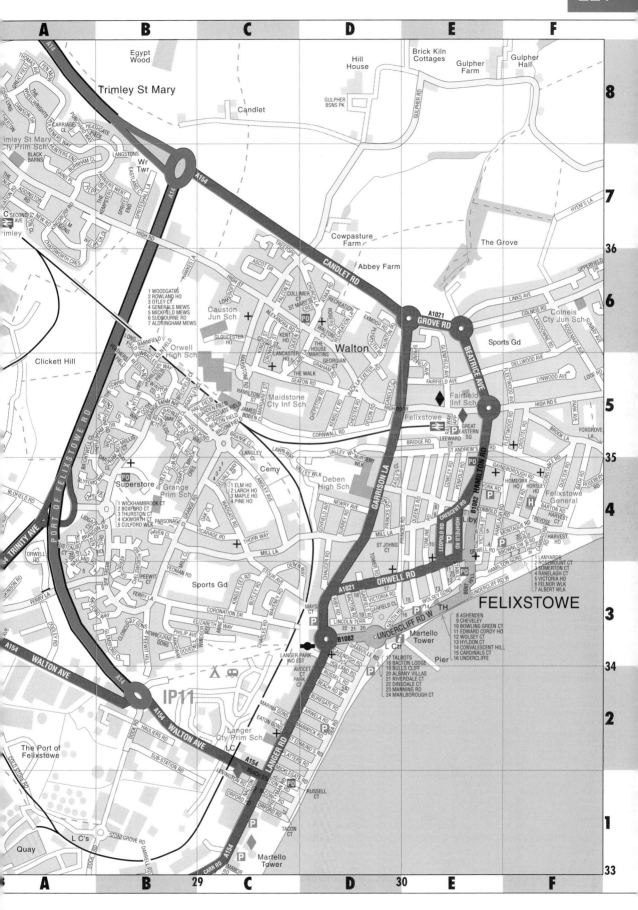

Index

Street names are listed alphabetically and show the locality, the Postcode District, the page number and a reference to the square in which the name falls on the map page

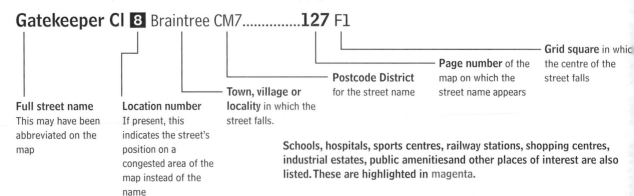

Gatekeeper Cl 8 Braintree CM7...............127 F1

Full street name
This may have been abbreviated on the map

Location number
If present, this indicates the street's position on a congested area of the map instead of the name

Town, village or locality in which the street falls.

Postcode District for the street name

Page number of the map on which the street name appears

Grid square in which the centre of the street falls

Schools, hospitals, sports centres, railway stations, shopping centres, industrial estates, public amenitiesand other places of interest are also listed. These are highlighted in magenta.

Abbreviations used in the index

App **Approach**	Cl **Close**	Espl **Esplanade**	Mans **Mansions**	Rdbt **Roundabout**
Arc **Arcade**	Comm **Common**	Est **Estate**	Mdw **Meadows**	S **South**
Ave **Avenue**	Cnr **Corner**	Gdns **Gardens**	N **North**	Sq **Square**
Bvd **Boulevard**	Cotts **Cottages**	Gn **Green**	Orch **Orchard**	Strs **Stairs**
Bldgs **Buildings**	Ct **Court**	Gr **Grove**	Par **Parade**	Stps **Steps**
Bsns Pk **Business Park**	Ctyd **Courtyard**	Hts **Heights**	Pk **Park**	St **Street, Saint**
Bsns Ctr **Business Centre**	Cres **Crescent**	Ho **House**	Pas **Passage**	Terr **Terrace**
Bglws **Bungalows**	Dr **Drive**	Ind Est **Industrial**	Pl **Place**	Tk **Track**
Cswy **Causeway**	Dro **Drove**	**Estate**	Prec **Precinct**	Trad **Trading Est**
Ctr **Centre**	E **East**	Intc **Interchange**	Prom **Promenade**	Wlk **Walk**
Circ **Circle**	Emb **Embankment**	Junc **Junction**	Ret Pk **Retail Park**	W **West**
Cir **Circus**	Ent **Enterprise**	La **Lane**	Rd **Road**	Yd **Yard**

Town and village index

Abberton 162 B3	Colchester 135 F7	Great Oakley 116 C4	Little Yeldham 30 E4	Stratford St Mary 58
Aldham 133 B8	Colne Engaine 77 F2	Great Sampford 47 B3	Littlebury 21 E4	Sturmer 9
Alphamstone 54 F3	Copford 133 D4	Great Tey 132 C8	Long Melford 15 D7	Stutton 61
Alresford 165 B8	Cressing 156 A6	Great Totham 196 B4	Maldon 210 A3	Sudbury 33
Ardleigh 111 E7	Danbury 218 F7	Great Waltham 190 F7	Manningtree 86 E4	Takeley 148
Arkesden 41 E2	Debden 68 B7	Great Wigborough 181 F2	Manuden 92 F2	Tattingstone 61
Ashdon 6 B1	Dedham 84 F7	Great Yeldham 30 A1	Margaretting 215 D1	Tendring 140
Ashen 11 D1	Duddenhoe End 41 A6	Greenstead Green 104 A5	Marks Tey 132 E3	Terling ....175 C
Bardfield Saling 99 C2	Earls Colne 105 B6	Hadstock 5 C6	Messing 159 D2	Thaxted 70
Barnston 151 A4	East Bergholt 59 C2	Halstead 76 D2	Mistley 86 F4	Thorington Street .....57 C
Bartlow 6 B7	East Mersea 184 E1	Harkstead 63 B2	Nayland 56 B1	Thorpe-le-Soken 142
Beaumont 141 F7	Easthorpe 160 A7	Harwich 91 E5	New Mistley 87 B4	Thorrington 166
Beazley End 101 C6	Eight Ash Green 134 A8	Hatfield Peverel 194 A4	Newport 43 A1	Tiptree 179
Belchamp St Paul 13 A2	Elder Street 44 E1	Haverhill 9 C7	North End 151 F2	Tollesbury 199
Belchamp Walter 31 F5	Elmdon 20 B4	Hazeleigh 220 A4	Nuthampstead 39 A2	Tolleshunt D'arcy ....198 D
Belstead 36 C7	Elmstead 138 A6	Helions Bumpstead ...26 C8	Panfield 127 A7	Tolleshunt Knights ...180
Bentley 60 E7	Elsenham 94 C1	Hempstead 25 F1	Pattiswick 129 F5	Tolleshunt Major 197
Berden 92 C8	Farnham 118 D6	Henham 94 F6	Peldon 182 E6	Toppesfield 50
Bicknacre 218 F2	Feering 158 E5	Heybridge 210 C5	Pentlow 13 F6	Trimley St Mary 221
Birch 161 A3	Felixstowe 221 A4	Heybridge Basin 210 E3	Point Clear Bay 186 A3	Ugley 93
Birchanger 119 D2	Felsted 152 B5	Highwoods 110 B4	Purleigh 220 D1	Ulting 208
Birdbrook 28 B7	Finchingfield 72 C5	Hinxton 3 B7	Quendon 66 F2	Wakes Colne 106
Bishop's Stortford ...145 E6	Fingringhoe 163 F5	Holbrook 62 C5	Radwinter 45 F8	Walton-on-the-Naze ..171
Black Notley 155 B5	Ford End 172 B6	Holland-on-Sea 189 E6	Ramsey 89 F1	Washbrook 35
Blackheath 163 A8	Fordham 107 D5	Howe Green 217 D3	Rayne 126 F2	Weeley 140
Boreham 206 E8	Fordham Heath 107 F1	Howe Street 172 F2	Rickling Green 93 D8	Weeley Heath 168
Borley 14 F3	Foxearth 14 C6	Ickleton 3 A4	Ridgewell 29 B7	Wendens Ambo 42
Boxted 82 F7	Frating 139 A3	Ipswich 17 C7	Rivenhall 177 B7	West Bergholt 108
Bradfield 87 F2	Frinton-on-Sea 170 F6	Jaywick 188 A1	Rowhedge 163 F8	West Mersea 201
Bradwell 129 D2	Galleywood 216 C3	Kelvedon 158 C2	Rushmere St Andrew 18 E8	Wethersfield 73
Bradwell Waterside ..214 F4	Gestingthorpe 31 E1	Kirby Cross 170 B6	Saffron Walden 22 D2	Wherstead 37
Braintree 128 B5	Glemsford 2 C4	Kirby-le-Soken 170 C8	Salcott-cum-virley ...199 B8	White Colne 105
Brantham 60 E1	Goldhanger 211 E7	Lamarsh 55 B4	Sandon 217 C6	White Notley 155
Brightlingsea 185 F6	Gosfield 102 E8	Langham 83 F4	Sewards End 23 E1	Wickham Bishops 195
Broomfield 191 B2	Great Baddow 216 F6	Langley 40 C2	Shalford 100 E7	Wickham St Paul 53
Bulmer 32 F5	Great Bardfield 72 C1	Lawford 86 B3	Shotley Gate 91 A8	Widdington 67
Bures 79 E8	Great Bentley 166 E8	Layer-de-la-Haye ...161 F5	Shudy Camps 7 B6	Wimbish 45
Canfield End 149 B7	Great Braxted 178 C1	Lindsell 98 A3	Sible Hedingham 51 E1	Witham 176
Capel St Mary 35 B2	Great Bromley 112 E1	Little Baddow 207 E3	Silver End 156 D4	Wivenhoe 137
Castle Camps 7 E3	Great Chesterford 3 D2	Little Bentley 139 F8	Sproughton 16 B6	Wix 115
Castle Hedingham 51 E4	Great Cornard 34 B5	Little Bromley 113 B6	St Lawrence 213 B1	Woodham Mortimer 219
Cavendish 1 C1	Great Dunmow 150 D8	Little Clacton 168 C3	St Osyth 187 A4	Woodham Walter 208
Chappel 106 C5	Great Easton 122 F7	Little Dunmow 151 D7	Stambourne 28 D3	Woolverstone 38
Chelmondiston 63 B8	Great Hallingbury ..146 E4	Little Easton 122 F5	Stansted 2 F7	Wormingford 80
Chelmsford 205 B2	Great Henny 54 C8	Little Horkesley 81 E4	Stansted Mountfitchet .119 C8	Wrabness 88
Chrishall 19 D3	Great Holland 170 A3	Little Leighs 173 E6	Stebbing 124 E5	Writtle 204
Clacton-on-Sea 189 B6	Great Horkesley 82 B1	Little Maplestead ...53 B4	Steeple Bumpstead ...27 B8	
Clare 12 C8	Great Leighs 173 F7	Little Oakley 117 B7	Stisted 129 C6	
Clavering 65 C5	Great Maplestead 52 D2	Little Totham 197 B4	Stoke by Clare 11 C4	
Coggeshall 131 A3	Great Notley 154 C6	Little Waltham 191 B6	Stoke by Nayland 56 E5	

A

Abberton Rd
Fringinghoe CO5 ....163 D3
Layer-de-l-H CO2 ......162 C5
Abberton Resr Nature
Reserve CO2 ....161 F2
Abberton Wildfowl Ctr
CO2 ....161 E1
Abbess Cl CM1 ....204 E2
Abbey Cres CO16 ......142 A1
Abbey Gate St ■ CO2 ..135 F6
Abbey La Coggeshall CO6 .131 A4
Saffron Walden CB10 ....22 D1
Abbey Mdw CO9 ....51 D2
Abbey Rd CO10 ....15 E1
Abbey St Ickleton CB10 ...3 A4
Thorpe-le-S CO16 ......142 A1
Abbey Turning CM9 ....209 D4
Abbey View CM6 ....96 E2
Abbot's Rd CO2 ....136 B3
Abbots Cl
Clacton-on-S CO15 ....188 E6
Manningtree CO11 ......115 C5
Abbots Gdns CO16 ....187 C4
Abbots La CO6 ....134 A7
Abbots Wick La CO5 ..181 B3
Abbotsbury Cl IP2 ......17 A1
Abbott Rd CO12 ....90 F2
Abbotts Cl CM2 ....205 D3
Abbotts Ct CB9 ....9 E5
Abbotts Way CM23 ....145 C5
Abdy Ave CO12 ....90 E2
Abell Way CM2 ....206 B4
Abels Rd CO9 ....103 D8
Abercorn Ct ■ CB9 ......8 F7
Abercorn Ho CM3 ......206 E8
Abercorn Way CM8 ....177 A2
Abingdon Cl IP2 ....17 A1
Abinger Cl CO16 ......188 C6
Abington Pl ■ CB9 ......9 A8
Abraham Dr CM8 ......156 E4
Abram's La SG8 ....19 C4
Acacia Ave CO4 ....136 E8
Acacia Cl IP3 ....18 E1
Acacia Ct CO11 ....60 D1
Acacia Dr CM9 ....209 F1
Acacia Gdns CM8 ......177 B4
Accommodation Rd CO4 109 D7
Acer Gr IP8 ....16 C1
Achilles Way CM7 ......128 B5
Achnacone Dr CO4 ....109 C3
Acland Ave CO3 ....135 B7
Acland Ct CO3 ....18 C2
Acorn Ave Braintree CM7 .127 E2
Halstead CO9 ....76 D1
Acorn Cl Colchester CO4 .110 D4
Harwich CO12 ....90 F1
Ipswich IP2 ....16 C2
Acorn Wlk CO7 ....166 A5
Acorns The CM24 ......119 E2
Acres End CM1 ....204 E4
Acton Cl CO10 ....33 F8
Acton Gn CO10 ....33 F8
Acton La CO10 ....33 E8
Acton Sq ■ CO10 ......33 E7
Adair Rd IP1 ....16 D8
Adams Cl IP2 ....17 A2
Adams Ct Halstead CO9 ..76 D2
Saffron Walden CB11 ....43 C8
Adderley Rd CM23 ....145 F7
Addington Rd IP11 ....221 A4
Addison Rd CO13 ......170 B5
Adelaide Dr CO2 ......136 A1
Adelaide Rd IP4 ....18 D6
Adelaide St CO12 ......90 F5
Admiral Rd IP8 ....36 E8
Admirals Wlk CM1 ....204 F3
Aetheric Rd CM7 ......127 E3
Affleck Rd CO4 ....136 E7
Agar Rd ■ CO14 ......171 C8
Agar Road App ■ CO14 .171 C8
Agate Rd CO15 ....188 F2
Agincourt Rd CO15 ....188 D4
Agricultural/Domestic
Mus CM9 ....211 E7
Ainger Rd CO12 ....90 F2
Aingers Green Rd CO7 .167 A5
Ainslie Rd IP1 ....17 A6
Aire Wlk CM8 ....176 E2
Aisne Rd CO2 ....135 D4
Ajax Cl CM7 ....128 B5
Alamein Rd
Chelmsford CM1 ......204 F6
Colchester CO2 ......135 C2
Alan Cl CO3 ....134 A4
Alan Dr CO16 ....168 D1
Alan Hasler Ho CM6 ..150 D7
Alan Rd Ipswich IP3 ....17 F4
Witham CM8 ....176 E1
Alan Way CO3 ....134 A4
Alanbrooke Rd CO2 ..136 D2
Albany Chase CO15 ..189 B4
Albany Cl Chelmsford CM1 .204 E5
West Bergholt CO6 ....108 D4
Albany Gdns E CO15 ..189 B3
Albany Gdns W CO15 ..189 B3
Albany Rd CO6 ....108 E4
Albany The IP4 ....17 E8
Albany Villas IP11 ....221 D3
Albemarle Gdns CM7 ..128 C5
Albemarle St CO12 ....91 D5
Albert Gdns
Clacton-on-S CO15 ....189 B3
Coggeshall CO6 ......131 A2
Albert Ho IP2 ....17 B4
Albert Pl CO6 ....131 A2
Albert Rd Braintree CM7 .128 A3

Albert Rd *continued*
Brightlingsea CO7 ....186 A6
Witham CM8 ....177 A3
Albert St Colchester CO1 .135 E8
Harwich CO12 ....91 D5
Albert Wlk IP11 ......221 E4
Albertine Cl CO3 ......134 C6
Albion Cl ■ CM2 ......205 B1
Albion Gr CO2 ....136 A5
Albion Hill IP4 ....17 F7
Albion St CO5 ....164 A8
Albra Mead CM2 ......206 B4
Albrighton Croft CO4 ..110 C4
Alconbury CM23 ......119 B1
Alde Rd CB9 ....9 A8
Aldeburgh Cl
Clacton-on-S CO16 ....188 B4
Haverhill CB9 ....8 E7
Aldeburgh Gdns CO4 ..110 B4
Aldeburgh Way CM1 ..205 D5
Alder Cl CM23 ....145 C4
Alder Dr CM2 ....216 B6
Alder Wlk CM8 ....177 B4
Alderbury Lea CM3 ....218 F1
Alderbury Rd CM24 ..119 C8
Aldercar Rd CO6 ......133 F1
Alderford St CO9 ......75 E8
Alderlee IP2 ....36 F8
Alderman Blaxhill Sch
CO2 ....135 B3
Alderman Howe Lodge
CO4 ....110 B4
Alderman Rd IP1 ......17 B5
Alderton Cl CM6 ......152 C6
Alderton Rd CO4 ......136 C8
Aldham Ct ■ CB9 ......8 E7
Aldon Cl CO12 ....90 F1
Aldous Cl CO7 ....59 C3
Aldridge Cl CM2 ......206 A4
Aldringham Mews IP11 .221 B5
Alec Hunter High Sch
The CM7 ....128 C1
Alec Kay Ct CO2 ......135 C2
Aletha Farm Pl CO9 ..29 D6
Alexander Cl ■ CM1 ..205 E7
Alexander Mews 217 D2
Alexander Rd CM7 ....127 E4
Alexandra Ave CO5 ..201 E6
Alexandra Dr CO7 ....137 C3
Alexandra Rd
Clacton-on-S CO15 ....188 F3
Colchester CO3 ......135 E6
Felixstowe IP11 ......221 C6
Harwich CO12 ....91 D5
Ipswich IP4 ....17 E6
Sible Hedingham CO9 ..51 D1
Sudbury CO10 ....34 A7
Weeley CO16 ....140 A7
Alexandra St CO12 ....91 D5
Alexandra Terr ■ CO3 .135 E6
Alf Eounder Cl CO4 ..136 E6
Alfells Rd CO7 ....137 F6
Alfred Terr CO14 ....171 C8
Alfreg Rd CM8 ....194 D8
Alienor Ave CM7 ......72 B1
All Hallows Ct IP3 ....18 A1
All Saints Ave CO3 ..135 A4
All Saints CE Prim Sch
Great Oakley CO12 ....116 C3
Harwich CO12 ....90 F3
Maldon CM9 ....209 E2
Maldon CM9 ....209 F2
All Saints CE Sch CM23 .146 B8
All Saints'
Bishop's Stortford CM23 ...146 A8
Chelmsford CM1 ......205 E4
All Saints' Rd IP1 ....17 A8
Allectus Way CM8 ....194 D8
Allen Cotts CO6 ......106 E5
Allen Way CO16 ......186 A3
Allenby Rd IP2 ....16 F6
Allendale Dr CO6 ....133 D4
Allens Cl CM3 ....192 F1
Alleyne Way CO15 ....203 G8
Allfields CO12 ....91 A2
Allington Cl IP4 ......17 F7
Allington Wlk CB9 ....8 E8
Alma Dr CM1 ....205 A2
Alma Sq ■ CO11 ......86 D4
Alma St CO7 ....164 B8
Almond Cl
Clacton-on-S CO15 ....188 C3
Tiptree CO5 ....179 C6
Wivenhoe CO7 ....137 C2
Almond Way CO4 ....136 E8
Almondhayes IP2 ....17 B3
Almshouses CO7 ....164 B8
Alpe St IP1 ....17 B7
Alpha Cl CM7 ....128 A2
Alpha Pl
■ Bishop's Stortford CM23 .145 F8
■ Saffron Walden CB11 ..22 E1
Alpha Rd CO16 ......186 B3
Alphamstone Rd CO8 ..55 B4
Alport Ave CO2 ......135 C4
Alresford Cty Prim
Sch CO7 ....165 B7
Alresford Rd CO7 ....164 E8
Alresford Sta CO7 ..165 A8
Alsa Bsns Pk CM24 ..93 F1
Alsa Gdns CM22 ......94 C2
Alsa Leys CM22 ......94 C2
Alsa St CM24 ....93 F1
Alston Rd IP3 ....17 F4
Alstone Ct IP3 ....18 D1
Altbarn Cl CO4 ......110 C4
Altbarn Rd CO2 ......136 D5
Alton Dr CO3 ....135 B6

Alton Hall La IP9 ......61 F3
Alton Park Cty Jun Sch
CO15 ....188 D2
Alton Park La CO15 ..188 B1
Alton Park Rd CO15 ..188 D3
Alton Rd CO15 ....188 E1
Alton Water (Nature
Reserve) IP9 ....62 A4
Aluf Cl CM8 ....194 E8
Alverton Cl CM7 ......154 B6
Alverton Way CO4 ....110 B3
Alvis Ave CO15 ......203 E6
Alyssum Cl CM1 ......206 A6
Alyssum Wlk CO4 ....136 D8
Amberley Ct CO7 ....137 D1
Ambridge Rd CO3 ....130 E3
Ambrose Ave CO3 ....134 F4
Ambrose Ct CO6 ......133 D4
Ambross Ho CO2 ....135 D2
America Rd CO6 ......105 C2
America St CM9 ......210 A2
Amos Hill CO10 ....54 E8
Amoss Rd CM2 ......216 F8
Ancaster Rd IP2 ......17 B4
Anchor End CO11 ......87 A4
Anchor Hill CO7 ......164 B7
Anchor Ho CO2 ......135 E2
Anchor La Heybridge CM9 .210 A5
New Mistley CO11 ....87 A4
Anchor Rd
Clacton-on-S CO15 ....188 E3
Tiptree CO5 ....179 C4
Anchor St
Bishop's Stortford CM23 .146 A6
Chelmsford CM2 ......205 B1
Anderson Ave CM1 ..204 F5
Anderson Cl CM23 ....92 F2
Andover Cl CO15 ....189 A6
Andrew Cl CM7 ......127 F5
Andrews Farm La CM6 .123 C8
Andrews Pl CM1 ......204 F3
Andros Cl IP3 ....38 A8
Anemone Ct CO4 ....109 C2
Angel La Glemsford CO10 ..2 B4
Great Dunmow CM6 ..150 D8
■ Ipswich IP4 ....17 D5
Angelgate CO12 ....91 E6
Angelgate Cotts CO12 ..91 E6
Angle Side CM7 ......128 B2
Anglefield CO15 ......188 F2
Anglesea Rd Ipswich IP1 ..17 B7
Wivenhoe CO7 ....164 C6
Anglesey Cl CM23 ....145 C7
Anglia Cl IP2 ....135 B3
Anglia Poly Univ CM1 .205 B4
Anglia Univ CM1 ......205 B2
Anglia Way CM7 ......128 B2
Anita Cl E IP2 ....16 E5
Anita Cl W IP2 ....16 E5
Ann Coles Cl CB9 ....27 C6
Ann St IP1 ....17 B7
Annbrook Rd IP2 ......16 E1
Anne Cl CO7 ....185 F6
Anne St IP11 ....221 C6
Ansgar Rd CB11 ......43 E7
Anson Cl CO12 ....91 B3
Anson Way CM7 ......128 C4
Anthony Cl CO4 ......110 D2
Antonia Cl CB9 ....9 E7
Antonio Wlk CO4 ....136 F7
Antonius Way CO4 ..110 B6
Anvil Way CM1 ......205 E8
Anzani Ave IP11 ......221 A4
Anzio Cres CO2 ......135 C3
Apollo Ho IP2 ....16 D1
Apollo Mews CO2 ....135 C1
Apple Ct CM1 ....204 F2
Apple Way CM2 ......216 B6
Appleby St IP2 ....16 D1
Appleton Fields CM23 .145 C6
Appletree Cl CM7 ....155 F5
Appletree Wlk CM7 ..128 A1
Approach The CO15 ..203 G8
Apsley Cl CM3 ......145 F4
Apsley Ct ■ IP1 ......17 A7
Apton Cl CM23 ......145 F7
Apton Fields ■ CM23 .145 F7
Apton Rd CM23 ......145 F7
Aquiline Ho CO15 ....203 J8
Aragon Cl CO15 ......203 F8
Aragon Rd CM3 ......173 F7
Arakan Cl CO2 ......135 C4
Arbour La Chelmsford CM1 205 D4
Wickham Bishops CM8 ..195 F4
Arbour Way CO4 ....110 C4
Arbutus Cl CM2 ......216 B6
Arcade St ■ IP1 ......17 C6
Arcade The CO15 ....188 F2
Archangel Gdns IP2 ..16 A6
Archers Way CM2 ....216 C2
Archery Fields CO15 ..189 A5
Arden Cl CO4 ....110 C3
Arderne Cl CO12 ......90 F2
Ardleigh Ct CO7 ....111 E8
Ardleigh Rd Dedham CO7 ..84 D3
Great Bromley CO7 ..112 B4
Little Bromley CO11 ..112 C5
Argents La CO3 ......108 C2
Argyle Ct CO5 ....158 C2
Argyle Rd
Thorpe-le-S CO16 ....141 F2
Thorpe-le-S CO16 ....142 A2
Argyle St IP4 ....17 D6
Argyll Cl ■ CB9 ....8 F7
Argyll Rd CM2 ......206 A5
Ariel Cl CO4 ....136 F7
Arkwright Rd IP2 ......16 E7

Armidale Wlk CO2 ....136 A2
Armiger Way CM8 ....177 B2
Armond Rd CM8 ......176 F3
Armonde Cl CM3 ....192 E1
Armour Rd CO6 ......108 F4
Armoury Rd CO6 ....108 F4
Armstrong Way CO9 ..30 A2
Arnhem Gr CM7 ......127 E5
Arnhem Rd CM1 ......204 E6
Arnold Dr CO4 ......136 E6
Arnold Rd CO15 ......188 D1
Arnold Villas CO5 ....179 C6
Arnold Way CM2 ....216 C3
Arnstones Cl CO4 ....136 C8
Arras Rd CO2 ....135 D3
Arras Sq ■ IP1 ....17 C6
Arrow Rd CO4 ....136 F7
Arthur Ct CM1 ......204 F5
Arthur St ■ CO2 ....135 F6
Arthur's Terr IP4 ....17 E6
Arthy Cl CO7 ....194 A4
Artillery St CO1 ....136 B6
Arun Cl CM1 ....205 C5
Arundel Way IP3 ....18 E3
Arundel Wlk ■ CB9 ..8 E8
Arwela Rd IP11 ......221 D2
Asbury Cl CO4 ......136 D8
Asbury Dr CO6 ......132 F3
Ascot Cl CM23 ......146 C8
Ascot Dr Felixstowe IP11 .221 C6
Ipswich IP3 ....18 B4
Ascot Gdns CO3 ....134 E7
Ash Cl Brightlingsea CO7 .185 E7
Clacton-on-S CO15 ....188 C3
Hatfield Peverel CM3 ..194 A4
Witham CM8 ....177 A5
Ash Ct CO12 ....90 E2
Ash Fall CM8 ....177 A5
Ash Gn CB10 ....3 D1
Ash Gr Blackheath CO2 .163 A8
Capel St M IP9 ....35 A2
Chelmsford CM2 ......216 D7
Great Bromley CO7 ..139 A6
Great Cornard CO10 ..34 C5
Great Dunmow CM6 ..150 D7
Heybridge CM9 ......210 C6
Wivenhoe CO7 ....137 C3
Ash Ground Cl CO11 ..86 D8
Ash Ho IP2 ....16 D2
Ash Rd CO7 ....165 B8
Ash Rise CO9 ....103 F8
Ash Tree Cl CM1 ....204 F2
Ash Tree Cnr CM3 ..191 B6
Ash Tree Cres CM1 ..204 F2
Ash Way CO3 ....134 F3
Ashby Rd CM8 ......195 A4
Ashby Rise CM23 ....119 B1
Ashdale CM23 ....145 C4
Ashdon Cty Prim Sch CB10 .6 B1
Ashdon Rd CB10 ......23 C3
Ashdown Rd CB10 ....24 E3
Ashdown Way
Colchester CO4 ......136 D7
Ipswich IP3 ....18 D3
Ashen Cl CO10 ....11 D1
Ashen Hill CO10 ......11 C3
Ashen La CO10 ......11 C3
Ashen Rd Ashen CO10 ..12 A1
Clare CO10 ....12 B5
Ridgewell CO9 ....29 B8
Ashenden IP11 ......221 E4
Ashes Cl CO14 ......170 F8
Ashes Rd CM7 ......155 F7
Ashfield Ct IP4 ......18 A6
Ashfield Farm Rd
Hatfield Peverel CM9 .194 E1
Ulting CM9 ....208 D8
Ashford Rd CM1 ....204 E2
Ashlea Cl CB9 ....9 B6
Ashlea Rd CB9 ....9 B6
Ashley Ct CO12 ......91 B3
Ashley Gdns CO3 ....135 C6
Ashley Rd CO12 ......91 B3
Ashley St IP2 ....17 C4
Ashlong Gr CO9 ......76 E3
Ashlyn's Rd CO13 ..170 E4
Ashmere Gr IP4 ......17 F6
Ashmere Rise CO10 ..34 A8
Ashmole Dr CO13 ..170 F6
Ashpole Rd CM7 ....102 B1
Ashstead Cl CO16 ..188 B6
Ashton Cl IP2 ....16 C2
Ashton Pl CM2 ......206 A3
Ashurst Cl CO5 ......163 F8
Ashurst Dr CM1 ....205 D7
Ashwells Mdw CO6 ..105 B6
Ashwin Ave CO6 ....133 D4
Askins Rd CO7 ....59 C3
Aspen Way
■ Colchester CO4 ....136 D8
Little Oakley CO12 ..117 B7
Aspens The CM23 ....119 B3
Aspin Mews CB10 ....22 E3
Asquith Dr CO10 ....110 C5
Astell Ct CO13 ......170 F4
Aster Cl
Bishop's Stortford CM23 .145 D6
■ Chelmsford CM1 ....205 E5
Clacton-on-S CO16 ....188 C4
Aster Rd IP2 ....16 E4
Astley Rd CO15 ......188 D3
Ataka Rd IP11 ......221 D6
Athelstan Rd CO3 ..135 C5
Atherton Rd IP2 ....16 F6
Atholl Rd CM2 ......205 F5
Atlantic Sq CM8 ....177 A3
Atlas Bglws CO6 ....105 A6

Abb-Bad 223

Atlas Ct CO6 ....105 A7
Atlas Ho ■ IP4 ......17 E6
Atlas Rd CO6 ....104 F7
Attlee Gdns ■ CO1 ..136 A6
Attwood Cl CO4 ......110 B5
Attwoods Cl CM4 ....216 C3
Aubrey Cl CM1 ......205 B7
Auckland Cl CM1 ....204 E5
Audley End Miniature
Rly CB11 ....43 A8
Audley End Rd CB11 ..43 C8
Audley End Sta CB11 ..42 F5
Audley Rd Colchester CO3 .135 C5
Great Leighs CM3 ....173 F7
Saffron Walden CB11 ..22 E1
Audley Way CO13 ....171 B6
Audrey Gdns CM23 ..145 F4
Audries Est CO14 ....171 A8
Augustine Way CM3 ..218 F2
Augustus Cl
Colchester CO4 ......110 B6
Haverhill CB9 ....9 D7
Augustus Way CM8 ..194 E8
Austen Cl CM7 ......155 A8
Austin Ave CO15 ....203 E6
Austin St IP2 ....17 C4
Auton Croft CB11 ..43 D7
Autoway CO4 ....110 C5
Autumn Cl CO16 ....188 C5
Aveley Way CM9 ....220 F8
Aveline Rd CO7 ......111 C7
Avenue Rd
Bishop's Stortford CM23 ..146 B6
Chelmsford CM2 ......216 D7
Witham CM8 ....177 A3
Avenue The Braintree CM7 127 F3
Clacton-on-S CO15 ..189 B7
Colchester CO3 ......135 C6
Danbury CM3 ....218 F7
Great Braxted CM8 ..178 A3
Great Dunmow CM6 ..150 E8
Great Oakley CO12 ..116 B3
Ipswich IP1 ....17 C8
Trimley St M IP11 ..221 A7
Washbrook IP8 ....35 F7
West Bergholt CO6 ..108 D3
Witham CM8 ....177 A2
Wivenhoe CO7 ....137 B1
Avignon Cl CO2 ....136 B4
Avila Chase CM2 ....216 B1
Avocet Cl
Frinton-on-S CO13 ..170 E6
Kelvedon CO5 ......158 D2
West Mersea CO5 ..201 D7
Avocet Ct IP11 ......221 B2
Avocet Way CM9 ....210 C5
Avon Rd CM1 ....204 C5
Avon Way CO4 ......136 F6
Avon Wlk CM8 ......176 E3
Avondale Ho CO15 ..189 A3
Avondale Rd
Clacton-on-S CO15 ..189 A3
Ipswich IP3 ....18 A2
Aylesbury Dr CO15 ..189 F6
Ayletts CM1 ....191 B3
Ayloffe Rd CO4 ......110 C1
Aynsworth Ave CM23 .119 B2
Azalea Ct CO4 ......136 D8
Azalea Way CO16 ....188 C4
Azelea Ct ■ CM1 ....205 F6

B

Back Hamlet IP3 ......17 E5
Back Hill CB1 ....5 B6
Back La Broomfield CM1 .191 D2
Colchester CO3 ......134 E7
Felixstowe IP11 ......221 D5
Ford End CM3 ......172 B6
Great Oakley CO12 ..116 C4
Ickleton CB10 ....3 A3
Little Waltham CM3 ..191 C4
Stisted CM7 ....129 C7
Tattingstone IP9 ......61 C6
Thaxted CM6 ....69 F3
Washbrook IP8 ....35 E8
Wickham Bishops CM8 ..195 F4
Back La E CO7 ......139 A6
Back La W CO7 ......138 F7
Back Rd Ardleigh CO7 ..112 B5
Tollesbury CM9 ......199 C4
Writtle CM1 ....204 A1
Back Waterside La CO7 .185 C5
Backwarden Nature
Reserve CM3 ....218 E5
Bacon's La CO6 ......106 C3
Bacton Lodge IP11 ..221 D3
Bacton Rd IP11 ......221 D3
Baddow Ct CM2 ....217 A6
Baddow Hall Ave CM2 .217 A7
Baddow Hall Cres CM2 .217 B7
Baddow Hall Cty Jun &
Inf Sch CM2 ....217 A6
Baddow Place Ave CM2 .217 A6
Baddow Rd
Chelmsford CM2 ....205 C1
Great Baddow CM2 ..216 E7
Baden Powell Dr CO3 .135 A4
Bader Cl IP2 ....18 C2
Badger Gr CM7 ......128 B3
Badgers CM23 ......145 E5
Badgers Bank IP2 ....16 E1
Badgers Cl CM2 ....216 B1

Badgers Gn CO6 ....132 E3
Badgers Gr CO6 ....82 B1
Badley Hall Rd CO7 ...112 F2
Badminton Rd CO15 ...203 G7
Badshah Ave IP3 ....18 B3
Bagshaw Rd CO12 ....91 D4
Bailey Bridge Rd CM7 ...127 E5
Bailey Cl Haverhill CB9 ....9 D7
  Ipswich IP2 ....16 E6
Bailey Dale CO3 ....134 C4
Bailey La CO10 ....12 C7
Bainbridge Dr CO5 .....179 D4
Baines Cl CO3 ....135 A5
Baird Cl IP2 ....16 F7
Baker Ave CM3 ....194 A3
Baker Mews CM9 ....210 A2
Baker Rd IP9 ....91 A8
Baker St CM2 ....205 A1
Baker's La Colchester CO4 ...135 E7
  Great Notley CM7 .....154 D6
  Tolleshunt Major CM9 ...197 D4
Baker's Rd CO10 ....12 F2
Bakers Ct CM23 ....146 A7
Bakers La Danbury CM3 ...218 E7
  Felsted CM6 ....152 C4
Bakers Mead CM3 ....190 F7
Bakers Terr CO7 ....85 A5
Bakery Ct CM24 ....119 D6
Baldry Cl IP8 ....16 C1
Baldwin's La CO6 ....131 E8
Bale Cl CO3 ....134 E4
Balfe Ct CO4 ....136 E6
Balkerne Gdns CO1 ....135 E7
Balkerne Hill CO3 ......135 E7
Balkerne Pas CO1 ......135 E7
Ball Alley CO3 ....135 E7
Ball La Abberton CO2 ...162 F5
  Blackheath CO2 ......163 B5
Ball's Chace CO6 ....79 F2
Ball's Chase CO9 ....76 F1
Ballast Quay Rd
  Fingringhoe CO5 ......164 B6
  Wivenhoe CO7 ....137 D1
Ballingdon Hill CO10 ...33 C5
Ballingdon Hill Ind Est
  CO10 ....33 C6
Ballingdon St CO10 ....33 D6
Ballingdon Trad Est CO10 33 C6
Balmoral Ave CO15 ....188 D3
Balmoral Cl IP2 ....16 F1
Balmoral Ct CM2 ....205 C2
Balmoral Dr CB9 ....8 E8
Balton Way CO12 ....90 F2
Banham Dr CO10 ....33 F8
Banister Cl CO16 ......188 C5
Bank Pas CO1 ....135 E7
Bank Rd IP4 ....17 E6
Bank St CM7 ....127 F3
Bankart La CM2 ....205 F4
Banks Ct CM6 ....150 D8
Bannister Green
  Villas CM6 ....152 E6
Banters La CM3 ....154 B1
Bantoft Terr IP3 ....18 C2
Barbary Lodge CM2 ....205 A2
Barbel Rd CO4 ....110 F1
Barbour Gdns CO2 .....134 F2
Barbrook La CO5 ....179 D6
Barbrook Way CM3 ....218 E1
Barclay Cl CM2 ....217 A6
Bardell Cl CM1 ....204 F6
Bardfield Cottage Mus
  CM7 ....72 A1
Bardfield Rd
  Bardfield Saling CM7 ...99 A1
  Colchester CO2 ....136 A1
  Thaxted CM6 ....70 D2
Bardfield Way CO13 ...170 F6
Bargate La CO7 ....85 C3
Baring-gould Cotts CO5 184 D1
Barker Cl Ipswich IP2 ...16 D5
  Lawford CO11 ....86 B4
  Steeple Bumpstead CB9 ...27 B6
Barker Rd CO10 ....15 E2
Barkers Mead CM22 ...146 B1
Barkis Cl CM1 ....204 D7
Barkstead Rd CO4 .....110 C1
Barlee Cl CB11 ....65 C3
Barley Cl CB11 ....22 C1
Barley Fields CM8 .....177 A1
Barley Hills CM23 .....145 E4
Barley Mead CM3 .....219 B6
Barley Way CO3 ....134 E5
Barlon Rd CO11 ......112 F4
Barlow Road Cotts CB10 ...6 B2
Barlow's Reach CM2 ...206 A4
Barn Gn CM1 ....205 E8
Barn Hall Ave CO2 ....136 C4
Barn La CO11 ....112 F7
Barn Mead CM7 ....128 D2
Barn View Rd CO6 .....131 A1
Barnaby Rudge CM1 ...204 F7
Barnard Cl CB11 ....66 F8
Barnard Rd CM2 ......216 C2
Barnardiston Rd CO4 ...110 C1
Barnardiston Way CM8 176 F3
Barnards Field CM6 ...70 B2
Barncroft Cl CO4 ......110 B3
Barnes Farm Cty Jun &
  Inf Sch CM2 ....206 A3
Barnes Mill Rd CM2 ...205 F2
Barnfield Capel St M IP9 ...35 B1
  Feering CO5 ....158 D3
  Felixstowe IP11 ......221 B6

Barnfield continued
  Manningtree CO11 .....86 D4
Barnfield Cotts CM9 ...210 B5
Barnfield Mews CM1 ...205 A6
Barnfield Pl CM8 ....176 F1
Barnfield Rd CO6 ......109 C6
Barnhall Rd CM9 ......180 D2
Barnham Pl IP5 ....18 F6
Barnston Gn CM6 ......151 A4
Baron's Ct CB9 ....8 E7
Baron's La CM3 ....220 E1
Baronia Croft CO4 ....110 C3
Barons The CM23 .....145 D5
Baronswood Way CO2 ...135 D2
Barr Cl CO7 ....137 C1
Barrack Cnr IP1 ....17 B6
Barrack La
  Great Waltham CM3 ...190 E4
  Harwich CO12 ....91 E4
  Ipswich IP1 ....17 B6
Barrack Sq CM2 ......205 B2
Barrack St Bradfield CO11 114 D8
  Colchester CO1 ......136 B6
Barrel Cl CO7 ....139 A3
Barrells Down Rd CM23 118 E1
Barrett La CM23 ......145 F7
Barrington Cl
  Great Baddow CM2 ...217 A6
  Little Clacton CO16 ...168 C2
Barrington Gdns CO15 189 C5
Barrington Rd CO2 ....136 A5
Barrow Marsh CM9 ...211 A4
Barryfields CM7 ......100 F1
Bartholomew Cl CB10 ...3 E2
Bartholomew Rd
  CM23 ....145 F6
Bartholomew St IP4 ...17 F6
Bartletts CB10 ....22 C1
Bartlow Rd Castle Camps CB17 7 D4
  Hadstock CB1 ....5 D7
Barton Cl IP2 ....16 E2
Barton Rd IP11 ....221 F4
Bartram Ave CM7 .....128 C3
Barwell Way CM8 .....177 B2
Basbow La CM23 .....145 F7
Basin Rd CM9 ....210 D3
Bassetts La CM3 CM9 ...208 A4
Bassingbourn Rd CM24 121 A3
Bateman Rd CO7 .....185 E8
Bateman's Rd CO16 ...168 B4
Bates Rd CM9 ....210 B4
Bath Ct CB9 ....8 F6
Bath Rd IP11 ....221 F4
Bath St Ipswich IP2 ...17 D3
  Wivenhoe CO7 ......164 B8
Bathurst Cl CO2 ......136 A1
Battery La IP9 ....91 B8
Battisford Dr CO16 ...188 A4
Battlesbrook Rd CO2 ...136 D2
Bawdsey Cl CO16 .....188 B3
Bawn Cl CM7 ....128 A4
Bawtree Way CO3 ....135 A5
Baxters CM3 ....219 A7
Bay Rd CO12 ....91 D4
Bay View Cres
  Harwich CO12 ....90 C1
  Little Oakley CO12 ...117 C8
Bayard Ave CO7 .....185 F7
Bayley St CO9 ....51 F4
Baynard's Cty Prim Sch
  CO5 ....179 B7
Baynards Cres CO13 ...170 E6
Bayning Ho CO7 ......139 F8
Baytree Ct CM7 ......126 F2
Beach App CO16 .....203 B6
Beach Cres CO15 .....203 F6
Beach Rd
  Clacton-on-S CO15 ...188 F2
  Harwich CO12 ....91 C2
  Point Clear B CO16 ...202 C7
  St Osyth CO16 ....187 B2
  West Mersea CO5 ....201 C5
Beach Rd W IP11 .....221 D2
Beach Station Rd IP11 221 C1
Beach Way CO15 .....203 F6
Beach's Dr CM1 ......204 D3
Beachcroft Ave CO13 ...170 A6
Beacon Cl CO7 ......185 E6
Beacon Field IP11 ....221 C5
Beacon Hill Maldon CM9 209 C2
  Wickham Bishops CM8 ...196 A6
Beacon Hill Ave CO12 ...91 E4
Beacon Hill Sch IP2 ...16 F3
Beacon Hts CO16 .....186 B5
Beacon Way
  Colchester CO3 ......134 C6
  Point Clear B CO16 ...186 B2
Beaconsfield Ave CO3 ...135 E6
Beaconsfield Cl CO10 ...33 E8
Beaconsfield Ct CB9 ...8 F7
Beaconsfield Rd
  Clacton-on-S CO15 ...188 F3
  Ipswich IP1 ....16 F7
  Sudbury CO10 ....33 E8
Beadel Cl CM8 ....194 E8
Beadle Way CM3 .....174 A6
Beadon Dr CM7 ......128 A1
Bear St CO6 ....56 A1
Beard's La CO11 ......41 A4
Beardsley Dr CM1 ....205 F7
Bearwalden Bsns Pk CB11 42 F5
Beatrice Ave IP11 ....221 E5
Beatrice Cl IP3 ....18 A3
Beatrice Rd
  Clacton-on-S CO15 ...188 E2
  Walton-on-t-N CO14 ...144 D2
Beatty Gdns CM7 .....128 C4
Beatty Rd IP3 ....18 B2

Beauchamps Cl CM1 ...205 F8
Beaufort Ct CB9 ....8 F7
Beaufort Gdns CM7 ...128 A4
Beaufort Rd CM2 .....206 A4
Beaufort St IP1 ....17 A7
Beaumont Ave
  Brightlingsea CO7 ....186 A7
  Clacton-on-S CO15 ...188 D3
Beaumont Cl
  Colchester CO4 ......109 F4
  Walton-on-t-N CO14 ...170 F7
Beaumont Ct CB9 ......9 B6
Beaumont Hill CM6 ...123 D2
Beaumont Pk CM3 ....218 C6
Beaumont Pl CM7 ....128 B3
Beaumont Rd CO12 ...116 C2
Beaumont Vale CB9 ....9 B6
Beaumont Way CM3 ...210 B1
Beaumont Wlk CM1 ...204 D5
Beaver Cl CO3 ....134 E7
Beche Rd CO2 ....136 B5
Beck Rd CB11 ....22 D1
Becker Rd CO3 ......134 E4
Beckers Green Cty Prim
  Sch CM7 ....128 D2
Beckers Green Rd CM7 128 D2
Becketts La IP7 ....57 D8
Beckford Rd CO11 ....87 A4
Beckingham Bsns Pk
  CM9 ....197 D3
Beckingham Rd
  Great Totham CM9 ...196 D5
  Tolleshunt D'arcy CM9 198 C4
Beckingham St CM9 ...197 D3
Becontree Cl CO15 ...188 F4
Bedells Ave CM7 ......155 B5
Bedford Cl Braintree CM7 128 B4
  Tiptree CO5 ....179 D5
Bedford Ct CB9 ....8 F7
Bedford Rd Colchester CO4 109 F5
  Holland-on-S CO15 ...189 D5
Bedford St IP1 ....17 B6
Bedwell Rd CM22 ......94 B3
Beech Ave Braintree CM7 127 F5
  Halstead CO9 ....77 A2
Beech Cl Sproughton IP8 ...16 A4
  Takeley CM22 ....148 C8
Beech Gn CM8 ....195 F5
Beech Gr
  Fordham Heath CO3 ...107 A1
  Haverhill CB9 ....8 E8
  Ipswich IP3 ....17 F3
  Little Oakley CO12 ...117 B7
  Sible Hedingham CO9 ...51 D1
Beech Hill CO3 ....135 A6
Beech Ho IP2 ....16 D2
Beech Rd
  Great Cornard CO10 ...34 B6
  Rivenhall CM8 ....177 B7
Beech Rise CM3 ......194 A3
Beeches Cl
  Chelmsford CM1 .....204 E2
  Saffron Walden CB11 ...43 C7
Beeches Rd
  Chelmsford CM1 .....204 E2
  Heybridge CM9 ......209 F5
Beeches The Ipswich IP3 ...17 F4
  Wendens Ambo CB11 ...42 F5
Beechholm IP4 ....17 E6
Beechlands CM23 .....145 F5
Beechwood Cl CO2 ...135 D2
Beehive La CM2 ......216 C5
Beehive Lane Cty Prim
  Sch CM2 ....216 D5
Beeleigh Chase CM9 ...209 D4
Beeleigh Cl CO2 ......136 A1
Beeleigh Link CM2 ...205 F3
Beeleigh Rd CM9 ....209 F3
Begonia Cl CM1 .....205 F6
Begonia Pl CO16 .....188 C4
Bekeswell La CM2 ...215 F2
Bekeswell Pl CM2 ...216 C2
Belcham's La CB11 ...93 E8
Belcham St Paul CE
  Prim Sch CO10 ....13 A1
Beldams Cl CO16 .....142 A1
Beldams La CM23 ....146 B5
Belgrave Cl
  Chelmsford CM2 .....216 D7
  Ipswich IP4 ....17 E8
Belgrave Ho CM23 ...146 B8
Bell Cl Colchester CO2 ...136 D2
  Ipswich IP2 ....17 C4
Bell Coll CB11 ....43 E8
Bell Farm Ind Est SG8 ...39 E2
Bell Hill Danbury CM3 ...218 C2
  Lamarsh CO8 ....55 C3
Bell La Great Bardfield CM7 72 A2
  Ipswich IP2 ....17 C4
  Nuthampstead SG8 ...39 B2
  Panfield CM7 ....127 A7
  Thaxted CM6 ....70 A3
Bell St CM2 ....216 F6
Bellamy Cl IP3 ....18 A3
Bellcroft CM8 ....177 A3
Belle Vue CM2 ....205 A1
Belle Vue Rd
  Colchester CO1 ......109 E1
  Ipswich IP4 ....17 F6
  Sudbury CO10 ....33 F7
  Wivenhoe CO7 ......137 C1
Bellevue Terr CO9 ....76 E2
Bellfield Ave CO7 ....186 A7
Bellfield Cl CO7 ......186 A8
Bellmead CM1 ....205 B2
Bells Chase CM2 .....216 E6
Bells Cl CB11 ....43 E8

Bells Hill
  Bishop's Stortford CM23 ...145 E7
  Bures CO8 ....80 A4
Bells La CO10 ....2 C5
Bells Rd CO10 ....31 F6
Belmans Ct CO12 .....91 A2
Belmonde Dr CM1 ...205 E7
Belmont Cl CM1 .....205 E7
Belmont Cres CO4 ...110 C3
Belmont Ct CB9 ....8 F7
Belmont Hill CB11 ....43 A1
Belmont Pl CO1 .....136 C5
Belmont Rd IP2 ......16 C1
Belsay Ct CB9 ....8 D8
Belsize Ave CO15 ....203 D6
Belstead Ave IP2 .....17 B3
Belstead Rd IP2 ......17 A3
Belstead Sch IP8 .....16 C2
Belsteads Farm La CM3 191 E2
Belvawney Cl CM1 ...204 E6
Belvedere Cl CM3 ...218 F7
Belvedere Ct CM2 ...215 F8
Belvedere Pl CM9 ...220 F8
Belvedere Rd
  Danbury CM3 ....218 F7
  Ipswich IP4 ....17 F7
Belvoir Ct CB9 ....8 E8
Bembridge Cl CO15 ...188 F8
Bemerton Ct CO13 ...170 B6
Bemerton Gdns CO13 170 C6
Benacre Rd IP3 ....18 A2
Bendalls Ct CO11 .....86 D4
Bendlowes Rd CM7 ...72 C1
Benedict Dr CM1 ....204 E2
Benezet St IP1 ....17 B6
Benfield Way CM7 ...128 B2
Benhooks Ave CM23 ...145 E5
Benhooks Pl CM23 ...145 E5
Bennet Ct CO4 ....136 E6
Bennett Cl Braintree CM7 155 A8
  Walton-on-t-N CO14 ...171 A8
Bennett Rd IP1 ....16 D8
Bennett Way CM3 ...194 A4
Bennett's La CM6 ...151 E2
Benskins Ct CM23 ....92 A8
Bensusan Ct CO2 ...135 B3
Bent Hill IP11 ....221 E3
Bent La IP4 ....18 E8
Bentall Cl CO9 ....103 F8
Bentfield Cty Prim Sch
  CM24 ....119 D8
Bentfield End Cswy
  CM24 ....119 D7
Bentfield Gdns CM24 ...119 D7
Bentfield Green CM24 119 D8
Bentfield Rd CM24 ...119 D7
Bentleigh Ct CO1 ...136 D7
Bentley Ave CO15 ...203 E6
Bentley CE Prim Sch IP9 60 F7
Bentley Ct CM23 ....145 E5
Bentley Ct CO3 .....135 C2
Bentley La Belstead IP8 ...36 C6
  Stutton IP9 ....61 E3
Bentley Rd
  Little Bromley CO11 ...113 D3
  Weeley Heath CO7, CO16 167 E6
  Witham CM8 ....176 E4
Benton Cl Cressing CM7 155 B4
  Witham CM8 ....195 A7
Berberis Wlk CO1 ...136 E7
Bercolta Ct CO6 .....108 E4
Berdale Rd IP3 ....18 A2
Bere Ct CO4 ....110 C4
Bergen Ct CM9 ......220 E8
Bergholt Rd Brantham CO11 86 B7
  Colchester CO4 ......109 D2
Beridge Rd CO9 ......76 D2
Beriffe Pl CO7 ....185 F7
Berkeley Cl IP4 ......17 E8
Berkeley Rd CO15 ...188 F5
Berkley Dr CM2 .....205 F2
Berkley Cl CO4 ......110 C4
Bermuda Rd IP3 ......38 E7
Bernard Ct CO13 ...170 E6
Bernard Cres IP3 ....18 B2
Berners End CM6 ...151 B4
Berners St IP1 ......17 B6
Bernside CM7 ....127 F2
Berrimans Cl CO4 ...136 D6
Berry Cl IP3 ....18 F1
Berryfield Cotts CO1 ...136 B7
Bertram Ave CO16 ...168 D1
Berwick Ave CM1 ....205 B7
Beryl Rd CO12 ....90 D1
Beslyns Rd CM7 .....72 A3
Bethany St CO7 .....164 B7
Betjeman Cl CM7 ...155 A8
Betony Wlk CB9 ......8 D8
Betts Green Rd CO16 ...168 D5
Betty Dent's Cnr CO16 ...141 C5
Beverley Ave CO5 ...201 E7
Beverley Ct IP4 ......17 D6
Beverley Dr CO13 ...170 E7
Beverley Rd
  Colchester CO3 ......135 D6
  Ipswich IP4 ....17 F8
Bevington Mews CM8 ...195 B2
Bewick Ct CO9 ....51 E2
Bexhill Cl CO15 .....203 I8
Bexley Ave CO12 ....90 F1
Bibb Way IP1 ....17 A5
Bicknacre Rd CM3 ...218 D1
Bignalls Croft CO4 ...110 C4
Bignells Croft CO4 ...110 C4
Bigods La CM6 ......123 D4
Bijou Cl CO5 ....179 D6

Bilberry End CB1 ....5 C
Billy's La CO7 ....58 D
Bilsdale Cl CO4 ....110 C
Bilton Rd CM1 ....204 F
Binley Rd CM2 ....205 F
Birch Ave
  Great Bentley CO7 ...166 A
  Harwich CO12 ....91 B
Birch CE Prim Sch CO2 161 A
Birch Cl Braintree CM7 ...127 C
  Brightlingsea CO7 ...185 E
  Clacton-on-S CO15 ...188 C
  Witham CM8 ....177 A
Birch Dr Brantham CO11 ...60 D
  Halstead CO9 ....77 A
Birch Rd CO2 ....161 E
Birch Rise CM8 ......195 E
Birch St Birch CO2 ...161 A
  Nayland CO6 ....56 A
Birch Wood Cl CO5 ...201 D
Birchalls CM24 ......119 E
Birchanger CE Prim Sch
  CM23 ....119 C
Birchanger Ind Est CM23 119 B
Birchanger La CM23 ...119 C
Birches The CO13 ...170 E
Birches Wlk CM2 ....216 A
Birchway CO2 ....161 A
Birchwood CM23 .....119 C
Birchwood Cl CO5 ...179 F
Birchwood High Sch
  CM23 ....146 C
Birchwood Rd
  Dedham CO7 ....84 B
  Hazeleigh CM3 ....219 F
  Langham CO4 ....84 A
  Purleigh CM3 ....220 B
Birchwood Way CO5 ...179 F
Bird La CO5 ....179 E
Birdbrook Rd CO9 ....28 A
Birdbush Ave CB11 ...43 D
Birds Cl CB10 ....3 A
Birk Beck CM1 ....205 C
Birkdale Rise CM8 ...194 E
Birkfield Cl IP2 ......17 A
Birkfield Dr IP2 ......16 F
Birkin Cl CO5 ....179 C
Biscay Cl CB9 ....9 C
Bishop Mews IP8 ....16 B
Bishop Rd Chelmsford CM1 205 B
  Colchester CO2 ......135 A
Bishop William Ward
  Sch CO6 ....109 A
Bishop's Ave CM23 ...145 E
Bishop's CE & RC Aided
  Prim Sch The CM1 ...205 E
Bishop's Cl CB9 ....8 E
Bishop's Ct CB9 ....8 E
Bishop's Hall La CM1 ...205 E
Bishop's Hill IP3 ......17 E
Bishop's La CO9 ......54 E
Bishop's Stortford Bsns
  Ctr CM23 ....146 A
Bishop's Stortford Coll
  CM23 ....145 E
Bishop's Stortford High
  Sch The CM23 ......145 F
Bishop's Stortford Sta
  CM23 ....146 A
Bishops Ave CM7 ....128 B
Bishops Dr CO16 ....203 B
Bishops Gdns CO16 ...203 A
Bishops La CO5 .....179 C
Bishops Park Way CM23 145 C
Bishopscourt Gdns CM2 205 E
Bishopsgarth IP3 .....17 F
Bisley Cl CO15 ......188 B
Bittern Cl Ipswich IP2 ...16 E
  Kelvedon CO5 ......158 D
Bixley Dr IP4 ....18 E
Bixley La IP4 ....18 F
Bixley Rd IP3 ....18 D
Black Barns IP11 ...221 A
Black Bouy Hill CO7 ...164 B
Black Boy La CO11 ...89 A
Black Chapel La CM6 ...151 E
Black Horse La IP1 ...17 C
Black La CM7 ....71 F
Blackberry Rd CO3 ...134 C
Blackbrook Rd CO6 ...109 C
Blackbushe CM23 ...119 C
Blackdown Ave IP5 ...18 F
Blackfriars CO10 .....33 D
Blackfriars Ct IP4 ...17 D
Blackheath CO2 .....163 A
Blackhouse La CO10 ...34 C
Blacklands Cl CB11 ...43 C
Blackley La Braintree CM7 153 F
  Great Notley CM7 ....154 A
Blacklock CM2 ......206 A
Blackman Way CM8 ...177 A
Blacksmith Cl CM1 ...205 E
Blacksmith's Corner CO4 83 D
Blacksmith's La CO12 ...90 F
Blacksmiths Cl CM23 ...145 E
Blacksmiths Hill CO10 ...11 B
Blacksmiths La
  Bulmer CO10 ....32 F
  Shudy Camps CB1 .....7 C
  Wickham Bishops CM8 ...195 E
Blackthorn Ave CO4 ...136 E
Blackthorn Cl Ipswich IP3 18 E
  Writtle CM1 ....204 A
Blackthorn Rd
  Harwich CO12 ....90 F
  Witham CM8 ....176 E
Blackthorn Way CM9 ...180 A
Blackwater Ave CO4 ...110 E

Blackwater Cl
Chelmsford CM1 .205 C6
Heybridge Basin CM9 .210 E3
Blackwater Dr CO5 .201 A6
Blackwater La CM8 .195 B8
Blackwater Way CM7 .128 A4
Blackwell Dr CM7 .127 C4
Bladen Dr IP4 .18 F5
Bladon Cl Braintree CM7 .127 E7
Tiptree CO5 .179 E5
Blaine Dr CO13 .170 F7
Blair Cl
Bishop's Stortford CM23 .145 C7
Rushmere St A IP4 .18 E5
Blair Par CB9 .8 E8
Blake Cl CO11 .86 B4
Blake Dr Braintree CM7 .128 C4
Clacton-on-S CO16 .188 D6
Blake Rd CM8 .176 F5
Blamsters Cres CO9 .103 D8
Blanchard Cl CO13 .170 A7
Blanche St IP4 .17 D6
Blandford Rd IP3 .18 D3
Blaxhall Ct 17 CB9 .8 E7
Blenheim Cl
Braintree CM7 .127 E7
Brantham CO11 .60 D1
Danbury CM3 .218 F2
Blenheim Ct
Bishop's Stortford CM23 .145 C7
Clacton-on-S CO15 .188 D2
4 Ipswich IP1 .17 A7
Blenheim Dr CO2 .163 A8
Blenheim Rd
Clacton-on-S CO15 .188 D2
Ipswich IP1 .17 A7
Blenheim Way CO5 .179 F5
Blickling Cl IP2 .17 B2
Blind La Easthorpe CO2 .160 B4
Eight Ash G CO6 .134 A8
Goldhanger CM9 .211 C7
Howe Green CM2 .217 F4
Tolleshunt Knights CM9 .180 B1
Blithe Ct CO7 .164 B8
Blofield Rd IP11 .221 A4
Blois Mdws CB9 .27 C7
Blois Rd
Steeple Bumpstead CB9 .27 D8
Sturmer CB9 .9 F1
Bloom Cl CO13 .170 F6
Bloomfield Ave CO13 .170 E7
Bloomfield St IP4 .18 B6
Blooms Hall La CO10 .2 F8
Blott Rise CM8 .194 F8
Blue Mill La CM9 .208 E4
Blue Mills Hill CM8 .195 B7
Blue Rd CO5 .179 C5
Bluebell Ave CO16 .188 C4
Bluebell Cl Ipswich IP2 .16 E4
Witham CM8 .176 E3
Bluebell Gn 5 CM1 .205 E7
Bluebell Way CO4 .109 C2
Bluebridge Cotts CO9 .77 A1
Bluebridge Ind Est CO9 .77 B1
Bluegate La IP9 .60 B7
Bluehouse Ave CO16 .188 A4
Bluestem Rd IP3 .38 E8
Blundens The CO6 .56 C6
Blunt's Hall Dr CM8 .176 D1
Blunts Hall Rd CM8 .176 D1
Blyford Rd CO16 .188 A4
Blyford Way IP11 .221 A4
Blyth Cl IP2 .17 A1
Blyth's Mdw CM7 .127 F3
Blyth's Way CM7 .126 F2
Blythe La CO7 .164 B8
Blythwood Gdns CM24 .119 D6
Boadicea Cotts CO6 .79 F6
Boadicea Way CO2 .135 C4
Boars Tye Rd CM8 .156 D6
Bobbits La IP9 .36 F8
Bobbits Way CO7 .164 C8
Bober Ct CO2 .163 B7
Bocking Church Street Cty Prim Sch CM7 .127 F8
Bocking End CM7 .127 F3
Bocking's Gr CO16 .188 B5
Bockings Elm Par CO16 .188 B5
Bodiam Cl IP3 .18 D4
Bodiam Rd IP3 .18 D4
Bodiam Wlk 3 CB9 .8 E8
Bodmin Rd CM1 .205 D5
Bogmoor Rd SG8 .39 A8
Bohun Cl CM3 .173 F7
Bois Field Terr CO9 .76 E2
Bois Hall Gdns CO9 .76 F3
Boley Dr CO15 .189 A4
Boley Rd CO6 .106 A8
Boleyn Way Boreham CM3 .192 F1
Clacton-on-S CO15 .203 F8
Boleyns Ave CM7 .127 F6
Bolford St CM6 .69 F2
Bolingbroke Cl CM3 .173 F7
Bolton La IP4 .17 D6
Bond St Chelmsford CM2 .205 C2
Ipswich IP4 .17 D5
Bonham Cl CO15 .189 A5
Bonington Chase CM1 .205 E6
Bonneting La CM23 .92 B8
Bonnington Rd IP3 .17 F1
Boone Pl CM8 .177 A2
Booth Ave CO4 .136 C8
Borda Cl CM1 .205 A5
Boreham Cty Prim Sch CM3 .206 F8
Boreham Ind Est CM3 .192 F2
Boreham Rd
Great Leighs CM3 .174 B7

Boreham Rd *continued*
Little Waltham CM3 .174 B2
Borehamgate CO10 .33 F7
Borley Rd CO10 .15 B4
Borough La CB11 .43 D8
Borradale Ct CB9 .27 B6
Borrowdale Ave IP4 .17 E8
Boscawen Gdns CM7 .128 C4
Boscombe Ct CO15 .189 F6
Boss Hall Bsns Pk IP1 .16 E7
Boss Hall Rd IP1 .16 E7
Bostock Rd IP2 .17 C1
Boston Rd IP4 .17 F7
Boswells Dr CM2 .205 C2
Boswells Sch The CM1 .205 D6
Botanical Way CO16 .187 A5
Botany La CO16 .168 B5
Bouchers Mead CM1 .205 F7
Bouchiers Barn Visitors Ctr CO6 .130 D7
Boudicca Wlk CO7 .137 C3
Boulton Cotts CM9 .210 B5
Boundary Rd
Bishop's Stortford CM23 .146 A5
Colchester CO4 .136 F4
Sturmer CB9 .9 D5
Wivenhoe CO7 .137 A4
Bounderby Gr CM1 .204 E7
Bounstead Hill CO2 .162 C5
Bounstead Rd CO2 .162 D7
Bourchier Ave CM7 .128 D5
Bourchier Way CO9 .103 D8
Bourne Cl CO9 .103 D8
Bourne Ct CO2 .136 A4
Bourne Hill IP2 .37 B7
Bourne Mill CO2 .136 B4
Bourne Rd Colchester CO2 136 B4
Haverhill CB9 .9 B8
West Bergholt CO6 .108 E2
Bourne The CM23 .146 A8
Bournebridge Hill CO9 .103 B6
Bournemouth Rd CO15 .189 F6
Bouverie Rd CM2 .216 B8
Bovills Way CO16 .168 C1
Bovingdon Rd CM7 .101 D2
Bowdens La CO6 .80 F7
Bower Gdns CM9 .209 F3
Bower Hall Dr CB9 .27 B6
Bower Hall La CO5 .183 F1
Bowers Cl CM8 .156 E3
Bowes Rd CO7 .137 D1
Bowland Dr IP8 .16 C1
Bowling Cl 14 CM23 .145 F6
Bowling Green Ct IP11 .221 E4
Bowmans Pk CO9 .51 E4
Bowsers La CB10 .5 C3
Bowthorpe Cl IP1 .17 B7
Box Mill La CO9 .76 E3
Boxford Ct
Felixstowe IP11 .221 A4
Haverhill CB9 .8 E7
Boxhouse La Dedham CO7 .84 C5
Langham CO7 .84 B6
Boxted Ave CO16 .188 C4
Boxted CE Prim Sch CO4 .82 F7
Boxted Church Rd CO6 .82 C5
Boxted Rd Colchester CO4 .109 E6
Great Horkesley CO6 .82 C3
Boxted Straight Rd CO4 .83 A5
Boyd Cl 1 CM23 .146 B8
Boydell's Dairy Farm CM7 .100 E8
Boydin Cl CM8 .194 E8
Boydlands IP9 .35 A1
Boyes Croft CM6 .123 D1
Boyles Ct CO2 .163 B7
Boyne Dr CM1 .205 D6
Boyton Rd IP3 .18 B1
Boyton's La CB10 .26 A1
Bracken Way CO5 .163 B2
Brackenbury Cl IP1 .17 B8
Brackenden Dr CM1 .205 D7
Brackenhayes Cl IP2 .17 B3
Brackens The CO4 .110 B3
Brackley Cl IP11 .221 C5
Bracks La CO6 .131 F3
Bradbrook Cotts CO6 .108 F4
Bradbury Dr CM7 .127 D3
Braddy Ct CO5 .158 C2
Bradfield Cty Prim Sch CO11 .87 E1
Bradfield Rd CO11 .115 B7
Bradford St Braintree CM7 128 A4
Chelmsford CM2 .205 A1
Bradfords Ct CM7 .128 A4
Brading Ave CO15 .189 A7
Bradley Cl CM6 .123 C2
Bradley Comm CM23 .119 C3
Bradley Mews 2 CB10 .22 F2
Bradley St 7 IP2 .17 C4
Bradwell Ct CM7 .155 C8
Braemar Ave CM2 .216 B8
Braemore Cl CO4 .110 D3
Braggon's Hill IP29 .2 B8
Brain Rd CM8 .176 E3
Brain Valley Ave CM7 .155 B6
Braintree Cnr CO9 .75 F6
Braintree Coll CM7 .128 A5
Braintree Ent Ctr CM7 .127 D5
Braintree Foyer The 3 CM7 .127 F2
Braintree Rd
Cressing CM7 .155 E7
Felsted CM6 .152 C6
Gosfield CO9 .102 E5
Great Bardfield CM7 .72 B1
Great Dunmow CM6 .124 A1
Great Dunmow CM6 .123 F1

Braintree Rd *continued*
Shalford CM7 .100 E6
Terling CM3 .174 E5
Wethersfield CM7 .73 D2
Witham CM8 .176 F3
Braintree Sta CM7 .128 A2
Braiswick CO4 .109 C2
Braiswick La CO4 .109 D4
Bramble Ct CM8 .176 E4
Bramble Dr IP3 .18 E1
Bramble La
Great Dunlow CM6 .124 E1
Little Dunmow CM6 .151 F8
Bramble Rd CM8 .176 E4
Brambledown CO5 .201 C7
Brambles CO14 .171 B7
Brambles The
Bishop's Stortford CM23 .145 C6
Colchester CO3 .134 F3
Bramblewood 1 IP8 .16 C2
Bramford La IP1 .16 F8
Bramford Rd IP1 .16 E8
Bramhall Cl IP2 .16 D1
Bramley Chase IP4 .18 B7
Bramley Cl Alresford CO7 .165 B8
Braintree CM7 .128 A1
Colchester CO3 .135 B7
Bramleys The CO6 .131 A3
Bramston Cl CM2 .216 F8
Bramston Gn CM8 .176 F4
Bramston Sports Ctr CM8 .176 F1
Bramston Wlk CM8 .176 F4
Bramwoods Rd CM2 .216 E8
Bran End Fields CM6 .124 D7
Brand Ct CM7 .127 F7
Brand Dr CO5 .163 B3
Brandon Rd
Braintree CM7 .127 D2
Felixstowe IP11 .221 A4
Brands Cl CO10 .34 C5
Bransby Gdns IP4 .17 E7
Branscombe Cl CO13 .170 E5
Branston Ct CO16 .188 C4
Branston Rd CO15 .188 D3
Brantham Hill CO11 .86 C8
Brantham Mill Ind Est CO11 .86 B7
Braxted La
Great Braxted CM8 .178 C1
Great Totham CM9 .196 D8
Braxted Rd Tiptree CO5 .178 E2
Wickham Bishops CM8 .196 A6
Brazier's Wood Rd IP3 .38 B8
Braziers Cl CM2 .216 C3
Braziers Quay CM23 .146 A6
Breach La CM6 .97 B2
Breachfield Rd CO2 .135 C2
Brecon Cl IP2 .17 B2
Bredfield Cl IP11 .221 B5
Bree Ave CO6 .132 E3
Brendon Dr IP5 .18 F6
Brendon Pl CM1 .204 E1
Brent Cl Frinton-on-S CO13 170 F7
Witham CM8 .176 E2
Brent Hall Rd CM7 .72 B6
Brentwood Rd CO15 .189 C6
Bretten Cl CO16 .188 A4
Brettenham Cres IP4 .17 D8
Bretts Cotts CM8 .178 F3
Brewers Cl CM23 .145 C5
Brewery Chapel Mus CO9 .76 D2
Brewery Fields CM2 .217 A5
Brewery La CM24 .119 E7
Brewery Yd CM24 .119 F7
Brian Bishop Cl CO14 .171 B8
Brian Cl CM2 .216 B6
Briar Rd CO7 .112 B4
Briardale Ave CO12 .90 F3
Briarfields CO13 .170 C8
Briarhayes Cl IP2 .17 B3
Briarsford Ind Est CM8 .177 B1
Briarswood CM1 .205 D7
Briarwood Ave CO15 .189 F6
Briarwood End CO4 .110 B3
Brices Way CO10 .2 B5
Brick Cotts IP9 .62 F4
Brick End Villas CM6 .121 E8
Brick House La CM3 .192 E1
Brick House Rd CM9 .197 B7
Brick Kiln Cl CO6 .131 A3
Brick Kiln La
Rickling Green CB11 .66 D1
Stebbing CM6 .124 D7
Thorrington CO7 .165 E5
Brick Kiln Rd
Colchester CO1 .109 E1
Great Horkesley CO6 .109 C7
Harkstead IP9 .63 C5
Sandon CM2 .217 C7
Brick Kiln Way CM7 .128 D2
Brick Row SG8 .19 D3
Brick St CO3 .108 B1
Brickburn Cl CM6 .152 C4
Brickfield Cl IP2 .17 D3
Brickhouse Cl CO5 .201 B7
Brickhouse Rd CO6 .78 A3
Brickmakers La CO4 .109 F2
Brickman's Hill CO11 .87 D3
Brickspring La CM9 .196 D7
Brickway Ct CO6 .105 B6
Bridewell St CO10 .12 C8
Bridge Cotts CO10 .1 D2
Bridge Croft CM3 .172 F2
Bridge Foot CO10 .33 D6
Bridge Hall Rd CM7 .129 C3
Bridge Hill CO6 .107 C7
Bridge Hospl CM8 .176 F1

Bridge Rd IP11 .221 E5
Bridge St
Bishop's Stortford CM23 .145 F7
Bures CO8 .55 F1
Coggeshall CO6 .130 F1
Finchingfield CM7 .72 C6
Great Bardfield CM7 .72 B2
Great Yeldham CO9 .30 A1
Halstead CO9 .76 E2
Ipswich IP1 .17 C4
Saffron Walden CB10 .22 D2
Witham CM8 .176 F1
Writtle CM1 .204 C1
Bridge Terr CO10 .33 F8
Bridgebrook Cl CO4 .110 D1
Bridgefield Cl CO4 .136 C7
Bridgeford Ho 13 CM23 .145 F6
Bridgwater Rd IP2 .16 D2
Bridlewalk CO3 .134 D6
Bridport Ave IP3 .18 D3
Bridport Rd CM1 .205 D5
Bridport Way CM7 .128 D4
Brierley Ave CO5 .201 E7
Bright Cl CO16 .188 D6
Brightlingsea Cl CO7 .136 F4
Brightlingsea Cty Inf Sch CO7 .185 E6
Brightlingsea Cty Jun Sch CO7 .185 E6
Brightlingsea Rd
Thorrington CO7 .165 E3
Wivenhoe CO7 .137 C4
Brighton Rd CO15 .189 F6
Brightside CO13 .170 E7
Brightwell Cl IP11 .221 A5
Brimstone Ct CM7 .154 E8
Brimstone Rd IP8 .36 E8
Brindley Rd CO15 .189 B8
Bringey The CM2 .217 A6
Brinkley Cres CO4 .110 D2
Brinkley Grove Prim Sch CO4 .110 B5
Brinkley Grove Rd CO4 .110 A5
Brinkley La CO4 .110 B5
Brinkley Pl CO4 .109 F3
Brisbane Rd IP4 .18 D6
Brisbane Way CO2 .136 A1
Brise Cl CM7 .128 A1
Bristol Ct CM8 .156 E3
Bristol Hill IP9 .91 B8
Bristol Rd Colchester CO1 .136 A8
Ipswich IP4 .18 A7
Bristowe Ave CM2 .217 A6
Britannia Cres CO7 .137 B1
Britannia Ct CO7 .137 B1
Britannia Pl 3 CM23 .145 E5
Britannia Rd IP4 .18 B6
Brittania Cty Prim Sch IP4 .18 B5
Brittany Way CO2 .136 B4
Britten Cl CO4 .136 E6
Britten Cres CM2 .216 F8
Brixham Cl CO15 .203 E8
Brixton La CB11 .93 B6
Broad La CO6 .82 C2
Broad Meadow 3 IP8 .16 C2
Broad Oaks Cl CB10 .44 E2
Broad Oaks Pk CO4 .110 E3
Broad Oke IP1 .17 B6
Broad Rd Braintree CM7 .128 B7
Wickham St P CO9 .53 B8
Broad St CB9 .8 F8
Broad Street Green Rd
Great Totham CM9 .196 B1
Heybridge CM9 .210 C7
Broadcroft Cres CB9 .8 F8
Broadfield CM23 .118 F2
Broadfield Rd CM22 .148 E7
Broadfields CO7 .137 C3
Broadlands CO13 .170 E3
Broadlands Way
Colchester CO4 .110 B1
Rushmere St A IP4 .18 F5
Broadleaf Ave CM23 .145 D4
Broadmead Rd CO4 .110 E1
Broadmere Cl CO15 .189 E7
Broadmere Rd IP1 .16 E8
Broadoaks Cres CM7 .128 D4
Broadstrood CO16 .187 B5
Broadwater Gdns IP9 .91 A8
Broadway
Clacton-on-S CO15 .203 G7
Glemsford CO10 .2 B5
Silver End CM8 .156 D4
Broadway Ct CM8 .156 D5
Broadway The CM6 .123 F3
Brock Cl CM8 .194 E8
Brockenhurst Way CM3 .218 F1
Brockham Cl CO16 .188 B6
Brockley Cres IP1 .16 D8
Brockley Rd CM2 .205 D2
Brocks Mead CM6 .122 E7
Brockwell La CO5 .158 C1
Brograve Cl CM2 .216 D3
Broke Hall Gdns IP3 .18 D4
Broke Hall Prim Sch IP4 .18 E5
Broman's La CO5 .185 A2
Bromfield CB11 .43 E8
Bromley Cl IP2 .17 C3
Bromley Cnr CO11 .86 A2
Bromley La CB11 .43 B1
Bromley Rd
Colchester CO7, CO4 .111 C2
Elmstead CO7 .138 B5
Frating CO7 .139 A4
Lawford CO11 .86 B2
Brompton Gdns CM9 .220 E8
Bronte Cl CM7 .155 A8

Bronte Rd CM8 .176 F5
Brook Cl Braintree CM7 .127 C2
Great Totham CM9 .196 A3
Tiptree CO5 .179 F3
Woodham Walter CM9 .208 D2
Brook Cotts Boxted CO4 .82 E5
Stansted Mountfitchet CM24 .119 E5
Brook End Rd
Chelmsford CM2 .206 A4
Chelmsford CM2 .206 B2
Brook Farm Cl CO9 .77 A1
Brook Farm La IP9 .62 D6
Brook Hall Rd CO5 .164 B5
Brook Hill
Little Waltham CM3 .191 B6
North End CM6 .151 F1
Brook La Chelmsford CM2 .206 B2
Felixstowe IP11 .221 F5
Galleywood CM2 .216 E3
Brook Mdw CO9 .51 D1
Brook Mead CM3 .190 E8
Brook Meadows CO5 .179 C4
Brook Rd Aldham CO6 .133 B7
Great Tey CO6 .132 C7
Stansted Mountfitchet CM24 .119 E6
Tiptree CO5 .179 F3
Tolleshunt Knights CO5 .180 A2
Brook Service Rd CB9 .9 A7
Brook St Chelmsford CM1 .205 B3
Colchester CO1 .136 B7
Colne Engaine CO6 .77 F1
Dedham CO7 .84 F7
Glemsford CO10 .2 B6
Great Bardfield CM7 .72 B2
Great Bromley CO7 .112 E1
Little Dunmow CM6 .151 D6
Manningtree CO11 .86 D4
Wivenhoe CO7 .164 C8
Brook Terr CO9 .51 E1
Brook Vale CO16 .187 B3
Brook View Sandon CM2 .217 C6
Thaxted CM6 .70 A3
Brook Wlk CM8 .194 F8
Brookbank CM2 .216 E8
Brooke Ave CB10 .22 E2
Brooke Gdns CM23 .146 C7
Brooke Sq CM9 .210 A1
Brookes Nature Reserve CM7 .103 E2
Brookfield Rd IP1 .16 F8
Brookfields CM6 .124 D7
Brookhampton St CB10 .3 A5
Brookhill Way IP4 .18 F4
Brookhouse Bsns Pk IP2 .16 F6
Brookhouse Pl 3 CM23 .145 F8
Brookhouse Rd CO6 .132 B8
Brookhurst Cl CM2 .205 D3
Brookland CO5 .179 C4
Brooklands
Clacton-on-S CO15 .203 E6
Colchester CO1 .136 B7
Brooklands Cty Prim Sch CO11 .86 D8
Brooklands Gdns CO15 .203 E6
Brooklands Rd CO11 .86 D8
Brooklands Rise CO11 .86 D8
Brooklands Wlk CM2 .216 A7
Brooklyn Ct CO12 .91 C3
Brooklyn Mews CO12 .91 C3
Brooklyn Rd CO12 .91 C3
Brooks Hall Rd IP1 .17 A7
Brooks Maltings 3 CO11 .86 D4
Brookside Cl CO2 .136 B4
Brooksies CB11 .40 F6
Brookview IP2 .36 E8
Broom Cres IP3 .17 F1
Broom Farm Rd CM22 .94 C2
Broom Field IP11 .221 C5
Broom Hill Rd IP1 .17 A8
Broom Knoll CO7 .60 C2
Broom St CO10 .34 B5
Broom Way Abberton CO5 .163 B2
Capel St M IP9 .35 B2
Broomclose Villas CM7 .100 E5
Broome Gr CO7 .137 B2
Broome Way CO15 .203 F6
Broomfield CM8 .156 C5
Broomfield Comm IP8 .16 B6
Broomfield Cres CO7 .137 B2
Broomfield Hospl CM1 .191 A3
Broomfield Prim Sch CM1 .191 B1
Broomfield Rd CM1 .205 A5
Broomgrove Cty Jun & Inf Schs CO7 .137 B2
Broomhall Cl CM1 .191 B2
Broomhall Rd CM1 .191 B2
Broomhayes IP2 .17 A2
Broomhills Ind Est CM7 .127 D2
Broomhills Rd CO5 .201 D5
Brotherton Ave IP11 .221 A8
Broton Dr CO9 .76 E2
Brougham Glades CO3 .134 D5
Broughton Cl CO2 .135 C4
Broughton Rd IP1 .17 B7
Brown's End Rd CM6 .121 F7
Browning Cl CO3 .134 F6
Browning Rd
Braintree CM7 .155 A8
Brantham CO11 .86 C7
Brownings Ave CM1 .205 A5
Brownlow Rd IP11 .221 F4
Brownsea Way CO3 .135 A4

Bruce Gr CM2 ....216 A7
Bruce Rd CM1 ....204 B1
Bruff Cl CO4 ....109 E2
Bruff Dr CO14 ....171 A7
Brundells Rd CO7 ....139 A5
Brundon La CO10 ....33 C7
Brunel Ct CO4 ....110 C6
Brunel Rd Braintree CM7 .128 A1
Clacton-on-S CO15 ....189 B8
Ipswich IP2 ....16 F6
Brunel Way CO4 ....110 C6
Brunswick House Cut
CO11 ....87 A3
Brunswick Rd IP4 ....17 F8
Brunwin Rd CM7 ....126 F2
Brussels Cl CO12 ....91 B1
Bryan Rd CM23 ....145 F8
Bryanstone Mews CO3 ..134 E5
Bryant's La CM9 ....219 D7
Bryon Ave IP11 ....221 A2
Buchan Cl CM7 ....155 A8
Buck Hill CM7 ....154 F6
Buck's Horns La IP8 ....36 B6
Buckenhoe Rd CB10 ....22 E3
Buckfast Ave CO13 ....170 D6
Buckfast Cl 5 IP2 ....17 A2
Buckingham Ct 2 CM2 ..205 F4
Buckingham Dr CO4 ....136 E7
Buckingham Rd CB9 ....8 E6
Bucklesham Rd IP3 ....18 E2
Buckley's La CO6 ....131 E6
Buckleys CM2 ....216 F7
Buckleys Cl CM8 ....195 E5
Bucks La CO10 ....12 B7
Buckwoods Rd CM7 ....128 A1
Buddleia Cl IP2 ....16 E4
Buddleia Ct CO7 ....137 A2
Buffett Way CO4 ....136 E6
Buglers Rise CM1 ....215 B8
Buick Ave CO15 ....203 D6
Building End Rd
Chrishall SG8 ....19 C1
Duddenhoe End SG8 ....40 B7
Duddenhoe End SG8 ....40 B8
Bulford La CM7 ....155 C5
Bulford Mill La CM7 ....155 D5
Bull Hill Rd CO15 ....188 F5
Bull La Langley CB11 ....40 C2
Long Melford CO10 ....15 E8
Long Melford CO10 ....15 F8
Maldon CM9 ....210 A3
Tiptree CO5 ....179 C3
Bull's Hill CO9 ....51 A4
Bullace Cl CO4 ....110 D3
Bullen Wlk CM2 ....216 C3
Bullfields CB11 ....67 A8
Bullfinch Cl CO4 ....136 F8
Bullock Wood Cl CO4 ..110 D4
Bullocks La CO10 ....33 E6
Bulls Cliff IP11 ....221 D3
Bulls Lodge Cotts CM3 ..192 B1
Bulmer Rd CO10 ....33 C6
Bulmer St CO10 ....32 D4
Bulstrode Rd IP2 ....17 D4
Bulwer Rd IP1 ....17 A6
Bumfords La CM3 CM9 ..208 A2
Bumpstead Rd CB9 ....9 B4
Bundick's Hill CM1 ....204 F3
Bung Row CM8 ....178 C1
Bungalows The CM8 ....176 F1
Bunting Cl CM2 ....216 B5
Bunting Rd IP2 ....16 D3
Buntingford Ct 2 CO2 ..136 A1
Bunyan Rd CM7 ....127 E3
Burdun Cl CM8 ....194 D8
Bure Dr CM8 ....176 D3
Buregate Rd IP11 ....221 D2
Bures CE Prim Sch CO6 ..79 B4
Bures Ct 16 CB9 ....8 E7
Bures Ho CO6 ....79 F8
Bures Rd
Great Cornard CO10 ....34 B3
Nayland CO6 ....81 B8
Bures Sta CO6 ....79 E8
Burgate Ct CO16 ....188 A4
Burgess Field CM2 ....205 F4
Burghley Ave CM23 ....145 C7
Burghley Cl
Great Notley CM7 ....154 B6
4 Ipswich IP2 ....17 A2
Burgundy Ct CM2 ....205 C2
Burkitts Ct 8 CO10 ....33 E7
Burkitts La CO10 ....33 E7
Burley Rd CM23 ....146 A4
Burlington Ho IP2 ....17 B4
Burlington Rd
Colchester CO3 ....135 E6
Ipswich IP1 ....17 B6
Burmanny Cl CO15 ....188 C3
Burnells Way CM24 ....119 E4
Burnham Cl Ipswich IP4 ..17 F7
Trimley St M IP11 ....221 A7
Walton-on-t-N CO14 ....171 B8
Burnham Rd
Chelmsford CM1 ....205 D5
Woodham Mortimer
CM9, CM3 ....219 E5
Burns Ave CO3 ....134 F6
Burns Cl CM9 ....210 A1
Burns Cres CM2 ....216 C8
Burnsall Cl CB11 ....43 F8
Burnside Cres CM1 ....205 B7
Burnstie Rd CM6 ....152 F6
Burnt Dick Hill CO4 ....82 D7

Burnt Oak Cnr CO7 ....59 D1
Burnthouse Rd CO6 ....105 E2
Burr Cl CO12 ....90 C1
Burrell Rd IP2 ....17 C4
Burroughs Piece Rd CO10 .33 F7
Burrows Cl
Clacton-on-S CO16 ....188 D6
Lawford CO11 ....86 B4
Burrows Rd CO6 ....105 B7
Burrs Rd CO15 ....189 A7
Burrsville Cty Jun & Inf
Schs 188 F6
Burrswood Pl CM9 ....210 E3
Burstall Cl CO16 ....188 B4
Burstall La IP8 ....16 A6
Burton Cl 7 CB9 ....8 E7
Burton End CB9 ....8 E7
Burton End Cty Prim Sch
CB9 ....8 D7
Burton Pl CM2 ....205 F4
Burton's Green Rd CO9 ..104 B4
Burwood Ct CM2 ....205 C1
Bury Cl Colchester CO1 ..136 A8
Marks Tey CO6 ....132 F4
Bury Fields CM5 ....152 A5
Bury La Chrishall SG8 ....19 D1
Great Waltham CM3 ....190 D8
Hatfield Peverel CM3 ....193 F4
Howe Street CM3 ....172 D1
Bury Lodge La
Great Hallingbury CM22 ..147 C7
Stansted
Mountfitchet CM24 ....120 A2
Bury The CO16 ....187 A4
Bury Water La CB11 ....42 E1
Burywater Cotts CB11 ....42 F1
Burywoods CO4 ....109 B3
Bush Gr CO10 ....33 C6
Bush La CB10 ....46 D2
Bush Rd CB10 ....46 E2
Bushell Way CO13 ....170 E6
Bushey Cl IP9 ....35 A1
Butcher Row CB10 ....22 D1
Butcher's Hill CB10 ....3 A4
Butcher's View CO5 ....182 E6
Butchers La Capel St M IP9 .35 B1
Walton-on-t-N CO14 ....171 B7
Butchers Pasture CM6 ..122 F5
Butchers Row CM2 ....22 D1
Bute Ct CB9 ....8 F6
Butler Cl CB11 ....22 E1
Butler Rd CO9 ....76 D2
Butler's La CO11 ....88 E1
Butlers Cl CM1 ....191 B2
Butlers La CB10 ....23 C5
Butlers Way CO9 ....30 A1
Butley Cl IP2 ....36 F8
Butley Ct 1 CB9 ....8 E6
Butley Rd IP11 ....221 C3
Butt La Maldon CM9 ....210 A3
Manuden CM23 ....92 E2
Butt Rd Colchester CO2 ..135 E5
Great Cornard CO10 ....34 B6
Stoke-by-N CO6 ....56 C5
Butt's Green Rd CM2 ..217 F3
Butter Market IP1 ....17 C6
Buttercup Cl IP8 ....16 C2
Buttercup Wlk CM8 ....176 E4
Butterfield Rd CM3 ....206 E8
Butterfly Gdns IP4 ....18 E5
Buttermarket Sh Ctr 3
IP1 ....17 C5
Buttermere CM7 ....154 C7
Buttleys La CM6 ....149 F8
Butts La CM3 ....218 F7
Butts Way CM2 ....215 E3
Buxey Cl CO5 ....201 B7
Buxton Rd Coggeshall CO6 .130 F3
Colchester CO2 ....136 A3
Bylam La IP9 ....63 C6
Byland Cl IP2 ....17 A2
Bylands Cl CM23 ....145 D6
Byng Cres CO16 ....142 B1
Byng Ct CO2 ....136 A1
Byng Gdns CM7 ....128 C4
Byng Ho CO16 ....142 B1
Bypass Rd CO16 ....187 B5
Byrd's Farm La CB10 ....22 E3
Byron Ave CO3 ....134 F7
Byron Cl CM7 ....155 A8
Byron Dr CM8 ....195 E5
Byron Rd CM2 ....205 D2
Byrony Cl CM8 ....176 D4

C

Cadenhouse Mews CO3 ..134 E7
Caernarvon Wlk CB9 ....8 E8
Cage La Boxted CO4 ....83 B4
Felixstowe IP11 ....221 D5
Cairns Rd CO2 ....136 B2
Caithness Cl IP4 ....18 B8
Calamint Rd CM7 ....176 D3
Caldbeck Way CM7 ....154 C6
Caledonia Rd IP9 ....91 B8
California Cl CO4 ....110 B4
California Rd CO11 ....87 A4
Callis Cl CO10 ....12 C8
Callis St CO10 ....12 C8
Callowood Croft CM3 ....220 D1
Calverley Cl CM23 ....145 E4
Calves La CO6 ....56 B8
Cam Way CM8 ....176 D2
Camberley Rd IP4 ....18 D7
Camberton Rd CM7 ....127 D6
Camborne Cl CM1 ....205 E5
Cambrai Rd CO2 ....135 D4

Cambria Cl CO11 ....87 B3
Cambridge Ave CO9 ....75 E8
Cambridge Ct
Clacton-on-S CO15 ....188 E4
Frinton-on-S CO13 ....171 A5
Cambridge Dr IP2 ....16 F1
Cambridge Rd
Clacton-on-S CO15 ....188 E4
Colchester CO3 ....135 C5
Felixstowe IP11 ....221 F4
Frinton-on-S CO13 ....171 A5
Littlebury CB11 ....21 F4
Newport CB11 ....43 A2
Stansted
Mountfitchet CM24 ....119 E8
Cambridge Way CO8 ....79 F8
Camden Rd IP3 ....18 B4
Camellia Ave CO16 ....188 C4
Camellia Cl 2 CM1 ....205 F6
Camellia Cres CO16 ....188 C5
Camellia Ct 5 CO4 ....136 D8
Camelot Cl CM1 ....204 F5
Cameron Cl CO10 ....15 C6
Camoise Cl CO9 ....50 B7
Camomile Way CO4 ....109 C2
Camp Rd CO7 ....139 A7
Campbell Cl CM2 ....216 A7
Campbell Ct CO3 ....135 D6
Campbell Dr CO4 ....110 C2
Campbell Rd Ipswich IP3 ..18 C1
Witham CM8 ....176 F5
Campernell Cl CO7 ....185 F8
Campion Rd
Colchester CO2 ....136 A5
Ipswich IP2 ....16 F4
Campion Way CM8 ....176 E3
Campions Hill CO6 ....81 D8
Campions The CM24 ....119 E8
Camps Rd Bartlow CB1 ....6 B7
Helions Bumpstead CB9 ....8 B1
Haverhill CB9 ....8 F8
Camulodunum Way CO2 .135 C1
Camulus Cl CM2 ....135 A2
Camwood Gdns CM1 ....18 B4
Can Bridge Way CM2 ..205 C1
Canberra Cl
Chelmsford CM1 ....204 E5
9 Colchester CO2 ....136 A1
Ipswich IP4 ....18 D6
Candlet Gr IP11 ....221 D5
Candlet Rd IP11 ....221 D6
Candytuft Rd CM1 ....205 F6
Canes Mill Ct CM7 ....128 A5
Canfield Cl CM23 ....145 E8
Canfield Rd CM6 ....149 D1
Canford Cl CM2 ....216 E7
Canham St 6 IP1 ....17 B6
Canhams Rd CO10 ....34 C5
Cann Hall Cty Prim Sch
CO16 ....188 D6
Canning St CO12 ....91 D5
Cannock Mill Ct CO2 ..136 C4
Cannon Circ CM7 ....73 D6
Cannon Leys CM2 ....216 D3
Cannon Rd CO1 ....136 B6
Cannon St CO1 ....136 B6
Cannons Cl
Bishop's Stortford CM23 ..119 A1
Colchester CO2 ....135 D4
Cannons Mead CM24 ....119 D7
Cannons Mill La CM23 ..119 A1
Cannons The CO2 ....135 D4
Canons Cl CM3 ....218 E1
Cansey La CO11 ....114 E6
Cant Way CM7 ....128 C1
Canterbury Cl IP2 ....36 F8
Canterbury Grange CM7 .127 F8
Canterbury Rd
Colchester CO2 ....136 A5
Holland-on-S CO15 ....189 E6
Sudbury CO10 ....15 C2
Canterbury Way CM1 ....204 E4
Canuden Rd CM1 ....204 E2
Canvey Wlk CM1 ....205 E6
Canwick Gr CO2 ....136 C4
Cap Pillar Cl CO7 ....137 B2
Cape Cl CO3 ....134 C5
Capel Cl Chelmsford CM1 .205 B7
Rayne CM7 ....126 F2
Capel Dr IP11 ....221 A4
Capel Pk CO13 ....170 E7
Capel Rd Colchester CO3 .135 C5
Rayne CM7 ....126 F2
Capel St Mary CE Prim
Sch IP9 ....35 A1
Caper La CO2 ....160 F4
Capons La CM3 ....219 A5
Captains Rd CO5 ....201 B6
Captains Wood Rd CM9 ..196 A3
Card's Rd CM2 ....217 C6
Cardiff Ave IP2 ....17 B2
Cardigan St IP1 ....17 B7
Cardinal Cl CO4 ....137 A7
Cardinal St IP1 ....17 C5
Cardinals Ct IP11 ....221 C5
Carisbrooke Ave CO15 ..189 A7
Carlisle Cl CO1 ....136 A8
Carlton Cl CO9 ....30 A2
Carlton Rd CO15 ....189 B5
Carlton Way IP4 ....17 E8
Carmarthen Cl IP2 ....17 A2
Carmel St CB10 ....3 C2
Carmelite Way CM9 ....209 C2
Carmen St CB10 ....3 D3
Carnaby Rd CO15 ....188 F3
Carnation Cl CM1 ....205 F6
Carnation Dr CB10 ....22 F5
Carolbrook Rd IP2 ....16 E1

Carolina Way CO5 ....179 D5
Caroline Cl CO7 ....137 C3
Carpenters The CM23 ..145 B5
Carr St IP4 ....17 D6
Carraways CM8 ....195 B8
Carriage Cl IP11 ....221 A8
Carriage Dr CM1 ....205 E7
Carriers Cl CO5 ....201 A7
Carrigans CM23 ....145 E8
Carrington Ct CO5 ....201 D7
Carrington Ho CO5 ....201 D7
Carrington Way CM7 ....127 F8
Carringtons Rd CO7 ....112 D4
Carrs Rd CO15 ....188 D3
Carsey Hill CB1 ....7 B6
Carshalton End CO3 ....134 F4
Carsons Dr CO10 ....34 D5
Carstone Pl CM1 ....204 F2
Cartbridge Cl CO14 ....171 B8
Carters Cl CO16 ....188 B3
Carters Croft CB10 ....6 B1
Carters Hill Boxted CO4 ....83 A6
Manuden CM23 ....93 A1
Carters La Henham CM22 ..94 F5
Wickham Bishops CM8 ..195 F6
Carters Leys CM23 ....145 D8
Cartwright Wlk CM2 ....205 F2
Case La IP9 ....60 D7
Cassino Rd
Chelmsford CM1 ....204 E6
Colchester CO2 ....135 C3
Castle Ave CB9 ....8 E7
Castle Bailey 17 CO1 ....135 F7
Castle Camps Prim Sch
CB1 ....7 E3
Castle Cl
Castle Hedingham CO9 ..51 E4
Great Leighs CM3 ....173 F6
Castle Cross CB10 ....22 E2
Castle Ct CO15 ....188 E3
Castle Hill Dedham CO7 ..84 F4
Haverhill CB9 ....8 D2
Castle Hill Mid Sch CB9 ..8 D8
Castle Hill Pk CO16 ....188 E7
Castle House CO7 ....85 A5
Castle La
Castle Hedingham CO9 ..51 E4
Haverhill CB9 ....8 F8
Castle Manor Upper Sch
CB9 ....8 E8
Castle Mdw CO9 ....51 D2
Castle Rd
Clacton-on-S CO15 ....188 E3
Colchester CO1 ....136 A7
Castle St
Bishop's Stortford CM23 ..145 F6
Saffron Walden CB10 ....22 D2
Castle View CM23 ....146 A7
Castle Way CO16 ....187 A4
Castle Wlk Haverhill CB9 ..8 E8
Stansted
Mountfitchet CM24 ....119 E6
Castlegate St CO12 ....91 E6
Castleward Cl CO7 ....164 C8
Caswell Mews CM2 ....205 F2
Cat's La CO10 ....34 A7
Catchpole Ct 12 CO10 ....33 E7
Catchpole La CM9 ....196 A4
Catchpool Rd CO1 ....135 F8
Caterham Cl CO16 ....188 C6
Cates Cnr CB10 ....22 E1
Cathedral Sch The CM1 .205 C3
Cathedral Wlk CM1 ....205 B3
Catherine Cl CO15 ....189 A5
Catherine Hunt Way CO2 135 C2
Catherine May Ct CO15 .188 F3
Catherines Cl CM3 ....174 A6
Catons La CB10 ....22 D2
Cattawade St CO11 ....86 C7
Cattermole Ct CO16 ....188 B3
Catts Cl IP9 ....61 F2
Cattsfield IP9 ....61 F2
Cauldwell Ave IP4 ....17 F7
Cauldwell Hall Rd IP4 ..18 A6
Causeway CM3 ....152 F1
Causeway Cl CO11 ....2 C5
Causeway End CO11 ....86 B5
Causeway End Rd CM6 ..152 C3
Causeway Reach CO15 ..188 E7
Causeway The
1 Bishop's Stortford CM23 146 A7
Braintree CM7 ....127 F4
Colchester CO4 ....110 C1
Finchingfield CM7 ....72 D6
Great Baddow CM2 ....216 F7
Great Dunmow CM6 ....123 D2
Great Horkesley CO6 ....82 B2
Halstead CO9 ....76 E1
Harkstead SG9 ....64 B1
Haverhill CB9 ....8 F8
Henham CB11 ....68 B7
Langley CB11 ....40 C3
Maldon CM9 ....210 A4
Ridgewell CO9 ....28 F8
Toppesfield CO9 ....50 B7
Ulting CM9 ....208 D5
Causton Jun Sch IP11 ..221 C6
Causton Rd CO1 ....135 E6
Caustons Cl CO10 ....34 C5
Cavendish Ave CO2 ....136 C3
Cavendish Ct
2 Haverhill CB9 ....8 E6
Saffron Walden CB10 ....22 F2
Cavendish Dr
Clacton-on-S CO16 ....188 A4
Lawford CO11 ....86 B3
Cavendish Gdns
Braintree CM7 ....128 C5

Cavendish Gdns continued
Chelmsford CM2 ....205 E2
Cavendish La CO10 ....1 C1
Cavendish Prim Sch CO10 ..1 C2
Cavendish Rd Clare CO10 ..12 C2
Felixstowe IP11 ....221 F5
Cavendish St IP3 ....17 F5
Cavendish Way CO10 ....33 F1
Cawkell Cl CM24 ....119 D2
Cawkwell Cl CM2 ....206 A4
Caxton Ct CO4 ....110 C6
Cecil Cl CM23 ....146 D2
Cecil Rd IP1 ....17 B2
Cecilia St IP1 ....17 C5
Cedar Ave
Brightlingsea CO7 ....185 E4
Chelmsford CM1 ....205 A3
Tiptree CO5 ....179 C2
Cedar Ave W CM1 ....205 A3
Cedar Chase CM9 ....210 C5
Cedar Cl Brantham CO11 ..60 D1
Great Dunmow CM6 ....123 A4
Walton-on-t-N CO14 ....171 A2
Cedar Cres CO11 ....86 C3
Cedar Ct
Bishop's Stortford CM23 ..118 F1
West Bergholt CO6 ....108 D1
Cedar Dr CM8 ....177 A5
Cedar Gr CM8 ....177 A4
Cedar Pk CM23 ....145 D4
Cedar Way CO7 ....166 E8
Cedars Rd 18 CO2 ....135 F6
Cedars The CO9 ....102 E2
Celandine Ct CO4 ....109 C2
Cemetery La
East Bergholt CO7 ....59 B2
Ipswich IP4 ....17 E7
Cemetery Rd
Bishop's Stortford CM23 ..145 F6
Ipswich IP4 ....17 E7
Centaury Cl CO3 ....134 C3
Centenary
Way CO15, CO16 ....168 E3
Central Arc CB10 ....22 D1
Central Ave
Frinton-on-S CO13 ....171 A4
Ipswich IP3 ....38 E4
Central Ho CO12 ....91 C7
Central Par CO15 ....188 F5
Central Sq 7 CM1 ....205 B3
Centre The
2 Colchester CO4 ....136 E2
Halstead CO9 ....76 E5
Ipswich IP2 ....17 A4
Tiptree CO5 ....179 D2
Centurion Ho 3 CO2 ....135 F6
Centurion Way CO2 ....135 A4
Chadburn Rd CO10 ....15 D9
Chaffinch Gdns CO4 ....136 F7
Chaffix CM6 ....152 C4
Chaffix Cl CM6 ....152 C6
Chainey Pieces 12 CB9 ....8 F7
Chalfont Rd CO4 ....110 C6
Chalfont Sq 13 IP4 ....17 D6
Chalklands
Saffron Walden CB10 ....22 E1
Sandon CM2 ....217 D2
Chalkners Cl 2 IP9 ....35 A1
Chalks Rd CM8 ....176 F4
Chalkstone Mid Sch CB9 ..9 A4
Chalkstone Way CB9 ....9 D1
Chalky La SG8 ....19 C1
Challenge Way CO1 ....136 B6
Challis La CM7 ....155 A4
Chalon St IP1 ....17 B
Chamberlain Ave CO14 ..171 B2
Chamberlain Way IP8 ....16 C
Chamley Ct CO15 ....189 D1
Chancellor Ave CM2 ....206 B6
Chancery Gr CO2 ....163 A4
Chancery Pl CM1 ....204 B3
Chancery Rd IP1 ....17 F5
Chandlers Cl
Bishop's Stortford CM23 ..145 C
Clacton-on-S CO16 ....188 E2
West Mersea CO5 ....201 C4
Chandlers Ct CO5 ....201 C
Chandlers Row CO1 ....136 C5
Chaney Rd CO7 ....137 A4
Chant Ct CO4 ....110 D
Chanterelle CO4 ....110 B
Chantry Cl
Bishop's Stortford CM23 ..145 E
Clacton-on-S CO16 ....188 E2
Chantry Gn IP2 ....16 D
Chantry High Sch IP2 ..16 E
Chantry Jun & Inf Sch IP2 16 E
Chantry La CM3 ....193 A
Chantry Mount CM23 ..145 E
Chantry Rd CM23 ....145 E
Chantry The
6 Bishop's Stortford CM23 145 F
Colchester CO3 ....135 C
Chantry View CM8 ....195 A
Chantry Villas CM3 ....193 A
Chanute Ave CM7 ....73 D
Chapel Cl IP9 ....35 A
Chapel Ct CO7 ....111 E
Chapel Cut CO11 ....87 A
Chapel Dr CM3 ....191 B
Chapel End Way CO9 ....28 B
Chapel Hill
Belchamp Walter CO10 ....31 D
Braintree CM7 ....128 B
Halstead CO9 ....76 D
Stansted
Mountfitchet CM24 ....119 E
Chapel Hill Bsns & Ret
Pk CM7 ....128 C

Chapel Hill Cty Prim Sch
CM7 ....128 B2
Chapel La Belstead IP8 ....36 C7
Boxted CO4 ....83 A3
Colchester CO7 ....111 B1
Elmstead CO7 ....138 C7
Great Bromley CO7 ....139 A5
Great Cornard CO10 ....34 C2
Heybridge Basin CM9 .....210 E2
Kirby Cross CO13 ....170 A6
Little Baddow CM3 ....207 B3
Newport CB11 ....67 A8
St Osyth CO16 ....187 A4
Tendring CO16 ....140 E8
Thorington Street CO6 ......57 D7
Thorrington CO7 ....166 B5
Washbrook IP8 ....16 A1
West Bergholt CO6 ....108 E4
Chapel Rd Beaumont CO16 141 E7
Boxted CO4 ....83 A3
Brightlingsea CO7 ....186 A7
Colchester CO3 ....134 C6
Fingringhoe CO5 ....163 F5
Great Totham CM9 ....196 D6
Langham CO4 ....83 D4
Ridgewell CO9 ....29 B7
Tiptree CO5 ....179 E4
Tolleshunt D'arcy CM9 ....198 F4
West Bergholt CO6 ....108 E4
Wivenhoe CO7 ....164 B8
Chapel Rise CM7 ....129 D2
Chapel Row ⑧ CM23 ......145 F6
Chapel St Halstead CO9 ....76 E2
Rowhedge CO5 ....164 A8
Steeple Bumpstead CB9 ....27 C7
Stoke by C CO10 ....11 A3
Chapel St N ② CO2 ....135 E6
Chapel St S ⑧ CO2 ....135 E6
Chapelfields CO13 ....170 E6
Chaplin Cl CM2 ....216 B2
Chaplin Dr CO4 ....110 D1
Chaplin Rd CO7 ....59 D3
Chaplin Wlk CO10 ....34 D5
Chaplins CO13 ....170 F7
Chapman Rd CO15 ....188 F3
Chapmans La CO5 ....201 F8
Chappel CE Prim Sch
CO6 ....106 D5
Chappel Cnr CO6 ....106 C5
Chappel Hill CO6 ....106 C5
Chappel Rd Bures CO6, CO8 .79 E3
Fordham CO6 ....107 D7
Great Tey CO6 ....106 C1
Chappel & Wakes Colne
Sta 106 D6
Charlecote Rd CM7 ....154 C7
Charles Ct Colchester CO3 134 D6
Wivenhoe CO7 ....137 C3
Charles Pell Rd CO4 ......136 E7
Charles Rd
Brightlingsea CO7 ....185 F6
Felixstowe IP11 ....221 C3
Charles St Colchester CO1 136 A6
Ipswich IP1 ....17 C6
Charles Wheeler Ho CO3 134 E6
Charleston Ct CO5 ....201 E6
Charlotte Dr CO10 ....170 E6
Charlotte Way CM8 ....177 B2
Charnock Cl CO10 ....170 F6
Charnwood Ave CM1 ......204 E1
Charnwood Cl IP2 ....17 A4
Charrington Cl CB9 ....9 C6
Charter Ct CO4 ....110 C4
Charter Ho CM9 ....210 A2
Charter Way CM7 ....128 C1
Charters The CM6 ....123 D2
Chartfield Dr CO13 ....170 D8
Chartwell Cl
Braintree CM7 ....127 E7
Ipswich IP4 ....18 A5
Chase Ct CO4 ....136 D7
Chase La CO12 ....90 E2
Chase Lane Prim Sch
CO12 ....90 E2
Chase Rd E CO7 ....139 C8
Chase Rd W CO7 ....139 A6
Chase The Aldham CO6 ...133 B8
Barnston CM6 ....151 A4
Bishop's Stortford CM23 145 F6
Boreham CM3 ....206 B8
Braintree CM7 ....128 A7
Brantham CO11 ....60 F1
⑥ Colchester CO1 ....136 C7
Dedham CO7 ....85 A4
Elmstead CO7 ....138 B6
Foxearth CO10 ....14 C4
Goldhanger CM9 ....212 A1
Great Baddow CM2 ....216 A6
Great Notley CM7 ....154 C5
Great Tey CO6 ....132 C8
Henham CM22 ....94 F6
Holland-on-S CO15 ....189 C6
Kelvedon CO5 ....158 C2
Mistley CO11 ....86 D3
Steeple Bumpstead CB9 ....27 B7
Tollesbury CM9 ....199 D2
Tolleshunt D'arcy CM9 ....198 A4
West Mersea CO5 ....201 C6
Chase Way The
Colchester CO3 ....109 B1
Colchester CO3 ....109 C1
Chaseway The CM7 ....128 C2
Chaters Hill CO10 ....11 A3
Chatham Hall La CM3 .....173 A1
Chatley Rd CM3 ....173 F7
Chatsworth Cl CM23 ......145 C7
Chatsworth Cres
Ipswich IP2 ....17 B2

Chatsworth Cres continued
Trimley St M IP11 ....221 A6
Chatsworth Dr IP4 ....18 E5
Chatsworth Gdns CO15 ..188 D2
Chatsworth Rd CO5 ....201 C7
Chattisham Rd IP8 ....35 C8
Chaucer Cl CO15 ....188 A1
Chaucer Cres CM7 ....155 A8
Chaucer Rd
Chelmsford CM2 ....205 D1
Felixstowe IP11 ....221 D3
Sudbury CO10 ....15 D2
Chaucer Way CO3 ....134 F6
Chauntry Rd CB9 ....8 F7
Chauntry The ② CB9 ....9 A7
Chedburgh Pl ⑧ CB9 ....9 A8
Chelmer Ave CM3 ....191 B5
Chelmer Cl
Kirby Cross CO13 ....170 E7
Little Totham CM9 ....197 B4
Chelmer Dr CM6 ....150 E8
Chelmer Lea CM2 ....216 E7
Chelmer Pl CM2 ....205 D3
Chelmer Rd
Braintree CM7 ....128 D1
Chelmsford CM2 ....205 D2
Haverhill CB9 ....9 B8
Witham CM8 ....176 F2
Chelmer Terr CM9 ....210 B8
Chelmer Valley High Sch
CM1 ....191 A2
Chelmer Valley Rd CM1 ..205 B5
Chelmer Village Ret Pk
CM2 ....205 E2
Chelmer Village Way
CM2 ....206 A3
Chelmerton Ave CM2 .....216 E7
Chelmondiston CE Prim
Sch IP9 ....63 E7
Chelmsford Coll F Ed
Chelmsford CM2 ....216 A8
Chelmsford CM2 ....216 C7
Chelmsford Cty High
Sch CM1 ....205 A4
Chelmsford & Essex
Regiment Mus CM2 ....216 A8
Chelmsford Ho CM6 ......150 E7
Chelmsford Rd
Barnston CM6 ....151 A4
Felsted CM6 ....152 B4
Great Dunmow CM6 ....150 E7
Great Waltham CM3 ....191 A7
Holland-on-S CO15 ....189 D6
Purleigh CM3 ....220 C3
Woodham Mortimer CM9 219 C6
Writtle CM1 ....204 C1
Chelmsford Road Ind Est
CM6 ....150 E7
Chelmsford Sta CM1 .....205 B3
Chelsea Cl CO10 ....33 F7
Chelsea Mews ⑥ CM7 ....127 F2
Chelsea Rd CO10 ....33 F7
Chelsworth Ave CO10 .....34 C4
Chelsworth Rd IP11 ....221 B3
Chelwater CM2 ....216 D8
Chenies Gn CM23 ....145 D6
Chepstow Rd IP11 ....221 D5
Chequers CM23 ....145 C8
Chequers Ct CM8 ....176 F2
Chequers La Glemsford CO10 2 C6
Great Dunmow CM6 ....150 D8
Maldon CM9 ....210 A2
Chequers Rd CO11 ....113 C6
Chequers The CO7 ....165 A7
Cheriton Rd CM7 ....128 C1
Cherry Bglws ① CM7 ......127 F3
Cherry Blossom Cl IP8 ....16 B3
Cherry Chase CO5 ....179 D4
Cherry Garden La
Danbury CM3 ....219 B7
Newport CB11 ....66 F8
Cherry Garden Rd
Great Waltham CM3 ....190 E2
Maldon CM9 ....209 E2
Cherry Gdns CM23 ....146 A8
Cherry La CO9 ....51 A8
Cherry Row CO3 ....134 F5
Cherry Tree Ave CO15 ...188 C1
Cherry Tree Cl
Halstead CO9 ....77 A2
Little Oakley CO12 ....117 B7
Cherry Tree Cty Prim Sch
CO2 ....163 A8
Cherry Tree Ho CO5 ......158 C3
Cherry Tree La
Abberton CO2 ....162 F6
Blackheath CO2 ....163 A4
Cherry Trees CO15 ....188 C1
Cherrygarden La ① CM2 216 A8
Cherrytree Ct CO3 ....134 F5
Cherrytree Rd CO10 ....34 B7
Cherrytree Rise CM8 .....177 A5
Cherrywood Dr CO3 ....134 F5
Cherrywoods CO7 ....166 D8
Chervil Cl CO5 ....179 C4
Cherwell Dr CM1 ....204 E5
Cheryl Ct CO15 ....188 D1
Chesapeake Cl IP9 ....63 F7
Chesapeake Rd IP3 ....38 A8
Chesfield Cl CM23 ....145 F5
Chesham Rd IP2 ....17 B4
Chess La CM8 ....177 A2
Chessington Gdns IP1 .....16 F8
Chester Ct ④ CB9 ....8 E6
Chester Pl CM1 ....205 A5
Chester Rd IP11 ....221 D5
Chesterton Cl IP2 ....16 F1

Chestnut Ave
Blackheath CO2 ....163 A8
Clacton-on-S CO15 ....188 C3
Gosfield CO9 ....102 E8
Hatfield Peverel CM3 .....194 A4
Heybridge CM9 ....210 C6
Jaywick CO16 ....188 A2
Kirby Cross CO13 ....170 C6
Littlebury CB11 ....21 C1
Chestnut Cl
Bishop's Stortford CM23 145 F4
Haverhill CB9 ....8 F7
Chestnut Ct CB11 ....67 A8
Chestnut Gr CM7 ....127 E2
Chestnut Rd
Alresford CO7 ....165 B8
Glemsford CO10 ....2 B5
Chestnut Terr CO10 ....15 C8
Chestnut Way
Brightlingsea CO7 ....185 E7
Takeley CM22 ....148 C7
Tiptree CO5 ....179 C7
Chestnut Wlk
Chelmsford CM1 ....205 A5
Felsted CM6 ....152 C6
Little Baddow CM3 ....207 A8
Witham CM8 ....177 B4
Chestnuts The IP2 ....16 C2
Chevalier Rd IP11 ....221 F4
Chevallier St IP1 ....17 A7
Cheveley IP11 ....221 E4
Cheveling Rd CO2 ....136 D2
Cheviot Dr CM1 ....204 D6
Chevy Ct CO12 ....90 C2
Chichester CO3 ....135 A7
Chichester Dr CM1 ....205 C4
Chichester Rd CB11 ....43 E8
Chickney Rd CM22 ....95 C7
Chigborough Rd CM9 .....210 F6
Chignall St CM1 ....204 D5
Chilburn Rd CO15 ....189 A7
Childers Field IP11 ....221 B5
Childwell Alley CO1 ....136 A6
Chilford Ct CM7 ....127 D3
Chiltern Cl CO1 ....109 E1
Chilton Cl Chelmsford CM2 216 D7
Great Horkesley CO6 ......109 B7
Chilton Cotts CO6 ....80 E4
Chilton Ct Ipswich IP2 .....17 B3
Sudbury CO10 ....34 A6
Chilton Ind Est
Sudbury CO10 ....34 A8
Sudbury CO10 ....34 B8
Chilton Lodge Rd CO10 ...34 A7
Chilton Rd IP3 ....18 C4
Chimney Pot La CM3 ......219 E3
Chimswell Way CB9 ....8 C8
Chingford Ave CO15 ......188 F8
Chinnel La CB11 ....42 D5
Chinnery Hill CM23 ....145 F5
Chinook CO7 ....110 B4
Chippetts La CO3 ....133 C7
Chipping Hill
② Halstead CO9 ....76 F2
Witham CM8 ....176 F3
Chipping Hill Cty Inf Sch
CM8 ....176 F3
Chippingdell CM8 ....176 F4
Chipstead Wlk CO16 ......188 C6
Chishill Rd SG8 ....19 A4
Chislett Row CM2 ....216 C8
Chitts Hill CO3 ....108 D1
Chivers Rd CO3 ....8 D7
Choat's Cotts CO6 ....107 E1
Choats Wood CO3 ....107 F1
Chrishall CE Prim Sch
SG8 ....19 C3
Chrismund Way CO6 ......106 C1
Christ Church Ct CO3 .....135 D5
Christchurch Ct ④ IP4 ....17 D6
Christchurch Mansion
(Mus) IP4 ....17 D6
Christchurch Park Hospl
(private) IP1 ....17 C7
Christchurch St IP4 ....17 D6
Christian Sch The CM22 148 B7
Christies Warehouse ⑮
IP4 ....17 D5
Christina Rd CM8 ....194 E8
Christine Chase CO3 ......134 F5
Christmas Field CO9 ....51 D2
Christopher Ct ⑨ CO10 ..33 E7
Christopher Dr CO16 .....168 D1
Christopher Jolly Ct CO2 135 F4
Christopher La CO10 ....33 E7
Christy Ave CM1 ....204 F4
Church Ave CM1 ....191 A2
Church Chase CM8 ....178 A3
Church Cl Cavendish CO10 ..1 D2
West Bergholt CO6 ....108 E4
Wickham Bishops CM8 ..195 D5
Church Cnr CM9 ....208 D2
Church Cotts CM8 ....195 D5
Church Cres
Clacton-on-S CO15 ....188 F2
Sproughton IP8 ....16 A6
Church Dr CM23 ....92 B8
Church End
Great Dunmow CM6 ....123 D4
Panfield CM7 ....127 B7
Church End Villas CM6 ...123 D4
Church Farm Way CO4 ...109 E4
Church Field CB11 ....43 E7
Church Field Rd CO10 .....34 C8
Church Fields CO9 ....29 F2
Church Gdns CM6 ....123 D2
Church Gn Boreham CM3 206 F8

Church Gn continued
Coggeshall CO6 ....131 A3
Hinxton CB10 ....3 F7
Little Yeldham CO9 ....30 D4
Wickham Bishops CM8 ..195 D5
Church Gr CO6 ....133 B8
Church Hill Ashdon CB10 ..24 A8
Earls Colne CO6 ....105 C6
Finchingfield CM7 ....72 D6
Harwich CO12 ....90 B1
Helions Bumpstead CB9 ..26 C8
Lawford CO11 ....85 F3
Little Waltham CM3 ....191 C6
Purleigh CM3 ....220 F1
Rowhedge CO5 ....163 F8
White Notley CM8 ....175 F8
Woodham Walter CM9 ...208 D2
Church Housen CM3 ......190 F7
Church La Beaumont CO16 142 A6
Bishop's Stortford CM23 145 D3
Braintree CM7 ....127 F6
Brantham CO11 ....60 E1
Canfield End CM6 ....149 B7
Castle Camps CB1 ....7 E3
Castle Hedingham CO9 ...51 E4
① Chelmsford,
Moulsham CM2 ....205 B2
Chelmsford,
Springfield CM1 ....205 D4
Clare CO10 ....12 B7
Colchester, Lexden CO3 135 A6
Colchester, Stanway CO3 134 A4
Debden CB11 ....68 A7
East Mersea CO5 ....184 E1
Elsenham CM22 ....120 E8
Felixstowe IP11 ....221 D6
Ford End CM3 ....172 B6
Great Henny CO10 ....54 D8
Great Holland CO13 ....170 B3
Great Leighs CM3 ....173 D7
Great Tey CO6 ....132 C4
Great Wigborough CO5 ..181 F4
Harkstead IP9 ....63 B3
Harwich CO12 ....91 E6
Heybridge CM9 ....211 A8
Little Totham CM9 ....197 B1
Marks Tey CO6 ....133 A4
Mistley CO11 ....86 E4
Nayland CO6 ....56 B1
Ridgewell CO9 ....29 B6
Sproughton IP8 ....16 B6
Takeley CM22 ....148 B7
Toppesfield CO9 ....50 C8
Washbrook IP8 ....35 D8
Weeley Heath CO16 ....168 A7
Widdington CB11 ....67 D4
Writtle CM1 ....204 B1
Church Manor CM23 ......146 B8
Church Mead CM8 ....155 F1
Church Path CB1 ....5 B6
Church Pk CO10 ....11 C3
Church Rd
Alphamstone CO10 ....54 C6
Alresford CO7 ....165 B7
Bentley IP9 ....60 F7
Black Notley CM7 ....155 A6
Boxted CO4 ....82 E6
Bradwell CM7 ....129 E1
Brightlingsea CO7 ....185 E8
Bulmer CO10 ....32 F4
Capel St M IP9 ....35 F1
Chrishall SG8 ....19 D3
Clacton-on-S CO15 ....189 A3
Copford CO6 ....133 E2
Cressing CM7 ....156 A5
Elmstead CO7 ....138 A7
Fingringhoe CO5 ....164 A5
Fordham CO6 ....107 D5
Frating CO7 ....138 D2
Gosfield CO9 ....102 E8
Great Cornard CO10 ....34 A5
Great Hallingbury CM22 146 D3
Great Notley CM7 ....154 F6
Great Totham CM9 ....196 E3
Great Yeldham CO9 ....29 F2
Greenstead Green CO9 ..104 A5
Hatfield Peverel CM3 .....194 A3
Hempstead CB10 ....46 F8
Holbrook IP9 ....62 D5
Kelvedon CO5 ....158 C2
Layer-de-l-H CO2 ....161 F2
Little Baddow CM3 ....207 A6
Little Bentley CO7 ....140 A5
Little Bromley CO11 ....113 B4
Pattiswick CM7 ....129 F5
Peldon CO5 ....182 D6
Rivenhall CM8 ....157 B1
Shudy Camps CB1 ....7 C5
Stambourne CO9 ....28 D2
Stansted
Mountfitchet CM24 ....119 F5
Stutton IP9 ....62 A2
Tattingstone IP9 ....61 C7
Terling CM3 ....175 B2
Thorrington CO7 ....166 B4
Tiptree CO5 ....179 D5
Tolleshunt Major CM9 ....197 D2
Ulting CM9 ....208 C6
Walton-on-t-N CO14 ......171 C8
West Mersea CO5 ....201 B6
Wickham Bishops CM8 ..195 D5
Wickham St P CO9 ....53 B6
Wormingford CO6 ....80 E5
Wrabness CO11 ....88 F4
Church Sq Bures CO8 ......55 F1
St Osyth CO16 ....187 A4
Church St
Belchamp St P CO10 ....13 B3

Church St continued
Bishop's Stortford CM23 145 F7
Boxted CO4 ....82 F7
Braintree CM7 ....102 B1
Chelmondiston IP9 ....63 E7
Chelmsford CM1 ....205 B2
Clare CO10 ....12 B7
Coggeshall CO6 ....131 A2
Colchester CO1 ....135 E7
Colne Engaine CO6 ....78 A1
Gestingthorpe CO9 ....31 E1
Goldhanger CM9 ....211 E7
Great Baddow CM2 ....217 A6
Great Chesterford CB10 ...3 D2
Great Dunmow CM6 ....123 D2
Great Maplestead CO9 ....52 D1
Harwich CO12 ....91 E6
Henham CM22 ....94 F6
Ickleton CB10 ....3 B4
Kelvedon CO5 ....158 B2
Maldon CM9 ....210 B2
Newport CB11 ....43 A1
Rowhedge CO5 ....164 A8
Saffron Walden CB10 ......22 D2
Sible Hedingham CO9 .....51 D1
Steeple Bumpstead CB9 ..27 B7
Stoke-by-N CO6 ....56 D5
Sudbury CO10 ....33 D6
Tollesbury CM9 ....199 D1
Tolleshunt D'arcy CM9 ....198 D4
Wendens Ambo CB11 ......42 E5
Witham CM8 ....176 F4
Church Terr CO10 ....10 D2
Church View Ardleigh CO7 111 E7
Stoke by C CO10 ....10 D3
Church Wlk
Colchester CO1 ....135 E7
Littlebury CB11 ....21 F4
Sturmer CB9 ....9 E4
⑤ Sudbury CO10 ....33 E7
Churchfield Rd
Coggeshall CO6 ....131 A3
Walton-on-t-N CO14 ......171 C8
Churchfields Stansted
Mountfitchet CM24 ....119 F6
Steeple Bumpstead CB9 ..27 B6
West Mersea CO5 ....201 B6
Churchfields Dr CB9 ....27 B6
Churchgate CO10 ....2 C5
Churchill Ave Halstead CO9 77 A3
Ipswich IP1 ....18 B5
Churchill Cl CO7 ....185 F8
Churchill Cl CO12 ....91 A4
Churchill Dr CO10 ....15 E2
Churchill Rd
Braintree CM7 ....127 E7
Tiptree CO5 ....179 F5
Churchill Rise CM1 ....205 B2
Churchill Terr CM7 ....127 E6
Churchill Way CO2 ....136 B4
Churchponds CO9 ....51 E4
Churchwell Ave CO5 ......160 A7
Churnwood Cl CO4 ....110 D1
Churnwood Rd CO4 ....110 D1
Chuzzlewit Dr CM1 ....204 E8
Cinque Port Rd CO7 ....185 F7
Circular Rd E CO2 ....135 F5
Circular Rd N CO2 ....135 F5
Circular Rd S CO2 ....135 E4
Circular Rd W CO2 ....135 E5
City Rd CO5 ....201 A6
Civic Dr IP1 ....17 B6
Civic Ind Est CB9 ....8 F5
Clachar Cl CM2 ....206 A3
Clacton Cty High Sch
CO15 ....189 A4
Clacton & District Hospl
CO15 ....188 E1
Clacton- on-Sea Sta
CO15 ....188 F3
Clacton Rd Bradfield CO11 114 A6
Elmstead CO7 ....137 C5
Elmstead CO7 ....138 C5
Great Holland CO13 ....170 A2
Holland-on-S CO15 ....189 F7
Little Oakley CO12 ....117 B5
Mistley CO11 ....86 E2
St Osyth CO16 ....187 B4
Thorrington CO7 ....166 C4
Weeley Heath CO16 ....168 A4
Wix CO11 ....115 C5
Wix CO11 ....115 D1
Claire Rd CO13 ....170 B6
Clairmont Cl ⑪ CM7 ......127 F2
Clairmont Rd CO3 ....134 E5
Clandon Ho CO13 ....170 F4
Clapgate Dr CO16 ....168 C2
Clapgate La IP3 ....18 A2
Clapton Hall La CM6 ......150 D6
Clara Reeve Cl CO3 ....134 F4
Clare Castle Ctry Pk CO10 12 C7
Clare Cl CO10 ....103 D7
Clare Ct CM6 ....69 F3
Clare Cty Prim Sch CO10 12 C8
Clare Mid Sch CO10 ....12 C8
Clare Priory (remains
of) CO10 ....12 C6
Clare Rd Braintree CM7 ..127 C2
Ipswich IP4 ....17 F8
Clare Way CO16 ....188 B5
Claremont Hts CO1 ....109 E1
Claremont Rd CO7 ....164 C8
Clarence Cl CM2 ....206 A4
Clarence Rd Clare CO10 ..12 B8
Ipswich IP3 ....18 B1

Clarence Rd *continued*
Stansted
Mountfitchet CM24 ......119 E7
Sudbury CO10 ....15 E1
Clarendon Pk CO15 ....189 B5
Clarendon Rd Haverhill CB9 .8 F6
Takeley CM6 ....148 E7
Clarendon Way CO1 ....109 E1
Clark Way CM1 ....191 A1
Clarke's Rd CO12 ......90 F3
Clarkesmead CO5 ......179 C4
Clarkia Wlk CO4 ......136 D7
Clarks Farm Rd CM3 ...218 F8
Clarkson St IP1 ......17 B6
Clatterbury La
Arkesden CB11 ....41 E1
Clavering CB11 ......65 D5
Claud Ince Ave CM7 ...155 E6
Claude Oliver Cl CO11 .86 A2
Claude St IP1 ....17 C6
Claudian Cl CB9 ......9 D7
Claudius Rd CO2 ......136 A5
Claudius Way CM8 .....194 E8
Clavering Cty Prim Sch
CB11 ....65 C4
Clavering Rd CM7 .....127 F6
Claverton Way IP4 ....18 E4
Clay Hill CO10 ....54 C8
Clay La St Osyth CO16 ..187 C7
Stebbing CM6 ....124 D7
Clay Lane Gr CO4 .....110 D4
Clay Pit Piece CB11 ...43 E6
Clay Pits Way CM7 ....128 D3
Claydon Cl CB1 ....7 E4
Clayhall Rd CO15 .....189 A5
Claypit Hill CM22 ....120 E5
Claypits Ave CO8 .....80 A8
Claypits La CO10 .....14 D5
Claypits Rd CM3 ......192 F1
Claypits Villas CM6 ...70 B2
Clayponds CM23 ....146 B2
Clays Rd CO14 ....171 B7
Clayshotts Dr CM8 ....195 B8
Clayton Rd CO12 ......90 C2
Claywall Bridge CB9 ...27 C7
Claywall Cotts CB9 ....27 C7
Clear Springs Chalet
Site 91 A1
Clearwater CO2 ....136 B3
Clematis Tye CM1 .....205 E7
Clematis Way CO4 .....136 E7
Clement Mellish Ho
CO1 ....135 F7
Clement's La CB9 ......8 F7
Clements Cl CB9 ....8 F7
Clements Cty Prim Sch CB9 8 F7
Clements Dr CB9 ....8 F7
Clench Cl IP4 ....17 D6
Clench Rd IP9 ....62 D7
Clermont Ave CO10 ....15 E2
Clevedon Cl CM7 ......154 C7
Cleveland Cl CO4 .....110 C4
Cleves Ct CM3 ....192 E1
Clicket Hill CO8 ......80 B8
Cliff Cres CM7 ....100 E7
Cliff Ct CO13 ....171 B6
Cliff La IP3 ....17 F3
Cliff Lane Prim Sch IP3 .17 E3
Cliff Par CO14 ....144 E2
Cliff Rd Harwich CO12 ...91 D3
Holland-on-S CO15 ....189 E5
Ipswich IP3 ....17 E3
Cliff Way CO13 ....171 B5
Cliffield CM7 ....100 E7
Clifford Ct CM23 .....146 A7
Clifford Rd IP4 ......17 F5
Clifford Road Prim Sch
IP4 ....17 F5
Clifton Terr CO7 .....164 B8
Clifton Way IP2 ......16 D2
Clifton Wood IP9 .....62 D6
Clive Rd CO1, CO2 ....136 A6
Cliveden Cl CM1 ......204 E3
Clobbs Yd CM1 ....205 B8
Clockhouse Way CM7 ..128 C2
Cloes La CO15 ....188 B4
Cloisters The
Braintree CM7 ....128 A5
Kelvedon CO5 ....158 B1
Cloncurry Gdns IP11 ...221 B3
Clopton Dr CO10 ......15 C6
Close The
Clacton-on-S CO15 ....203 H7
Colchester CO3 ......134 C6
Cressing CM7 ....155 E6
Debden CB11 ....68 B7
Frinton-on-S CO13 ...170 E5
Great Dunmow CM6 ...150 D4
Great Holland CO13 ..170 A3
Harwich CO12 ....91 A3
Sudbury CO10 ....33 F8
Tattingstone IP9 ....61 D7
Clouded Yellow Cl CM7 .154 E8
Clough Rd CO2 ....110 D6
Clovelly Cl IP4 ....18 F4
Clover Ave CM23 .....145 B6
Clover Cl IP2 ....16 F4
Clover Ct Colchester CO3 .134 C6
Great Cornard CO10 ..34 C6
Clover Dr CO7 ....166 A5
Clover Way CO7 ......111 B5
Cloverlands CO4 .....110 C2
Clovers CO9 ....76 D1

Cluanie Orch CO10 .....1 E1
Club Par CO16 ....203 B6
Clump Field IP2 ......16 F2
Clyde Cres CM1 ....204 D4
Clydesdale Rd CM7 ....127 E2
Coach House Way
CM8 ....177 A2
Coach La CM9 ....209 F3
Coach Rd Alresford CO7 .165 B8
Great Horkesley CO6 ..109 A7
Hempstead CB10 ......25 F2
Coachman's Paddock IP9 62 D6
Coachmans Ct IP4 .....17 C5
Coan Ave CO5 ....188 D1
Coast Rd CO5 ....201 A6
Coastguard Cotts CO14 .144 D1
Coates Cl CM23 ......210 B4
Coats Hutton Rd CO2 ..135 B3
Coats Quay CM2 ......205 C2
Cobbold Mews IP4 ....17 D6
Cobbold Rd IP11 .....221 E4
Cobbold St IP4 ....17 D6
Cobbs La CM22 ....121 F3
Cobbs Pl CM1 ....205 D3
Cobden Pl IP4 ....17 D6
Cobham Rd IP3 ....18 C2
Cock & Bell La CO10 ..15 C8
Cock La CB11 ....64 F3
Cock & Pye Ct CO1 ...135 E7
Cock Rd IP9 ....53 B1
Cockaynes La CO7 ....138 A1
Cockett Wick La CO16 .187 C1
Cockrell's Rd CO6 ....81 B4
Codham Little Park Dr
CM7 ....101 C6
Cody Rd IP3 ....18 C1
Coeur De Lion CO4 ...109 F2
Coggeshall Pieces CO9 .77 A2
Coggeshall Rd
Ardleigh CO7 ....84 F2
Braintree CM7 ....128 C3
Coggeshall CO6 ......131 F3
Coggeshall CO6 ......131 F7
Earls Colne CO6 ......105 B3
Great Tey CO6 ....132 B7
Kelvedon CO5 ....158 B5
Marks Tey CO6 ....132 C3
Coggeshall Rd
(Feering) CO5 ....158 D7
Coggeshall Road
(Feering) CO6 ....131 B1
Coggeshall Way CO9 ...77 A2
Cogmore CB11 ....41 B8
Cohort Dr CO2 ....135 A2
Coke St CO12 ....91 D5
Cokers Cl CM7 ....155 C5
Colam La CM3 ....207 C3
Colbayns High Sch CO15 188 D4
Colchester Boys High
Sch CO3 ....135 E6
Colchester Bsns Pk CO4 .110 C6
Colchester Castle CO1 .135 F7
Colchester Castle Mus
CO1 ....135 F7
Colchester Cty High Sch
for Girls CO3 ......135 B6
Colchester General
Hospl CO4 ....109 E3
Colchester Inst CO15 ..189 A3
Colchester Institute 135 D8
Colchester Oaks Hospl
CO3 ....135 D7
Colchester Rd
Abberton CO5 ....163 B1
Ardleigh CO7 ....111 C6
Bures CO8 ....79 F8
Chappel CO6 ....106 E5
Chelmsford CM2 ......206 A6
Coggeshall CO6 ......131 D2
Dedham CO7 ....84 E6
Elmstead CO7 ....137 F6
Frating CO7 ....139 E3
Great Bentley CO7, CO16 ..186 F8
Great Bromley CO7 ..112 A3
Great Totham CM9 ...196 D7
Great Wigborough
CO5, CM9 ....181 C2
Halstead CO9 ....77 A1
Heybridge CM9 ......210 B5
Holland-on-S CO15 ...189 D6
Ipswich IP4 ....18 B8
Lawford CO11 ....86 C3
Little Horkesley CO6 ..81 B1
Peldon CO5 ....183 B6
Salcott-cum-virley CM9 .199 A5
St Osyth CO16 ....187 A4
St Osyth CO16 ....187 A7
Thorpe-le-S CO16 ...141 D2
Tiptree CO5 ....179 D7
Weeley CO16 ....140 C2
West Bergholt CO6 ..108 D6
West Mersea CO5 ....201 C7
White Colne CO6 ....105 E6
Witham CM8 ....177 B3
Wivenhoe CO7 ....137 B4
Wix CO11 ....114 E4
Wix CO12 ....115 B3
Wormingford CO8 ....80 A6
Colchester Royal Gram
Sch CO3 ....135 D6
Colchester Sta CO1 ...109 E1
Colchester Zoo CO3 ...134 C1
Cold Hall Chase CO7 ...138 E6
Cold Store Rd IP11 ....221 A1
Coldhanger Ct CM7 ....155 D8
Coldnailhurst Ave CM7 .127 F5
Cole End La CB10 .....44 D6
Cole Hill CM3 ....174 B5

Cole Ness Rd IP3 .....38 A8
Colehills Cl CB11 .....65 C4
Colemans La CM3 .....218 D7
Coleridge Rd CM9 ....210 A1
Coles La CO14 ....144 A1
Coles Oak La CO7 .....84 C6
College Cl CM23 ......145 D7
College Ct CO11 ......86 C4
College Ho CM7 ......127 E2
College Rd Braintree CM7 .127 E2
Clacton-on-S CO15 ...189 A3
College St IP4 ....17 C5
Coller Rd CO12 ....90 F5
Colles Brook Rd CO7 ..166 F4
Colletts Chase CO6 ...80 F4
Colley Rd CM2 ....217 A6
Colliers The CM9 .....210 E3
Collimer Cl IP9 ....63 E7
Collimer Ct IP11 .....221 C6
Collindale Gdns CO15 ..189 C5
Collingwood Ave IP3 ..18 B3
Collingwood Cl CM7 ..128 C5
Collingwood Fields CO7 .59 B4
Collingwood Rd
Clacton-on-S CO15 ...188 D1
Colchester CO3 ......134 E6
Witham CM8 ....177 A2
Collins Cl CM7 ....127 F2
Collins Cross CM23 ...119 B1
Collins Rd CM9 ....53 C1
Collinson's IP2 ....16 D5
Collops Villas CM6 ....125 A4
Colne Bank Ave CO1 ...109 C1
Colne Bank Avenu CO3 .135 D8
Colne Chase CM8 .....176 E2
Colne Com Sch & Colne
Coll The CO7 ....185 E8
Colne Cswy CO2 ......136 D5
Colne Ct CM7 ....127 F1
Colne Engaine Prim CE
Sch CO6 ....78 A2
Colne Park Rd CO6 ...105 D7
Colne Rd
Brightlingsea CO7 ...185 E6
Bures CO8 ....79 E8
Clacton-on-S CO15 ...188 F2
Coggeshall CO6 ......131 A6
Halstead CO9 ....77 A2
Sible Hedingham CO9 .75 C8
Colne Rise CO5 ....163 F8
Colne Springs CO9 ....29 B6
Colne Terr CO7 ....164 B8
Colne Valley Cl CO9 ...76 D2
Colne Valley Railway CO9 .51 C5
Colne Valley Rd CB9 ...9 A7
Colne View
Colchester CO2 ......136 D2
Point Clear B CO16 ..186 A2
Colne View Ret Pk CO1 .110 A1
Colne Way CO15 ......185 F4
Colneford Hill CO6 ...105 D7
Colneis Cty Jun Sch IP11 221 F6
Colneis Rd CO15 .....221 E6
Colneys Cl CO10 ......15 D1
Colthorpe Rd CO15 ...188 C5
Colts The CM23 ......145 E4
Coltsfield CM24 ......119 E8
Coltsfoot Ct CO4 .....109 C2
Coltsfoot Rd IP2 ......16 E4
Columbine Gdns
Ipswich IP2 ....16 E5
Walton-on-t-N CO14 ..171 B7
Columbine Mews CO3 ..134 C7
Columbines The CO10 ...1 E2
Colvin Chase CM2 .....216 B1
Colvin Cl CO3 ....134 F7
Colyers Reach CM2 ...206 A2
Colyn Pl CB10 ....22 E3
Comac Yd CO15 ......188 B5
Comma Cl CM7 ....127 E1
Commerce Pk CO2 ....136 D4
Commerce Way
Colchester CO2 ......136 D4
Lawford CO11 ....86 C5
Commercial Rd IP1 ....17 B4
Common Hill CB10 ....22 D2
Common La
Duddenhoe End SG8 ..40 B7
Little Baddow CM3 ...207 E4
Woodham Walter CM9 .208 B3
Common St CO10 .....12 B8
Common The CM3 .....218 E6
Commons The CO3 ....135 A5
Compasses Rd CM7 ...129 F5
Compton Mews CM6 ...136 C8
Compton Rd CM2 .....136 C8
Comyns Pl CM1 ....204 B1
Conan Doyle Cl CM7 ..155 A8
Concil Houses CM7 ...156 A4
Conder Way CO2 .....216 B1
Conduit La CM9 ......219 E6
Conduite St CM1 .....205 B2
Conies Rd CM9 ....103 D7
Conifer Cl Alresford CO7 .164 F7
Colchester CO4 ......136 E8
Conifer Ct CM23 .....145 F8
Coniston Cl CM7 .....154 C6
Coniston Rd IP3 ......18 B2
Coniston Sq IP3 ......18 B2
Connaught Ave CO13 ..170 F4
Connaught Cl CO15 ...189 B3
Connaught Ct CO15 ...189 B3
Connaught Gdns CM7 ..128 B4
Connaught Gdns E CO15 189 B3
Connaught Gdns W CO15 189 B3
Connaught Ho
Clacton-on-S CO15 ...189 B4
Frinton-on-S CO13 ...170 F5

Connaught Rd Haverhill CB9 .8 E7
Weeley Heath CO16 ..168 C5
Conquerors Cl CM3 ...194 B3
Conrad Rd CM8 ....176 F5
Constable Ave CO16 ..188 C6
Constable Cl
Colchester CO4 ......109 E4
Lawford CO11 ....86 B4
West Mersea CO5 ....201 D7
Constable Ct CO2 .....135 B3
Constable Ho CM7 ....127 E3
Constable Rd
Felixstowe IP11 .....221 F4
Ipswich IP4 ....17 D8
Sudbury CO10 ....33 E8
Constable View CM1 ..205 F6
Constance Cl
Broomfield CM1 .....191 A3
Witham CM8 ....195 B8
Constantine Rd
Colchester CO3 ......135 D5
Ipswich IP1 ....17 B5
Witham CM8 ....194 E8
Constitution Hill
Ipswich IP1 ....17 B8
Sudbury CO10 ....33 F8
Convalescent Hill IP11 .221 E3
Convent Hill CM7 .....128 A5
Convent La CM7 ......128 A5
Conway Cl Halstead CO9 .103 D8
Haverhill CB9 ....8 E8
Ipswich IP2 ....17 B2
Wivenhoe CO7 ....164 C8
Conyer Cl CM9 ....220 F8
Cook Cl CO12 ....90 F1
Cook Cres CO4 ....136 E7
Cook Pl CM2 ....205 F3
Cook's Corner CO11 ...88 E2
Cook's Hall Rd CO6 ...108 C3
Cook's La Colchester CO3 .134 E8
Colchester CO3 ......134 F7
Great Bardfield CM7 ..71 E4
Cooks Hill CO4 ....83 B6
Coolyne Way CO15 ...189 B7
Coombe Lodge CO6 ...105 B6
Coombe Rise CM1 ....205 B7
Cooper Dr CM7 ....127 D4
Cooper's La CO7 .....84 F5
Cooper's Row CM1 ...205 A5
Coopers CM23 ....206 E8
Coopers Ave CM9 ....210 D5
Coopers Cl CM23 .....145 B4
Coopers Cres CO6 ....108 F4
Coopers End Rd CM24 .121 A3
Coopers End Rdbt CM24 121 B3
Coopers La
Clacton-on-S CO15 ...188 C3
Great Leighs CM3 ...173 F7
Coopers Villas CM21 ..121 B2
Copdock Cty Prim Sch
IP8 ....35 F8
Copford CE Prim Sch
CO6 ....133 D2
Copland Cl
Broomfield CM1 .....191 A1
Great Baddow CM2 ..216 F8
Copleston High Sch IP4 .18 C5
Copleston Rd IP4 .....18 B5
Coploe Rd CB10 ....3 A2
Copper Beeches CO3 ..134 D5
Copper Ct CM7 ....127 E1
Copperas Rd CO7 .....185 F5
Copperfield Rd
Chelmsford CM1 .....204 E7
Ipswich IP2 ....16 E5
Copperfields CB11 ....43 C8
Coppice Cl CM6 ......123 D1
Coppice End CO4 .....110 B3
Coppice Rd CO7 ......165 B8
Coppice The CO15 ....188 D1
Coppins Cl CM2 ......205 E4
Coppins Green Prim Sch
CO15 ....188 D4
Coppins Rd CO15 .....188 D4
Coprolite St IP3 ......17 E5
Copse The
Bishop's Stortford CM23 .146 C8
Colchester CO4 ......109 F3
Felsted CM6 ....152 F6
Copt Hall La CO5 ....182 C3
Copt Hill CM3 ....218 E6
Copthall Cl CM22 ....146 F4
Copthall La CM6 .....70 B3
Copy Hill CB9 ....8 E3
Coral Dr IP1 ....16 D8
Coralin Wlk CO3 .....134 C6
Cordell Pl CO10 ......15 D8
Cordell Rd CO10 .....15 D8
Corder Rd IP4 ....17 D8
Cordwinders CO7 .....59 F1
Coriander Rd CO5 ....179 C4
Corinda Ho CO3 ......170 F4
Coriolanus Cl CO2 ...135 A3
Cormorant Wlk CM7 ..216 C5
Corn Mill Ct CB11 ....43 E8
Cornard Rd CO10 .....33 F7
Cornel Cl CM8 ....176 D4
Cornelius Vale CM2 ..206 B4
Cornells La CB11 .....67 E3
Corner Pk CB10 ......22 E3
Cornerth Cres CO10 ..34 B6
Cornflower Cl
Colchester CO3 ......134 C7
Ipswich IP2 ....16 E4
Cornflower Dr CM1 ...205 F6
Cornflower Rd CO15 ..203 G7

Cornford Way CO11 ...86 B4
Cornhill
4 Chelmsford CM1 ...205 B2
16 Ipswich IP1 ......17 C6
Cornish Hall End Rd
Stambourne CO9 ......28 A1
Steeple Bumpstead CO9 .48 E1
Cornwall Cl CO11 .....86 B3
Cornwall Cres CM1 ...205 A2
Cornwall Gdns CM7 ...128 B4
Cornwall Ho CM23 ...145 E4
Cornwall Rd IP11 .....221 D5
Cornwallis Pl CB10 ...22 E3
Cornwallis Rd CB9 ....8 E4
Cornwalls Dr CO6 ....132 E4
Coronation Ave
Braintree CM7 ....127 E4
Colchester CO2 ......136 A2
Coronation Dr IP11 ...221 C3
Coronation Rd
Bishop's Stortford CM23 .145 E8
Clacton-on-S CO15 ...188 C3
Ipswich IP4 ....18 B5
Coronation Villas CO16 .141 E4
Coronation Way CM7 ..155 D5
Corporation Ave IP2 ..37 A4
Corporation Rd CM1 ..205 A4
Corriander Dr CM22 ..94 D2
Corry Ct CO4 ....136 D6
Corton Rd IP3 ....18 B3
Cortoncroft Cl CO13 ..170 F4
Cotman Ave CO11 .....86 B4
Cotman Rd
Clacton-on-S CO16 ...188 D6
Colchester CO3 ......135 A5
Ipswich IP3 ....18 A3
Cotswold Cres CM1 ...204 C1
Cotswold Ct
Clacton-on-S CO15 ...189 A3
Highwoods CO4 ......110 C4
Cotswold Dr CO10 ....15 C6
Cotswold Rd CO15 ....188 F5
Cottage Dr CO2 ......136 D3
Cottage Gn CO16 .....188 C6
Cottage Gr CO16 .....188 C6
Cottage Pl
Chelmsford CM1 .....205 B3
3 Ipswich IP1 ......17 B6
Cottage Wlk CO16 ....188 C6
Cottey Ho CM2 ....216 B2
Cottingham Rd IP8 ....16 B3
Cottonwood Cl CO2 ...135 C4
Coulsdon Cl CO16 ....188 C6
Council Bglws
Braintree CM7 ....127 F2
Hazeleigh CM3 ......220 A4
Council Cotts
Great Holland CO13 ..169 F3
Helions Bumpstead CB9 ..8 E1
Council Hos
Bicknacre CM3 ......218 A1
Chelmondiston IP9 ..63 E2
Great Bromley CO7 ..139 A4
Hadstock CB1 ....5 B6
Holbrook IP9 ....62 D7
Peldon CO5 ....182 B5
Thorington Street CO6 .57 B3
Thorpe-le-S CO16 ...141 E2
Tolleshunt Major CM9 .197 D2
Wakes Colne CO6 ....79 C1
Council Rd CM23 .....146 A8
Counting House La CM6 .123 D4
County Pl CM2 ....205 B3
Coupals Cl CB9 ....9 C6
Coupals Cty Prim Sch CB9 .9 D7
Coupals Rd CB9 ....9 C6
Court Cl CM23 ....145 E4
Court Eight CM8 .....176 E1
Court Eighteen CM8 ..176 E1
Court Eleven CM8 ....176 E1
Court Farm CO11 .....61 A1
Court Fifteen CM8 ....176 E1
Court Five CM8 ......176 E1
Court Four CM8 ......176 E1
Court Fourteen CM8 ..176 E1
Court Nine CM8 ......176 E1
Court Nineteen CM8 ..176 E1
Court One CM8 ......176 E1
Court Rd CM1 ....191 A1
Court Seven CM8 .....176 E1
Court Seventeen CM8 .176 E1
Court Six CM8 ....176 E1
Court Sixteen CM8 ...176 E1
Court St CO6 ....56 A1
Court Ten CM8 ....176 E1
Court Thirteen CM8 ..176 E1
Court Three CM8 .....176 E1
Court Twelve CM8 ....176 E1
Court Twenty CM8 ...176 E1
Court Two CM8 ......176 E1
Courtauld Cl CO9 .....76 F1
Courtauld Homes of
Rest CO9 ....76 E1
Courtauld Rd CM7 ....128 A4
Courtenay Cl CO10 ...15 C2
Courtland Mews CM9 ..220 F4
Courtland Pl CM9 ....220 F4
Courtlands
Chelmsford CM1 .....205 A4
Halstead CO9 ....103 D8
Coval Ave CM1 ....205 A3
Coval La CM1 ....205 A2
Covehite Ct CB9 ......9 D7
Coventry Cl CO1 .....136 A4
Coverdale CM8 ....176 E1
Coverts The
West Mersea CO5 ....201 D4
Writtle CM1 ....204 B1

Cow La
Great Chesterford CB10 4 A5
Point Clear B CO16 186 C3
Cow Watering La CM1 204 A3
Cowdray Ave CO1 109 F1
Cowdray Cres CO1 135 F7
Cowdray Ctr The CO1 110 A1
Cowell Ave CM1 204 E5
Cowell St IP2 17 C3
Cowels Farm La CM6 97 E5
Cowley Rd IP11 221 E4
Cowpar Mews CM7 155 A8
Cowper St IP4 18 B6
Cowslip Cl IP2 16 E4
Cowslip Ct CO3 134 C7
Cox La IP4 17 D5
Cox Rd CO7 165 B8
Cox's Hill CO11 86 B4
Coxhall Rd IP9 36 E1
Coytes Gdns 2 IP1 17 C5
Crabb's Hill CM3 193 F2
Crabb's La CO5 178 A8
Crabbe St IP4 18 A6
Crabs Croft CM7 128 D3
Crabtree CO13 170 C8
Crabtree Hill CB11 67 C3
Crabtree La CO6 81 C1
Cracknell Cl CO7 137 B2
Craig Ct CO2 135 B3
Craig Ho CM7 128 A3
Craig's Hill CO6 79 E6
Craigfield Ave CO15 189 A6
Craigs La CO6 79 E6
Craiston Way CM2 216 F5
Cramphorn Wlk CM1 204 F3
Cranbrook La CO10 2 F1
Crane Hill IP2 16 E4
Cranford Cl CO13 170 E5
Cranham Rd CM6 95 F3
Cranleigh Cl CO16 188 B6
Cranmer Ho CM2 215 F7
Cranmer's La CO6 131 E6
Cranmere Ct CO1 136 A7
Cranmore Cl CM22 94 C2
Cranmoregreen La CO10 2 F3
Cranwell Cres IP3 18 C1
Cranwell Gdns CM23 119 C1
Craven Dr CO4 110 C3
Crawley End SG8 19 D4
Crayfields CM6 123 E1
Crayford Cl CM9 220 E8
Crayford Rd CO10 15 D2
Creance Ct CM2 205 A2
Creasen Butt Cl CM9 210 A4
Credon Cl CO15 188 F7
Credon Dr CO15 188 F7
Creek Cotts CO14 144 E4
Creek View CO5 181 F2
Creekhurst Cl CO7 186 A6
Creffield Rd CO3 135 D6
Crepping Hall Dr IP9 61 F1
Crescent Rd
Bishop's Stortford CM23 146 A6
Felixstowe IP11 221 E4
Great Baddow CM2 217 A7
Heybridge CM9 209 F5
Ipswich IP1 17 B6
Tollesbury CM9 199 E1
Walton-on-t-N CO14 171 C8
Crescent The
Clacton-on-S CO15 189 B7
Colchester CO4 110 C7
Frinton-on-S CO13 170 F4
Great Holland CO13 170 A4
Great Horkesley CO6 82 B1
Great Leighs CM3 173 E5
Marks Tey CO6 133 A3
Steeple Bumpstead CB9 27 B7
Thorpe-le-S CO16 141 F2
West Bergholt CO6 108 D5
Cress Croft CM7 128 D1
Cressages Cl CM6 152 F6
Cressing Cty Prim Sch
CM7 155 E6
Cressing Rd
Braintree CM7 128 C2
Witham CM8 176 D6
Cressing Sta CM7 155 D5
Cressing Temple Barns
CM7 156 B2
Crestlands CO7 165 B7
Cricket Hill Rd IP11 221 B5
Cricketers Cl
Broomfield CM1 191 C1
Sudbury CO10 33 E6
Cricketfield La CM23 145 E8
Crispin Cl CB9 8 D7
Critchett Terr 1 CM1 205 A3
Crittall Cl CM8 156 E4
Crittall Dr CM7 127 D4
Crittall Rd CM8 177 B3
Crix Green Villas CM6 153 D6
Croasdaile Rd CM24 119 E8
Croasdale Cl CM24 119 E8
Crocklands CO9 104 A5
Crocus Cl IP2 16 F4
Crocus Fields CB10 22 E3
Crocus Way CM1 205 E7
Croft Cl CM7 128 A3
Croft Ct CM1 205 E8
Croft Ho 3 CO9 76 F2
Croft La CB9 9 B6
Croft Rd
Clacton-on-S CO15 188 D4
Kelvedon CO5 158 B2
Sudbury CO10 33 E8
Croft St IP2 17 C3
Croft The Bures CO8 55 F1

Croft The *continued*
Earls Colne CO6 105 A6
Elsenham CM22 94 C1
Glemsford CO10 2 C4
Great Yeldham CO9 30 A2
Croft Way CM8 177 A3
Crofton Cl IP4 18 B7
Crofton Rd IP4 18 B7
Cromarty Rd IP4 18 B8
Crome Cl CO3 135 A5
Crome Rd CO16 188 D5
Cromer Rd IP1 16 F8
Cromhurst Ct CO3 135 E7
Crompton Rd IP2 16 F7
Crompton St CM1 204 F1
Cromwell Cl
Bishop's Stortford CM23 145 B7
Boreham CM3 206 D8
Cromwell Ct
11 Ipswich IP1 17 C5
Maldon CM9 210 A3
Cromwell Ctr CM8 177 B2
Cromwell Hill CM9 209 F3
Cromwell La CM9 209 F3
Cromwell Pk CM6 152 B5
Cromwell Rd
16 Colchester CO2 135 F6
Saffron Walden CB11 43 E7
Cromwell Sq 8 IP1 17 C5
Cromwell Way CM8 176 F2
Croquet Gdns CO7 137 C1
Cross Cotts CO4 83 B6
Cross Field Way CO4 83 B5
Cross Hill CO12 116 D1
Cross La CO5 201 F7
Cross Rd Maldon CM9 210 A1
Witham CM8 176 F5
Cross St Felixstowe IP11 221 C6
Saffron Walden CB10 22 D1
Sudbury CO10 33 D7
Cross The CO5 201 E7
Cross Way CO5 201 E7
Crossfield Rd CO15 188 E3
Crossfield Way CO13 170 B6
Crossfields CO6 56 C5
Crossgate Field IP11 221 C5
Crossley Ave CO15 203 E7
Crosstree Wlk CO2 136 A3
Crossways
Chelmsford CM2 216 C7
Clacton-on-S CO15 203 G8
Colne Engaine CO6 77 F1
Crotchets Cl IP9 35 A1
Crouch Ct CM7 128 D1
Crouch Dr CM8 176 E2
Crouch St CO3 135 E6
Crouchman's Farm Rd
CM9 208 C7
Croutel Rd IP11 221 F5
Crow La CO16 141 A3
Crow Pond Rd CM3 175 C3
Crow St CM22 94 F5
Crowe Hall La IP9 62 A1
Crowhall La CO11 87 E1
Crowhurst Rd CO3 135 E7
Crowland Cl 7 IP2 17 A2
Crowland Rd CB9 8 F8
Crown Bays Rd CO4 136 C8
Crown Gate CO4 110 D6
Crown La Harwich CO12 91 D4
Tendring CO16 140 D3
Crown La N CO7 110 F7
Crown La S CO7 111 A4
Crown Meadow CM7 128 D4
Crown Rd CO15 188 C1
Crown St
Castle Hedingham CO9 51 E4
Dedham CO7 84 F6
Felixstowe IP11 221 C6
Great Bardfield CM7 72 B2
Ipswich IP1 17 C6
Crown Terr CM23 146 A7
Crownfield Rd CO10 2 B6
Crownfields CO7 84 F6
Croxall Ct CM8 176 F2
Crozier Ave CM23 145 C8
Cruce Way CO16 185 F3
Crummock Cl CM7 154 C6
Crunch Croft CB9 9 E5
Crusader Way CM7 128 D2
Cuckfield Ave IP3 18 E3
Cuckoo Hill Bures CO8 55 F1
Sible Hedingham CO9 75 B8
Cuckoo Way CM7 154 C7
Cuckoos La
Great Dunmow CM6 149 A3
Takeley CM6 148 F2
Cudmore Grove Ctry Pk
CO5 185 A1
Culford Pl IP3 17 F4
Culford Wlk IP11 221 A3
Cullingham Rd IP1 17 A5
Culver St E CO1 135 F7
Culver St W CO1 135 F7
Culver Wlk 23 CO1 135 F7
Culvert Cl CO6 130 F2
Cumberland Ave CM9 209 E1
Cumberland Cl CM7 128 B4
Cumberland Cres CM1 205 A7
Cumberland Ct
Clacton-on-S CO15 189 B5
Colchester CO3 135 D6
Cumberland St IP1 17 B7
Cumberland Towers IP1 17 A7
Cunningham Cl CO2 136 A4
Cunnington Rd CM7 128 C3
Cunobelin Way CO2 135 A2
Cuppers Cl CM8 176 E1

Curds Rd CO6 105 A4
Curlew Cl
Clacton-on-S CO15 188 F6
Heybridge CM9 210 C5
Kelvedon CO5 158 D2
Curlew Croft CO4 136 F8
Curlew Rd IP2 16 D4
Curling Tye La
Maldon CM9 209 A3
Woodham Walter CM9 208 F3
Currants Farm Rd CM7 127 E5
Currents La CO12 91 E6
Curriers' La IP1 17 C5
Curtis Cl
Clacton-on-S CO16 188 B3
Ipswich IP8 16 C1
Curzon Rd CO10 34 B8
Curzon Way CM2 206 A2
Cusak Rd CM2 205 F3
Custerson Ct CB11 22 D1
Custom House La CO12 91 D6
Cut Hedge CM7 154 C6
Cut The CO5 179 C5
Cut Throat La CM8 177 A4
Cut-A-Thwart La CM9 209 C4
Cuthedge La CO6 157 D7
Cutler St IP1 17 C5
Cutlers La CO7 59 D5
Cutmaple CO9 75 E4
Cutmore Pl CM2 215 F8
Cuton Hall La CM2 206 A5
Cutting Dr CO9 76 E1
Cygnet Ct
11 Bishop's Stortford CM23 145 F6
Sible Hedingham CO9 51 E1
Cymbeline Way
(Colchester By Pass)
CO3 135 B8
Cypress Cl CO15 188 E7
Cypress Ct CM6 123 B1
Cypress Dr CM2 216 C6
Cypress Gr 5 CO4 136 F8
Cypress Mews CO5 201 B7
Cypress Rd CM8 177 A4
Cyril Child Cl CO4 136 E7
Cyril Dowsett Ct CM9 209 E2

D

D'arcy Ave CM9 210 B1
D'arcy Cl CO13 170 F6
D'Arcy Ho CO14 144 D2
D'arcy Hts CO2 136 C3
D'arcy Rd Colchester CO2 136 C3
St Osyth CO16 187 B4
Tiptree CO5 179 F2
D'arcy Way
Brightlingsea CO7 185 E7
Tolleshunt D'arcy CM9 198 E4
Daen Ingas CM3 218 D7
Daffodil Cl IP2 16 E3
Daffodil Way CM1 205 E7
Dagnets La CM7 154 D3
Dahlia Cl
2 Chelmsford CM1 205 F5
Clacton-on-S CO16 188 C4
Dahlia Wlk CO4 136 D7
Daimler Ave CO15 203 D6
Dains Pl IP11 221 A7
Dairy Rd CM2 205 F4
Dairyhouse La CO11 114 F7
Daisleys La CM3 174 A2
Daisy Ct CM1 206 A6
Daisy Green Rd CO3 133 E8
Daisyley Rd CM6 98 B4
Dale Cl CO3 134 B7
Dale Hall La IP1 17 C8
Dale Ho CM7 127 E4
Dale The CO7 164 C8
Dales The CO12 90 F1
Dales View IP8 35 E8
Dales View Rd 1 IP1 17 A8
Daleview Ave CO11 115 C5
Dalham Pl 4 CB9 9 A8
Dallwood Way CM7 128 B3
Dalrymple Cl CM1 205 D3
Daltes La CO16 187 C3
Dalton Gdns CM23 145 E4
Dalton Rd IP1 17 B6
Damant's Farm La CO16 142 D1
Damases La CM3 193 C1
Damask Rd CO3 134 C7
Dame Elizabeth Ct CM1 190 F3
Dame Johane Bradbury's
Sch CB10 22 F2
Dammant Ct 8 CO4 136 D8
Dampier Rd CO6 130 F3
Danbury Cl CO6 132 F3
Danbury Ctry Pk CM3 218 B7
Danbury Park Cty Prim
Sch CM3 218 C7
Danbury Vale CM3 219 A6
Dancing Dicks La CM8 176 A2
Dandalan Cl IP1 16 E8
Dane Acres CM23 145 D8
Dane House CM23 145 D8
Dane O'Coys Rd CM23 118 E1
Dane Pk CM23 145 D8
Dane Rd CM1 204 E2
Dane St CM23 146 A7
Danes Ct CO10 34 B4
Daneum Holt CO10 12 A6
Daniel Cole Rd CO2 135 F4
Daniel Way CM8 156 E4
Daniell Cl CO16 188 C6
Daniell Dr CO2 135 B2
Dansie Ct 7 CO4 136 C8

Daphne Cl CM7 154 C7
Daphne Ct 4 CO4 136 D8
Dapier Dr CM7 128 D3
Darcy Rise CM3 207 E1
Darkhouse La CO5 164 A8
Darnay Rise CM1 204 D6
Darnel Way CO3 134 B7
Darnet Rd CM9 199 E1
Darrell Cl CM1 205 B6
Darrell Rd IP11 221 B1
Darsham Cl IP11 221 B4
Dart Cl CM8 176 D2
Dartmouth Rd CM1 205 E6
Darwin Cl
5 Braintree CM7 127 F1
Colchester CO2 136 B1
Darwin Rd IP4 17 F5
Dashwood Cl IP8 16 D1
Datchet Ho CO3 134 F7
Daundy Cl IP2 16 D5
Davall Cl CO12 90 C1
Davey Cl Colchester CO1 136 D6
Ipswich IP3 17 F1
Davidson Cl CO10 34 D4
Davy Rd CO15 189 C8
Daw St Birdbrook CO9 28 B7
Finchingfield CM7 72 E4
Daw's Hall (Wildfowl
Farm) CO8 55 B6
Dawes La CO5 201 E8
Dawlish Rd CO15 203 I8
Dawnbrook Cl 1 IP2 16 E1
Dawnford Cl CO3 134 C7
Dawnford Ct CO3 134 C7
Dawson Cl CB10 22 F2
Dawson Dr IP11 221 A8
Days Cl CM1 205 B8
Dazeley's La CO7 85 F8
De Bohun Ct CB10 22 E2
De Burgh Rd CO3 134 E6
De Greys Cl CO10 34 C5
De Mandeville Rd CM22 94 C2
De Staunton Cl CO7 165 B7
De Vere Ave CM9 210 B1
De Vere Cl
Hatfield Peverel CM3 194 B3
Wivenhoe CO7 164 B8
De Vere Cty Prim Sch CO9 51 E4
De Vere Est CO7 166 D8
De Vere La CO7 164 B8
De Vere Rd
Colchester CO3 135 A5
Earls Colne CO6 104 F7
De Vere Way CO12 90 F2
De Veres Rd 7 CO9 76 D1
De Vigier Ave CB10 23 A2
Dead La Ardleigh CO7 111 C8
Great Bentley CO7 166 F2
Lawford CO11 86 C2
Little Clacton CO16 168 B2
Wix CO11 115 D5
Deadman's La CM2 216 C4
Deal Cl Braintree CM7 127 E6
Clacton-on-S CO15 203 J8
Deal Way CO7 185 E8
Dean Rd CB1 6 B8
Dean Rogers Pl CM7 127 F7
Dean St CO7 185 E7
Dean Wlk CM1 204 E1
Deane's Cl CO12 91 A2
Deanery Gdns CM7 127 F7
Deanery Hill CM7 127 E7
Deanes Ct CO12 91 A2
Deanhill Ave CO15 189 C5
Deans Wlk CM7 127 F8
Debden CE Prim Sch
CB11 68 B7
Debden Dr CB10 44 E2
Debden Rd Newport CB11 67 C8
Saffron Walden CB11 43 D8
Saffron Walden CB11 43 E6
Deben Cl CM8 176 E2
Deben Ct CM7 128 D1
Deben Dr CO10 34 C6
Deben High Sch IP11 221 D4
Deben Rd Colchester CO4 110 F1
Haverhill CB9 9 B8
Deben Way IP11 221 C3
Deben Wlk CO16 188 C6
Dedham Ave CO16 188 B5
Dedham CE Prim Sch CO7 85 A6
Dedham Ct CO2 136 B4
Dedham Meade CO7 84 F3
Dedham Pl 7 IP4 17 D5
Dedham Rd Ardleigh CO7 84 D1
Boxted CO4 83 B6
Lawford CO11 85 E4
Stratford St M CO7 58 E1
Deepdale Rd CO12 91 A4
Deeping Wlk CO16 187 B5
Deerhurst Chase CM3 218 F1
Deerleap Way CM7 128 D4
Defoe Cres CO4 109 E4
Deford Rd CM8 194 D8
Delamere Rd
Chelmsford CM1 204 E1
Colchester CO4 110 D3
Delius Wlk CO4 136 E6
Dell La Bishop's Stortford,
Hockerill CM23 146 A7
Bishop's Stortford,
Latchmore Bank CM22 146 B1
Dell The Colchester CO1 136 A6
Great Baddow CM2 216 F6
Great Cornard CO10 34 A6
Great Dunmow CM6 123 E1
Dellows La CM22 94 A2
Dells The 11 CM23 145 F7

Dellwood Ave IP11 221 F5
Delvyn's La CO9 52 C6
Dene Ct CM1 204 D5
Dengie Cl CM8 194 F8
Denham Cl CO7 164 C8
Denholm Ct CM8 194 F8
Denmark Gdns IP9 62 D6
Denmark Ho CM2 216 D8
Denny Ct CM23 119 B2
Denton Cl IP2 16 D2
Denton's Terr CO7 164 B8
Derby Cl IP4 18 A5
Derby Rd IP3 18 A4
Derby Road Sta IP3 18 A4
Dereham Ave IP3 17 F3
Dereham Cl CO2 135 C3
Derwent Gdns CO15 189 C6
Derwent Rd
Highwoods CO4 110 C4
Ipswich IP3 17 F3
Derwent Way
Chelmsford CM1 204 D4
Great Notley CM7 154 C7
Devereaux Cl CO14 170 F8
Devereaux Pl CO4 109 C3
Devereux Ct CO15 188 F3
Devereux Pl CO4 109 C3
Devlin Rd IP8 16 B1
Devoils La 9 CM23 145 F7
Devon Rd Colchester CO2 135 B3
Felixstowe IP11 221 D5
Devon Way Harwich CO12 90 D2
Holland-on-S CO15 189 E7
Devonshire Gdns CM7 128 B4
Devonshire Rd IP3 17 F5
Dewberry Cl 3 CO4 136 D7
Dewes Green Rd
Berden CM23 92 A8
Clavering CM23 64 F1
Dewlands CM7 155 B6
Deynes Rd CB11 68 B7
Dial Cnr CO7 166 E3
Dial La IP1 17 C6
Dial Rd CO7 166 E3
Diana Ho CO13 170 E5
Diana Way CO15 188 C2
Dickens Cl CM7 155 A8
Dickens Pl CM1 204 D7
Dickens Rd IP2 16 F5
Dicksons Cnr IP1 16 C7
Dicky Moors CM3 190 F7
Didsbury Cl IP2 16 D2
Digby Mews CO5 201 C6
Digby Rd IP4 18 C7
Dilbridge Rd E CO4 136 C8
Dilbridge Rd W CO4 136 C8
Dillestone Ct CB9 9 E5
Dillwyn St IP1 17 A6
Dillwyn St W IP1 17 A6
Dilston CM3 219 A6
Dimsdale Cres CM23 146 B6
Dinants Cres CO6 132 E3
Dinsdale Cl 1 CO4 136 C8
Dinsdale Ct IP11 221 D3
Dismals The CM3 175 B2
Distillery La CO2 136 C4
Ditchingham Gr IP5 18 F6
Dixon Ave Chelmsford CM1 204 F4
Clacton-on-S CO16 188 C6
Dixon Cl CO11 86 B4
Dixon Way CO7 137 A2
Dobbies La CO6 132 F3
Dock La CO12 117 A4
Dock Rd IP11 221 B2
Dock St IP2 17 C4
Docker Ct CO2 136 B4
Dockfield Ave CO12 90 F3
Dockwra La CM3 218 F7
Doctor's La CO10 11 D2
Docwra Rd CO5 158 C2
Doddenhill Cl CB10 22 E3
Dodmans 7 IP9 35 A1
Doe's Cnr Halstead CO9 76 D5
Hatfield Peverel CM9 194 F1
Dog Chase CM7 73 C3
Dogden La CM23 92 E2
Doggetts La CO6 132 F2
Doghouse Rd CM7 129 F4
Dogs Head St 4 IP4 17 C5
Dogwood Cl IP3 18 D2
Dolby Rise CM2 205 F2
Dolphin Ct CO13 171 B6
Dolphin Way CM23 146 A8
Dombey Cl CM1 204 F7
Dombey Rd IP2 16 F5
Doms La CM3 175 B2
Domsey Bank CO6 132 E3
Domsey Chase CO5 159 C8
Domsey La CM3 191 F5
Don Ct CM8 176 D2
Donald Way CM2 216 C7
Donard Dr CO6 108 D4
Donne Dr CO15 203 G8
Donyland Way CO5 163 F8
Dooley Rd Felixstowe IP11 221 A3
Halstead CO9 76 D1
Dorchester End CO2 136 B3
Dorchester Rd IP3 18 D3
Dordell Ct CO9 50 B8
Dorewards Ave CM7 127 F7
Dorking Cres CO16 188 C6
Dorking Wlk CM2 216 E7
Dorothy Curtice Ct CO6 133 E5
Dorothy Sayers Dr CM8 177 A5
Dorset Ave CM2 216 E6

Dorset Cl
Great Baddow CM2 . . . . . .**216** E6
Halstead CO9 . . . .**76** E1
Holland-on-S CO15 . . . . . .**189** E6
Dorset Ho 18 CM23 . . . . . .**145** F7
Dorset Rd CM9 . . . .**220** F8
Dorvis La CB10 . . . .**6** B1
Doubleday Cnr CO6 . . . . .**130** F2
Doubleday Dr CM9 . . . . . .**209** F5
Doubleday Gdns CM7 . . . .**128** B5
Doucecroft Sch CO5 . . . . .**158** C3
Douglas Cl CM2 . . . .**216** D3
Douglas Gr CM8 . . . .**176** D2
Douglas Rd
Clacton-on-S CO15 . . . . . .**188** C4
Harwich CO12 . . . .**91** B3
Douglas Wlk 3 CM2 . . . .**216** A8
Dove Cl
Bishop's Stortford CM23 . .**145** E3
Stansted
Mountfitchet CM24 . . . . .**119** E8
Dove Cres CO13 . . . .**90** D2
Dove House Rd CB9 . . . .**9** A8
Dove La CM2 . . . .**216** A6
Dove St IP4 . . . .**17** E5
Dove Tree Ct CO3 . . . .**134** C5
Dovedale Gdns CO15 . . . .**189** C6
Dover Cl Braintree CM7 . . .**127** E6
Clacton-on-S CO15 . . . . . .**203** J8
Dover Rd
Brightlingsea CO7 . . . .**185** F8
Ipswich IP3 . . . .**18** B4
Dovercourt Sta CO12 . . . . .**91** D4
Doves La CM6 . . . .**150** B2
Dowches Cotts CO5 . . . . .**158** C2
Dowches Dr CO5 . . . .**158** C3
Dowches Gdns CO5 . . . . .**158** C3
Dowding Cl CO2 . . . .**136** A4
Dowling Rd CO6 . . . .**79** F3
Downing Cl IP2 . . . .**16** F2
Downing Prim Sch IP2 . . .**16** F2
Downs Cres
Great Dunmow CM6 . . . . .**123** C1
Haverhill CB9 . . . .**8** F8
Downs Pl 2 CB9 . . . .**8** F8
Downs Rd CM9 . . . .**210** B3
Downs The
Felixstowe IP11 . . . .**221** B5
Great Dunmow CM6 . . . . .**123** D1
Downside Cl IP2 . . . .**36** F8
Downsway CM1 . . . .**205** D6
Downton Dr CB9 . . . .**8** E8
Downton Wlk CO5 . . . . . .**179** D6
Dragon's Gn CB10 . . . .**23** D1
Drake Ave IP3 . . . .**18** B2
Drake Gdns CM7 . . . .**128** C4
Drake Sq N IP3 . . . .**18** B2
Drake Sq S IP3 . . . .**18** B2
Drakes App CO15 . . . .**188** A1
Drakes Cnr CO5 . . . .**181** F2
Drakes La Boreham CM3 . .**192** B7
Little Waltham CM3 . . . . . .**191** F7
Drapers Chase
Heybridge CM9 . . . .**210** D4
Rayne CM7 . . . .**153** D8
Drapers La CB9 . . . .**8** B2
Drapery Comm CO10 . . . . . .**2** B4
Dray Ct **108** F4
Drayman's Cl CM23 . . . . . .**145** B5
Drays The CO10 . . . .**15** B5
Drayton Cl CM9 . . . .**210** A1
Dreys The CB10 . . . .**44** D8
Driberg Way CM7 . . . .**128** A1
Driffield Cl CO5 . . . .**158** C4
Drift The
Great Cornard CO10 . . . . . .**34** C5
Ipswich, Priory Heath IP3 . .**18** C1
Ipswich, Rose Hill IP4 . . . . .**18** A6
Stutton IP9 . . . .**62** C2
Driftway The IP4 . . . .**18** B6
Drive The Chelmsford CM1 **205** A6
Clacton-on-S CO15 . . . . . .**189** B7
Harwich CO12 . . . .**91** B2
Rivenhall CM8 . . . .**177** E6
Thaxted CM6 . . . .**69** F3
Drood Cl CM1 . . . .**204** F7
Drovers Way CM23 . . . . . .**145** C5
Druce The CB11 . . . .**65** D4
Drum Field CO7 . . . .**58** D1
Drury La 4 Braintree CM7 .**127** F3
Ridgewell CO9 . . . .**29** A6
Drury Rd CO2 . . . .**135** C5
Du Cane Pl 3 CM8 . . . . . .**177** A2
Duchess CM23 . . . .**145** C7
Duck St Little Easton CM6 .**122** F6
Wendens Ambo CB11 . . . . .**42** E5
Ducketts Wharf 10 CM23 .**145** F6
Duddery Hill CB9 . . . .**9** A7
Duddery Rd CB9 . . . .**9** A7
Dudley Cl Boreham CM3 . .**192** E1
Colchester CO2 . . . .**136** A4
Dudley Rd
Clacton-on-S CO15 . . . . . .**188** D3
Earls Colne CO6 . . . .**104** F7
Fingringhoe CO5 . . . .**163** E3
Duffield Dr CO4 . . . .**136** E7
Duffield Rd CM2 . . . .**216** D6
Duffries Cl CM3 . . . .**190** E7
Duffs Hill CO10 . . . .**12** B8
Dugard Ave CO3 . . . .**134** E4
Duggers La CM7 . . . .**128** A1
Dugmore Ave CO13 . . . . .**170** C8
Duke St Brightlingsea CO7 .**185** E6
Chelmsford CM1 . . . .**205** B2

Duke St continued
Ipswich IP3 . . . .**17** E4
Dukes La 5 CM2 . . . .**205** F4
Dukes Orch CM1 . . . .**204** B1
Dukes Park Ind Est CM2 . .**206** A4
Dukes Priory Hospl The
CM1 . . . .**205** D4
Dukes Rd CM7 . . . .**127** F5
Dukes Ride CM23 . . . .**145** C7
Dulverton Cotts CO3 . . . .**134** C4
Dulwich Ct CO15 . . . .**189** D4
Dulwich Rd CO15 . . . .**189** D5
Dumbarton Rd IP4 . . . .**18** C8
Dumfries Rd IP4 . . . .**18** C8
Dumney La Braintree,
Hornells Corner CM3 . . . . .**153** E2
Braintree, Thistley
Green CM3 . . . .**153** B3
Great Leighs CM3 . . . .**173** E8
Dumont Ave CO16 . . . .**186** B2
Duncan Rd CO2 . . . .**135** B4
Duncan Rise CO9 . . . .**29** F2
Dunlin Cl CM9 . . . .**210** C5
Dunlin Ct CO5 . . . .**158** C2
Dunlin Rd IP2 . . . .**16** E2
Dunlop Rd IP2 . . . .**16** F6
Dunmore Rd CM2 . . . .**206** A3
Dunmow Inf Sch CM6 . . . .**123** D1
Dunmow Rd
Bishop's Stortford CM23 . .**146** C7
Felsted CM6 . . . .**125** F2
Great Bardfield CM7 . . . . . .**98** F8
Great Hallingbury CM22 . . .**147** C7
Rayne CM7 . . . .**126** B2
Takeley CM22 . . . .**148** C7
Thaxted CM6 . . . .**97** A7
Dunning Cl CO11 . . . .**114** C8
Dunnock Way CO4 . . . . . .**137** A7
Dunoon Cl CM7 . . . .**128** D4
Dunster Dr CB9 . . . .**8** E8
Dunthorne Rd CO4 . . . . . .**110** E2
Dunthorpe Rd CO16 . . . . .**188** D6
Duntons Almshouses CO7 .**84** F6
Dunwich Ct
Colchester CO2 . . . .**135** F4
Ipswich IP1 . . . .**16** E8
Dupont Cl CO16 . . . .**188** D6
Durham Cl CM7 . . . .**72** A1
Durham Sq CO1 . . . .**136** A7
Duxford Rd CB10 . . . .**3** A7
Dyer's Rd Colchester CO3 . .**134** C3
Maldon CM9 . . . .**210** A2
Dyers Rd CO9 . . . .**28** E1
Dyke St IP1 . . . .**17** C7
Dykes Chase CM9 . . . .**209** F3
Dyne's Hall Rd CO9 . . . . . .**76** C8

E

Eagle Ave CO14 . . . .**144** D1
Eagle La CM7 . . . .**127** F6
Eagle St 3 IP4 . . . .**17** D5
Eaglegate CO1 . . . .**136** A7
Eagles Cl IP11 . . . .**221** D4
Earlhams Cl CO12 . . . .**90** F1
Earls Cl CM23 . . . .**145** D6
Earls Colne Prim Sch
CO6 . . . .**105** C6
Earls Colne Rd CO6 . . . . . .**106** A1
Earls Hall Dr CO16 . . . .**187** E5
Earlsfield Dr CM2 . . . .**205** F3
Earlsmead CM8 . . . .**176** F3
Earlswood Way CO2 . . . . .**135** D2
East Anglian Rly Mus
CO6 . . . .**106** D6
East Area IP1 . . . .**16** C7
East Bay CO1 . . . .**136** B7
East Bergholt CE Prim
Sch CO7 . . . .**59** B3
East Bergholt High Sch
CO7 . . . .**59** D3
East Bergholt Place Gdns
CO7 . . . .**59** F1
East Dock Rd CO12 . . . .**90** F6
East Donyland CE Prim
Sch CO2 . . . .**163** F8
East End Rd CO7 . . . .**60** A3
East Essex Aviation Mus
CO16 . . . .**185** E4
East Gores Rd CO6 . . . . . .**131** F5
East Hanningfield Rd
CM2 . . . .**217** E2
East Haven CO15 . . . .**188** E5
East Hill CO1 . . . .**136** A7
East La CO7 . . . .**85** B5
East Lawn IP4 . . . .**18** C8
East Mersea Rd CO5 . . . . .**183** E1
East Mill CO9 . . . .**76** F2
East Mill Gn IP9 . . . .**60** E6
East Rd
Bishop's Stortford CM23 . .**146** B7
East Mersea CO5 . . . .**184** D1
West Mersea CO5 . . . .**201** E7
East Row IP9 . . . .**62** D6
East Side CO5 . . . .**83** A4
East St Braintree CM7 . . . . .**128** A3
Coggeshall CO6 . . . .**131** A2
Colchester CO1 . . . .**136** B7
Harwich CO12 . . . .**91** D4
Saffron Walden CB10 . . . . .**22** E1
Sudbury CO10 . . . .**33** F8
Tollesbury CM9 . . . .**199** D1
Wivenhoe CO7 . . . .**164** B7
East Stockwell St CO1 . . .**135** F7
East Terr CO14 . . . .**144** D1
East View CM22 . . . .**148** C8
East View 6 CB10 . . . .**45** F8

Eastacre CB10 . . . .**22** E2
Eastby Cl CB11 . . . .**43** F8
Eastcliff Ave CO15 . . . . . .**189** B4
Eastend La CM24 . . . .**121** C8
Easterford Rd CO5 . . . .**158** C2
Easterling Cl CO12 . . . .**91** A4
Eastern App CM2 . . . .**205** F5
Eastern Ave CB9 . . . .**8** F8
Eastern Cl IP4 . . . .**18** F4
Eastern Cres CM1 . . . .**204** F5
Eastern Prom CO16 . . . . . .**185** F3
Eastern Rd CO7 . . . .**185** E6
Eastgate
Great Chesterford CB10 . . . .**3** D2
17 Ipswich IP4 . . . .**17** D6
Eastgate St CO12 . . . .**91** D6
Easthorpe Rd
Easthorpe CO5 . . . .**159** D7
Messing CO5 . . . .**159** F5
Eastland Ct IP11 . . . .**221** B7
Easton Cl CM8 . . . .**177** A3
Easton Way CO13 . . . .**171** B6
Eastway Ent Ctr IP1 . . . . . .**16** D8
Eastways CM8 . . . .**177** B4
Eastwood Dr CO4 . . . .**110** B3
Eaton Cl IP11 . . . .**221** C2
Eaton Cotts CO5 . . . .**179** D7
Eaton Gdns IP11 . . . .**221** C2
Eaton Ho 6 CM2 . . . .**146** B8
Eaton Mews CO2 . . . .**136** B3
Eaton Way CM9 . . . .**196** E7
Ebenezer Cl CM8 . . . .**176** E5
Ebenezer Terr CM2 . . . . . .**216** F7
Ebony Cl CO2 . . . .**135** D2
Eccles Rd IP2 . . . .**16** D1
Eckersley Rd CM1 . . . .**205** C3
Eden Cl CM8 . . . .**176** E3
Eden Rd Haverhill CB9 . . . . . .**9** A7
Ipswich IP4 . . . .**18** B5
Eden Way CM1 . . . .**204** C5
Edens Cl CM23 . . . .**146** B7
Edenside CO13 . . . .**170** E7
Edgefield Ave CO11 . . . . . .**86** B3
Edgeworth Rd IP2 . . . .**16** E2
Edgworth Rd CO10 . . . .**33** E7
Edgware Rd CO16 . . . .**188** D5
Edinburgh Cl CM8 . . . .**195** A8
Edinburgh Gdns
Bishop's Stortford CM23 . .**145** E6
Braintree CM7 . . . .**128** C4
Edison Cl 3 CM7 . . . .**127** F1
Edison Gdns CO4 . . . .**110** C1
Edith Borthwick Sch The
CM7 . . . .**127** F8
Edith Cavell Way CB9 . . . . .**27** C6
Edith Rd
Clacton-on-S CO15 . . . . . .**188** E5
Kirby-le-S CO13 . . . .**170** D8
Edmund Cl CB9 . . . .**8** F8
Edmund Gn CO9 . . . .**102** E8
Edmund Rd CM8 . . . .**194** E8
Edward Ave CO7 . . . .**185** F7
Edward Bright Cl CM2 . . . .**210** A2
Edward Cl Ipswich IP1 . . . . .**16** F8
Edward Cordy Ho IP11 . . .**221** E3
Edward Dr CM2 . . . .**216** C7
Edward Marke Dr CO5 . . .**163** B3
Edward Rd CO16 . . . .**168** F7
Edward St CO12 . . . .**90** E5
Edward Terr CO16 . . . .**168** E5
Edwards Wlk CM9 . . . .**209** F3
Egerton Green Rd CO2 . . .**135** A3
Egglestone Cl IP2 . . . .**16** F1
Eggshall La CM7 . . . .**27** E2
Eglinton Dr CM2 . . . .**206** B4
Egremont St CO10 . . . .**2** B3
Egremont Way CO3 . . . . . .**134** C4
Egret Cres CO4 . . . .**137** A8
Ehringshausen Way CB9 . . .**9** B7
Eight Acre La CO2 . . . .**135** C2
Eight Ash Green CE
Prim Sch CO3 . . . .**107** F1
Eld La CO1 . . . .**135** F7
Elder Field CM7 . . . .**154** B5
Elderberry Gdns CM8 . . . .**177** B4
Eldon Cl CO4 . . . .**110** E1
Eldred Ave CO2 . . . .**135** B3
Eldred Dr CO10 . . . .**34** C4
Eleanor Cl CO5 . . . .**179** D6
Eleanor Wlk CO5 . . . .**179** D6
Eleventh Ave CM24 . . . . . .**120** B2
Elgin Ave CM1 . . . .**205** A2
Elianore Rd CO3 . . . .**135** B7
Eliot Way CM9 . . . .**210** A1
Elisabeth Ct CO14 . . . .**144** E3
Elizabeth Ave CM8 . . . . . .**195** A8
Elizabeth Cl
Highwoods CO4 . . . .**110** C4
Saffron Walden CB10 . . . . .**22** F2
Elizabeth Rd
Bishop's Stortford CM23 . .**145** E5
Harwich CO12 . . . .**91** A3
Elizabeth Villas CM9 . . . . .**180** A2
Elizabeth Way
Brightlingsea CO7 . . . .**185** F6
Felixstowe IP11 . . . .**221** C3
Halstead CO9 . . . .**76** E2
Hatfield Peverel CM3 . . . . .**194** A4
Heybridge CM9 . . . .**210** A5
Saffron Walden CB10 . . . . .**22** F2
Sudbury CO10 . . . .**33** E4
Wivenhoe CO7 . . . .**137** C3
Ellen Friend Ho CM23 . . .**146** B6
Ellen Way CM7 . . . .**154** D7
Ellenborough Cl CM23 . . .**145** D5
Ellenbrook Gn IP2 . . . .**16** D1

Ellenbrook Rd IP2 . . . .**16** D1
Elliots Dr CO14 . . . .**171** B8
Elliott St IP1 . . . .**17** A6
Ellis Rd Boxted CO4 . . . .**82** F3
Bradfield CO11 . . . .**114** D8
Clacton-on-S CO15 . . . . . .**188** E2
Elm Ave CM9 . . . .**210** C5
Elm Bglws CM3 . . . .**127** D4
Elm Cl Alresford CO7 . . . . .**165** B8
Brantham CO11 . . . .**60** D1
Chelmsford CM1 . . . .**205** A8
Elsenham CM22 . . . .**94** C2
Great Baddow CM2 . . . . . .**216** F6
Great Bentley CO7 . . . .**166** E8
Haverhill CB9 . . . .**8** F8
Sible Hedingham CO9 . . . . .**51** D2
Takeley CM22 . . . .**148** C7
Tiptree CO5 . . . .**179** C7
Elm Close Extension
CM22 . . . .**148** C7
Elm Cres CO4 . . . .**136** D7
Elm Dr Brightlingsea CO7 . .**185** D7
Sturmer CB9 . . . .**9** E5
Elm Ho IP11 . . . .**221** C4
Elm La Capel St M IP9 . . . . .**35** A1
Marks Tey CO5 . . . .**132** B2
Washbrook IP8 . . . .**35** E8
Elm Rd
Bishop's Stortford CM23 . .**145** F8
Chelmsford CM2 . . . .**216** A8
East Bergholt CO7 . . . .**59** C3
Little Clacton CO16 . . . . . .**168** C3
Rushmere St A IP5 . . . .**18** F7
Sudbury CO10 . . . .**34** A7
Wivenhoe CO7 . . . .**137** B1
Elm Green La CM3 . . . .**218** C8
Elm Green Sch CM3 . . . . . .**207** D3
Elm Ho IP11 . . . .**221** C4
Elm Rise CM8 . . . .**177** A5
Elm St IP1 . . . .**17** C6
Elm Tree Ave CO13 . . . . . .**170** F7
Elm Tree Cl CO13 . . . .**170** F7
Elm Way CM3 . . . .**192** E1
Elm Wlk CM7 . . . .**126** F2
Elmbrook Dr CM23 . . . . . .**145** E3
Elmcroft CO7 . . . .**138** A6
Elmdale Dr CO11 . . . .**86** D3
Elmden Ct CO15 . . . .**188** E5
Elmdon Pl 1 CB9 . . . .**9** B8
Elmfield Cl CO15 . . . .**189** E7
Elmhurst Cl CB9 . . . .**9** B7
Elmhurst Dr IP3 . . . .**17** F3
Elmhurst Rd CO12 . . . .**91** C3
Elms Dr CM1 . . . .**205** A4
Elms Hall Rd CO6 . . . .**104** C8
Elms The East Bergholt CO7 **60** C3
Frinton-on-S CO13 . . . .**170** F6
Great Chesterford CB10 . . . .**3** E3
Elmstead Prim Sch CO7 . .**137** F6
Elmstead Rd
Colchester CO4 . . . .**136** E5
Wivenhoe CO7 . . . .**137** D4
Elmwood Ave CO2 . . . .**135** B2
Elmwood Dr CO5 . . . .**201** D7
Elsenham CE Prim Sch
CM22 . . . .**94** D1
Elsenham Sta CM22 . . . . . .**94** C3
Elsham Dr CM7 . . . .**154** B6
Elsmere Rd IP1 . . . .**17** C8
Elthorne Pk CO16 . . . .**188** D4
Elton Park Bsns Ctr IP2 . . .**16** D6
Elton Pk IP2 . . . .**16** D6
Elton Wlk CO5 . . . .**179** D6
Elvina Ho CO15 . . . .**203** F6
Elwes Cl CO4 . . . .**110** D1
Elwin Rd CO5 . . . .**179** D5
Elysian Gdns CM9 . . . .**199** C1
Embassy Ct CM9 . . . .**210** A2
Emberson Ct CM2 . . . .**205** F4
Emblems CM6 . . . .**123** C1
Embra Ct CO2 . . . .**136** B5
Emily May Ct CO12 . . . .**91** A3
Emlen St IP1 . . . .**17** A6
Emmanuel Cl IP2 . . . .**16** F3
Empire Ct CO15 . . . .**188** E3
Empire Rd CO12 . . . .**91** D3
Empire Wlk 2 CM2 . . . . . .**205** C2
Empress Ave CO15 . . . . . .**201** E6
Empress Dr CO5 . . . .**201** D6
Emson Cl CB10 . . . .**22** D2
Endean Ct CO7 . . . .**137** A2
Endeavour Ct CM9 . . . . . .**199** D2
Endsleigh Ct CO3 . . . .**135** C7
Endway The
Great Easton CM6 . . . .**122** F8
Steeple Bumpstead CB9 . . . .**27** C8
Engleric SG8 . . . .**19** D5
Enid Way CO4 . . . .**109** D2
Ennerdale Ave CM7 . . . . . .**154** C6
Enterprise Ct
Braintree CM7 . . . .**128** B2
Witham CM8 . . . .**177** A3
Enville Way CO4 . . . .**110** B4
Epping Cl Chelmsford CM1 **204** E1
Clacton-on-S CO15 . . . . . .**188** F8
Epping Way CM8 . . . .**176** E1
Epsom Cl CO16 . . . .**188** D6
Erbury Pl CO10 . . . .**12** B8

Erica Wlk CO4 . . . .**136** D7
Erick Ave CM1 . . . .**205** B4
Eridge Cl CM1 . . . .**205** D7
Eriswell Rd CB9 . . . .**9** B8
Erle Havard Rd CO6 . . . . .**108** E4
Ernest Rd CO7 . . . .**137** C1
Ernleigh Rd IP4 . . . .**18** B6
Errington Rd CO3 . . . .**135** D5
Erskine Rd CO11 . . . .**86** D4
Esplanade
Frinton-on-S CO13 . . . .**170** F3
Harwich CO12 . . . .**91** E4
Esplanade Ct
Frinton-on-S CO13 . . . .**171** A5
Harwich CO12 . . . .**91** E6
Esplanade The CO15 . . . . .**189** G6
Essex Ave Chelmsford CM1 **205** A7
Clacton-on-S CO15 . . . . . .**203** E6
Sudbury CO10 . . . .**15** F2
Essex Cty Hospl CO3 . . . . .**135** D6
Essex Hall Rd CO1 . . . .**109** E1
Essex Hill CB11 . . . .**20** B2
Essex Knowle CO8 . . . .**55** F1
Essex Rd Braintree CM7 . . .**128** B3
Maldon CM9 . . . .**209** F1
Essex Regiment Way
Howe Street CM3 . . . .**173** A2
Little Waltham CM3 . . . . . .**191** D5
Essex Show Ground CM3 **154** A2
Essex Way IP3 . . . .**18** E1
Essex Yeomanry Way
CO3 . . . .**134** B7
Estella Mead CM1 . . . .**204** B8
Estuary Cl CO4 . . . .**109** C4
Estuary Cres
Clacton-on-S CO15 . . . . . .**188** D3
Shotley Gate IP9 . . . .**91** B8
Estuary Mews CM9 . . . . . .**199** D3
Estuary Park Rd CO5 . . . . .**201** E6
Estuary Rd IP9 . . . .**91** B8
Eton Cl CO13 . . . .**171** A5
Eton Rd Clacton-on-S CO15 **188** F4
Frinton-on-S CO13 . . . .**171** A5
Eudo Rd CO2 . . . .**135** C4
Euro Ret Pk IP3 . . . .**18** D1
Europa Way Harwich CO12 .**90** F4
Ipswich IP1 . . . .**16** D7
Eustace Rd IP1 . . . .**16** E8
Euston Ave IP4 . . . .**18** F6
Euston Ct IP11 . . . .**221** A4
Evabrook Cl IP2 . . . .**16** E1
Evelyn Rd CM3 . . . .**153** C2
Evelyn Wood Rd CM7 . . . .**155** E6
Everest Way CM9 . . . .**210** B5
Everett Ho CO1 . . . .**136** B6
Everett Way CO9 . . . .**51** E2
Evergreen Dr CO4 . . . .**110** D4
Everitt Rd CO10 . . . .**22** F2
Eves Cnr CM3 . . . .**218** E7
Eves Cres CM1 . . . .**205** A5
Eves Ct CO12 . . . .**90** C1
Eves Orch CO8 . . . .**55** F1
Evesham Cl IP2 . . . .**17** A2
Ewan Cl CO3 . . . .**134** C6
Ewan Way CO3 . . . .**134** C7
Ewell Hall Chase CO5 . . . .**158** C4
Exchange Way 5 CM1 . . . .**205** B2
Exeter Cl Braintree CM7 . . .**128** B5
Great Horkesley CO6 . . . . .**109** C7
Exeter Ct 6 CB9 . . . .**8** E6
Exeter Dr CO1 . . . .**136** A7
Exeter Rd Chelmsford CM1 **205** C6
Felixstowe IP11 . . . .**221** D5
Ipswich IP3 . . . .**18** B4
Exmoor Cl CM1 . . . .**204** D1
Exmoor Rd IP11 . . . .**221** D6

F

Faber Rd CM8 . . . .**194** E8
Fabians Cl CO6 . . . .**131** A3
Factory Hill CO5 . . . .**179** E3
Factory La CO11 . . . .**86** C7
Factory La E CO7 . . . .**76** E1
Factory La W CO9 . . . .**76** E1
Factory Terr CO9 . . . .**76** E2
Faggot Yd CM7 . . . .**127** F5
Fair Cl CO7 . . . .**186** A6
Fair Leas CB10 . . . .**22** E3
Fairbrother Ct 1 CO4 . . . .**136** D7
Fairclough Ave CO16 . . . . .**188** B3
Fairfax Mead CM2 . . . .**206** A2
Fairfax Rd 17 CO2 . . . .**135** F6
Fairfield Ave IP11 . . . .**221** E5
Fairfield Cl CO7 . . . .**139** C4
Fairfield Gdns 2 CO4 . . . .**136** C8
Fairfield Inf Sch IP11 . . . . .**221** E5
Fairfield Rd Braintree CM7 **127** F2
Chelmsford CM1 . . . .**205** B3
Clacton-on-S CO15 . . . . . .**188** E4
Ipswich IP3 . . . .**18** A2
Fairfield Way CO9 . . . .**76** D1
Fairfields CM3 . . . .**220** D1
Fairhaven Ave CO5 . . . . . .**201** E6
Fairhead Rd N CO4 . . . . . .**136** C8
Fairhead Rd S 6 CO4 . . . . .**136** C8
Fairleads CM3 . . . .**218** F8
Fairlop Cl CO15 . . . .**188** F8
Fairstead Hall Rd CM3 . . .**175** C5
Fairstead Rd CM3 . . . .**175** C5
Fairway
Bishop's Stortford CM23 . .**146** C6
Chelmsford CM2 . . . .**216** D7
Fairways CO4 . . . .**109** B3
Fairways The IP4 . . . .**18** E5
Fairy Hall La CM7 . . . .**127** A1
Fairycroft Rd CB10 . . . .**22** E1

Fal Dr CM8 ....176 E2
Falcon Cl CB9 ......9 C8
Falcon Cres CO1 ....136 B5
Falcon Fields CM9 ....220 F8
Falcon Mews CM9 ....220 F8
Falcon Sq CO9 ....51 F4
Falcon St Felixstowe IP11 .221 C6
　Ipswich IP1 ....17 C5
Falcon Way
　Chelmsford CM2 ....216 A6
　Clacton-on-S CO15 ...188 F6
Falcon Yd CO7 ......164 B8
Falconer Rd CB9 .....9 C5
Falconer St CM23 ...145 C5
Falkland Cl CM3 ....206 E8
Falkland Ct CM7 ....128 B4
Falkland Gn CM7 ....219 E6
Falklands Dr 7 CO11 ..86 D4
Fallowden La CB10 ...23 F8
Fallowfield CO12 .....90 F3
Fallowfield 14 CB9 ...8 E7
Fallowfield Rd CO2 ..135 C2
Falmouth Rd CM1 ...205 E5
Fambridge Chase CM8 ..155 F2
Fambridge CM9 .....210 A1
Fambridge Rd
　Maldon CM9 ....209 F2
　Maldon CM9 ....220 F6
Fanner's Green Cotts
　CM3 ....190 C5
Fanny's La CO16 ....167 D2
Faraday Cl Braintree CM7 .127 F1
　Clacton-on-S CO15 ...169 A1
Faraday Rd IP4 ....17 F5
Farford Field CO10 ...34 C5
Farm Rd CO12 ......116 D3
Farm Wlk CO7 ......185 E8
Farmadine CB11 .....22 E1
Farmadine Ct 3 CB11 ..22 E1
Farmadine Gr CB11 ..22 E1
Farmadine Ho 5 CB11 ..22 E1
Farmers Way CO16 ..188 B3
Farmfield Rd CO6 ....106 B1
Farmleigh Ave CO15 ..188 F8
Farnham CE Prim Sch
　CM23 ....118 D6
Farnham Rd CM23 ...118 F3
Farriers End CO3 ....134 D5
Farriers Went IP11 ..221 B7
Farrington Cl 3 CO1 .136 C6
Farrow Rd CM1 ......215 E7
Farthing Cl CM7 ....128 D4
Farthing Rd IP1 ......16 C7
Farthing Road Ind Est IP1 16 C7
Farthings Went IP9 ..35 B2
Fastnet Cl CB9 ....9 D8
Faulds Wlk CO2 .....136 A3
Faulkbourne Rd CM8 ..176 A4
Faulkeners Way IP11 ..221 A8
Fawkner Cl CM2 .....205 F2
Fawley Cl IP4 ....18 C7
Feathers Field IP11 ..221 B5
Feedhams Cl CO7 ...137 C3
Feering CE Prim Sch
　CO5 ....158 E4
Feering Hill CO5 ....158 D3
Feering Mus CO5 ....158 B1
Felaw St IP2 ....17 D4
Felix Rd Felixstowe IP11 .221 F4
　Ipswich IP3 ....18 C2
Felixstowe Rd CO16 ..188 A4
Felixstowe General
　Hosp IP11 ....221 F4
Felixstowe Rd IP3 ....18 B3
Felixstowe Sta IP11 ..221 E5
Fell Christy CM1 ....205 B5
Fell Rd CO9 ....28 B8
Fellbrigg Ave IP5 .....18 F6
Felnor Wlk IP11 .....221 E4
Felstead Cl CO2 ....163 A8
Felsted Almshouses CM6 152 B6
Felsted Cty Prim Sch
　CM6 ....152 D7
Felsted Sch CM6 ....152 C6
Feltwell Pl 2 CB9 .....9 B8
Fen La CO7 ....84 D1
Fen Mdw IP11 ....221 A8
Fen St CO6 ....56 B1
Fen View IP8 ....35 E8
Fenbridge La CO7 ....59 B1
Fenman Ct CM22 .....94 C2
Fenn Cl CO7 ....139 A3
Fenn Rd CO9 ....77 A1
Fennell Cl CO5 .....179 C5
Fennels Cl CB9 ....9 A7
Fennes Rd CM7 ....102 A3
Fennings Chase CO1 ..136 A7
Fenno Cl CO3 ....134 F4
Fenton Rd CB9 ....9 B8
Ferdinand Wlk CO4 ..136 F7
Ferguson Cl CB11 ....23 A2
Fern Gr CB9 ....8 E8
Fern Hill CO10 ....2 B7
Fern Way CO15 .....203 F7
Ferndale Cl CO15 ...188 F7
Ferndale Rd IP1 .....18 D5
Ferndown Rd CO13 ..170 C5
Ferndown Rd CM3 ..194 B4
Fernhayes Cl IP2 .....17 A2
Fernie CM7 ....127 D2
Fernlea CO4 ....109 C2
Fernlea Rd CO12 .....91 D5
Ferry La Felixstowe IP11 .221 A3
　Felixstowe IP11 ....221 B3
Ferry Rd CO5 ....164 B6
Festival Gdns CM9 ..198 D4
Feverills Rd CO16 ...168 D4

Fiat Ave CO15 ......203 D6
Fiddlers Folly CO3 ..107 E1
Fiddlers Hill CO3 ...107 E2
Fiddlers La CO7 ......59 C3
Field Ct CO4 ....136 E8
Field Gate La CM22 ...94 A3
Field View Dr CM9 ..197 C4
Field Way CO7 ......137 C2
Fieldgate Dock CO7 ..185 E5
Fields Cl CO16 ......167 F6
Fields Farm Rd CO2 ..162 B4
Fieldside CB11 ....43 E7
Fifth Ave Chelmsford CM1 .205 B6
　Frinton-on-S CO13 ...170 E5
　Halstead CO9 ......77 B1
　Stansted
　Mountfitchet CM24 ...120 B2
Finbars Wlk IP4 ......17 F5
Finborough Cl IP4 ....18 F6
Finch Dr Braintree CM7 ..127 D4
　Great Bentley CO7 ..139 D1
Finch Hill CO10 ......33 A7
Finch's CM8 ....195 F6
Finchdale CO15 .....188 F6
Finchingfield CE Prim
　Sch CM7 ....72 D6
Finchingfield Guildhall
　Mus CM7 ....72 D6
Finchingfield Rd
　Stambourne CO9 ....49 C7
　Steeple Bumpstead CB9 .27 C6
Finchingfield Way CO2 .163 A8
Finchley Ave CM2 ...216 A8
Finchley Rd IP4 ......17 E6
Findley Cl IP9 ....61 F2
Finer Cl CO16 ......188 E5
Fingringhoe CE Prim
　Sch CO5 ....163 F5
Fingringhoe Rd
　Abberton CO5 ......163 B3
　Colchester CO2 ....136 D1
Fingringhoe Wick
　Nature Reserve &
　Visitor Ctr CO5 ....164 D3
Finham CO15 ....136 F7
Finsbury Pl CO9 .....76 F2
Fir Tree Cl CO4 ....110 B4
Fir Tree Hill IP9 .....62 E4
Fir Tree La CM3 ....207 E1
Fir Tree Rise
　Chelmsford CM2 ...216 B6
　Ipswich IP8 ....16 C2
Fir Tree Wlk CM9 ...210 C5
Fir Way CO15 ......203 G6
Firebronds Rd IP9 ....62 D5
Firecrest Rd CM2 ...216 C5
Firlands CM23 ......145 E6
Firlands Ho CM23 ...145 E6
Firlie Wlk CO2 ......136 A2
Firmins Ct CO6 .....108 D4
Firs Chase CO5 .....201 A6
Firs Dr CM1 ....204 B1
Firs Hamlet CO5 ....201 A6
Firs Jun & Mid Sch The
　CM23 ....145 E6
Firs Rd Tiptree CO5 ..179 D4
　West Mersea CO5 ...201 B7
First Ave Chelmsford CM1 .205 B5
　Clacton-on-S CO15 ..189 B4
　Frinton-on-S CO13 ..170 E4
　Glemsford CO10 .....2 C5
　Halstead CO9 ......77 B1
　Harwich CO12 ......91 C3
　St Osyth CO16 .....203 C6
　Stansted
　Mountfitchet CM24 ...120 B2
　Walton-on-t-N CO14 ..144 E3
　Weeley CO16 ......140 F1
Firstore Dr CO3 ....134 E7
Firwood's Rd CO9 ...103 E8
Fish Pond Hill IP9 ....63 C3
Fish St CM9 ....211 E6
Fishbane Cl IP3 ......38 B8
Fisher Cl CB9 ....9 D8
Fisher Way CM7 ....128 C4
Fisher's La CO7 ......60 C1
Fishmarket St CM6 ...70 A2
Fishponds Hill CO6 ...81 F4
Fishponds La IP9 .....62 E5
Fisin Wlk CO3 ......134 E3
Fiske Ct CO15 ......188 F2
Fitches Cres CM9 ...210 B1
Fitches Croft CO6 ...133 C4
Fitzgerald Cl CO11 ...86 B4
Fitzgerald Cotts CO12 ..90 F1
Fitzgilbert Rd CO2 ...135 C4
Fitzmaurice Rd IP3 ...18 B3
Fitzpiers CB10 ....22 E2
Fitzroy St 2 IP1 .....17 C6
Fitzwalter La CM3 ...218 D6
Fitzwalter Pl
　Chelmsford CM1 ....204 E3
　Great Dunmow CM6 ..150 A4
Fitzwalter Rd
　Boreham CM3 ......206 F8
　Colchester CO3 ....135 B6
Fitzwilliam Cl IP2 ....16 F2
Fitzwilliam Rd CO3 ..135 B6
Five Acres Danbury CM3 .218 F3
　Holbrook IP9 ....62 D5
　Stansted
　Mountfitchet CM24 ...119 E8
　Walton-on-t-N CO14 ..171 B8
Five Ways CO3 ......134 D4
Fiveash La CM7 .....129 E1
Flag Hill CO7 ....186 F8
Flagstaff Rd CO2 ...135 F6
Flail Cl CO7 ....137 C2

Flanders Cl CM7 ....127 E5
Flanders Field CO2 ..136 B3
Flatford Dr CO16 ...188 B5
Flatford Mill CO7 .....85 D7
Flatford Rd CO7 .....85 C8
Flavian Cl CB9 ....9 D7
Flax La CO10 ....2 C3
Fleetwood Ave
　Felixstowe IP11 ...221 F5
　Holland-on-S CO15 ..189 E7
Fleetwood Cl CO15 ..189 E7
Fleetwood Rd IP11 ..221 F5
Fleming Cl 7 CM7 ..127 F1
Flemish Ct CO1 .....135 F8
Fletcher Rd IP3 ......18 A1
Flint Cl IP2 ....17 B2
Flintwich Manor CM1 .204 E7
Flitch Ind Est The CM6 .150 D7
Flitch La CM6 ....150 E7
Flixton CO16 ....188 A4
Flora Rd CM8 ....176 D4
Florence Cotts CO7 ..185 F6
Florence Rd CO14 ...144 E2
Florence Wlk 8 CM23 ..145 F8
Florie's Rd CO5 .....131 F8
Flowers Way CO15 ..203 G7
Flumsey Row CM1 ..204 B1
Foley Cotts CM7 ....102 D3
Folkards La CO7 ....185 F8
Folly La CO7 ....35 A2
Folly Mill La CM6 .....96 E6
Folly The Layer-de-l-H CO2 .162 A5
　Tiptree CO5 ....179 F2
　Wivenhoe CO7 .....164 C7
Fonnereau Rd IP1 ....17 C6
Ford End CE Prim Sch
　CM3 ....172 B6
Ford La Aresford CO7 ..165 A5
　Colchester CO5 ....109 D5
Ford Rd CO15 ......188 D3
Ford St CO6 ....107 C2
Fordham CE Prim Sch
　CO6 ....107 D4
Fordham Pl IP4 ......18 F5
Fordham Rd Bures CO6, CO8 79 F2
　Wormingford CO6 ...80 E2
Fordson Rd CM2 ...206 B6
Fordstreet Hill CO6 ..107 C2
Fordwich Rd CO7 ...165 E1
Fore Field CM7 .....128 D3
Fore Hamlet IP3 .....17 E5
Fore St IP4 ....17 D5
Forefield Gn CM7 ...205 F7
Foresight Rd CO2 ...136 E2
Forest Dr CM1 ......204 E1
Forest Park Ave CO15 .188 F7
Forest Rd Colchester CO4 .136 D7
　Witham CM8 ......177 A5
Foresthall Rd CM24 ..119 E4
Forfar Ct IP4 ....18 B8
Forfields Way CM7 ..155 E6
Forge Cotts CO10 ....13 E6
Forge Cres CM7 ....129 D3
Forge St CO7 ....85 A6
Forres CO13 ....170 F4
Forsyth Dr CM7 ....155 A8
Forsythia Cl CM1 ...205 E7
Forties Cl CB9 ....9 D8
Fortinbras Way CM2 .216 B8
Fortis CM8 ....194 E8
Fortune Cl CM3 ....174 A7
Fossetts La CO6 ....107 F4
Foster Ct 2 CM8 ...177 A2
Foster Rd
　Great Totham CM9 ..196 A4
　Harwich CO12 ......90 E5
Foster's Cotts CM7 ..129 D2
Foundation St 18 IP4 .17 C5
Foundry La Copford CO6 .133 D5
　Earls Colne CO6 ...105 B6
　Ipswich IP2 ....17 C5
Fountain Ct CO12 ....91 E5
Fountain La CM7 ....134 A1
　Easthorpe CO6 .....160 F8
Fountains Rd IP2 ....16 F1
Four Acres
　Great Chesterford CB10 ..3 E3
　Saffron Walden CB11 ..22 E1
Four Ash Hill CO9 ...10 E1
Four Ashes CM7 .....74 C1
Four Sisters CO7 .....59 B5
Fourth Ave
　Chelmsford CM1 ....205 B5
　Clacton-on-S CO15 ..189 B4
　Frinton-on-S CO13 ..170 E4
　Glemsford CO10 .....2 B5
　Halstead CO9 ......77 B1
　St Osyth CO16 .....203 B6
Fourways CM22 ......94 C1
Fowe's La CO10 ......31 B8
Fowler Ct CM2 ......216 A4
Fowlers Arc CO13 ...170 F4
Fowlmere Rd SG8 ....19 A6
Fox Burrows La CM1 .204 B2
Fox Cres CM1 ......204 F4
Fox Yd CO9 ....53 C5
Fox's Ave CO10 .....11 C1
Foxburrow Rd IP3 ...18 F1
Foxdells La CM23 ...118 F2
Foxden CM8 ....177 D6
Foxendale Folly CO3 ..134 C7
Foxes La CO3 ....133 D8
Foxglove Cl
　Bishop's Stortford CM23 .145 C6
　Clacton-on-S CO15 ..188 F7
　Witham CM8 ....176 D3
Foxglove Cres IP3 ....18 A5

Foxglove Way CM1 ..205 F6
Foxglove Wlk 4 CO4 .136 E7
Foxglove Way IP11 ..221 F5
Foxhall Cl CO7 ....59 C4
Foxhall Fields CO7 ...59 C3
Foxhall Rd IP3 ....18 D5
Foxholes Rd CM2 ...216 F6
Foxley Dr CM23 ....146 B8
Foxmead CM8 ......177 D6
Foxtail Rd IP3 ....38 E8
Foxwood Cl CO11 ...85 C2
Foxwood Cres IP4 ...18 F5
Frambury La CB11 ...66 F8
Framlingham Ct 5 IP1 .17 A8
Framlingham Way CM7 .154 C7
Frampton Rd IP3 .....38 A8
Frances Cl CM7 .....137 B2
Francis Cl Haverhill CB9 ..8 F1
　Tiptree CO5 ....179 C4
Francis Rd Braintree CM7 .127 D2
　Sudbury CO10 ......33 E7
Francis St CO7 .....185 F5
Francis Way
　Colchester CO4 ....110 D1
　Silver End CM8 ....156 C4
Franciscan Way IP1 ..17 C5
Frank Clater Cl CO4 ..136 C8
Frank Naylor Ct 12 CO1 ..135 F7
Franklin Rd IP3 ......18 B2
Fraser Cl CM2 ......216 C8
Fraser Rd IP1 ....16 F7
Frating Abbey Farm Rd
　CO7 ....166 C6
Frating Cross CO7 ...166 B7
Frating Ct CM7 .....128 C1
Frating Hill CO7 ....138 D3
Frating Rd Ardleigh CO7 .111 F6
　Great Bromley CO7 ..138 F6
　Thorrington CO7 ...166 A7
Fredrick J French Meml
　Homes CM1 ....205 B6
Fredricks Cl CO7 ....115 B5
Freebournes Ct 5 CM8 ..177 A2
Freebournes Rd CM8 .177 B2
Freehold Rd IP4 ......18 B6
Freeland Rd CO15 ...188 E1
Freelands CO7 ....186 C6
Freewood La CB11 ...20 B3
Fremantle Rd CO2 ...136 B1
Frenche's Sq 1 CM2 .205 C2
Frenche's Wlk 4 CM2 .205 C2
Frensham Cl CO3 ....134 D7
Frere Ct CM23 ......118 F1
Frere Way CO5 .....164 B6
Freshfields CO12 .....90 F1
Freshwater Cres CM9 .210 C4
Freshwell Gdns CB10 ..22 C2
Freshwell St CB10 ...22 D2
Fresian Cl CM7 .....127 D2
Freston Hill IP9 ......37 E4
Freston St IP9 ....37 E3
Friars IP9 ....60 B8
Friars Bridge Rd IP1 ..17 B5
Friars Cl
　Clacton-on-S CO15 ..188 E6
　Colchester CO4 ....110 C4
　Sible Hedingham CO9 ..51 D2
　Wivenhoe CO7 .....164 C6
Friars Ct CO2 ......136 C3
Friars Ctyd 16 1 IP1 ..17 C5
Friars Grove Jun & Inf
　Schs CO4 ....110 C4
Friars La Braintree CM7 .127 F4
　Maldon CM9 ....209 F2
Friars St Ipswich IP1 ..17 C5
　Sudbury CO10 ......33 E7
Friars Wlk CM2 .....205 B1
Friars Wood CM23 ..146 C8
Friday Wood Gn CO2 .162 F8
Friedberg Ave CM23 .145 D4
Friends Field CO8 ....55 F1
Friends Wk CB11 ....43 D7
Frietuna Rd CO13 ...170 E6
Frinton Cl CO13 ....170 D3
Frinton Park Ct CO14 .171 A6
Frinton Rd
　Holland-on-S CO15 ..189 D6
　Kirby Cross CO13 ..170 D6
　Thorpe-le-S CO16 ..142 B1
Frinton-on-Sea Cty
　Prim Sch CO13 ....170 E5
Frinton-on-Sea Sta
　CO13 ....170 F5
Fritillary Cl IP8 ......36 E8
Fritton Cl IP2 ....17 A1
Fritton Ct 19 CB9 .....8 E7
Frobisher Cty Prim Sch
　CO15 ....187 F1
Frobisher Dr CO15 ..187 F1
Frobisher Rd Harwich CO12 90 F1
　Ipswich IP3 ....18 E2
Frobisher Way CM7 ..128 C4
Frog Hall Cl CO5 ....164 B6
Frog Mdw CO7 ......84 F7
Frogge St CB10 ....3 B3
Fronk's Ave CO12 ....91 C2
Fronk's Rd CO12 .....91 B2
Front Rd IP3 ....18 D8
Frowick La CO16 ...167 B2
Fryatt Ave CO12 .....91 A4
Fuchsia Cl 6 CO4 ...136 E7
Fuchsia La IP4 ....18 A5
Fuchsia Way CO16 ..188 C5
Fulcher Ave CM2 ...205 F3
Fulfen Way CB11 ....43 D7
Fullbridge CM9 .....210 A3

Fuller Ct 3 CM23 ...146 A7
Fuller's Cl CO5 .....158 B2
Fullers Rd CO2 .....136 D2
Fulmar Cl CO4 .....137 A8
Fulton Cres CM23 ..146 C8
Furneaux La CO5 ...163 F5
Furness Cl IP2 ....36 F8
Furriers Cl CM23 ...145 C5
Furrow Cl CO3 .....134 C5
Further Meadow CM1 .215 A8
Furze Cres CO7 ....165 A7
Furze La CO7 ......139 A5

G

Gablefields CM2 ....217 D6
Gaces Acre CB11 ....43 A1
Gadwall Reach CO5 .158 D2
Gage's Rd
　Belchamp St P CO10 ..13 A1
　Little Yeldham C10 ..30 F8
Gager Dr CO5 ......179 E5
Gaiger Cl CM1 .....205 D7
Gainsborough Cl
　Clacton-on-S CO16 ..188 B6
　West Mersea CO5 ..201 D6
Gainsborough Cres CM23 .205 E3
Gainsborough Dr CO11 .86 C4
Gainsborough La IP3 ..37 F7
Gainsborough Rd
　Colchester CO3 ....135 B5
　Felixstowe IP11 ...221 F4
　Ipswich IP4 ....17 D8
　Sudbury CO10 ......33 E8
Gainsborough St CO10 ..33 E7
Gainsborough's House
　Mus CO10 ....33 E7
Gainsford Ave CO15 .189 B4
Gainsford End Rd CO9 ..50 B6
Galiots CO5 ....201 A6
Gall End La CM24 ..119 F7
Galleydene Ave CM2 .216 C3
Galleywood Cty Inf Sch
　CM2 ....216 C2
Galleywood Rd
　Chelmsford CM2 ...216 A5
　Great Baddow CM2 .216 E5
Galliford Rd CM9 ...210 A4
Galloway Cl 1 CM23 .145 F8
Galloway Dr CO16 ..168 D3
Galloway Rd CM23 ..118 F1
Gallows Green Rd CM6 .97 F2
Gallows Hill CB11 ...43 C7
Galsworthy Cl CM7 .155 A7
Gandish Cl CO7 ......59 D1
Gandish Rd CO7 .....59 C2
Ganges Rd IP9 ......91 B8
Gannet Cl CB9 ....9 C8
Gannet Rd IP2 ....16 E3
Gaol La CO10 ....33 E7
Gap The Arkesden CB11 ..41 F1
　Holland-on-S CO15 ..189 G6
Garden Ct CO13 ....170 E4
Garden Farm CO5 ..201 D7
Garden Field
　Felixstowe IP11 ...221 C5
　Hatfield Peverel CM3 .193 H4
Garden Field Cotts CO6 ..81 E5
Garden Fields
　Great Tey CO6 .....132 C8
　Stebbing CM6 ......124 D6
Garden Pl CO10 ......33 D7
Garden Rd
　Clacton-on-S CO15 ..203 G7
　Walton-on-t-N CO14 .171 A7
Garden Terr CO9 .....76 F2
Gardeners CM2 .....216 D5
Gardeners Rd CO9 ...76 F1
Gardenia Pl CO16 ..188 B4
Gardenia Wlk CO4 ..136 E7
Garfield Cl IP11 ....221 D3
Garfield Rd CO12 ....90 F5
Garland Rd CO12 ....90 F5
Garnetts CM22 .....148 B8
Garnetts Bglws CM6 .152 C5
Garnetts La CM6 ...152 C6
Garnetts Villas CM6 .152 C5
Garnons Chase CO6 ..81 A5
Garrettlands CM2 ...217 F6
Garrison La IP11 ...221 D4
Garrod Ct CO2 .....163 B7
Garrods IP9 ....35 B1
Garthwood Cl CO6 ..108 E4
Gascoigne Rd CO4 ..136 C8
Gasfield 18 CO11 .....86 D4
Gaston End CO7 .....59 C3
Gaston St CO7 ......59 C3
Gatacre Ct CO2 .....135 B3
Gatacre Rd IP1 .....17 A7
Gate St CM9 ....209 F3
Gate Street Mews CM9 .209 F3
Gatefield Cl CO14 ..170 F7
Gatekeeper Cl
　8 Braintree CM7 ...127 F1
　Ipswich IP8 ....36 E8
Gatwick Cl CM23 ...119 B1
Gauden Rd CM7 ....127 F7
Gavin Way CO4 .....110 B5
Gay Bowers La CM3 .218 D4
Gay Bowers Rd CM3 .218 C4
Gay Bowers Way CM8 .195 A4
Gaye St 1 IP1 ....17 B6
Gazelle Ct CO4 .....110 C4
Generals La CM3 ...192 B2

Generals Mews IP11 ...221 B5
Genesta Cl CM9 ...199 D2
Geneva Rd IP1 ...17 B7
Gentian Ct CO4 ...109 C2
Geoff Seaden Cl **2** CO1 ...136 C6
George Ave CO7 ...185 F7
George Cl CO15 ...188 C2
George Cut CO7 ...185 F6
George Frost Cl IP4 ...17 D7
George Gent Cl CB9 ...27 B6
George Green CM22 ...146 B1
George La CO10 ...2 B3
George Rd CM7 ...127 D2
George St Chelmsford CM2 205 B1
  13 Colchester CO1 ...135 F7
  Harwich CO12 ...91 D6
  Saffron Walden CB10 ...22 D1
George Yd **7** CM7 ...127 F3
Georgian Ct IP11 ...221 D5
Geralds Ave IP4 ...18 A5
Geranium Cl CO16 ...188 C4
Geranium Wlk CO4 ...136 D7
Gerard Ave CM23 ...145 E4
Gerard Rd CO16 ...188 C6
Gernon Cl CM1 ...191 B3
Gernon Rd CO7 ...111 E7
Gestingthorpe Rd CO10 ...31 F4
Gibbons Ct CM6 ...123 D1
Gibbons St **3** IP1 ...17 A6
Gibbs Field CM23 ...145 D5
Gibson Cl CB10 ...22 D1
Gibson Gdns CB10 ...22 D1
Gibson Rd CO9 ...51 D1
Gibson Way CB10 ...22 D1
Giffins Cl CM7 ...127 F1
Gifford Cl IP9 ...62 D5
Giffords Pl IP4 ...18 F6
Gilberd Ct CO4 ...110 C6
Gilberd Ho CO3 ...135 A7
Gilberd Rd CO2 ...136 B4
Gilberd Sch The CO4 ...110 B5
Gilbert Rd CO10 ...12 B8
Gilbert Way CM7 ...128 C5
Gilbey Ave CM23 ...146 B6
Gilbey Cotts CM22 ...94 C1
Gilbey Cres CM24 ...119 E8
Gilbey Gn CB11 ...42 F1
Gilchrist Way CM7 ...127 E4
Gilda Terr CM7 ...127 B2
Gilderslee Cl CO4 ...110 D3
Gilders Way CO16 ...188 C5
Gill Cl CM9 ...209 F6
Gilmore Way CM2 ...217 B6
Gilpin Way CM7 ...154 C7
Gilson Cl CM2 ...205 F2
Gilwell Park Cl CO3 ...135 A4
Gimson Ct CM8 ...176 F2
Gippeswyk Ave IP2 ...17 A4
Gippeswyk Rd IP2 ...17 B4
Gipping Cl CB9 ...8 E6
Gipping Way IP8 ...16 B6
Gipsy La CM23 ...119 C4
Girling St CO10 ...33 E8
Girton Rd CB9 ...9 B7
Girton Way IP2 ...16 F1
Glade The CO4 ...110 F2
Gladeview CO15 ...188 F7
Gladiator Way CO2 ...135 A2
Gladstone Ct CM2 ...205 B1
Gladstone Rd
  Colchester CO1 ...136 B5
  Ipswich IP3 ...17 F5
  Tiptree CO5 ...179 D4
Gladwin Rd CO2 ...135 D4
Glamis Cl CB9 ...8 D8
Glamorgan Rd IP2 ...17 B1
Glastonbury Cl IP2 ...16 F1
Glebe Ave CM7 ...127 F6
Glebe Cl Elmstead CO7 ...138 A6
  Sproughton IP8 ...16 B6
  Tattingstone IP9 ...61 C7
  Wix CO11 ...115 C5
Glebe Cres
  Broomfield CM1 ...191 B1
  Witham CM8 ...176 E4
Glebe Ct CM23 ...146 B8
Glebe End Capel St M IP9 ...35 B2
  Elsenham CM22 ...94 D1
Glebe Gdns CO5 ...158 E5
Glebe La Chelmondiston IP9 63 A8
  Little Easton CM6 ...122 F5
  Woolverstone IP9 ...38 B1
Glebe Meadow CM3 ...190 E7
Glebe Rd Chelmsford CM1 ...205 B3
  Colchester CO2 ...135 C2
  Heybridge CM9 ...210 C5
  Kelvedon CO5 ...158 B2
  Tiptree CO5 ...179 C5
Glebe The Elsenham CM22 ..94 C1
  Peldon CO5 ...182 E5
  Purleigh CM3 ...220 D1
  Saffron Walden CB11 ...43 E7
Glebe View CM2 ...216 B3
Glebe Way
  Clacton-on-S CO15 ...203 G7
  Frinton-on-S CO13 ...170 F5
Glebefield Rd CM3 ...194 B4
Glebelands CO6 ...82 B5
Glemham Dr IP4 ...18 F4
Glemsford Cl IP11 ...221 B3
Glemsford Cty Prim Sch
  CO10 ...2 B5
Glemsford Pl **3** CB9 ...9 B8
Glen Ave CO3 ...135 B7
Glenavon Rd IP4 ...18 D7

Glencoe Rd IP4 ...18 C8
Glendale Gr CO4 ...110 C3
Gleneagles Dr IP4 ...18 D5
Gleneagles Way CM3 ...194 B4
Glenfield Ave IP11 ...221 E5
Glenhurst Ave IP4 ...18 B8
Glenside CO10 ...34 A6
Glentress Cl CO4 ...110 D3
Glenway Ct CO6 ...82 B1
Glisson Sq CO2 ...135 B4
Globe Cl CO5 ...179 D6
Globe Cres CM23 ...118 D6
Globe Wlk CO5 ...179 D6
Globe Yd **4** CO10 ...33 E8
Gloucester Ave
  Chelmsford CM2 ...216 C6
  Colchester CO2 ...135 C3
  Maldon CM9 ...209 F1
Gloucester Cres CM1 ...205 A5
Gloucester Gdns CM7 ...128 B4
Gloucester Ho IP11 ...221 C6
Gloucester Rd Haverhill CB9 .8 F6
  Ipswich IP3 ...18 B2
Gloucester Way CO10 ...15 D2
Goat Hall La
  Chelmsford CM2 ...215 F3
  Galleywood CM2 ...216 A3
Goat House La CM3 ...219 F4
Goat Lodge Rd CM9 ...196 A5
Goda Cl CM8 ...194 D8
Goddard Way
  Chelmsford CM2 ...205 F2
  Saffron Walden CB10 ...22 E3
Godfrey Way CM6 ...123 C1
Godfreys Mews CM2 ...205 B1
Godlings Way CM7 ...127 F2
Godmans La CO6 ...132 E3
Godric Pl CM7 ...127 E3
Godric Rd CM8 ...194 E8
Godwin Cl CO9 ...76 D1
Godwit Ct CO5 ...158 D2
Goff's La CO16 ...141 F8
Goings La CO5 ...201 D6
Gold Cl CM22 ...94 B3
Gold St CB10 ...22 D1
Goldcrest Cl CO4 ...137 A8
Goldcrest Ct IP2 ...16 D3
Goldcrest Rd IP2 ...16 C3
Golden Dawn Way CO4 ...109 E2
Golden La Radwinter CB10 ..22 E7
  Thorpe-le-S CO16 ...141 F3
Golden Noble Hill CO1 ..136 A6
Goldenacres CM1 ...205 F8
Goldenlond CO4 ...56 C5
Goldfinch Ct CO4 ...136 F7
Goldhanger Ct CM7 ...128 D1
Goldhanger Rd CM9 ...210 D4
Golding Thoroughfare
  CM2 ...205 F3
Golding Way Glemsford CO10 2 B4
  St Osyth CO16 ...187 A5
Goldingham Dr CM7 ...155 A7
Goldings CM23 ...146 B8
Goldlay Ave CM2 ...216 C8
Goldlay Gdns CM2 ...205 C1
Goldlay Rd CM2 ...205 C1
Golds Nursery Bsns Pk
  CM22 ...94 C3
Golf Green Rd CO15 ...203 G8
Goodchild Way CO9 ...30 A2
Goodey Cl CO1 ...136 A6
Goodlake Cl CO12 ...90 F2
Goodliffe Pk CM23 ...119 B2
Goodmans La CM3 ...173 F4
Goodwin Stile CM23 ...145 D5
Goodwins Cl CB11 ...21 E3
Goojerat Rd CO2 ...135 D5
Gordon Dr CO4 ...110 C5
Gordon Rd
  Chelmsford CM2 ...216 A6
  Harwich CO12 ...91 B2
  Ipswich IP4 ...18 A7
Gordon Way CO12 ...91 B2
Gore La CM7 ...127 A2
Gore Rd CM7 ...127 A2
Gore Terr CM7 ...127 A2
Gorefield Rd CM22 ...121 B5
Gorefield Rdbt CM24 ...121 B4
Goring Rd Colchester CO4 .110 C1
  Ipswich IP4 ...18 C6
Gorse La
  Clacton-on-S CO15 ...189 A8
  Tiptree CO5 ...179 D4
Gorse Lane Ind Est CO15 189 B8
Gorse Rd IP3 ...18 B2
Gorse Way
  Clacton-on-S CO15 ...203 F7
  Colchester CO3 ...134 D4
Gorse Wlk CO4 ...136 D7
Gorsehayes IP2 ...17 B3
Gosbecks Cty Prim Sch
  CO2 ...135 A3
Gosbecks Rd CO2 ...135 A2
Gosbecks View CO2 ...135 A2
Gosfield Cty Prim Sch
  CO9 ...102 E8
Gosfield Hall CO9 ...102 C8
Gosfield Rd
  Blackheath CO2 ...163 A8
  Braintree CM7 ...102 D3
Gosfield Sch CO9 ...75 F2
Gosford Cl CO10 ...12 B8
Goshawk Dr CM2 ...216 B5
Goslings The CM8 ...156 C5
Goul La CB10 ...22 D1
Gouldings Ave CO14 ...171 B8
Goulds Rd CO8 ...54 F2
Goulton Rd CM1 ...191 A1

Government Flats CO12 ...91 E5
Gower St IP2 ...17 C4
Gowers Ave CM2 ...216 E6
Gowers End CO10 ...2 C5
Goyfield Ave IP11 ...221 D4
Grace Gdns CM23 ...145 F4
Grace's Cross CM2 ...217 C7
Graces Cl CM8 ...195 A4
Graces La CM3 ...207 B1
Graces Wlk CO13 ...171 A6
Grafton Pl CM2 ...206 A4
Grafton Rd CO12 ...91 D4
Grafton Way IP1 ...17 C5
Graham Ave IP1 ...17 B8
Graham Rd
  Felixstowe IP11 ...221 D5
  Ipswich IP1 ...17 B7
Grailands CM23 ...145 D8
Grammar School Pl **11**
  CO10 ...33 E7
Grampian Gr CM1 ...204 D6
Granary Barn Mus The
  CO7 ...85 D7
Granary Ct CM6 ...150 D7
Granary The CO10 ...12 B6
Grange Cl Felixstowe IP11 221 C5
  Halstead CO9 ...103 E7
  Walton-on-N CO14 ...171 A7
Grange Ct Chelmsford CM2 215 F7
  Clacton-on-S CO16 ...188 A4
Grange Farm Ave IP11 ...221 B5
Grange Farm Rd CO2 ...136 C4
Grange Hill CO6 ...130 F1
Grange La CM6 ...151 C7
Grange Mill CO6 ...130 F2
Grange Pk CM23 ...118 F1
Grange Prim Sch IP11 ...221 B4
Grange Rd
  Bishop's Stortford CM23 .146 A7
  Felixstowe IP11 ...221 B4
  Great Horkesley CO6 ...109 B7
  Harwich CO12 ...91 A3
  Ickleton CB10 ...20 A8
  Lawford CO11 ...85 F1
  Little Bromley CO11 ...112 E7
  Tiptree CO5 ...179 A6
  Wickham Bishops CM8 ...195 E4
Grange The CM23 ...118 F1
Grange Way CO2 ...136 D3
Grange Way Bsns Pk
  CO2 ...136 D3
Grange Wlk CM23 ...146 A4
Granger Ave CM9 ...209 F1
Grangeside CM23 ...119 A2
Granta Cl CB10 ...3 D1
Granta Cotts CB10 ...3 C2
Grantham Cres IP2 ...17 A4
Grantham Ct CO1 ...136 A7
Grantham Rd CO6 ...109 B7
Grantley Cl CO6 ...133 D5
Grants Ct CO14 ...171 C8
Granville Cl CO6 ...108 E3
Granville Rd
  Clacton-on-S CO15 ...188 F3
  Colchester CO1 ...136 B5
  Felixstowe IP11 ...221 D3
Granville St **2** IP1 ...17 B6
Granville Way CO7 ...186 A7
Grasby Cl CO7 ...137 B2
Grasmere Cl
  Great Notley CM7 ...154 C6
  Ipswich IP3 ...18 B1
Grasmere Gdns CO13 ...170 F7
Grassfields CO13 ...170 E6
Grassmere CO4 ...110 B5
Gravel Hill CO6 ...56 A2
Gravel Hill Way CO12 ...90 F1
Gravel Pit La CO11 ...60 E2
Gravel The CO6 ...130 F2
Gray Rd CO3 ...135 D6
Gray's Cotts CO1 ...136 B7
Gray's La CM7 ...73 E4
Grayling Cl CM7 ...127 E1
Grayling Dr CO4 ...110 F1
Grayling Rd IP8 ...36 E8
Grays Cl CO5 ...201 C6
Grays Ct CM23 ...145 E8
Grays Mead CO9 ...51 D2
Great Baddow Sch CM2 .216 D6
Great Bardfield Cage CM7 72 B2
Great Bardfield Cty Prim
  Sch CM7 ...72 B2
Great Bentley Cty Prim
  Sch CO7 ...166 E7
Great Bentley Rd CO7 ..166 A8
Great Bentley Sta CO7 ..166 E7
Great Bradfords Cty Jun
  & Inf Sch CM7 ...128 B4
Great Canfield Rd CM22 .148 D5
Great Chesterford CE
  Prim Sch CB10 ...3 D2
Great Chesterford Ct CB10 .3 C2
Great Chesterford Sta
  CB10 ...3 C1
Great Cob CM7 ...205 E5
Great Colman St **14** IP4 ...17 D6
Great Cornard Ctry Pk
  CO10 ...34 C4
Great Cornard Mid Sch
  CO10 ...34 C4
Great Cornard Upper Sch
  CO10 ...34 A4
Great Dunmow CE Jun
  Sch CM6 ...150 C8
Great Eastern Cl CM23 .146 A6
Great Eastern Rd CO10 ...33 F7
Great Eastern Sq IP11 ..221 E5

Great Easton CE Prim
  Sch CM6 ...123 A8
Great Field IP11 ...221 A8
Great Gibcracks Chase
  CM3 ...218 A2
Great Gipping St IP1 ...17 B5
Great Hadham Rd CM23 .145 C5
Great Harrods CO14 ...171 A7
Great Holland Common
  Rd CO13 ...169 D2
Great House Farm Rd
  CO2 ...162 A5
Great Leighs Cty Prim
  Sch CM3 ...174 A7
Great Notley Ave CM7 ..154 C6
Great Oak Ct CO9 ...30 A1
Great Sampford Cty Prim
  Sch CB10 ...47 A3
Great Sq **9** CM7 ...127 F3
Great Tey CE Prim Sch
  CO6 ...106 C1
Great Tey Rd CO6 ...132 C4
Great Totham Prim Sch
  CM9 ...196 A5
Great Totham Rd CM8 ..195 F5
Great Tufts IP9 ...35 B1
Great Waltham CE Prim
  Sch CM3 ...190 E7
Great Whip St IP2 ...17 C4
Great Yeldham Rd CO9 ...50 D7
Grebe Cl IP2 ...16 E2
Green Acres Rd CO2 ...162 A5
Green Cl Chelmsford CM1 .205 D4
  Hatfield Peverel CM3 ...194 C3
  Writtle CM1 ...204 B1
Green Cnr CO7 ...139 E1
Green Ct CO6 ...104 F7
Green End La CO13 ...170 B5
Green Farm Rd CO6 ...78 B2
Green La Aldham CO6 ...107 C1
  Ardleigh CO7 ...111 D6
  Black Notley CM8 ...155 A4
  Boxted CO4 ...82 D5
  Colchester CO4 ...110 E2
  Colchester, Crockleford
  Heath CO7 ...111 C1
  Great Horkesley CO6 ...109 C6
  Great Notley CM7 ...154 F2
  Little Totham CM9 ...197 C4
  Stratford St M CO7 ...58 C4
  Tattingstone IP9 ...61 D7
  Tiptree CO5 ...179 D6
  Tiptree CO5 ...179 E1
  Walton-on-N CO14 ...144 D2
  Weeley Heath CO16 ...168 A6
Green Man La CM8 ...195 F7
Green Mdws CM3 ...219 A6
Green St CM6 ...148 F2
Green The
  Bishop's Stortford CM23 .145 F4
  Chelmsford CM1 ...204 F4
  Chrishall SG8 ...19 D3
  Clacton-on-S CO16 ...188 B2
  Great Bentley CO7 ...166 D8
  Mistley CO11 ...86 F4
  St Osyth CO16 ...203 B6
  Writtle CM1 ...204 B1
Green Way CO6 ...78 A2
Green's Yd CO1 ...135 E7
Greenacres
  Clacton-on-S CO15 ...189 A5
  Coggeshall CO6 ...130 F1
  Colchester CO4 ...109 E3
Greene View CM7 ...155 B8
Greenfield CM7 ...177 A1
Greenfield Cotts CO4 ...82 E6
Greenfield Dr CO6 ...106 B1
Greenfields
  Galleywood CM2 ...216 C2
  Gosfield CO9 ...102 F7
  Stansted
  Mountfitchet CM24 ...119 E7
Greenfields Way CB9 ...8 E6
Greenfinch Ave IP2 ...16 D3
Greenfinch End CO4 ...136 F8
Greenford Rd CO15 ...188 C3
Greengates Mobile
  Home Pk CO16 ...168 C4
Greenhill Pk CM23 ...145 D5
Greenhurst Rd CO7 ...186 A6
Greenhythe Ct CO4 ...136 D6
Greens The IP4 ...18 F4
Greens Yd CO13 ...170 F5
Greensmill CO11 ...86 C5
Greenspire Gr IP8 ...16 B2
Greenstead Ct CO1 ...136 D6
Greenstead Rd CO1 ...136 D7
Greenstead Rdbt CO4 ...136 D6
Greenview Pk CO15 ...189 A4
Greenway
  Bishop's Stortford CM23 .146 C6
  Frinton-on-S CO13 ...170 F5
Greenway Cl CO15 ...189 B7
Greenway Gdns CM7 ...154 D7
Greenway The CO15 ...189 B7
Greenways
  Chelmsford CM1 ...205 B6
  Feering CO5 ...158 D3
  Gosfield CO9 ...102 F7
  Maldon CM9 ...209 F2
  Saffron Walden CB11 ...43 E7
Greenways Cl IP1 ...17 B8
Greenways The CO15 ...189 B7
Greenwich Bsns Pk IP3 ..17 E2
Greenwich Rd IP3 ...17 E2
Greenwood Cl CB9 ...8 E7
Greenwood Gr CO4 ...110 C3

Greenwood Sch CO9 ...76 F2
Gregory St CO10 ...33 E7
Grendel Way CO15 ...189 F6
Grenfell Ave CO15 ...189 E6
Grenfell Cl CO4 ...110 C2
Grenville Rd
  Braintree CM7 ...127 B4
  Sudbury CO10 ...15 F2
Gresley Cl CO4 ...109 F2
Gresley Gdns IP2 ...17 C3
Gretna Gdns IP4 ...18 B8
Greville Cl CO14 ...144 E2
Grey Friars Rd **10** IP1 ...17 C5
Grey Ladys CM2 ...216 B2
Greyhound Hill CO4 ...83 E5
Greyhound Rd CO10 ...2 B3
Greys Cl CO10 ...1 C1
Greys Hollow CB11 ...93 D8
Greystones Cl CO3 ...135 A3
Grieves Ct CO3 ...134 C4
Grimston Rd CO2 ...136 A4
Grimston Way CO14 ...171 B7
Grimwade Cl CO11 ...86 C5
Grimwade St IP4 ...17 D5
Grindle The IP8 ...16 A7
Groom Ho CO15 ...188 E4
Groom Pk CO15 ...188 E4
Groome Ct **2** CO4 ...136 D7
Grooms La CM8 ...156 E4
Groomside CM7 ...128 A2
Grosvenor Cl
  Bishop's Stortford CM23 .145 C4
  Chelmsford CM2 ...216 C1
  Ipswich IP4 ...18 E8
  Tiptree CO5 ...179 D5
Grosvenor Ct IP3 ...18 B1
Grosvenor Ho **4** CO4 ...146 B8
Grosvenor Rd CO10 ...15 C2
Grove Ave
  Walton-on-N CO14 ...171 B1
  West Mersea CO5 ...201 C5
Grove Cotts **1** CM8 ...177 A4
Grove Ctr The CM8 ...177 A1
Grove Farm Rd
  Tiptree CO5 ...179 A1
  Tolleshunt Major CM9 ...197 C4
Grove Field CM7 ...102 C1
Grove Hill Belstead IP8 ...36 C7
  Dedham CO7 ...84 D4
  Ipswich IP8 ...16 E1
  Langham CO4 ...83 F5
  Stansted
  Mountfitchet CM24 ...119 E7
Grove La Chelmondiston IP9 63 D3
  Ipswich IP5 ...17 E5
Grove Orch CM7 ...102 C1
Grove Pl **10** CM23 ...145 F7
Grove Rd Bentley IP9 ...60 E1
  Brantham CO11 ...86 D8
  Chelmsford CM2 ...205 B4
  Felixstowe IP11 ...221 E6
  Little Clacton CO16 ...168 D5
  Tiptree CO5 ...179 D5
Grove The Bicknacre CM3 .218 F1
  Clacton-on-S CO15 ...188 F2
  Earls Colne CO6 ...105 B6
  Great Hallingbury CM22 .146 F4
  Witham CM8 ...177 A2
Grove Villas CM7 ...126 A8
Gryme's Dyke Ct CO3 ...134 E3
Gryme's Dyke Way CO3 .134 E3
Guelph's La CM6 ...70 A3
Guernsey Way CM7 ...127 D2
Guildford Rd CO1 ...136 A8
Guildhall Way CB10 ...24 A7
Guinea Ct CM7 ...128 D4
Guithavon Ct CM8 ...176 F1
Guithavon Rd CM8 ...176 F1
Guithavon Rise CM8 ...176 F2
Guithavon St CM8 ...176 F2
Guithavon Valley CM8 ...176 F2
Gull Cotts CO16 ...142 D4
Gull Ct CO16 ...141 F1
Gull's La CO7 ...85 A3
Gulls Croft CM7 ...128 D3
Gulpher Bsns Pk IP11 ...221 E8
Gulpher Rd IP11 ...221 E8
Gun Hill CO7 ...84 C7
Gunfleet Cl CO15 ...201 B7
Gunfleet Ct CO15 ...189 E4
Gurdon Rd CO2 ...135 F3
Gurney Benham Cl CO2 ..135 B4
Gurton Rd CO6 ...131 A3
Gusford Prim Sch IP2 ...16 D1
Gutteridge Hall La CO16 .167 F7
Gutters La CM1 ...205 C7
Guy Cook Cl CO10 ...34 C4
Guys Farm CM1 ...204 B1
Gwendoline Rd IP4 ...18 F4
Gwyn Cl CM3 ...192 E1
Gwynne Rd CO12 ...91 D4
Gymnasium St IP1 ...17 D7
Gypsy La CO5 ...159 C6

H

Ha'penny Field IP9 ...62 D5
Hackmans La CM3 ...219 E2
Haddon Pk CO1 ...136 C6
Hadfelda Sq CM3 ...194 A4
Hadham Ct CM23 ...145 E8
Hadham Gr CM23 ...145 C8
Hadham Ho CM23 ...145 D8
Hadham Rd CM23 ...145 D8
Hadleigh Ct
  Clacton-on-S CO15 ...189 A3
  5 Saffron Walden CB10 ...22 F2

adleigh Rd
Clacton-on-S CO16 . . . . . .**188** B4
East Bergholt CO7 . . . .**59** B3
Frinton-on-S CO13 . . . . . .**171** A5
Ipswich IP2 . . . .**16** D5
Stratford St M CO7 . . . .**58** A6
adleigh Road Ind Est IP2 **16** F7
adley Cl CM7 . . . .**102** B1
adrian Cl Colchester CO4 **136** B4
Haverhill CB9 . . . .**9** D7
adrians Cl CM8 . . . .**194** E8
adstock Rd CB1 . . . .**5** B8
aggars La CO7 . . . .**138** F3
aglemere Dr IP4 . . . .**17** E7
aig Ct CM2 . . . .**205** A1
ailes Wood CM22 . . . .**94** D1
ainault Gr CM1 . . . .**204** E1
ale Cl IP2 . . . .**16** D2
alesowen Ct IP2 . . . .**36** F8
alf Acres CM23 . . . .**145** F8
alf Moon Yard CO10 . . . .**12** B7
alfacres CM8 . . . .**195** A7
alford Ct 6 IP8 . . . .**16** C2
alfway Cotts CO5 . . . . . .**158** B6
alifax Prim Sch IP2 . . . . . .**17** B2
alifax Rd IP2 . . . .**17** B2
all Barn CO5 . . . .**201** B6
all Bridge Rise CM9 . . . .**210** C4
all Chase CO6 . . . .**133** B3
all Cl Great Baddow CM2 **217** A6
Henham CM22 . . . .**94** F5
Holland-on-S CO15 . . . . .**189** F6
all Cut CO7 . . . .**185** F6
all Dr CO9 . . . .**102** D8
all Est CM9 . . . .**211** E2
all Farm Cl CO5 . . . .**158** E4
all Field IP11 . . . .**221** C5
all La Harwich CO12 . . . . .**91** A2
Ridgewell CO9 . . . .**29** B6
Sandon CM2 . . . .**217** C6
Thorpe-le-S CO16 . . . . . .**169** B8
Walton-on-t-N CO14 . . . .**144** D2
all Pond Way IP11 . . . . . .**221** C5
all Rd
Belcham Walter CO10 . . . . .**32** A6
Borley CO10 . . . .**15** A3
Bures CO8 . . . .**79** E5
Copford CO6 . . . .**133** E4
Elsenham CM22 . . . .**94** D1
Fordham CO6 . . . .**107** D5
Great Bromley CO7 . . . . . .**112** C2
Great Totham CM9 . . . . . .**196** D6
Maldon CM9 . . . .**210** B4
Panfield CM7 . . . .**127** A6
Tiptree CO5 . . . .**179** C3
Tollesbury CM9 . . . .**199** D1
West Bergholt CO6 . . . . . .**108** D5
all Rise Sudbury CO10 . . . .**33** A8
Witham CM8 . . . .**194** F8
all Road Cotts CO6 . . . . .**108** D6
all St Chelmsford CM2 . . .**205** B1
Long Melford CO10 . . . . . .**15** C8
all View Rd CO7 . . . .**166** E7
all Villas CM7 . . . .**72** B4
allcroft Chase CO4 . . . . .**110** C4
allingbury Cl CM22 . . . .**146** A5
allingbury Rd CM22 . . . .**146** B4
alliwell Rd IP4 . . . .**18** B6
alstead Hospl CO9 . . . . . .**76** E3
alstead Rd
Braintree CM7 . . . .**102** E3
Colchester CO3 . . . .**134** D7
Earls Colne CO6 . . . .**104** F7
Eight Ash G CO6 . . . .**134** A8
Fordham CO6 . . . .**107** B3
Fordham Heath CO6 . . . . .**107** E1
Gosfield CO9 . . . .**75** F1
Kirby Cross CO13 . . . . . .**170** B7
Kirby-le-S CO13 . . . .**170** C8
Sible Hedingham CO9 . . . . .**76** B6
alston Pl CM9 . . . .**220** F8
alton Cres IP3 . . . .**18** C1
amble Cl CM8 . . . .**176** E2
amel Way CB11 . . . .**67** D4
amford Ct CO14 . . . .**144** D2
amford Cty Prim Sch
CO13 . . . .**170** F7
amford Dr CO12 . . . .**116** C3
amilton Cl CO15 . . . . . .**189** E6
amilton Cty Prim Sch
CO3 . . . .**135** D5
amilton Gdns IP11 . . . . .**221** F3
amilton Ho IP4 . . . .**18** A7
amilton Mews 4 CB10 . . .**22** F2
amilton Rd
Colchester CO3 . . . .**135** D4
Felixstowe IP11 . . . .**221** E4
Great Holland CO13 . . . . .**170** A5
Ipswich IP3 . . . .**18** B3
Sudbury CO10 . . . .**33** E7
Takeley CM6 . . . .**148** F7
Wivenhoe CO7 . . . .**164** B8
amilton St
Felixstowe IP11 . . . .**221** C5
Harwich CO12 . . . .**90** F5
amlet Ct CO8 . . . .**79** E8
amlet Dr CO4 . . . .**136** F7
amlet Rd
Chelmsford CM2 . . . .**205** B1
Haverhill CB9 . . . .**9** B7
ammonds Rd CM3 . . . . .**206** E3
ampit Cl CB11 . . . .**41** D2
ampstead Ave CO16 . . . .**188** D5
ampton Rd
Great Baddow CM2 . . . . .**216** E6
Ipswich IP1 . . . .**16** F7
amsters Cl CO9 . . . .**77** F8

Hanbury Gdns CO4 . . . . .**110** B5
Hanbury Rd CM1 . . . .**215** E8
Hance La CM7 . . . .**126** F2
Hanchetts Orch CM6 . . . . .**70** A3
Handel Wlk CO4 . . . .**136** E6
Handford Cut IP1 . . . .**17** A6
Handford Hall Prim Sch
IP1 . . . .**17** A6
Handford Rd IP1 . . . .**17** A6
Hankin Ave CM7 . . . .**90** C1
Hanlee Brook CM2 . . . . .**216** F5
Hanover Bridge CO5 . . . .**158** F5
Hanover Ct
Ipswich IP4 . . . .**17** E6
Sudbury CO10 . . . .**33** D6
Walton-on-t-N CO14 . . . .**171** A8
Witham CM8 . . . .**177** A1
Hanover Pl CB10 . . . .**22** C1
Hanover Sq CO5 . . . .**158** F6
Hanwell Cl CO16 . . . .**188** D5
Happy Gdns CO5 . . . .**179** A8
Harborough Hall Rd CO5 **159** E2
Harbour Cres CO12 . . . . . .**91** E5
Harcourt Ave CO12 . . . . . .**91** A4
Hardings Cl CO6 . . . .**133** B8
Hardwick Cl IP4 . . . .**18** E5
Hardwick Rd CB9 . . . .**9** B8
Hardy Cl Braintree CM7 . .**155** A8
Brantham CO11 . . . .**86** C7
Hardy Ct CO10 . . . .**15** F2
Harebell Cl CO4 . . . .**110** B3
Harebell Dr CM8 . . . .**176** B3
Harebell Rd IP2 . . . .**16** F4
Harewood Rd CM1 . . . . . .**204** E1
Harewood Terr 20 CB9 . . . .**8** E7
Harfred Ave CM9 . . . .**210** E3
Hargrave Cl CM24 . . . . . .**119** E8
Harkilees Way CM7 . . . . .**127** F5
Harkstead La
Chelmondiston IP9 . . . .**63** A7
Woolverstone IP9 . . . .**38** A1
Harkstead Rd IP9 . . . .**62** F3
Harlings Gr CM1 . . . .**205** C3
Harman Wlk CO16 . . . . . .**188** C5
Harness Cl CM1 . . . .**205** E7
Harnham Dr CM7 . . . .**154** C7
Harold Cl CM7 . . . .**76** F1
Harold Gr CO13 . . . .**170** F4
Harold Rd Braintree CM7 .**127** E2
Clacton-on-S CO15 . . . . .**188** F3
Frinton-on-S CO13 . . . . .**170** F4
Harold Way CO13 . . . . . .**170** F4
Harpclose Rd CO10 . . . . . .**33** F8
Harpur's Rd CO10 . . . .**2** B4
Harrington Cl
8 Bishop's Stortford CM23 **146** A7
Tiptree CO5 . . . .**179** C5
Harrison Ct CM1 . . . .**204** F3
Harrison Dr CM7 . . . .**128** A1
Harrison Rd CO2 . . . .**135** F3
Harrisons CM23 . . . .**119** D2
Harrold Ct CO15 . . . .**189** A3
Harrow Cl IP4 . . . .**18** B5
Harrow Hill CO9 . . . .**49** F6
Harrow Rd
Clacton-on-S CO15 . . . . .**188** F4
Haverhill CB9 . . . .**8** E7
Harrow Way CO4 . . . .**217** A6
Harsnett Rd CO1 . . . .**136** B5
Hart St CO7 . . . .**205** A1
Hart's La CO7 . . . .**84** B7
Hartest Way CO10 . . . .**34** B6
Hartley Cl CM2 . . . .**206** A4
Hartley St IP2 . . . .**17** C4
Harvard Ct CO4 . . . .**110** B4
Harvest Ct Feering CO5 . .**158** E4
Felixstowe IP11 . . . .**221** F4
Harvest End CO3 . . . .**134** D5
Harvest Ho IP11 . . . .**221** F4
Harvest Way CO7 . . . .**137** F6
Harvesters' Way CO6 . . . .**132** B8
Harvey Cl CO11 . . . .**86** C4
Harvey Cres CO3 . . . .**134** C4
Harvey Rd Colchester CO2 **135** B2
Great Totham CM9 . . . . . .**196** A4
Wivenhoe CO7 . . . .**137** C1
Harvey St CO9 . . . .**76** F1
Harvey Way
Hempstead CB10 . . . .**25** F1
Saffron Walden CB10 . . . .**22** F2
Harwich Crane The CO12 **191** E5
Harwich Ct CO7 . . . .**136** F4
Harwich Cty Prim Sch
CO12 . . . .**91** D5
Harwich & District Hospl
CO12 . . . .**91** A3
Harwich International
Port CO12 . . . .**90** F6
Harwich Parkeston Quay
Sta CO12 . . . .**90** F6
Harwich Rd Ardleigh CO7 **110** F3
Ardleigh CO7 . . . .**111** F8
Beaumont CO16 . . . .**141** F4
Bradfield CO11 . . . .**87** C4
Colchester CO4 . . . .**136** C8
Dedham CO7 . . . .**84** F1
Great Bromley CO7 . . . . .**139** C6
Great Oakley CO12 . . . . .**116** A4
Great Oakley CO12 . . . . .**116** C1
Great Oakley CO12 . . . . .**116** D5
Lawford CO11 . . . .**85** C2
Little Bentley CO7 . . . . . .**113** E1
Little Bentley CO7 . . . . . .**113** F3
Little Oakley CO16 . . . . .**168** E6
Little Oakley CO12 . . . . .**117** C7
New Mistley CO11 . . . .**87** B3
Ramsey CO11 . . . .**89** A2

Harwich Rd continued
Wix CO11 . . . .**115** D5
Wix CO11 . . . .**115** F6
Wrabness CO11 . . . .**88** D7
Harwich Sch The CO12 . . .**91** A2
Harwich Town Sta CO12 . .**91** D5
Harwood Cl CO2 . . . .**136** A4
Haselfoot Rd CM3 . . . . . .**206** F8
Haselmere Gdns CO13 . . .**170** F4
Haskell Mews CM7 . . . . . .**155** A8
Haslemere Dr IP4 . . . .**17** E6
Hasler Rd CM9 . . . .**199** D2
Hastings Ave CO15 . . . . .**203** A8
Hastings Pl CO7 . . . .**185** F8
Hastings Rd CO3 . . . .**135** A4
Hatchcroft Gdns CO7 . . . .**138** A4
Hatchfields CM3 . . . .**190** F7
Hatfield Forest (Cntry Pk)
CM22 . . . .**147** D6
Hatfield Gr CM1 . . . .**204** D1
Hatfield Peverel Sta CM3 **193** F5
Hatfield Rd
Hatfield Peverel CM8 . . . .**194** F4
Heybridge CM9 . . . .**209** B7
Ipswich IP3 . . . .**18** A3
Terling CM3 . . . .**175** D2
Witham CM8 . . . .**194** E7
Hatherley Ct CB10 . . . .**22** C1
Haubourdin Ct CO9 . . . . . .**77** A2
Haughley Dr IP4 . . . .**18** F4
Hauliers Rd IP11 . . . .**221** B2
Haven Ave CO15 . . . .**189** G1
Haven Cl IP11 . . . .**221** B4
Haven Ct CM3 . . . .**193** F4
Haven Rd CO2 . . . .**136** D4
Haven The CO12 . . . .**90** F3
Havencroft Ct 3 CO14 . . .**171** C8
Havengore CM1 . . . .**205** F5
Havens Par CM23 . . . .**145** F4
Havens The IP3 . . . .**38** E7
Haverhill Rd
Castle Camps CB1 . . . .**7** E5
Helions Bumpstead CB9 . . .**8** D1
Steeple Bumpstead CB9 . . .**27** C8
Havering Rd
Clacton-on-S CO15 . . . . .**188** D4
Colchester CO4 . . . .**110** B1
Havers Inf Sch The CM23 **145** E5
Havers La CM23 . . . .**145** F4
Havisham Way CM1 . . . . .**204** E7
Hawbridge IP9 . . . .**35** A4
Hawbush Gn CM7 . . . . . .**155** F5
Hawes St IP2 . . . .**17** D3
Hawfinch Rd CO2 . . . . . .**162** A5
Hawfinch Wlk CM2 . . . . .**216** B5
Hawke Rd IP3 . . . .**17** E1
Hawkendon Rd CO16 . . . .**188** A4
Hawkes La CO7 . . . .**185** F6
Hawkesway CO15 . . . . . .**188** F6
Hawkhurst Cl CM1 . . . . . .**204** E2
Hawkins Cl CM3 . . . .**219** E2
Hawkins Ct CO10 . . . .**15** F2
Hawkins Rd Alresford CO7 **165** B8
Colchester CO2 . . . .**136** D5
Sudbury CO10 . . . .**15** F2
Hawkins Way CM7 . . . . . .**128** C4
Hawks Cl CM3 . . . .**219** A4
Hawkwood Rd CO9 . . . . . .**75** D8
Hawlmark End CO6 . . . . .**132** E3
Hawthorn Ave CO4 . . . . .**136** D7
Hawthorn Cl
Chelmsford CM2 . . . .**216** C6
Halstead CO9 . . . .**77** A2
Takeley CM22 . . . .**148** C7
Hawthorn Dr IP2 . . . .**16** E3
Hawthorn Rd
Clacton-on-S CO15 . . . . .**188** E6
Great Cornard CO10 . . . . .**34** B7
Hatfield Peverel CM3 . . . .**194** A4
Tolleshunt Knights CM9 . .**180** A2
Hawthorn Rise CM23 . . . .**145** F3
Hawthorne Rise CM8 . . . .**177** A5
Hawthornes CM3 . . . .**220** D1
Hawthorns
Kirby Cross CO13 . . . . . .**170** F7
Sible Hedingham CO9 . . . .**51** D2
Hawthorns The CM3 . . . . .**219** A4
Hay Gn CM3 . . . .**218** D7
Hay La CM7 . . . .**128** C3
Haycocks La CO5 . . . .**183** F1
Haycroft CM23 . . . .**146** C7
Haye La CO5 . . . .**163** C4
Hayes Cl CM2 . . . .**205** B1
Hayes Rd CO15 . . . .**188** E3
Hayhill Rd IP4 . . . .**17** F7
Hayhouse Rd CO6 . . . . . .**105** A6
Haylands Sch CM1 . . . . . .**204** D1
Hayley Bell Gdns CM23 . .**145** F3
Hayman Rd IP3 . . . .**17** F1
Haymeads La CM23 . . . . .**146** C6
Haynes Green Rd CO5 . . .**180** A8
Haytor Cl CM7 . . . .**128** C2
Haywain The CO3 . . . . . .**134** D5
Hayward Ct CO1 . . . .**136** C7
Hayward Sch The CM1 . . .**205** A4
Hazel Cl Haverhill CB9 . . . .**8** E7
Thorrington CO7 . . . .**166** A5
Witham CM8 . . . .**177** A4
Hazel Dr IP3 . . . .**18** C1
Hazel Gr CM7 . . . .**127** E1
Hazeldon Cl CM3 . . . .**191** C6
Hazeleigh Hall La CM9 . . .**220** C4
Hazelend Rd CM23 . . . . . .**119** B4
Hazell Ave CO2 . . . .**135** B2
Hazelton Rd CO4 . . . .**110** D1
Hazelville Cl CO12 . . . . . .**90** E1

Hazelwood Cres CO16 . . .**168** C1
Hazelwood Ct CM9 . . . . .**210** B6
Hazlemere Cty Jun & Inf
Schs CO4 . . . .**136** E8
Hazlemere Rd CO15 . . . . .**189** C4
Head Ct CM24 . . . .**119** D7
Head La CO10 . . . .**34** B5
Head St Colchester CO1 . .**135** E7
Goldhanger CM9 . . . .**211** E6
Halstead CO9 . . . .**76** F2
Rowhedge CO5 . . . .**163** F8
Headgate Bldg 1 CO2 . . .**135** E6
Headgate Ct CO1 . . . .**135** E7
Headingham Cl 3 IP2 . . . .**17** A2
Headland Ave CB9 . . . .**8** E7
Heard's La CM7 . . . .**48** C5
Heards La CM7 . . . .**48** C6
Hearsall Ave CM1 . . . . . .**205** B7
Heath Cl CO7 . . . .**59** D3
Heath Cotts CO3 . . . .**107** F1
Heath Dr CM2 . . . .**216** B6
Heath La IP4 . . . .**18** C5
Heath Rd Alresford CO7 . .**165** B8
Bradfield CO11 . . . .**114** D8
Colchester CO3 . . . .**134** F5
Colchester, Stanway
Green CO3 . . . .**134** D4
East Bergholt CO7 . . . .**59** D3
Fordham Heath CO3 . . . . .**108** A1
Ipswich IP4 . . . .**18** D6
New Mistley CO11 . . . .**87** B2
Rowhedge CO5 . . . .**163** F8
St Osyth CO16 . . . .**167** E1
Tendring CO16 . . . .**140** E7
Wivenhoe CO7 . . . .**137** E2
Heath Row CM23 . . . .**119** B1
Heath Sch The CO3 . . . . .**134** D5
Heath The Dedham CO7 . . .**85** A4
Layer-de-l-H CO2 . . . .**162** A6
Heathcote Sch CM3 . . . . .**218** E7
Heather Ave IP3 . . . .**18** C3
Heather Cl
Bishop's Stortford CM23 . .**145** D6
Clacton-on-S CO15 . . . . .**189** B7
Layer-de-l-H CO2 . . . .**161** C5
Heather Ct 10 CM1 . . . . .**205** E6
Heather Dr CO3 . . . .**134** F5
Heatherhayes Ipswich IP2 **17** A3
Ipswich IP2 . . . .**17** B3
Heathfield Rd
Chelmsford CM1 . . . .**205** B2
Holbrook IP9 . . . .**62** D5
Heathfields CO6 . . . .**134** B8
Heathfields Ho CO6 . . . . .**136** C3
Heathgate CM8 . . . .**195** D6
Heathgate Piece IP11 . . . .**221** A8
Heathlands CO7 . . . .**166** A5
Heathlands CE Prim
Sch CO6 . . . .**108** E4
Heathlands Pk IP4 . . . . . .**18** D6
Heathside Spec Sch IP4 . .**18** D6
Heatley Way CO4 . . . .**136** F8
Heckford's Rd CO7 . . . . . .**139** E2
Heckworth Cl CO4 . . . . . .**110** C6
Hedge Dr CO2 . . . .**135** B3
Hedgelands CO6 . . . .**133** D5
Hedingham Castle
(remains of) CO9 . . . .**51** F4
Hedingham Rd
Bulmer CO10 . . . .**32** C1
Gosfield CO9 . . . .**75** E3
Halstead CO9 . . . .**76** E3
Wickham St P CO9 . . . . . .**53** A7
Hedingham Sch The CO9 . .**51** D1
Heights The CM3 . . . .**218** D7
Helen How CM3 . . . .**173** F7
Helena Rd IP3 . . . .**17** E3
Helena Romanes Sch
CM6 . . . .**123** C3
Helford Ct CM3 . . . .**206** A4
Helions Bumpstead Rd CB9 **9** A5
Helions Park Ave CB9 . . . . .**9** A7
Helions Park Gdns CB9 . . . .**9** A7
Helions Park Gr CB9 . . . . . .**9** A7
Helions Rd CB9 . . . .**27** A6
Helions Service Rd CB9 . . . .**9** A7
Helions Wlk CB9 . . . .**9** A7
Helm Cl CO6 . . . .**109** C7
Helston Rd CM1 . . . .**205** E6
Hemingway Rd CM8 . . . . .**176** F5
Hemlock Cl CM8 . . . .**177** A4
Hemmings Ct CM9 . . . . . .**220** E8
Hendon Cl CO16 . . . .**188** D5
Hendy Fisher Ct CO3 . . . .**135** B4
Hengrave Cl IP2 . . . .**17** A2
Henham Rd Debden CB11 . .**68** C3
Elsenham CM22 . . . .**94** E3
Henham & Ugley Cty
Prim Sch CM22 . . . .**94** F5
Henley Ct Colchester CO3 **134** F6
Manningtree CO11 . . . .**86** C4
Henley Rd IP1 . . . .**17** C8
Henniker Gate CM2 . . . . .**206** A4
Henniker Rd IP1 . . . .**16** D8
Henny Back Rd CO8 . . . . . .**54** E4
Henny Rd CO8 . . . .**55** B5
Henrietta Cl CO7 . . . .**137** C3
Henry Cl CO15 . . . .**188** C2
Henry Dixon Rd CM8 . . . .**177** D6
Henry Rd Chelmsford CM1 **205** B4
Ipswich IP3 . . . .**18** B1
Henslow Rd IP4 . . . .**18** B5
Henstead Gdns IP3 . . . . . .**18** A2
Herald Cl CM23 . . . .**145** D6
Herbage Park Rd CM9 . . .**208** D1
Herbert Rd CO15 . . . .**188** E3

Hereford Ct
Clacton-on-S CO15 . . . . .**189** E5
Great Baddow CM2 . . . . .**217** A5
Hereford Rd
Colchester CO1 . . . .**136** A8
Holland-on-S CO15 . . . . .**189** E6
Hereward Cl CO7 . . . .**137** C3
Hereward Way CM7 . . . . . .**73** C3
Heriot Way CM9 . . . .**196** B4
Hermitage Ct CM24 . . . . .**119** D7
Heron Ct CM23 . . . .**146** A7
Heron Glade CO15 . . . . . .**188** F7
Heron Rd Ipswich IP2 . . . . .**16** E3
Kelvedon CO5 . . . .**158** D2
Heron Way
Frinton-on-S CO13 . . . . .**170** F6
Heybridge CM9 . . . .**210** C5
Heronsgate CO13 . . . .**170** F6
Herrick Pl CO3 . . . .**135** A6
Herringham Gn CM2 . . . .**206** A4
Herrings' Way CO6 . . . . . .**107** D6
Hertford La CB11 . . . .**19** E5
Hertfordshire & Essex
High Sch CM23 . . . .**146** B7
Herts & Essex Comm
Hospl CM23 . . . .**146** B6
Herts & Essex High Sch
CM23 . . . .**146** B6
Hervey St IP4 . . . .**17** D7
Hervilly Way CO14 . . . . .**171** B7
Heseltine Ct CO15 . . . . . .**189** B3
Hetherington Cl CO2 . . . .**163** A8
Hewes Cl CO4 . . . .**136** F7
Hewitt Ct CO12 . . . .**90** C1
Hewitt Wlk CM8 . . . .**177** A2
Hexham Cl 6 IP2 . . . .**17** A2
Heybridge App CM9 . . . . .**209** F5
Heybridge Cl CO15 . . . . .**189** B3
Heybridge House Ind
Est CM9 . . . .**210** B4
Heybridge Prim Sch
CM9 . . . .**210** C5
Heybridge St CM9 . . . . . .**210** B5
Heycroft Rd CM7 . . . .**155** E5
Heycroft Way
Great Baddow CM2 . . . . .**216** F5
Tiptree CO5 . . . .**179** D6
Heydon La Chrishall SG8 . .**19** A5
Elmdon CB11 . . . .**19** F4
Heythrop The CM2 . . . . . .**205** D4
Heywood Cl IP2 . . . .**16** E1
Heywood Ct CM9 . . . .**210** B6
Heywood Way CM9 . . . . .**210** B6
Hickford Hill CO10 . . . . . .**12** D6
Hickory Ave CO4 . . . .**136** D7
Hicks Way CO9 . . . .**9** E5
Hidcote Way CM7 . . . . . .**154** B7
High Bridge Rd CM2 . . . .**205** C1
High Chelmer 8 CM1 . . . .**205** B2
High Cl SG8 . . . .**19** A5
High Croft CO6 . . . .**78** A2
High Cross La CM6 . . . . . .**149** E6
High Cross Villas CM6 . . .**149** B6
High Easter Rd CM6 . . . . .**150** F2
High Fields CM6 . . . .**150** D8
High Garrett CM7 . . . .**102** C2
High La
Bishop's Stortford CM24 . . .**119** D7
Stansted Mountfitchet CM24 **93** E1
High Lift Villas CO4 . . . . . .**83** D8
High Meadow CM6 . . . . . .**150** C8
High Rd CO2 . . . .**161** F5
High Rd E IP11 . . . .**221** E4
High Rd W IP11 . . . .**221** D5
High St
Bishop's Stortford CM23 . . .**145** F7
Braintree CM7 . . . .**127** F3
Brightlingsea CO7 . . . . . .**185** F6
Bures CO8 . . . .**55** F1
Castle Camps CB1 . . . .**7** E3
Cavendish CO10 . . . .**1** D2
Chelmsford CM1 . . . .**205** B2
Chrishall SG8 . . . .**19** D3
Clacton-on-S CO15 . . . . .**188** F2
Clare CO10 . . . .**12** B7
Clavering CB11 . . . .**65** D4
Colchester CO1 . . . .**135** F7
Debden CB11 . . . .**68** B7
Dedham CO7 . . . .**84** F7
Earls Colne CO6 . . . .**105** B6
Elsenham CM22 . . . .**94** D1
Felixstowe IP11 . . . .**221** C6
Great Baddow CM2 . . . . .**216** F6
Great Bardfield CM7 . . . . .**72** A1
Great Chesterford CB10 . . . .**3** E2
Great Chesterford CB10 . . .**21** F8
Great Dunmow CM6 . . . .**150** D8
Great Oakley CO12 . . . . .**116** C4
Great Yeldham CO9 . . . . . .**30** A1
Halstead CO9 . . . .**76** E2
Harwich CO12 . . . .**91** D4
Haverhill CB9 . . . .**9** A7
Hempstead CB10 . . . .**25** F1
Henham CM22 . . . .**94** F5
Hinxton CB10 . . . .**3** B7
Ipswich IP1 . . . .**17** C6
Kelvedon CO5 . . . .**158** C2
Langham CO4 . . . .**83** D4
Littlebury CB11 . . . .**21** F4
Maldon CM9 . . . .**210** A2
Manningtree CO11 . . . .**86** D4
Mistley CO11 . . . .**86** F4
Nayland CO6 . . . .**56** B1
Newport CB11 . . . .**67** A8
Rowhedge CO5 . . . .**164** A8

High St continued
Saffron Walden CB10 . . . . . **22** D1
Sproughton IP8 . . . . **16** A6
Stebbing CM6 . . . . **124** E5
Thorpe-le-S CO16 . . . . . . **141** F1
Tollesbury CM9 . . . . **199** D1
Walton-on-t-N CO14 . . . . **171** C8
West Mersea CO5 . . . . . . **201** B6
Wethersfield CM7 . . . . **73** C3
Widdington CB11 . . . . **67** D4
Wivenhoe CO7 . . . . **164** B8
High St N CO5 . . . . **201** C7
High Stile CM6 . . . . **150** C8
High Tree La CO14 . . . . . **144** D2
High View CM23 . . . . . . **119** D3
High View Ave CO15 . . . **188** E6
High View CO15 . . . . . . **188** E6
High View Rd IP1 . . . . . . **16** D8
High Woods Ctry Pk CO4 **110** A4
Higham Hill IP7 . . . . **58** A8
Higham Rd CO7 . . . . **58** B3
Highams Chase CM9 . . . **212** A8
Highbank CO10 . . . . **2** B5
Highbirch Rd CO16 . . . . **167** D3
Highbury Terr 1 CO9 . . . **76** F2
Highbury Way CO10 . . . . **34** B5
Highclere Rd
Colchester CO4 . . . . **110** B4
Great Notley CM7 . . . . . **154** B6
Highfield CO10 . . . . **12** D7
Highfield Ave
Bishop's Stortford CM23 . **146** C6
Harwich CO12 . . . . **91** B3
Highfield Cl
Braintree CM7 . . . . **128** A6
Danbury CM3 . . . . **218** D6
Highfield Ct CO12 . . . . . . **91** B3
Highfield Dr CO3 . . . . . . **135** C7
Highfield Holiday Pk
CO16 . . . . **188** E8
Highfield Rd
Chelmsford CM1 . . . . . . **204** E4
Felixstowe IP11 . . . . **221** D4
Sudbury CO10 . . . . **34** A8
Highfield Stile Rd CM7 . **128** A6
Highfields Bentley IP9 . . **60** E6
Debden CB11 . . . . **68** B7
Great Yeldham CO9 . . . . **30** A2
Halstead CO9 . . . . **103** F8
Henham CM22 . . . . **94** F6
Langley CB11 . . . . **40** D2
Saffron Walden CB10 . . . **22** E2
Highfields Cty Prim Sch
CO11 . . . . **86** C4
Highfields La CO5 . . . . . **178** E7
Highfields Rd CM8 . . . . **176** E1
Highland Rd CM23 . . . . **145** F3
Highlands CO9 . . . . **75** E1
Highlands Chalet Pk
CO15 . . . . **188** F7
Highlands Dr CM9 . . . . . **209** E2
Highmead CM24 . . . . . . **119** E8
Highview CO10 . . . . **15** E2
Highwoods App CO4 . . . **110** C4
Highwoods Cty Prim Sch
CO4 . . . . **110** B4
Highwoods Sq CO4 . . . . **110** B4
Hildabrook Cl 2 IP2 . . . . **16** E1
Hill Cl CO10 . . . . **15** D8
Hill Cotts CO7 . . . . **166** E2
Hill Cres CM2 . . . . **205** D2
Hill Farm La IP9 . . . . **63** F7
Hill Fields CM3 . . . . **219** A6
Hill House Ct CO7 . . . . . **186** A7
Hill House Pk CM9 . . . . **209** F3
Hill House Rd IP3 . . . . . . **17** E5
Hill La CB9 . . . . **9** F4
Hill Rd Chelmsford CM2 . **205** D2
Clacton-on-S CO15 . . . . **188** E6
Coggeshall CO6 . . . . . . **131** B2
Harwich CO12 . . . . **91** C4
Hempstead CB10 . . . . . . **46** D8
Ramsey CB10 . . . . **116** E8
Hill Road S CM2 . . . . . . **205** D2
Hill St CB10 . . . . **22** D1
Hill Top La CB11 . . . . . . **43** E7
Hill View CM3 . . . . **218** F1
Hill View Cl CO5 . . . . . . **163** F8
Hill View Rd CM1 . . . . . **205** C4
Hillary Cl Bradwell CM7 . **129** D2
Chelmsford CM1 . . . . . . **205** D4
Heybridge CM9 . . . . **210** B5
Ipswich IP4 . . . . **18** A5
Hillcrest
Clacton-on-S CO15 . . . . **189** A6
Kirby-le-S CO13 . . . . . . **170** D8
Hillcrest Cotts CO4 . . . . **83** E6
Hillcrest Ct CO12 . . . . . . **91** C3
Hillcrest Rd CO10 . . . . . **15** E2
Hillhouse La CO16 . . . . **141** B3
Hilliards Rd CO7 . . . . . . **113** C2
Hillie Bunnies CO6 . . . . **105** B7
Hillman Ave CO15 . . . . **203** E6
Hillmead JMI Sch
CM23 . . . . **119** C1
Hillridge CO4 . . . . **110** B3
Hills Cl CM7 . . . . **127** F4
Hills Cres CO3 . . . . **135** A5
Hills Rd CO9 . . . . **75** D8
Hillside CO13 . . . . **170** E4
Hillside Ave CM23 . . . . **146** A7
Hillside Cotts
Birchanger CM23 . . . . . . **119** C3
Sudbury CO10 . . . . **34** A7
Thorpe-le-S CO16 . . . . . **142** A2

Hillside Cres
Holland-on-S CO15 . . . . **189** C5
Ipswich IP3 . . . . **18** C3
Hillside End CM23 . . . . . **119** C3
Hillside Gdns CM7 . . . . **127** F1
Hillside Gr CM2 . . . . **216** A7
Hillside Ho 2 CM7 . . . . **127** F1
Hillside Mews CM7 . . . . **216** A7
Hillside Prim Sch IP2 . . . **17** C3
Hillside Rd CO10 . . . . . . **34** A7
Hillside Specl Sch CO10 . **15** F1
Hillside Terr 1 CM7 . . . **127** F1
Hillston Cl CO2 . . . . **136** B2
Hilltop Cl CO2 . . . . **136** D4
Hilltop Cres CO16 . . . . . **140** F1
Hilltop Rise CO16 . . . . . **140** E1
Hilton Cl CO11 . . . . **86** A4
Hilton Rd IP3 . . . . **18** C1
Hilton Way CO9 . . . . **75** E8
Hilton Wlk CO9 . . . . **75** E8
Hines Cl CO6 . . . . **133** B8
Hintesham Cl IP4 . . . . . . **18** F5
Hintlesham Dr IP11 . . . . **221** B5
Hinxton Rd CB10 . . . . **3** A7
Hipkins CM23 . . . . **145** E4
Histon Cl IP5 . . . . **18** F7
Hitch Common Rd CB11 **66** F8
Hitcham Rd CO6 . . . . . . **130** F3
Hitchcock Pl CO10 . . . . . **15** E1
Hitchin Mews CM7 . . . . **155** B8
Hitherwood Rd CO2 . . . **135** C2
Hobart Cl CM1 . . . . **204** E5
Hobbs Dr CO4 . . . . **83** A5
Hobbs La CO10 . . . . **2** D2
Hockerill
Anglo-European Sch
CM23 . . . . **146** B7
Hockerill Ct 7 CM23 . . . **146** A7
Hockerill St CM23 . . . . . **146** A7
Hockney Gdns IP3 . . . . . **38** A8
Hodges Holt CM8 . . . . . **195** A7
Hodgkinson Rd IP11 . . . **221** A3
Hoe Dr CO3 . . . . **135** A5
Hoe La Great Waltham CM3 **190** E6
Pentlow CO10 . . . . **13** F8
Hoe Mill Rd CM9 . . . . . **208** E4
Hoffmans Way CM1 . . . **205** B4
Hog's La SG8 . . . . **19** D3
Hogarth Cl CO5 . . . . **201** D6
Hogarth Ct CM1 . . . . . . **205** E6
Hogarth End CO13 . . . . **170** E7
Hogarth Rd IP3 . . . . **18** A1
Hogarth Sq IP3 . . . . **18** A1
Holborough Cl CO4 . . . . **136** F7
Holbrook Cl CO16 . . . . . **188** B4
Holbrook Cres IP11 . . . . **221** D4
Holbrook High Sch IP9 . . **62** D6
Holbrook Prim Sch IP9 . . **62** D6
Holbrook Rd Harkstead IP9 **63** A2
Haverhill CB9 . . . . **8** E6
Ipswich IP3 . . . . **17** F1
Stutton IP9 . . . . **62** A2
Holcombe Cres IP2 . . . . **16** D2
Holden Cl IP2 . . . . **17** D3
Holden Rd CO4 . . . . **109** F2
Holdsworth Cl CO10 . . . . **2** B3
Holkham Cl IP4 . . . . **18** F5
Holland Haven Ctry Pk
CO15 . . . . **189** I8
Holland Haven Prim Sch
CO15 . . . . **189** E6
Holland Ho CO15 . . . . . **189** A3
Holland Lodge CO15 . . . **188** F3
Holland Park Prim Sch
CO15 . . . . **189** B5
Holland Pk CO15 . . . . . . **189** B4
Holland Rd Clacton-on-S,
Clacton-on-S, Rush
Green CO15 . . . . **188** F2
Felixstowe IP11 . . . . **221** D3
Frinton-on-S CO13 . . . . **170** E3
Ipswich IP4 . . . . **17** F6
Kirby Cross CO13 . . . . . **170** B6
Little Clacton CO16 . . . . **168** E2
Hollands Rd CB9 . . . . **9** A6
Holledge Cres CO13 . . . **170** E6
Hollies Rd CM7 . . . . **129** C3
Holliland Croft CO6 . . . **132** C8
Hollington Gr CO2 . . . . **161** A3
Hollis Lock CM2 . . . . . . **206** A3
Holliwel Cl CO3 . . . . . . **134** D6
Hollow La Broomfield CM1 **204** E8
Bures CO8 . . . . **55** F3
Chelmondiston IP9 . . . . **63** F7
Hollow Rd Ashen CO10 . . **11** C3
Braintree CM6 . . . . **153** B4
Chrishall SG8 . . . . **19** D2
Elmdon CB11 . . . . **20** C4
Kelvedon CO5 . . . . **157** F2
Washbrook IP8 . . . . **35** D8
Widdington CB11 . . . . . **67** C3
Holloway Rd CM3 . . . . . **210** A5
Holly Bush Cnr CO7 . . . . **58** C5
Holly Cl CO2 . . . . **135** C2
Holly Ct CO15 . . . . **188** E4
Holly La Belstead IP8 . . . . **36** C7
Great Horkesley CO6 . . . **82** C4
Stutton IP9 . . . . **61** D3
Holly Oaks CO6 . . . . **80** E4
Holly Rd Colchester CO3 . **134** C4
Ipswich IP1 . . . . **17** B7
Rushmere St A IP5 . . . . . **18** F7
Holly Way
Chelmsford CM2 . . . . . . **216** D7
Elmstead CO7 . . . . **138** A6
Tiptree CO5 . . . . **179** C5

Holly Wlk CM8 . . . . **177** B5
Hollybank CM8 . . . . **176** F1
Hollybush Hill CO7 . . . . **166** E3
Hollyhock Rd CB10 . . . . . **22** E2
Hollymead Cl CO4 . . . . **109** F3
Hollytree Ct CO2 . . . . . . **135** C3
Hollyview Cl CO16 . . . . **140** F5
Hollywood Cl CM2 . . . . **216** C6
Holm Oak CO2 . . . . **136** A3
Holman Cres CO3 . . . . . **135** A4
Holman Rd CO9 . . . . . . **103** E8
Holmans CM3 . . . . **206** B8
Holmbrook Way CO13 . . **170** E5
Holmes Rd CO9 . . . . . . **103** E8
Holmoak IP9 . . . . **62** D6
Holmswood House
Prep Sch CO3 . . . . **134** D8
Holmwood Cl CO16 . . . **188** B6
Holmwood House Prep
Sch CO3 . . . . **134** D8
Holt Dr Blackheath CO2 . **163** A7
Wickham Bishops CM8 . . **195** E5
Holt's Rd CO6 . . . . **81** B3
Holy Family RC Prim
Sch CM8 . . . . **194** F8
Holy Trinity CE Prim Sch
CO9 . . . . **76** D2
Holybread La CM3 . . . . . **207** C4
Holyrood CO12 . . . . **90** F2
Holyrood Cl IP2 . . . . **16** F1
Holywells Cl IP3 . . . . **17** E4
Holywells High Sch IP3 . . **18** C1
Holywells Rd IP3 . . . . . . **17** E3
Home Cl CB9 . . . . **27** C7
Home Farm Cty Prim Sch
CO3 . . . . **134** F6
Home Farm La
Ardleigh CO7 . . . . **112** A8
Dedham CO7 . . . . **85** A1
Home Mead
Galleywood CM2 . . . . . . **216** C2
Writtle CM1 . . . . **204** A1
Homebridge CB10 . . . . . **47** A3
Homedale Cotts CO4 . . . **83** B6
Homefield IP9 . . . . **35** B1
Homefield Cl CM1 . . . . . **204** D5
Homefield Rd
Colchester CO2 . . . . **135** C1
Haverhill CB9 . . . . **8** E7
Witham CM8 . . . . **177** A4
Homefield Way
Cressing CM7 . . . . **155** D7
Earls Colne CO6 . . . . . . **105** B7
Homelands Ct CO14 . . . **171** A7
Homelye Chase CM6 . . . **124** B1
Homeorr Ho IP11 . . . . . . **221** F4
Homerton Cl CO15 . . . . **188** F8
Homestead CM1 . . . . . . **205** B7
Homestead Sch CO4 . . . **83** E4
Homey Bridge Rd CO6 . . **56** C8
Homing Rd CO16 . . . . . **168** C4
Honey Cl CM2 . . . . **216** D6
Honey La CB11 . . . . **64** F3
Honeybourne CM23 . . . **145** E4
Honeypot La
Little Clacton CO16 . . . . **168** C4
Tolleshunt Knights CM9 . **180** C3
Weeley Heath CO16 . . . . **168** A4
Wix CO11 . . . . **114** F3
Honeypots CM2 . . . . . . **216** C6
Honeysuckle Cl CM23 . . **145** C6
Honeysuckle Gdns IP2 . . **16** E4
Honeysuckle Path 9
CM1 . . . . **205** F6
Honeysuckle Way
Colchester CO4 . . . . **136** E8
Thorrington CO7 . . . . . . **166** A5
Witham CM8 . . . . **176** D4
Honeywood Ave CO6 . . . **131** A3
Honeywood Rd CO9 . . . . **77** A3
Honywood Cl CO6 . . . . . **132** C3
Honywood Rd CO3 . . . . **135** D6
Honywood Sch The CO6 . **131** A3
Honywood Way CO13 . . **170** F7
Hood Gdns CM7 . . . . . . **128** C4
Hood Rd IP3 . . . . **17** E1
Hop Gardens La CO9 . . . **208** F4
Hopgrounds The CM7 . . . **72** D6
Hopkin's La CO12 . . . . . . **91** D6
Hopkins Cl
Chelmsford CM2 . . . . . . **206** A3
Kirby Cross CO13 . . . . . **170** F6
Hopkins Mead CM2 . . . **206** A2
Hopkirk Cl CM3 . . . . **218** F8
Hopping Jacks La CM3 . **218** F7
Hoppit Mead CM7 . . . . **127** F1
Hopton Rise CB9 . . . . **8** B8
Horace Eves Cl 1 CB9 . . . **8** F8
Hordle Pl CO12 . . . . **91** D4
Hordle St CO12 . . . . **91** D4
Horkesley Hill CO6 . . . . . **82** A7
Horkesley Rd
Great Horkesley CO4 . . . **109** E8
Nayland CO6 . . . . **56** A1
Horley IP2 . . . . **16** E4
Horley Cl CO16 . . . . **188** C6
Horn Hill CO9 . . . . **75** C5
Hornbeam Cl
Chelmsford CM2 . . . . . . **216** A6
Colchester CO2 . . . . **135** D2
Hornbeam Wlk CM7 . . . **127** A4
Hornbeams The CO12 . . **117** B7
Horne Row CM3 . . . . . . **218** D5
Horner Pl 4 CM8 . . . . . **177** A2
Hornsea Villas CM6 . . . **124** D7
Horrocks Cl CO2 . . . . . . **136** A4
Horse & Groom La CM2 . **216** A3
Horse Pond Cl CO10 . . . . **34** C4

Horseshoe Cl CB11 . . . . . **20** B4
Horseshoe La CB9 . . . . **8** E7
Horsey Rd CO13 . . . . . . **170** C8
Horsham Ave IP3 . . . . . . **18** D3
Horsley Ho IP11 . . . . . . **221** F4
Hospital App CM1 . . . . . **191** B3
Hospital La CO3 . . . . . . **135** D6
Hospital Rd CO3 . . . . . . **135** D6
Hossack Rd IP3 . . . . **38** A8
Houblon Dr CM2 . . . . . . **216** C2
Houchin's La CO6 . . . . . **131** E3
Houghton Pl IP4 . . . . **18** F5
House Martins The IP11 . **221** D6
Hove Ct CO15 . . . . **189** F6
Howard Ave CO12 . . . . . . **90** F2
Howard Rd
Holland-on-S CO15 . . . . **189** C4
Saffron Walden CB10 . . . **22** C2
Howard St IP4 . . . . **18** B6
Howard Vyse Ct CO15 . . **188** E5
Howards Cl CM3 . . . . . . **206** B8
Howards Croft CO4 . . . . **109** D5
Howbridge CE Jun Sch
CM8 . . . . **194** F8
Howbridge Hall Rd
Witham CM8 . . . . **194** F6
Witham CM8 . . . . **194** F7
Howbridge Inf Sch The
CM8 . . . . **194** F8
Howbridge Rd CM8 . . . . **194** F8
Howe Ave IP3 . . . . **18** C3
Howe Chase CO9 . . . . . . **76** E4
Howe Cl CO4 . . . . **136** D7
Howe Green House Sch
CM22 . . . . **146** D2
Howe La CB10 . . . . **47** A5
Howlets Terr IP3 . . . . **63** E7
Hoxter Way CO10 . . . . . . **15** E2
Hoxton Cl CO16 . . . . . . **188** D5
Hoynors CM3 . . . . **219** A4
Hubbards Chase CO14 . . **171** B8
Hubert Rd CO3 . . . . **135** B8
Hudson Cl
Clacton-on-S CO16 . . . . **188** C5
Haverhill CO12 . . . . **91** A1
Haverhill CB9 . . . . **9** C6
Hudson's Hill CM7 . . . . . **73** D4
Hudsons La CO6 . . . . . . **57** B5
Hugh Dickson Rd CO4 . . **109** F2
Hugh Villas CM23 . . . . . **146** A5
Hughes Cnr CO7 . . . . . . **59** A4
Hughes Rd CO7 . . . . **59** A4
Hughes Stanton Way
CO11 . . . . **86** B4
Hull La CM3 . . . . **175** A6
Hull's La CM2 . . . . **217** E7
Hulton Cl CM3 . . . . **206** E8
Hulver Ct IP3 . . . . **18** B2
Humber Ave CO15 . . . . . **203** E6
Humber Doucy La IP4 . . . **18** D8
Humber Rd
Chelmsford CM1 . . . . . . **205** C5
Witham CM8 . . . . **176** D2
Humphrey's Farm La
CM3 . . . . **190** C7
Humphry Rd CO10 . . . . . **33** E8
Hundon Pl 4 CB9 . . . . **9** B8
Hundred La CO4 . . . . . . **83** C4
Hungerdown La CO11, CO7 **85** E1
Hunnable Rd CM7 . . . . . **127** E2
Hunt Ave CM9 . . . . **210** B5
Hunt Cl CO5 . . . . **158** D4
Hunt Dr CO16 . . . . **188** D6
Hunt Rd CO6 . . . . **105** A6
Hunt Way CO13 . . . . . . **170** E6
Hunt's Cl CM1 . . . . **215** B8
Hunt's Dr CM1 . . . . **215** B8
Hunter Dr CO11 . . . . **86** A3
Hunter Rd CM7 . . . . **128** C2
Hunter's Chase CO7 . . . . **84** E2
Hunters Cnr CO3 . . . . . . **134** F5
Hunters Ct CM22 . . . . . . **94** C2
Hunters End IP11 . . . . . **221** A7
Hunters Ridge CO4 . . . . **110** B4
Hunters Way
Chelmsford CM1 . . . . . . **205** F7
Saffron Walden CB11 . . . **43** D7
Hunting Gate CO1 . . . . . **136** C7
Huntingdon Way CO15 . . **188** E6
Hunts Farm Cl CM9 . . . . **199** D3
Hunts Hill CO10 . . . . **2** B4
Hunts La CB10 . . . . **3** B7
Hunwicke Rd CO4 . . . . . **136** E7
Hurnard Dr CO3 . . . . . . **135** A4
Hurrell Down
Boreham CM3 . . . . **192** F1
Highwoods CO4 . . . . . . **110** A4
Hurrells La CM3 . . . . . . **206** F3
Hurst Cl
Bishop's Stortford CM23 . **145** E7
Brightlingsea CO7 . . . . . **186** A6
Hurst Way CM2 . . . . . . **205** F2
Hutland Rd IP4 . . . . **17** F7
Huxtables La CO3 . . . . . **108** A1
Hyacinth Cl
Clacton-on-S CO16 . . . . **188** C4
Tollesbury CM9 . . . . . . **199** E1
Hyacinth Ct 4 CM1 . . . . **205** E7
Hyam's La IP9 . . . . **61** F1
Hyams La CB9 . . . . **8** A8
Hyde Chase Danbury CM3 . **219** B4
Woodham Mortimer CM9 . **219** C4
Hyde Gn CM3 . . . . **219** B7
Hyde La Danbury CM3 . . **219** B6
Wethersfield CM7 . . . . . **74** B2

Hyde Rd CO10 . . . . **33** E4
Hydewood Rd CO9 . . . . . . **30** B3
Hyem's La IP11 . . . . **221** F7
Hylands CM6 . . . . **151** A4
Hylands Par CM2 . . . . . **216** A4
Hyldon Ct IP11 . . . . **221** E3
Hyll Cl CB10 . . . . **3** B6
Hyntle Cl IP2 . . . . **16** E5
Hythe Cl Braintree CM7 . **127** E4
Clacton-on-S CO15 . . . . **203** J8
Hythe Gr CO7 . . . . **165** E1
Hythe Hill CO1 . . . . **136** C6
Hythe Quay CO2 . . . . . . **136** D5
Hythe Sta CO4 . . . . **136** D6
Hythe Station Rd CO2 . . **136** D6
Hythe The CM9 . . . . **210** B2

I

Iceni Way CO2 . . . . **135** B3
Ickleton Pl 5 CB9 . . . . **9** B8
Ickleton Rd Elmdon CB11 . **20** A4
Great Chesterford CB10 . . . **3** C2
Hinxton CB10 . . . . **3** B6
Icknield Cl CB10 . . . . **3** A3
Ickworth Cres IP4 . . . . . . **18** F5
Ickworth Cl IP11 . . . . . . **221** A3
Ilex Cl CO2 . . . . **135** D2
Imogen Cl 4 CO4 . . . . . **136** F7
Imphal Cl CO2 . . . . **135** C1
Ingarfield Rd CO15 . . . . **189** E6
Ingelrica Ave CM3 . . . . **194** B3
Ingestre St CO12 . . . . . . **91** D4
Ingham Rd CB9 . . . . **9** B8
Inglenook CO15 . . . . . . **189** B7
Ingleside Ct CB10 . . . . . . **22** D5
Inglis Rd CO3 . . . . **135** C6
Ingram Mews CM7 . . . . **155** B8
Ingram's Piece CO7 . . . . **111** C6
Ingram's Well CO10 . . . . **33** F7
Ingram's Well Rd CO10 . . **33** F7
Inkerman Row 3 CO10 . . **33** E8
Inkerpole Pl CM2 . . . . . **205** F4
Innes End 4 IP8 . . . . . . **16** C2
Innham Hill CO9 . . . . . . **75** C6
Inverness Cl CO1 . . . . . **136** A4
Inworth La CO6 . . . . **79** D2
Inworth Rd CO5 . . . . . . **158** E3
Inworth Wlk 6 CO2 . . . . **136** A1
Ipswich Airport IP3 . . . . **38** C1
Ipswich High Sch IP9 . . . **38** E1
Ipswich Hospl IP4 . . . . . . **18** C6
Ipswich Mus IP1 . . . . . . **17** C4
Ipswich Prep Sch IP1 . . . **17** B7
Ipswich Rd Ardleigh CO7 . **83** F1
Brantham CO11 . . . . . . **60** E2
Colchester CO4 . . . . **110** C3
Dedham CO7 . . . . **84** B6
Harkstead IP9 . . . . **63** B3
Holbrook IP9 . . . . **62** E6
Holland-on-S CO15 . . . . **189** D6
Ipswich IP10 . . . . **38** F6
Stratford St M CO7 . . . . . **58** E2
Ipswich Sch Ipswich IP1 . . **17** B8
Ipswich IP1 . . . . **17** C7
Ipswich Sta IP2 . . . . **17** B4
Ipswich Transport Mus
IP3 . . . . **18** C2
Ireland Rd IP3 . . . . **17** F1
Ireton Rd CO3 . . . . **135** D5
Iris Cl Chelmsford CM1 . . **205** F5
Ipswich IP2 . . . . **16** F5
Irlam Rd IP2 . . . . **16** D1
Iron Latch La CO3 . . . . . **134** C4
Irvine Rd CO3 . . . . **135** C5
Irving Cl CM23 . . . . **145** D4
Isbourne Rd CO4 . . . . . . **136** F7
Ishams Chase CM8 . . . . **195** C7
Island La CO13 . . . . **143** E1
Island Rd CO14 . . . . **143** E4
Ivor Brown Ct CO4 . . . . **110** B4
Ivry St IP1 . . . . **17** B7
Ivy Cotts CM6 . . . . **123** B4
Ivy La CO5 . . . . **185** B3
Ivy Lodge Rd CO6 . . . . . **109** C4
Ivy Todd Hill CB11 . . . . . **68** A8
Ixworth Rd CB9 . . . . **8** A7

J

Jacaranda Cl CM1 . . . . . **206** A4
Jack Andrews Ave CO4 . . **110** C5
Jack Branch Ct CO15 . . . **188** E2
Jack Hatch Way CO7 . . . **137** A3
Jack's La CM22 . . . . **148** D7
Jackson Pl CM2 . . . . . . **216** D6
Jackson Rd CO15 . . . . . **188** E2
Jackson Sq 10 CM23 . . . **145** F7
Jackson Wlk CO2 . . . . . **136** B3
Jackson's La CB10 . . . . **3** D3
Jackson's Sq CB10 . . . . . . **3** D3
Jacobs Ct CO7 . . . . **185** F6
Jacquard Way CM7 . . . . **128** A2
Jacqueline Ct CO3 . . . . **135** A7
Jaggard's Rd CO6 . . . . . **131** A3
James Boden Cl IP11 . . . **221** C5
James Carter Rd CO3 . . . **134** F3
James Cl CO7 . . . . **137** C3
James Croft CM2 . . . . . **216** B2
James Gdns CO16 . . . . . **187** B5
James Hatfield Ho IP2 . . . **17** A2
James Rd CO15 . . . . **188** C2
James St
Brightlingsea CO7 . . . . . **185** F6
Colchester CO1 . . . . **136** A6
Jameson Pl CO10 . . . . . . **33** E8

Jameson Rd CO15 ......188 C3
Janebrook Rd IP2 ......16 E2
Janmead CM8 ......177 A3
Janus Cl CB9 ......9 D6
Japonica Ct CO15 ......189 C4
Jaques Cl CO10 ......2 C5
Jarmin Rd CO1 ......135 F8
Jarndyce CM1 ......204 F6
Jarvis Field CM3 ......207 D5
Jasmin Cl CM23 ......145 C6
Jasmine Cl
 [2] Chelmsford CM1 ......205 E7
 Colchester CO4 ......136 E8
 Ipswich IP2 ......16 F3
Jasmine Way CO15 ......203 G7
Jaspers Green CM7 ......100 E2
Jay Cl CB9 ......9 C7
Jaymar Cl CM7 ......127 F2
Jayrest Ctr CO3 ......134 E4
Jays La CO14 ......132 F3
Jays The CO4 ......110 C3
Jaywick La CO15 ......188 A3
Jaywick Rd CB9 ......9 A8
Jeans La CM23 ......145 E7
Jeffcut Rd CM2 ......205 E2
Jefferies Rd IP4 ......17 E6
Jefferson Cl CO3 ......134 E5
Jeffery Rd CM2 ......217 A7
Jeffrey Cl CO3 ......134 F5
Jeffrey's Rd CM7 ......155 E6
Jekylls La CM7 ......48 D4
Jellicoe Way CM7 ......128 C4
Jenkins Dr CM22 ......94 C3
Jenkins La CM22 ......146 C5
Jenner Cl CM7 ......127 F1
Jenner Mead CM2 ......206 A3
Jennings Cl [1] CO1 ......136 C6
Jermyns IP9 ......35 B2
Jersey Rd CM9 ......210 B1
Jersey Way CM7 ......127 D2
Jervis CI IP9 ......62 D5
Jervis Rd CM23 ......145 C6
Jessica Cl CO4 ......136 F7
Jimmy's La CO11 ......60 F2
Joes Rd CO10 ......34 F6
John Ball Wlk [2] CO1 ......135 F7
John Bird Ct CO1 ......109 F1
John Bramston Sch &
 Sixth Form Ctr The
 CM8 ......176 F1
John Bunyan Cty Jun &
 Inf Sch CM7 ......127 E4
John Dane Player Ct [4]
 CB11 ......22 E1
John English Ave CM7 ......127 C4
John Harper St [4] CO1 ......135 E8
John Henry Keene
 Meml Homes CM1 ......205 A4
John Kavanagh Ct [1]
 CO1 ......136 A6
John Kent Ave CO2 ......135 B2
John King Ct CO7 ......185 F6
John Raven Ct CO5 ......158 D3
John Ray Cty Jun & Inf
 Schs CM7 ......154 F8
John Ray Gdns CM7 ......155 B5
John Ray St CM7 ......128 A3
John St CO7 ......185 F6
John Tibauld Ct CB9 ......27 B6
Johns Rd CM23 ......119 A1
Johnson Cl Braintree CM7 ......155 A4
 Ipswich IP2 ......17 C3
Johnson Rd
 Great Baddow CM2 ......217 A5
 St Osyth CO16 ......187 B4
Johnson's Dr CO7 ......138 A6
Johnston Cl Halstead CO9 ......103 F8
 Holland-on-S CO15 ......189 B5
Jollyboys La CM6 ......152 C6
Jollyboys La S CM6 ......152 C6
Jonathan Feedham Ct
 CO7 ......137 B1
Jonquil Way CO4 ......109 C2
Joseph Gdns CM8 ......156 E4
Josse Lyns The IP11 ......221 A8
Josselin Cl CO6 ......105 B7
Joyce's Chase CM9 ......212 A8
Jubilee Ave
 Broomfield CM1 ......191 B2
 Clacton-on-S CO16 ......188 E8
Jubilee Cl CO12 ......90 E1
Jubilee Ct
 Great Dunmow CM6 ......123 C1
 Sible Hedingham CO9 ......75 E8
 Walton-on-t-N CO14 ......171 C7
Jubilee End CO11 ......86 C5
Jubilee La CO7 ......111 C3
Jubilee Rd CO10 ......33 F8
Jubilee Rise CM3 ......219 A6
Jubilee Terr CM1 ......205 A4
Jubilee Way CO13 ......170 E6
Jubilee Wlk [3] CB9 ......9 A7
Julian Ave CO4 ......110 B6
Julian Cl Broomfield CM1 ......191 B1
 Haverhill CB9 ......9 D7
Julien Court Rd CM7 ......128 A4
Jun Sch Felsted The
 CM6 ......152 B5
Juniper Cl CO9 ......103 D8
Juniper Cres CM8 ......177 A4
Juniper Ct CM6 ......123 C1
Juniper Rd Boreham CM3 ......206 F8
 Colchester CO3 ......134 D5
Juniper Way CO4 ......136 D8
Juno Mews CO2 ......135 C1
Jupe's Hill CO8 ......79 D1

Jupes Hill CO7 ......85 C4
Jupiter Cl CB9 ......9 D6
Jupiter Rd IP4 ......18 B7
Justinian Cl CB9 ......9 D6
Juvina Cl CM8 ......194 F7

K

Kale Croft CO3 ......134 D5
Kangels The CB11 ......40 D2
Kate Daniels Ho CO16 ......140 F1
Kate's La CB10 ......24 C8
Katherine Semar Cty Inf
 Sch CB11 ......43 E6
Katherine Semar Jun Sch
 CB11 ......43 E6
Kay Cl CM3 ......174 A7
Kayla Ct [6] CO3 ......135 E6
Keable Rd CO6 ......132 E3
Keating Cl CO11 ......86 B4
Keats Ave CM7 ......154 F8
Keats Rd CO3 ......134 F6
Kebbles CO10 ......2 B6
Keble Cl CO3 ......135 D6
Kedington Hill CO10 ......34 B2
Keeble Cl CO5 ......179 E5
Keeble Ct CO7 ......166 F7
Keeble Pk CM7 ......220 F8
Keeble Way CM7 ......128 A3
Keeble's Yd [7] CB9 ......9 A8
Keelars La CO7 ......137 E2
Keelers Way CO6 ......109 B7
Keene Way CM2 ......216 B3
Keep The [3] CB9 ......8 E7
Keepers Gn CO4 ......109 B3
Keith Cl CO5 ......189 B8
Kelly Rd IP2 ......16 E5
Kelso Cl CO6 ......109 C6
Kelvedon Cl CM1 ......205 A6
Kelvedon Dr IP4 ......18 F5
Kelvedon Hall La CO5 ......178 E5
Kelvedon Rd
 Coggeshall CO6 ......158 A8
 Messing CO5 ......159 C2
 Tiptree CO5 ......179 B7
 Tolleshunt D'arcy CM9 ......198 C6
 Wickham Bishops CM8 ......195 F5
Kelvedon Sta CO5 ......158 C3
Kelvin Ct CO13 ......170 F3
Kemball St IP4 ......18 A5
Kempe Rd CM7 ......72 D6
Kempson Dr CO10 ......34 C5
Kempsters The IP11 ......221 B7
Kempton Pk CO16 ......168 B5
Kemsley Rd
 Earls Colne CO6 ......105 A6
 Felixstowe IP11 ......221 D5
Ken Cooke Ct [4] CO1 ......135 F7
Kendall CE Prim Sch
 CO1 ......136 C4
Kendall Rd CO1 ......136 A6
Kendall's
 Almshouses CO1 ......136 A6
Kenilworth Gr CO16 ......142 A2
Kenilworth Rd CO15 ......189 A6
Kennedy Cl IP4 ......18 A6
Kennedy Way CO15 ......189 A5
Kennet Way CO1 ......204 D5
Kensington Rd IP1 ......17 A8
Kenston Ct CO5 ......201 B6
Kent Cl CO7 ......185 F7
Kent Cres CM23 ......145 A4
Kent Gdns CM7 ......128 B4
Kent Ho IP11 ......221 C6
Kent's Ave CO15 ......189 E6
Kentford Rd IP11 ......221 A4
Kentings The CM7 ......127 E2
Kentmere CO4 ......110 E2
Kents Grass CM9 ......199 D2
Kents Yd CB11 ......21 F4
Kentwell Cl IP4 ......18 F4
Kenworthy Rd CM7 ......127 F2
Kenyon Cl CO7 ......58 D1
Kenyon St IP2 ......17 C4
Kerby Rise CM2 ......205 F2
Kerridge's Cut CO11 ......87 A4
Kerry Ct CO1 ......136 C7
Kersey Ave CO4 ......34 B6
Kersey Ct CO2 ......135 C2
Kersey Dr CO16 ......188 B5
Kersey Rd IP11 ......221 B3
Kessler Ave CM7 ......73 D7
Kesteven Rd IP2 ......17 B4
Kestrel Gdns CM23 ......145 C6
Kestrel Rd Haverhill CB9 ......9 C7
 Ipswich IP2 ......16 E2
Kestrel Way CO15 ......188 F6
Kestrel Wlk CM2 ......216 B5
Keswick Ave CO15 ......189 C6
Keswick Cl CO13 ......170 F7
Ketleys CM2 ......216 C3
Ketleys View CM7 ......127 A7
Kettlebaston Way IP4 ......17 D8
Kew La CO13 ......170 A4
Key Rd CO15 ......188 E3
Key St IP4 ......17 D5
Keyes Way CM7 ......128 C4
Keymer Way CO3 ......134 F4
Keynes Way CO12 ......90 F1
Khartoum Rd IP4 ......17 F7
Kidder Rd CM7 ......126 F1
Kilburn Gdns CO16 ......188 D5
Kildermorie Cl CO4 ......110 D3
Kilmaine Rd CO12 ......90 F2
Kiln Barn Ave CO15 ......188 F7
Kiln Cotts Danbury CM3 ......218 D6
 Dedham CO7 ......84 F5

Kiln Dr CO10 ......34 B6
Kiln Field IP11 ......221 B5
Kilns CO15 ......130 F5
Kimberley Cl CM23 ......146 A5
Kimberley Rd CO1 ......136 B5
Kincaid Rd CO16 ......187 A4
King Charles Rd CO5 ......201 D6
King Coel Rd CO3 ......134 D7
King Edward Ind Pk CO2 ......136 D5
King Edward IV's
 Almshouses CB11 ......22 C1
King Edward Quay CO2 ......136 D5
King Edward Rd IP3 ......18 B3
King Edward VI Gram
 Sch CM1 ......205 A3
King Edward Vii Dr IP9 ......91 C8
King Edward Way CM8 ......194 E8
King George Rd CO2 ......135 F4
King George V Memorial
 Homes IP3 ......17 F3
King George's Ave CO12 ......91 B4
King Harold Rd CO3 ......135 A4
King St
 Bishop's Stortford CM23 ......145 F7
 Bradfield CO11 ......114 C3
 Castle Hedingham CO9 ......51 F4
 Felixstowe IP11 ......221 C6
 [14] Ipswich IP1 ......17 C6
 Maldon CM9 ......210 A1
 Saffron Walden CB10 ......22 E1
 Sudbury CO10 ......33 E7
King Stephen Rd CO1 ......136 B6
King Street Mews [1]
 CM23 ......145 F7
King's Cl CO16 ......187 A3
King's Cotts CM23 ......146 A6
King's Ct CM6 ......123 D1
King's Ford Cty Jun &
 Inf Schs CO2 ......135 C3
King's Head St CO12 ......91 E6
King's La Elmdon CB11 ......20 A3
 Long Melford CO10 ......15 F3
King's Quay St CO12 ......91 E6
King's Rd
 Clacton-on-S CO15 ......188 D1
 Harwich CO12 ......91 B3
King's Way IP3 ......18 C2
Kingfisher Ave IP2 ......16 E3
Kingfisher Cl
 Colchester CO4 ......136 F8
 Haverhill CB9 ......9 C8
 Heybridge CM9 ......210 C5
Kingfisher Gate CM7 ......128 C6
Kingfisher Lodge CM2 ......216 F7
Kingfisher Way
 Bishop's Stortford CM23 ......146 A7
 Kelvedon CO5 ......158 C2
Kingfishers CO15 ......188 F6
Kings Acre CO6 ......130 F2
Kings Ave
 Clacton-on-S CO15 ......189 D5
 Ipswich IP4 ......17 E5
Kings Chase CM8 ......177 A1
Kings Cl CO11 ......86 C4
Kings Ct
 Bishop's Stortford CM23 ......146 A8
 Holland-on-S CO15 ......189 D5
Kings Fleet Rd IP11 ......221 C3
Kings Ford Ct CO2 ......135 B3
Kings Head Ct [1] CO1 ......135 E8
Kings Head Wlk [6] CM2 ......205 C2
Kings Hill CO10 ......34 A6
Kings Ho CO13 ......171 A4
Kings La CM7 ......129 A6
Kings Mead CO9 ......78 A7
Kings Meadow CO10 ......34 A6
Kings Meadow Ct CO5 ......158 C4
Kings Meadow Rd CO1 ......135 F8
Kings Mews CO7 ......137 C4
Kings Par CO15 ......189 E5
Kings Prom CO15 ......203 J8
Kings Quay St CO12 ......91 E6
Kings Rd Braintree CM7 ......127 E6
 Chelmsford CM1 ......204 F4
 Glemsford CO10 ......2 B5
 Great Totham CM9 ......196 A5
 Halstead CO9 ......76 E1
Kings Reach CO14 ......144 D1
Kings Road Cty Jun &
 Inf Sch CM1 ......204 F4
Kings Wlk CM9 ......199 E1
Kingsbridge Cl CM7 ......127 F8
Kingsbridge Rd CM23 ......146 A8
Kingsbury Cl CO6 ......132 F3
Kingsbury Rd IP11 ......221 A7
Kingsdale Ind Est The
 CM1 ......205 C3
Kingsfield Ave IP1 ......17 D8
Kingsgate Dr IP4 ......17 F8
Kingsland Beach CO5 ......201 C5
Kingsland Cl CO5 ......201 C5
Kingsland Rd CO5 ......201 C5
Kingsman Dr CO16 ......188 C5
Kingsmead Rd CM23 ......146 A8
Kingsmere Cl CO5 ......201 D7
Kingston Ave CM2 ......205 E3
Kingston Chase CM9 ......209 F5
Kingston Cres CM2 ......205 E3
Kingston Rd IP1 ......16 E5
Kingsway Harwich CO12 ......91 D4
 Tiptree CO5 ......179 C4
Kingswode Hoe Specl
 Sch CO3 ......135 C7
Kingswood Rd CO4 ......109 F4
Kingwell Ave CO15 ......188 E5
Kinlett Cl CO5 ......110 B4
Kinloch Chase CM8 ......194 F7
Kino Rd CO14 ......171 D8

Kipling Cl CM1 ......205 A5
Kipling Way CM7 ......155 A8
Kirby Cl IP4 ......18 A7
Kirby Cross Sta CO13 ......170 B6
Kirby Hall Rd CO9 ......51 D5
Kirby Rd
 Great Holland CO13 ......170 B5
 Walton-on-t-N CO14 ......171 B8
Kirby St IP4 ......18 A6
Kirby-le-Soken Cty
 Prim Sch CO13 ......170 B7
Kirk Pl CM2 ......205 F3
Kirkbaye CO13 ......170 E6
Kirkham Cl IP2 ......17 A2
Kirkhurst Cl CO7 ......186 A6
Kirklees CM1 ......204 F4
Kirkmans Rd CM2 ......216 D3
Kirkton Cl IP9 ......91 A8
Kirtling Pl [12] CB9 ......9 B8
Kitchen Field CM7 ......128 D3
Kitchener Rd IP1 ......16 F8
Kitchener Way IP9 ......91 A8
Kittiwake Cl IP2 ......16 E3
Kittiwake Dr CM9 ......210 C5
Knapton Cl CM1 ......205 D7
Knebworth Ct CM23 ......145 D6
Knight's Ct [2] CB9 ......8 E7
Knights Cl
 Bishop's Stortford CM23 ......145 C8
 Lawford CO11 ......86 C4
 Tiptree CO5 ......179 F3
Knights Rd
 Braintree CM7 ......128 D1
 Coggeshall CO6 ......130 F2
Knights Way CM23 ......123 D1
Knightsbridge Cl CM2 ......135 C3
Knightsbridge Ct CO15 ......189 B3
Knole La CB11 ......41 A7
Knowles Ct CO9 ......76 E1
Knox Cl CO15 ......188 E5
Knox Gdns CO15 ......188 E5
Knox Rd CO15 ......188 E5
Knutsford Cl IP8 ......16 C1
Kohima Rd CO2 ......135 B1
Kreswell Gr CO12 ......91 B2
Kynaston Pl CM8 ......177 B2
Kynaston Rd CM7 ......127 A7

L

Laburnum CM3 ......194 A3
Laburnum Cl
 Clacton-on-S CO15 ......188 C3
 Great Bentley CO7 ......166 F8
 [2] Ipswich, Chantry IP8 ......16 C2
 Ipswich, Warren Heath IP3 ......18 E2
Laburnum Cres CO13 ......170 D6
Laburnum Dr CM2 ......216 B8
Laburnum Gr CO4 ......136 E8
Laburnum Way CM8 ......177 A5
Lacey St IP4 ......17 E6
Ladbrook Dr CO2 ......136 A3
Ladbrooke Rd CO16 ......188 D6
Ladell Cl CO3 ......134 E3
Lady D'Arcy Charity
 Almshouses [3] CO1 ......135 F6
Lady La Chelmsford CM2 ......216 C8
 [6] Ipswich IP1 ......17 B6
Ladygate CB9 ......9 B8
Ladysmith Ave CO7 ......185 E6
Ladysmith Cotts CM6 ......152 E4
Ladywell La CM2 ......217 B5
Ladywood Rd IP4 ......18 C7
Laing Rd CO4 ......136 E6
Lake Ave CO15 ......188 C3
Lake Way CO15 ......203 F6
Lake Wlk CO15 ......188 C3
Lakes Mdw CO6 ......131 A2
Lakes Rd CM7 ......128 B2
Lakeside Cl IP2 ......16 E2
Lakeside Rd IP2 ......16 E2
Lakforth CO10 ......15 D8
Lakin Cl CM2 ......206 A3
Lamarsh Hill Bures CO8 ......55 E1
 Lamarsh CO8 ......55 B6
Lamarsh Rd CO8 ......55 A4
Lamb La CO9 ......75 D7
Lambert Cross CB10 ......22 E1
Lambert's Rd CO6 ......105 F3
Lambeth Wlk CO15 ......188 E5
Lambourne Cl
 Clacton-on-S CO15 ......188 F8
 Colchester CO3 ......134 D4
Lambourne Gr CM9 ......220 F8
Lammas Way CO7 ......137 C2
Lancaster Gdns E CO15 ......189 A3
Lancaster Gdns W CO15 ......189 A3
Lancaster Ho IP11 ......221 C5
Lancaster Rd
 [6] Ipswich IP4 ......17 E6
 Sudbury CO10 ......15 D2
Lancaster Way
 Bishop's Stortford CM23 ......145 C8
 Braintree CM7 ......127 E4
 Earls Colne CO6 ......104 C3
Lanchester Ave CO15 ......203 D6
Lancing Ave IP4 ......18 A8
Land Cl CO15 ......188 C5
Land La CO1 ......136 A7
Landermere Rd CO16 ......142 B2
Landermere View CO16 ......142 A2
Landers Ct CM1 ......204 D5
Landisdale CM3 ......219 A7
Landscape View CB11 ......43 D6
Landsdown Rd CO10 ......34 A8
Landseer Rd IP3 ......18 A1

Landseer Ct
 Clacton-on-S CO15 ......188 F2
 Haverhill CB9 ......8 F6
Landseer Rd
 Colchester CO3 ......135 B5
 Ipswich IP3 ......17 E2
Lane Rd CO6 ......106 B7
Lane The Mistley CO11 ......86 B4
 West Mersea CO5 ......201 A4
Lanercost Way IP2 ......17 A1
Langdale CM7 ......154 C7
Langdale Dr CO4 ......110 B4
Langdale Gdns CM2 ......216 D8
Langenhoe Cty Prim
 Sch CO5 ......163 B2
Langenhoe Hall La CO5 ......183 C7
Langenhoe Pk CO5 ......163 B2
Langer Cty Prim Sch
 IP11 ......221 C2
Langer Rd IP11 ......221 C2
Langford Rd
 Heybridge CM9 ......209 F6
 Wickham Bishops CM8 ......195 C2
Langham Court Prim
 Sch CO4 ......83 E4
Langham Dr CO16 ......188 B4
Langham La CO4 ......83 B2
Langham Rd CO4 ......82 F1
Langley Ave
 Felixstowe IP11 ......221 C4
 Wethersfield CM7 ......73 D7
Langley Cl Felixstowe IP11 ......221 C5
 Harwich CO12 ......91 C3
Langley Hill CO8 ......55 C3
Langleys CO6 ......106 C1
Langstons IP11 ......221 B7
Langton Ave CO4 ......204 E5
Languidec Cl CO10 ......34 C6
Langwood CO5 ......201 C7
Lanham Green Rd CM7 ......156 A7
Lansdowne CO5 ......179 C6
Lansdowne Rd
 Felixstowe IP11 ......221 F6
 Ipswich IP2 ......18 A5
Lanvalley Rd CO3 ......134 C6
Lanyards IP11 ......221 F4
Lapwing Dr
 Heybridge CM9 ......210 C5
 Kelvedon CO5 ......158 C2
Lapwing Rd IP2 ......16 D3
Larch Cl CO4 ......136 D8
Larch Gr Chelmsford CM2 ......216 C8
 Nayland CO6 ......56 A1
 Witham CM8 ......177 A5
Larch Ho IP11 ......221 C6
Larch Way CM6 ......123 B1
Larch Wlk CM9 ......210 C5
Larches The CM3 ......206 E8
Larchwood CM23 ......145 D5
Larchwood Cl IP2 ......16 C5
Lark Rise CO10 ......33 D5
Lark's La Broomfield CM3 ......191 A6
 Great Waltham CM3 ......190 F5
Larkfield Rd CO7 ......139 D1
Larkhill Way IP11 ......221 B5
Larkrise Cty Prim Sch
 CM2 ......216 E6
Larks Cl CB9 ......9 C7
Larksfield Cres CO12 ......91 B4
Larksfield Rd IP9 ......62 A2
Larkspur Cl
 Bishop's Stortford CM23 ......145 D6
 Witham CM8 ......176 E4
Larkspur Ct [3] CM1 ......205 F6
Larkspur Rd IP2 ......16 F3
Larksway
 Bishop's Stortford CM23 ......145 C6
 Felixstowe IP11 ......221 B3
Larkway CO13 ......170 E7
Larman Ct CO11 ......86 C7
Larneys The CO13 ......170 E7
Latchmore Bank CM22 ......146 B2
Lathcoates Cres CM2 ......216 E8
Lattice Ave IP4 ......18 C6
Launceston Cl CO2 ......136 B1
Laundry Gdns CO10 ......33 D6
Laurel Ave CO12 ......90 F2
Laurel Cl CO15 ......189 B7
Laurel Ct CO4 ......136 E8
Laurel Dr
 Great Dunmow CM6 ......123 B1
 Long Melford CO10 ......15 C7
Laurel Gr [4] CM2 ......216 A8
Laurelhayes IP2 ......17 A3
Laurels The Braintree CM7 ......128 A3
 Great Notley CM7 ......154 C6
Laurence Ave CM8 ......195 A8
Laurence Cl CO7 ......137 F6
Laurence Croft CM1 ......204 B1
Lavender Cl
 Bishop's Stortford CM23 ......145 D6
 Tiptree CO5 ......179 C4
 Witham CM8 ......176 E4
Lavender Ct [1] CM1 ......205 F5
Lavender Hill IP2 ......16 F4
Lavender Way CO4 ......109 C2
Lavender Wlk CO15 ......203 G7
Lavenham Cl CO16 ......188 B4
Lavenham Ct CO2 ......135 C2
Lavenham Rd IP2 ......16 C2
Lawford CE Prim Sch
 CO11 ......86 B2
Lawford La
 Chelmsford CM1 ......204 D3
 Writtle CM1 ......204 C1

Lawford Mead Cty Inf
Sch CM1 . . . . .204 D5
Lawford Mead Cty Jun
Sch CM1 . . . . .204 D5
Lawling Ave CM9 . . . . .210 C5
Lawn Chase CM8 . . . . . .176 F1
Lawn La CM1 . . . . .205 D6
Lawn Way IP11 . . . . . . .221 C5
Lawns Cl CO5 . . . . .201 C7
Lawns The
  Chelmsford CM1 . . . . . .205 D5
  Ipswich IP4 . . . . .18 C8
Laws Cl CB11 . . . . .43 D7
Lawshall's Hill CO6 . . . . .78 D1
Laxton Cl CO3 . . . . . . .135 A4
Laxton Gr CO13 . . . . . .170 A5
Laxton Rd CO7 . . . . . . .165 B8
Layender Field **7** CB10 . .22 F2
Layer Breton Hill CO2 . .161 B1
Layer Cross CO2 . . . . . .161 F5
Layer Ct CO2 . . . . .135 D4
Layer Marney Tower
  CO5 . . . . .180 D8
Layer Rd Abberton CO5 . .162 E4
  Abberton CO5 . . . . .163 A3
  Colchester CO2 . . . . . . .135 C3
  Great Wigborough CO5 . .181 E5
  Haverhill CB9 . . . . .8 E7
Layer-de-la-Haye CE
  Prim Sch CO2 . . . . . . .161 F5
Layzell Croft CO10 . . . . .34 C4
Le Cateau Rd CO2 . . . . .135 E6
Lea Cl
  Bishop's Stortford CM23 . .119 B1
  Braintree CM7 . . . . . . .128 D1
Lea Gr
  Bishop's Stortford CM23 . .119 B1
  Hatfield Peverel CM9 . . .194 F1
Lea La CM8 . . . . .177 F2
Lea Side CO5 . . . . .201 D6
Leach Cl CM2 . . . . .217 B7
Leam Cl CO4 . . . . .136 F7
Leapingwell Cl CM2 . . . .206 A3
Leas La CO2 . . . . .161 D6
Leas Rd Clacton-on-S CO15 188 D2
  Colchester CO2 . . . . . . .135 C1
Leas Sch The CO15 . . . .188 D2
Leas The CO13 . . . . . . .171 B6
Leather La
  5 Braintree CM7 . . . . . .127 F3
  Great Yeldham CO9 . . . . .30 A1
  Haverhill CB9 . . . . .8 E7
Lee Ct CM2 . . . . .216 E7
Lee Rd Harwich CO12 . . . .91 C3
  Ipswich IP3 . . . . .17 F3
Lee Wick La CO16 . . . . .186 D2
Leech's La CO4 . . . . . . .109 D4
Leeward Ct IP11 . . . . . .221 E5
Leeway The CM3 . . . . . .218 F7
Leez La CM3 . . . . .152 E2
Leez Priory CM3 . . . . . .153 A2
Legerton Cotts CO8 . . . . .79 C1
Legg St CM1 . . . . .205 B3
Legions Way CM23 . . . . .146 A8
Leicester Cl
  Colchester CO1 . . . . . . .136 A8
  Ipswich IP2 . . . . .16 F1
  Jaywick CO15 . . . . . . .187 F1
Leicester Ct CM8 . . . . . .156 D3
Leigh Dr Elsenham CM22 . .94 F1
  Wickham Bishops CM8 . .195 D5
Leighs Rd CM3 . . . . . . .191 E6
Leighton Rd IP3 . . . . . . .38 A8
Leighton Sq IP3 . . . . . . .38 A8
Leiston Rd CB9 . . . . .8 E7
Lely Rd IP3 . . . . .37 F8
Lemons Hill IP9 . . . . . . .61 D8
Leonard Mews CM7 . . . .155 B8
Leopold Gdns IP4 . . . . . .18 B8
Leopold Rd
  Felixstowe IP11 . . . . . .221 E4
  Ipswich IP4 . . . . .18 A8
Les Bois CO2 . . . . .162 A5
Leslie Rd IP3 . . . . .18 D1
Lethe Gr Blackheath CO2 . .163 A8
  Colchester CO2 . . . . . . .162 F8
Letton Cl IP9 . . . . .35 A1
Levens Way CM7 . . . . . .154 C6
Levington Rd
  Felixstowe IP11 . . . . . .221 C1
  Ipswich IP3 . . . . .18 A3
Lewes Cl IP3 . . . . .18 E3
Lewin Pl CM3 . . . . .206 E8
Lewis Dr CM2 . . . . .216 B6
Lewis La IP9 . . . . .61 E2
Lexden Ct CO3 . . . . . . .135 C7
Lexden Cty Prim Sch
  CO3 . . . . .134 E6
Lexden Gr CO3 . . . . . . .134 F7
Lexden Mews CO3 . . . . .134 F7
Lexden Park Ho CO3 . . . .135 A7
Lexden Rd Colchester CO3 135 B7
  West Bergholt CO6 . . . .108 D4
Lexden Springs Sch CO3 134 C7
Lexdon Pl CO3 . . . . .134 E7
Ley Field Marks Tey CO6 . .132 C3
  Takeley CM22 . . . . . . .148 C7
Ley The CM7 . . . . .128 D1
Leybourne Dr CM1 . . . . .205 D2
Leyfields CM7 . . . . .126 F1
Leys Dr CO16 . . . . .168 C2
Leys Rd CO7 . . . . .137 C3
Leys The Chelmsford CM2 . .205 F5
  Wimbish CB10 . . . . .45 C3
Leyside CM7 . . . . .126 F2

Leyton Ct CO15 . . . . . .188 F8
Leywood Cl CM7 . . . . . .128 D2
Lichfield Cl
  Chelmsford CM1 . . . . . .204 E4
  Colchester CO1 . . . . . . .136 A8
Lidgate Ct IP11 . . . . . . .221 A4
Lifchild Cl CM8 . . . . . . .195 A7
Lilac Ave CO16 . . . . . . .203 B6
Lilac Cl CM2 . . . . .216 C6
Lilac Ct CO7 . . . . .137 A2
Lilac Tree Ct CO4 . . . . . .136 E8
Lilley's La CO7 . . . . .112 D4
Lillies The CM7 . . . . . . .102 B1
Lilly Cnr CB9 . . . . .27 B6
Lily Cl CM1 . . . . .205 F6
Limbourne Dr CM9 . . . .210 D5
Lime Ave Colchester CO4 . .136 D8
  Harwich CO12 . . . . .91 B3
Lime Cl Clacton-on-S CO15 188 C3
  Witham CM8 . . . . .177 A5
Lime Gr CO10 . . . . .33 C5
Lime St CO7 . . . . .185 F5
Lime Wlk CM2 . . . . .216 C6
Limebrook Way CM9 . . .220 E7
Limefields CB10 . . . . . . .22 C4
Limekiln La CM24 . . . . .119 C5
Limes Cres CM23 . . . . . .146 A7
Limes The Ardleigh CO7 . .111 F8
  Clacton-on-S CO15 . . . .189 A3
  Galleywood CM2 . . . . . .216 B2
  Gosfield CO9 . . . . .102 E7
  Long Melford CO10 . . . . .15 C7
Limetree Dr IP3 . . . . . . .18 D2
Lincoln Ave CO15 . . . . .203 D6
Lincoln Cl CM23 . . . . . .145 D5
Lincoln La CO6 . . . . .82 C1
Lincoln Terr IP11 . . . . . .221 D3
Lincoln Way CO1 . . . . . .136 A8
Lindbergh Rd IP3 . . . . . .18 C2
Linden Cl Chelmsford CM2 216 C7
  Colchester CO4 . . . . . . .110 E1
  Lawford CO11 . . . . .86 B3
Linden Dr CO15 . . . . . . .188 E7
Lindens The
  Bishop's Stortford CM23 . .145 F6
  Braintree CM7 . . . . . . .128 A1
Lindisfarne Cl IP2 . . . . . .17 A1
Lindisfarne Ct CM9 . . . .220 E8
Lindsell La CM6 . . . . . . .98 B2
Lindsey Ave CO10 . . . . . .34 B6
Lindsey Cl CM23 . . . . . .118 F1
Lindsey Rd
  Bishop's Stortford CM23 . .118 F1
  Ipswich IP4 . . . . .18 C7
Line Cotts CO4 . . . . .83 A4
Linfold Cl CM7 . . . . . . .128 D4
Linford Mews CM9 . . . . .220 E8
Ling's La IP9 . . . . .63 D5
Lingwood Cl CM3 . . . . . .218 E7
Link Cl CO4 . . . . .109 E4
Link La IP9 . . . . .60 D1
Link Rd
  Bishop's Stortford CM23 . .145 F8
  Brightlingsea CO7 . . . . .186 A6
  Capel St M IP9 . . . . .35 A1
  Clacton-on-S CO15 . . . .188 D2
  Halstead CO9 . . . . .103 D8
Link The IP9 . . . . .60 D6
Link Way CM23 . . . . . . .145 E6
Links Ave IP11 . . . . . . .221 F6
Links Bsns Ctr The CM23 146 C7
Links Dr CM2 . . . . .215 F7
Links Rd Bradwell CM7 . .129 C1
  Cressing CM7 . . . . .156 C7
  St Osyth CO16 . . . . . . .203 B6
Linksfield IP5 . . . . .18 E7
Linksfield Gdns IP5 . . . . .18 F7
Linkside CO13 . . . . .170 E3
Linley Gdns CO15 . . . . .188 D2
Linnet Dr CM2 . . . . . . .216 B6
Linnet Rd IP2 . . . . .16 D4
Linnet Way CO7 . . . . . . .166 D8
Linnets CO15 . . . . .188 F6
Linnets The CO13 . . . . . .170 B6
Linnetts La CB9 . . . . .10 A4
Linstead Cl CO16 . . . . . .188 A4
Linton Cl CB11 . . . . .43 F8
Linton Pl **18** CB9 . . . . . . .9 B8
Linton Rd CB1 . . . . .5 B7
Lintons The CM2 . . . . . .217 D6
Lion Meadow CB9 . . . . . .27 B7
Lion Rd CO10 . . . . .2 B5
Lion St IP1 . . . . .17 C6
Lion Wlk **22** CO1 . . . . . .135 F7
Lionel Hurst Cl CO10 . . . .34 C5
Lionfield Terr CM1 . . . . .205 D3
Lisle Ho CO3 . . . . .135 A7
Lisle Rd CO2 . . . . .136 A5
List Ho CO10 . . . . .15 C8
Lister Rd CM7 . . . . .154 F8
Lister Tye CM2 . . . . . . .216 C7
Liston La CO10 . . . . .15 B6
Listonhall Chase CO9 . . . .75 B5
Litchborough Pk CM3 . . .218 F8
Litchfield CO12 . . . . .90 E2
Litchfield Cl CO15 . . . . .188 E5
Littell Tweed CM2 . . . . .206 A3
Little Baddow Rd
  Danbury CM3 . . . . .218 E7
  Woodham Walter CM9 . . .208 C3
Little Bakers CM24 . . . . .171 A7
Little Bentley Rd CO16 . . .114 B1
Little Bradfords CM7 . . . .128 A4
Little Braxted La CM8 . . .177 C3
Little Bromley Rd
  Ardleigh CO7 . . . . .112 B7
  Great Bromley CO7 . . . .112 F3
  Little Bentley CO7 . . . . .113 E1

Little Chishill Rd SG8 . . . .39 C8
Little Church St CO12 . . . .91 D6
Little Clacton Engaines
  Prim Sch CO16 . . . . . .168 C2
Little Clacton Rd
  Clacton-on-S CO16 . . . .188 B7
  Great Holland CO13 . . . .169 E2
Little Croft St IP2 . . . . . .17 C3
Little Dorrit CM1 . . . . . .204 E7
Little Fields CM3 . . . . . .219 A7
Little Gipping St **7** IP1 . .17 B6
Little Gr **4** IP9 . . . . .35 A1
Little & Great Sir
  Hughes La CM2 . . . . . .217 B2
Little Gulls **6** IP9 . . . . . .35 A1
Little Harrods CO14 . . . .171 A7
Little Horkesley Rd CO6 . .81 A4
Little Hyde Cl CO9 . . . . . .30 A2
Little Hyde Rd CO9 . . . . . .30 A2
Little Larchmount CM11 . .43 D8
Little London Hill CM7 . . .72 D8
Little London La CM9 . . .208 D4
Little Meadow CM1 . . . .204 A1
Little Meadows CM9 . . . .219 E6
Little Nell CM1 . . . . . . .204 E7
Little Oakley CE Inf Sch
  CO12 . . . . .117 B7
Little Sq **6** CM7 . . . . . .127 F3
Little St Mary's CO10 . . . .15 C7
Little Stile CM1 . . . . . . .215 A8
Little Stone Ct CO15 . . . .203 J8
Little Tey Rd CO5 . . . . . .158 F7
Little Totham Rd
  Goldhanger CM9 . . . . . .211 D8
  Little Totham CM9 . . . . .197 C1
Little Tufts IP9 . . . . .35 B1
Little Walden Rd CB10 . . .22 E5
Little Waltham CE Prim
  Sch CM3 . . . . .191 B7
Little Waltham Rd CM1 . .191 D1
Little Whip St **7** IP2 . . . .17 C4
Little Wood CO13 . . . . . .170 E6
Little Yeldham Rd CO9 . . .30 C3
Little's Cres IP2 . . . . . . .17 C4
Littlebury Gdns CO2 . . . .136 C4
Littlebury Green Rd CB11 .21 D3
Littlecotes CO4 . . . . . . .109 D4
Littlefield Rd CO2 . . . . . .135 C2
Livery Mews CM6 . . . . . .124 E5
Llewellyn Cl CM1 . . . . . .205 D3
Lloyd Rd IP9 . . . . .91 A8
Lloyds Ave **7** IP1 . . . . . .17 C6
Loamy Hill Rd
  Great Braxted CO5 . . . . .178 F1
  Tolleshunt Major CM9 . . .197 A2
Loates Pasture CM24 . . .119 D8
Lobelia Cl CM1 . . . . . . .206 A6
Locarno Rd IP3 . . . . . . .18 B3
Lock Rd CO9 . . . . .103 E8
Lockhart Ave CO3 . . . . .135 C7
Lockram La CM8 . . . . . .177 A2
Lodge Ave CM2 . . . . . . .216 F7
Lodge Cl
  Clacton-on-S CO15 . . . .188 E4
  Little Oakley CO12 . . . . .117 C8
Lodge Cres CM3 . . . . . .206 E7
Lodge Ct CO6 . . . . .108 F4
Lodge Farm La CO16 . . . .187 D4
Lodge Farm Rd CO10 . . . .2 C3
Lodge La Abberton CO5 . .163 D1
  Ardleigh CO7 . . . . .111 B6
  Ardleigh CO7 . . . . .111 C6
  Brightlingsea CO7 . . . . .185 E7
  Langham CO4 . . . . . . .110 D8
  Peldon CO5 . . . . .182 E7
  Purleigh CM3 . . . . .220 C2
  Tendring CO16 . . . . . . .140 F6
Lodge Rd Braintree CM7 . .127 F1
  Brightlingsea CO7 . . . . .185 E8
  Hazeleigh CM3 . . . . . . .220 B5
  Little Clacton CO16 . . . .169 A5
  Little Oakley CO12 . . . . .117 C8
  Maldon CM9 . . . . .209 F3
  Messing CO5 . . . . .159 D3
  Thorpe-le-S CO16 . . . . .168 F6
  Writtle CM1 . . . . .215 A8
Lodge The CO15 . . . . . .189 F6
Loftin Way CM2 . . . . . . .216 D7
Lombard Ct IP4 . . . . . . .17 F7
Lombarday Pl CM1 . . . . .205 B3
Lombardy Rd CO10 . . . . .15 C2
Lonbarn Hill CO11 . . . . . .88 A2
London Hill
  Chelmsford CM2 . . . . . .215 F2
  Galleywood CM2 . . . . . .216 A2
London Land Cotts CO6 . . .80 E4
London Rd
  Bishop's Stortford CM23 . .146 A5
  Braintree CM7 . . . . . . .127 C1
  Capel St M IP9 . . . . .35 B1
  Chelmsford CM2 . . . . . .215 E6
  Clacton-on-S CO15 . . . .188 E7
  Colchester CO3 . . . . . . .134 D6
  Copford CO6 . . . . .133 D4
  Feering CO5 . . . . .159 B7
  Great Chesterford CB10 . . .3 D2
  Great Horkesley CO6 . . . .81 F7
  Great Notley CM7 . . . . .154 C5
  Ipswich IP2 . . . . .16 C3
  Ipswich IP2 . . . . .16 F5
  Ipswich IP1 . . . . .17 A6
  Kelvedon CO5 . . . . . . .158 B1
  Littlebury CB11 . . . . . . .21 F7
  Maldon CM9 . . . . .209 D3
  Marks Tey CO6 . . . . . . .133 A3
  Newport CB11 . . . . .67 A6
  Saffron Walden CB11 . . . .43 D8
  Washbrook IP8 . . . . . . .35 E6

London Rd continued
  Wendens Ambo CB11 . . . .42 F4
  Wendens Ambo CB11 . . . .42 F7
Lone Barn Ct IP1 . . . . . .16 D8
Long Acres CO5 . . . . . . .158 F6
Long Border Rd CM24 . . .120 E1
Long Brandocks CM1 . . .204 A1
Long Comm CM9 . . . . . .209 F5
Long Croft CM24 . . . . . .119 D8
Long Field IP11 . . . . . . .221 B6
Long Gdns CO9 . . . . .53 F5
Long Gn CM7 . . . . .155 E8
Long Green La CM7 . . . . .99 C2
Long Horse Croft CB11 . . .43 E7
Long La Arkesden CB11 . . .41 E5
  Great Holland CO13 . . . .170 C3
  Rayne CM7 . . . . .153 F8
Long Ley CB11 . . . . .40 D2
Long Meadow
  Bishop's Stortford CM23 . .145 D6
  Great Notley CM7 . . . . .154 B5
Long Meadows CO12 . . . .90 F2
Long Melford Prim Sch
  CO10 . . . . .15 C7
Long Pastures CO10 . . . . .2 C3
Long Perry IP9 . . . . .35 B1
Long Rd CO11 . . . . .86 C3
Long Rd E CO7 . . . . .85 B3
Long Rd W CO7 . . . . .84 E3
Long St IP3 . . . . .17 E5
Long Wyre St CO1 . . . . .135 F7
Longacre Chelmsford CM1 .215 E8
  Colchester CO4 . . . . . . .109 E2
Longacre Rd CM7 . . . . . .155 E6
Longacres CM7 . . . . . . .128 A1
Longcroft Felixstowe IP11 .221 C6
  Hempstead CB10 . . . . . .46 E8
  Takeley CM22 . . . . . . .148 C7
Longcroft Rd CO4 . . . . . .136 C8
Longedryve CO2 . . . . . .135 C4
Longfellow Rd CM9 . . . . .210 A1
Longfield CM8 . . . . .176 E5
Longfield Rd Capel St M IP9 35 B2
  Great Baddow CM2 . . . .216 E8
Longfields CO16 . . . . . .187 B4
Longhedges CB11 . . . . . .22 E1
Longleaf Dr CM7 . . . . . .155 A8
Longleat Cl CM1 . . . . . .204 F7
Longmead Ave CM2 . . . .216 E8
Longmeads CM8 . . . . . .195 E5
Longmeads Cl CM1 . . . .204 A1
Longmore Ave CM2 . . . .216 E8
Longridge CO4 . . . . . . .136 F8
Longs CM3 . . . . .173 F1
Longship Way CM9 . . . . .220 E8
Longshots Cl CM1 . . . . .191 A1
Longstomps Ave CM2 . . .216 A7
Longstraw Cl CO3 . . . . .134 D6
Lonsdale **4** IP2 . . . . . . .17 C4
Lonsdale Cl IP4 . . . . . . .17 F7
Lonsdale Rd CO16 . . . . .142 A2
Looe Rd IP11 . . . . .221 F5
Loompits Way CB11 . . . . .43 D7
Loraine Way IP8 . . . . . . .16 A8
Lord Holland Rd CO2 . . .135 F3
Lord's Croft La CB9 . . . . . .9 A8
Lords Ave CM23 . . . . . .145 B7
Lords Cl CB10 . . . . .23 D1
Lordship Rd CM1 . . . . . .204 B3
Lordsland La CM7 . . . . .103 C1
Lordswood Rd CO2 . . . . .135 C2
Lorkin Way CO6 . . . . . .108 F4
Lorkin's La CO10 . . . . . . .54 C4
Lort's Rd CO10 . . . . . . .168 B4
Louise Cl CO14 . . . . . . .144 E3
Louse La CO7 . . . . .84 E4
Louvain Rd CO12 . . . . . .91 A1
Love La CO7 . . . . .185 F8
Love Way CO16 . . . . . . .188 C6
Loveday Cl SG8 . . . . . . .19 D3
Lover's La CO7 . . . . . . .167 A7
Lovers La IP9 . . . . .63 C4
Loves Wlk CM1 . . . . . . .204 B1
Lovibond Pl **4** CM2 . . . .205 F4
Low Lighthouse Maritime
  Mus CO12 . . . . .91 E5
Lower Anchor St CM2 . . .205 A1
Lower Brook St IP4 . . . . .17 C5
Lower Cotts SG9 . . . . . . .64 A2
Lower Dales IP1 . . . . . . .16 F8
Lower Dales View Rd **8**
  IP1 . . . . .17 A8
Lower Downs Slade IP9 . .61 E7
Lower Farm Rd CO4, CO6 . .57 B1
Lower Gn Galleywood CM2 216 B1
  Galleywood CM2 . . . . . .216 C2
  Wakes Colne CO6 . . . . . .79 C1
Lower Harlings IP9 . . . . . .91 A8
Lower Holt St CO6 . . . . .105 D6
Lower Houses Rd IP9 . . . .63 D2
Lower King CM7 . . . . . .128 D1
Lower Langley CO6 . . . . .106 C1
Lower Marine Par CO12 . .91 C3
Lower Mill Field CM6 . . . .150 E7
Lower Orwell St **1** IP4 . . .17 D5
Lower Park Cres CM23 . .145 F5
Lower Park Rd CO7 . . . . .185 E6
Lower Rd Birch CO2 . . . .161 A5
  Birch CO2 . . . . .181 A8
  Borley CO10 . . . . .15 B3
  Glemsford CO10 . . . . . . .2 B2
  Peldon CO5 . . . . .182 D5
  Wormingford CO5, CO6 . . .80 B5
Lower St Cavendish CO10 . .1 D1

Lower St continued
  Sproughton IP8 . . . . . . .16 A
  Stanstead CO10 . . . . .2 E
Stansted
  Mountfitchet CM24 . . . . .119 A
  Stratford St M CO7 . . . . .84 C
  Stutton IP9 . . . . .62 B
Lowry Gdns IP3 . . . . . . .38 A
Luard Way Birch CO2 . . . .161 A
  Witham CM8 . . . . .176 F
Lubberhedges La CM6 . . .125 B
Lucas Ave Chelmsford CM2 216 C
  Fordham CO6 . . . . .107 D
Lucas Ho CO3 . . . . .135 A
Lucas Rd Colchester CO2 . .136 A
  Sudbury CO10 . . . . .33 F
Lucas's La CO16 . . . . . . .141 D
Lucerne Rd CO7 . . . . . . .138 A
Lucerne Way CM1 . . . . . .215 B
Luces La CO9 . . . . .51 F
Luck's La CM3 . . . . .172 F
Lucksfield Way CM2 . . . .216 F
Lucy Cl CO3 . . . . .134 C
Lucy La N CO3 . . . . . . .134 B
Lucy La S CO3 . . . . . . .134 C
Ludgores La CM3 . . . . . .218 D
Ludham Hall La CM7 . . . .154 D
Luff Way CO14 . . . . . . .170 F
Lufkin Rd CO4 . . . . .109 F
Lugar Cl CO4 . . . . .136 E
Lukin's Dr CM6 . . . . . . .150 D
Lulworth Ave IP3 . . . . . .18 D
Lulworth Cl CO15 . . . . . .203 I
Lulworth Dr CB9 . . . . . . .8 E
Lumber Leys CO14 . . . . .171 A
Lundy Cl CB9 . . . . .9 D
Lunnish Hill CO12 . . . . . .89 F
Lupin Dr CM1 . . . . .205 F
Lupin Mews **1** CM1 . . . .205 F
Lupin Rd IP2 . . . . .16 E
Lupin Way CO16 . . . . . .188 C
Lushington Ave CO13 . . .170 E
Lushington Rd CO11 . . . .86 C
Luther Rd IP2 . . . . .17 C
Lutus Cl CO10 . . . . .12 A
Lydgate Cl CO11 . . . . . . .86 B
Lydia Dr CO16 . . . . .186 A
Lymington Ave CO15 . . . .189 A
Lyndhurst Ave IP4 . . . . . .18 D
Lyndhurst Dr CM3 . . . . . .218 F
Lyndhurst Rd CO15 . . . . .189 C
Lynmouth Ave CM2 . . . .205 C
Lynmouth Gdns CM2 . . . .205 C
Lynne Cl CO13 . . . . .170 E
Lynton Cl CO12 . . . . . . .91 B
Lynton Ct CM23 . . . . . . .145 E
Lynton Dr CM1 . . . . . . .205 E
Lynwood Ave IP11 . . . . .221 F
Lyon Cl Clacton-on-S CO15 189 A
  Galleywood CM2 . . . . . .216 B
Lyons Hall Cty Prim
  Sch CM7 . . . . .128 C
Lyons Hall Rd CM7 . . . . .128 D
Lyster Ave CM2 . . . . . . .217 A

M

Mabbitt Way CO4 . . . . . .110 B
Maberly Ct CB10 . . . . . .22 C
Macbeth Cl CO4 . . . . . . .136 F
Mace Wlk CM1 . . . . . . .204 F
Mackay Ct CO2 . . . . . . .136 B
Maclarens CM8 . . . . . . .196 A
Macmillan Ct **4** CM2 . . . .205 B
Madeira Rd CO15 . . . . . .189 D
Madeline Pl CM1 . . . . . .204 E
Madgements Rd CM7 . . .129 C
Magazine Farm Way
  CO3 . . . . .135 A
Magdalen Cl CO15 . . . . .188 E
Magdalen Ct CO15 . . . . .188 E
Magdalen Gn
  Colchester CO1 . . . . . . .136 C
  Thaxted CM6 . . . . .70 B
Magdalen Rd CO15 . . . . .188 E
Magdalen St CO1 . . . . . .136 A
Magdalene Cl IP2 . . . . . .16 F
Magdalene Cres CM8 . . .156 D
Magingley Cres IP5 . . . . .18 F
Magnaville Rd CM23 . . . .145 E
Magnolia Cl
  Chelmsford CM2 . . . . . .216 B
  Witham CM8 . . . . .177 A
Magnolia Dr CO4 . . . . . .136 F
Magpie Cl IP8 . . . . .16 C
Magwitch Cl CM1 . . . . . .204 F
Maidenburgh St CO1 . . . .135 F
Maidenhall App IP2 . . . . .17 B
Maidenhall Gn IP2 . . . . .17 B
Maidment Cres CM8 . . . .194 F
Maidstone Cty Inf Sch
  IP11 . . . . .221 C
Maidstone Rd IP11 . . . . .221 C
Mailers La CM23 . . . . . .92 F
Main Rd Bicknacre CM3 . .218 F
  Boreham CM3 . . . . .192 F
  Braintree CM3 . . . . . . .153 D
  Broomfield CM1 . . . . . .191 B
  Danbury CM3 . . . . .218 A
  Danbury CM3 . . . . .218 D
  Frating CO7 . . . . .138 E
  Great Holland CO13 . . . .170 A
  Great Leighs CM3 . . . . .173 F
  Harwich, Bath Side CO12 . .91 E
  Harwich, Dovercourt CO12 . .91 B
  Ramsey CO12 . . . . .90 A

Main Rd *continued*
Rushmere St A IP5 . . . . .18 F8
Sandon CM2 . . . . .217 F7
St Lawrence CM0 . . . . . .213 C1
Woolverstone IP9 . . . . .38 B2
Wormingford CO6 . . . . .80 F4
Main St CB1 . . . . .6 F6
Mais Ct IP2 . . . . .16 F2
Maitland Ct CO13 . . . . . . .170 F4
Maitland Rd CM24 . . . . . .119 E6
Makemores CM7 . . . . . . .126 F2
Makins Rd CO12 . . . . .90 F5
Maldon Court Sch CM9 .209 F3
Maldon Ct
8 Colchester CO3 . . . . . . .135 E6
Great Cornard CO10 . . . . .34 B7
Maldon Cty Prim Sch
CM9 . . . . .210 A2
Maldon District Mus
CM9 . . . . .210 B2
Maldon Rd Birch CO2 . . . .160 E4
Bradwell Waterside CM0 . .214 F1
Colchester, Abbey Field
CO3 . . . . .135 D5
Colchester, Stanway Green
CO3 . . . . .134 D1
Danbury CM3 . . . . .219 B5
Danbury CM3 . . . . .219 B7
Goldhanger CM9 . . . . . . .211 E2
Great Baddow CM2 . . . . .217 C7
Great Totham CM9 . . . . . .196 B4
Great Wigborough CO5 . . .181 E2
Hatfield Peverel CM3 . . . .194 C1
Hatfield Peverel CM8 . . . .194 F5
Heybridge CM9 . . . . . . .209 D6
Kelvedon CO5 . . . . .158 C1
Margaretting CM4 . . . . . .215 D1
Tolleshunt D'arcy CM9 . . .198 C2
Witham CM8 . . . . .195 A6
Woodham Mortimer CM9 . .219 E6
Maldon Way CO16 . . . . . .188 B4
Malin Cl CB9 . . . . .9 D7
Mallard Cl
Great Notley CM7 . . . . . .154 C5
Kelvedon CO5 . . . . .158 C3
Layer-de-l-H CO2 . . . . . .162 A5
Tollesbury CM9 . . . . . . .199 D2
Mallard Ct IP2 . . . . .16 F3
Mallard Rd CM2 . . . . . . .216 A5
Mallard Way
Great Cornard CO10 . . . . .34 C5
Ipswich IP2 . . . . .16 E3
Mallow Wlk CB9 . . . . .8 D8
Mallowhayes Cl IP2 . . . . .17 B3
Mallows Field CO9 . . . . . .76 F2
Mallows Green Rd CM23 . .92 D1
Mallows La CO9 . . . . .49 F3
Malmesbury Cl IP2 . . . . . .17 A1
Maltese Rd CM1 . . . . . . .205 A4
Malthouse Rd CO11 . . . . . .86 D4
Malting Farm La CO7 . . . .84 D2
Malting Green Rd CO2 . .162 A5
Malting La Clare CO10 . . . .12 B7
Kirby-le-S CO13 . . . . . . .143 C1
Malting Rd Colchester CO2 135 C1
Peldon CO5 . . . . .182 E6
Malting Terr IP2 . . . . .17 D4
Malting Yd CO7 . . . . . . .164 B8
Maltings Cl CO8 . . . . .55 E1
Maltings Ct CM8 . . . . . . .194 F8
Maltings La CM8 . . . . . . .194 F8
Maltings Rd
Brightlingsea CO7 . . . . . .165 E1
Great Baddow CM2 . . . . .217 A5
Maltings The
Cavendish CO10 . . . . .1 D2
Great Dunmow CM6 . . . . .123 D1
Ramsey CO12 . . . . .116 E8
Rayne CM7 . . . . .127 A2
Saffron Walden CB10 . . . . .22 C1
Thaxted CM6 . . . . .70 A2
Maltings View CM7 . . . . . .128 A3
Maltings Park Rd CO6 . . .108 F4
Malvern Cl
Chelmsford CM1 . . . . . . .204 D6
Ipswich IP3 . . . . .18 B4
Rushmere St A IP5 . . . . . .18 F7
Malvern Way CO6 . . . . . .109 B7
Malyon Rd CM8 . . . . . . .194 F8
Manchester Rd
Holland-on-S CO15 . . . . .189 E6
Ipswich IP2 . . . . .16 D2
Mandeville Rd
Marks Tey CO6 . . . . .132 E3
Saffron Walden CB11 . . . . .43 D8
Mandeville Way
Broomfield CM1 . . . . . . .191 B3
Kirby Cross CO13 . . . . . .170 F6
Mandy Cl IP4 . . . . .18 A6
Manfield Gdns CO16 . . . .187 B5
Manning Rd IP11 . . . . . . .221 D3
Mannings Cl CB11 . . . . . . .43 E7
Mannings La IP2 . . . . .38 A2
Mannington Cl IP4 . . . . . .18 F5
Manningtree Ct CO7 . . . .136 F4
Manningtree Rd
Brantham CO11 . . . . .86 A8
Dedham CO7 . . . . .85 B6
East Bergholt CO7 . . . . . . .59 F1
Little Bentley CO7 . . . . . .139 F8
Stutton IP9 . . . . .61 F2
Manningtree Sch CO11 . . . .86 B3
Manningtree Sta CO11 . . . .86 A5
Manor Cl Cavendish CO10 . . .1 C2
Great Horkesley CO6 . . . .109 C7
Manor Cres CM3 . . . . . . .191 B5
Manor Dr CM2 . . . . .216 F7

Manor Fields JMI Sch
CM23 . . . . .145 D5
Manor House Way CO7 . .185 E8
Manor La
Great Chesterford CB10 . . . .3 D2
Harwich CO12 . . . . .91 B2
Stutton IP9 . . . . .61 E2
Manor Links CM23 . . . . . .146 C7
Manor Rd
Bishop's Stortford CM23 . .146 A7
Chelmsford CM2 . . . . . . .205 A5
Colchester CO3 . . . . .135 E7
Felixstowe IP11 . . . . . . .221 C1
Great Holland CO13 . . . . .170 A3
Harwich CO12 . . . . .91 B3
Hatfield Peverel CM3 . . . .194 C1
Haverhill CB9 . . . . .9 B7
Ipswich IP4 . . . . .17 D8
Little Easton CM6 . . . . . .122 F5
Maldon CM9 . . . . .209 A4
Stansted
Mountfitchet CM24 . . . . .119 E5
Sudbury CO10 . . . . .15 E1
West Bergholt CO6 . . . . . .108 E5
Witham CM8 . . . . .177 A4
Wivenhoe CO7 . . . . .137 C1
Woodham Walter CM9 . . . .208 E5
Manor St CM7 . . . . .128 A3
Manor Way CO15 . . . . . .189 G6
Manors CM8 . . . . .156 D4
Manors Way CM8 . . . . . .156 C4
Mansard Ct CO5 . . . . .189 C5
Manse Chase CM9 . . . . .210 A1
Mansfield Twrs CM15 . . . .188 F2
Manston Dr CM23 . . . . . .119 B1
Manudent Cty Prim Sch
CM23 . . . . .93 A2
Manwick Rd IP11 . . . . . . .221 D2
Maple Ave
Bishop's Stortford CM23 . .145 D8
Braintree CM7 . . . . .127 D2
Heybridge CM9 . . . . . . .210 C6
Maple Cl
Bishop's Stortford CM23 . .145 D8
Clacton-on-S CO15 . . . . .188 C3
Halstead CO9 . . . . .77 A2
Harwich CO12 . . . . .91 B3
Ipswich IP2 . . . . .17 A3
Maple Dr
Chelmsford CM2 . . . . . . .216 B6
Kirby Cross CO13 . . . . . .170 D6
Witham CM8 . . . . .177 A5
Maple Gr CM23 . . . . .145 D8
Maple Ho IP11 . . . . .221 C4
Maple La CB10 . . . . .45 C5
Maple Leaf CO5 . . . . . . .179 C7
Maple Rd CO10 . . . . .34 B5
Maple Spring CM23 . . . . .145 D8
Maple Way CO2 . . . . . . .136 A4
Maples The IP4 . . . . .18 E8
Maplin Ct CO15 . . . . .189 D4
Marasca End CO2 . . . . . .163 A7
Maraschino Cres CO2 . . .163 A7
Marauder Way CO6 . . . . .104 F2
Marconi Rd CM1 . . . . . . .205 B3
Marcus Ct CB9 . . . . .9 D7
Marennes Cres CO7 . . . . .185 C7
Mareth Rd CO2 . . . . .135 C2
Margaret Cl CO7 . . . . . . .186 A6
Margaret Rd CO1 . . . . . . .135 F8
Margaret St
Felixstowe IP11 . . . . . . .221 C5
Thaxted CM6 . . . . .70 A3
Margaret Way CB10 . . . . . .22 D1
Margaretting Rd
Chelmsford CM2 . . . . . . .215 F1
Galleywood CM2 . . . . . . .216 A2
Writtle CM1 . . . . .215 A6
Margate Rd IP3 . . . . .18 C3
Margrave Gdns **4** CM23 .145 B7
Marguerite Way CM23 . . .145 C6
Marigold Ave
Clacton-on-S CO16 . . . . .188 C4
Ipswich IP2 . . . . .16 E3
Marigold Cl
Chelmsford CM1 . . . . . . .205 F6
Colchester CO4 . . . . .136 E8
Marina Gdns
Clacton-on-S CO15 . . . . .189 C5
Felixstowe IP11 . . . . . . .221 C2
Marina Mews **1** CO14 . . .171 A5
Marina Point CO15 . . . . . .188 D1
Marina Rd CM3 . . . . .194 A4
Marine Ct
Clacton-on-S CO15 . . . . .188 E1
Frinton-on-S CO13 . . . . . .170 F4
Marine Par CO12 . . . . .91 D3
Marine Par E CO15 . . . . .189 B3
Marion Ave CO15 . . . . . .188 E6
Maritime Ave CM9 . . . . . .210 E3
Maritime Ct **12** IP4 . . . . . .17 D5
Market End CO6 . . . . . . .130 C4
Market Field Sch CO7 . . . .138 A5
Market Hill Clare CO10 . . . .12 B7
Coggeshall CO6 . . . . . . .131 A2
Halstead CO9 . . . . .76 E2
Haverhill CB9 . . . . .9 A8
Maldon CM9 . . . . .210 A3
Saffron Walden CB10 . . . . .22 D2
Sudbury CO10 . . . . .33 E7
Market Pl
11 Braintree CM7 . . . . . .127 F3
Great Dunmow CM6 . . . . .123 D1
Saffron Walden CB10 . . . . .22 D2
Market Rd CM1 . . . . .205 B2
Market Row CB10 . . . . . . .22 D1
Market Sq **6** CM23 . . . . .145 F7

Market St
7 Bishop's Stortford CM23 .145 F7
10 Braintree CM7 . . . . . .127 F3
Harwich CO12 . . . . .91 E6
Saffron Walden CB10 . . . . .22 D2
Market Wlk CB10 . . . . .22 C1
Marking's Field CB10 . . . . .22 E2
Markland Cl CM2 . . . . . . .216 C3
Markland Dr CM9 . . . . . . .209 E1
Marks Gdns CM7 . . . . . . .128 C3
Marks Hall Rd CO6 . . . . .130 E6
Marks Tey Rdbt CO6 . . . . .133 A4
Marks Tey Sta CO6 . . . . .133 B4
Markshall Ctry Est
Arboretum CO6 . . . . .130 E7
Markwells CM22 . . . . .94 C2
Marlborough Cl
Bishop's Stortford CM23 . .145 F5
Clacton-on-S CO15 . . . . .188 C3
Marlborough Ct
Felixstowe IP11 . . . . . . .221 D2
Haverhill CB9 . . . . .8 E7
Marlborough Dr CO10 . . . . .33 F8
Marlborough Rd
Braintree CM7 . . . . .128 A4
8 Chelmsford CM2 . . . . .205 A1
Ipswich IP4 . . . . .18 A6
Marlowe Cl CM7 . . . . .155 A8
Marlowe Rd
Clacton-on-S CO15 . . . . .203 G8
Jaywick CO15 . . . . .188 A1
Marlowe Way CO3 . . . . . .134 F6
Marlpits Rd CM3 . . . . . . .219 E4
Marne Rd CO2 . . . . .135 E4
Marney Cl CM2 . . . . .216 C2
Marney Way CO13 . . . . . .171 B6
Marquis Cl CM23 . . . . . . .145 B7
Marram Ct CO3 . . . . .134 B6
Marsden Ct CO3 . . . . .134 C4
Marsh Cres CO5 . . . . .164 A8
Marsh Farm La CO7 . . . . .166 D3
Marsh Rd CO6, CO7 . . . . . .57 E6
Marsh Way CO7 . . . . .185 E6
Marshall Cl CO5 . . . . .158 D4
Marshalls Piece CM6 . . . .124 D6
Marshalls Rd CM7 . . . . . .127 E1
Marshbarns CM23 . . . . . .145 C8
Marshy La C09, C10 . . . . . .30 C7
Marston Beck CM2 . . . . . .206 A2
Martello **8** CO14 . . . . . .171 C8
Marten's La CO6 . . . . .56 F8
Martens Mdw CM7 . . . . . .128 D3
Martin End CO2 . . . . .162 A5
Martin Mews CB9 . . . . .8 C8
Martin Rd IP2 . . . . .17 C4
Martin's Rd CO9 . . . . .76 E1
Martingale Dr CM1 . . . . . .205 F7
Martinsdale CO15 . . . . . . .188 F6
Martyns Rise CO10 . . . . . .15 C5
Marvens CM2 . . . . .216 D3
Mary La N CO7 . . . . .139 A8
Mary La S CO7 . . . . .139 B6
Mary McArthur Pl CM24 . .119 E8
Mary Park Gdns CM24 . . .145 F4
Mary Warner Rd CO7 . . . .111 E7
Maryborough Gr CO2 . . . .136 B2
Maryland Ct **1** CO2 . . . . .136 A1
Maryon Rd IP3 . . . . .18 B1
Mascalls The CM2 . . . . . .216 E8
Mascalls Way CM2 . . . . . .216 E8
Masefield Dr CO3 . . . . . . .134 F6
Masefield Rd CM7 . . . . . .155 A8
Mashbury Rd CM3 . . . . . .190 B7
Mashey Rd CO9 . . . . .30 D5
Mason Cl CO2 . . . . .135 B3
Mason Rd
Clacton-on-S CO16 . . . . .188 B3
Colchester CO1 . . . . .109 F1
Masons Ct CM23 . . . . . . .145 E7
Masterman Wharf
12 Bishop's Stortford,
Hockerill CM23 . . . . .146 A3
12 Bishop's Stortford, New
Town CM23 . . . . .145 F7
Matching La CM23 . . . . . .145 D8
Matfield Cl CM1 . . . . .205 D7
Mathams Dr CM23 . . . . . .145 D5
Mather Way IP2 . . . . .17 D4
Mathews Cl Halstead CO9 . .77 A3
Stratford St M CO7 . . . . . .58 C1
Matlock Cl **8** IP2 . . . . . . .16 C2
Matson Rd IP4 . . . . .16 F8
Maudlyn Rd CO1, CO4 . . . .136 C6
May Rd IP3 . . . . .18 C2
May Wlk Chelmsford CM2 .216 C7
Elsenham CM24 . . . . .94 A1
May's La CO7 . . . . .84 E4
Mayberry Wlk CO2 . . . . . .136 A3
Maybury Cl CO5 . . . . .179 E4
Maybury Rd IP3 . . . . .18 B1
Mayda Cl CO9 . . . . .76 D1
Mayes Cl CM23 . . . . .146 D8
Mayes La Danbury CM3 . . .218 A6
Harwich CO12 . . . . .90 C1
Sandon CM2 . . . . .217 E5
Mayes Pl CM6 . . . . .97 A6
Mayfield Cl CO4 . . . . .110 C2
Mayfield Pk CO5 . . . . . . .179 E4
Mayfield Rd Ipswich IP4 . . .18 C7
Writtle CM1 . . . . .204 A2
Mayflower Ave CO12 . . . . .91 E5
Mayflower Cl CO3 . . . . . . .134 D6
Mayflower Cty Prim Sch
The CO12 . . . . .91 B4
Mayflower Gdns CM23 . . .145 B6
Mayflower Ho CO12 . . . . . .91 D6
Mayflower Way CO10 . . . . .15 F2
Mayford Way CO16 . . . . . .188 B6

Mayland Cl CM9 . . . . . . .210 D4
Mayland Rd CM8 . . . . . . .177 A2
Maylands Dr CM7 . . . . . . .154 D8
Maynard Cl CM6 . . . . . . .123 C1
Mayne Crest CM1 . . . . . . .205 E6
Maynard Villas CM6 . . . . .122 F5
Maypole Cl CB11 . . . . .43 C7
Maypole Dr CO16 . . . . . . .187 B4
Maypole Green Rd CO2 . .135 C2
Maypole Rd Tiptree CO5 . .179 C6
Wickham Bishops CM8 . . .195 F2
Maypole The CM6 . . . . . . .69 F3
Mays Cl IP11 . . . . .221 D3
Maysent Ave CM7 . . . . . . .127 F5
Maytree Gdns CM23 . . . . .94 B3
Maze Green Hts CM23 . . .145 C7
Maze Green Rd CM23 . . . .145 D7
Mazers Ct **5** CM7 . . . . . .127 F2
Mazoe Cl CM23 . . . . .145 F5
Mazoe Rd CM23 . . . . .145 F5
Mead Ct CO15 . . . . .188 E3
Mead Monks CM3 . . . . . . .218 F2
Mead Pastures CM9 . . . . .208 D3
Mead Path CM2 . . . . .215 F8
Mead The
Great Cornard CO10 . . . . .34 B4
Great Dunmow CM6 . . . . .123 C2
Thaxted CM6 . . . . .70 A3
Meadgate Ave CM2 . . . . . .216 D8
Meadgate Cty Prim Sch
CM2 . . . . .216 E8
Meadow Brown Ct CM7 . . .127 E5
Meadow Cl
Chelmondiston IP9 . . . . . .63 F7
Clacton-on-S CO15 . . . . .189 B7
Elmstead CO7 . . . . .137 F6
Great Bromley CO7 . . . . .139 A6
Halstead CO9 . . . . .103 F8
Panfield CM7 . . . . .127 A4
Meadow Clays CB11 . . . . . .21 F4
Meadow Grass Cl CO3 . . . .134 B6
Meadow La Sudbury CO10 . .33 C7
West Mersea CO5 . . . . . .201 C5
Meadow Rd
Colchester CO3 . . . . .135 D1
Great Chesterford CB10 . . . .3 D3
Meadow Side CM1 . . . . . .205 B3
Meadow View
Bicknacre CM3 . . . . .218 E1
Great Bardfield CM7 . . . . .72 B2
Kirby-le-S CO13 . . . . . . .143 D1
Tiptree CO5 . . . . .179 B5
Meadow View Cl CO3 . . . .134 B5
Meadow View Rd CO10 . . . .33 D5
Meadow Way
Abberton CO5 . . . . .163 B2
Black Notley CM7 . . . . . .155 C5
Clacton-on-S CO15 . . . . .203 G7
Meadow Wlk **5** CM2 . . . . .205 C2
Meadowbrook Ct CO1 . . . .136 B2
Meadowcroft CM24 . . . . . .119 E7
Meadowcroft Way CO13 . .170 F7
Meadowford CB11 . . . . . . .42 F1
Meadowlands CM23 . . . . .119 A2
Meadows Cl CO7 . . . . . . .137 F6
Meadows The
Bishop's Stortford CM23 . .145 E5
3 Chelmsford CM2 . . . . .205 C2
Meadowside
Braintree CM7 . . . . .127 E5
Chelmsford CM2 . . . . . . .205 C3
Meadowside Ct CM3 . . . . .192 E1
Meadowside Gdns IP4 . . . .18 E8
Meadowsweet CM23 . . . . .145 C6
Meadowvale Cl IP4 . . . . . .17 F7
Meads The CM24 . . . . . . .119 F6
Meadway Gosfield CO9 . . .102 E8
Lawford CO11 . . . . .86 B3
Maldon CM9 . . . . .210 B1
Mearns Pl **3** CM2 . . . . . .205 F4
Mede Way CO7 . . . . .137 C3
Medlar Cl CM8 . . . . .177 A4
Medley Rd CM7 . . . . .126 F2
Medusa Cl CO15 . . . . .189 E5
Medway Ave CM8 . . . . . . .176 D2
Medway Cl CM1 . . . . .204 D4
Medway Rd IP3 . . . . .17 F2
Meekings Rd CO10 . . . . . . .34 B8
Meers The CO13 . . . . .170 E6
Meeson Meadows CM9 . .220 E8
Meeting Field CO10 . . . . . .15 C7
Meeting La
East Mersea CO5 . . . . . . .184 C1
Ridgewell CO9 . . . . .29 D7
Meeting Wlk CB9 . . . . .9 B7
Megs Way CM7 . . . . .128 B2
Melba Ct CM1 . . . . .204 E5
Melbourne Ave CM1 . . . . .204 E5
Melbourne Chase CO2 . . .136 B1
Melbourne Cl CM1 . . . . . .204 E5
Melbourne Par CM1 . . . . .204 E5
Melbourne Park Cty
Prim Sch CM1 . . . . .204 D5
Melbourne Rd
Clacton-on-S CO15 . . . . .188 E4
Ipswich IP4 . . . . .18 D7
Melford Cl IP4 . . . . .18 F5
Melford Rd Cavendish CO10 . .1 C4
Sudbury CO10 . . . . .15 D2
Melford Way IP11 . . . . . . .221 A3
Mell Rd CM9 . . . . .199 E1
Mellis Ct IP11 . . . . .221 B5
Mellor Chase CO3 . . . . . . .134 E7
Melplash Cl IP3 . . . . .18 E4
Melplash Rd IP3 . . . . .18 E4
Melrose Gdns
Clacton-on-S CO15 . . . . .189 C5

Melrose Gdns *continued*
Ipswich IP4 . . . . .18 B8
Melrose Rd CO5 . . . . .201 C6
Melton Cl CO16 . . . . .188 A4
Melville Rd IP4 . . . . .17 F5
Menai Ct IP1 . . . . .17 B7
Mendip Dr IP5 . . . . .18 F6
Mendip Rd CM1 . . . . .204 D6
Mendlesham Cl CO16 . . . .188 B4
Menin Rd CO2 . . . . .135 D4
Menish Way CM2 . . . . . . .206 A3
Meon Cl CM1 . . . . .205 C6
Meopham Ct CO2 . . . . . . .136 B4
Mercantile Ho **1** CO1 . . . .135 F6
Mercers Ave CM23 . . . . . .145 B4
Mercers Row CB10 . . . . . . .22 D1
Mercers Way **2** CO1 . . . . .135 E8
Mercia Cl CM2 . . . . .217 A5
Mercury Cl CO2 . . . . .135 A3
Meredith Rd CO15 . . . . . .188 E3
Meres Cl CM8 . . . . .176 F1
Meriden Ct CO15 . . . . . . .189 A5
Merivale Cl CO11 . . . . .86 C3
Merivale Rd CO11 . . . . . . .86 B3
Merlin End CO4 . . . . .110 F1
Merlin Pl CM1 . . . . .204 F5
Merlin Rd IP2 . . . . .16 C3
Merriam Cl CO11 . . . . .86 D8
Merrilees Cres CO15 . . . . .189 D6
Merrill Pl **2** CM23 . . . . . .145 E5
Merrion Cl **7** IP2 . . . . . . .16 C2
Merrymount Gdns CO15 . .189 B5
Mersea Ave CO5 . . . . .201 B6
Mersea Cl CO5 . . . . .201 B7
Mersea Fleet Way CM7 . . .128 C1
Mersea Mus CO5 . . . . . . .201 B6
Mersea Point Nature
Reserve CO5 . . . . .185 C3
Mersea Rd Abberton CO5 . .163 B5
Colchester CO2 . . . . .136 A3
Peldon CO5 . . . . .182 F5
Mersea View CO16 . . . . . .186 A3
Mersey Rd Ipswich IP3 . . . .17 F2
Witham CM8 . . . . .176 E2
Mersey Way CM1 . . . . . . .204 C5
Merstham Dr CO16 . . . . . .188 C6
Merton Ct CO2 . . . . .163 A7
Messines Rd CO2 . . . . . . .135 D5
Messing-cum-Inworth
Cty Prim Sch CO5 . . . . .159 C2
Meteor Way CM1 . . . . . . .204 F2
Mews Ct CM2 . . . . .205 B1
Mews The
Bishop's Stortford CM22 . .146 A3
Frinton-on-S CO13 . . . . . .171 A5
Panfield CM7 . . . . .126 A7
Stansted
Mountfitchet CM24 . . . . .119 F7
Meyrick Cres CO2 . . . . . . .135 F5
Micawber Way CM1 . . . . .204 D7
Michaels Rd CM23 . . . . . .119 A2
Michaelstowe Cl CO12 . . . .90 C2
Michaelstowe Dr CO12 . . . .90 C2
Mickfield Mews IP11 . . . . .221 B5
Micklegate Rd IP11 . . . . . .221 C1
Middle Gn CO6 . . . . .79 C1
Middle King CM7 . . . . . . .128 D1
Middle Mill Rd CO1 . . . . . .135 F8
Middle Row **5** CM23 . . . . .145 F6
Middle St CB11 . . . . .65 C4
Middle Way CO10 . . . . . . .15 D8
Middleborough CO1 . . . . . .135 E8
Middlefield CO9 . . . . .76 F1
Middlefield Rd CO11 . . . . . .87 A3
Middleton Cl
Clacton-on-S CO16 . . . . .188 D6
Ipswich IP2 . . . . .16 C2
Middleton Rd CO10 . . . . . .33 D5
Middlewick Cl **4** CO2 . . . .136 A1
Midguard Way CM9 . . . . .220 F8
Midland Cl CO2 . . . . .135 F4
Midway CO15 . . . . .203 E6
Midway Rd CO2 . . . . .135 C2
Milburn Cres CM1 . . . . . . .204 D1
Milch La CM3 . . . . .153 E6
Milden Rd IP2 . . . . .16 E5
Mildenhall Pl **14** CB9 . . . . .9 B8
Mildmay Ct **2** CM2 . . . . . .205 B1
Mildmay Cty Jun & Inf
Sch CM2 . . . . .216 B5
Mildmay Rd
Chelmsford CM2 . . . . . . .205 B1
Ipswich IP3 . . . . .18 B1
Mildmays CM3 . . . . .218 C7
Mile End Rd CO4 . . . . . . .109 E3
Miles Cl CO3 . . . . .134 C6
Milestones The CM3 . . . . .194 A4
Milford Cl CO7 . . . . .137 C1
Military Ct **10** CO1 . . . . . .136 A6
Military Rd CO1 . . . . .136 A5
Mill Chase Halstead CO9 . . .76 F2
Steeple Bumpstead CB9 . . .27 C5
Mill Cl Elsenham CM22 . . . .94 C1
Felixstowe IP11 . . . . . . .221 B4
Great Bardfield CM7 . . . . .72 B2
Tiptree CO5 . . . . .179 C6
Mill Cotts CO2 . . . . .217 C8
Mill Cswy SG8 . . . . .19 C5
Mill Ct Braintree CM7 . . . .128 B2
Takeley CM6 . . . . .149 B7
Mill End CM6 . . . . .70 A2
Mill Hill Braintree CM7 . . . .128 B2
Chelmondiston IP9 . . . . . .63 E8
Mill Hill Barnston CM6 . . . .151 A4
Chelmsford CM2 . . . . . . .215 F2

Mill Hill *continued*
Farnham CM23 ....118 E5
Harwich CO12 ....91 C3
Haverhill CB9 ....9 A7
Lawford CO11 ....85 D4
Manningtree CO11 ....86 C4
Purleigh CM3 ....220 C1
Stansted
Mountfitchet CM24 .....119 E6
Sudbury CO10 ....33 D7
Wormingford CO8 ....80 E6
Mill House Cotts CO12 ..116 D4
Mill La Ardleigh CO7 ....112 B4
Birch CO2 ....161 A3
Bradfield CO11 ....87 D2
Broomfield CM1 ....191 C1
Cavendish CO10 ....13 B8
Coggeshall CO5 ....131 F1
Colne Engaine CO6 .....105 B8
Cressing CM7 ....155 D5
Danbury CM3 ....219 A6
Dedham CO7 ....84 F7
Felixstowe IP11 ....221 C4
Finchingfield CM7 ....48 F3
Ford End CM3 ....172 D7
Great Dunmow CM6 ....123 D1
Great Holland CO13 ....169 E3
Great Leighs CM3 ......174 B7
Great Maplestead CO9 ..76 E8
Harkstead SG9 ....64 A5
Harwich CO12 ....91 D3
Hinxton CB10 ....3 A7
Ickleton CB10 ....3 B4
Layer-de-l-H CO2 ......162 B5
Little Baddow CM3 .....207 E3
Little Yeldham CO9 ......30 A3
Littlebury CB11 ....21 F4
Maldon CM9 ....210 A3
Manningtree CO11 ....86 D4
Pebmarsh CO9 ....78 A7
Purleigh CM3 ....220 C1
Rayne CM7 ....153 E8
Saffron Walden CB10 ....22 F2
Salcott-cum-virley CM9 .199 B8
Stebbing CM6 ....124 E5
Stoke-by-N CO6 ....56 D7
Sudbury CO10 ....33 D7
Terling CM3 ....175 A3
Thorpe-le-S CO16 ......141 F1
Tolleshunt Major CM9 ..197 E3
Walton-on-t-N CO14 ....171 C8
Washbrook IP8 ....16 A1
Weeley Heath CO16 ....168 A6
Witham CM8 ....176 F1
Mill Lane Cl CO16 .....168 A6
Mill Park Dr CM7 ......128 B1
Mill Rd Birdbrook CO9 ..10 C2
Boxted CO4 ....82 F4
Clare CO10 ....12 C7
Colchester CO4 ....109 F4
Debden CB11 ....68 B8
East Bergholt CO7 ....59 E2
Elder Street CB10 ....45 B3
Felsted CM6 ....152 A4
Finchingfield CM7 ....72 D5
Fordham CO6 ....107 D4
Foxearth CO10 ....14 C5
Great Bardfield CM7 .....72 B2
Great Totham CM9 .....196 D7
Haverhill CB9 ....9 A7
Helions Bumpstead CB9 ..26 C8
Henham CM22 ....94 E4
Ipswich IP3 ....18 F1
Maldon CM9 ....210 B2
Marks Tey CO6 ....133 C4
North End CM6 ....151 F2
Ridgewell CO9 ....29 B6
Stambourne CO9 ....28 C3
West Mersea CO5 ......201 D7
Mill Rise IP9 ....62 D5
Mill Side CM24 ....119 E6
Mill St
Bishop's Stortford CM23 .146 A5
Brightlingsea CO7 ......186 A6
Colchester CO1 ....136 A6
Nayland CO6 ....56 B1
St Osyth CO16 ....186 F4
Stoke-by-N CO6 ....56 D8
Mill Tye CO10 ....34 A4
Mill Vale Lo CM8 ......176 F2
Mill View CM7 ....129 D3
Mill Vue Rd CM2 ......205 F2
Mill Wlk CO5 ....179 C6
Millars The CM1 ....191 A3
Millbridge Rd CM8 ....176 F2
Millcroft CM23 ....119 A1
Milldene Cty Prim Sch
The CO5 ....179 D6
Millenium Way CM7 ...155 D8
Miller's Barn Rd CO15 .188 A1
Miller's Cl CM6 ....151 A4
Millers Cl
Bishop's Stortford CM23 ..145 C5
Braintree CM7 ....128 A8
Colchester CO3 ....134 C6
Great Horkesley CO6 ...109 B7
Millers Croft
Great Baddow CM2 .....216 F6
Great Dunmow CM6 ....123 E1
Millers La CO3 ....134 D6
Millers Mead CO5 .....158 E4
Millers Row CM7 ......48 C6
Millfield Gdns IP4 .....18 A6
Millfields Stansted
Mountfitchet CM24 .....119 E6

Millfields *continued*
Writtle CM1 ....204 A1
Millfields Prim Sch CO7 .137 D1
Millfields Way CB9 ......9 B8
Millhouse Villas CM6 ...151 A4
Milligans Chase CM2 ...216 B1
Milliners Way CM23 ....145 C4
Mills La CO10 ....15 C4
Mills Rd CO10 ....34 A8
Mills The IP4 ....18 E8
Millside CM23 ....146 A5
Millson Bank CM2 .....206 A4
Millways CM9 ....196 B4
Millwrights CO5 ....179 C6
Milner Rd Sudbury CO10 ..34 B8
Sudbury CO10 ....34 C8
Milner St IP4 ....17 E5
Milnrow IP2 ....16 C2
Milton Ave CM7 ....155 A8
Milton Cl CO3 ....134 F6
Milton Ct CO15 ....189 E6
Milton Pl CM1 ....205 A5
Milton Rd Harwich CO12 ..91 D4
Lawford CO11 ....86 B2
Witham CM8 ....176 F5
Milton St IP4 ....18 B6
Mimosa Cl CM1 ....205 F6
Mimosa Ct CO4 ......136 E8
Minden Rd CO10 ....33 F7
Minerva Cl Harwich CO12 ..90 F1
Haverhill CB9 ....9 D6
Minerva End CO2 ......135 C1
Minsmere Dr CO16 ....188 C6
Minsmere Way CO10 ...34 C6
Minster Way CM9 .....220 E8
Minters Cotts CO11 ...115 C5
Miranda Wlk CO4 .....136 E7
Mirosa Dr CM9 ....210 B1
Mission La CO7 ....60 B3
Mistley Norman CE Prim
Sch CO11 ....87 A4
Mistley Place Park CO11 .86 E4
Mistley Sta CO11 ....86 F4
Mistley Towers CO11 ...86 F4
Mitchell Ave CO9 ......76 E1
Mitchell Circ CM7 ......73 C6
Mitre Gdns CM23 .....146 A4
Mitton Vale CM2 ......205 F2
Moat Farm CO9 ....28 B7
Moat Farm Chase CM8 .176 F3
Moat Farm Cl CM7 .....17 F8
Moat Fields CO6 ....107 D6
Moat La CO8 ....55 A4
Moat Rd Birdbrook CO9 ..28 C7
Fordham CO6 ....107 D6
Moat Wlk CB9 ....8 E8
Modlen Rd CO14 ......171 B7
Moffat Ave IP4 ....18 B8
Mole Hall La CB11 ......67 F3
Mole Hall Wildlife Pk
CB11 ....67 F3
Molehill Green Cotts
CM22 ....121 C6
Molehill Green Rdbt
CM22 ....121 C5
Molrams La CM2 ......217 B6
Monk's Cnr CB10 ......47 B4
Monk's La CO7 ....84 D4
Monkdowns Rd CO6 ...131 B3
Monklands Ct CO9 .....76 D1
Monks Ct CM8 ....176 E3
Monks Gate IP8 ....16 A6
Monks Hill CB11 ....43 F8
Monks Lodge Rd CO9 ...52 D2
Monks Rd CO6 ....105 B7
Monks Wlk CM9 ....213 E8
Monkswood Dr CM23 ..145 D6
Monkwick Ave CO2 ....135 F1
Monkwick Cty Jun & Inf
Schs CO2 ....136 A2
Monmouth Cl IP2 ....17 B1
Mons Rd CO2 ....135 D4
Montague Rd IP11 ....221 F4
Montbretia Cl CO3 .....134 D6
Montbretia Ct CO16 ...188 C4
Montfort Ct CB9 ....8 F7
Montgomery Cl
Chelmsford CM1 ....205 E7
Colchester CO2 ....136 B4
Montgomery Cty Jun &
Inf Sch CO2 ....135 D2
Montgomery Rd IP2 ....17 B1
Monton Rise IP2 ....16 D2
Montrose Ct IP3 ....17 F4
Montrose Ho CO1 ......135 F7
Montrose Rd CM2 .....206 A4
Moon Hall La CB9 ....9 A5
Moor Hall La CM3 .....218 C2
Moor Rd Great Tey CO6 ..132 C8
Langham CO4 ....83 D4
Moor's Farm Chase CM9 .197 A3
Moor's La CO7 ....139 E1
Moore Cl CO5 ....158 E5
Moorfield Ct CM8 ......176 F1
Moorhouse Gn CO7 ....111 E8
Moorings The CM23 ...146 A5
Moors Cl CO7 ....139 E1
Moors La
Little Dunmow CM6 ....151 D7
Rayne CM7 ....126 A3
Moors The CM6 ....151 D7
Moorsfield CO10 ....34 B4
Moorside CO1 ....136 B7
Mope La CM8 ....195 D6
Moran Ave CM1 ....205 B7
Morant Rd CO1 ....136 B5
Morebarn Rd CO7 .....112 E2
Morecambe Ct IP4 .....18 A7

Morella Cl CO7 ....166 E8
Morello Ct CO2 ....163 A7
Moretons CM2 ....216 B2
Morland Ct CM6 ....82 B1
Morland Prim Sch IP3 ...38 A8
Morland Rd IP3 ....37 F8
Morley Rd Halstead CO9 ..76 F2
Tiptree CO5 ....179 D4
Morleys Rd CO6 ....105 A6
Mornington Ave IP1 ....17 A8
Morris Ave CO15 ......203 E6
Morris Harp CB10 ......22 E3
Morris Rd CM2 ....205 D2
Morrow La CO7 ....112 A6
Mors End CO7 ....58 D2
Morses La CO7 ....165 F1
Mortimer Rd CM3 .....194 A4
Morton Rd CM9 ....196 A4
Morton Way CO9 ....77 A3
Moss Path CM2 ....216 C3
Moss Rd Colchester CO3 ..134 E4
Witham CM8 ....177 B3
Moss Way CO5 ....108 E3
Moss Wlk CM2 ....216 B6
Mossfield Cl CO3 ......135 C6
Mott's La CO6 ....132 D4
Mottram Cl IP2 ....16 C2
Motts Cl CM7 ....127 E4
Motts La CM8 ....177 B4
Motts Yd CM6 ....124 E5
Moules La CB1 ....5 C6
Moulsham Chase CM2 ..216 C8
Moulsham Cty Jun & Inf
Sch CM2 ....216 B7
Moulsham Dr CM2 .....216 B8
Moulsham Hall La
Braintree CM3 ....153 F2
Great Leighs CM3 .....154 A1
Moulsham High Sch
CM2 ....216 B7
Moulsham St
Chelmsford CM1 ....205 B2
Chelmsford, Moulsham CM2 205 B1
Moulsham Thrift CM2 ..216 A6
Mount Dr Ipswich IP3 ...18 F1
Stansted
Mountfitchet CM24 .....119 C5
Mount Hill CO9 ....76 D1
Mount Lodge Chase CM9 196 E6
Mount Pleasant
Halstead CO9 ....76 E1
Maldon CM9 ....209 F2
Mount Pleasant Cotts
CB11 ....43 D8
Mount Pleasant Est CM9 .196 E6
Mount Pleasant Rd CB11 .43 E8
Mount Rd Braintree CM7 .128 A3
Coggeshall CO6 ....131 B2
Haverhill CB9 ....9 B7
Mount Rise CO9 ....76 D1
Mount The Colchester CO3 134 F6
Tollesbury CM9 ....199 D1
Mountain Ash Cl CO4 ..110 C2
Mountain's Farm Rd
CM6 ....150 C3
Mountains Rd CM6 ....196 C7
Mountbatten Cl CO10 ..15 F2
Mountbatten Ct IP1 ....17 A7
Mountbatten Dr CO2 ...136 B4
Mountbatten Rd
Braintree CM7 ....128 C4
Sudbury CO10 ....15 F2
Mountbatten Way CM1 .205 E7
Mountfitchet Castle &
Norman Village CM24 ..119 F6
Mountfitchet High Sch
The CM24 ....119 E5
Mountfitchet Rd CM24 .119 E5
Mounthill Ave CM2 ....205 D3
Mountview Cres CM0 ..213 C1
Mountview Rd CO15 ...189 A5
Moverons La CO7 ......165 C2
Mowden Hall La CM3 ..193 D1
Mowlands IP9 ....35 B1
Moy Rd CO2 ....136 A1
Moze Cross CO12 ......116 D1
Mulberries The CM7 ...128 A2
Mulberry Ave CO2 .....136 A4
Mulberry Ct CO3 ......133 A6
Mulberry Gdns CM8 ...177 A4
Mulberry Way CM1 ....205 D4
Mullins Rd CM7 ....127 F6
Mumford Cl CO6 ......108 E4
Mumford Rd Ipswich IP1 ..16 E8
West Bergholt CO6 ....108 D4
Mumfords La CO13 ....170 A7
Mundon Rd Braintree CM7 128 C4
Maldon CM9 ....210 A1
Munnings Cl IP3 ....38 B8
Munnings Dr CO16 ....188 D6
Munnings Rd CO3 .....135 A5
Munnings Way CO11 ....86 B5
Munro Rd CM8 ....176 F5
Murchison Cl CM1 .....204 E5
Murray Cl CM7 ....127 F6
Murray Rd IP3 ....18 A3
Murrayfield Prim Sch IP3 18 A2
Murrell Lock CM2 .....206 A4
Murrills Rd IP3 ....18 E5
Murton Slade CB9 ....9 A8
Muscade Cl CO5 ....179 D6
Museum St
Colchester CO1 ....135 F7
Ipswich IP1 ....17 C6
Saffron Walden CB10 ...22 D2
Musgrave Cl CO12 ......90 F1
Musk Cl CO3 ....134 D7

Muswell Wlk CO16 ....188 D5
Mutlow Cl CB11 ....42 F5
Mutlow Hill CB11 ......42 F5
Mychett Cl CO16 ......188 B6
Myddlyton Pl CB10 .....22 D2
Myland Cty Prim Sch
CO4 ....109 E4
Myland Hall Chase CO4 .110 C3
Mynards Way CM3 ....218 C2
Myneer Pk CO6 ....131 B2
Myrtle Gr CO2 ....136 B5
Myrtle Rd IP3 ....17 E4

N

Nabbott Rd CM1 ....204 E2
Nabbotts Cty Jun & Inf
Sch CM1 ....205 E7
Nacton Cres IP3 ....18 B2
Nacton Rd Felixstowe IP11 221 C1
Ipswich, Racecourse IP3 ...18 B2
Ipswich, Rose Hill IP3 .....18 A3
Nails La CM23 ....145 F7
Nalla Gdns CM1 ....205 A6
Nancy Smith Cl CO2 ...135 F5
Nansen Rd
Holland-on-S CO15 ....189 D6
Ipswich IP3 ....18 B2
Napier Ave CO15 ......203 D6
Napier Ct CM1 ....204 E5
Napier Rd CO2 ....135 F6
Narvik Cl CM9 ....220 E8
Nash Cl Colchester CO3 ..135 B5
Lawford CO11 ....86 B5
Nash Dr CM1 ....191 A3
Nash Gdns IP3 ....38 B8
Nassau Rd CO16 ......187 B4
Nathan Ct CO2 ....163 B8
Nathan's La CM1 ......215 A6
Nats La CB11 ....42 E6
Navarre St IP1 ....17 C6
Navigation Rd CM2 ...205 C2
Nayland Cty Prim Sch
CO6 ....56 A1
Nayland Rd Bures CO8 ..79 F8
Colchester CO6 ....109 D6
Felixstowe IP11 ....221 A4
Great Horkesley CO6 ...82 B4
Haverhill CB9 ....8 E6
Little Horkesley CO6 ....81 F6
West Bergholt CO6 ....108 D7
Nayling Rd CM7 ....127 C2
Naze Nature Reserve
The CO14 ....144 D6
Naze Nature Trail The
CO14 ....144 E4
Naze Park Rd CO14 ...144 E2
Neale Rd CO9 ....76 E1
Neale St IP1 ....17 C6
Neasden Ave CO16 ....188 D5
Neath Dr IP2 ....17 A1
Nelson Gdns CM7 .....128 C4
Nelson Gr CM1 ....204 F3
Nelson Rd
Bishop's Stortford CM23 .146 A5
Clacton-on-S CO15 ....188 E1
Colchester CO3 ....134 E6
Harwich CO12 ....91 D4
Ipswich IP4 ....18 A6
Nelson St CO7 ....185 F6
Neptune Ct CO1 ....136 C6
Ness Wlk CM8 ....176 D2
Nethaniah Home For The
Aged IP2 ....17 C4
Nether Cl CO9 ....77 A1
Nether Hill CO9 ....31 D3
Nether Rd CO10 ....1 D2
Nethergate St CO10 ....12 B7
Netley Cl IP2 ....36 F8
Neville Rd CB10 ....22 E7
New Barn La CM22 ....146 D1
New Bowers Way CM1 .205 F6
New Captains Rd CO5 ..201 B6
New Cardinal St IP1 ....17 B5
New Church Rd CO6 ...108 E4
New Cotts Great Tey CO6 .132 C8
Wakes Colne CO6 .....106 C6
New Cut Bures CO8 .....79 E8
Glemsford CO10 ....2 B3
Great Bentley CO7 ....166 E8
Layer-de-l-H CO2 ......161 F5
New Cut E IP2, IP3 .....17 D4
New Cut W IP3 ....17 D4
New Dukes Way CM2 ..205 F4
New England Cl CM3 ..218 F1
New Farm Lodge CO3 ..134 D5
New Farm Rd CO3 ....134 D6
New Hall Cotts CO7 .....58 F7
New Hall Vineyard CM3 .220 D2
New House La CB10 ....24 C3
New Kiln Rd CO3 ......135 C2
New La CO5 ....158 F5
New Lodge Chase CM3 .207 B2
New London Rd CM2 ..205 A1
New Meadgate Terr
CM2 ....216 D8
New Nabbotts Way CM1 205 F6
New Orleans Flats CO5 .201 B5
New Park Rd CO9 ....51 F3
New Park St CO1 ......136 B6
New Pier St CO14 .....171 C8
New Pond La CB10 .....22 C2
New Queens Rd CO10 ..15 E1
New Rd Aldham CO6 ...107 B2
Broomfield CM1 ....191 B1
Colchester CO3 ....134 D6

New Rd *continued*
Elsenham CM22 ....94 C2
Gosfield CO9 ....102 E2
Great Baddow CM2 ....217 A4
Hatfield Peverel CM3 ..194 A4
Hinxton CB10 ....3 Be
Holbrook IP9 ....63 A7
Kelvedon CO5 ....158 C5
Long Melford CO10 .....15 Cc
Messing CO5 ....159 C7
Mistley CO11 ....86 Ec
Rayne CM7 ....127 A
Saffron Walden CB10 ...22 E
Shudy Camps CB1 ......7 C
Terling CM3 ....175 C7
Tiptree CO5 ....179 D2
Tollesbury CM9 ....199 D2
New Road Terr CM7 ....126 F7
New St Braintree CM7 ..127 F4
Brightlingsea CO7 ....185 Fe
Chelmsford CM1 ......205 B3
Glemsford CO10 ....2 A1
Great Dunmow CM6 ...150 D8
Halstead CO9 ....76 Ei
Ipswich IP4 ....17 D5
Maldon CM9 ....209 F2
Sudbury CO10 ....33 E8
New Street Fields CM6 .150 D8
New Thorpe Ave CO16 .142 A4
New Town Rd
Colchester CO1 ....136 A6
Thorpe-le-S CO16 .....141 F2
New Village CO11 ....86 C7
New Way Ipswich IP2 ...16 Fe
Point Clear B CO16 ....185 F3
New Writtle St CM2 ....205 B2
Newark Cl IP2 ....16 F1
Newbarn Rd CO6 ......106 B1
Newbiggen St CM6 .....69 F3
Newbourne Gdns IP11 .221 B3
Newbridge Hill CO6 ....108 D2
Newbridge Rd Birch CO5 .180 A6
Tiptree CO5 ....179 C5
Newbury Cl CM23 .....145 E8
Newbury Ho IP4 ....18 B4
Newbury Rd IP4 ....18 C6
Newby Dr IP4 ....18 B5
Newcastle Ave CO3 ...134 F4
Newcomen Way CO4 ..110 C4
Newcourt Rd CM2 ....205 D3
Newcroft CB10 ....22 E1
Newgate St CO14 .....171 C8
Newhaven La CO12 .....91 D6
Newhouse Rd CO6 ....104 F5
Newhythe CO3 ....134 E7
Newington Gdns CO15 .188 F8
Newland Ave CM7 ......72 B1
Newland Pl CM8 ....177 A1
Newland St CM8 ......177 A2
Newlands Dr CM8 .....177 A2
Newlands La CO6 ....56 B1
Newlands Prec CM8 ...177 A2
Newlands Spring Prim
Sch CM1 ....204 D7
Newman's Rd CO10 ....33 F8
Newmarket Rd CB10 ....3 C3
Newmill La Brantham CO11 61 A1
Stutton CO11 ....87 A8
Newnham Cl CM7 .....127 C2
Newnham Ct IP2 ....16 E2
Newnham Gn CM9 ....209 E3
Newpasture La CM6 ...125 C5
Newport Cl
Great Baddow CM2 ....217 B4
Harwich CO12 ....91 A1
Newport Cty Prim Sch
CB11 ....66 F7
Newport Dr
Clacton-on-S CO15 ....189 A7
Rickling Green CB11 ....66 F4
Newport Free Gram Sch
CB11 ....42 F1
Newport Rd CB11 ....43 C7
Newport Sta CB11 .....67 A8
Newport Way CO13 ...171 A6
Newpots Cl CO5 ....182 D5
Newpots La CO5 ......182 D5
Newquay Ct IP5 ....18 F6
Newry Ave IP11 ....221 D4
Newson St IP1 ....17 B7
Newton Cl CM7 ....127 F1
Newton Croft CO10 .....34 A7
Newton Gdns CO16 ...187 A5
Newton Pl CB9 ....9 B8
Newton Rd Harwich CO12 .91 A3
Ipswich IP3 ....18 A4
Sudbury CO10 ....34 A7
Newton St IP4 ....17 D6
Newton Way CO16 ....187 B5
Newtown Rd CM23 ....145 C4
Nicholas Cl CM1 ......204 B1
Nicholas Ct
Chelmsford CM1 ....204 D6
Chelmsford,
Moulsham CM2 ....205 A1
Witham CM8 ....176 F2
Nicholas Rd IP11 ......221 A4
Nichols Cl CO11 ....86 B3
Nichols Cnr CO7 ......112 A5
Nickleby Rd CM1 .....204 D6
Nickolsons Gr CO1 ....136 A6
Nien-Oord CO16 ......188 C4
Nightingale Cl
Clacton-on-S CO15 ....188 F5
Colchester CO4 ....137 A8
Harwich CO12 ....90 F1
Witham CM8 ....194 B8

Nightingale Hill CO4 ......83 F6
Nightingale Mews 3 CB10 22 F2
Nightingale Rd IP3 ......38 A8
Nightingale Sq IP3 ......38 A8
Nightingale Way CO15 ...188 F5
Nine Acres IP2 ......16 D5
Nineacres CM7 ......128 A1
Ninth Ave CM24 ......120 B2
Noah's Ark La CO10 ......33 D7
Noak's Cross CM8 ......178 B2
Noakes Ave CM2 ......216 E6
Noaks Rd IP7 ......58 D8
Nobles The CM23 ......145 D6
Nonsuch Meadow CO10 ...33 E7
Nook The CO7 ......164 C8
Norbury Cl CO6 ......132 F3
Norbury Rd IP4 ......18 B8
Nordic Lodge CM9 ......220 F8
Norfolk Ave
Clacton-on-S CO15 ......189 E7
West Mersea CO5 ......201 D7
Norfolk Cl CM9 ......209 E1
Norfolk Cres CO4 ......110 B1
Norfolk Dr CM1 ......205 A7
Norfolk Gdns CM7 ......128 B4
Norfolk Rd Ipswich IP4 ...17 D6
Maldon CM9 ......209 E1
Norfolk Way CM23 ......145 F5
Norman Ave CM23 ......145 D6
Norman Cl Marks Tey CO6 .132 E3
St Osyth CO16 ......187 A4
Norman Cres IP3 ......18 A2
Norman Ct CM24 ......119 E7
Norman Hill CM3 ......175 B2
Norman Rd
Clacton-on-S CO15 ......189 E6
Manningtree CO11 ......86 D4
Norman Way
Colchester, Lexton CO3 ...135 B6
Colchester, Shrub End CO3 .135 B4
Point Clear B CO16 ......185 F3
Norman's Way CM24 ......119 E7
Normandie Way CO8 ......79 E8
Normandy Ave CO2 ......136 A3
Normanhurst CO15 ......188 E1
Normansfield CM6 ......150 E7
Norris Cl
Bishop's Stortford CM23 ...146 C7
Braintree CM7 ......128 C5
North Ave Chelmsford CM1 204 F5
Haverhill CB9 ......8 E8
North Cl IP4 ......17 E8
North Cres CB9 ......27 B7
North Cty Prim Sch CO1 .135 E8
North Dell CM1 ......205 E7
North Dr CM2 ......216 F7
North End Rd
Gestingthorpe CO9 ......31 C2
Hinxton CB10 ......3 B8
Little Yeldham CO9 ......30 E8
North Hall Rd CB11 ......67 A2
North Hill Colchester CO1 .135 E7
Little Baddow CM3 ......207 D5
North Hill Gdns 1 IP4 ...17 E6
North Hill Rd IP4 ......17 E6
North Ho CO13 ......170 F4
North La CO6 ......133 B5
North Lawn IP4 ......18 C8
North Mill Pl CO9 ......76 E3
North Rd
Belchamp Walter CO10 ......31 F6
Brightlingsea CO7 ......185 F7
Clacton-on-S CO15 ......188 F6
Great Yeldham CO9 ......30 A2
Takeley CM22 ......148 C8
Tollesbury CM9 ......199 C2
North Rise CO10 ......34 A6
North St
4 Bishop's Stortford CM23 .145 F7
Great Dunmow CM6 ......123 D1
Maldon CM9 ......210 B2
Manningtree CO11 ......86 D4
Steeple Bumpstead CB9 ....27 B7
Sudbury CO10 ......33 E8
Tolleshunt D'arcy CM9 ....198 E5
Walton-on-t-N CO14 ......171 C8
North Station Rd CO1 ...135 E8
North Street Par 1 CO10 .33 E7
North Terr 5 CM23 ......145 F8
North View Cotts CO6 ...109 D7
North Wall CO16 ......186 A3
Northampton Mdw CM7 ..72 B2
Northbourne Rd CO15 ...188 F4
Northcroft CO10 ......33 E7
Northfield CM7 ......72 B3
Northfield Gdns CO4 ....110 A4
Northfield Rd CB11 ......43 E8
Northgate End CM23 ....145 F8
Northgate JMI Sch CM23 145 E8
Northgate St
Colchester CO1 ......135 F8
Ipswich IP1 ......17 C6
Northolt Ave CM23 ......145 D5
Northumberland Cl CM7 .128 B4
Northumberland Ct 1
CM2 ......205 F4
Norton Rd
Chelmsford CM1 ......205 A3
Haverhill CB9 ......8 E6
Norway Cres CO12 ......90 F3
Norwich Cl
Clacton-on-S CO16 ......188 E6
Colchester CO1 ......136 A8
Norwich Ct 2 IP1 ......17 A7
Norwich Rd IP1 ......17 A7
Norwood Ave CO15 ......189 B5
Norwood Way CO14 ......171 A7
Notcutts CO7 ......59 E1
Notley Gn CM7 ......154 B6
Notley High Sch The
CM7 ......154 F8
Notley Rd CM7 ......154 F8
Nottidge Rd IP4 ......17 E6
Nottingham Rd CO15 ....189 E6
Nounsley Rd CM3 ......194 B1
Nun's Meadow CO9 ......102 E7
Nunn's Rd CO1 ......135 E7
Nunnery St CO9 ......51 D4
Nunns Cl CO6 ......131 A2
Nuns Wlk CO9 ......29 F1
Nunty's La
Greenstead Green CO9 ....104 A1
Pattiswick CM7 ......129 E7
Nursery Cl
Bishop's Stortford CM23 ...145 F6
Colchester CO3 ......134 C5
Nursery Dr CM7 ......128 A5
Nursery La CM3 ......218 F8
Nursery Rd
Bishop's Stortford CM23 ...145 F6
Chelmsford CM2 ......216 B8
Great Cornard CO10 ......34 B5
Nursery Rise CM6 ......150 D7
Nursery Wlk IP11 ......221 D5
Nyedale Dr CO3 ......134 E5

O

Oak Ave CO16 ......188 A2
Oak Bglws CM7 ......127 E3
Oak Cl Felixstowe IP11 ...221 C4
Rushmere St A IP4 ......18 E7
Thorpe-le-S CO16 ......142 A1
West Bergholt CO6 ......108 E4
Oak Cnr Beaumont CO16 ..141 F8
Woodham Mortimer CM9 ..219 D6
Oak Cotts CM3 ......206 E8
Oak Fall CM8 ......177 A5
Oak Farm Rd CM9 ......208 E1
Oak Hall CM23 ......145 E8
Oak Haven CO12 ......90 F1
Oak Hill Beazley End CM7 .101 A8
Wethersfield CM7 ......73 F1
Oak Hill La IP2 ......17 B3
Oak Ho IP2 ......16 D2
Oak Lodge Tye CM1 ......206 A6
Oak Rd Chappel CO6 ......106 B3
Great Cornard CO10 ......34 B6
Halstead CO9 ......103 D7
Heybridge CM9 ......210 B6
Little Maplestead CO9 ......77 A8
Pebmarsh CO9 ......77 F8
Rivenhall CM8 ......177 C6
Tiptree CO5 ......179 C7
Oak Ridge CO12 ......117 B7
Oak St CM23 ......145 F6
Oak Tree Cotts CO6 ......133 B8
Oak Tree Rd CO7 ......165 B8
Oak Wlk CO9 ......51 D2
Oak Yd CO9 ......76 E2
Oakapple Cl CO2 ......135 D1
Oakfield La CM3 ......175 A2
Oakfield Rd Belstead IP8 ..36 A7
Washbrook IP8 ......35 F6
Oakland Rd CO12 ......91 C3
Oaklands Ave CO3 ......134 E5
Oaklands Cl
Bishop's Stortford CM23 ...119 B2
Great Notley CM7 ......154 D8
Oaklands Cres CM2 ......216 B8
Oaklands Cty Inf Sch
CM2 ......216 B8
Oaklands Dr CM23 ......119 B2
Oaklands Pk CM23 ......119 B2
Oaklands Way CM3 ......207 E2
Oaklea Ave CM2 ......205 E3
Oaklee IP2 ......17 A1
Oakleigh Rd CO15 ......188 F8
Oakley Cross CO12 ......117 B7
Oakley Rd Braintree CM7 ..127 F7
Harwich CO12 ......90 D1
Wix CO11 ......115 E5
Oakmead Rd CO16 ......186 B3
Oakroyd Ave CM6 ......150 E8
Oaks Dr CO3 ......135 D7
Oaks Hospl The CO4 ......109 E3
Oaks Pl CO4 ......109 E2
Oaks The CO13 ......170 F6
Oaksmere Gdns IP2 ......17 A2
Oakstead Cl IP4 ......18 A6
Oaktree Cl 14 CM23 ......145 F7
Oakview CO12 ......90 F1
Oakwood Ave
Clacton-on-S CO15 ......189 E7
West Mersea CO5 ......201 D7
Oakwood Cl CO13 ......170 E6
Oakwood Cty Inf Sch
The CO15 ......188 D2
Oakwood Dr CO5 ......201 D7
Oakwood Gdns CO5 ......201 D7
Oasis Ct CM1 ......205 F5
Oasthouse Ct CB10 ......22 D1
Oatfield Cl CO3 ......134 D6
Oatlands CO7 ......137 F6
Oban St IP1 ......17 B7
Oberon Cl CO4 ......136 F7
Obrey Way CM23 ......145 E3
Observation Ct IP1 ......17 B5
Observer Way CO5 ......158 C4
Ockelford Ave CM1 ......204 F5
Ockendon Way CO14 ......171 A8
Octavia Dr CM8 ......194 E7
Oddcroft CO6 ......77 F1
Odin Lodge CM9 ......220 F8
Office La CM9 ......197 A4
Old Barn Rd CO8 ......80 A6
Old Bell Cl CM24 ......119 D6
Old Burylodge La CM24 ..120 A4
Old Cattle Market 5 IP4 ..17 C5
Old Chapel The CO6 ......56 B1
Old Church La Bulmer CO10 32 F2
Bulmer CO10 ......32 F3
West Bergholt CO6 ......108 D5
Old Clements La CB9 ......8 F7
Old Coach Rd CO1 ......136 B7
Old Coastguard Cotts
CM0 ......214 E4
Old Court Rd CM2 ......205 D3
Old Ct CM2 ......205 D3
Old Forge CO7 ......137 C2
Old Forge Rd
Boreham CM3 ......206 E8
Layer-de-l-H CO2 ......161 F5
Old Foundry Rd IP4 ......17 D6
Old Hall Cl CB9 ......27 C7
Old Hall La Capel St M IP9 ..35 F3
Tolleshunt D'arcy CM9 ....199 C5
Walton-on-t-N CO14 ......144 E3
Old Heath Rd CO1 ......136 C4
Old House La CO4 ......83 B2
Old House Rd CO6 ......109 A8
Old Ipswich Rd CO7 ......110 E7
Old London Rd
Capel St M IP9 ......59 F7
Woodham Walter CM9 ......208 E1
Old Maltings The 2
CM23 ......146 A7
Old Market Ct 3 CO10 ....33 E7
Old Market Pl 2 CO10 ....33 E7
Old Mead La CM22 ......94 D4
Old Mead Rd CM22 ......94 C5
Old Mill Chase CM7 ......73 C4
Old Mill La CO5 ......158 D7
Old Mill Rd Langham CO4 ..83 D5
Saffron Walden CB11 ......43 E8
Old Parsonage Ct CM8 ..176 F2
Old Parsonage Way
CO13 ......170 F5
Old Pier St CO14 ......171 C8
Old Rd Clacton-on-S CO15 .188 E4
Coggeshall CO6, CO5 ......131 E1
Frinton-on-S CO13 ......170 F4
Pattiswick CM7 ......129 F5
Wickham St P CO9 ......53 D5
Old River La CM23 ......145 F7
Old Rope Wlk CB9 ......8 E7
Old Rose Gdns CO4 ......109 D4
Old School Cl CO16 ......187 A4
Old School Ct CM3 ......194 B3
Old School Field CM1 ...205 E4
Old School Ho The
Rowhedge CO5 ......164 A8
Shotley Gate IP9 ......91 B8
Old School La CO7 ......138 A6
Old School Yard CB11 ...43 D8
Old Southend Rd CM2 ...217 D1
Old St The IP9 ......35 B1
Old Vicarage Rd CO12 ....91 C3
Old Vicarage The CM7 ....72 D6
Old Way CO13 ......170 F4
Oldbury Ave CM2 ......216 F8
Olde Forge CO7 ......165 E1
Oldfield Rd IP8 ......16 B1
Oldhouse Villas CM22 ....148 C8
Olive Gr CO2 ......135 D2
Oliver Pl CM8 ......177 B2
Oliver Way CM1 ......204 F7
Olivers Cl
Clacton-on-S CO15 ......188 E4
Long Melford CO10 ......15 D7
Olivers Ct CO15 ......188 E4
Olivers Dr CM8 ......195 A7
Olivers La CO2 ......135 A1
Olivers Rd CO15 ......188 E4
Oliveswood Rd CM6 ......150 D7
Ongar Cl CO16 ......188 B4
Ongar Rd
Great Dunmow CM6 ......150 D6
Writtle CM1 ......204 A1
Ongar Road Trad Est
CM6 ......150 E7
Ongark Rd CM1 ......204 B1
Onslow Cotts CO5 ......160 A7
Onslow Cres CO2 ......136 B1
Opal Ave IP1 ......16 D8
Ophir Rd CO7 ......185 F5
Orange St CM6 ......70 A2
Orange Tree Cl CM2 ......216 C6
Orchard Ave CO9 ......76 D2
Orchard Cl
Chelmsford CM2 ......216 C6
Clacton-on-S CO16 ......188 C5
Copford CO6 ......133 D2
Elmstead CO7 ......138 A6
Great Oakley CO12 ......116 C3
Hatfield Peverel CM3 ......194 A4
Haverhill CB9 ......8 F7
Maldon CM9 ......209 F2
Newport CB11 ......66 F8
Ramsey CO12 ......90 A2
Ridgewell CO9 ......29 B6
Saffron Walden CB11 ......43 D7
Thaxted CM6 ......70 A3
Tollesbury CM9 ......199 E1
Writtle CM1 ......204 B1
Orchard Cotts
Langham CO4 ......83 F3
Little Horkesley CO6 ......81 E5
Orchard Ct CO3 ......135 C7
Orchard Dr
Braintree CM7 ......128 A1
Great Holland CO13 ......170 A4
Orchard Gate IP2 ......16 C5
Orchard Gdns CO4 ......136 B8
Orchard Gr IP5 ......18 F7
Orchard Lodge CO5 ......179 D4
Orchard Mews CO5 ......179 C4
Orchard Pightle CB1 ......5 C6
Orchard Rd Alresford CO7 .165 B8
Bishop's Stortford CM23 ...119 B1
3 Colchester CO1 ......135 E8
Kelvedon CO5 ......158 C3
Maldon CM9 ......209 F2
Orchard St
Chelmsford CM2 ......205 B1
9 Ipswich IP4 ......17 D6
Orchard The CM6 ......152 C5
Orchard Way CO10 ......2 B3
Orchards CM8 ......176 F1
Orchid Ave CM8 ......176 E4
Orchid Cl IP2 ......16 E4
Orford Cres CM1 ......205 D5
Orford Rd
Felixstowe IP11 ......221 C1
Haverhill CB9 ......8 F6
Orford St IP1 ......17 B7
Oriel Cl CO10 ......34 B6
Oriole Way CM23 ......145 C6
Orion Way CM7 ......128 B4
Orkney Cl CB9 ......9 D7
Orlando Ct CO14 ......171 C8
Ormonde Cl CO6 ......108 E4
Orpen Cl CO6 ......108 D4
Orpen's Hill CO2 ......161 A5
Orplands Cotts CM0 ......214 F1
Orsino Wlk CO4 ......136 F7
Orvis La CO7 ......59 E1
Orwell Cl CO4 ......110 E1
Orwell Ct 1 IP4 ......17 D5
Orwell Gdns IP2 ......17 A3
Orwell High Sch IP11 ...221 C5
Orwell Ho IP11 ......221 A4
Orwell Hts IP2 ......16 E2
Orwell Jun Sch IP3 ......17 F1
Orwell Pl
Chelmondiston IP9 ......63 F7
2 Ipswich IP4 ......17 D5
Orwell Rd
Clacton-on-S CO15 ......188 F2
Felixstowe IP11 ......221 D3
Harwich CO12 ......91 D4
Ipswich IP3 ......18 A4
Orwell Ret Pk IP2 ......16 F5
Orwell Rise IP9 ......63 F8
Orwell Way CO16 ......188 C6
Orwell Wlk CM8 ......176 E3
Osbert Rd CM8 ......194 E8
Osborne Cl CO15 ......189 A7
Osborne Rd Ipswich IP3 ...18 A4
West Mersea CO5 ......201 E6
Osborne St CO2 ......135 F6
Osbourne Gdns 5 CM23 .145 E5
Osbournes Ct CO7 ......185 F6
Osea Rd CM9 ......211 B3
Osea Way CM1 ......205 F5
Osier Pl 3 CB9 ......8 F8
Osprey Rd CB9 ......9 C7
Osprey Way CM2 ......216 A5
Ospreys CO15 ......188 F6
Ostler Cl CM23 ......145 C4
Othello Cl CO4 ......136 F8
Otley Ct IP11 ......221 B5
Otten Rd CO10 ......13 B1
Ottershaw Way CO16 ......188 B6
Oulton Cl CO12 ......90 F3
Oulton Rd IP3 ......17 E2
Our Lady Immaculate
RC Prim Sch CM2 ......205 A1
Ouse Chase CM8 ......176 D2
Outpart Eastward CO12 ...91 E6
Over Hall La CB10 ......6 D2
Overchurch Cl CB9 ......8 F7
Overhall Hill CO6 ......78 C2
Overstone Ct CO2 ......135 C3
Ovington Pl 16 CB9 ......9 B8
Owen Ward Cl CO2 ......135 A3
Owl's Hill CM3 ......175 B3
Owls Retreat 1 CO4 ......136 F8
Ox Yd CO9 ......102 E7
Oxcroft CM23 ......145 F3
Oxenford Cl CO12 ......90 F1
Oxford Cl CO10 ......34 A6
Oxford Cres CO15 ......188 F4
Oxford Ct
Chelmsford CM2 ......205 E4
Colchester CO3 ......135 D6
Earls Colne CO6 ......105 B6
Oxford La CO9 ......51 D2
Oxford Mdw CO9 ......51 D2
Oxford Pl CO6 ......105 B6
Oxford Rd
Clacton-on-S CO15 ......188 F4
Colchester CO3 ......135 D6
Frinton-on-S CO13 ......171 A5
Halstead CO9 ......76 D1
Ipswich IP4 ......17 E5
Manningtree CO11 ......86 D4
Oxley Hill Abberton CO5 ..163 A3
Tolleshunt D'arcy CM9 ....198 B8
Tolleshunt Knights CM9 ...180 A1
Oxley Ho CM7 ......155 B5
Oxley Parker Sch The
CO4 ......110 A6
Oxlip Rd CM8 ......176 E4
Oxney Villas CM6 ......152 D6
Oyster Cl CO5 ......201 C7
Oyster Pk CO1 ......136 D6
Oyster Pl CM2 ......205 F4
Oyster Tank Rd CO7 ......185 E5
Ozier Ct CB11 ......43 E7
Oziers CM22 ......94 C2

P

Packard Ave IP3 ......18 B2
Packards La CO6 ......80 F1
Packe Cl CO5 ......158 D4
Paddock Cl CO12 ......91 C4
Paddock Dr CM1 ......205 E8
Paddock The CM23 ......145 D3
Paddock Way CO7 ......137 C3
Paddocks The Bures CO8 ...79 E8
Great Bentley CO7 ......166 F5
Great Totham CM9 ......196 A4
West Mersea CO5 ......201 D6
Witham CM8 ......177 A2
Page Cl CM8 ......194 D8
Page Rd CO15 ......188 E3
Pages Cl CM23 ......145 D5
Pages La CM9 ......198 F1
Paget Ct CM22 ......94 C1
Paget Rd Ipswich IP1 ......17 B7
Rowhedge CO5 ......163 F8
Wivenhoe CO7 ......164 C8
Paignton Ave CM1 ......205 D5
Pakenham Pl 18 CB9 ......9 B8
Palace Gdns CM23 ......145 E5
Palfrey Hights CO11 ......86 D8
Pallister Rd CO15 ......188 F2
Palm Cl Chelmsford CM2 ..216 C6
Witham CM8 ......177 A5
Palmers Croft CM2 ......206 A2
Palmers La
8 Bishop's Stortford CM23 .145 F7
Chrishall SG8 ......19 C3
Palmerston Lodge CM2 ..216 F7
Palmerston Rd Ipswich IP4 17 E6
Thorpe-le-S CO16 ......142 A2
Pampas Cl CO4 ......110 A4
Panfield La CM7 ......127 E5
Pannells Ash CO10 ......11 D1
Pannels Cl CO10 ......2 B4
Pantile Cl CM8 ......195 A7
Pantlings La CO5 ......158 A5
Panton Cres 7 CO4 ......136 E7
Panton Mews CM7 ......155 A8
Papermill Cotts CO9 ......76 E2
Papillon Rd CO3 ......135 E7
Parade Rd IP4 ......17 F7
Parade The
Colchester CO2 ......136 A1
Kirby Cross CO13 ......170 B6
Walton-on-t-N CO14 ......171 C8
Paradise Rd CM1 ......215 B8
Pardoe Pl IP4 ......18 E5
Park Ave
Bishop's Stortford CM23 ...145 F3
Chelmsford CM1 ......204 F4
Felixstowe IP11 ......221 F5
Park Bvd CO15 ......189 E6
Park Chase CO16 ......187 C5
Park Cl CO10 ......34 A8
Park Cotts Gosfield CO9 ..102 E8
Manningtree CO11 ......86 D3
Park Ct Felixstowe IP11 ...221 D2
Sible Hedingham CO9 ......51 D1
Park Dr Braintree CM7 ....155 A8
Brightlingsea CO7 ......185 E7
Halstead CO9 ......76 E1
Maldon CM9 ......210 B1
Park Drive Par CO7 ......185 E7
Park Farm Ind Est SG8 ...39 C2
Park Farm La SG8 ......39 C2
Park Gate Cotts CM7 ......101 C6
Park Gate Rd CM8 ......157 B3
Park La
Bishop's Stortford CM23 ...145 F4
Bulmer CO10 ......32 F2
Castle Camps CB1 ......7 F3
Earls Colne CO6 ......105 B6
Glemsford CO10 ......2 D4
Gosfield CO9 ......102 F7
Langham CO4 ......83 E3
Langley CB11 ......40 A3
Saffron Walden CB10 ......22 D1
Tolleshunt Knights CM9 ....180 B3
Toppesfield CO9 ......50 B7
Park Lane Cl CO6 ......105 B6
Park North IP4 ......17 D8
Park Rd Ardleigh CO7 ......111 F3
Chelmsford CM1 ......205 B2
Clacton-on-S CO15 ......188 D2
Colchester CO3 ......135 C6
East Bergholt CO7 ......60 B2
Elsenham CM22 ......94 D1
Ford End CM3 ......172 A3
Great Chesterford CB10 ......3 E5
Harwich CO12 ......91 D4
Haverhill CB9 ......8 D8
Ipswich IP1 ......17 C8
Little Bentley CO7 ......139 D8
Little Easton CM6 ......122 F3
Little Horkesley CO6 ......82 B8
Maldon CM9 ......209 F2
Rivenhall CM8 ......157 A2
Stansted
Mountfitchet CM24 ......119 E6
Stoke-by-N CO6 ......56 E4
Sudbury CO10 ......34 A8
Wivenhoe CO7 ......164 C8
Wivenhoe, Wivenhoe
Park CO4 ......137 A4
Park Side CM6 ......124 D6
Park Sq E
Clacton-on-S CO15 ......203 G8
Jaywick CO15 ......188 A1

Park Sq W
Clacton-on-S CO15 . . . . . . .203 F8
Jaywick CO15 . . . . .187 F1
Park St Stoke-by-N CO6 . . .56 D5
Thaxted CM6 . . . . .70 A2
Park Terr Harwich CO12 . . .91 D4
Long Melford CO10 . . . . . . .15 C7
Park The CO11 . . . . .86 D3
Park Vale Cl CO9 . . . . .51 E4
Park View CO10 . . . . .12 C8
Park View Cres CM2 . . . . .216 F5
Park View Rd IP1 . . . . .17 B8
Park Way CO15 . . . . .188 D1
Park Wood La CM9 . . . . . .197 A3
Parkdale CM3 . . . . .218 C7
Parker Ct CM0 . . . . .214 F4
Parker Rd CM2 . . . . .205 C1
Parker Way CO9 . . . . .103 E8
Parker's Way CO6 . . . . . . .56 A1
Parkeston Rd
Felixstowe IP11 . . . . .221 B4
Harwich, Parkeston CO12 . . .90 F4
Harwich, Upper
Dovercourt CO12 . . . . .91 A4
Parkfield St CO5 . . . . .163 F7
Parkfields CO9 . . . . .51 D1
Parkgate Cnr CO16 . . . . . .169 A2
Parkhall Rd
Beazley End CM7 . . . . .101 E7
Gosfield CO9 . . . . .102 B7
Parkland Ct CO1 . . . . .136 C5
Parklands CM7 . . . . .155 A8
Parklands Cl CO10 . . . . . . .2 C5
Parklands Ct CO16 . . . . . .188 B3
Parklands Dr CM7 . . . . . . .205 D3
Parklands Way CM2 . . . . . .216 C2
Parkside Haverhill CB9 . . . . .8 F6
Saffron Walden CB10 . . . . . .22 C1
Parkside Ave IP4 . . . . .17 D7
Parkway
Chelmsford CM1 CM2 . . . . .205 B2
Shudy Camps CB1 . . . . .7 C6
Parkwood IP1 . . . . .17 C7
Parkwood Ave CO7 . . . . . .137 B1
Parkwood Dr CO10 . . . . . . .15 E2
Parliament Rd IP4 . . . . .18 B5
Parmenter Dr CO10 . . . . . . .34 C5
Parnell Cl CO2 . . . . .136 A2
Parnham Pl IP4 . . . . .18 F5
Parr Cl CM7 . . . . .128 D4
Parr Dr CO3 . . . . .134 E4
Parrington Way CO11 . . . . .86 A3
Parry Dr CO16 . . . . .188 C5
Parson's Field CO7 . . . . . . .85 A6
Parson's Heath CO4 . . . . .110 E2
Parson's Hill CO3 . . . . . . .135 C6
Parsonage Cl
Broomfield CM1 . . . . .191 A1
Felixstowe IP11 . . . . .221 B4
Parsonage Farm La CB10 .47 B4
Parsonage Farm Trad
Est CM24 . . . . .119 F3
Parsonage Gdns [6] CB9 . . . .8 E7
Parsonage Gr CO8 . . . . . . .79 E8
Parsonage La
Barnston CM6 . . . . .151 D3
Bishop's Stortford CM23 . . .146 C8
Clavering CB11 . . . . .65 B3
Elder Street CB10 . . . . .44 F3
Howe Street CM3 . . . . .172 F2
Little Baddow CM3 . . . . . . .207 D2
Stansted
Mountfitchet CM24 . . . . . .119 F4
Tendring CO16 . . . . .140 E8
Parsonage Rd CM24 . . . . .148 C8
Parsonage St CO9 . . . . . . .76 F1
Parsons Ct [4] CO9 . . . . . . .76 F2
Parsons Heath CE Prim
Sch CO4 . . . . .110 E2
Parsons Hill CO7 . . . . .138 F8
Parsons La CO1 . . . . .136 C6
Parsons Yd [9] CO10 . . . . . .86 D4
Partridge Ave CM1 . . . . . .204 F6
Partridge Cl CO12 . . . . . . .116 D4
Partridge Dr CO6 . . . . .107 D5
Partridge Rd IP2 . . . . .16 E3
Paschal Way CM2 . . . . . . .216 F8
Pashlers Alley CO10 . . . . . .12 B7
Paske Ave CB9 . . . . .8 F7
Pasture High CM3 . . . . . . .207 D3
Pastures The IP4 . . . . .18 F5
Patching Hall La CM1 . . . .205 A6
Paternoster Row [6]
CO14 . . . . .171 C8
Path The CO7 . . . . .166 E8
Pathfields Rd CO15 . . . . . .188 D4
Pathway The CO13 . . . . . .170 E6
Patmore Cl CM23 . . . . . . .145 C8
Patmore Fields CM22 . . . . .93 E6
Patmore Rd CO4 . . . . .110 D1
Patricia Gdns CM23 . . . . .145 E5
Patten Cl CO6 . . . . .132 F3
Pattern Bush Cl CO11 . . . . .86 D8
Patteson Rd IP3 . . . . .17 E4
Patticroft CO10 . . . . .2 B6
Pattison Cl CM8 . . . . .195 A8
Pattocks La CO6 . . . . .106 C2
Pattrick's La CO12 . . . . . . .91 C4
Paul Spendlove Ct CO4 . .110 E1
Paul's Rd IP2 . . . . .16 F5
Pauline Cl CO15 . . . . .189 B6
Pauline St [8] IP2 . . . . .17 C4
Pauls Cres CO7 . . . . .137 F6
Pauls Way CO15 . . . . .188 A1
Pavilion Ct CB9 . . . . .9 B7

Pavitt Mdw CM2 . . . . .216 C2
Pawle Cl CM2 . . . . .217 A7
Paxman Ave CO2 . . . . . . .135 A3
Paxton Rd CO15 . . . . .189 B8
Paycocke Way CO6 . . . . . .131 A3
Paycocke's House CO6 . . .130 F2
Payne's La CO11 . . . . .113 C3
Peace Rd CO3 . . . . .134 D7
Peacock Cl Braintree CM7 .127 F1
[5] Ipswich IP8 . . . . .16 C2
Peacocks Cl CO10 . . . . .1 C2
Peacocks Rd CO10 . . . . . . .1 C2
Peakes Cl CO5 . . . . .179 B4
Peal Rd CB11 . . . . .43 F7
Pearce Manor CM2 . . . . . .215 F8
Pearce Rd IP3 . . . . .18 A5
Pearl Rd IP1 . . . . .16 D8
Pearmain Way CO3 . . . . . .134 C4
Pearse Way IP3 . . . . .18 E1
Pearson Rd IP3 . . . . .18 C5
Pearsons Cl CO10 . . . . .2 A4
Peartree Bsns Ctr CO3 . . .134 E4
Goldhanger CM9 . . . . .211 E6
Peartree Hill Bures CO8 . . .80 A5
Bures CO8 . . . . .80 B4
Peartree La CM3 . . . . .218 F3
Peartree Rd CO3 . . . . .134 E4
Peartree Way CO16 . . . . . .168 C2
Peaslands Rd CB11 . . . . . .43 E8
Pebmarsh Cl CO2 . . . . . . .163 A8
Pebmarsh Rd
Alphamstone CO8 . . . . .54 E2
Colne Engaine CO6 . . . . . . .77 F2
Pecocks Cl CO10 . . . . .34 C5
Pedder's Cl CM3 . . . . .134 F3
Pedlars Cl CM3 . . . . .219 A6
Pedlars Path CM3 . . . . . . .219 A6
Pedler's Cnr CO11 . . . . . . .86 D2
Peek's Cnr CO6 . . . . .105 D5
Peel Cres CM7 . . . . .127 E3
Peel Rd CM2 . . . . .205 F4
Peel St [5] IP1 . . . . .17 C6
Peersway Rd CO2 . . . . . . .135 D2
Peewit Cl IP11 . . . . .221 B3
Peewit Hill IP11 . . . . .221 B3
Peewit Rd IP2 . . . . .16 C3
Peg Millar's La CM3 . . . . .175 E5
Pegasus Way
Braintree CM7 . . . . .127 C5
Colchester CO4 . . . . .110 C1
Peggotty Cl CM1 . . . . .204 F6
Peggy's Wlk CB11 . . . . .21 E3
Pelham Cl CO12 . . . . .90 F2
Great Wigborough CO5 . . . .182 A3
Pelham Rd CB11 . . . . .65 C4
Pelham's La [20] CO1 . . . . .135 F7
Pelican Cl IP2 . . . . .16 E3
Pelly Ave CM8 . . . . .195 A8
Pembroke Ave CM9 . . . . . .209 F1
Pembroke Cl
Colchester CO2 . . . . .136 C3
Ipswich IP2 . . . . .17 B3
Pembroke Gdns CO15 . . . .189 E6
Pembroke Pl
Chelmsford CM1 . . . . .205 B7
Sudbury CO10 . . . . .15 C2
Pen Wlk CM1 . . . . .204 D5
Pendleton Rd IP2 . . . . .16 D1
Penfold Rd
Clacton-on-S CO15 . . . . . .188 E2
Felixstowe IP11 . . . . .221 E4
Penhaligon Ct [9] CM8 . . . .177 A4
Penlan Hall La CO6 . . . . . .107 B5
Penn Cl IP9 . . . . .35 B2
Penn Mews CM7 . . . . .155 A8
Pennine Rd CM1 . . . . .204 D5
Pennington La CM24 . . . . . .93 D2
Penningtons CM23 . . . . . .145 C5
Pennsylvania La CO5 . . . . .179 C5
Penny Cnr IP1 . . . . .16 C8
Penny La IP3 . . . . .18 F1
Penny Meadow IP9 . . . . . . .35 A1
Penny Royal Rd CM3 . . . . .218 D6
Pennyroyal Cres CM8 . . . .176 E4
Pennyroyal Gdns IP2 . . . . . .16 E4
Pennystone Rd CB11 . . . . . .43 E8
Penrice Cl CO4 . . . . .136 E6
Penrose Mead CM1 . . . . . .215 B8
Penshurst Pl CM7 . . . . . . .154 B6
Penshurst Rd IP3 . . . . .18 D4
Penticton Rd CM7 . . . . . . .127 D2
Pentland Ave CM1 . . . . . . .205 A6
Pentlow Dr CO10 . . . . .1 E1
Pentlow Hawke Cl CB9 . . . .9 B7
Pentlow Hill CO10 . . . . .14 A8
Penzance Cl
Chelmsford CM1 . . . . .205 E5
Clacton-on-S CO15 . . . . . .203 I8
Penzance Rd IP5 . . . . .18 F6
Pepper's Rd CO4 . . . . .82 E1
Peppercorn Cl CO4 . . . . . .109 F2
Peppercorn Way IP2 . . . . . .17 D3
Pepples La Debden CB10 . . .69 A8
Elder Street CB10 . . . . .45 A1
Pepys St CO12 . . . . .91 D5
Percival Rd
Kirby-le-S CO13 . . . . .143 D1
Walton-on-N CO14 . . . . . . .144 D2
Peregrine Cl
Bishop's Stortford CM23 . . .145 D6
Clacton-on-S CO15 . . . . . .188 F7
Peregrine Ct CO4 . . . . .136 F8
Peregrine Dr CM2 . . . . . . .216 A4
Perkins Way IP3 . . . . .17 F1
Perriclose CM1 . . . . .205 D7

Perrin Pl CM2 . . . . .205 A1
Perry Hill CM1 . . . . .205 D3
Perry La CO4 . . . . .84 A4
Perry Rd Tiptree CO5 . . . . .179 C5
Witham CM8 . . . . .177 B1
Perry Way CM8 . . . . .177 B1
Perryfield CO10 . . . . .34 B4
Perryfields Jun & Inf
Sch CM1 . . . . .205 D6
Persardi Ct CO2 . . . . .163 A7
Pershore End CO3 . . . . . . .134 E5
Perth Cl CO2 . . . . .136 A1
Pertwee Cl CO7 . . . . .185 E8
Pertwee Dr CM2 . . . . .216 F6
Pertwee Way CO5 . . . . . . .163 B2
Pesthouse La CO12 . . . . . .116 D3
Peter Bruff Ave CO16 . . . .188 C5
Peter Kirk Sch CM24 . . . . .119 F6
Peter's Gr IP9 . . . . .35 A1
Peterfield's La CO9 . . . . . .102 F5
Peterhouse Cl IP2 . . . . .16 F2
Peters Ho CO5 . . . . .158 C2
Petersfield CM1 . . . . .205 B7
Peto Ave CO4 . . . . .109 F2
Petrebrook CM2 . . . . .206 A3
Petrel Way CM2 . . . . .216 C6
Petrolea Cl CO4 . . . . .109 F1
Pettit La CM7 . . . . .156 A4
Petts La CB10 . . . . .4 E1
Petunia Cres CM1 . . . . . . .205 F6
Petworth Cl
Great Notley CM7 . . . . .154 B7
Wivenhoe CO7 . . . . .164 C8
Pevensey Dr CO15 . . . . . . .203 I8
Peverel Ave CM3 . . . . .194 C1
Peverells Rd CB10 . . . . .44 D1
Pewterers Ave CM23 . . . . .145 C4
Pharos La CO5 . . . . .201 C6
Pheasant Rd IP2 . . . . .16 E3
Pheasant Rise IP8 . . . . .35 F8
Philip Ave IP11 . . . . .221 B3
Philip Cl CO14 . . . . .171 A8
Philip Morant Sch The
CO3 . . . . .135 B5
Philip Rd Ipswich IP2 . . . . .17 C4
Witham CM8 . . . . .194 E8
Philips Cl CM7 . . . . .126 F2
Philips Rd CM7 . . . . .126 F2
Phillip Rd CO7 . . . . .164 B8
Phillips Chase CM7 . . . . . .128 A5
Phillips Field Rd CO10 . . . .34 A5
Philpot End La CM6 . . . . . .150 B4
Phoenix Ct CO2 . . . . .136 D5
Phoenix Gr CM2 . . . . .216 A8
Phoenix Rd IP4 . . . . .18 A7
Piccotts La CM7 . . . . .126 B8
Pickers Way CO15 . . . . . . .189 E7
Pickford Wlk CO4 . . . . . . .136 F7
Pickpocket La CM7 . . . . . .154 D6
Pickwick Ave CM1 . . . . . . .204 D6
Pickwick Rd IP2 . . . . .16 E5
Pier App CO14 . . . . .171 C8
Pier Ave CO15 . . . . .188 E2
Pier Gap CO15 . . . . .188 F2
Pierce Glade CO5 . . . . . . .179 C5
Pierrefitte Way CM7 . . . . .127 E3
Pig La CM22 . . . . .146 A3
Pigeon's La IP8 . . . . .16 A3
Pightle The Capel St M IP9 .35 B2
Finchingfield CM7 . . . . .72 D6
Haverhill CB9 . . . . .9 A8
Pightle Way CO14 . . . . . . .171 A7
Pilborough Way CO3 . . . . .134 C4
Pilcox Hall La CO16 . . . . . .140 D8
Pilgrim Cl CM7 . . . . .127 F5
Pilgrims Cl CB10 . . . . .3 D2
Pimblett Row CM22 . . . . . . .94 F5
Pimpernel Rd IP2 . . . . .16 F3
Pin Mill Cl IP2 . . . . .16 C1
Pincey Rd CM24 . . . . .120 F3
Pincey Rdbt CM24 . . . . . . .121 A3
Pinchpools Rd CM23 . . . . . .93 A3
Pine Ave
Great Dunmow CM6 . . . . . .123 B1
Ipswich IP1 . . . . .17 B8
Pine Cl Brantham CO11 . . . .86 D8
Great Bentley CO7 . . . . . . .166 F8
Pine Gr
Bishop's Stortford CM23 . . .146 B6
West Mersea CO5 . . . . . . .201 B7
Witham CM8 . . . . .177 A5
Pine Ho IP11 . . . . .221 C4
Pine Tree Ct CO4 . . . . .136 E8
Pine View Rd IP1 . . . . .17 A8
Pinetree Cl IP5 . . . . .18 F7
Pinewood Cl
Clacton-on-S CO15 . . . . . .188 E7
Kirby Cross CO13 . . . . . . .170 D6
Pink La CM3 . . . . .175 D7
Pinkham Dr CM8 . . . . .194 F8
Pinkney Cl CB10 . . . . .44 E2
Pinkuah La CO10 . . . . .13 F6
Pinmill Rd IP9 . . . . .63 F8
Pintail Cl IP2 . . . . .16 E3
Pintail Cres CM7 . . . . .154 C6
Pioneer Pl [8] CO1 . . . . . . .136 A6
Pipchin Rd CM1 . . . . .204 F6
Piper Rd CO3 . . . . .135 B7
Piper's Tye CM2 . . . . .216 D3
Piperell Way CB9 . . . . .9 A5

Pipers Cl CB9 . . . . .9 C6
Pippins The Glemsford CO10 .2 C4
Halstead CO9 . . . . .76 D2
Pirie Rd CO6 . . . . .108 E3
Pit La CO5 . . . . .179 C6
Pitcairn Rd IP1 . . . . .16 E8
Pitmire La CO8 . . . . .55 B6
Pitt Ave CM8 . . . . .195 A8
Pitt Chase CM2 . . . . .216 E5
Pitt Gn CM8 . . . . .195 A8
Pitts End CO7 . . . . .59 D3
Place Farm Ct CO2 . . . . . .136 D2
Place Farm Cty Prim Sch
CB9 . . . . .8 F8
Plains Farm Cl CO7 . . . . . .110 D6
Plains Field CM7 . . . . .128 D1
Plains Rd
Great Totham CM9 . . . . . . .196 F6
Little Totham CM9 . . . . . . .197 A6
Plaistow Green Rd CO9 . . .103 C1
Plane Tree Cl CM2 . . . . . . .216 B6
Plane View Cl CO16 . . . . . .188 B2
Plantation Cl CO4 . . . . . . .109 F1
Plantation Rd CM3 . . . . . . .192 F1
Planton Way CO7 . . . . . . .185 E6
Platters Cl IP3 . . . . .38 B7
Platters Rd IP11 . . . . .221 C2
Plaw Hatch Cl CM23 . . . . .146 B8
Plaw Hatch La CM23 . . . . .146 D8
Players Ct CM6 . . . . .152 C6
Playfield Rd IP9 . . . . .35 B1
Playford Rd [2] CO10 . . . . . .33 E8
Playford Rd IP4 . . . . .18 E8
Playle Chase CM9 . . . . . . .196 B4
Pleasant Rd CM23 . . . . . . .145 E8
Pleasant Row [13][4] IP9 . . . .17 D5
Pleasant Valley CB11 . . . . . .43 D7
Pleasants Mews CO5 . . . . .201 C6
Pleshey Rd CM3 . . . . .172 B5
Plough Cnr CO16 . . . . .168 C4
Plough Dr CO3 . . . . .135 A5
Plough La CO10 . . . . .33 D7
Plough Rd CO7 . . . . .166 E6
Plough St IP3 . . . . .17 E4
Ploughmans Cl CM23 . . . . .145 C5
Ploughmans
Headland CO3 . . . . .134 E5
Plover Cl CO13 . . . . .170 E6
Plover Rd IP2 . . . . .16 E3
Plover Wlk CM7 . . . . .216 B5
Plowright Ho [5] CO1 . . . . .135 E8
Plum St CO10 . . . . .2 A6
Plume Ave Colchester CO3 135 A4
Maldon CM9 . . . . .209 F1
Plume Sch (Lower Sch)
The CM9 . . . . .210 A2
Plume Sch (Upper Sch)
The CM9 . . . . .209 F2
Plummers Rd CO6 . . . . . . .107 E7
Plumptre La CM3 . . . . .218 D5
Plums La CM7 . . . . .99 E4
Plumtree Ave CM2 . . . . . . .216 F6
Plymouth Rd
Chelmsford CM1 . . . . .205 E5
Clacton-on-S CO15 . . . . . .203 J8
Felixstowe IP11 . . . . .221 D6
Pochard Way CM7 . . . . . . .154 C5
Pocklington Cl CM2 . . . . . .206 A3
Pods La CM7 . . . . .126 D2
Point Clear Rd CO16 . . . . .186 D3
Pointwell La CO6 . . . . .158 A8
Pole Barn La CO13 . . . . . . .170 F5
Pole La CM5 . . . . .155 C3
Polecat Rd CM7 . . . . .155 F5
Pollard Ct IP2 . . . . .16 D2
Pollard Wlk CO16 . . . . . . .188 C5
Pollard's Gn CM2 . . . . . . .205 F3
Pollards Villas CM7 . . . . . . .99 D2
Polley Cl CO3 . . . . .170 E7
Polstead St CO6 . . . . .56 D5
Polstead Way CO16 . . . . . .188 B4
Pond Chase CO3 . . . . .135 B4
Pond Cl IP11 . . . . .221 B5
Pond Cross Cotts CB11 . . . .67 A8
Pond Cross Farm CB11 . . . .67 A8
Pond Cross Way CB11 . . . . .67 A8
Ponders Rd CO6 . . . . .107 C4
Pondfield Rd CO4 . . . . .110 D1
Pondholton Dr CM8 . . . . . .194 F7
Ponds Rd CM2 . . . . .216 B1
Pondtail Ct CO13 . . . . .170 C6
Poney Chase CM8 . . . . . . .195 F5
Poney's CM8 . . . . .195 F5
Pontisbright Cotts CO6 . . .106 E6
Poole Cl IP3 . . . . .18 D3
Poole St Cavendish CO10 . . .1 C1
Great Yeldham CO9 . . . . . . .51 B6
Poore St CB11 . . . . .65 F8
Pope's La CO3 . . . . .135 E7
Pope's Rd CO6 . . . . .106 D4
Poperinghe Rd CO2 . . . . . .135 F4
Popes Cl CB9 . . . . .9 E5
Poplar Ave CO16 . . . . .188 A2
Poplar Cl Chelmsford CM2 .216 C6
Clacton-on-S CO15 . . . . . .188 B2
Great Yeldham CO9 . . . . . . .30 A1
Halstead CO9 . . . . .103 F8
Witham CM8 . . . . .177 A5
Poplar Ct CO10 . . . . .34 B7
Poplar Grove Chase CM9 .210 B8
Poplar La IP8 . . . . .16 B3
Poplar Rd CO10 . . . . .34 B7
Poplar Way CO13 . . . . .170 D6
Poplars Cl CO7 . . . . .165 B7
Poplars The
Brantham CO11 . . . . .60 D2
Great Dunmow CM6 . . . . . .123 C2
Great Hallingbury CM22 . . .146 F4

Poppy Cl IP2 . . . . .16 F4
Poppy Gdns CO2 . . . . .136 C3
Pork La CO13 . . . . .169 E5
Port La
Bishop's Stortford CM22 . . .146 F2
Colchester CO1 . . . . .136 A5
Port Of Felixstowe Rd
IP11 . . . . .221 A4
Portal Prec CO1 . . . . .135 F7
Porter Rd IP3 . . . . .18 F1
Porter Way CO16 . . . . .188 B3
Porter's Cl CO3 . . . . .107 F2
Porter's Cotts CO3 . . . . . . .107 F1
Porter's La CO3 . . . . .107 F2
Porters Brook Wlk CO4 . . .110 C2
Porters Pk CM3 . . . . .193 A2
Portland Ave CO12 . . . . . . .91 C3
Portland Cl CM7 . . . . .128 B3
Portland Cres CO12 . . . . . . .91 C3
Portland Ho CO13 . . . . . . .170 F5
Portland Pl [17] CM23 . . . . .145 F7
Portland Rd
Bishop's Stortford CM23 . . .145 F7
[15] Colchester CO2 . . . . . .135 F6
Portlight Cl CO11 . . . . .87 A4
Portman Rd IP1 . . . . .17 B6
Portman Road (Ipswich
Town FC) IP1 . . . . .17 B5
Portman's Wlk IP1 . . . . . . .17 B5
Portmans Walk Ind Ctr
IP1 . . . . .17 A5
Portobello Rd CO14 . . . . . .171 C8
Portreath Pl CM1 . . . . .205 A4
Portsmouth Rd CO15 . . . . .203 J8
Portway Cl CO9 . . . . .76 F3
Posford Ct CO4 . . . . .109 F4
Post Mill Cl IP4 . . . . .17 F5
Post Office Cnr IP9 . . . . . . .61 C2
Post Office La
Glemsford CO10 . . . . .2 B5
Little Totham CM9 . . . . . . .197 A6
Post Office Rd
Broomfield CM1 . . . . .205 B8
Woodham Mortimer CM9 . .219 E3
Postman's La CM3 . . . . . . .207 E3
Pot Kiln Chase CO9 . . . . . . .31 F2
Pot Kiln Cty Prim Sch
CO10 . . . . .34 B6
Pot Kiln Rd CO10 . . . . .34 C6
Pot Kilns The CO10 . . . . . . .34 C6
Potash Cotts IP9 . . . . .60 E3
Potash La IP9 . . . . .60 E3
Potter St
Bishop's Stortford CM23 . . .145 F7
Sible Hedingham CO9 . . . . . .75 E7
Potters Cl CM3 . . . . .219 A6
Pottery La
Castle Hedingham CO9 . . . . .51 F3
Chelmsford CM1 . . . . .205 A5
Poulk Hall La CM3 . . . . . . .174 A5
Poulteney Rd CM24 . . . . . .119 C6
Pound Farm Dr CO12 . . . . .91 A3
Pound Fields CM1 . . . . . . .215 D8
Pound Gate CM6 . . . . .124 D6
Pound La Belstead IP8 . . . . .36 A4
Capel St M IP9 . . . . .59 F8
Washbrook IP8 . . . . .35 F7
Pound Wlk CB10 . . . . .22 C2
Poundfield Cl CO7 . . . . . . .165 B7
Poundfield Ho CO7 . . . . . . .138 C4
Powers Hall Cty Inf
Sch CM8 . . . . .176 D3
Powers Hall Cty Jun
Sch CM8 . . . . .176 D3
Powers Hall End CM8 . . . . .176 D3
Powling Rd IP3 . . . . .18 A2
Pownall Cres CO2 . . . . . . .135 F4
Poynter Pl CO13 . . . . .170 E7
Prail Ct CO6 . . . . .130 F2
Pratt's La IP9 . . . . .38 A2
Pratts Farm La CM3 . . . . . .191 D4
Prentice Hall La CM9 . . . . .213 B8
President Rd CO3 . . . . .134 E5
Preston Rd CO15 . . . . .189 D5
Prestwick Dr CO15 . . . . . .119 B1
Pretoria Rd CO9 . . . . .76 F2
Prettygate Jun & Inf
Sch CO3 . . . . .135 A4
Prettygate Rd
Colchester CO3 . . . . .135 A4
Colchester CO3 . . . . .135 A5
Pretyman Rd
Felixstowe IP11 . . . . .221 C1
Ipswich IP3 . . . . .18 B3
Prime's Cl CB10 . . . . .22 D1
Primrose Cl CM23 . . . . . . .145 C5
Primrose Hill
Chelmsford CM1 . . . . .204 F3
Haverhill CB9 . . . . .8 F7
Holbrook IP9 . . . . .62 D4
Ipswich IP2 . . . . .16 F4
Primrose La
Ramsey CO12 . . . . .89 A1
Tiptree CO5 . . . . .179 C6
Primrose Pl CM8 . . . . .176 E4
Primrose Rd CO15 . . . . . . .189 E6
Primrose Wlk
Colchester CO4 . . . . .136 E7
Maldon CM9 . . . . .210 B1
Primula Cl CO16 . . . . .188 C4
Primula Way CM1 . . . . . . .206 A6
Prince Albert Rd CO5 . . . . .201 D6
Prince Charles Cl
Clacton-on-S CO15 . . . . . .188 C1
Sudbury CO10 . . . . .33 F8
Prince Charles Rd CO2 . . .136 A2
Prince Of Wales Dr IP2 . . . .17 B2
Prince Of Wales Rd CM9 196 A4

Prince of Wales Rdbt
CO6 ...133 B4
Prince Philip Ave CO15 ..188 C1
Prince Philip Rd CO2 ...136 A1
Prince St CO10 ...33 E8
Prince's Espl CO14 ...144 D1
Princel La CO7 ...84 F7
Princes Ct CM23 ...145 C7
Princes Gate CM23 ...145 C7
Princes Gdns IP11 ...221 D4
Princes Rd
Chelmsford CM2 ...216 B7
Clacton-on-S CO15 ...189 D5
Felixstowe IP11 ...221 E4
Harwich CO12 ...91 B3
Maldon CM9 ...210 A2
Princes St Ipswich IP1 ...17 B5
Maldon CM9 ...209 F3
Princess Anne Cl CO15 ..188 C1
Princess Dr CO4 ...110 C5
Princess St CO12 ...90 F5
Princess Way CB9 ...8 E8
Princethorpe Rd IP3 ...18 C4
Princeton Mews CO4 ...110 B4
Prior Cl CO9 ...103 D8
Prior Way CO4 ...109 E2
Prior's Hall Barn CB11 ...67 D4
Prior's Wood Rd CM22 ..148 C7
Priors 9 CM23 ...146 A7
Priors Way CO6 ...131 A3
Priory Ave CB9 ...8 F7
Priory Cl Chelmsford CM1 .204 E2
Hatfield Peverel CM3 ...194 B1
Ickleton CB10 ...3 A3
St Osyth CO16 ...203 A6
Priory Ct
Bishop's Stortford CM23 ..145 F7
Hatfield Peverel CM3 ...194 A4
Priory Cty Prim Sch The
CM3 ...218 F2
Priory Dr CM24 ...119 E5
Priory Farm Rd CM3 ...194 B2
Priory Heath Prim Sch
IP3 ...18 C1
Priory La CM3 ...218 F1
Priory Mews CM3 ...194 C2
Priory Rd Bicknacre CM3 ..218 E1
Chappel CO6 ...106 B3
Clacton-on-S CO15 ...188 E3
Sudbury CO10 ...15 D1
Tiptree CO5 ...178 F3
Priory St Colchester CO1 ..136 A7
Earls Colne CO6 ...105 B7
Priory The CM1 ...215 B8
Priory Wlk
26 Colchester CO1 ...135 F7
Sudbury CO10 ...33 E7
Priory Wood CO9 ...51 E4
Priory Wood Rdbt CM22 .147 A8
Prittlewell Cl IP2 ...16 F1
Proctor Cl CO5 ...163 B2
Proctor Way CO6 ...132 E3
Proctors Way CM23 ...146 A4
Progress Ct CM7 ...127 E3
Progress Way CO16 ...168 C1
Promenade
Clacton-on-S CO15 ...203 D6
Harwich CO12 ...91 C2
Harwich CO12 ...91 E4
Promenade Way CO7 ...185 E5
Prospect Cl CM3 ...194 A3
Prospect Hill CO10 ...34 D3
Prospect Pl CB11 ...22 F1
Prospect Rd IP1 ...17 A7
Prospect St 1 IP1 ...17 A6
Prospero Cl CO4 ...136 F8
Provence Cl CO3 ...134 C7
Providence La IP1 ...17 A7
Providence Pl CO1 ...136 B6
Providence St 6 IP1 ...17 C6
Provident Sq CM2 ...205 C2
Prunus Ct CO2 ...163 A7
Prykes Dr CM1 ...205 A2
Pryor Cl CM8 ...177 A1
Pryors Cl CM23 ...146 A6
Pryors Rd CM2 ...216 C2
Pudding La CO2 ...161 B3
Puffinsdale CO15 ...188 F5
Pulford Pl CM6 ...124 D7
Pulpitfield Cl CO14 ...171 A8
Pump Hill
Great Baddow CM2 ...216 F6
Harkstead SG9 ...64 A2
St Osyth CO16 ...187 D4
Pump La Chelmsford CM1 .205 E6
Danbury CM3 ...218 D5
Purleigh CM3 ...220 D1
Punchard Way IP11 ...221 A8
Punders Field CM7 ...128 D1
Purbeck Ct
4 Colchester CO1 ...136 D7
Great Baddow CM2 ...216 E6
Purcell Cl Colchester CO4 .136 E6
Writtle CM1 ...204 A1
Purdis Ave IP3 ...18 F2
Purdis Farm La IP3 ...18 F2
Purleigh Cty Prim Sch
CM3 ...220 D1
Purley Way CO16 ...188 B6
Purplett Ho IP2 ...17 D4
Purplett St IP2 ...17 D4
Purvis Way CO4 ...110 B5
Putticks La CO7 ...59 E3
Pye Cnr CO9 ...51 E4
Pyecat''s Cnr CO7 ...137 C7
Pyefleet Cl
Brightlingsea CO7 ...185 E7
Fingringhoe CO5 ...164 C6
Pyefleet Ho CO5 ...201 D7
Pyefleet View CO5 ...163 B3
Pyesand CO13 ...170 C8
Pygot Pl CM7 ...127 E4
Pyms Rd CM2 ...216 B3
Pynchbek CM23 ...145 E3
Pynchon Mews CM1 ...205 D3
Pyne Gate CM2 ...216 B1

Q

QM Ind Pk IP3 ...18 C1
Quadling St IP1 ...17 C5
Quadrangle Ctr The IP3 ..18 C1
Quaker's La CB9 ...9 A7
Quale Rd CM2 ...206 B4
Quantock Cl IP5 ...18 F7
Quay Court Yd 2 CO11 ..86 D4
Quay La Beaumont CO16 .142 B5
Kirby-le-S CO13 ...143 D1
Sudbury CO10 ...33 E6
Quay St
1 Manningtree CO11 ...86 D4
Wivenhoe CO7 ...164 B8
Quay The CO12 ...91 D6
Quay Theatre CO10 ...33 E6
Queech La IP9 ...87 C8
Queech The IP9 ...35 B2
Queen Anne Dr CO5 ...201 D6
Queen Anne Gdns CO5 ..201 D6
Queen Anne Rd CO5 ...201 D7
Queen Edith Dr CB9 ...27 B6
Queen Elizabeth Ave
CO15 ...188 C1
Queen Elizabeth Way
CO2 ...136 A2
Queen Mary Ave CO2 ...135 F4
Queen St
Brightlingsea CO7 ...185 F6
Castle Hedingham CO9 ...51 E3
Chelmsford CM2 ...205 A1
Coggeshall CO6 ...131 A2
Colchester CO1 ...135 F7
Felixstowe IP11 ...221 C6
Great Oakley CO12 ...116 C4
Ipswich IP1 ...17 C5
Maldon CM9 ...210 A2
Sible Hedingham CO9 ...75 F6
Queen Victoria Dr CO12 ..91 B8
Queen's Ave CM9 ...210 A1
Queen's Cotts CO6 ...105 B6
Queen's Ct
Clacton-on-S CO15 ...189 D4
6 Haverhill CB9 ...8 E8
Queen's Gdns CM7 ...127 B7
Queen's Head Rd CO4 ...82 E3
Queen's Ho CO13 ...170 F4
Queen's Rd
Chelmsford CM2 ...205 D2
Clacton-on-S CO15 ...188 D1
Colchester CO3 ...135 C6
Earls Colne CO6 ...105 B7
Felixstowe IP11 ...221 E4
Frinton-on-S CO13 ...170 F4
Harwich CO12 ...91 A2
West Bergholt CO6 ...108 D3
Wivenhoe CO7 ...164 C8
Queen's Sq IP3 ...18 B2
Queen's Way IP3 ...18 B2
Queenborough La
Great Notley CM7 ...154 D8
Rayne CM7 ...154 B8
Queenbury Cl CO5 ...201 E6
Queens Cl Stansted
Mountfitchet CM24 ...119 E8
Sudbury CO10 ...33 E8
Queens Cnr CO5 ...201 D7
Queens Cres CM23 ...145 E5
Queens Ct CO5 ...201 D7
Queens Mews CO5 ...201 B6
Queens Rd Braintree CM7 .127 F5
Sudbury CO10 ...33 E8
Queens Sq 5 CB9 ...9 A8
Queens St CB9 ...9 A8
Queens Terr CO10 ...34 A7
Queensberry Rd IP3 ...18 A1
Queensbury Ave CO6 ...133 D5
Queenscliffe Rd IP2 ...17 A3
Queensgate Dr IP4 ...17 F8
Queensland Cres CM1 ..204 E5
Queensland Dr CO2 ...136 A1
Queensway
Clacton-on-S CO15 ...189 D5
Great Cornard CO10 ...34 B5
Haverhill CB9 ...8 E8
Lawford CO11 ...86 C4
Tiptree CO5 ...179 C6
Quendon Pl 17 CB9 ...9 B8
Quendon Way CO13 ...171 A6
Quentin Cl IP1 ...16 E8
Quickset Rd CB11 ...20 C5
Quicksie Hill CB11 ...41 E2
Quilp Dr CM1 ...204 F7
Quilter Dr IP8 ...16 C1
Quilter Rd IP11 ...221 F4
Quilters Cl CO15 ...189 F6
Quince Cl CO11 ...60 D1
Quinion Cl CM1 ...204 D7
Quintons Cnr CO7 ...59 D4
Quintons Rd CO7 ...59 D4

R

RA Butler Cty Prim & Inf
Sch CB11 ...22 E1
Rachael Ct 1 CM2 ...205 B1
Rachael Gdns CM8 ...156 E4
Rachel Ct 6 IP4 ...17 D6
Radcliffe Dr IP2 ...16 D2
Radiator Rd CO10 ...34 A5
Radwinter Rd Ashdon CB10 24 B7
Saffron Walden CB10 ...23 B1
Sewards End CB10 ...23 F1
Raeburn Cl CO13 ...170 F7
Raeburn Inf Sch IP3 ...17 F1
Raeburn Rd IP3 ...18 A1
Raeburn Rd S IP3 ...37 F8
Raglan Mews CO15 ...188 C3
Raglan Rd CO13 ...171 A5
Ragley Cl CM7 ...154 B6
Raile Wlk CO10 ...15 D8
Railey Rd CB11 ...43 E8
Railway App IP11 ...221 E5
Railway Cotts CB11 ...42 F5
Railway Sq CM1 ...205 A3
Railway St Braintree CM7 .128 A3
Chelmsford CM1 ...205 A3
Manningtree CO11 ...86 D4
Railway Terr
Clacton-on-S CO15 ...188 F3
10 Manningtree CO11 ...86 D4
Rainbow Mead CM3 ...194 A5
Rainbow Mews CM9 ...209 F5
Rainbow Rd CO5 ...201 D6
Rainbow Way CO6 ...77 F1
Rainham Way CO13 ...171 B6
Rainsborowe Rd CO2 ...135 C4
Rainsford Ave CM1 ...204 F3
Rainsford High Sch CM1 .204 E4
Rainsford La CM1 ...204 F2
Rainsford Rd
Chelmsford CM1 ...204 F3
Stansted
Mountfitchet CM24 ...119 E8
Rambler Cl CO3 ...134 D7
Rampart Cotts CO6 ...109 D7
Ramparts Cl CO6 ...109 B7
Ramplings Ave CO15 ...188 E5
Ramsden Cl CO15 ...189 A5
Ramsey Cl Heybridge CM9 210 D4
Ipswich IP2 ...17 A1
Ramsey Cty Prim Sch
CO12 ...89 F1
Ramsey Mews CO2 ...136 A4
Ramsey Rd Halstead CO9 .103 D8
Harwich CO12 ...90 C2
Ramsey Sch The
Halstead CO9 ...76 F2
Halstead CO9 ...77 A2
Ramsgate Dr IP3 ...18 B3
Ramshaw Dr CM2 ...205 F3
Rana Ct CM7 ...127 F4
Rana Dr CM7 ...127 F4
Randall Cl CM6 ...123 D1
Randolph Ave CM7 ...73 C6
Randolph Cl CM9 ...220 F8
Rands Way IP3 ...18 B2
Randulph Terr CM1 ...205 D3
Randwell Cl IP4 ...18 B5
Ranelagh Ct IP11 ...221 E4
Ranelagh Prim Sch IP2 ..16 F5
Ranelagh Rd
Felixstowe IP11 ...221 E4
Ipswich IP2 ...17 A5
Ranger Wlk CO2 ...136 B3
Rangoon Cl CO2 ...135 B1
Ransom Rd CO5 ...179 C5
Ransome Cl IP8 ...16 A6
Ransome Cres IP3 ...18 B2
Ransome Rd IP3 ...18 B3
Ransomes Europark IP3 ..38 E8
Ransomes Way
Chelmsford CM1 ...205 B4
Ipswich IP3 ...38 D8
Ranulph Way CM3 ...194 B3
Raphael Dr CM1 ...205 F7
Rapier St IP2 ...17 C3
Rat Hill IP9 ...63 F2
Ratcliffe Ct
Frinton-on-S CO13 ...170 F5
Kelvedon CO5 ...158 C2
Ratcliffe Rd CO3 ...134 E6
Raven Way CO4 ...109 E4
Ravens Ave CO9 ...76 F1
Ravens Cres CM6 ...152 E6
Ravensbourne Dr CM1 ...204 E2
Ravenscroft Cty Prim
Sch CO16 ...188 B4
Ravensdale CO15 ...188 F6
Ravenswood 11 CO1 ...136 A6
Rawden Cl CO12 ...91 B4
Rawhedge Ct CO7 ...136 F4
Rawlings Cres CO4 ...110 B5
Rawstorn Rd CO3 ...135 E7
Ray Ave CO12 ...91 A3
Ray Ho CO5 ...201 D7
Ray La Harwich CO12 ...90 E5
Ramsey CO12 ...90 A3
Ray Mead CM3 ...190 F7
Ray The CM1 ...205 E5
Raycliff Ave CO15 ...188 E7
Raydon Way CO10 ...34 C6
Rayfield Cl CM6 ...151 A4
Rayhaven CO12 ...90 D2
Rayleigh Cl Braintree CM7 128 C4
Colchester CO4 ...110 B1
Rayment's Bungalows
CB10 ...45 E3
Raymouth Ho CO2 ...135 E2
Rayne Cty Prim Sch CM7 126 F2
Rayne Rd CM7 ...127 D3
Rayner Rd CO2 ...135 B4
Rayner Way CO9 ...76 E1
Raynham Rd CM23 ...146 B8
Reaburn Ct CM1 ...205 E6
Reade Rd IP9 ...62 D5
Reader's Cnr CM2 ...216 E5
Readers Ct CM2 ...216 E6
Reading Rd IP4 ...18 B7
Reaper Rd CO3 ...135 A5
Rebecca Gdns CM8 ...156 E4
Rebecca Meade CM6 ...122 F8
Rebow Rd Harwich CO12 ..91 A2
Wivenhoe CO7 ...164 B8
Rebow St CO1 ...136 B6
Reckitts Cl CO15 ...189 B4
Recreation Cl IP11 ...221 D6
Recreation Ground CM24 119 E6
Recreation La IP11 ...221 D6
Recreation Rd
Clacton-on-S CO15 ...188 F3
Colchester CO1 ...136 C5
Haverhill CB9 ...8 F7
Sible Hedingham CO9 ...75 D8
Recreation Way
Brightlingsea CO7 ...185 F7
Ipswich IP3 ...18 B2
Recreation Wlk CO10 ...34 B5
Rectory Cl
Bishop's Stortford CM23 ..145 D3
Colchester CO4 ...109 E2
Glemsford CO10 ...2 B5
Little Waltham CM3 ...191 C6
Littlebury CB11 ...21 F4
Rectory Field IP9 ...63 E7
Rectory Hill
East Bergholt CO7 ...59 C1
Stoke-by-N CO6 ...56 D7
Wivenhoe CO7 ...137 C1
Rectory La Abberton CO5 .163 A3
Ashdon CB10 ...6 A1
Brantham CO11 ...60 E1
Chelmsford CM1 ...205 B4
Farnham CM23 ...118 D6
Great Leighs CM3 ...173 D7
Ramsey CO12 ...90 A1
Rivenhall CM8 ...177 A6
Wickham St P CO9 ...53 C6
Woodham Mortimer CM9 ..219 F6
Rectory Mdw CM7 ...129 C2
Rectory Rd Aldham CO6 ..132 F7
Copford CO6 ...133 C1
Frating CO7 ...138 F1
Great Henny CO10 ...33 E4
Great Holland CO13 ...170 A3
Harkstead IP9 ...63 C2
Ipswich IP2 ...17 C4
Langham CO4 ...83 F7
Little Bentley CO7 ...139 E8
Little Oakley CO12 ...117 A7
Rowhedge CO5 ...163 E8
Sible Hedingham CO9 ...51 D1
Stisted CM7 ...129 B7
Tiptree CO5 ...179 C5
Tolleshunt Knights CM9 ...180 C1
Weeley Heath CO16 ...167 F3
Wivenhoe CO7 ...137 C2
Woodham Walter CM9 ...208 D3
Wrabness CO11 ...89 A3
Writtle CM1 ...215 B8
Red Barn La CO12 ...116 B2
Red Barn Rd CO7 ...185 F8
Red House La CO10 ...34 A4
Red La IP9 ...60 A8
Red Lion Ct 5 CM23 ...146 A7
Red Lion Yd 19 CO1 ...135 F7
Red Sleeve 5 IP9 ...35 A1
Redan St IP1 ...17 B7
Redbridge Rd CO15 ...188 F8
Redcliffe Rd 4 CM2 ...205 A1
Reddings Cl CB11 ...43 E7
Rede Way CO10 ...34 C6
Redgate La IP9 ...37 D5
Redgates La CB10 ...23 E3
Redgates Pl CM2 ...205 D4
Redhouse La
Great Horkesley CO4 ...82 D2
Sudbury CO10 ...33 E7
Redmayne Dr CM2 ...215 F8
Redmill CO3 ...135 A3
Redrose Wlk CO16 ...188 C4
Redruth Cl CM1 ...205 E5
Redshank Cl CB9 ...9 C7
Redshank Dr CM9 ...210 C5
Redvers Cl CM23 ...119 A2
Redwing Cl IP2 ...16 D3
Redwood Cl
Colchester CO4 ...110 E1
Witham CM8 ...177 A5
Redwood Ct 2 CO4 ...136 E8
Redwood Dr CM1 ...204 A1
Reed Cl CO16 ...188 C5
Reed Hall Ave
Colchester CO2 ...135 C3
Colchester CO2 ...135 D3
Reedland Way IP11 ...221 B5
Reeds La CB9 ...9 A8
Refinery Rd CO12 ...90 E5
Regal Cl CM2 ...216 D8
Regency Cl
Bishop's Stortford CM23 ..145 E7
Chelmsford CM2 ...205 D3
Regency Ct CM9 ...210 A5
Regency Gn CO3 ...135 A4
Regency Lodge CO15 ...188 E5
Regent Cl CO7 ...185 F8
Regent Ct CO5 ...164 A8
Regent Rd CO7 ...185 F7
Regent St Ipswich IP4 ...17 E6
8 Manningtree CO11 ...86 D4
Rowhedge CO5 ...164 A8
Regents Cl CO4 ...110 C5
Regina Cl IP4 ...18 B5
Regina Rd CM1 ...205 C3
Reigate Ave CO16 ...188 D6
Reigate Cl IP3 ...18 B3
Rembrandt Gr CM1 ...205 E6
Rembrandt Way CO3 ...135 B5
Rembrow Rd IP9 ...35 A1
Remembrance Ave CM3 .194 A3
Remercie Rd CO11 ...87 A4
Remus Cl CO4 ...109 F5
Rendlesham Ct 8 IP1 ...17 A7
Rendlesham Rd
Felixstowe IP11 ...221 B5
Ipswich IP1 ...17 A6
Renoir Pl CM1 ...205 F7
Retreat The
West Bergholt CO6 ...108 D3
Witham CM8 ...177 A1
Reverdy Ho CO2 ...135 E2
Reydon Ho IP3 ...18 A2
Reymead Cl CO5 ...201 C6
Reynard Copse CM23 ...118 F1
Reynard Ct CM2 ...216 F6
Reynards Cl CO13 ...170 D6
Reynards Copse CO4 ...110 A3
Reynolds Ave
Colchester CO3 ...135 B5
Ipswich IP3 ...38 A8
Reynolds Ct IP11 ...221 B5
Reynolds Rd IP3 ...18 A1
Rhodes Ave CM23 ...145 F5
Rhodes Meml Mus &
Commonwealth Ctr
CM23 ...146 A6
Riby Rd IP11 ...221 D3
Rice Bridge Ind Est CO16 169 A7
Rich Cl CM3 ...173 F7
Richard Avanue CO7 ...137 C3
Richard Ave CO7 ...185 F6
Richard Burn Way CO10 ..15 E2
Richard De Clare Cty
Prim Sch CO9 ...76 F1
Richard Wittington JMI
Sch CM23 ...145 E4
Richards Wlk CO15 ...188 E6
Richardson Pl CM1 ...204 F4
Richardson Rd CO7 ...59 D3
Richardson Wlk
Colchester CO3 ...134 F5
Witham CM8 ...177 B2
Richardsons La IP9 ...63 D8
Riche Cl CM6 ...152 B5
Richmond Cl CM23 ...145 C7
Richmond Cres CO12 ...91 B2
Richmond Dr CO15 ...188 A1
Richmond Ho 20 IP4 ...17 D5
Richmond Rd
Chelmsford CM2 ...206 A4
Ipswich IP1 ...16 F8
West Mersea CO5 ...201 D6
Rickling CE Prim Sch
CB11 ...93 E8
Rickling Green Rd
Quendon CB11 ...66 E1
Rickling Green CB11 ...93 E8
Rickling Rd CB11 ...66 B6
Rickstones Rd CM8 ...177 A6
Rickstones Sch The CM8 .176 F6
Riddiford Dr CM1 ...204 F4
Riddles Dr CO4 ...109 F2
Ridge The
Little Baddow CM3 ...207 E2
Walton-on-t-N CO14 ...171 B8
Ridgeway CO4 ...110 A4
Ridgeway The
Braintree CM7 ...128 A1
Harwich CO12 ...91 B3
Ridgewell Ave CM1 ...204 F4
Ridgewell CE Prim Sch
CO9 ...29 B6
Ridgewell Rd
Birdbrook CO9 ...10 E2
Great Yeldham CO9 ...29 E3
Ridgewell Way CO2 ...135 F1
Ridings The
Bishop's Stortford CM23 ..145 D4
Great Baddow CM2 ...216 D7
Ridlands Cl CM7 ...155 E6
Ridley Gdns CM22 ...94 C2
Ridley Rd CM1 ...205 B8
Riffhams Chase CM3 ...207 D2
Riffhams Dr CM2 ...217 A7
Riffhams La Danbury CM3 .218 C8
Little Baddow CM3 ...207 C1
Rifle Hill CM7 ...127 F1
Rifle Hill Works CM7 ...127 F1
Rigby Ave CO11 ...87 A3
Rignal's La CM2 ...216 D3
Riley Ave CO15 ...203 E6
Rimini Cl CO2 ...135 C3
Ringham Rd IP4 ...18 A6
Ripley Cl CO16 ...188 B6
Ripple Way CO4 ...110 B1
Risby Cl Clacton-on-S CO16 188 A4
Ipswich IP4 ...18 B6
Rise The CO6 ...134 A8
Ritabrook Rd IP2 ...16 E1
Rivenhall CE Prim Sch
CM8 ...177 B8
River Cl CO9 ...76 F1
River Cotts CM3 ...206 F8
River Hill CM3 ...175 B3
River Mead CM7 ...128 A5
River View Braintree CM7 .127 F1
Holbrook IP9 ...62 D5

River View continued
Manningtree CO11 . . . . .86 C4
Witham CM8 . . . . .195 A8
River View Rd IP9 . . . . .63 B2
Riverbank Cl CO10 . . . . . . .12 C7
Riverdale Ct IP11 . . . . .221 D3
Rivermead Gate CM1 . . . .205 B4
Rivermead Ind Est CM1 . .205 B4
Rivers Ho CO14 . . . . .144 D2
Rivers St IP4 . . . . .17 F7
Riverside
Bishop's Stortford CM23 . .145 F7
Bradwell CM7 . . . . .129 D3
Chelmsford CM1 . . . . . . .205 C3
Great Dunmow CM6 . . . . .123 E1
Riverside Ave E CO11 . . . .86 C5
Riverside Ave W CO11 . . . .86 C5
Riverside Cotts CO11 . . . . .86 C7
Riverside Ind Pk IP2 . . . . .17 D3
Riverside Pk CM1 . . . . . .205 C3
Riverside Rd IP1 . . . . .16 F7
Riverside Way CO5 . . . . . .158 C2
Riverside Wlk
10 Bishop's Stortford CM23 .145 F7
Colchester CO1 . . . . .135 E8
Riverton Dr CM0 . . . . . . .213 B1
Rivish La CO10 . . . . .15 C7
Roach Vale CO4 . . . . .110 E1
Roach Vale Cty Prim
Sch CO4 . . . . .110 E1
Robeck Rd IP3 . . . . .17 F1
Robert Cl CM2 . . . . .205 F4
Robert Wallace Cl CM23 .118 F1
Robert's Hill CO6 . . . . .79 F3
Roberts Ct CM2 . . . . .216 E7
Roberts Rd CO1, CO2 . . . .136 A5
Robin Cl
Great Bentley CO7 . . . . . .166 D8
Haverhill CB9 . . . . .9 C7
Robin Dr IP2 . . . . .16 D3
Robin Hood Rd CM22 . . . .94 C1
Robin Way
Chelmsford CM2 . . . . . . .216 B5
Sudbury CO10 . . . . .33 C5
Robinia Cl **1** CO4 . . . . . .136 E7
Robinsbridge Rd CO6 . . . .130 F2
Robinsdale CO15 . . . . . . .188 F6
Robinson Cl CM23 . . . . . .145 F5
Robinson Rd CO7 . . . . . . .186 A7
Robjohns Rd CM1 . . . . . .215 E8
Robletts Way CO6 . . . . . . .80 E4
Rochdale Way CO4 . . . . . .136 E6
Rochelle Cl CM6 . . . . .70 A3
Rochester Cl CM7 . . . . . .128 D4
Rochester Ct **6** CB10 . . . .22 F2
Rochester Way CO10 . . . . .15 D2
Rochford Cl CM24 . . . . . .119 E5
Rochford Rd
Bishop's Stortford CM23 . .119 C1
Chelmsford CM2 . . . . . . .205 C1
St Osyth CO16 . . . . .187 B4
Rochford Way
Frinton-on-S CO13 . . . . . .170 F7
Walton-on-t-N CO14 . . . .171 A7
Rockall Cl CB9 . . . . .9 D7
Rockhampton Wlk 10
CO2 . . . . .136 A1
Rockingham Cl CO4 . . . . .110 D3
Rodbridge Hill CO10 . . . . .15 B5
Roddam Cl CO3 . . . . .135 C6
Roding Ct CM7 . . . . .128 D1
Rodney Gdns CM7 . . . . . .128 C4
Rodney Way CM1 . . . . . .215 E7
Rogation Cl CO3 . . . . . . .134 D6
Rogers Cl IP11 . . . . .221 D6
Rokell Way CO13 . . . . . . .170 F6
Rolands Cl CM1 . . . . .205 B7
Rollerworld CO1 . . . . . . .136 B7
Rolley La CO5 . . . . .158 C2
Rolph CE Prim Sch CO16 141 F1
Rolph Cl CO16 . . . . .142 A2
Roman Ct Braintree CM7 . .128 C1
Saffron Walden CB11 . . . . .43 E7
Roman Ho **3** CM2 . . . . . .205 B1
Roman Rd Colchester CO1 136 A7
Little Waltham CM3 . . . . . .191 B5
Roman Way Haverhill CB9 . . .9 D7
Littlebury CB11 . . . . .21 F4
Long Melford CO10 . . . . . .15 C6
Point Clear B CO16 . . . . . .186 A3
Romans Pl CM1 . . . . .204 B1
Romans Way CM1 . . . . . .204 B1
Romford Cl CO4 . . . . .136 B8
Romney Cl Braintree CM7 .127 E6
Brightlingsea CO7 . . . . . .165 E1
Clacton-on-S CO16 . . . . . .188 D5
Kirby Cross CO13 . . . . . . .170 E7
Romney Rd IP3 . . . . .38 A8
Romulus Cl CO4 . . . . .109 F5
Ronald Rd CO9 . . . . .103 E8
Rook End La CB11 . . . . . . .68 B5
Rookeries The CO6 . . . . . .133 B4
Rookery Chase CO7 . . . . . .84 C2
Rookery Cl
Great Chesterford CB10 . . . .3 D3
Hatfield Peverel CM3 . . . .194 A5
Rookery La
Great Totham CM9 . . . . . .196 E7
Tiptree CO5 . . . . .179 C7
Wendens Ambo CB11 . . . . .42 F4
Rookery The Lawford CO11 .86 C4
Stansted
Mountfitchet CM24 . . . . . .119 E8
Rookes CB10 . . . . .22 D3
Rookwood Cl CO15 . . . . .188 D7

Rookwood Way CB9 . . . . . . .9 A6
Roos Hill Debden Rd CB11 43 E5
Roosevelt Way CO2 . . . . .136 B4
Roothings The CM9 . . . . .210 B5
Roots La CM8 . . . . .195 E5
Rope Wlk Ipswich IP4 . . . . .17 C5
Maldon CM9 . . . . .210 A1
Roper Ct IP4 . . . . .18 C5
Roper's Chase CM1 . . . . .215 A3
Ropers La CO10 . . . . .15 B5
Rosabelle Ave CO7 . . . . . .137 B1
Rosalind Cl CO4 . . . . .136 F7
Rose Acre CO7 . . . . .58 F6
Rose Ave CO3 . . . . .134 C4
Rose Cotts SG9 . . . . .64 A5
Rose Cres CO4 . . . . .109 D2
Rose & Crown Wlk CB10 . .22 D2
Rose Gdns Braintree CM7 .128 A2
St Osyth CO16 . . . . .203 B6
Rose Glen CM2 . . . . .216 C7
Rose Hill CM7 . . . . .128 A2
Rose Hill Cty Prim Sch
IP3 . . . . .18 A4
Rose Ho **12** CO1 . . . . . . .136 A6
Rose La
Great Chesterford CB10 . . . .3 E2
Ipswich IP1, IP4 . . . . .17 C5
Salcott-cum-virley CM9 . . .199 B8
Wivenhoe CO7 . . . . .164 B7
Rose Wlk CO9 . . . . .29 B6
Roseacres CM2 . . . . .148 C7
Rosebank CO12 . . . . .91 A3
Rosebank Ct CO15 . . . . . .189 A3
Rosebank Rd CO5 . . . . . . .201 B6
Rosebay Cl CM8 . . . . .176 D3
Rosebery CM23 . . . . .146 C6
Rosebery Ave CO1 . . . . . .136 A7
Rosebery Rd
Chelmsford CM2 . . . . . . .216 B8
Felixstowe IP11 . . . . .221 F4
Ipswich IP4 . . . . .17 F5
Rosecroft Cl CO15 . . . . . .188 E6
Rosedale Cotts CO3 . . . . .133 F5
Rosefinch Cl CB9 . . . . .9 C7
Rosehill Cres IP3 . . . . .17 F4
Rosehill Rd IP3 . . . . .17 F4
Rosemary Ave
Braintree CM7 . . . . .127 F4
Felixstowe IP11 . . . . .221 F6
Rosemary Cl
Great Dunmow CM6 . . . . .123 C1
Tiptree CO5 . . . . .179 C5
Rosemary Cotts CM3 . . . .192 E1
Rosemary Cres
Clacton-on-S CO15 . . . . . .188 F2
Great Dunmow CM6 . . . . .123 C1
Tiptree CO5 . . . . .179 C5
Rosemary Ct **2** CO4 . . . . .136 D8
Rosemary Gdns CO10 . . . .15 C7
Rosemary La
Castle Hedingham CO9 . . . .52 A4
Great Dunmow CM6 . . . . .123 C1
Halstead CO9 . . . . .76 E2
Stebbing CM6 . . . . .124 C7
Thorrington CO7 . . . . . . .166 B5
Rosemary Rd CO15 . . . . .188 F2
Rosemary Rd W CO15 . . .188 E2
Rosemary Way CO15 . . . .203 G7
Rosemount Ct IP11 . . . . . .221 F4
Rosery Mews CO13 . . . . .170 A4
Rosewood Cl CO4 . . . . . . .110 A4
Roslings Cl CM1 . . . . .204 D5
Ross Cl Saffron Walden CB9 . . .9 D7
Saffron Walden CB11 . . . . .43 E6
Round Cl CO3 . . . . .135 B7
Round Coppice Rd
Great Hallingbury CM24 . . .147 A8
Stansted
Mountfitchet CM24 . . . . . .120 B1
Roundacre CO9 . . . . .103 E8
Roundbush Cnr
Birch CO5 . . . . .160 D3
Great Totham CM9 . . . . . .196 D6
Roundbush Rd CO5 . . . . .160 D2
Roundridge Rd IP9 . . . . . . .35 B2
Roundwood Rd IP4 . . . . . .18 A7
Rous Chase CM2 . . . . . . .216 B1
Routh Ave IP3 . . . . .18 F1
Rover Ave CO15 . . . . .203 E6
Row The CO7 . . . . .58 C2
Rowallan Cl CO3 . . . . . . .135 A3
Rowan Chase CO5 . . . . . .179 C6
Rowan Cl
Clacton-on-S CO15 . . . . . .188 C3
Colchester CO3 . . . . .134 D4
Great Bentley CO7 . . . . . .166 F8
Harwich CO12 . . . . .91 B3
Ipswich IP3 . . . . .18 D2
Rowan Dr CM9 . . . . .210 C5
Rowan Way
Hatfield Peverel CM3 . . . .194 A3
Witham CM8 . . . . .177 A5
Rowanhayes Cl IP2 . . . . . .17 B3
Rowhedge Ferry Rd CO7 164 A8
Rowhedge Rd CO2, CO5 . .136 E1
Rowherns La
Great Bentley CO7 . . . . . .139 E4
Great Bentley CO7 . . . . . .139 F4
Rowland Ho IP11 . . . . . . .221 B5

Rowland's Yd CO12 . . . . . .90 E2
Rowley Cl CO11 . . . . .86 D8
Rowley Ct CB9 . . . . .9 F5
Rowley Hill CB9 . . . . .9 E5
Rowney Ave CB10 . . . . . . .44 E2
Rowntree Way CB11 . . . . . .43 D7
Roxborough Cl CO6 . . . . .132 E3
Roxburghe Rd CO16 . . . . .167 F6
Roxwell Ave CM1 . . . . . . .204 D3
Roxwell Rd
Chelmsford CM1 . . . . . . .204 C4
Writtle CM1 . . . . .204 A4
Roy Ave IP3 . . . . .18 B5
Royal Ct Colchester CO4 . . .110 E1
Maldon CM9 . . . . .210 A1
Royal Oak Gdns **6** CM23 .145 F6
Royal Sq CO7 . . . . .84 F7
Roydon Way CO15 . . . . . .170 F6
Royston Dr IP2 . . . . .16 D3
Royston La CB11 . . . . .20 C6
Royston Rd CB11 . . . . .42 C5
Ruaton Dr CO16 . . . . .188 C4
Rubens Gate CM1 . . . . . .205 F7
Rubens Rd IP3 . . . . .18 A1
Rudkin Rd CO4 . . . . .109 F5
Rudland Way CO3 . . . . . .134 F5
Rudsdale Way CO3 . . . . . .134 F5
Rue De Jeunes **2** CM7 . . .127 F2
Ruffels Field CM6 . . . . . . .124 E4
Rugby Rd CO10 . . . . .34 B4
Rugosa Cl CO3 . . . . .134 C7
Rumsey Fields CM3 . . . . .218 F2
Runnacles St CM8 . . . . . .156 C5
Runnacles Way IP11 . . . . .221 B5
Running Mare La CM2 . . . .216 A3
Runsell Cl CM3 . . . . .218 F7
Runsell La CM3 . . . . .218 F8
Runsell View CM3 . . . . . .219 A7
Rurik Ct CM9 . . . . .220 E8
Rush Green Rd CO16 . . . .188 B2
Rush La CM22 . . . . .94 C1
Rushbury Cl IP4 . . . . .18 B8
Rushes Ct CM23 . . . . .146 A5
Rushleigh Gn CM23 . . . . .145 D4
Rushleydale CM1 . . . . . . .205 E5
Rushmere Cl CO5 . . . . . . .201 D6
Rushmere Pl **11** CB9 . . . . . .9 B8
Rushmere Rd IP4 . . . . .18 B7
Rushmere St Ipswich IP4 . .18 D8
Rushmere St A IP5 . . . . . . .18 E8
Ruskin Cl CO13 . . . . .170 E7
Ruskin Rd Chelmsford CM2 205 E2
Ipswich IP4 . . . . .17 F5
Ruskins The CM7 . . . . . . .126 F1
Russell Ct Colchester CO2 .136 B4
Felixstowe IP11 . . . . .221 C1
Russell Gdns CM2 . . . . . .216 A4
Russell Rd
Clacton-on-S CO15 . . . . . .189 A3
Felixstowe IP11 . . . . .221 D2
Ipswich IP1 . . . . .17 B5
Russell Way CM1 . . . . . . .215 E7
Russell's Rd Gosfield CO9 . .76 A1
Halstead CO9 . . . . .103 B8
Russet Cl CM7 . . . . .128 A1
Russets CM2 . . . . .216 D3
Rutherfords CM1 . . . . . . .191 B1
Rutland Ave CO2 . . . . . . .135 B3
Rutland Ct **11** CB9 . . . . . . .8 E7
Rutland Gdns CM7 . . . . . .128 A4
Rutland Pl CM7 . . . . .72 B2
Rutland Rd CM1 . . . . .205 A7
Rydal Way CM7 . . . . .154 C6
Rydal Wlk IP3 . . . . .18 C2
Ryde Ave CO15 . . . . .189 A8
Rye Cl Brightlingsea CO7 . .165 E1
Colchester CO3 . . . . .134 E5
Hatfield Peverel CM3 . . . .194 A3
Ipswich IP3 . . . . .18 D4
Rye Ct **3** CB9 . . . . .8 F7
Rye Field The CM3 . . . . . .207 D3
Rye Hills CO9 . . . . .103 F8
Rye La CO2 . . . . .162 A4
Rye Mill La CO5 . . . . .158 D4
Rye St CM23 . . . . .118 F1
Ryes La CO10 . . . . .33 A2
Rygate Rd CO1 . . . . .135 F7
Rylands IP9 . . . . .35 A2
Ryle The CM1 . . . . .215 A8
Rylstone Way CB11 . . . . . .43 F8
Rysley CM3 . . . . .207 D4

S

Sackville Cl CM1 . . . . . . .204 E3
Sackville Way CO6 . . . . . .108 D4
Saddle Mews CO3 . . . . . .134 E6
Saddle Rise CM1 . . . . . . .205 E8
Saddlers Cl CM23 . . . . . . .145 C4
Sadds Yd CO15 . . . . .188 F3
Sadler Cl CO2 . . . . .136 B4
Sadlers Cl CO13 . . . . .170 C6
Saffron Bsns Ctr 11 CB10 .22 F2
Saffron Cl CM7 . . . . .73 C3
Saffron Ct CM7 . . . . .73 C3
Saffron Walden Cty High
Sch CB11 . . . . .43 C8
Saffron Walden Mus CB10 22 D1
Saffron Waldon Hospl
CB10, CB11 . . . . .23 A2
Saffron Way CO5 . . . . . . .179 C4
Saffron Wlk CM7 . . . . .73 D4
Sage Rd CO2 . . . . .136 A2
Sage Wlk CO5 . . . . .179 C4
Sages CM22 . . . . .94 F5
Sages End Rd CB9 . . . . . . .26 B8
St Agnes Way IP5 . . . . . . .18 F6

St Alban's Cath Sec Sch
IP4 . . . . .18 C7
St Alban's Rd
Clacton-on-S CO15 . . . . . .189 A3
Colchester CO3 . . . . .135 D7
St Andrew's Ave CO4 . . . .137 A5
St Andrew's Ave
(Colchester By-Pass
Rd) CO4 . . . . .136 D7
St Andrew's CE Jun Sch
& Hatfield Peverel Cty
Inf Sch CM3 . . . . .194 B3
St Andrew's CE Prim Sch
Bulmer CO10 . . . . .32 E4
Great Yeldham CO9 . . . . . .29 F2
Halstead CO9 . . . . .77 A3
Wormingford CO6 . . . . . . .80 E5
St Andrew's Cotts CM3 . .194 B3
St Andrew's Cty Jun &
Inf Schs CO4 . . . . .136 D7
St Andrew's Dr IP9 . . . . . .63 E7
St Andrew's Prim Sch
CO6 . . . . .132 E3
St Andrew's Rd
Clacton-on-S CO15 . . . . . .188 E3
Felixstowe IP11 . . . . .221 E5
Hatfield Peverel CM3 . . . .194 A4
Weeley CO16 . . . . .140 F1
St Andrew's Rise CO10 . . . .32 E5
St Andrews Cl
Alresford CO7 . . . . .165 B7
Ipswich IP4 . . . . .18 D5
St Andrews Ct **3** CO4 . . .136 C8
St Andrews Gdns CO4 . . .136 C8
St Andrews Pl CO7 . . . . . .165 E1
St Andrews Rd
Boreham CM3 . . . . .192 F1
Great Cornard CO10 . . . . . .34 A6
Halstead CO9 . . . . .76 F1
St Anne's Cty Prim Sch
CO4 . . . . .110 C1
St Anne's Prep Sch CM2 .205 A1
St Anne's Rd CO4 . . . . . .136 C8
St Annes Cl CO6 . . . . . . .131 B2
St Annes Ct CM1 . . . . . . .205 C3
St Anns Rd CO15 . . . . . . .188 E4
St Anthony's Dr CM2 . . . .216 C7
St Aubins Ct CO15 . . . . . .189 B4
St Aubyns Rd IP4 . . . . .18 A5
St Augustine Mews CO1 .136 A7
St Augustine Rd IP3 . . . . . .18 D4
St Augustine's Gdns IP3 . .18 C3
St Austell Rd CO4 . . . . . .110 D2
St Austin's La CO12 . . . . . .91 E6
St Barbara's Rd CO2 . . . .135 D4
St Bartholomew Cl CO4 . .110 C3
St Bartholomews La CO10 15 D2
St Benedict RC Coll CO3 .135 B6
St Bernard Rd CO4 . . . . . .136 A7
St Bodolph's Pl **1** CO8 . . . .8 F7
St Botolph's Church Wlk
7 CO2 . . . . .135 F6
St Botolph's Cir **8** CO2 . .135 F6
St Botolph's St **6** CO2 . . .135 F6
St Botolph's Sta CO2 . . . .136 A6
St Botolph's Terr 11
CO13 . . . . .171 C8
St Botolph's Way CB9 . . . . .8 F8
St Brelades Ct CO15 . . . . .189 B5
St Bride Ct CO4 . . . . .110 D2
St Bridewells Ind Est
CO10 . . . . .12 C8
St Catherine's Ct IP2 . . . . .16 E1
St Catherine's Rd
Chelmsford CM1 . . . . . . .204 E2
Long Melford CO10 . . . . . .15 C7
St Catherines Cl CO2 . . . .135 D1
St Catherines Ct CM23 . . .145 E7
St Cedd's Sch CM1 . . . . . .205 A3
St Christopher Ct CO4 . . .110 D2
St Christopher Rd CO4 . . .110 D2
St Christophers Way
CO15 . . . . .203 G7
St Clair Cl CO15 . . . . .188 F8
St Clair's Dr CO16 . . . . . . .187 B5
St Clair's Rd CO16 . . . . . .187 B5
St Clare Dr CO3 . . . . .135 A7
St Clare Rd CO3 . . . . .135 A6
St Clare's RC Prim Sch
CO16 . . . . .188 B4
St Clement Rd CO4 . . . . .110 D2
St Clement's Church La
IP4 . . . . .17 D5
St Clement's Cl CO15 . . . .188 B5
St Clement's Hospl IP3 . . .18 B4
St Clements CM6 . . . . .70 A2
St Cleres Hall La CO16 . . .187 B3
St Cleres Way CM3 . . . . . .218 D7
St Columb Ct CO4 . . . . . .110 C2
St Cyrus Rd CO4 . . . . . . .110 D3
St David's Rd IP3 . . . . .18 B3
St Davids Cl CO4 . . . . . . .136 C7
St Denis Cl CO12 . . . . .91 A1
St Dominic Rd CO4 . . . . .110 D2
St Edmund's Ct CO4 . . . . .136 C8
St Edmund's Hill CO8 . . . . .55 D6
St Edmund's Pl IP1 . . . . . .17 C8
St Edmund's Rd
Felixstowe IP11 . . . . .221 D2
Ipswich IP1 . . . . .17 B8
St Edmunds Cl CO4 . . . . . .91 C1
St Edmunds Croft CM6 . .123 E1
St Edmunds Fields CM6 . .123 E1
St Edmunds La Bures CO8 .55 F1
Great Dunmow CM6 . . . . .123 E1
St Edmundsbury Ho IP4 . .17 F6
St Fabian's Dr CM1 . . . . .204 E4
St Faith CO4 . . . . .110 D2

St Felix RC Prim Sch CB9 . .8 D3
St Fillan Rd CO4 . . . . .110 D2
St Francis RC Prim Sch
Braintree CM7 . . . . .127 E4
Maldon CM9 . . . . .209 F3
St George's Ave CO12 . . . .91 C2
St George's CE Prim
Sch CO7 . . . . .112 E1
St George's Cl CO7 . . . . . .112 E1
St George's Inf Sch CO2 .136 A4
St George's Jun
Sch CO2 . . . . .136 A5
St George's St IP1 . . . . . .17 C6
St Giles CE Prim Sch CO9 52 D2
St Giles Cl
Great Maplestead CO9 . . . .52 D2
Maldon CM9 . . . . .209 F3
St Giles Cotts CO9 . . . . . .52 D2
St Giles Cres CM9 . . . . . .209 E2
St Gregory Prim Sch
CO10 . . . . .33 D7
St Gregory's Ct CO10 . . . . .33 D8
St Helen's Church La **6**
IP4 . . . . .17 E6
St Helen's Gn CO12 . . . . . .91 E5
St Helen's La **8** CO1 . . . .135 F7
St Helen's Prim Sch IP4 . .17 E6
St Helen's St IP4 . . . . .17 D6
St Helena Mews CO3 . . . .135 D5
St Helena Rd CO3 . . . . . .135 D5
St Helena Sch CO3 . . . . . .135 D8
St Helens Ave CO15 . . . . .189 A8
St Helier Ct CO15 . . . . . . .189 B5
St Ives Cl CO16 . . . . .188 B3
St Ives Rd CO5 . . . . .182 C6
St James' CE Prim Sch
CO1 . . . . .136 B7
St James Ct
Brightlingsea CO7 . . . . . .185 E6
Clacton-on-S CO15 . . . . . .188 E1
Haverhill CB9 . . . . .8 E8
St James Pk CM1 . . . . . . .204 D4
St James Rd CM7 . . . . . . .127 F5
St James Way CM23 . . . . .145 C3
St James's St
Castle Hedingham CO9 . . . .51 F4
Castle Hedingham CO9 . . . .52 C2
St Jean Wlk CO5 . . . . .179 D6
St John Payne RC
Comp Sch CM1 . . . . . . .205 A4
St John The Baptist CE
Sch CO9 . . . . .78 D3
St John's Ave
Chelmsford CM2 . . . . . . .216 B8
12 Colchester CO2 . . . . . .135 F6
St John's CE Prim Sch
Colchester CO4 . . . . .110 D4
Ipswich IP4 . . . . .18 A7
St John's Cl CO4 . . . . . . .110 D4
St John's Cres CM23 . . . .119 E7
St John's Ct Ipswich IP4 . . .18 A7
Tollesbury CM9 . . . . .199 C1
St John's Danbury CE
Prim Sch CM3 . . . . .218 F7
St John's Gn CM1 . . . . . .204 B1
St John's Green Cty
Prim Sch CO2 . . . . .135 F6
St John's Hospl CM2 . . . .215 F7
St John's La CM24 . . . . . .119 E7
St John's Pl **14** CO2 . . . .135 F6
St John's Rd
Chelmsford CM2 . . . . . . .216 B8
Clacton-on-S CO16 . . . . . .188 C5
Colchester CO4 . . . . .110 D3
Ipswich IP4 . . . . .18 A4
Stansted
Mountfitchet CM24 . . . . . .119 E7
Wivenhoe CO7 . . . . .164 C7
Writtle CM1 . . . . .204 B1
St John's St
Colchester CO2 . . . . .135 F6
Tollesbury CM9 . . . . .199 C1
St John's Terr CM7 . . . . . .72 B2
St Johns Ave CM7 . . . . . .127 F2
St Johns Cl CB11 . . . . .43 D7
St Johns Ct IP11 . . . . .221 D4
St Joseph Rd CO4 . . . . . . .110 C3
St Joseph's Coll IP2 . . . . . .17 A3
St Joseph's Jun Sch IP2 . .17 B3
St Joseph's Prim Sch
CO10 . . . . .33 D8
St Joseph's RC JMI Sch
CM23 . . . . .145 E2
St Joseph's RC Prim Sch
CO12 . . . . .91 B2
St Jude Gdns CO4 . . . . . .110 E2
St Judes Cl CO4 . . . . .110 D2
St Julian Gr CO1 . . . . . . .136 A6
St Lawrence Ct **3** CM7 . .127 F3
St Lawrence Dr CM0 . . . .213 B3
St Lawrence Rd CO4 . . . .110 D2
St Lawrence St **11** IP1 . . .17 C5
St Leonard's Hospl CO10 . .33 F7
St Leonard's Rd CO1 . . . .136 C6
St Leonards Cl CB11 . . . . .43 A2
St Leonards Rd IP3 . . . . . .18 B3
St Leonards School Ho
CO1 . . . . .136 C6
St Leonards Terr **7** CO1 .136 C6
St Luke's Chase CO5 . . . .179 D5
St Luke's Church Sch
CO5 . . . . .179 D5
St Luke's Ct CO4 . . . . . . .110 D2
St Margaret's CE Prim
Sch Ipswich IP4 . . . . .17 D6
Toppesfield CO9 . . . . .50 C7
St Margaret's Ct CO16 . . .188 C4
St Margaret's Gn **2** IP4 . .17 D6

St Margaret's Plain **1**
1P4 . . . . .17 D6
St Margaret's Rd CM2 . .205 E3
St Margaret's Sch CO9 . .102 D8
St Margaret's St 1P4 . . . .17 D6
St Mark Dr CO4 . . . . . .110 D2
St Marks RC Prim Sch IP2 16 F3
St Marks Rd CO15 . . . . .188 E4
St Martins Cl CO15 . . . . .188 E4
St Mary Magdalen Ho
CO1 . . . . .136 B6
St Mary's Art Ctr CO1 . .135 E7
St Mary's Cath CM1 . . . .205 B2
St Mary's CE Prim Sch
Ardleigh CO7 . . . . . . .111 E7
Kelvedon CO5 . . . . . .158 C2
Stansted
Mountfitchet CM24 . . . .119 E7
St Mary's Cl
Great Baddow CM2 . . . .216 F6
Great Bentley CO7 . . . .166 F5
Panfield CM7 . . . . . . .127 B7
St Mary's Convent Sch
CO1 . . . . .136 B7
St Mary's Cres IP11 . . . .221 D6
St Mary's Dr CM24 . . . .119 F5
St Mary's Hospl
Colchester CO3 . . . . .135 E7
Tattingstone IP9 . . . . . .61 D7
St Mary's La CM9 . . . . .210 B2
St Mary's Pl CM7 . . . . .151 D7
St Mary's Prim Sch CB10 .22 D2
St Mary's RC Prim Sch
IP4 . . . . .17 F7
St Mary's RC Sch CM23 .145 E7
St Mary's Rd
Braintree CM7 . . . . . .128 B3
Clacton-on-S CO15 . . . .188 E4
Frinton-on-S CO13 . . . .171 A5
Great Bentley CO7 . . . .166 F6
Kelvedon CO5 . . . . . .158 C2
Rivenhall CM8 . . . . . .177 B7
St Mary's Sch
Colchester CO3 . . . . .135 C7
Copford CO3 . . . . . . .133 F5
St Mary's Sq CO5 . . . . .158 B1
St Mary's Villas CM7 . . . .72 B1
St Mary's Wlk CO6 . . . . .27 B6
St Marys Mead CM1 . . . .191 A1
St Marys Mews
Frinton-on-S CO13 . . . .171 A5
Tollesbury CM9 . . . . . .199 D2
St Mathew's Ho **4** IP1 . .17 B6
St Matthew's CE Prim
Sch IP1 . . . . .17 B6
St Matthew's St IP1 . . . .17 B6
St Michael's CE Prim
Sch
Bishop's Stortford CM23 .145 F7
Braintree CM7 . . . . . .127 F2
St. Michael's Chase CO6 133 D2
St Michael's Ct **4** CM7 . .127 F2
St Michael's Cty Prim
Sch CO2 . . . . .135 C1
St Michael's Hospl CM7 .127 F1
St Michael's La CM7 . . . .127 F2
St Michael's Prim Sch
CM23 . . . . .145 E7
St Michael's Rd
Braintree CM7 . . . . . .127 F2
Chelmsford CM2 . . . . .216 B8
Harwich CO12 . . . . . . .91 B2
Thorpe-le-S CO16 . . . .141 F2
St Michaels Ct **5** CO11 . .86 D4
St Michaels Rd CO2 . . . .135 D1
St Michaels Wlk CM2 . . .216 C2
St Mildreds Rd CM2 . . . .216 B8
St Monance Way CO4 . . .110 D2
St Nazaire Rd CM1 . . . .204 E6
St Neots Cl CO4 . . . . . .110 D2
St Nicholas Cl CM8 . . . .176 E4
St Nicholas Ct CO12 . . . .91 D6
St Nicholas Field CM23 . .92 E8
St Nicholas' Gdns CM7 . .127 F8
St Nicholas Pas **18** CO1 . .135 F7
St Nicholas Rd CM8 . . . .176 E4
St Nicholas St
25 Colchester CO1 . . . .135 F7
Ipswich IP1 . . . . .17 C5
St Nicholas Way CO6 . . .131 A3
St Osyth CE Prim Sch
CO16 . . . . .187 B4
St Osyth CE Sch CO15 . .188 E3
St Osyth Cl IP2 . . . . . . .36 F8
St Osyth Priory CO16 . . .187 A4
St Osyth Rd Alresford CO7 165 D7
Clacton-on-S CO15 . . . .188 D3
Little Clacton CO16 . . . .168 B1
St Osyth Rd E CO16 . . . .168 C2
St Osyth Rd W CO16 . . .168 C1
St Paul's Rd
Clacton-on-S CO15 . . . .189 A3
Colchester CO1 . . . . .135 E8
St Peter's Ave CM9 . . . .209 F2
St Peter's CE Prim Sch
Coggeshall CO6 . . . . .131 B2
Sible Hedingham CO9 . . .75 D8
St Peter's Cl CM7 . . . . .127 F4
St Peter's Hospl CM9 . . .209 F2
St Peter's Rd
Braintree CM7 . . . . . .127 F4
Chelmsford CM1 . . . . .204 E2
Coggeshall CO6 . . . . .131 B2
West Mersea CO5 . . . .201 B6
St Peter's St
Colchester CO1 . . . . .135 F8
Ipswich IP1 . . . . .17 C5
St Peter's Wlk CM7 . . . .127 F3

St Peter's-in-the-Fields
CM7 . . . . .127 F4
St Peters Ct
Clacton-on-S CO15 . . . .189 B5
Clare CO10 . . . . .12 B7
Colchester CO1 . . . . .135 E8
10 Sudbury CO10 . . . . .33 E7
St Philip's Priory Sch
CM2 . . . . .216 A8
St Philomena's Sch CO13 170 F5
St Pius X RC Prim Sch
CM1 . . . . .204 F6
St Runwald St **10** CO1 . .135 F7
St Saviour Cl CO4 . . . . .110 D2
St Stephens La **9** IP1 . . .17 C6
St Swithins Cotts CM2 . .217 C3
St Teresa's RC Prim
Sch CO3 . . . . .134 E5
St Thomas Cl CO4 . . . . .110 E2
St Thomas More RC Prim
Sch CB11 . . . . .43 E8
St Valery CM22 . . . . . .148 C2
St Vincent Chase CM7 . .128 B5
St Vincent Rd CO15 . . . .188 E1
St Vincents Rd CM2 . . . .216 B8
Sainty Cl CO7 . . . . . . .164 C8
Salary Cl CO4 . . . . . . .110 F1
Salcombe Rd CM7 . . . . .128 C1
Salcott Creek Ct CM7 . . .128 D1
Salcott St CM9 . . . . . .199 C8
Salehurst Rd IP3 . . . . . .18 E3
Salerno Cres CO2 . . . . .135 C2
Salerno Way CM1 . . . . .204 E6
Saling Hall Gardens CM7 126 A8
Salisbury Ave CM2 . . . .135 E6
Salisbury Cl CM23 . . . . .145 F5
Salisbury Ct
Clacton-on-S CO15 . . . .189 D5
2 Haverhill CB9 . . . . . .8 F7
Salisbury Rd
Clacton-on-S CO15 . . . .189 D5
Ipswich IP3 . . . . .18 A4
Salisbury Terr **1** CO10 . . .33 E8
Sallows Cl IP1 . . . . . . .16 F1
Salmon Cl CO3 . . . . . .134 F4
Salmon Parr CM2 . . . . .205 B3
Salmon's La CO6 . . . . .132 A4
Salmons Cl CM6 . . . . . .151 A5
Saltcote Maltings CM9 . .210 E4
Salter Pl CM2 . . . . . . .205 F2
Salter's Mdw CM9 . . . . .198 D4
Salters CM23 . . . . . . .145 F6
Salters Hall Mews CO10 . .33 D7
Salthouse St **17** 1P4 . . . .17 D5
Salvia Cl CO15 . . . . . .188 C4
Samford Cl IP9 . . . . . . .62 D7
Samford Pl IP8 . . . . . . .16 B6
Samphire Cl CM8 . . . . .176 D3
Sampson's La CO5 . . . . .182 F3
Samson's Cnr CO7 . . . . .165 D1
Samson's Rd CO7 . . . . .165 L1
Samsons Cl CO7 . . . . . .185 E8
Samuel Ct 1P4 . . . . . . .17 D6
Samuel Manor CM2 . . . .205 F3
Sanderling Gdns CM9 . . .210 C5
Sanders Dr CO3 . . . . . .135 B7
Sanderson Mews **7** CO1 .135 F7
Sandford Cl CO7 . . . . . .164 C8
Sandford Mill Rd
Chelmsford CM2 . . . . .206 B2
Great Baddow CM2 . . . .217 C8
Sandford Rd CM2 . . . . .205 E3
Sandhurst Ave IP3 . . . . .17 F4
Sandle Rd CM23 . . . . . .146 A7
Sandling Cres CM4 . . . . .18 E5
Sandlings The IP3 . . . . . .18 D1
Sandon Cl CO6 . . . . . .109 C7
Sandon Hall
Bridleway CM2 . . . . .217 D4
Sandon Hill CM3 . . . . . .172 A6
Sandon Sch The CM2 . . .217 B6
Sandown Cl CO15 . . . . .189 D4
Sandpiper Cl
Colchester CO4 . . . . .137 A8
Haverhill CB9 . . . . . . .9 C8
Heybridge CM9 . . . . . .210 C5
Sandpiper Rd IP2 . . . . . .16 E2
Sandpiper Wlk CM2 . . . .216 C6
Sandpit Cl IP4 . . . . . . .18 F5
Sandpit La **8** CM7 . . . . .127 F3
Sandra Ct **5** CO2 . . . . .135 E6
Sandringham Cl IP2 . . . .16 F2
Sandringham Ct CO10 . . .34 A7
Sandringham Gdns **6**
CM23 . . . . .145 E5
Sandringham Pl CM2 . . .205 D5
Sandwich Cl CM7 . . . . .127 E6
Sandwich Rd
Brightlingsea CO7 . . . .185 F8
Clacton-on-S CO15 . . . .203 J8
Sandy Hill CO8 . . . . . . .80 D5
Sandy La Bulmer CO10 . .32 F5
Sudbury CO10 . . . . . . .33 B5
Sandyhill La IP3 . . . . . .17 E1
Sapling Pl IP4 . . . . . . .18 E5
Saran Ct **5** CO7 . . . . . .137 A2
Sarcel CM7 . . . . .129 C6
Sargeant Cl CO2 . . . . . .136 B3
Sarre Way CO7 . . . . . .185 E8
Sassoon Way CM9 . . . . .210 A1
Saul's Ave CM8 . . . . . .195 A8
Sauls Bridge Cl CM8 . . . .195 A8
Saunders Ave CM7 . . . .127 E3
Saunders Cl CM22 . . . . .94 C1
Savernake Rd CM1 . . . .204 E1
Savill Rd CO2 . . . . . . .136 C2
Saville Cl CB11 . . . . . . .65 C4

Saville St CO14 . . . . . .144 C1
Sawkins Ave CM2 . . . . .216 D6
Sawkins Cl Abberton CO5 .163 B2
Chelmsford CM2 . . . . .216 D6
Sawkins Gdns CM2 . . . .216 D6
Sawney Brook CM1 . . . .204 A1
Sawpit La CM23 . . . . . .92 D7
Sawston IP2 . . . . .17 A2
Sawyer's Rd CM9 . . . . .197 C5
Sawyers Cl **3** IP9 . . . . . .35 A1
Saxmundham Way CO16 .188 A3
Saxon Bank CM7 . . . . . .128 B2
Saxon Cl Colchester CO3 .134 F4
Halstead CO9 . . . . . . .76 F2
Saxon Ct CM9 . . . . . . .210 A4
Saxon Dr CM8 . . . . . . .176 B2
Saxon La IP8 . . . . .35 D7
Saxon Way
Broomfield CM1 . . . . .205 B7
Holland-on-S CO15 . . . .189 F6
Maldon CM9 . . . . . . .210 B1
Point Clear B CO16 . . . .185 F3
Saffron Walden CB11 . . .22 C1
Saxstead Dr CO16 . . . . .188 A4
Saywell Brook CM2 . . . .206 A2
Scarfe Way CO4 . . . . . .136 E6
Scarfe's Cnr CO6 . . . . . .82 B4
Scarletts Cl CM8 . . . . . .195 A7
Scarletts Rd CO1 . . . . . .136 C4
Sceptre Cl CM9 . . . . . .199 D2
School Barn Cotts CO10 . .13 F7
School Chase CO9 . . . . .103 E8
School Cl IP9 . . . . .35 A1
School Ct CO12 . . . . . . .91 D4
School Hill Birch CO2 . . .161 A4
Washbrook IP8 . . . . . . .35 F8
School Ho
13 Colchester CO1 . . . .136 A6
Shalford CM7 . . . . . . .100 E5
School La Birch CO2 . . . .161 A3
Brantham CO11 . . . . . .60 D1
Broomfield CM1 . . . . .191 A1
Chelmsford CM1 . . . . .204 F8
Dedham CO7 . . . . . . .84 F7
Duddenhoe End CB11 . . .41 A7
East Bergholt CO7 . . . . .59 B3
Great Bentley CO7 . . . .166 A8
Great Horkesley CO6 . . .81 D5
Great Horkesley CO6 . . .82 A2
Great Leighs CM3 . . . . .173 F8
Great Wigborough CO5 . .181 F3
Haverhill CB9 . . . . .8 E7
Henham CM22 . . . . . . .94 F5
Lawford CO11 . . . . . . .86 A2
Mistley CO11 . . . . . . .86 F4
Newport CB11 . . . . . . .42 F1
Stratford St M CO7 . . . . .58 D2
Takeley CM22 . . . . . . .121 D6
West Bergholt CO6 . . . .108 E4
School Mews CO6 . . . . .130 F2
School Rd Colchester CO2 .136 A2
Copford CO6 . . . . . . .133 D3
Elmstead CO7 . . . . . . .138 A4
Frinton-on-S CO13 . . . .170 E5
Great Oakley CO12 . . . .116 A3
Great Totham CM9 . . . .196 B3
Langham CO4 . . . . . . .83 E4
Little Horkesley CO6 . . . .81 D4
Little Maplestead CO9 . . .77 B8
Little Totham CM9 . . . . .197 B3
Little Yeldham CO9 . . . . .30 D3
Messing CO5 . . . . . . .159 D2
Pentlow CO10 . . . . . . .13 F6
Rayne CM7 . . . . .153 E8
Shotley Gate IP9 . . . . . .91 B8
Sible Hedingham CO9 . . .75 D8
Silver End CM8 . . . . . .156 E3
Tattingstone IP9 . . . . . .36 D1
Tendring CO16 . . . . . .140 E6
Wickham Bishops CM8 . .195 F5
Wickham St P CO9 . . . . .53 C5
School St Foxearth CO10 . .14 D6
Great Chesterford CB10 . .3 D2
Stoke-by-N CO6 . . . . . .56 D5
Sudbury CO10 . . . . . . .33 E7
School View Rd CM1 . . .204 F3
School Villas
Great Easton CM6 . . . .123 A8
Henham CM22 . . . . . . .95 F2
Lindsell CM6 . . . . .97 F4
Takeley CM22 . . . . . . .121 C6
School Wlk CM7 . . . . . .127 F3
Schoolfield CO10 . . . . . .2 B5
Schreiber Rd IP4 . . . . . .18 B7
Scofield Ct CO10 . . . . . .34 A6
Scotland St CO6 . . . . . .56 E6
Scott Ave CM7 . . . . . . .73 D6
Scott Cl CM7 . . . . .155 A8
Scott Dr CO3 . . . . .134 F6
Scott Rd
Bishop's Stortford CM23 . .145 A6
Ipswich IP3 . . . . .18 B1
Scotts Wlk CM1 . . . . . .204 D5
Scraley Rd CM9 . . . . . .210 E6
Scrip's Rd CO6 . . . . . . .158 A7
Scrivener Dr IP2 . . . . . .16 C2
Scurvy Hall La CM3 . . . .173 C1
Scylla Cl CM9 . . . . . . .210 C6
Scythe Way CO3 . . . . . .134 F4
Sea Cornflower Way
CO15 . . . . .203 G7
Sea Cres CO15 . . . . . .203 F6
Sea Flowers Way CO15 . .203 G7
Sea Glebe Way CO15 . . .203 G7
Sea Holly Way CO15 . . . .203 G6
Sea King Cres CO4 . . . . .110 B4
Sea Lavender Way CO15 .203 G7
Sea Pink Way CO15 . . . .203 G6

Sea Rd IP11 . . . . .221 D2
Sea Rosemary Way CO15 203 G7
Sea Shell Way CO15 . . . .203 G7
Sea Thistle Way CO15 . . .203 G7
Sea View Par CM0 . . . . .213 C1
Sea View Prom CM0 . . . .213 B1
Sea Way CO15 . . . . . . .203 F6
Seabrook Gdns CM3 . . . .192 F1
Seabrook Rd CM2 . . . . .217 A6
Seafield Ave CO11 . . . . .87 B4
Seafield Rd CO12 . . . . . .91 B2
Seafields Gdns CO15 . . . .189 C5
Seafields Rd CO15 . . . . .189 C5
Seagers CM9 . . . . . . .196 B4
Searle Way CO6 . . . . . .108 B1
Seaton Cl CO11 . . . . . . .86 B3
Seaton Rd IP11 . . . . . .221 D5
Seaview Ave
Little Oakley CO12 . . . .117 C7
West Mersea CO5 . . . .201 C6
Seaview Hts CO14 . . . . .171 C7
Seaview Rd
Brightlingsea CO7 . . . .185 F7
St Osyth CO16 . . . . . .203 B7
Seaview Terr CO16 . . . . .186 A3
Seawick Rd CO16 . . . . .203 B6
Sebastian Cl CO4 . . . . .136 F7
Seckford Cl IP4 . . . . . . .18 F5
Second Ave
Chelmsford CM1 . . . . .205 B5
Clacton-on-S CO15 . . . .189 B4
Frinton-on-S CO13 . . . .170 E3
Glemsford CO10 . . . . . .2 C5
Halstead CO9 . . . . . . .77 B1
Harwich CO12 . . . . . . .91 C3
St Osyth CO16 . . . . . .203 C6
Stansted
Mountfitchet CM24 . . . .120 B2
Sudbury CO10 . . . . . . .15 F1
Trimley St M IP11 . . . . .221 A7
Walton-on-t-N CO14 . . .144 C3
Weeley CO16 . . . . . . .167 F8
Seden Ct CO15 . . . . . .169 B1
Sedgefield Way CM7 . . . .128 B1
Sedop Cl CB11 . . . . . . .43 D7
Seedbed Ctr CO4 . . . . .110 C6
Selby Cl CO2 . . . . . . .135 D1
Seldon Rd CO5 . . . . . .179 D5
Seldon Cl CO5 . . . . . . .179 D5
Selhurst Ct CO14 . . . . . .170 F7
Selkirk Rd IP4 . . . . .18 B8
Selsey Ave CO15 . . . . .203 I8
Selvale Way IP11 . . . . .221 C4
Selwyn Cl IP2 . . . . .17 C4
Serpentine Rd IP3 . . . . .18 B3
Serpentine Wlk CO1 . . . .109 E1
Servite Ho IP4 . . . . . . .17 F6
Seven Ash Gn CM1 . . . .205 C5
Seven Devils La CB11 . . .43 D6
Seventh Ave
Chelmsford CM1 . . . . .205 B6
Stansted
Mountfitchet CM24 . . . .120 B2
Severalls Hospl CO4 . . . .109 E5
Severalls La CO4 . . . . . .110 B6
Severn Rd
Clacton-on-S CO15 . . . .188 F5
Ipswich IP3 . . . . .17 F3
Sewell's La CO10 . . . . . .13 B1
Sexton Cl CO2 . . . . . . .163 B8
Sextons La CM8 . . . . . .178 B1
Seymour Rd Ipswich IP2 . .17 C4
Seymour St CM2 . . . . .205 A1
Shackleton Cl CO12 . . . . .90 F1
Shackleton Rd IP3 . . . . .18 B3
Shackleton Sq IP3 . . . . .18 B3
Shaftenhoe End Rd SG8 . .39 B8
Shaftesbury Ave CO12 . . .91 B4
Shaftesbury Ct **10** CB9 . . .8 E7
Shaftesbury Sq **4** 1P4 . . .17 D5
Shafto Rd IP1 . . . . .16 E2
Shair La CO16 . . . . . . .140 B2
Shakespeare Cl CM7 . . . .155 A7
Shakespeare Dr CM9 . . .210 A1
Shakespeare Rd CO3 . . .134 F6
Shakeston Cl CM1 . . . . .215 B8
Shalford Cty Prim Sch
CM7 . . . . .100 E5
Shalford Lodge CM1 . . . .205 B8
Shalford Rd CM7 . . . . . .126 E3
Shamrock Ave IP2 . . . . .16 E4
Shamrock Cl CM9 . . . . .199 D2
Shamrock Ho CO15 . . . .203 J8
Shangani Rd CM23 . . . . .145 F5
Shanklin Cl CO15 . . . . .189 A8
Shannon Cl CB9 . . . . . . .9 D7
Shannon Rd IP3 . . . . . .38 A8
Sharlands Row CM9 . . . .199 A8
Sharpington Cl CM2 . . . .216 C3
Shatters Rd CO2 . . . . . .161 A1
Shaw Cl CO13 . . . . . . .170 F7
Shaw Dr CM7 . . . . .73 D7
Shaw Rd Long Melford CO10 15 D8
Witham CM8 . . . . .176 F5
Shawlands Ave CO10 . . . .34 F1
Shearers The CM23 . . . .145 C4
Shearers Way CM3 . . . . .192 F1
Shearman Ct **1** CB9 . . . . .9 A7
Shears Cres CO5 . . . . . .201 D5
Shears Ct CO5 . . . . . . .201 D5
Sheds La CB10 . . . . . . .22 E4
Sheepcoates La CM9 . . . .196 F2
Sheepcot Rd CO9 . . . . . .51 D3
Sheepcote La CM23 . . . .92 D3
Sheepcotes La
Little Waltham CM3 . . . .191 C7
Silver End CM8 . . . . . .156 E5
Sheepen Pl CO3 . . . . . .135 E8

Sheepen Rd CO3 . . . . .135 D8
Sheepshead Hill CO10 . . .34 C6
Sheering Wlk CO4 . . . . .135 F2
Sheerwater Mews CO4 . .137 A8
Sheldrake Dr **7** IP2 . . . . .16 E2
Shellcroft CO6 . . . . . . .77 F1
Shellduck Cres CM7 . . . .154 C5
Shelley Ave CO10 . . . . . .34 B6
Shelley La CO16 . . . . . .168 F2
Shelley Rd
Chelmsford CM2 . . . . .205 D2
Colchester CO3 . . . . .134 F6
Shelley St **6** IP2 . . . . . .17 C4
Shenley Rd IP3 . . . . . . .18 B1
Shepherd Dr IP8 . . . . . .16 C2
Shepherds Cl CM23 . . . .145 C4
Shepherds Croft CO3 . . .134 D5
Shepherds Ct **15** CB9 . . . .8 E7
Shepherds La CO15 . . . . .2 A6
Shepherds Way CB10 . . .22 F2
Sheppard Cl CO16 . . . . .188 D6
Sheppard Dr CM2 . . . . .206 A4
Sherborne Rd CM1 . . . .205 D5
Sherbourne Cl CO13 . . . .170 F7
Sherbourne Rd CO4 . . . .136 F7
Sheriffs Way CO15 . . . . .188 E2
Sherrington Rd IP1 . . . . .17 A8
Sherwood Cl CO4 . . . . .136 D7
Sherwood Ct **20** CM23 . .145 F7
Sherwood Dr
Chelmsford CM1 . . . . .204 D1
Clacton-on-S CO15 . . . .188 E6
Sherwood Way CO5 . . . .158 D4
Shetland Cl IP4 . . . . . . .18 A8
Shetland Rd CB9 . . . . . .9 D8
Shillito Cl CO3 . . . . . . .134 F3
Ship La CO11 . . . . .87 E3
Ship Launch Rd IP3 . . . . .17 E3
Shipyard Est CO7 . . . . .185 F5
Shire Cl CM1 . . . . .205 F7
Shire Cl **18** CB9 . . . . . . .8 E7
Shire Hall Yd **4** IP4 . . . . .17 D5
Shire Hill La CB10 . . . . . .44 A8
Shire La CO6 . . . . .108 F4
Shirley Ct CO15 . . . . . .188 A1
Shoebridge's Hill CO7 . . .84 E6
Shop La CO5 . . . . .184 F3
Shop Rd CO11 . . . . . . .113 B6
Shops The CM8 . . . . . .156 D4
Shore La Bradfield CO11 . .87 E3
Harkstead IP9 . . . . . . .63 A2
Shoreham Rd CO15 . . . .203 I8
Short Cut Rd CO1 . . . . .135 E7
Short Wyre St **27** CO1 . . .135 F7
Shortcroft CM23 . . . . . .146 D7
Shortgate IP8 . . . . .16 D1
Shortlands Pl CM23 . . . .145 F8
Shortridge Ct CM8 . . . . .194 F8
Shotley Cl
Clacton-on-S CO16 . . . .188 A3
Felixstowe IP11 . . . . . .221 B4
Ipswich IP2 . . . . .16 C2
Shropshire Cl CM2 . . . . .216 F5
Shrub End Rd CO2 . . . . .135 B4
Shrubland Cl CO15 . . . . .189 B5
Shrubland Dr IP4 . . . . . .18 F5
Shrubland Rd
6 Colchester CO2 . . . .136 A6
New Mistley CO11 . . . . .87 A3
Shrublands CB10 . . . . . .22 E3
Shrublands Cl CM2 . . . . .205 C2
Shums Hill CO13 . . . . . .170 C8
Shut La CO6 . . . . .105 B6
Siam Pl CO10 . . . . .33 E7
Sidegate Ave IP4 . . . . . .18 A8
Sidegate La IP4 . . . . . . .18 A8
Sidegate Prim Sch IP4 . . .18 A8
Sidmouth Rd CM1 . . . . .205 C6
Sidney Terr CM23 . . . . .145 F6
Siena Mews CO4 . . . . . .136 B4
Siggin's La CB1 . . . . . . .5 D7
Silcock Cl CO4 . . . . . . .110 C2
Silcott St CO7 . . . . . . .185 E6
Silent St IP1 . . . . .17 C5
Silk Factory Row CO10 . . .2 B6
Silk Mus CM7 . . . . . . .127 F2
Silks Way CM7 . . . . . . .127 F2
Sillett Cl CO16 . . . . . . .188 D6
Silvanus Cl CO3 . . . . . .135 D6
Silver End Cty Prim Sch
CM8 . . . . .156 E3
Silver Leys IP9 . . . . . . .60 E6
Silver Row CB11 . . . . . .42 F5
Silver St Maldon CM9 . . .209 F3
Silver End CM8 . . . . . .156 D4
Stansted
Mountfitchet CM24 . . . .119 D6
Wethersfield CM7 . . . . .73 B3
Silverdale Ct CO15 . . . . .189 B5
Silverthorne Cl CO2 . . . .136 A3
Simmonds Way CM3 . . . .218 F8
Simons La CO1 . . . . . . .136 B6
Simpson Cl IP3 . . . . . . .17 F1
Simpsons La CO5 . . . . .179 A3
Sims Cl CO6 . . . . .105 B7
Sinclair Cl CO4 . . . . . . .109 F2
Sinclair Dr IP2 . . . . . . .17 C3
Singer Ave CO15 . . . . . .203 E7
Singleton Ct CO4 . . . . . .34 A5
Sinnington End CO4 . . . .110 C4
Sioux Cl CO4 . . . . .110 C4
Sir Charles Lucas Sch
The CO4 . . . . .136 E8
Sir Isaac's Wlk CO1 . . . .135 F7

Sir John Payne RC
Comp Sch CM1 . . . . .204 F6
Sirdar Rd IP1 . . . . .17 A7
Siskin Cl CO4 . . . . .136 F8
Sittang Cl CO2 . . . . .135 C1
Sitwell Cl CO11 . . . . .86 B4
Siward Rd CM8 . . . . .194 D8
Six Bells Ct CM7 . . . . .127 F5
Sixth Ave Chelmsford CM1 .205 B6
  Stansted
  Mountfitchet CM24 . . . . . .120 C3
Sixth Form Coll The CO1 .135 E7
Skate's Hill CO10 . . . . .2 B2
Skeins Way CB11 . . . . .65 C4
Skelmersdale Rd CO15 . . .188 F3
Skelton Cl CO11 . . . . .86 C4
Skerry Rise CM1 . . . . .205 B7
Skiddaw Cl CM7 . . . . .154 D7
Skinner's La CM2 . . . . .216 B3
Skinners St CM23 . . . . . . .145 C4
Skipper Ct CM7 . . . . .154 F8
Skitts Hill CM7 . . . . .128 A1
Skitts Hill Ind Est CM7 . .128 B1
Skreens Ct CM1 . . . . .204 D4
Sky Hall Hill CO4 . . . . .83 D7
Skylark La IP8 . . . . .16 C2
Skylark Wlk CM2 . . . . .216 B5
Skyrmans Fee CO13 . . . . .170 E6
Sladbury's La CO15 . . . . .189 C6
Sladburys La CO15 . . . . . .189 D8
Slade Rd CO15 . . . . .189 C6
Slade St CM 1P4 . . . . .17 D5
Slade The CB10 . . . . .22 F7
Slade's La CM2 . . . . .216 A3
Slades Cl CO10 . . . . .2 C5
Slate CO9 . . . . .76 F1
Slaters Cl CO13 . . . . .170 E6
Sleaford Cl IP2 . . . . .17 A3
Slippers The CM9 . . . . . . .199 D1
Sloe Hill CO9 . . . . .76 C2
Slough Farm Rd CO9 . . . . .76 D2
Slough House Cl CM7 . . . .128 D1
Slough La Ardleigh CO7 . . .111 D4
  Elmstead CO7 . . . . .137 B6
  Purleigh CM3 . . . . .219 D3
Slough Rd Danbury CM3 . .219 C3
  East Bergholt CO7 . . . . .60 D2
Slushy La IP9 . . . . .63 B3
Smaley La CO10 . . . . .15 C8
Smallbridge Entry CO8 . . .80 D8
Smallwood Rd CO2 . . . . . .135 B3
Smart St CM 1P4 . . . . .17 D5
Smeaton Cl CO4 . . . . .110 C6
Smeetham Hall La CO10 . .32 E6
Smith's End La SG8 . . . . . .39 A8
Smithers Cl IP9 . . . . .35 A1
Smithers Dr CM2 . . . . .217 A6
Smiths Cotts CM22 . . . . . . .93 E4
Smiths Field
  Colchester CO1 . . . . .136 C5
  Rayne CM7 . . . . .126 F2
Smythe Cl CO16 . . . . .188 C6
Smythies Ave CO1 . . . . . .136 A7
Snakes La
  Stansted Mountfitchet CM24 .93 F2
  Ugley CM22 . . . . .94 A2
Snape Cl CO16 . . . . .188 A4
Snape Way CO13 . . . . . . .170 F7
Sneating Hall La CO13 . . .169 E8
Snelling Gr CM2 . . . . .216 F6
Sniveller's La CO5 . . . . . . .157 D3
Snow Hill La CO6 . . . . .57 D5
Snowberry Ct CM7 . . . . . .128 D4
Snowberry Gr CO2 . . . . . .136 A3
Snowcroft IP9 . . . . .35 A1
Snowdon Ct CM CB9 . . . . . .8 E6
Snowdon Rd IP2 . . . . .17 B8
Snowdrop Cl
  Bishop's Stortford CM23 . .145 C6
  Chelmsford CM1 . . . . .205 E7
  Witham CM8 . . . . .176 E4
Snowley Par CM23 . . . . . .119 B1
Snows Way CO11 . . . . .86 D8
Soane St 1P4 . . . . .17 D6
Soft Rd CO10 . . . . .31 F5
Soils The CO12 . . . . .116 E5
Solway Ct CO4 . . . . .136 E8
Somers Rd CO3 . . . . .135 A4
Somerset Cl CO2 . . . . .135 B3
Somerset Ct CM CB9 . . . . . .8 E7
Somerset Pl CM1 . . . . .205 A7
Somerset Rd IP4 . . . . .17 F8
Somerset Way CO15 . . . . .187 F1
Somerton Ct IP11 . . . . . . .221 F4
Somme Rd CO2 . . . . .135 E4
Sonell Ct CO7 . . . . .137 B2
Songers Cotts CO4 . . . . . . .83 B6
Sorrel Cl Colchester CO4 . .109 C2
  Ipswich IP2 . . . . .16 F3
Sorrel Horse Mews CM
  1P4 . . . . .17 D5
Sorrell Cl
  Goldhanger CM9 . . . . .211 E7
  Little Waltham CM3 . . . . . .191 B6
South Area IP1 . . . . .16 C7
South Cl Halstead CO9 . . .103 E8
  Ipswich IP4 . . . . .17 E8
  St Osyth CO16 . . . . .187 B4
South Gn CB11 . . . . .67 D4
South Green Rd CO5 . . . . .163 F3
South Heath Rd CO7 . . . . .166 F3
South Hill IP11 . . . . .221 D3
South Hill Cl CM3 . . . . . . .218 D6
South Ho CO13 . . . . .170 F4
South Primrose Hill CM1 204 F3

South Rd
  Bishop's Stortford CM23 . . .146 A5
  Saffron Walden CB11 . . . . . .22 E1
  Takeley CM22 . . . . .148 C8
South St
  Bishop's Stortford CM23 . . .145 F6
  Braintree CM7 . . . . .127 F2
  Colchester CO2 . . . . .135 E6
  Great Chesterford CB10 . . . . .3 D2
  Great Waltham CM3 . . . . . .190 E7
  Ipswich IP1 . . . . .17 B7
  Manningtree CO11 . . . . .86 D4
  Tolleshunt D'arcy CM9 . . . .198 D4
South St Commercial
  Ctr CM23 . . . . .145 F6
South Strand CO11 . . . . . . .86 C5
South Suffolk Bsns Pk
  CO10 . . . . .34 A7
South View CM6 . . . . .150 C8
South View Gr IP9 . . . . .60 E6
Southborough Rd CM2 . . .216 A8
Southcliff CO14 . . . . .171 C7
Southcliff CO15 . . . . .189 B4
Southcliff Hall CO15 . . . . .188 F2
Southcliff Pk CO15 . . . . . .189 A4
Southcliff Prom CO14 . . . .171 C7
Southcote Rd CM8 . . . . . .176 F4
Southcroft Cl CO13 . . . . . .170 C6
Southend Rd
  Great Baddow CM2 . . . . . .217 B4
  Howe Green CM2 . . . . . . .217 D2
  Woodham Mortimer CM9 . .219 C5
Southey Cl CM9 . . . . .210 C4
Southfield CB10 . . . . .3 A3
Southfields CO7 . . . . .84 F6
Southgate Gdns CO10 . . . .15 C6
Southgate Rd IP8 . . . . .16 B1
Southgate St CO10 . . . . . . .15 C6
Southgates Ind Pk CB10 . .43 F7
Southgreen Gdns CO16 . .188 C4
Southland Cl CO4 . . . . . . .110 C1
Southlands Chase CM2 . . .217 E2
Southmill Rd CM23 . . . . . .146 A5
Southmill Trad Ctr CM23 .146 A6
Southview Dr
  Holland-on-S CO15 . . . . . .189 F6
  Walton-on-t-N CO14 . . . . .171 C7
Southview Rd CM3 . . . . . .218 D6
Southview Terr CM3 . . . . .218 D6
Southway
  Brightlingsea CO7 . . . . . . .185 F7
  Colchester CO1, CO3 . . . . .135 E6
Southwold Way CO16 . . . .188 A5
Southwood Chase CM3 . . .219 A4
Sovereign Cl CM7 . . . . . . .128 D4
Sovereign Cres CO3 . . . . .135 C6
Sovereign Ctr IP1 . . . . .16 C7
Sowerberry Cl CM1 . . . . . .204 F7
Spa Dr CM0 . . . . .213 B1
Spa Rd Feering CO5 . . . . . .158 E4
  Witham CM8 . . . . .176 E2
Spalding Ave CM1 . . . . . . .204 E5
Spalding Cl CM7 . . . . .127 E4
Spalding Way CM2 . . . . . .216 F8
Spanbies Rd CO7 . . . . .58 D2
Spansey Ct CM CO9 . . . . . .76 D1
Sparkey La N CB10 . . . . . .47 A4
Sparkey La S CB10 . . . . . .47 B4
Sparkey Cl CM8 . . . . .195 A7
Sparks La CO9 . . . . .29 A6
Sparling Cl CO2 . . . . .135 C2
Sparlings The CO13 . . . . . .170 C8
Sparrow Cl CO9 . . . . .75 D8
Sparrow Rd CO10 . . . . .34 B6
Sparrows Herne CO15 . . . .188 F6
Sparrowsend Cotts CB11 . .43 A4
Sparrowsend Hill CB11 . . .43 A5
Speckled Wood Ct CM7 . .154 E8
Speedwell Cl CM8 . . . . . . .176 D4
Speedwell Rd
  Colchester CO2 . . . . .136 D2
  Ipswich IP2 . . . . .16 F4
Spencer Cl Elsenham CM22 .94 C3
  Stansted
  Mountfitchet CM24 . . . . . .119 E6
Spencer Rd
  Great Chesterford CB10 . . . .3 D3
  Thorpe-le-S CO16 . . . . . . .142 A2
Spencer Sq CM7 . . . . .127 F8
Spencers Piece CO4 . . . . . .83 E4
Spendells Cl CO14 . . . . . . .144 D2
Spenlow Dr CM1 . . . . .204 D7
Spennells The CO16 . . . . .142 A2
Spenser Way CO15 . . . . . .187 F1
Spicers La CO10 . . . . .15 C8
Spindle Rd CB9 . . . . .8 D8
Spindle Wood CO4 . . . . . .110 B4
Spinks La CM8 . . . . .176 F1
Spinnaker Cl CO15 . . . . . .203 J8
Spinnaker Dr CM9 . . . . . . .210 E3
Spinnel's Hill CO11 . . . . . .88 B1
Spinnel's La Wix CO11 . . . .115 D7
  Wrabness CO11 . . . . .88 C1
Spinner Cl IP1 . . . . .16 D8
Spinney The
  Braintree CM7 . . . . .128 C1
  Earls Colne CO6 . . . . .105 A6
  Newport CB11 . . . . .67 A7
  Rushmere St A IP4 . . . . . . .18 F4
  Stansted
  Mountfitchet CM24 . . . . . .119 E6
Spinneyfields CO5 . . . . . . .179 D6
Spires The CM2 . . . . .216 F6
Spital Rd Maldon CM9 . . . .209 F2
  Maldon CM9 . . . . .220 D7
Sporehams La
  Danbury CM3 . . . . .218 C4
  Howe Green CM2, CM3 . . .217 F4

Sportsmans La CM3 . . . . .194 A2
Sportsway CO1 . . . . .135 F8
Spots Wlk CM2 . . . . .216 D3
Spout La CO10 . . . . .55 D7
Spratts La CO11 . . . . .113 B4
Spring Chase
  Brightlingsea CO7 . . . . . . .185 E7
  Wivenhoe CO7 . . . . .137 B2
Spring Cl
  Clacton-on-S CO16 . . . . . .188 C5
  Colchester CO4 . . . . .110 C3
  Little Baddow CM3 . . . . . .207 D5
Spring Elms La CM3 . . . . .207 F3
Spring Gardens Rd CO6 . .106 E6
Spring Hill CB11 . . . . .22 A1
Spring La Colchester CO3 . .135 A7
  Colchester CO3 . . . . .135 A8
  Eight Ash G CO3 . . . . .108 B1
  Great Totham CM9 . . . . . .196 D7
  Hatfield Peverel CM3 . . . . .194 F2
  Maldon CM9 . . . . .210 A4
  West Bergholt CO6 . . . . . .108 E3
  Witham CM8 . . . . .195 A7
  Wivenhoe CO7 . . . . .137 B2
Spring Lane Rdbt CO3 . . . .135 A7
Spring Meadow CO10 . . . . .2 B6
Spring Meadow Prim
  Sch CO12 . . . . .91 A3
Spring Pond Cl CM2 . . . . .216 E8
Spring Rd
  Brightlingsea CO7 . . . . . . .185 F7
  Ipswich IP4 . . . . .18 A4
  St Osyth CO16 . . . . .187 A3
  Tiptree CO5 . . . . .179 C4
Spring Rise CM2 . . . . .216 C2
Spring Sedge Cl CO3 . . . .134 C7
Spring Way CO9 . . . . .51 E1
Springbank Ave CO11 . . . . .86 B3
Springbook Ho CM2 . . . . .216 F5
Springett's Hill CO8 . . . . . .55 D2
Springfield Ave IP11 . . . . .221 E5
Springfield Cotts CM9 . . . .210 B5
Springfield Ct CM23 . . . . .145 E8
Springfield Gn CM1 . . . . . .205 E4
Springfield Inf Sch IP1 . . . .16 F8
Springfield Jun Sch IP1 . . .16 F8
Springfield La IP1 . . . . .16 F8
Springfield Park Ave
  CM2 . . . . .205 E2
Springfield Park Hill
  CM2 . . . . .205 D2
Springfield Park La CM2 .205 E2
Springfield Park Par
  CM2 . . . . .205 D2
Springfield Park Rd CM2 .205 E2
Springfield Pl CM1 . . . . . . .205 E5
Springfield Rd
  Chelmsford CM1 . . . . .205 E4
  Sudbury CO10 . . . . .15 E1
Springfield Terr CO10 . . . . .33 F8
Springfields
  Brightlingsea CO7 . . . . . . .185 F7
  Great Dunmow CM6 . . . . .150 D8
Springfields Dr CO2 . . . . . .135 A3
Springfields CM7 . . . . .127 C2
Springhill Cl CO7 . . . . .138 E8
Springhill Rd CB11 . . . . . . .43 D8
Springhurst Cl IP4 . . . . . . .17 F6
Springland Cl IP4 . . . . .18 A6
Springlands Way CO10 . . . .15 F2
Springmead CM7 . . . . .154 D7
Springvalley La CO7 . . . . .111 C4
Springwell Rd CO10 . . . . . .22 A5
Springwood Ct CM7 . . . . .127 D3
Springwood Dr CM7 . . . . .127 C4
Springwood Ind Est CM7 .127 D3
Sprites End IP11 . . . . .221 B7
Sprites Jun & Inf Sch IP2 .16 C2
Sprites La IP8, IP2 . . . . . . .16 C2
Spriteshall La IP11 . . . . . .221 B7
Sproughton Bsns Pk IP1 . .16 C8
Sproughton CE Prim Sch
  IP8 . . . . .16 B6
Sproughton Ct IP8 . . . . . . .16 A6
Sproughton Rd IP1 . . . . . . .16 D7
Spruce Ave CO4 . . . . .136 E8
Spruce Cl
  West Mersea CO5 . . . . . . .201 B7
  Witham CM8 . . . . .177 A4
Spurgeon Cl CO9 . . . . .51 E1
Spurgeon Pl CO5 . . . . .158 C2
Spurgeon St CO1 . . . . .136 C6
Square The
  Colchester CO2 . . . . .135 B3
  West Mersea CO5 . . . . . . .201 B6
Squire's Ct CM CB9 . . . . . . .8 E7
Squires Cl CM23 . . . . .145 C8
Squirells Ct CM1 . . . . .204 F5
Squirrels Cl CM CM23 . . . .145 F8
Squirrels Field CO4 . . . . . .109 F5
Squirrels The IP9 . . . . .35 A2
Stable Mews CO5 . . . . . . .201 E8
Stable Mews CO5 . . . . . . .201 E8
Stablecroft CM1 . . . . .205 E8
Stablefield Rd CO4 . . . . . .171 A7
Stacey Ct CM CM23 . . . . . .145 F6
Stackyard The CB10 . . . . . .3 A3
Staff Hos CM1 . . . . .190 F4
Stafford Cl CO13 . . . . .170 E6
Stafford Cres CM7 . . . . . . .128 D4
Stafford Ho CM23 . . . . . . .145 F5
Stalin Rd CO2 . . . . .136 B4
Stallards Cres CO13 . . . . .170 E6
Stambourne Rd
  Great Yeldham CO9 . . . . . .29 D3
  Ridgewell CO9 . . . . .28 F5
  Toppesfield CO9 . . . . .50 B7

Stambridge Rd CO15 . . . . .188 C4
Stamford Cl IP2 . . . . .36 F8
Stammers Rd CO4 . . . . . . .109 F4
Standard Ave CO15 . . . . . .203 D6
Standard Rd CM CO1 . . . . .136 C6
Standley Rd CO14 . . . . . . .144 D1
Standrums CM6 . . . . .150 D8
Stane Cl CM23 . . . . .118 F1
Stane Field CO6 . . . . .132 E3
Stanes Rd CM7 . . . . .127 F6
Stanfield Cl CO3 . . . . .134 E3
Stanfield Mdw CM8 . . . . . .155 F1
Stanley Ave
  Brightlingsea CO7 . . . . . . .186 A7
  Ipswich IP3 . . . . .18 A4
Stanley Rd
  Clacton-on-S CO15 . . . . . .188 C2
  Felixstowe IP11 . . . . .221 E3
  Great Chesterford CB10 . . . .3 E3
  Halstead CO9 . . . . .76 D2
  Sudbury CO10 . . . . .33 E8
  Wivenhoe CO7 . . . . .137 C1
Stanley Rise CM2 . . . . . . .205 F3
Stanley Wood Ave CO10 . .15 F1
Stanley Wooster Way
  CO4 . . . . .136 E7
Stanleys Farm Rd CB11 . . .43 B8
Stanmore Cl CO16 . . . . . . .188 D5
Stanmore Way CO16 . . . . .187 B4
Stannard Way CO10 . . . . . .34 A6
Stanstead Rd CO9 . . . . . . .103 F8
Stansted Airport Sta
  CM24 . . . . .121 B4
Stansted Cl CM1 . . . . .204 E1
Stansted Mountfitchet
  Sta CM24 . . . . .119 E6
Stansted Rd
  Birchanger CM23 . . . . . . .119 C4
  Bishop's Stortford CM23 . .119 B2
  Colchester CO2 . . . . .136 A1
  Elsenham CM22 . . . . .94 C1
Stansted Way CO13 . . . . . .171 A6
Stanstrete Field CM7 . . . . .154 B5
Stanton Pl CM CB9 . . . . .9 B8
Stanway Cl CO10 . . . . .2 C5
Stanway Cty Prim Sch
  CO3 . . . . .134 C6
Stanway Fiveways Cty
  Prim Sch CO3 . . . . .134 D5
Stanway Sch CO3 . . . . . . .134 D5
Stanwell St CM CO2 . . . . . .135 F6
Stanwyn Ave CO15 . . . . . .188 E3
Stapleford Cl CM2 . . . . . . .205 A1
Staplers Cl CM9 . . . . .196 B4
Staplers Heath CM9 . . . . . .196 B4
Staplers Wlk CM9 . . . . . . .196 B4
Star La Great Dunmow CM6 123 D1
  Ipswich IP4 . . . . .17 D5
Star Mead CM6 . . . . .70 A2
Starfield Cl IP4 . . . . .18 B6
Starling's Hill CO9 . . . . . . .75 E4
Starr Rd CM22 . . . . .94 B4
Station App Braintree CM7 128 A2
  Frinton-on-S CO13 . . . . . .170 F5
Station Cotts CO6 . . . . . . .133 D2
Station Hill CO8 . . . . .79 E8
Station La CO12 . . . . .91 C4
Station Rd Alresford CO7 . .165 A8
  Ardleigh CO7 . . . . .111 E7
  Bentley IP9 . . . . .60 E6
  Birdbrook CO9 . . . . .10 D1
  Bishop's Stortford CM23 . .146 A1
  Bradfield CO11 . . . . .87 E3
  Braintree CM7 . . . . .127 F2
  Brightlingsea CO7 . . . . . . .185 E6
  Clacton-on-S CO15 . . . . . .188 F3
  Clare CO10 . . . . .12 C7
  Colne Engaine CO6 . . . . . . .77 F1
  Cressing CM8 . . . . .156 A3
  Earls Colne CO6 . . . . .105 A7
  Elsenham CM22 . . . . .94 C2
  Felsted CM6 . . . . .151 F6
  Great Bentley CO7 . . . . . . .166 A8
  Great Bentley CO7 . . . . . . .166 E8
  Great Dunmow CM6 . . . . .150 B8
  Harwich, Bath Side CO12 . . .91 E5
  Harwich, Dovercourt CO12 . .91 D4
  Harwich, Parkeston CO12 . . .90 F5
  Hatfield Peverel CM3 . . . . .193 F5
  Haverhill CB9 . . . . .9 A8
  Kelvedon CO5 . . . . .158 C3
  Kirby Cross CO13 . . . . . . .170 B6
  Long Melford CO10 . . . . . .15 C5
  Maldon CM9 . . . . .210 A3
  Manningtree CO11 . . . . .86 C5
  Marks Tey CO6 . . . . .133 B4
  Newport CB11 . . . . .67 A8
  Rayne CM7 . . . . .126 F1
  Saffron Walden CB11 . . . . . .22 D1
  Sible Hedingham CO9 . . . . .51 E2
  Stansted
  Mountfitchet CM24 . . . . . .119 E6
  Sudbury CO10 . . . . .33 E7
  Takeley CM22 . . . . .148 C2
  Thorpe-le-S CO16 . . . . . . .168 F8
  Thorrington CO7 . . . . .166 A6
  Tiptree CO5 . . . . .179 C4
  Tollesbury CM9 . . . . .199 D2
  Tolleshunt D'arcy CM9 . . . .198 D5
  Trimley St M IP11 . . . . . . .221 A7
  Wakes Colne CO6 . . . . . . .106 D6
  Wendens Ambo CB11 . . . . .42 F5
  White Colne CO6 . . . . .105 E8
  White Notley CM8 . . . . . . .155 F2
  Wickham Bishops CM8 . . . .195 C4
  Witham CM8 . . . . .177 A3
  Wivenhoe CO7 . . . . .164 B8
  Wrabness CO11 . . . . .88 A3

Station Road Ind Est
  CM6 . . . . .150 E
Station St Ipswich IP2 . . . . .17 C
  Saffron Walden CB11 . . . . . .22 D
  Walton-on-t-N CO14 . . . . .171 C
Station Villas CM3 . . . . . . .193 F
Station Way CO1 . . . . .109 E1
Station Yd IP2 . . . . .17 B
Steam Mill Rd CO11 . . . . .114 B8
Steamer Terr CM CM1 . . . .205 A
Stebbing Cty Prim Sch
  CM6 . . . . .124 E!
Stebbing Rd CM6 . . . . .152 B2
Steeds Meadow CO10 . . . .15 C8
Steele Cl CO6 . . . . .132 F3
Steele Ho CO12 . . . . .91 C3
Steeple Bumpstead Cty
  Prim Sch CB9 . . . . .27 B6
Steeple Bumpstead Rd
  CB9 . . . . .26 E1
Steeple Cl CM9 . . . . .210 D5
Steeple View CM23 . . . . . .145 FE
Steerforth Cl CM1 . . . . . . .204 D2
Stella Maris IP2 . . . . .16 D5
Stepfield CM8 . . . . .177 B2
Stephen Cl Haverhill CB9 . . .8 F1
  Long Melford CO10 . . . . . .15 D5
Stephen Cranfield Cl
  CO5 . . . . .164 A7
Stephen Marshall Ave
  CM7 . . . . .72 C6
Stephen Neville Ct CB11 . .43 D8
Stephen's Ct IP4 . . . . .18 B4
Stephenson Rd
  Braintree CM7 . . . . .128 A1
  Clacton-on-S CO15 . . . . . .189 B8
  Colchester CO2 . . . . .110 C6
Stephenson Rd W CO15 . .169 A1
Sterling Cl CO3 . . . . .134 E5
Sterling Complex IP1 . . . . .16 F7
Stevens La CM6 . . . . .152 F6
Stevens Rd CM8 . . . . .176 E1
Stevens Wlk CO4 . . . . .136 F7
Stevenson Rd IP1 . . . . .17 B6
Stewards Cl CO13 . . . . . . .170 F7
Stewart Rd CM2 . . . . .216 A4
Stewarts The CM23 . . . . . .145 E4
Stewarts Way CM23 . . . . . .92 F2
Stilemans Wood CM7 . . . .128 D1
Stiles The CM23 . . . . .210 E3
Stirling Dr CB9 . . . . .8 E8
Stirrup Cl CM1 . . . . .205 E7
Stirrup Mews CO3 . . . . . . .134 E6
Stisted CE Prim Sch CM7 129 B6
Stivvy's Rd CM9 . . . . .208 C3
Stock Chase CM9 . . . . . . .210 B5
Stock Rd CM2 . . . . .216 B2
Stock Terr CM9 . . . . .210 B5
Stockhouse Cl CM9 . . . . . .180 B2
Stockhouse Rd CM9 . . . . .180 B2
Stocking La SG8 . . . . .39 C1
Stockley Cl CB9 . . . . .9 C7
Stockmen Field CM23 . . . .145 C6
Stockmers Rd CM IP9 . . . . .35 A1
Stockwell CM CO1 . . . . . . .135 F7
Stoke Coll CO10 . . . . .11 C3
Stoke Hall Rd IP2 . . . . .17 C4
Stoke High Sch IP2 . . . . . .17 C2
Stoke Park Dr IP2 . . . . . . .17 A1
Stoke Rd Clare CO10 . . . . . .12 A6
  Nayland CO6 . . . . .56 B2
Stoke St IP2 . . . . .17 C4
Stoke-by-Nayland Mid
  Sch CO6 . . . . .56 C6
Stoke-by-Nayland Prim
  Sch CO6 . . . . .56 C6
Stokeash Cl CO16 . . . . . . .188 A3
Stokebridge Maltings CM
  IP2 . . . . .17 C4
Stokes The CO14 . . . . .171 B8
Stone La Tiptree CO5 . . . . .179 A2
  Wrabness CO11 . . . . .88 F5
Stone Lodge La IP2 . . . . . .17 A3
Stone Lodge La W IP2 . . . .16 F3
Stone Lodge Wlk IP2 . . . . .17 B3
Stone Path Dr CM3 . . . . . .193 F3
Stone Rd CO7 . . . . .113 B1
Stone's Green Rd CO12 . .115 E2
Stonebridge Hill CO6 . . . . .104 E7
Stonechat Rd IP2 . . . . .16 D2
Stonecrop CO4 . . . . .109 C2
Stonegrove Rd IP11 . . . . . .221 B1
Stonehall CO10 . . . . .12 B7
Stonehall Dr CO16 . . . . . . .168 D1
Stonehall La CO12 . . . . . . .115 B1
Stoneham St CO6 . . . . .130 F2
Stonehill Way CO5 . . . . . . .201 A6
Stoneleigh Pk CO3 . . . . . . .134 F4
Stoney Comm CM24 . . . . .119 E5
Stoney Common Rd
  CM24 . . . . .119 D5
Stoney La CO7 . . . . .186 A8
Stoney Pl CM24 . . . . .119 E5
Stoneyfield Dr CM24 . . . . .119 E6
Stonham Ave CO16 . . . . . .188 A4
Stony La CM6 . . . . .70 A2
Stopford Ct CM IP1 . . . . . . .17 A6
Stores Rd CO5 . . . . .179 C6
Storms Way CM2 . . . . .206 B2
Stort Lodge CM23 . . . . . . .145 D8
Stort Rd CM23 . . . . .145 F6
Stortford Hall Ind Pk
  CM23 . . . . .146 B7
Stortford Hall Pk CM23 . . .146 B8
Stortford Hall Rd CM
  CM23 . . . . .146 B8
Stortford Rd
  Clavering CB11 . . . . .65 C4

tortford Rd continued
Great Dunmow CM6 ......123 C1
Takeley CM6 ....149 D7
tour Ave IP11 ....221 C1
tour Cl Glemsford CO10 ...2 C2
Harwich CO12 ....90 D2
tour Ct CM7 ....128 D1
tour Gdns CO10 ......34 B4
tour Gn CO10 ....12 B6
tour Rd CO12 ....91 D5
tour St Cavendish CO10 ...13 C8
Manningtree CO11 .....86 D4
Sudbury CO10 ....33 E7
tour Vale Clare CO10 ....12 A6
Stoke by C CO10 ......10 D2
tour Valley Rd CB9 ....9 B7
tour View Ct CO12 ......91 D5
tour Wlk CO4 ....110 E2
tour Wood Nature
Reserve CO12 ....89 C3
tourdale Cl CO11 ....86 A3
tourside IP9 ....91 A8
tourton Rd CM8 ......176 E3
tourview Ave CO11 .....87 A4
tourview Ct CO11 ......87 B4
tow Ct CO4 ....109 F5
tradbroke Rd IP4 .....18 A2
traight Rd Boxted CO4 ...82 F2
Bradfield CO11 ......87 C1
Colchester CO3 ......134 F5
Great Bentley CO7 ....167 A4
traight Way CO2 .....161 A2
trand The IP2 ....37 C8
trasbourg Sq 6 CB9 ......9 B8
tratford Pl 4 CO14 ...171 C7
tratford Rd
Clacton-on-S CO15 ...189 D6
Dedham CO7 ....84 D7
tratford St Mary Prim
Sch CO7 ....58 C1
traw La CO10 ....33 D7
trawberry Cl CM7 ....128 A1
trawberry Fields CB9 ...8 D7
trawberry La CO5 ....179 F3
trawbrook Hill CM3 ...173 E4
treet The Ardleigh CO7 ..111 C6
Ashen CO10 ....11 D1
Belchamp Walter CO10 ..31 C8
Belstead IP8 ....36 C6
Berden CM23 ....92 B8
Birdbrook CO9 ......28 B7
Bradfield CO11 ......87 E1
Bradwell CM7 ......129 D3
Brantham CO11 ......61 A1
Bulmer CO10 ....32 E5
Capel St M IP9 ......35 A1
Chappel CO6 ......106 D5
Cressing CM7 ......156 A6
East Bergholt CO7 ....59 B2
Feering CO5 ....158 E5
Foxearth CO10 ......14 C6
Galleywood CM2 .....216 B2
Gosfield CO9 ......102 E7
Great Hallingbury CM22 ..147 B4
Great Henny CO10 ....33 E3
Great Tey CO6 ......132 C8
Harkstead IP9 ......63 B2
Hatfield Peverel CM3 ...193 F4
Holbrook IP9 ....62 D6
Kirby-le-S CO13 ......143 B1
Little Clacton CO16 ....168 C3
Little Dunmow CM6 ...151 D7
Little Totham CM9 ...197 B5
Little Waltham CM3 ...191 B6
Manuden CM23 ......92 F2
Messing CO5 ......159 D2
Pebmarsh CO9 ......78 A8
Pentlow CO10 ......14 A8
Purleigh CM3 ......220 F1
Ramsey CO12 ......90 A1
Rayne CM7 ......126 F2
Salcott-cum-virley CM9 ..199 B8
Ststed CM7 ......129 C6
Stoke by C CO10 ......11 B3
Tendring CO16 ......140 E5
Terling CM3 ......175 C2
Toppesfield CO9 ......50 B7
Washbrook IP8 ......35 F8
Weeley CO16 ......140 F1
Wherstead IP9 ......37 B6
White Notley CM8 ...155 E1
Wickham Bishops CM8 ..195 F5
Woodham Walter CM9 ..208 D2
Stretford CM3 ......156 D3
Strethall Rd CB11 ......21 C4
Strickmere CO7 ......58 D2
Strood Cl CO5 ......201 B7
Strood The CO5 ......183 C3
Strudwick Cl 10 CM7 ..127 F2
Strutt Cl CM3 ......194 A4
Stuart Cl
Great Baddow CM2 ...217 B6
Ipswich IP4 ......17 F7
Stuart Pawsey Ct CO7 ..137 C1
Stuarts Way CM7 ......128 B2
Stubbs Cl Ipswich IP3 ..18 A1
Kirby Cross CO13 ....170 E7
Lawford CO11 ......86 B4
Stubbs La CM7 ......128 C1
Studd's La CO4 ......109 D4
Stump Cross CB10 ......3 C5
Stump La CM1 ......205 D4
Sturdee Ave IP3 ......18 B3
Sturmer Ct 3 CO2 ...136 A1
Sturmer Rd Haverhill CB9 ...9 F7
Haverhill, Calford Green CB9 ...9 F7
Sturrick La CO7 ......139 D1
Stutton Cl IP9 ......62 A2

Stutton Gn IP9 ....62 C1
Stutton La IP9 ....61 C5
Stutton Rd IP9 ....61 A2
Stylemans La CM22 ...146 B5
Styles CM7 ....71 D2
Sub-Station Rd IP11 ...221 B2
Sudbourne Ave CO16 ...188 A4
Sudbourne Rd IP11 ...221 B5
Sudbury Rd Bulmer CO10 ..32 F6
Bures CO8 ....55 F1
Castle Hedingham CO9 ..52 B4
Felixstowe IP11 ......221 A4
Gestingthorpe CO9 ...31 F2
Great Cornard CO10 ...34 F7
Great Maplestead CO9 ..53 C2
Halstead CO9 ......76 F3
Long Melford CO10 ...15 C3
Stoke-by-N CO6 ......56 C6
Sudbury Sta CO10 ...33 F7
Sudbury Upper Sch CO10 ..15 F1
Sue Ryder Mus CO10 ...1 D1
Suffolk Ave CO5 ......201 D7
Suffolk Cl
Clacton-on-S CO15 ...189 E7
Colchester CO4 ......110 B1
Suffolk Cres CM9 ......209 E1
Suffolk Dr CM2 ......206 A4
Suffolk Ent Pk IP1 ......17 B5
Suffolk Knowle CO8 ...55 F1
Suffolk Rd Ipswich IP4 ..17 D7
Maldon CM9 ......209 E1
Sudbury CO10 ......33 E8
Suffolk Ret Pk IP1 ......17 A6
Suffolk Ski Ctr IP2 ....37 B8
Suffolk Sq CO10 ......33 E8
Suffolk St CO14 ......171 C8
Sugar La CO9 ......74 E7
Sulleys Hill IP7 ......58 B8
Sullivan Cl CO4 ......136 E6
Summer Garden Ct CO9 ..51 E1
Summer Hill Rd CB11 ...43 D8
Summercroft Jun & Inf
Schs CM23 ......146 C8
Summerfield Cl IP4 ...18 D8
Summerfield Ct IP4 ...18 D8
Summerfields CO9 ...51 E1
Sun Lido Square Gdns
CM7 ....127 C2
Sunbank CM6 ......150 E7
Sunbeam Ave CO15 ...203 E6
Sunbury Way CM9 ...220 F8
Sundale Cl CO15 ......189 F6
Sunfield Cl IP4 ......18 B6
Sunflower Cl 5 CM1 ..205 F6
Sunningdale Ave IP4 ..18 D5
Sunningdale Dr IP11 ..221 F6
Sunningdale Fall CM3 ..194 B4
Sunningdale Rd CM1 ..204 E4
Sunningdale Way CO13 .170 E4
Sunny Point CO14 ...144 E3
Sunnyfields Rd CM7 ..102 D2
Sunnyside Braintree CM7 .127 E3
Stansted
Mountfitchet CM24 ...119 B4
Sunnyside Rd CO6 ...107 D5
Sunnyside Way CO16 ..168 C1
Sunnyway Cotts CM3 ..218 E3
Sunray Ave IP11 ......221 F6
Sunrise Ave CM1 ......205 A5
Surbiton Rd IP1 ......16 F8
Surrey Ct CO15 ......189 A3
Surrey La CO5 ......206 F8
Surrey Rd Felixstowe IP11 221 C4
Ipswich IP1 ......17 A6
Sussex Cl CM3 ......206 F8
Sussex Gdns CO15 ...189 E6
Sussex Rd CO3 ......135 C7
Sutherland Ho CM1 ...205 A4
Sutor Cl CM8 ......176 E1
Sutton CE Prim Sch IP9 .62 A2
Sutton Mead CM2 ...206 A4
Sutton Park Ave CO3 ..135 A3
Swallow Cl CO2 ......162 A5
Swallow Field CO6 ...105 B6
Swallow Path CM2 ...216 B5
Swallow Rd IP2 ......16 C3
Swallow's Row CO7 ..140 B1
Swallowdale
Clacton-on-S CO15 ...188 F6
Colchester CO2 ......136 C3
Swan Chase CO5 ......75 E8
Swan Cl Colchester CO4 .136 E5
Hatfield Peverel CM3 ..193 F4
Swan Cotts CM3 ......193 F4
Swan Ct
2 Bishop's Stortford CM23 .145 F6
14 Colchester CO1 ...135 F7
Maldon CM9 ......210 B4
New Mistley CO11 ...87 A3
Sible Hedingham CO9 ..75 E8
Swan Dale CO15 ......188 F6
Swan Farm Mews IP8 ..16 A1
Swan Gr CO6 ......106 C5
Swan Hill IP8 ......16 A1
Swan La Haverhill CB9 ...9 A8
Long Melford CO10 ...15 C7
Margaretting CM4 ...215 D1
Swan Pas 15 CO1 ...135 F7
Swan Rd CO16 ......141 D5
Swan Side CO7 ......127 E5
Sible Hedingham CO9 ..51 E1
Swan Yd CO6 ......131 A2
Swanfield CO10 ......15 C7
Swanscomb Rd CO6 ...105 F5
Swansea Ave IP2 ......17 B1

Swatchway Cl IP3 ......38 B8
Swaynes CO7 ......58 C2
Sweden Cl CO12 ......90 F4
Swedish Est CO11 ...115 B5
Sweet Briar CM23 ...145 B6
Sweet Briar Rd CO3 ..134 C7
Sweet Mead CB10 ......22 B3
Swift Ave CO15 ......203 F6
Swift Cl CM7 ......155 A7
Swinbourne Dr CM7 ..127 D3
Swinton Cl IP2 ......16 E1
Swiss Ave CM1 ......205 A4
Sworders Rd 8 CM23 ..145 F7
Sycamore Cl Ipswich IP8 .16 C1
Takeley CM22 ......148 C2
Witham CM8 ......177 A5
Sycamore Ct CM7 ...127 E1
Sycamore Pl CO7 ...166 E8
Sycamore Rd
Colchester CO4 ......136 D8
Great Cornard CO10 ...34 B7
Heybridge CM9 ......210 C6
Sycamore Way
Brantham CO11 ......60 D1
Chelmsford CM2 ...216 C6
Clacton-on-S CO15 ...188 C3
Kirby Cross CO13 ...170 D6
Sycamores The CM23 ..146 B6
Sydner Cl CM2 ......217 A5
Sydney St
Brightlingsea CO7 ...185 F6
Colchester CO1 ......136 B1
Syers Field CM7 ......74 B2
Sylvan Cl CM7 ......216 B6
Symmons Cl CM7 ...126 F1
Syringa Ct 6 CO4 ...136 E7

T

Taber Pl CM8 ......177 B3
Tabor Ave CM7 ......127 E3
Tabor High (Mid) Sch
CM7 ....127 E3
Tabor High Sch (Upper
Sch) The CM7 ......127 D4
Tabor Rd CO1 ......136 C7
Tabor's Hill CM2 ...216 F7
Tabors Ave CM2 ...216 F8
Tacket St IP4 ......17 D5
Tacon Cl IP11 ......221 C1
Tacon Rd IP11 ......221 C1
Tailors CM23 ......145 B5
Talbot Ave CO15 ...203 F6
Talbot Rd
Little Clacton CO16 ...168 C4
Sudbury CO10 ......15 F2
Talbot St CO12 ......91 D5
Talbots IP11 ......221 B3
Talcott Rd CO4 ......136 A2
Talisman Cl CO5 ...179 D6
Talisman Wlk CO5 ...179 D6
Tall Trees CO4 ......109 E3
Tally Ho CO4 ......110 B4
Tallyho Cnr CO7 ......58 D1
Tamar Rise CM1 ...205 C6
Tamarisk Way
Clacton-on-S CO15 ...203 F6
Colchester CO4 ......136 E8
Tambour Cl CO4 ......136 C8
Tamdown Way CM7 ..127 C4
Tamworth Chase CO2 ..136 A2
Tan La CO16 ......168 F4
Tangerine Cl CO4 ...136 D6
Tanner Cl CO16 ......188 B3
Tanners Mdw CM7 ...128 D2
Tanners Way CB10 ...22 E1
Tanyard The CM6 ...70 A2
Tapestry Ct CO6 ...105 B6
Tapestry Wlk CM7 ...128 D2
Tapley Rd CM3 ......204 F7
Tapsworth Cl CO16 ..188 B5
Tapwoods CO3 ......135 A7
Tara Cl CM7 ......179 D4
Tarragon Cl CO5 ...179 C4
Tarragona Mews CO2 ..136 B4
Tasman Ct CM1 ......204 E5
Tasman Rd 8 ......9 C7
Tasmania Rd IP4 ...18 D6
Tattersall Way CM1 ..215 E7
Tattingstone CE Prim
Sch IP9 ....61 D7
Taunton Rd
Chelmsford CM1 ...205 E5
Felixstowe IP11 ...221 D6
Tavern St IP1 ......17 C6
Taverners Wlk CM8 ..176 F4
Tavistock Rd CM1 ...205 E5
Tawney Cl IP9 ......35 A1
Tawneys Ride CO8 ...80 A8
Taylor Ave CM1 ...204 E5
Taylor Ct CO11 ......135 F7
Taylor Dr CO11 ......86 C4
Taylor's Rd CO5 ...163 F8
Tayspill Ct CO10 ......33 B3
Teak Wlk CM8 ......177 A4
Teal Cl Colchester CO4 .137 A8
Great Notley CM7 ...154 B5
Ipswich IP2 ......16 D3
Teal Way CO5 ......158 D2
Teapot Cnr IP7 ......57 E8
Tedder Cl CO2 ......136 A4
Tees Cl CM8 ......176 E2
Tees Rd CM7 ......205 C6
Teign Dr CM8 ......176 D2

Telford Way CO4 ......110 D6
Temperance Yd CO6 ...105 B6
Templar Rd CM7 ...128 D2
Templar's Ct CB9 ......8 E7
Templars Cl CM8 ...176 F4
Templars Cty Inf Sch
CM8 ....176 F5
Templars Cty Jun Sch
CM8 ....176 F5
Temple Cl CO13 ......171 A6
Temple Ct CO4 ......110 D2
Temple La CM8 ......156 C3
Temple Pattle CO11 ...86 C7
Temple Rd
Colchester CO2 ......135 A2
Ipswich IP3 ......18 C4
Templemead CM8 ...176 F4
Templewood Rd
CO4 ....110 E1
Ten Acre App CM9 ...209 F5
Tenby Rd IP2 ......17 B1
Tendring Cyt Prim Sch
CO16 ....140 F6
Tendring Rd
Little Bentley CO7 ...140 A8
Tendring CO12 ......114 C2
Thorpe-le-S CO16 ...141 D4
Tendring Tech Coll
CO16 ....142 A1
Tendring Tech & Sixth
Form Coll CO14 ...171 A7
Tennyson Cl CM7 ...154 F8
Tennyson Rd
Chelmsford CM1 ...204 F5
Ipswich IP4 ......17 F5
Maldon CM9 ......210 A1
Tenpenny Hill CO7 ...165 E5
Tenter Cl CM7 ......127 F5
Tenter Field CO7 ......58 D1
Tenterfield CM6 ...150 E8
Tenterfield Rd CM9 ..210 A2
Tenterfields CB11 ...42 F1
Tenth Ave CO12 ......120 C2
Terling CE Prim Sch
CM3 ....175 C3
Terling Cl CO2 ......136 A1
Terling Hall Rd
Hatfield Peverel CM3 .193 C7
Terling CM3 ......174 F1
Terling Rd
Hatfield Peverel CM3 .193 F6
Witham CM8 ......176 B3
Terminal Rd N CM24 ..121 B4
Terminal Rd S CM24 ..121 B4
Termitts Chase CM3 ..194 A7
Tern Cl
Haverhill CB9 ......9 C7
Kelvedon CO5 ......158 D3
Tern Rd IP2 ......16 E2
Terndale CO15 ......188 F6
Terra Cotta Pl CO10 ...2 E8
Terrace Hall Chase
CO6 ....109 D6
Terrace The CO10 ...1 D7
Terrace The CM6 ...152 B5
Terrace The CM4 ...194 B5
Tewkesbury Rd CO15 .188 F6
Tey Rd
Aldham CO6 ......106 E1
Coggeshall CO6 ...131 C4
Earls Colne CO6 ...105 D4
Tey Road Cl CO6 ...105 D6
Thackeray Cl CM7 ...155 A8
Thames Ave CM1 ...204 D5
Thames Cl CM7 ......128 D1
Thanet Rd IP4 ......18 B6
Thatchers Dr CO7 ...137 F6
Thatchers The CM23 .145 C5
Thaxted Prim Sch
CM6 ....70 A2
Thaxted Rd
Debden CM6 ......68 C6
Elder Street CB10 ...44 C4
Saffron Walden CB10 .43 F8
Thaxted CB10 ......69 E8
Thaxted Wlk CO2 ...163 A8
The Bungalows CM7 ..100 F5
Theberton Rd IP3 ...18 B1
Thelsford Wlk CO4 ..136 F7
Thetford Cl CM1 ...204 E1
Thetford Rd 1 IP1 ...17 A7
Thieves' Cnr CM1 ...204 A4
Third Ave
Chelmsford CM1 ...205 B5
Clacton-on-S CO15 ..189 C4
Frinton-on-S CO13 ..170 E4
Glemsford CO10 ......2 C5
Halstead CO9 ......77 B1
Harwich CO12 ......91 C3
St Osyth CO16 ......203 B6
Stansted
Mountfitchet CM24 ..120 B2
Walton-on-t-N CO14 .144 E3
Thirlmere Cl CM7 ...154 D7
Thirslet Dr CM9 ...210 C4
Thirtieth St CM24 ...120 F3
Thirtle Cl CO16 ......188 D6
Thistle Cl IP2 ......16 F4
Thistle Down CM7 ...127 A7
Thistledown CO4 ...110 B3
Thistley Cl CM9 ...211 E6
Thistley Cres CB11 ...66 E1
Thistley Green Rd CM7 .128 B2
Thomas Ave IP11 ...221 A8
Thomas Bell Rd CO6 ..105 A6
Thomas Cl CM2 ...205 F3
Thomas Heskin Ct 11
CM23 ....146 A7

Thomas, Lord Audley
Sch CO2 ....135 F2
Thomas Rd CO15 ...188 D4
Thomas St CO7 ......185 F6
Thomas Wakley Cl CO4 .109 F5
Thompson Ave CO3 ...134 F6
Thompson Rd IP1 ...16 F8
Thorley Ctr CM23 ...145 D4
Thorley High CM23 ..145 F2
Thorley Hill CM23 ...145 F2
Thorley Hill JMI Sch
CM23 ....145 F4
Thorley La
Bishop's Stortford CM23 .145 B4
Bishop's Stortford CM23 .145 D3
Thorley Park Rd CM23 .145 C4
Thorn Gr CM23 ......146 B6
Thorn Grove JMI Sch
CM23 ....146 B6
Thorn Way IP11 ...221 C4
Thornbera Cl CM23 ..145 E4
Thornbera Gdns CM23 .145 E4
Thornbera Rd CM23 ..145 E4
Thornberry Ave CO16 .140 F1
Thornbury Rd CO15 ..188 F4
Thornbush La IP8 ...16 A8
Thorncroft CB10 ......22 F2
Thorndon Cl CO16 ...188 A4
Thorne Rd CO5 ......158 B2
Thorney Rd IP9 ......35 A1
Thornfield Ct CO2 ...136 D2
Thornfield Rd CM23 ..145 E8
Thornhayes Cl IP2 ...17 A3
Thornhill CM3 ......220 D1
Thornhill Cl CO13 ...170 F7
Thornley Dr IP4 ......18 C8
Thorns Way CO14 ...171 A8
Thornton Dr CO4 ...109 F2
Thornton Rd CM6 ...148 F7
Thornwood CO4 ...109 F4
Thornwood Cl CO5 ..201 D6
Thoroughfare 9 IP1 ..17 C6
Thoroughgood Rd CO15 188 F3
Thorpe Cross CO16 ..169 D8
Thorpe Park La CO16 .169 B7
Thorpe Rd Beaumont CO16 141 B5
Clacton-on-S CO15 ..188 F6
Kirby Cross CO13 ...169 E7
Weeley CO16 ......141 A2
Thorpe Wlk CO4 ...136 F7
Thorpe-le-Soken Sta
CO16 ....168 F7
Thorrington Cross CO7 .165 F5
Thorrington Rd
Great Bentley CO7 ...166 C8
Little Clacton CO16 ..168 C4
Thorrington Tide Mill
CO7 ....165 E3
Thracian Cl CO2 ...135 A3
Threadneedle St
2 Chelmsford CM1 ..205 B2
Dedham CO7 ......84 F7
Three Acres CO16 ...187 A4
Three Crowns Rd CO4 .109 E2
Three Gates Cl CO9 ..103 D8
Three Mile Hill CM4 ..215 C2
Thremhall Ave
Bishop's Stortford CM23 .146 F8
Great Hallingbury CM24 .147 C8
Takeley CM24 ......121 A2
Thresher Cl CM23 ...145 C5
Threshers End CO3 ..134 D5
Thrift Wood CM3 ...218 F1
Thriftwood Sch The CM2 216 B3
Thrushdale CO15 ...188 F6
Thurlow Pl 10 CB9 ...9 B8
Thurlston Cl CO4 ...110 D1
Thurstable Cl CM9 ...199 E2
Thurstable Rd CM9 ..199 D2
Thurstable Sch CO5 ..179 D6
Thurstable Way CM9 .199 E2
Thurston IP11 ......221 A3
Thyme Mews CM8 ...176 E3
Thyme Rd CO5 ......179 C5
Tiberius St 8 ......9 D7
Tiberius Gdns CM8 ..194 E8
Tideswell Cl CM7 ...128 D4
Tidings Hill CO9 ...103 D8
Tilbury Rd
Great Yeldham CO9 ...30 A3
Ridgewell CO9 ......29 C7
Tile Barn La CO11 ...85 C2
Tile House Rd CO6 ..109 B8
Tilkey Rd CO6 ......130 C3
Tillwicks Cl CO6 ...105 A7
Timber Hill CO1 ...136 C6
Timbers Cl CM7 ...154 B7
Timsons La CM2 ...205 E4
Tinabrook Cl IP2 ...16 E1
Tindal Sq 3 CM1 ...205 B2
Tindal St CM1 ......205 B2
Tindon End Rd CB10 ..46 D2
Tinker Ave CM7 ......73 C6
Tinker St CO12 ......116 D8
Tinnocks La CM0 ...213 B1
Tintagel Way CM9 ...220 E8
Tintern Cl IP2 ......17 A2
Tippett Cl CO4 ......136 E6
Tiptree Hall La CO5 ..179 B2
Tiptree Heath Cty Prim
Sch 179 B3
Tiptree Rd
Great Braxted CM8 ...196 B8
Wickham Bishops CM8 .195 F6

Titania Cl CO4 . . . . .136 F7
Tithe Ct CM8 . . . . .176 E3
Titus Way CO4 . . . . .110 B6
Tobruk Rd
  Chelmsford CM1 . . . . . .204 F6
  Colchester CO2 . . . . . . .135 D3
Tofts Chase CM3 . . . . . . .207 E6
Tofts Wlk 12 CM7 . . . . . . .127 C6
Tog La Great Horkesley CO6 .82 A3
  Little Horkesley CO6 . . . . .81 F3
Toga Ct CO2 . . . . .135 A2
Tokely Rd CO7 . . . . .139 A3
Tokio Rd IP4 . . . . .18 A6
Toll Gate Rd IP9 . . . . .35 A1
Toller Rd IP3 . . . . .17 E3
Tollesbury Cty Prim Sch
  CM9 . . . . .199 D1
Tollesbury Rd CM9 . . . . .198 F3
Tolleshunt D'arcy Prim
  Sch CM9 . . . . .198 D4
Tolleshunt D'arcy Rd
  CM9 . . . . .197 F3
Tollgate Ct CO3 . . . . .134 C6
Tollgate Dr CO3 . . . . .134 C6
Tollgate E CO3 . . . . .134 C6
Tollgate Rbt CO3 . . . . . . .134 C6
Tollgate W CO3 . . . . .134 B5
Tolliday Ct CO7 . . . . .137 A2
Tolworth Rd IP4 . . . . .18 A6
Tom Davies Ho 8 CM7 . . .127 F2
Tom Tit La CM9 . . . . .219 E7
Tom's La CM7 . . . . .72 A6
Tomline Rd
  Felixstowe IP11 . . . . . . .221 E4
  Ipswich IP3 . . . . .18 A4
Tony Webb Cl CO4 . . . . . .110 C4
Tooley's Ct
  (Almshouses) 9 IP4 . . . .17 D5
Top Rd
  Tolleshunt Knights CM9 . .180 A2
  Wimbish CB10 . . . . .45 E3
  Woodham Walter CM9 . . .208 D2
Toppesfield Rd CO9 . . . . . .50 F8
Torquay Rd CM1 . . . . .205 D5
Torrington Ct CM1 . . . . . .205 E5
Tortoiseshell Way CM7 . . .127 E1
Torver Cl CO4 . . . . .154 C6
Tot La CM23 . . . . .119 D4
Totham Hill Gn CM9 . . . . .196 E6
Totlands Dr CO15 . . . . . . .189 A7
Totnes Wlk CM1 . . . . .205 C6
Totteridge Cl CO16 . . . . . .188 D5
Toucan Way CO15 . . . . . . .188 F6
Toulmin Rd CM3 . . . . .194 A4
Tovell's Rd IP4 . . . . .17 F4
Tower Ave CM1 . . . . .204 F4
Tower Ct 4 CB9 . . . . .8 E7
Tower Cut CO7 . . . . .185 E6
Tower Est CO16 . . . . .185 E4
Tower Hill Redoubt
  Fort CO12 . . . . .91 E5
Tower Mill Rd IP1 . . . . .16 F7
Tower Ramparts IP1 . . . . . .17 C6
Tower Ramparts Ctr
  8 IP1 . . . . .17 C6
Tower Rd
  Clacton-on-S CO15 . . . . .188 E1
  Felixstowe IP11 . . . . . . .221 D3
  Wivenhoe CO7 . . . . .137 B2
Tower St Brightlingsea CO7 185 F6
  Ipswich IP1 . . . . .17 C6
Towers Rd CM9 . . . . .210 C5
Town Croft CM1 . . . . .205 A5
Town End Field CM8 . . . . .194 F8
Town St CM6 . . . . .70 A2
Townfield St CM1 . . . . . . .205 B3
Townsend Rd CO5 . . . . . .179 C7
Towse Cl CO16 . . . . .188 C5
Traddles Ct CM1 . . . . .204 F6
Trafalgar Cl IP4 . . . . .17 F6
Trafalgar Cotts CO12 . . . . .90 F3
Trafalgar Ct CM7 . . . . . . .128 B4
Trafalgar Rd
  Clacton-on-S CO15 . . . . .188 E1
  Colchester CO3 . . . . . . .134 E6
Trafalgar Way CM7 . . . . . .128 B4
Trajan Cl CO4 . . . . .110 B6
Tree Cl CO15 . . . . .188 F7
Treetops IP11 . . . . .221 C6
Treetops Ct CO4 . . . . .109 F5
Trefoil Cl IP2 . . . . .16 F4
Trefoil Ct 4 CB9 . . . . .8 F7
Trelawn CM3 . . . . .206 E8
Trenchard Cres CM1 . . . . .205 D8
Trenchard Lodge CM1 . . . .205 D7
Trent Rd Chelmsford CM1 .204 D5
  Ipswich IP3 . . . . .17 F2
  Witham CM8 . . . . .176 E2
Trevose IP11 . . . . .221 F4
Trews Gdns CO5 . . . . .158 C3
Triangle Sh Ctr CO14 . . . .170 F7
Trickett Ct CO7 . . . . .137 B1
Trimley Cl CO16 . . . . .188 B4
Trimley St Mary Cty
  Prim Sch IP11 . . . . .221 A7
Trimley Sta IP11 . . . . .221 A7
Trinity Ave IP11 . . . . .221 E4
Trinity Cl
  Bishop's Stortford CM23 .145 F6
  Manningtree CO11 . . . . . .86 D3
  Rushmere St A IP5 . . . . . .18 F7
  West Mersea CO5 . . . . . .201 C7
  Wivenhoe CO7 . . . . .137 C1

Trinity Ct CO9 . . . . .76 E2
Trinity Farm Ct 11 CO11 . . .86 D4
Trinity Mews CO5 . . . . . . .201 C7
Trinity Rd Chelmsford CM2 205 D2
  Halstead CO9 . . . . .76 D1
  Manningtree CO11 . . . . . .86 D3
Trinity Road Cty Prim
  Sch CM2 . . . . .205 D2
Trinity Sq 21 CO1 . . . . . . .135 F7
Trinity St
  Bishop's Stortford CM23 .145 F6
  Colchester CO1 . . . . . . .135 F7
  Halstead CO9 . . . . .76 D2
  Ipswich IP3 . . . . .17 E4
Trinity Terr 3 CO9 . . . . . . .76 D1
Trinity Way CM23 . . . . . . .145 F6
Triumph Ave CO15 . . . . . .203 E7
Troon Gdns IP4 . . . . .18 B8
Trotters Field CM7 . . . . . .128 B3
Trotwood Cl CM1 . . . . . . .204 E7
Troys Chase CM3 . . . . . . .175 C6
Trunette Rd CO15 . . . . . . .188 C3
Trusses Rd CM0 . . . . .214 F3
Truswell Terr CO11 . . . . . .86 D7
Tryon Ct 5 CO9 . . . . .76 D1
Tucker Dr CM8 . . . . .176 F1
Tucker's Row 4 CM23 . . . .145 F6
Tuddenham Ave IP4 . . . . . .17 A4
Tuddenham Rd IP4 . . . . . . .17 C5
Tudor Cl Brightlingsea CO7 185 E8
  Jaywick CO15 . . . . .188 A1
  Sudbury CO10 . . . . .15 E1
  Walton-on-t-N CO14 . . . .144 D2
  Witham CM8 . . . . .176 F1
Tudor Ct CO5 . . . . .201 C7
Tudor Gn
  Clacton-on-S CO15 . . . . .203 F8
  Jaywick CO15 . . . . .187 F1
  Sudbury CO10 . . . . .15 E2
Tudor House Mus CM7 . . .128 A5
Tudor Par CO15 . . . . .203 G8
Tudor Pl 3 IP4 . . . . .17 D6
Tudor Prim Sch CO10 . . . . .15 F1
Tudor Rd CO10 . . . . .15 E1
Tudor Rose Cl CO3 . . . . . .134 C7
Tudor Works 12 IP4 . . . . . .17 C5
Tudwick Rd CO5 . . . . .197 E6
Tufnell Way CO4 . . . . .109 D2
Tufted Cl CM7 . . . . .154 C5
Tugby Pl CM1 . . . . .204 E6
Tukes Way CB11 . . . . .43 F7
Tulip Cl CM1 . . . . .205 E7
Tulip Way CO16 . . . . .188 C4
Tulip Wlk CO4 . . . . .136 D7
Tumulus Way CO4 . . . . . .134 F2
Tunstall Cl CO16 . . . . .187 B5
Tupman Cl CM1 . . . . .204 D6
Turin St IP2 . . . . .17 C4
Turkentine Cl CO10 . . . . . .34 D5
Turkey Cock La CO3 . . . . .133 E7
Turkey Oaks CM1 . . . . . . .205 D3
Turner Ave CO11 . . . . .86 B5
Turner Ct CO7 . . . . .137 C1
Turner Rd Colchester CO4 .109 F3
  Ipswich IP3 . . . . .38 A8
Turner Village Hospl
  CO4 . . . . .109 F3
Turners Cres CM23 . . . . . .145 C4
Turnpike Ct CM7 . . . . . . .110 E8
Turnstone End 3 CO4 . . . .136 F8
Turpins Ave CO15 . . . . . . .189 C5
Turpins Cl CO15 . . . . .189 C5
Turpins Ct CO15 . . . . .189 C5
Turpins La
  Kirby Cross CO13 . . . . . .170 D7
  Kirby-le-S CO13 . . . . . . .170 D7
Turret Green Ct 7 IP1 . . . .17 C5
Turret La IP4 . . . . .17 C5
Tursan Rd CM8 . . . . .194 E8
Tusser Cl CM8 . . . . .177 B7
Tusser Ct CM2 . . . . .216 B8
Tusser Mews CO3 . . . . . . .134 E7
Tweed Cl CO9 . . . . .103 D8
Twelve Acres CM2 . . . . . .128 D3
Twentyfirst St CM24 . . . . .120 F3
Twin Oaks CM2 . . . . .206 A4
Twining Rd CO3 . . . . .134 E4
Twitten La CM2 . . . . .216 B2
Twitty Fee CM3 . . . . .219 A8
Two Acres IP9 . . . . .35 B2
Twyford Bsns Ctr The
  CM23 . . . . .146 A4
Twyford Bury La CM22 . . .146 A4
Twyford Ct CM23 . . . . . . .146 A5
Twyford Gdns CM23 . . . . .145 F4
Twyford Mill CM22 . . . . . .146 A3
Twyford Rd CM23 . . . . . . .146 A5
Tyburn Hill CO6 . . . . .106 A6
Tydeman Cl CO4 . . . . .134 C4
Tye Gn CO10 . . . . .2 B5
Tye Green Rd CM22 . . . . .120 D6
Tye La CO7 . . . . .137 E3
Tye Rd CO7 . . . . .137 E7
Tye Rd The CO7 . . . . .167 B7
Tyehurst Cres CO4 . . . . . .110 C2
Tyler St Harwich CO12 . . . .90 F5
  Ipswich IP4 . . . . .17 D4
Tylers CB10 . . . . .23 C1
Tylers Cl CM2 . . . . .216 B6
Tylers Gn IP11 . . . . .221 B5
Tylneys Rd CO9 . . . . .77 A3
Tymperley Ct 9 CO1 . . . . .136 A6
Tymperleys Clock Mus
  CO1 . . . . .135 F7
Tyndale Dr CO15 . . . . .188 A1
Tyndales La CM3 . . . . .219 B5
Tyne Way CM1 . . . . .204 D5

Tynedale Ct CO4 . . . . .110 B4
Tynedale Sq CO4 . . . . .110 B4
Tyrells Cl CM2 . . . . .205 E4
Tyrells Way CM2 . . . . .216 F2
Tyrrells Cty Prim Sch
  The CM1 . . . . .205 E5
Tyssen Mead CM3 . . . . . . .206 E8
Tythe Cl CM1 . . . . .205 E8
Tythings The CO9 . . . . . . .103 D8

U

Ufford Pl 6 CB9 . . . . .9 B8
Ullswater Cl CM7 . . . . .154 C6
Ulting Hall Rd CM9 . . . . . .208 E7
Ulting La CM9 . . . . .208 E6
Ulting Rd CM3 . . . . .194 C2
Una Rd CO12 . . . . .90 F5
Undercliff Rd W IP11 . . . . .221 D3
Union Rd CO15 . . . . .203 G8
Union St 11 IP4 . . . . .17 D6
Unity Cl CO2 . . . . .136 B4
Unity St IP3 . . . . .17 E4
Univ Coll Suffolk IP4 . . . . .17 E5
Univ of Essex CO4 . . . . . .136 F4
Upland Cres CO5 . . . . .201 C7
Upland Dr CO4 . . . . .110 C2
Upland Rd Ipswich IP4 . . . .18 A6
  West Mersea CO5 . . . . . .201 C7
Uplands Cres CO10 . . . . . .15 E1
Uplands Ct CO15 . . . . .188 D1
Uplands Dr CM1 . . . . .205 D7
Uplands Mid Sch CO10 . . .15 F1
Uplands Rd
  Clacton-on-S CO15 . . . . .188 D1
  Sudbury CO10 . . . . .15 E1
Upper Acres CM8 . . . . . . .176 F5
Upper Barclay St 12 IP4 . .17 D6
Upper Branston Rd CO15 188 D4
Upper Bridge Rd CM2 . . . .205 A1
Upper Brook St IP4 . . . . . .17 C5
Upper Cavendish St IP3 . . .18 A5
Upper Chapel St CO9 . . . . .76 E2
Upper Chase 2 CM2 . . . . .216 A8
Upper East St CO10 . . . . . .33 F8
Upper Farm Rd CO10 . . . . .29 D8
Upper Fenn Rd CO9 . . . . . .77 A2
Upper Fourth Ave CO13 . .170 F5
Upper High St 1 IP1 . . . . .17 C6
Upper Holt St CO6 . . . . . .105 C6
Upper Mill Field CM6 . . . . .150 E7
Upper Moors CM3 . . . . . . .190 F7
Upper Orwell St IP4 . . . . . .17 D5
Upper Park Rd
  Brightlingsea CO7 . . . . . .185 E7
  Clacton-on-S CO15 . . . . .188 D3
Upper Rd CO10 . . . . .55 E8
Upper Roman Rd CM2 . . . .205 B1
Upper Second Ave CO13 .170 E5
Upper St Stanstead CO10 . . .2 E8
  Stratford St M CO7 . . . . . .58 D1
Upper Third Ave CO13 . . . .170 E5
Upper Trinity Rd CO9 . . . . .76 E1
Upperfield Dr IP11 . . . . . . .221 F6
Upsheres IP11 . . . . .43 F8
Upton Cl Ipswich IP4 . . . . .17 E6
  West Bergholt CO6 . . . . .108 D4
Urban Rd CM23 . . . . .146 B7
Usterdale Rd CB10 . . . . . . .22 E3
Uxbridge Cres IP3 . . . . . . .18 C1

V

Valance Rd CB11 . . . . .65 A6
Vale Cl CO4 . . . . .110 E2
Vale End CM2 . . . . .216 C3
Vale La IP9 . . . . .61 B4
Valentine Ct CM7 . . . . . . .127 E4
Valentine Way CM8 . . . . . .156 D3
Valentines Dr CO4 . . . . . . .110 C1
Valfreda Way CO7 . . . . . . .137 B2
Valkyrie Cl CM9 . . . . .199 D2
Valletta Cl CM1 . . . . .205 A3
Valley Bridge CM1 . . . . . . .205 B6
Valley Cl Brantham CO11 . . .60 D1
  Colchester CO3 . . . . . . .134 E3
Valley Cres CO6 . . . . .108 E3
Valley La Tattingstone IP9 . .36 F4
  Wherstead IP9 . . . . .37 A3
Valley Rd Braintree CM7 . .128 A4
  Clacton-on-S CO15 . . . . .189 A5
  Colchester CO4 . . . . . . .136 F4
  Harwich CO12 . . . . .90 D2
  Ipswich IP1 . . . . .17 B8
  Sudbury CO10 . . . . .34 F8
  Wivenhoe CO7 . . . . .164 C8
Valley View
  Finchingfield CM7 . . . . . .72 D6
  Stanstead CO10 . . . . .2 F7
  West Bergholt CO6 . . . . .108 E3
Valley View Cl CO4 . . . . . .110 A4
Valley Wlk IP11 . . . . .221 D5
Valleybridge Rd CO15 . . . .189 A5
Valleyview Dr IP4 . . . . .18 F4
Van Dieman's La CM2 . . . .216 C8
Van Dieman's Rd CM2 . . . .216 C8
Van Dyck Rd CO3 . . . . . . .135 B5
Vandenbury Circ CM7 . . . . .73 D6
Vandyck Rd IP3 . . . . .38 A8
Vane Ct CM8 . . . . .177 A5
Vane La CO6 . . . . .131 A2
Vanessa Dr CO7 . . . . .137 B1
Vanguard Way 7 CB9 . . . . .9 B8
Vanners Rd CB9 . . . . .9 A7
Vansittart St CO12 . . . . . . .91 D5

Varden Cl CM1 . . . . .204 F6
Vaughan Cl CM7 . . . . .126 F2
Vaughan St 9 IP2 . . . . .17 C4
Vaux Ave CO12 . . . . .90 F1
Vauxhall Ave CO15 . . . . . .203 E6
Vauxhall Dr CM7 . . . . .127 D2
Vellacotts CM1 . . . . .205 B7
Venmore Dr CM6 . . . . .150 E8
Ventnor Dr CO15 . . . . .189 A8
Ventris Cl IP2 . . . . .16 D5
Vermeer Ride CM1 . . . . . .205 D7
Vermont Cl CO15 . . . . .189 A4
Vermont Rd IP4 . . . . .17 D7
Vernon Cl CM23 . . . . .145 E4
Vernon St IP2 . . . . .17 C4
Vernon Way CM7 . . . . .128 C5
Vernon's Cl CM22 . . . . .94 F4
Veronica Wlk CO4 . . . . . . .136 E7
Vesta Cl CO6 . . . . .130 F2
Veyses End CO7 . . . . .58 D2
Viaduct Rd CM1 . . . . .205 A2
Viborg Gdns CM9 . . . . . . .220 E8
Vicarage Ave CM8 . . . . . . .155 F1
Vicarage Cl
  18 Bishop's Stortford CM23 .145 F7
  Panfield CM7 . . . . .126 A8
  Tolleshunt D'arcy CM9 . . .198 D4
Vicarage Cres CM3 . . . . . .194 B4
Vicarage Field CO10 . . . . . .34 B5
Vicarage Gdns CO15 . . . . .188 E2
Vicarage La Berden CM23 . .92 B8
  Great Baddow CM2 . . . . .216 F5
  Thaxted CM6 . . . . .70 A3
  Thorpe-le-S CO16 . . . . . .141 F2
  Ugley CM22 . . . . .93 E5
  2 Walton-on-t-N CO14 . . .171 C8
  Wherstead IP9 . . . . .37 B5
Vicarage Mead CM6 . . . . . .70 A3
Vicarage Meadow CO9 . . . .76 E1
Vicarage Mews CM2 . . . . .216 F4
Vicarage Rd
  Belchamp St P CO10 . . . .13 A1
  Chelmsford CM2 . . . . . . .216 B8
  Felixstowe IP11 . . . . . . .221 C4
  Finchingfield CM7 . . . . . .72 D6
Vicars Orch CO10 . . . . .32 E5
Vicerons Pl CM23 . . . . . . .145 D4
Viceroy Cl CO2 . . . . .136 B3
Victor Rd CO1 . . . . .136 B6
Victoria Ave
  Kirby-le-S CO13 . . . . . . .170 D8
  Saffron Walden CB11 . . . .22 E1
Victoria Chase CO1 . . . . . .135 E8
Victoria Cl CO7 . . . . .137 B2
Victoria Cres
  Chelmsford CM1 . . . . . . .205 A3
  Lawford CO11 . . . . .86 C4
Victoria Ct
  Clacton-on-S CO15 . . . . .188 F3
  Colchester CO3 . . . . . . .134 F7
  Harwich CO12 . . . . .91 C3
Victoria Espl CO5 . . . . . . .201 E5
Victoria Gdns
  Colchester CO4 . . . . . . .110 B3
  Saffron Walden CB11 . . . .22 E1
Victoria Ho
  Felixstowe IP11 . . . . . . .221 E4
  Ipswich IP2 . . . . .17 B4
Victoria Pl
  Brightlingsea CO7 . . . . . .185 F6
  Colchester CO1 . . . . . . .136 B6
Victoria Rd
  Chelmsford CM1 . . . . . . .205 B3
  Clacton-on-S CO15 . . . . .189 A3
  Colchester CO3 . . . . . . .135 C6
  Felixstowe IP11 . . . . . . .221 D3
  Haverhill CB9 . . . . .8 D7
  Maldon CM9 . . . . .210 A2
  Walton-on-t-N CO14 . . . .171 C8
  Weeley Heath CO16 . . . . .168 B5
  Writtle CM1 . . . . .204 A1
Victoria Rd S CM1 . . . . . . .205 B2
Victoria St Braintree CM7 .128 A2
  Felixstowe IP11 . . . . . . .221 E4
  Harwich CO12 . . . . .91 D4
  Ipswich IP1 . . . . .17 A6
Victory Gdns CM7 . . . . . . .128 B4
Victory Rd
  Clacton-on-S CO15 . . . . .188 D3
  Ipswich IP4 . . . . .18 A7
  West Mersea CO5 . . . . . .201 A6
Vienna Ct CO12 . . . . .91 A1
Viking Rd CM9 . . . . .209 E1
Viking Way CO15 . . . . .189 F6
Villa Ct 4 CO1 . . . . .136 C6
Villa Ho CO3 . . . . .134 C6
Villa Rd CO3 . . . . .134 C5
Village Cl
  Kirby Cross CO13 . . . . . .170 D7
  Little Clacton CO16 . . . . .168 D1
Village Gate CM2 . . . . .206 A2
Village Sq CM2 . . . . .206 A3
Village Way CO15 . . . . . . .170 D6
Villiers Pl CM3 . . . . .206 E8
Villiers-Sur-Marne
  Ave CM23 . . . . .145 D4
Vince Cl CO5 . . . . .201 C6
Vincent Cl IP1 . . . . .16 E8
Vine Ct CO7 . . . . .137 C3
Vine Dr CO7 . . . . .137 C3
Vine Farm Rd CO7 . . . . . . .137 C3
Vine Par CO7 . . . . .137 C3
Vine St CM7 . . . . .72 B2
Vine Wlk IP9 . . . . .35 A1
Vinesse Rd CO6 . . . . .81 D3

Vineway The CO12 . . . . . . .91 E7
Vineyard Gate 4 CO2 . . . .135 E7
Vineyard St CO2 . . . . .135 E7
Vineyards The
  Braintree CM7 . . . . .153 C6
  Great Baddow CM2 . . . . .216 F6
Vinnicombe Ct 3 IP2 . . . . .16 E3
Vint Cres CO3 . . . . .135 C6
Viola Wlk CO4 . . . . .136 E6
Violet Cl Chelmsford CM1 .205 E7
  Ipswich IP2 . . . . .16 F1
Virgil Rd CM8 . . . . .176 F1
Virginia Cl CO15 . . . . .188 A4
Virley Cl CM9 . . . . .210 C8
Viscount Dr CO4 . . . . .110 C4
Vista Ave CO13 . . . . .143 C5
Vista Rd CO15 . . . . .189 A3
Vitllus Cl CO4 . . . . .110 B4
Vivian Ct CO14 . . . . .171 C4

W

Waddesdon Rd CO12 . . . . .91 D3
Wade Rd CO15 . . . . .189 B6
Wade Reach CO14 . . . . . . .171 B6
Wadgate Rd IP11 . . . . .221 C6
Wadhurst Rd IP3 . . . . .18 D3
Wagtail Dr CM9 . . . . .210 C6
Wainsfield Villas CM6 . . . . .70 B3
Wakefield Cl
  Colchester CO1 . . . . . . .136 A4
  Great Chesterford CB10 . . .3 D7
Wakelin Way CM8 . . . . . . .177 B8
Wakes St CO6 . . . . .106 C2
Wakeshall La C10 . . . . .30 C5
Waldeck Ct CB11 . . . . .43 D7
Waldegrave Cl CO11 . . . . . .86 B5
Waldegrave Rd CO11 . . . . .86 C5
Waldegrave Way CO11 . . . .86 B5
Waldegraves La CO5 . . . . .201 G5
Waldegraves The CO8 . . . . .79 F7
Walden Ave CO15 . . . . .44 E
Walden Castle CB10 . . . . . .22 D
Walden Cl CM3 . . . . .196 A4
Walden Ho CO13 . . . . .170 F
Walden House Rd CM9 . . .196 A4
Walden Pl CB10 . . . . .22 D
Walden Rd Ashdon CB10 . .23 C3
  Great Chesterford CB10 . . .3 E
  Hadstock CB1 . . . . .5 B
  Littlebury CB10 . . . . .21 F
  Radwinter CB10 . . . . .45 D
  Sewards End CB10 . . . . . .23 D
  Thaxted CM6 . . . . .69 F
  Wendens Ambo CB11 . . . .42 F
  Wendens Ambo CB11 . . . .43 A
Walden Way CO13 . . . . . . .171 A4
Waldgrooms CM6 . . . . . . .123 C
Waldingfield Rd CO10 . . . . .33 F
Walford Pl CM2 . . . . .205 F2
Walford Way CO6 . . . . . . .131 A4
Walk The Eight Ash G CO6 .134 A4
  Felixstowe IP11 . . . . . . .221 C
  10 Ipswich IP1 . . . . .17 C
Walker Cl IP3 . . . . .18 C
Walkers Cl CM1 . . . . .205 D
Wall Ct 6 CM7 . . . . .127 F
Wall La CM7 . . . . .88 D
Wall St CO16 . . . . .202 E
Wallace Binder CM9 . . . . . .209 F1
Wallace Cres CM2 . . . . . . .216 B8
Wallace La CM3 . . . . .172 B2
Wallace Rd IP1 . . . . .16 E
Wallace's La CM3 . . . . .192 F
Wallasea Gdns CM1 . . . . . .205 F
Waller's Gr IP2 . . . . .16 F
Wallflower Ct 11 CM1 . . . .205 E
Wallis Ct CO3 . . . . .134 E
Walls The CO11 . . . . .86 E
Walnut Dr
  Bishop's Stortford CM23 .145 D
  Witham CM8 . . . . .177 A4
Walnut Gr CM7 . . . . .127 E
Walnut Tree Cotts CM3 . . .190 E
Walnut Tree La
  Farnham CM23 . . . . .118 E4
  Harkstead IP9 . . . . .63 B2
  Sudbury CO10 . . . . .33 D
Walnut Tree Way
  Colchester CO2 . . . . . . .135 B3
  Tiptree CO5 . . . . .179 C4
Walnut Way
  Brightlingsea CO7 . . . . . .185 E4
  Clacton-on-S CO15 . . . . .188 C4
Walnuttree Hospl CO10 . . .33 D2
Walsingham Cl CO10 . . . . .34 C5
Walsingham Rd CO2 . . . . .135 F6
Walter Porter Ct CO4 . . . . .110 D
Walter Radcliffe Way
  CO7 . . . . .164 C7
Walter Way CM8 . . . . .156 D4
Walters Cl IP2 . . . . .216 C3
Walters Yd 6 CO1 . . . . . . .135 F
Waltham Cl IP2 . . . . .17 A2
Waltham Glen CM2 . . . . . .216 C
Waltham Rd
  Boreham CM3 . . . . .193 A3
  Terling CM3 . . . . .175 A2
Waltham Way CO13 . . . . . .171 A4
Walton Ave IP11 . . . . .221 A4
Walton Ct Colchester CO7 .136 F4
  Felixstowe IP11 . . . . . . .221 A4
Walton Ho 4 Ipswich IP1 . .17 C
  Walton-on-t-N CO14 . . . .171 B
Walton Maritime Mus
  CO14 . . . . .144 D1
Walton Prim Sch CO14 . . .144 D1

Walton Rd
Clacton-on-S CO15 ....189 A3
Frinton-on-S CO13 ....170 F6
Kirby-le-S CO13 ....143 A1
Kirby-le-S CO13 ....170 E8
Thorpe-le-S CO13, CO16 ..142 D2
Walton-on-t-N CO13 ....171 B7
Walton-On-Naze Sta
CO14 ....171 C7
Wantz Chase CM9 ....210 A2
Wantz Haven CM9 ....210 A2
Wantz Rd CM9 ....210 A2
Wapping La CO7 ....165 B2
Warburton Ave CO9 ....75 D8
Ward Cres CM23 ....145 E6
Ward Rd IP8 ....16 B2
Warde Chase CO14 ....171 B8
Wardle Way CM1 ....204 E7
Wardley Cl IP2 ....16 D1
Wards Croft CB11 ....43 D7
Wareham Ave IP3 ....18 C2
Warehouse Ct CM6 ....124 F4
Warehouse Villas CM6 ..125 A4
Wargrave Rd CO15 ....188 D4
Warham Rd CO12 ....90 F1
Warley Cl CM7 ....128 C3
Warley Way CO13 ....171 B6
Warner Cl CM7 ....126 F1
Warner Dr CM7 ....127 D4
Warner Way CO10 ....34 A8
Warners CM6 ....150 D8
Warnham Cl CO16 ....188 B6
Warren Cl Broomfield CM1 191 B3
Takeley CM22 ....148 D2
Warren Ct 12 CB9 ....8 E7
Warren Heath Ave IP3 ..18 D2
Warren Heath Rd IP3 ..18 D2
Warren La CO3 ....134 C2
Warren Rd Braintree CM7 .128 C2
Halstead CO9 ....76 D1
Warrens The
Kirby Cross CO13 ....170 E6
Wickham Bishops CM8 ..195 F6
Warrenside CM7 ....155 A8
Warrington Rd IP1 ....17 E7
Warwick Bailey Cl CO4 .109 D2
Warwick Cl Braintree CM7 128 B4
Little Easton CM6 ....122 F5
Maldon CM9 ....210 A1
Warwick Cres
Clacton-on-S CO15 ....188 E3
Maldon CM9 ....210 A1
Warwick Ct 2 CB9 ....8 E8
Warwick Dr CM9 ....210 A1
Warwick Rd
Bishop's Stortford CM23 .146 B6
Clacton-on-S CO15 ....188 E3
Ipswich IP4 ....17 E6
Takeley CM6 ....148 E7
Warwick Sq CM1 ....204 F4
Wash Cnr CO6 ....107 C3
Wash La
Clacton-on-S CO15 ....188 D1
Little Totham CM9 ....211 B7
Washford Gdns CO15 ..188 D2
Washington Cl CM9 ....209 E1
Washington Ct
Colchester CO3 ....134 E5
Maldon CM9 ....209 E1
Washington Rd
Harwich CO12 ....91 A2
Maldon CM9 ....209 F1
Wasses Cnr CO16 ....141 D5
Wat Tyler Wlk 1 CO1 ..135 F7
Watch House La CM6 ..124 F5
Watchouse Rd CM2 ....216 C3
Water La
Bishop's Stortford CM23 .145 F8
Bures CO8 ....55 E1
Cavendish CO10 ....1 D2
Colchester CO3 ....135 D8
Debden CB11 ....44 B1
Great Easton CM6 ....122 C7
Helions Bumpstead CB9 ..26 D7
Little Horkesley CO6 ....81 F8
Newport CB11 ....43 A1
Pebmarsh CO9 ....78 A7
Radwinter CB10 ....45 E8
Shalford CM7 ....100 F3
Stansted
Mountfitchet CM24 ....119 E6
Steeple Bumpstead CB9 ..27 B6
Ststed CM7 ....129 C5
Stoke-by-N CO6 ....56 E8
Sturmer CB9 ....9 F5
Waterglade Pk CO15 ..188 E2
Waterhouse La
Ardleigh CO7 ....112 B5
Chelmsford CM1 ....204 F1
Waterhouse St CM1 ....204 F1
Waterloo La CM1 ....205 C2
Waterloo Rd IP1 ....17 A7
Watermill Rd CO5 ....158 E4
Waterside
Brightlingsea CO7 ....185 F5
Stansted
Mountfitchet CM24 ....119 E6
Waterside Rd CM0 ....214 F3
Waterson Vale CM2 ....216 C8
Waterville Mews CO2 ..136 B3
Waterwick Hill CB11 ....40 B1
Waterworks Cl CO2 ....163 A8
Waterworks Dr CO16 ..188 B5
Waterworks St 1 IP4 ..17 D5
Watery La Bradwell CM7 .129 C1
Coggeshall CO6 ....130 A1
Great Dunmow CM6 ....150 A2

Watery La *continued*
Manuden CM23 ....92 C1
Watling La CM6 ....69 F3
Watling St CM6 ....70 F3
Watson Rd CO15 ....188 E3
Watson's Cl CB10 ....47 B4
Watts Cl CM6 ....151 B4
Watts Rd CO2 ....135 B2
Watts Yd CM23 ....93 A2
Wave Bridge Cl CM9 ....210 B5
Wavell Ave CO2 ....135 C4
Wavell Cl CM1 ....205 D8
Waveney Dr CM1 ....205 C6
Waveney Rd
Felixstowe IP11 ....221 C3
Ipswich IP1 ....16 E8
Waveney Terr CB9 ....9 A7
Way Bank La CO10 ....10 E7
Wayback The CB10 ....22 E2
Wayside CM3 ....218 E8
Waytemore Rd CM23 ..145 E6
Waytmore Castle CM23 .146 A7
Wear Dr CM1 ....205 D6
Weathervane Cotts CM7 .72 B1
Weaver Cl IP1 ....16 D8
Weaver St CM23 ....145 C4
Weaverhead Cl CM6 ....70 A3
Weaverhead La CM6 ....70 A3
Weavers Cl Braintree CM7 127 F3
Colchester CO3 ....134 F5
Weavers Ct Halstead CO9 .76 E1
6 Sudbury CO10 ....33 E7
Weavers Dr CO10 ....2 B4
Weavers Gn CO6 ....107 D6
Weavers La CO10 ....33 E7
Weavers Row CO9 ....76 F1
Weavers Terr 7 CO10 ..33 E7
Weaversfield CM8 ....156 C5
Webb St IP2 ....17 C3
Webster Cl CO9 ....75 D8
Weddell Rd CB9 ....9 C6
Wedgewood Dr CO4 ....109 E2
Wedow Rd CM6 ....70 A3
Weeley By-Pass Rd
CO16 ....140 E1
Weeley CE Prim Sch
CO16 ....167 F8
Weeley Rd
Great Bentley CO7 ....166 F5
Great Bentley CO7 ....166 F6
Little Clacton CO16 ....168 C4
Weeley Sta CO16 ....167 F8
Weggs Willow CO4 ....136 C7
Weighbridge Ct CB11 ..43 D8
Weight Rd CM2 ....205 C2
Weir La CO2,CO5 ....163 C7
Welhams Way CO11 ....86 D7
Well Field Halstead CO9 .103 F8
Writtle CM1 ....204 A1
Well La Clare CO10 ....12 B7
Danbury CM3 ....218 C2
Easthorpe CO5 ....160 A6
Galleywood CM2 ....216 B2
Well Side CO6 ....132 E3
Well St CO7 ....185 E7
Well Terr CM9 ....210 B5
Well's St 3 CM1 ....205 A3
Well-Green Cl CB11 ....43 E7
Welland Ave CM1 ....204 C5
Wellands CM8 ....195 E5
Wellands Cl CM8 ....195 D5
Weller Gr CM1 ....204 E7
Wellesley Cl CO3 ....134 F5
Wellesley Ho 7 CO3 ..135 E6
Wellesley Rd
Clacton-on-S CO15 ....188 E4
Colchester CO3 ....135 E6
Ipswich IP4 ....17 F5
Wellfield Way CO13 ....170 D7
Wellington Cl
Braintree CM7 ....128 C4
Chelmsford CM1 ....204 D5
Wellington Ct 5 IP1 ..17 A7
Wellington Rd
Harwich CO12 ....91 E6
Maldon CM9 ....209 F2
Wellington St
Brightlingsea CO7 ....185 F6
4 Colchester CO2 ....135 E6
Ipswich IP1 ....17 A7
Wellington Terr 7 CB9 ..8 E7
Wellmeads CM2 ....216 B8
Wells Cl 4 IP4 ....17 E6
Wells Ct Chelmsford CM1 .205 D5
Great Dunmow CM6 ....123 C1
Wells Hall Cty Prim Sch
CO10 ....34 B5
Wells Hall Rd CO10 ....34 C4
Wells Mead CB11 ....67 D4
Wells Rd CO1 ....136 B8
Wellum Cl 8 CB9 ....9 A7
Welshwood Park Rd CO4 110 F2
Wenden Rd CB11 ....43 B7
Wendy Cl IP9 ....63 D7
Wenham La CO7 ....59 D6
Wenham Rd IP8 ....35 C7
Wenlock Rd CO16 ....167 F6
Wents Cl CO7 ....139 E1
Wentworth Cl CM3 ....194 B4
Wentworth Cres CM7 ..127 F3
Wentworth Cty Prim
Sch CM9 ....209 F1
Wentworth Dr
Bishop's Stortford CM23 .145 D6
Ipswich IP9 ....16 C2
Wentworth
Meadows CM9 ....209 F2
Wentworth Terr 5 CB9 ..8 E8

Wesel Ave IP11 ....221 B3
Wesley Ave CO4 ....136 C8
Wesley End Rd CO9 ....28 C4
West Acre Ct CO3 ....135 B7
West Area IP1 ....16 C7
West Bank
Clacton-on-S CM1 ....204 F5
Clacton-on-S CO15 ....188 E2
West Bank Ferry
Terminal IP2 ....17 C7
West Belvedere CM3 ....218 F7
West Bowers Rd CM9 ..208 A2
West Chase CM9 ....209 F3
West Ct CO3 ....134 F7
West Dock Rd CO12 ....90 E5
West Dr 73 C3
West End La CO12 ....91 B1
West End Rd Ipswich IP1 .17 A5
Tiptree CO5 ....179 A3
West Fields CB11 ....43 E8
West Green Cotts CO16 ..86 A7
West Hanningfield Rd
CM2 ....217 A3
West Lawn
Galleywood CM2 ....216 C2
Ipswich IP4 ....18 C8
West Lodge Rd CO3 ....135 D6
West Mersea Cty Prim
Sch 201 C6
West Mill Gn IP9 ....60 E6
West Rd
Bishop's Stortford CM23 .145 F4
Clacton-on-S CO15 ....203 H8
Halstead CO9 ....76 E1
Ipswich IP3 ....38 E8
Saffron Walden CB11 ....43 D8
Stansted
Mountfitchet CM24 ....119 E6
West Sq
6 Chelmsford CM1 ....205 B2
Maldon CM9 ....209 F3
West St Coggeshall CO6 .130 E1
Colchester CO2 ....135 E6
Harwich CO12 ....91 D6
Rowhedge CO5 ....163 F8
Tollesbury CM9 ....199 C1
Walton-on-t-N CO14 ....171 C1
Wivenhoe CO7 ....164 B8
West Station Ind Est
CM9 ....220 E8
West Station St CM9 ....209 E1
West Stockwell St CO1 .135 F7
West View CM22 ....148 C8
West View Cl CO4 ....110 B3
West Wood Hill CO4 ....109 B3
West Yd CO9 ....103 E8
Westbourne Ct 1 CB9 ..9 A8
Westbourne Gr CM2 ....216 D7
Westbourne Rd IP1 ....16 E8
Westbury Cl CO6 ....133 D5
Westbury Rd
Great Holland CO13 ....170 A5
Ipswich IP4 ....18 B8
Westcliff Ct CO15 ....188 E1
Westcott Cl CO16 ....188 D6
Westerdale CM1 ....205 D7
Westerfield La CM7 ....17 D7
Westerfield Rd IP4 ....17 D8
Westergreen Meadow
CM7 ....127 E1
Westerings Danbury CM3 .218 F2
Purleigh CM3 ....220 D1
Westerings The CM2 ....216 F5
Westerlings The CM7 ..155 E6
Western Cl
Rushmere St A IP4 ....18 F4
Silver End CM8 ....156 E3
Western Ho CO5 ....158 C2
Western La CM8 ....156 E3
Western Prom CO16 ....185 E5
Western Rd
Brightlingsea CO7 ....185 E6
Silver End CM8 ....156 F3
Western's End CO11 ....86 D8
Westfield CO10 ....12 A6
Westfield Ave CM1 ....205 A4
Westfield Cl CM23 ....145 E8
Westfield Cty Prim Sch
CB9 ....9 B7
Westfield Dr CO6 ....131 A3
Westfield Rd CM23 ....145 E8
Westgate St IP1 ....17 C6
Westholme Rd IP1 ....17 A8
Westlake Cres CO7 ....137 A2
Westlands Cty Inf Sch
CM1 ....204 E2
Westlands Prim Sch
CM1 ....204 E2
Westleton Way IP11 ....221 B5
Westley La CB10 ....22 D5
Westminster Cl IP4 ....18 B5
Westminster Ct
Clacton-on-S CO15 ....189 B3
Colchester CO2 ....136 C4
Westminster Gdns CM7 .128 B4
Westmorland Cl CO11 ..87 B3
Weston Rd CO2 ....136 B4
Westridge Rd CO15 ....189 A6
Westropps CO10 ....15 C5
Westside Ctr CO3 ....134 A4
Westway
Chelmsford CM1 ....215 E8
Colchester CO1, CO3 ....135 E8
Westwood Ave IP1 ....17 A8
Westwood Dr CO5 ....201 E4
Wet La CO4 ....82 E6
Wetherfield CM24 ....119 D7
Wetherfield CE Prim
Sch CM7 ....73 C3

Wethersfield Rd
Blackheath CO2 ....163 A8
Sible Hedingham CO9 ....51 C1
Wetzlar Cl CM1 ....136 B4
Weymouth Cl CO15 ....203 J8
Weymouth Rd
Chelmsford CM1 ....205 E6
Ipswich IP4 ....17 F6
Whalebone Cnr CO4 ....83 F7
Whaley Rd CO4 ....136 C8
Wharf La CO6 ....79 F8
Wharf Rd
12 Bishop's Stortford CM23 .145 F6
Chelmsford CM2 ....205 C2
Heybridge Basin CM9 ....210 F4
Wharfe Cl CM1 ....176 E2
Wheat Croft CM23 ....145 E4
Wheater Ind Est CM7 ..177 B1
Wheatfield Rd CO3 ....134 D5
Wheatfield Way CM1 ..204 F3
Wheatlands CO7 ....137 F6
Wheatley Ave CM7 ....128 C3
Wheaton Rd CM8 ....177 B2
Wheatsheaf Cl CO10 ..88 D3
Wheatsheaf Ct 14 CO1 .136 A6
Wheatsheaf La CO11 ..88 D3
Wheeler Cl CO4 ....136 E6
Wheeler's Hill CM3 ....191 D6
Wheelwrights CO3 ....134 C8
Wheelwrights The IP11 .221 A8
Wherry La 18 IP4 ....17 D5
Wherstead Rd Ipswich IP2 .17 C2
Ipswich IP2 ....17 C3
Whinchat Cl CM18 ....16 D3
Whinfield Ave CO12 ....90 F1
Whitbreads Farm La
CM3 ....173 D4
Whitby Rd IP4 ....17 F8
White Arch Pl CO4 ....83 B6
White Barns CM3 ....172 B6
White Bear CM24 ....119 E8
White Cotts CM3 ....174 E5
White Court Cty Prim
Sch 154 C6
White Elm Rd CM3 ....219 A2
White Elm St IP3 ....17 E4
White Hart La
Chelmsford CM1 ....205 F8
West Bergholt CO6 ....108 E5
White Horse Ave CO9 ..103 D8
White Horse Hill IP9 ....36 D1
White Horse La
Maldon CM9 ....209 F2
Newport CB11 ....43 A1
Witham CM8 ....176 F3
White Horse Rd
Capel St M IP9 ....35 B1
East Bergholt CO7 ....59 E1
White Lodge Cres CO16 .142 C1
White Mead CM1 ....191 B3
White Notley CE Prim
Sch CM8 ....155 F1
White Notley Sta CM8 ..155 F2
White St CM6 ....150 D8
Whitebeam Cl CM2 ....215 F7
Whiteditch La CB11 ....42 F2
Whitefriars Way CO3 ..135 A5
Whitegate Rd CO7 ....186 A6
Whitegates CM6 ....97 F4
Whitehall Cl CO2 ....136 C4
Whitehall Coll CO12 ....118 E1
Whitehall Ct CM8 ....177 A2
Whitehall Ind Est CO2 .136 D4
Whitehall La
Bishop's Stortford CM23 .118 F1
Thorpe-le-S CO16 ....141 C3
Whitehall Rd
Bishop's Stortford CM23 .118 E1
Colchester CO2 ....136 D4
Whitehart Ct CO12 ....91 C4
Whitehouse Cres CM2 .216 D8
Whitehouse Hill CM9 ..199 A7
Whitehouse La
Belchamp St P CO10 ....13 B2
West Bergholt CO6 ....108 D3
Whitehouse Rd CM6 ..124 F5
Whites Field CO7 ....59 B3
Whites La CM3 ....173 A6
Whitesbridge La CM4 ..215 D1
Whitesheet Way CB10 ..22 D2
Whitethorn Gdns CM2 .216 C7
Whitethorn Rd IP3 ....18 F1
Whiteways CB10 ....3 C2
Whiteways CM8 ....176 E3
Whitewell Rd 10 CO2 ..135 F6
Whitland Cl IP2 ....37 A8
Whitlands CO10 ....2 B6
Whitlock Dr CO9 ....29 F1
Whitlock Gr CO9 ....30 A1
Whittaker Way CO5 ....201 B7
Whittington Way CM23 .145 F3
Whittle Rd IP2 ....16 F6
Whitworth Cl IP2 ....16 D2
Whybrews 4 CO4 ....136 C5
Whyverne Cl CM1 ....205 E6
Wick La Ardleigh CO7 ..111 B8
Fingringhoe CO5 ....164 C3
Harwich CO12 ....91 B2
St Osyth CO7, CO16 ....167 C3
Wick Rd Colchester CO2 .136 D2
Great Bentley CO7 ....167 B5
Langham CO4 ....83 F3
Thorington Street CO4, CO6 .57 C2
Wicken Rd Arkesden CB11 ..41 F1
Newport CB11 ....66 F8
Wickfield Ash CM1 ....204 D6
Wickham Bishop Rd
CM3 ....194 D4

Wickham Hall La CM8 ..195 D3
Wickham Rd
Colchester CO3 ....135 D6
Witham CM8 ....194 F8
Wickham's Chase CM3 ..219 C2
Wickhambrook Ct IP11 .221 A4
Wickhay Cotts CM3 ....207 D5
Wicklow Ave CM1 ....204 D6
Wicks Cl CM7 ....127 C4
Widford Chase CM2 ....215 F7
Widford Cl CM2 ....215 F7
Widford Gr CM2 ....215 F7
Widford Ind Est CM1 ..215 E8
Widford Lodge Boys
Prep Sch CM2 ....215 F7
Widford Park Pl CM2 ..215 F7
Widford Rd CM2 ....215 F7
Widgeon Cl IP2 ....16 F3
Widgeon Pl CO5 ....158 C2
Widleybrook CM7 ....74 A3
Widleybrook La
Wethersfield CM7 ....73 F3
Wethersfield CM7 ....74 A2
Wigboro Wick La CO16 .186 F2
Wigborough Rd
Layer-de-l-H CO2 ....161 E2
Peldon CO5 ....182 C5
Wigeon Cl CM7 ....154 C5
Wigmore Cl IP2 ....16 F1
Wignall St CO11 ....85 F3
Wilberforce St IP1 ....17 A6
Wilbye Cl CO2 ....135 A3
Wilbye Ho CO3 ....135 A7
Wilding Rd IP8 ....16 B1
Wilkin Cl CO3 ....135 A4
Wilkinsons Mead CM2 .206 A4
Will's Ayley La CB10 ....23 F2
Willets Pond CO7 ....59 E1
Willett Rd CO3 ....135 B3
Willetts Field CB10 ....47 A3
William Booth Way IP11 .221 B5
William Boys Cl 1 CO4 .136 D8
William Cl CO7 ....137 C4
William Dr CO15 ....188 D2
William Groom Ave CO12 .91 A2
William Ho 7 IP4 ....17 D6
William Julien
Courtauld Hospl CM7 .127 E2
William Paul Housing
Trust 3 CM7 ....17 C4
William Sparrow Ct CO7 .137 C2
William St 3 IP1 ....17 C6
William's Wlk 9 CO1 .135 F7
Williams Rd CM1 ....191 B1
Williamson Ho 2 CO1 .136 A6
Willingale Rd CM7 ....128 D4
Willingham Way CO4 ..136 C5
Willoughby Ave CO1 ....201 D6
Willoughby Dr CM2 ....205 F2
Willoughby Rd IP2 ....17 B4
Willoughby's La CM7 ..128 C8
Willow Ave
Kirby Cross CO13 ....170 C6
St Osyth CO16 ....203 B6
Willow Cl Ardleigh CO7 .110 C6
Bishop's Stortford CM23 .145 E8
Brightlingsea CO7 ....185 D6
Broomfield CM1 ....191 B1
Willow Cres CM3 ....194 A3
Willow Hall La CO11 ..115 D8
Willow Mdws CO9 ....75 E8
Willow Pk CO6 ....133 E6
Willow Rise CM3 ....177 A5
Willow Springs CM23 ..145 D8
Willow Tree Cl 1 CO4 .136 E8
Willow Tree Way CO5 ..105 B6
Willow Way
Clacton-on-S CO15 ....203 G7
Halstead CO9 ....76 D1
Harwich CO12 ....90 F2
Willow Wlk Tiptree CO5 .179 C7
Weeley CO16 ....167 F8
Willowbank CM2 ....216 B3
Willowdene CO9 ....51 D2
Willows The Boreham CM3 206 F8
Colchester CO6 ....136 A3
Frinton-on-S CO13 ....170 F5
Great Chesterford CB10 ..3 D3
Wills Gn CO5 ....158 F6
Wilmington Rd CO4 ....110 C2
Wilmslow Dr IP2 ....16 C2
Wilshire Ave CM2 ....205 F3
Wilson Cl
Bishop's Stortford CM23 .145 F5
Wivenhoe CO7 ....137 A2
Wilson Ct CO15 ....188 F3
Wilson Marriage Rd CO4 110 C1
Wilson Rd IP8 ....16 B1
Wilson's Ct CM9 ....210 B3
Wilson's La CO10 ....132 E3
Wilton Cl CM23 ....146 E3
Wimbish Wlk CB10 ....44 E2
Wimborne Ave IP3 ....18 E4
Wimbourne Gdns CO13 .170 F5
Wimpole Cl IP5 ....18 F6
Wimpole Rd CO1 ....136 B5
Wimsey Ct CM3 ....177 A5
Wincelow Hall Rd CB10 .25 E2
Winchelsea Dr CM2 ....216 E7
Winchelsea Pl CO7 ....185 F8
Winchester Cl CM23 ....145 D4
Winchester Rd
Colchester CO2 ....136 B5
Frinton-on-S CO13 ....171 A5
Winchester Way IP2 ....36 F8

Winckford Cl CM3 ....191 B6
Windermere Cl IP3 ....38 B8
Windermere Ct CO15 ....189 A3
Windermere Dr CM7 .....154 C6
Windermere Rd
  Clacton-on-S CO15 .....189 C6
  Great Notley CM7 ....154 C7
  Sudbury CO10 ....34 A8
Windham Rd CO10 ....34 B8
Windhill CM23 ....145 E7
Windhill Old Rd CM23 ...145 E7
Winding Piece IP9 ....35 A1
Windmill Cl Boxted CO4 ...82 F4
  Great Dunmow CM6 .....123 E1
  Ramsey CO12 ....89 F1
Windmill Ct
  Clacton-on-S CO15 .....188 F5
  Colchester CO4 ....109 A8
  Copford CO6 ....133 D4
Windmill Fields CO6 .....130 F3
Windmill Gdns CM7 .....128 A8
Windmill Hill CB10 ......22 B3
Windmill Pk CO15 ....188 F5
Windmill Rd Bradfield CO11 87 C1
  Halstead CO9 ....76 D1
Windmill Row CO10 ......2 C5
Windmill View CO5 ......179 C6
Windmills CO6 ....106 C1
Windmills The CM1 ......191 B3
Windrush Dr CM1 ....205 C6
Windsor Ave CO15 ....188 D3
Windsor Cl CO2 ....136 A2
Windsor Ct
  Brightlingsea CO7 ......185 F6
  6 Colchester CO1 ......136 C6
Windsor Gdns
  Bishop's Stortford CM23 ..145 C7
  Braintree CM7 ....128 B4
Windsor Ho CO5 ....201 D7
Windsor Pl CO10 ....34 A7
Windsor Rd
  Clacton-on-S CO15 .....188 D3
  Felixstowe IP11 ....221 C3
  Ipswich IP1 ....16 F7
  West Mersea CO5 ....201 D7
Windsor Sch CO15 ......189 B4
Windsor Terr CB9 ....8 E8
Windsor Way CM1 ......204 E1
Winfield Terr CO14 ......144 D2
Winfrith Rd IP3 ....18 D4
Wingate Cl CM7 ....127 C6
Wingfield St IP4 ....17 D5
Wingrove Ct CM1 ....205 A6
Winnock Rd CO1 ....136 A6
Winnock's
  Almshouses CO1 ....136 A6
  Winnocks **6** CO1 ......136 A6
Winsey Chase CM7 ......72 C6
Winsford Way CM2 .....206 C6
Winsgate Ho **6** IP1 .....17 A7
Winsley Rd CO1 ....136 B6
Winsley Sq CO1 ....136 B4
Winstanley Rd CB11 ....43 E7
Winston Ave
  Colchester CO3 ....135 B4
  Ipswich IP4 ....18 C8
  Tiptree CO5 ....179 E5
Winston Cl Braintree CM7 .127 E6
  Felixstowe IP11 ....221 B5

Winston Ct CO13 ....170 F4
Winston Way CO9 ....77 A3
Winstree Ct CO3 ....134 C4
Winstree Rd CO3 ....134 D5
Winstreet Cl CO2 ....161 F5
Winter's Hill CO2 ....160 F1
Winter's Rd CO5 ....160 E1
Winterbournes CO14 ....171 A7
Wintermere CO14 ....131 B3
Wisdoms Gn CO6 ....131 B3
Wistaria Ct **3** CO4 ......136 E7
Wistaria Pl CO16 ....188 C5
Wisteria Lodge **7** CM1 ..205 F6
Wiston Rd CO6 ....81 D8
Witch Elm CO12 ....90 F2
Witch La CO6 ....131 B8
Witchtree La CB10 ......25 F3
Witham Lodge CM8 .....194 D7
Witham Rd
  Black Notley CM7 ....155 B5
  Cressing CM7 ....156 B3
  Heybridge CM9 ....209 D7
  Terling CM3 ....175 E2
  Tolleshunt Major CM9 ...197 D5
  Wickham Bishops CM8 ..195 E6
  Witham Sta CM8 ....177 B2
Withersfield Rd CB9 ....8 F8
Withipoll St IP4 ....17 D6
Withrick Wlk CO16 ......187 A5
Witting Cl CO16 ....188 D5
Witton Wood Rd CO13 ..170 E5
Wivenhoe Cross CO7 ....137 C2
Wivenhoe Rd
  Alresford CO7 ....165 B7
  Colchester CO7 ....111 C1
  Wivenhoe Sta CO7 .....164 B8
Wix By-Pass CO11 ......115 C6
Wix Cty Prim Sch CO11 .115 B5
Wix Rd Beaumont CO16 ..141 E8
  Bradfield CO11 ....87 C1
  Great Oakley CO12 .....116 B3
  Ramsey CO12 ....89 F1
  Tendring CO11 ....114 F8
  Wix CO11 ....115 C3
Woburn Ave
  Bishop's Stortford CM23 ..145 C7
  Kirby Cross CO13 ....170 D7
Woburn Cl **1** CM2 ......205 A1
Wolfe Ave CO1, CO2 .....136 A5
Wolmers Hey CM3 ......190 F7
Wolseley Ave CO15 ......203 E6
Wolseley Rd CM2 ....205 A1
Wolsey Art Gall IP4 .....17 D6
Wolsey Ct IP11 ....221 B4
Wolsey Gdns IP11 ......221 E3
Wolsey St **9** IP1 ....17 C5
Wolton Rd CO2 ....135 B2
Wolves Hall La CO16 ....114 F1
Wood Barn La CO11 ....85 D1
Wood Cnr CM9 ....209 B2
Wood Dale CM2 ....216 E6
Wood End CB11 ....67 D3
Wood Field End CO2 ....162 A5
Wood La
  Birchanger CM23 ....119 E2
  Fordham Heath CO3 ....107 A7
  Harkstead SG9 ....64 A6
  Heybridge CM9 ....210 A5
Wood Rd CM9 ....210 B6
Wood St CM2 ....216 A7
Wood Way CM7 ....154 B6
Woodberry Way CO14 ...171 C7
Woodbridge Gr CO16 ...188 A4

Woodbridge Rd
  Ipswich IP4 ....17 E6
  Rushmere St A IP5 .....18 E7
Woodbridge Rd E IP4 ...18 D7
Woodcock Cl
  Colchester CO4 ....136 E6
  Haverhill CB9 ....9 C7
Woodcock Rd IP2 ....16 E2
Woodfield Cl Stansted
  Mountfitchet CM24 .....119 E6
  Walton-on-t-N CO14 ....171 A7
Woodfield Cotts CM9 ...210 C6
Woodfield Dr CO5 ......201 B7
Woodfield La IP9 ....61 E3
Woodfield Rd CM7 .....128 A3
Woodfield Terr CM24 ...119 E6
Woodfield Way CM3 ....194 A4
Woodfields CM24 ....119 E6
Woodford Cl CO15 .....188 F8
Woodgates IP11 ....221 B6
Woodgates Rd CO7 .....59 D5
Woodhall Bsns Pk CO10 .15 F2
Woodhall Cty Prim Sch
  CO10 ....15 F2
Woodhall Gr CM23 .....145 D6
Woodhall Hill CM1 .....190 C2
Woodhall Par CM1 .....205 A7
Woodhall Rd
  Chelmsford CM1 ....205 A7
  Sudbury CO10 ....15 E1
Woodham Dr CM3 .....194 B4
Woodham Mortimer Rd
  CM9 ....219 E8
Woodham Walter Prim
  Sch CM9 ....208 D3
Woodhill Rd Danbury CM3 218 B6
  Sandon CM2 ....217 E6
Woodhouse La CM3 ....191 A4
Woodhouse Sq **5** IP4 ..17 D5
Woodland Chase CO3 ..107 F1
Woodland Cl CM3 ......194 A5
Woodland Dr CO3 .....134 F5
Woodland Rd CM1 .....205 A4
Woodland Way
  Gosfield CO9 ....102 E8
  Wivenhoe CO7 ....137 B1
Woodlands
  Bishop's Stortford CM23 ..146 C8
  Braintree CM7 ....128 C3
  Broomfield CM1 ....191 A4
  Chelmondiston IP9 .....63 E7
  Colchester CO4 ....110 F2
  Great Oakley CO12 ....116 B2
  Ipswich IP8 ....16 C1
  Jaywick CO16 ....188 A1
Woodlands Cl CO15 ....189 A8
Woodlands Park Dr CM6 .123 B1
Woodlands Rd IP9 .....62 D7
Woodlands Rise CO16 ..140 F1
Woodlands Sch CM1 ...204 F6
Woodlands The CO7 ...185 E8
Woodlands Wlk CM6 ...123 B1
Woodlark Cl IP2 ....16 E1
Woodlyn Ct CO15 .....189 E6
Woodpecker Cl
  Bishop's Stortford CM23 ..145 C6
  2 Colchester CO4 ....136 F8
Woodpecker Rd IP2 ....16 D3
Woodroffe Cl CM2 .....206 A3
Woodrolfe Farm La CM9 .199 E1

Woodrolfe Pk CM9 ......199 F2
Woodrolfe Rd CM9 .....199 E2
Woodrose Lodge **6** CM1 .205 F6
Woodrow Way CO4 .....136 E7
Woodrows La CO16 .....188 B5
Woodrush End CO3 ....134 B6
Woodrush Rd IP3 ......18 E2
Woods Rd CM3 ....172 B6
Woodside
  Bishop's Stortford CM23 ..146 D8
  Great Totham CM9 .....196 B3
  Little Baddow CM3 .....207 F1
  Walton-on-t-N CO14 ....171 B7
Woodside Cl CO4 ......110 E1
Woodside Way CM6 ....123 A1
Woodspring Cl **2** IP2 ..17 A2
Woodstock CO5 ....201 C7
Woodview Cl CO4 ......110 D4
Woodview Cotts CO5 ...180 C8
Woodview Dr CM3 .....174 A7
Woodview Rd CM6 .....150 D8
Woodville Rd IP4 ......17 F5
Woodyards CM0 ....214 F3
Woollards Cl IP1 ....17 A6
Woollards Gdns CO10 ..15 C8
Woolner Rd CO16 ......188 D6
Woolnough Cl CB9 ....27 B6
Woolpack La CM7 .....127 F5
Woolpit Downs CO6 ...79 E8
Woolpit's Rd CM7 .....99 E1
Woolverstone Cl IP2 ...16 C1
Woolwich Rd CO16 ....188 C5
Worcester CM7 ....128 A1
Worcester Cres CO7 ...165 B8
Worcester Ct
  Clacton-on-S CO15 ....188 E1
  Great Baddow CM2 ...217 A5
Worcester Rd
  Colchester CO1 ....136 A8
  Ipswich IP3 ....38 B8
Wordsworth Ct CM1 ..205 A5
Wordsworth Rd
  Braintree CM7 ....127 F7
  Colchester CO4 ....134 F6
Workhouse Corner CO12 116 C3
Workhouse Hill CO4 ...82 E5
Workhouse Rd CO6 ....81 C2
Worlds End La CO5 ....158 D3
Worsdell Way CO4 ....109 F2
Worsley Cl IP2 ....16 D2
Wortham Pl CB9 ......9 A8
Worthing Mews CO15 .203 I8
Worthington Way CO3 .134 F4
Wrabness Local Nature
  Reserve CO11 ....88 D4
Wrabness Rd Ramsey CO12 89 D3
  Ramsey CO12 ....90 A2
Wrabness Sta CO11 ...89 A4
Wraglins The CM23 ...146 B5
Wratting Rd CB9 .....9 A8
Wren Ave IP2 ....16 D3
Wren Cl CO7 ....139 D1
Wrenbrook Rd CM23 ..145 F6
Wrendale CO15 ....188 F6
Wright Ct **2** CM7 ....127 F3
Wright Rd IP3 ....18 C2
Wright's Ave CM7 .....155 E6
Wright's Piece CM22 ..95 A6
Writtle Cl CO16 ....188 B4
Writtle Coll CM1 ......204 B3
Writtle Cty Jun & Inf
  Schs CM1 ....215 A1

Writtle Rd CM1 ....215 A5
Wroxham Cl CO3 ......135 C6
Wroxham Rd IP3 ......17 F3
Wryneck Cl CO4 ......109 F3
Wulvesford CM8 ......194 D8
Wyatts La CO10 ......55 D8
Wych Elm CO2 ....136 A3
Wycke Hill CM9 ......220 D8
Wycke Hill Bsns Pk CM9 .220 E8
Wycke La CM9 ....213 E8
Wycliffe Gr CO1 ......109 E1
Wye Rd IP3 ....18 A3
Wykeham Rd CM1 ....204 B1
Wykes Bishop St IP3 ..17 E4
Wyncolls Rd CO4 .....110 D6
Wyndam Cl CO2 .....163 B8
Wyndham Cres CO15 .189 A5
Wynterton Cl IP3 .....18 B1
Wynyard Rd CB10 ....22 E2
Wyseman Pl CO11 ....86 C7
Wyvern Ct CO7 ......137 B5
Wyverne CM6 ....151 A5

Y

Yale Mews CO4 ....110 A4
Yardley Hall La CM6 ...69 D6
Yare Ave CM8 ....176 D2
Yarmouth Cl CO16 ....188 E6
Yarmouth Pl CB9 .....9 A8
Yarmouth Rd IP1 .....17 C6
Yarwood Rd CM2 ....205 E2
Yeldham Lock CM2 ...206 A2
Yeldham Pl CB9 ......9 A8
Yeomans CO9 ....51 D3
Yeomans Cl CM23 ....145 D6
Yeoman Rd IP11 .....221 B6
Yerril Garden CB9 ....8 E7
Yew Ct IP2 ....17 B3
Yew Tree Cl
  Colchester CO4 ....136 E8
  Hatfield Peverel CM3 ...194 A5
Yew Tree Gdns CM2 ..216 C6
Yew Tree Pl CM23 ....145 F8
Yew Way CO15 ....203 F7
Yewtree Gr IP5 ....18 F7
Yewtree Rise IP8 .....16 C1
Yorick Ave CO5 ......201 C6
Yorick Rd CO5 ....201 C6
York Cl CO10 ....33 E8
York Gdns CM7 ......128 B4
York Mans CO15 .....189 C5
York Pl CO1 ....136 A8
York Rd
  Brightlingsea CO7 .....185 E6
  Chelmsford CM2 ......216 A8
  Clacton-on-S CO15 ....189 E5
  Earls Colne CO6 ....105 A6
  Felixstowe IP11 ....221 E4
  Haverhill CB9 ....8 E7
  Ipswich IP3 ....18 A4
York St **6** CO11 .....86 D7
Young Cl CO16 ....188 C5
Ypres Rd CO2 ....135 E4

Z

Zambesi Rd CM23 .....145 F5